The Michigan
DIVORCE BOOK
A guide to doing an uncontested divorce without an attorney

with minor children

By Michael Maran • Michigan Attorney

Grand River Press
P.O. Box 1342
E. Lansing, MI 48826

The Michigan Divorce Book: A Guide to Doing an Uncontested Divorce without an Attorney (with minor children) by Michael Maran

Published by:
Grand River Press
P.O. Box 1342
E. Lansing, MI 48826

Printing history:
First edition: January 1986
Second edition:
  First printing: June 1989
  Second printing: September 1990
Third edition:
  First printing: May 1993
  Second printing: October 1994
  Third printing: January 1996
  Fourth printing: June 1997
Fourth edition:
  First printing: February 1998
  Second printing: November 1999
  Third printing: October 2000
Fifth edition:
  First printing: March 2001
  Second printing: March 2002
  Third printing: June 2003
Sixth edition: January 2004

ISBN 0-936343-17-6
Printed in the United States of America

Order Form

- **The Michigan Divorce Book: A Guide to Doing an Uncontested Divorce without an Attorney (without minor children)** $24.95

    Update $1.00

- **The Michigan Divorce Book: A Guide to Doing an Uncontested Divorce without an Attorney (with minor children)** $29.95

    Update $1.50

ALSO AVAILABLE:

- **The Michigan Estate Planning Book: A Complete Do-It Yourself Guide to Planning an Estate in Michigan** $29.95

- **After the Divorce: A Do-It-Yourself Guide to Enforcing or Modifying a Divorce Judgment in Michigan** $29.95

TITLE	PRICE	QUANTITY	TOTAL

Subtotal	
Add 6% Sales Tax	
Postage	$2.50
TOTAL	

Method of Payment:

☐ Check or money order (payable to **Grand River Press**)

☐ Charge: ☐ Visa ☐ MasterCard

Account # ☐☐☐☐☐☐☐☐☐☐☐☐☐☐☐☐☐☐

Expiration Date _____ Signature _____

Name _____

Address _____

City _____ State _____ Zip _____

Please send form to: Grand River Press, P.O. Box 1342, East Lansing, Michigan 48826

Dedication:
V. Cramer

Illustrations:
Patric Fourshe

Lettering and layout:
Altese Graphic Design

Editing:
Mark Woodbury

Contents

Preface

Chapter 1

Part I: Introduction to Divorce

Do-It-Yourself Divorce   6

II: Uncontested Divorce

Divorce Issues   8

End of Marriage   8

Custody   9
Types of Custody • Court-Ordered Custody • Uncontested Custody

Parenting Time   15
Types of Parenting Time • Court-Ordered Parenting Time
Uncontested Parenting Time

Residence of Children   17
Establishing Residences of Children • Court-Ordered
Change of Residence • Uncontested Change of Residence

Child Support   21
Child Support Formula • Payment of Child Support
Centralization of Child Support Services • Health Care,
Child Care and Educational Expenses • Court-Ordered
Child Support • Uncontested Child Support

Property Division   27

Court-Ordered Property Division • Uncontested Property Division

Alimony   29

Types of Alimony • Payment of Alimony • Court-Ordered Alimony • Uncontested Alimony

Other Divorce Issues   33

Name Change • Dependency Exemptions

III: Doing an Uncontested Divorce Yourself

Am I Married?   35

Do I Really Want to End My Marriage?   37

Is Divorce the Best Way to End My Marriage?   38

Annulment • Separation

Can I Get a Divorce in Michigan?   43

Residence • Divorce Jurisdiction • Custody Jurisdiction

Can I File the Divorce in My County?   45

What If My Spouse and I File for Divorce at the Same Time?   45

Can My Spouse Be Served with the Divorce Papers?   46

What If My Spouse or I Am Imprisoned?   46

Divorce by an Imprisoned Plaintiff • Filing against a Defendant-Prisoner

What If My Spouse or I Am in the Military?   48

How Long Will My Divorce Take?   48

How Much Will My Divorce Cost?   49

Which Children Must Be Included in My Divorce?   51

Minor Children • Adult Children

Must I Have the Friend of the Court in My Case?   52

Can I Get a Fair Property Division?   53

Inventorying Property • Valuing Property • Dividing Property

Does My Property Need Protection?   58

Do I Need to Change My Estate Plan?   58

Do I Need "Preliminary Relief"?   59
Alternatives to Preliminary Relief

Can I Socialize during the Divorce?   61

Can I Keep the Divorce Secret?   61

Will I Have Tax Problems from the Divorce?   61

What If My Spouse Is Mentally Incompetent?   62

What If I Need to File for Bankruptcy?   63

What If I Want to Dismiss the Divorce?   63

What If My Spouse Abuses Me?   64
Keeping Personal Information away from a Spouse-Abuser

Where Can I File If My Spouse or I Am Native American?   65

What If My Spouse or I Am an "Alien" (Non-citizen)?   66
Can an Alien Get a Divorce in Michigan? • Divorce by a Plaintiff-Alien • Plaintiff-Citizen Filing Divorce against a Defendant-Alien

Do You Need Legal Help?   67

Chapter 2

Legal Basics   71
Court System • Papers • Fees • Time • Courthouse Appearances • Local Rules and Forms • New Laws, Rules, Forms and Fees • Sample Forms

Overview of Divorce Procedure   85
Flowchart

Part I: Starting Your Divorce

1 Filing   87
Preparing Your Initial Divorce Papers • Filing Your Divorce • Getting Preliminary Relief • Sample Forms

2 Service   99
Serving the Defendant • Preparing for Service • Service by Acknowledgment • Service by Mail • Service by Delivery • Service Problems • Filing the Proof of Service Special Notice of Your Divorce

Part I Checklists   **109**

II: Finishing Your Divorce

3 Default   111
Getting the Default • After the Default • Sample Forms

4 Waiting for Final Hearing   121
Friend of the Court Investigation • Case Conference
Prosecuting Attorney

5 Final Hearing   123
Final Divorce Papers • Preparing for the Final Hearing
Attending the Final Hearing • After the Final Hearing
Sample Forms

Part II Checklist   140

After Your Divorce   141
Transferring Property • Health Care Coverage • Estate
Planning • Name Change • Credit Problems

Appendices

Appendix A: Fee Exemption   149
Obtaining a Fee Exemption • Sample Form

Appendix B: Preliminary Relief   153
Interim vs. Temporary Relief • Preparing a Request for In-
terim Relief • Getting an Interim Order • Court Hearing
Preparing for a Court Hearing • Making Your Case in
Court • Court Hearing Itself • After You Get Interim
Relief • Sample Forms

Appendix C: Opting Out of the Friend of the Court System   177
Types of Opt-Outs • Total Opt-Out • Partial Opt-Out
Limited Opt-Out • Sample Forms

Appendix D: Alternate Service   193
Forms of Alternate Service • Alternate Service for an
Elusive Defendant • Alternate Service for a Disappeared
Defendant • Sample Forms

Appendix E: Giving Special Notice of Your Divorce   209
Special Notice to a Third Party with Custody • Special
Notice to a Prior Court • Sample Form

Appendix F: Divorce and the Military   213

Military Relief Laws • Divorce by a Plaintiff-Servicemember • Divorcing a Defendant-Servicemember • Sample Forms

Appendix G: Dismissing Your Divorce   223

Sample Form

Appendix H: Additional Judgment Provisions   225

Property Division Provisions   225

Dividing Real Property • Joint Real Property • Solely-Owned Real Property • Dividing Personal Property Dividing Retirement Benefits, Businesses and Other New Property • Division of Debts

Alimony Provisions   234

Short-Term Alimony • Long-Term Alimony • Choosing an Alimony Payment Method

Custody Provisions   236

Joint Physical Custody • Split Custody • Mixed Custody Third-Party Custody

Parenting Time Provisions   240
Change of Children's Residence Provisions   241
Child Support Provisions   242

Providing for Child Support • Using the Formula and Child Support Schedules • Adding to Base Child Support Reserving Child Support • Adjusting the Child Support Schedules • Departing from the Child Suppprt Formula Health Care • Payment of Child Support • Assigning Dependency Exemptions

Michigan Child Support Formula Manual

Forms

Regular Forms
Optional Forms
Local Forms

Preface

Do your own divorce? The idea may sound crazy to many people. After all, doesn't everyone need a lawyer to get a divorce?

The fact is, you have the right to do your own divorce, just as you have the right to represent yourself in any legal matter. The right of legal self-representation is so important it's protected by the Bill of Rights in the U.S. Constitution (it falls under the First Amendment's right of petition for redress of grievances). In Michigan, legal self-help is also guaranteed by Sec. 13 of Art. 1 of the Michigan Constitution of 1963, which says: "a suitor in any court of this state has the right to prosecute or defend his suit, either *in his own proper person* or by an attorney." (Emphasis added.)

Despite these guarantees, the right to represent yourself in court doesn't mean very much if you don't know what you're doing once you get there. That's where this book comes in.

Chapter 1 describes divorce, tells you what an uncontested divorce is and helps you decide whether you can handle it yourself. Chapter 2 has instructions and sample forms to guide you through a divorce. And last but not least, blank forms are included in the back of the book which you can tear out and use to file your own divorce case.

PART I: Introduction to Divorce

PART II: Uncontested Divorce

PART III: Doing an Uncontested Divorce Yourself

PART I:
Introduction to Divorce

Asked about the origin of divorce, the French philosopher Voltaire said he didn't know exactly, but assumed that divorce was invented a few weeks after marriage. His reasoning? A couple married, quarreled and were ready for divorce a few weeks later.

Although it was meant as a joke, Voltaire's remark wasn't that far from the truth. Divorce *has* been around almost as long as marriage. The Babylonian Code of Hammurabi, the oldest known code of law, authorized divorce on several grounds, including a wife's barrenness, disloyalty, neglect or disease. According to the Bible, a Hebrew husband could divorce his wife for "uncleanness" by handing her a "bill of divorcement" and sending her away.

It was this law that Jesus was quizzed about by the Pharisees when they asked him: "Is it lawful for a man to divorce his wife?" The Gospel of St. Mark says Jesus condemned the practice, adding: "What therefore God hath joined together, let not man put asunder." Yet St. Matthew's account of this incident is different. It says that Jesus permitted divorce on grounds of wives' "fornication." Other New Testament scripture is also contradictory; some passages are hostile to divorce, while others seem to tolerate it.

With all this confusion, the Bible can be interpreted to either allow or disallow divorce. Catholic countries sided with the Mark Gospel and forbade divorce. But Protestant countries—with the notable exception of England—followed Matthew and allowed divorce on grounds of adultery and sometimes desertion.

When it came to law, America usually took its cue from England, so it should have observed the English ban on divorce. But divorce became firmly established in this country after the first American divorce was granted in

1639 by the Massachusetts Bay Colony to Mrs. James Luxford for her husband's bigamy.

There were several reasons for that. In a way, America itself was the child of divorce: the "divorce," in the guise of the American Revolution, from England. It's even possible to read the Declaration of Independence as the petition for that divorce. This interpretation isn't as far-fetched as it seems.

Thomas Jefferson, the author of the Declaration of Independence, had handled divorce cases as a young lawyer, and the catalog of grievances and wrongs found in the declaration echoed those from his divorce practice.

There were also practical reasons for the American love affair with divorce. During the colonial era, divorce was forbidden in England, France, Italy and several other European countries. Many immigrants to America were fleeing these repressive divorce laws as much as religious or political persecution. Once here, they were in no mood for tough European-style divorce laws.

By the mid-19th century, almost all the states had divorce laws. Typically, these laws permitted divorce on a variety of fault grounds. According to this fault system, divorce was available only when one spouse had committed marital misconduct. This gave the faultless spouse grounds for a divorce.

On the other hand, an at-fault spouse wasn't entitled to get a divorce. A peculiar divorce doctrine called recrimination prevented anyone with "unclean hands" from asking for a divorce. Recrimination effectively barred an at-fault spouse (who often wanted out of the marriage the most) from getting a divorce, unless the faultless spouse was willing to excuse the marital misconduct. By using this divorce veto, the faultless spouse could blackmail the at-fault spouse—by demanding extra property, support or other concessions—as the price for the divorce.

During this era, Michigan divorce law was typical of the fault divorce laws. The 1846 divorce law had seven fault grounds for divorce: 1) adultery 2) physical incompetence 3) imprisonment 4) desertion 5) husband's drunkenness 6) extreme cruelty 7) husband's neglect. It also had a strict recrimination doctrine.

But not every state was as generous with divorce grounds as Michigan. Before 1967, New York had a notoriously tough divorce law, which allowed divorce only on grounds of adultery. South Carolina was even worse. Divorce was legalized in that state after the Civil War and then abolished in 1878. Divorce was finally re-established in South Carolina in 1949, after an absence of 71 years!

When people were frustrated by strict divorce laws in their home states, they often fled to other states with better laws. This so-called migratory divorce was possible because the United States, unlike most countries, doesn't have a uniform national divorce law. Instead, divorce is regulated by each state. With 50 different divorce laws, it's no wonder that migratory divorce has been a problem in America since colonial times.

Many states tried to stop migratory divorce by adopting divorce residence requirements or erecting other barriers. But a handful of states encouraged divorce migration as a boost to local tourism. Nevada even managed to make migratory divorce its largest industry for a while. In 1907, William Schnitzer, a sharp New York lawyer, noticed that Nevada had a lax divorce law, with a short residence period, seven grounds for divorce and no recrimination doctrine. Schnitzer opened an office in Reno and soon divorce migrants flocked there. Other lawyers followed in Schnitzer's footsteps and migratory divorce flourished in Nevada.

As easy as migratory divorce was, it was still very expensive. There was the cost of getting the divorce, not to mention the expense of traveling to another state and living there during the residence period. As a result, migratory divorce was a luxury only the wealthy could afford.

Among those making the trek to Nevada was Nelson Rockefeller, then governor of New York. Millionaire Rockefeller got a Nevada divorce in 1962 while thousands of his fellow New Yorkers were stuck at home without a divorce remedy. Rockefeller's divorce caused a furor, and many think it cost him the Republican presidential nomination in 1964.

By the 1960s, all the controversy over migratory divorce had created the mood for change. California took the first step in 1969 when it adopted a "no-fault" divorce law. Previously, California had had a fault divorce law with several fault grounds (adultery, extreme cruelty, willful neglect, etc.). It replaced these with two no-fault grounds: incurable insanity and irreconcilable differences. What's more, the new California law banished fault from the other divorce issues of alimony, child support and property division.

The California no-fault law revolutionized divorce in America, as other states rushed to enact similar no-fault laws. Within five years, 45 states had adopted no-fault divorce. By 1986, when final holdout South Dakota gave in, every state had some type of no-fault divorce.

Michigan was among the first states to adopt no-fault divorce in the early 1970s. But in Michigan the transition from fault to no-fault divorce wasn't as smooth as it was in other states. At first, Michigan lawmakers were poised to adopt a sweeping California-style no-fault divorce law removing fault from divorce entirely. Michigan lawyers were horrified at this idea because they feared that no-fault divorce meant no-lawyer divorce. The lawyers lobbied furiously against the no-fault proposal. Ultimately, a deal was reached providing for no-fault divorce grounds, but with fault left intact for most of the other divorce issues. This no-fault divorce law took effect on Jan. 1, 1972, and is still the law today.

In the last few years, no-fault divorce has stirred up new controversy. Feminists have complained that no-fault divorce can be unfair to women. Their reasoning: no-fault destroyed the divorce leverage women once had, leading to smaller property division and support settlements for them. Some conservatives argue that no-fault divorce actually encourages divorce, bringing more of the social problems associated with divorce.

In Michigan, no-fault critics have introduced bills in the legislature to repeal parts of the no-fault law, and re-introduce fault into divorce grounds. These proposals got a lot of press, but haven't gone anywhere as legislators have shied away from re-opening the debate on no-fault divorce.

Do-It-Yourself Divorce

During the era of fault divorce, few dared to do their own divorces because they were hard to handle. But a no-fault divorce is really just a clerical task, which even a nonlawyer can manage. As soon as no-fault laws were adopted, nonlawyer entrepreneurs set up do-it-yourself divorce services to help people do their own divorces.

In Michigan, two such operations sprang up in 1972 after the no-fault divorce law went into effect: Harry Gordon Associates in Oak Park and Gordon, Graham and Cramer in Detroit. Harry Gordon Associates sold a divorce kit with forms and instructions. Gordon, Graham and Cramer offered personalized services, including preparation of papers, filing and help with court appearances.

Alarmed at this threat to their business, Michigan lawyers sought to enforce the unauthorized practice of law statute against their new rivals. Like most states, Michigan has an unauthorized practice law barring non-lawyers from practicing law. This law permits you to represent yourself, but you must be a lawyer to represent others.

In 1972, courts invoked this law and ordered Harry Gordon Associates and Gordon, Graham and Cramer out of business. Facing jail if they disobeyed, most of the firms' operators reluctantly closed. But Virginia Cramer, one of the partners in Gordon, Graham and Cramer, refused to be intimidated. She re-emerged with a new divorce service similar to her old one. Just like before, lawyers tried to stop her claiming that she was engaged in the unauthorized practice of law.

After battling in court for several years, the parties ended up before the Michigan Supreme Court in the case known as *State Bar of Michigan v. Cramer*. The issue in the case was whether Cramer had violated the unauthorized practice law by providing personalized legal services. The court decided that she had when she gave clients *specific* legal information (telling them what to do in their particular situations). On the other hand, the court said that nonlawyers like Cramer could offer *general* legal information in the form of books or legal kits.

Thanks to the apparent ban on nonlawyer divorce services, few such firms exist in Michigan. Without this option, most divorce do-it-yourselfers have had to rely on self-help divorce books or kits. Since the 1970s, several legal aid organizations and women's groups have offered do-it-yourself divorce kits. This book has its genesis in one such kit published in 1981. It was enlarged into book form in 1986, and has been revised several times since then.

PART II: Uncontested Divorce

Before you start your divorce, it's important to talk with your spouse and see if you agree on the divorce issues. This will determine whether your divorce will be contested or uncontested.

A disagreement over the divorce issues usually means a contested divorce. You are entitled to represent yourself in a contested divorce. But your spouse would probably get a lawyer, providing an edge over you during the divorce. That's why you shouldn't represent yourself in a contested case.

On the other hand, if you and your spouse agree on all the divorce issues, you have an uncontested divorce. You ought to be able to handle this kind of divorce yourself without a lawyer. But see Part III for several situations in which even an uncontested divorce may be too complicated for you to do yourself.

What sort of agreement do you need for an uncontested divorce? A formal written agreement—called a separation or settlement agreement—won't be necessary. Michigan doesn't require these in uncontested cases, as some states do. Instead, an informal agreement or understanding should be enough.

Sometimes you may not need an agreement at all. Needless to say, it's impossible to discuss divorce with a spouse who has disappeared. In that case, the spouse's absence should permit you to go ahead and get an uncontested divorce just as if s/he were agreeing to it.

Divorce Issues

During your talk, you and your spouse may quickly agree that your marriage must end. But a divorce is far more than simply ending a marriage. That's especially true when you have minor children. With that type of divorce, there are no less than seven important divorce issues:

- end of marriage
- custody
- parenting time
- residence of children
- child support
- property division
- alimony

These are the issues you and your spouse must agree on to have an uncontested divorce. To help you reach agreement, the rest of this chapter examines these issues in detail.

End of Marriage

Above all else, a divorce means ending your marriage. To accomplish that, you need specific grounds (reasons). As explained in Part I, Michigan once had fault grounds, such as adultery, desertion, extreme cruelty, etc., for divorce. But in 1972, Michigan adopted these no-fault grounds for divorce:

There has been a breakdown of the marriage relationship to the extent that the objects of matrimony have been destroyed and there remains no reasonable likelihood that the marriage can be preserved.

If you look at these grounds closely, you see that three things must exist to get a divorce: 1) a marital breakdown ("breakdown of the marriage relationship") 2) that is serious ("to the extent that the objects of matrimony have been destroyed") 3) and permanent ("there remains no reasonable likelihood that the marriage can be preserved").

At first, when the no-fault law was new, courts had trouble applying the no-fault grounds. Judges continued to probe into the reasons for marital breakdowns, as they had under the old fault law. Some judges even denied divorces when they felt that a marriage hadn't really broken down or could be saved.

By the late 1970s, courts were applying the no-fault law more liberally. These days, courts don't investigate the marital breakdown very much, and divorces are granted for almost any reason. As a result, the end-of-marriage issue is seldom contested in divorces any more.

Glossary

Uncontested divorce–divorce where spouses agree on all the divorce issues.

No-fault divorce–all Michigan divorces, whether contested or uncontested, are no-fault divorces since they must use no-fault grounds.

Custody

If end of marriage is the easiest divorce issue, custody is the most difficult because it's so emotional for parents. Fairly or not, parents regard custody as a test of their worth as parents. With the stakes so high, courts have struggled to find a custody formula that satisfies parents while looking out for children.

In the beginning, custody was simple. According to old English law, children were the property of their fathers and they could do with them what they liked. As for mothers, they were "entitled to no power [over their children] but only to reverence and respect," according to Blackstone's influential *Commentaries on the Law of England*.

In America, courts were more sympathetic to mothers, and seldom gave custody to fathers as easily as the English did. By the 19th century, that sympathy had evolved into an actual preference for maternal custody, known as the tender years doctrine. This doctrine gave custody to mothers of young children (of "tender years") unless they were unfit parents.

Michigan once had a tender years doctrine that gave mothers custody of children under the age of 12, except when they were unfit. This preference put fathers at a severe disadvantage when they sought custody. According to a 1948 Michigan custody survey, mothers got custody 95% of the time when the issue was contested.

By the 1960s, the unfairness of Michigan's custody law was plain, leading to adoption of a new law in 1970. The child custody act of 1970 abolished the tender years doctrine and assigned custody according to the "best interests of the children." These best interests were defined as the sum of several factors listed in the act (see below).

The new custody law may have changed how custody was awarded, but it didn't alter the type of custody courts ordered. The one-parent custody known as sole custody remained the favorite type of custody after passage of the act in 1970.

But by the 1970s, families were changing rapidly and many parents had become dissatisfied with sole custody. Many fathers disliked sole custody because it confined them to a limited weekend daddy role. Some working mothers found it difficult to cope with sole custody and new-found job responsibilities. And most children wanted more contact with their noncustodial parents than sole custody provided.

Parents displeased with sole custody wanted more flexible arrangements, such as joint custody. There are several forms of joint custody, also known as shared custody or coparenting. But whatever the form, joint custody tries to give parents control of their children in many of the same ways they had before the divorce.

Parents and children arranging custody amicably? You would think that the legal system would have encouraged joint custody. On the contrary, most legal experts were against the idea. Judges feared joint custody because they were convinced that it would disrupt families. Lawyers dreaded it because they thought that it would hurt business. Custody cases produced big fees for lawyers, so the idea of joint custody made many nervous.

Despite the hostility, by the late 1970s parents were seeking and winning joint custody in isolated cases, including several landmark cases in Michigan. But the event that really turned the tide was California's passage of the first comprehensive joint custody law in 1979. Not only did this law permit joint custody, it created a legal presumption in favor of it.

During the next several years, most states followed California's example and adopted similar joint custody laws. Michigan joined their ranks when it added joint custody provisions to its custody law in 1980.

Types of Custody

Before the introduction of joint custody, custody was all or nothing. One parent got it, leaving the other parent with nothing except a custody substitute in the form of visitation (now called parenting time). The 1980 joint custody law redefined custody by dividing it into two parts: legal custody and physical custody. These two elements can be combined in various ways to provide for several types of custody:

Sole custody. Sole custody assigns both legal and physical custody of the children to a custodial parent. Since the custodial parent has physical custody, the children live with him/her. The noncustodial parent ordinarily has periodic parenting time.

As the children's legal custodian, the custodial parent makes all important decisions about the children. Routine decisions are made by the parent in whose care the children are when the routine decision has to be made (usually this is the custodial parent, but it could be the noncustodial parent during a period of parenting time).

Joint legal custody. With this arrangement, one parent has physical custody of the children, but both parents share legal custody. Like sole custody, the children live with the custodial parent (parent with physical custody); the noncustodial parent ordinarily has parenting time.

Because legal custody is joint, both parents must agree about important aspects of the children's health care, education, religion, etc. For example, if a child wanted to transfer from a public to a private school, both parents must consent to the transfer. But if the child needed a routine school permission form signed, the parent taking care of the child at the time could sign the form.

Joint physical custody. When parents have joint physical custody, they share physical and usually legal custody of the children. As joint legal custodians, the parents share decision-making for the children, as described above. And as joint physical custodians, both parents also share physical control of the children. But how can that be accomplished? After all, you can't physically divide the children in two as King Solomon proposed in the Bible story. As it happens, there are several ways for parents to share physical custody of children:

¶ *Split-time custody.* With split-time custody, the children live with each parent for fairly short periods of time. For example, the children might reside with one parent for a week, then move to the other for the next week, and so on. Parents of young children have been known to exchange custody every few days or even every other day.

¶ *Block-time custody.* Block-time custody allows the children to spend large amounts of time with the parents. Typically, block-time custody is scheduled around the children's school year. In this arrangement, the children might reside with one parent for the nine-month school year and with the other parent during the three-month summer vacation.

¶ *"Bird's nest" custody.* Just as birds tend to their young in the nest, the children can stay in the home and the parents take turns moving in and out. Each parent exercises physical custody while living in the home with the children.

Split custody. Split custody divides the children between the parents so that each parent has custody of one or more. You can split sole custody or joint legal custody by assigning physical custody of the children to different parents. In a way, joint physical custody is already split because the parents share custody of the children. But you can split joint physical custody even more by putting the children on different custody schedules, so they don't move together as their physical custody changes.

Mixed custody. Ordinarily, parents get one type of custody for all their children. But it's possible to mix custody so there are different types of custody for the children of a family. For example, one parent might have sole custody of two children and joint physical custody of a third child with the other parent.

Third-party custody. When you divorce, you lose natural custody of your children to the court, which becomes their guardian. Ordinarily, the court gives custody back to you or your spouse. As a matter of fact, Michigan

More Information

About custody for fathers, contact one of these fathers' rights groups:

National Congress for Fathers & Children (NCFC)
9554 Wilshire Blvd.
Suite 907
Beverly Hills, CA 90212
(310) 247-6051
www.ncfc.net.

Dads of Michigan
26677 W. 12 Mile Rd.
Southfield, MI 48034
(248) 559-3237
www.dadsofmichigan.org

Fathers for Equal Rights of America
P.O. Box 2272
Southfield, MI 48037
(248) 354-3080

There are several excellent books about joint custody:

Joint Custody and Co-Parenting, Miriam Galper, Philadelphia: Running Press, 1980

The Disposable Parent, Mel Roman and William Haddad, New York: Holt, Rinehard and Winston, 1978

Sharing Parenthood after Divorce, Ciji Ware, New York: Viking Press, 1982

custody law favors parental custody (see below for more about this so-called parental presumption). Nevertheless, a court can award custody to a third party, instead of parents, when the parents aren't fit to care for the children. Parents can also agree to turn over custody to third parties. Third-party custodians might be relatives, such as grandparents, or even nonrelatives like a foster parent or child welfare agency.

After its debut in 1980, joint custody quickly became established in Michigan. A 1984 survey of Michigan judges found that they were routinely ordering joint legal custody, although many were still skeptical about joint physical custody. Nationally, it's been estimated that joint legal custody is awarded in 81% of cases.

Despite this popularity, joint custody has critics. They complain that joint legal custody gives noncustodial parents mostly symbolic power, but no real parental authority. They also cite studies showing that joint legal custody doesn't seem to improve compliance with parenting time or child support orders.

Joint physical custody poses practical problems. Split-time custody, particularly for short intervals, is disruptive for parents and children alike. Block-time custody is more sensible because it can be scheduled around work and school schedules. Bird's nest custody offers even greater stability for children, although not for parents. Yet all these types of joint physical custody are expensive, as the parents must have separate living accommodations, clothing, toys, etc., for the children.

Split custody is often perceived as unfair or even cruel, because it separates children. For this reason, courts normally frown on split custody of young children. But they may allow it for adolescents, particularly when they have strong custody preferences.

What all this shows is that there is no magic custody formula. Each type has its pluses and minuses. You must be aware of these and choose the type of custody that is best for you.

Court-Ordered Custody

Because all children must have caretakers, a court can make a preliminary custody order during a divorce to settle the custody issue until the end of the divorce (see "Do I Need 'Preliminary Relief'?" on page 59 for more about preliminary custody). With or without a preliminary custody order, the court always makes a final custody order in the Judgment of Divorce at the end of the divorce. This order continues, subject to future modification, until the children reach the age of 18.

When custody is contested during a divorce, the court must decide the issue according to the best interests of the children. The child custody act of 1970 defines children's best interests as the sum of the following factors:

- love, affection and other emotional ties existing between the parties involved and the child
- capacity and disposition of the parties involved to give the child love, affection and guidance, and to continue the education and raising of the child in his or her religion or creed, if any
- capacity and disposition of the parties involved to provide the child with food, clothing, medical care or other remedial care recognized and permitted under the laws of this state in place of medical care, and other material needs
- length of time the child has lived in a stable, satisfactory environment, and the desirability of maintaining continuity
- permanence, as a family unit, of the existing or proposed custodial home or homes
- moral fitness of the parties involved
- mental and physical health of the parties involved
- home, school and community record of the child
- reasonable preference of the child, if the court considers the child to be of sufficient age to express preference
- willingness and ability of each of the parties to facilitate and encourage a close and continuing parent-child relationship between the child and the other parent or the child and the parents
- domestic violence, regardless of whether the violence was directed against or witnessed by the child
- any other factor considered by the court to be relevant to a particular child custody dispute
- when joint custody is also at stake, the judge must also consider an extra factor: whether the parents will be able to cooperate and generally agree concerning important decisions affecting the welfare of the child

Note: In most cases, custody must be withheld from a parent who has committed criminal sexual conduct against any children in the family.

During a custody trial, the judge must address *all* of these best interest factors. The judge must make specific factual findings and reach legal concludions about each factor, even when it doesn't seem to apply.

Besides the best-interest factors, courts deciding custody are guided by two legal presumptions: custodial presumption and parental presumption.

To provide stability for children, the custodial presumption gives current custodians of children preference over noncustodians seeking custody. The presumption applies when children are living in an "estab-

---

Glossary

Legal presumption–a rule of evidence helping a party to prove something, or which makes it more difficult for another party to prove something.

lished custodial environment." According to the custody law, a custodial environment exists when "over an appreciable time the child naturally looks to the custodian in that environment for guidance, discipline, the necessities of life, and parental comfort."

The custodial presumption doesn't always figure in contested divorce cases because usually not enough time has passed to establish a custodial environment. But it may apply when the parents have been separated awhile and one parent alone has cared for the children.

Sometimes, two custodial environments coexist. Michigan courts have ruled that joint physical custody can establish custodial environments with both parents, and each may invoke the custodial presumption. This creates a kind of custody stalemate that is difficult to change.

The parental presumption gives parents a custody edge over non-parents. The parental presumption seldom applies in divorce cases because it's usually the parents who are vying for custody. Nevertheless, third parties can sometimes intervene in divorces and seek custody. And in some divorce cases, the custody of children may already be in the hands of third parties, such as relatives, foster parents or child welfare agencies. In these situations, parents can invoke the parental presumption to get custody away from third-party custodians, or fend off custody claims of intervening third parties.

Even when these custody presumptions apply, contesting custody is still painful and messy. To begin with, a custody battle is expensive. Lawyer fees for each spouse may be $5,000 or more. Added to this is the cost of having child psychologists or other expert witnesses testify during the custody hearing. What with lawyers, expert witnesses and other fees, a custody fight can cost many thousands of dollars.

Fighting over custody can also take a huge emotional toll. As explained in Part I, when Michigan's no-fault divorce law was adopted, fault was removed from the grounds for divorce, but left intact for all the other divorce issues. In custody law, fault appears in the guise of the "moral fitness of the parties." This leaves the door open for evidence of many kinds of marital misconduct.

As bad as a custody fight is for parents, it can be even worse for children. Contesting custody pits parent against parent, and can be extremely upsetting for children. The custody law also requires most children to declare their parental preference, forcing them to make a painful choice about which parent they like best.

A custody fight can also jeopardize joint custody. When joint custody is at stake, the court must consider the 13th custody factor of parental cooperation. Rightly or wrongly, some courts believe a custody battle shows a lack of parental cooperation, ruling out joint custody. As a result, custody contests often become winner-take-all, with the victors getting sole custody as the prize.

Uncontested Custody

If you and your spouse agree on custody, the court should approve your custodial arrangement. If you've chosen some form of joint custody, your agreement will carry even greater weight, because the custody law says that there is a presumption in favor of joint custody when both spouses have agreed to it. The forms in this book have provisions for sole custody, several forms of joint custody, split, mixed and third-party custody (see "Custody Provisions" in Appendix H for more about these custody choices and how to provide for them).

Whatever you and your spouse agree to, keep in mind that the court always has the final say on custody. In an uncontested divorce, you have a lot of room to bargain over property division and alimony. But the court keeps more control over the divorce issues directly affecting the welfare of minor children: custody, parenting time and child support. Therefore, the court has the right to reject your custody agreement when it isn't in your children's best interests.

Parenting Time

Until 1996, when the terminology changed, parenting time was known as visitation (some older divorce forms may still use this name). Whichever name it goes by, parenting time gives the children access to the noncustodial parent so the parent-child relationship can continue after the divorce. Parenting time is actually a right possessed by children. This fact often gets lost when parents fight over it, trying to assert their parenting time "rights."

Ordinarily, parenting time is given to noncustodial parents whenever sole custody or joint legal custody is ordered. But parenting time might be necessary for custodial parents in some long-term joint physical custody arrangements. For example, parents with split- or block-time custody where custody is exchanged infrequently might need parenting time. On the other hand, frequent split-time or bird's nest custody probably doesn't require parenting time.

Courts can order parenting time during a divorce as a form of preliminary relief, settling the issue until the end of the divorce (see "Do I Need 'Preliminary Relief'?" on page 59 for more about preliminary parenting time orders). At the end of the divorce, the court will make a final parenting time order in the Judgment of Divorce. This order will continue, subject to future modification, until the children reach the age of 18.

Types of Parenting Time

Many states have just one kind of parenting time: specific parenting time. In Michigan, you can choose from several types of parenting time:

Reasonable parenting time. Reasonable parenting time is a flexible arrangement allowing parents to schedule parenting time as they please, at times and on terms that are convenient for them.

Specific parenting time. Specific parenting time fixes parenting time according to specific times, terms and conditions.

Supervised parenting time. If a parent is irresponsible, the parenting time can be supervised by a responsible third party, such as a grandparent.

Long-distance parenting time. When face-to-face contact is too risky (for an irresponsible parent) or impossible (for a faraway parent), courts are allowing long-distance parenting time by telephone, video-conferencing or the Internet.

Court-Ordered Parenting Time

When one parent contests whether the children should have parenting time with the other parent, the court must decide the issue during a trial or hearing. Since parenting time is really a right of children, it's provided to them according to their best interests. That's determined by the same 12-factor test used to decide custody cases (see above for the full list).

Michigan law presumes that parenting time is in the best interests of children, and can only be taken away from them when parenting time endangers their mental, emotional or physical health. Judges also favor parenting time and are reluctant to withhold it. Even when a noncustodial parent is irresponsible, a court will often order supervised or long-distance parenting time, rather than deny it completely.

Thanks to this preference for parenting time, contesting *whether* parenting time should be ordered is unusual. Instead, most parenting time battles are fought over the type, frequency or duration of parenting time. In these disputes, the parenting time law says that the court may consider the following factors in making a parenting time order:

- existence of any special circumstances or needs of the child
- whether the child is a nursing child less than six months of age, or less than one year of age if the child receives substantial nutrition through nursing
- reasonable likelihood of abuse or neglect of the child during parenting time
- reasonable likelihood of abuse of a parent resulting from the exercise of parenting time
- inconvenience to, and burdensome impact or effect on, the child traveling to and from the parenting time
- whether the noncustodial parent can reasonably be expected to exercise parenting time in accordance with the court order
- threatened or actual detention of the child with the intent to retain or conceal the child from the other parent or from a third person who has legal custody. A custodial parent's temporary residence with the child in a domestic violence shelter may not be construed as evidence of the custodial parent's intent to retain or conceal the child from the other parent
- any other relevant factors

Michigan law says that a court must order specific parenting time when a party asks for it. Even without such a request, courts often order specific parenting time in contested cases. Reasonable parenting time demands a good deal of give-and-take, making reasonable parenting time unsuitable for feuding parents.

Uncontested Parenting Time

If you and your spouse agree on parenting time, the court will almost always approve your arrangement. In fact, the parenting time law says that parental agreements about parenting time carry great weight. The forms in this book have provisions for both reasonable and specific parenting time (see "Parenting Time Provisions" in Appendix H for suggestions about specific parenting time choices). But like other divorce issues affecting child welfare, courts get the final word on parenting time, and they can reject your parenting time agreement when it isn't in your children's best interests.

Residence of Children

The residence (also known as domicile) of minor children used to be a minor issue during divorce. Divorce judgments did bar custodial parents from moving children out of state. But otherwise, divorced parents were free to move around the state with their children as they pleased.

This freedom of movement worked all right in an era when sole custody was the norm. But as joint custody became more common, it was difficult to reconcile freedom of movement with joint custody rights. Imagine a parent moving with children from Detroit to Copper Harbor in the Upper Peninsula (a distance of over 600 miles), and the effect this move would have on the other parent's joint custody or parenting time back in Detroit.

As a result, in 2001 Michigan adopted a new law governing children's residence. The law tries to harmonize—not always successfully—parents' rights of movement and custody and parenting time arrangements for children.

Establishing Residences of Children

The 2001 law establishes local residences of minor children during divorce. These residences are created when the case is filed. A divorce-filing actually creates two local residences of the children: one with each parent, at the parental homes (the Summons and Complaint (MC 01) will list these addresses). Twin residences exist even if one parent ends up with most, or all, custody later. At this point, residence is a totally separate issue from custody, and is fixed without regard to custody.

Ultimately, your divorce judgment will re-affirm the children's residences established during divorce (the original or newer ones). Like a custody or parenting time order, a divorce judgment's residence order covers the minor children until they reach the age of 18, and then expires for each of them. On its face, the residence order applies to the children only. But it also applies indirectly to the parents, since the parents mustn't move the children's residences, which are also their own.

All this may sound rather restrictive and confining. But in fact, parents have a great deal more freedom to move, thanks to an elaborate system of exclusions and exceptions under the 2001 law.

Exclusions

Some kinds of intrastate moves are excluded outright from the 2001 law. Parents covered by these exclusions are free to move around the state without prior court approval. These moveaways are excluded from the residence law:

- move anywhere in Michigan by a custodial parent after receiving sole custody (sole legal and sole physical custody)*
- move by a parent in Michigan when the other parent consents to the move
- move in Michigan caused by a flight from domestic violence

Exceptions

Besides excluded moves, other moves are excepted from the residence law. Moveaways covered by these exceptions are based on distance, so you must know the children's two current local residences (see above for more about these). It's also helpful to have a good map of Michigan (such as a road map or atlas) and an inexpensive compass, like the ones geometry students use. Like excluded moves, these moves are exempted from the 2001 residence law and may take place without court review:

- move by a parent anywhere in Michigan if the children's local residences are more than 100 miles apart

On your map, you can use the scale to measure the distance in miles from the children's two residences. If these residences are more than 100 miles apart, you can move anywhere in Michigan.

- move by a parent inside his/her own 100-mile local residence zone in Michigan

---

*   Curiously, the 2001 law only mentions sole legal custody. But since sole legal custody is incompatible with any kind of joint custody, this limits the exclusion to sole custody cases; and by implication, this exclusion also makes the 2001 law apply to joint custody cases only.

This exception can be a little difficult to judge. On your map, find the local residence of the relocating parent. Using the map scale, measure a 100 miles on the compass and lock it. Put the pointed end on the residence and draw a 100-mile circle around this point. A move within this circle or zone is permissible under this exception.

> *Example*: A wife files for divorce in Lansing against her husband living in Mt. Pleasant. Dual residences for the children exist in both cities. Thanks to this exception, the wife could move inside a zone of 100 miles radius around Lansing (or the husband, if he wished to move, could move within a 100-mile zone around Mt. Pleasant).

• move in Michigan if the move actually brings the local residences closer together; a move creating more distance is barred

This is exception is even harder to visualize. Using a map and compass, place the two ends (pointed and pencil) of the compass on each parent's residence, and lock the compass. Then, put the pointed end on the stay-be-hind parent's residence and draw a pencil circle around this residence. This is the area in which the relocating parent can move under this exception.

> *Example*: A wife files for divorce in Lansing against her husband in Clare. The distance between these two local residences is 80 miles. The wife could move into a zone 80 miles around Clare, because this move wouldn't create more distance than existed before. Similarly, the husband could move into an 80-mile zone around Lansing.

Limits on Exclusions and Exceptions

Before the 2001 residence law was adopted, Michigan had a court rule preventing a custodial parent from moving out of state with the children, except with court approval. This approval was required so courts wouldn't lose control of the children, making it more difficult to enforce the custody-related provisions of divorce judgments.

It's not entirely clear how the 2001 law and the old court rule mesh. But it seems that they fit together in such a way that custodial parents who wish to move with children out of state must *always* obtain court permission, even when the move would normally be excluded or excepted under the 2001 law.

> *Example*: A couple divorces in Menominee, Michigan, and the mother gets sole custody of the children. She wants to move a few miles across the river to adjacent Marinette, Wisconsin.

Ordinarily, an exclusion (sole custody exclusion) and an exception (moving within one's 100-mile local residence zone) would exempt this move from court review. But because it's across state lines, prior court permission is necessary for the move.

Court-Ordered Change of Residence

When a parent wants to change the children's residence, and none of the exclusions or exceptions applies, s/he must file a change-of-residence motion. The motion must be filed before the move takes place; you can't move first and seek approval later.* At the hearing on the motion, the court must consider the following factors:

- whether the legal residence change has the capacity to improve the quality of life for both the child and the relocating parent
- the degree to which each parent has complied with, and utilized his or her time under, a court order governing parenting time with the child, and whether the parent's plan to change the child's legal residence is inspired by that parent's desire to defeat or frustrate the parenting time schedule
- the degree to which the court is satisfied that, if the court permits the legal residence change, it is possible to order a modification of the parenting time schedule and other arrangements governing the child's schedule in a manner that can provide an adequate basis for preserving and fostering the parental relationship between the child and each parent; and whether each parent is likely to comply with the modification
- the extent to which the parent opposing the legal residence change is motivated by a desire to secure a financial advantage with respect to a support obligation
- domestic violence, regardless of whether the violence was directed against or witnessed by the child

When parents want to take children not just out of state but outside the country, extra factors must be considered. For international moves, courts look at international relations between the U.S and the destination foreign county, cultural factors, the severe impact the move will likely have on joint custody and parenting time and the enforceability of custody orders in the foreign county.

Whether the move is intrastate, interstate or even overseas, courts frequently allow changes of residence for children. After all, parents often have good reasons for moving—to remarry, take a new job, return to school to acquire new job skills—and courts don't want to stand in the way of these opportunities.

---

*   There is an exception to this rule when the relocating spouse is fleeing the threat of domestic violence. In that case, the spouse can move while the motion is pending.

Uncontested Change of Residence

You may want to move the residence of children around the time of the divorce. The moveaway may be permissible without the approval of the defendant and the court, or you may need the consent of both to move.

The timing of your move is important. If you want to move early in the divorce, consider moving before you file the case. Remember, the residence of children is established at divorce-filing. So if you move to where you want to go beforehand, you won't have to deal with the issue during the divorce.*

After divorce-filing, when children's residences are established, a local residence can be changed if covered by one of the exclusions and exceptions. One exclusion allows a change of residence with the consent of a defendant-joint custodian. The trouble is, you need a special change-of-residence order for a pending-divorce moveaway. The defendant must also consent to the order which is legally awkward if s/he has defaulted and is out of the case. As a result, the forms in this book don't provide for a pending-divorce move with the consent of the defendant. In addition, out-of-state moves during this time are discouraged since courts want children nearby while the case is pending.

You have more flexibility at the end of the divorce. Sometimes, parents want to finish their divorce and then move, perhaps even out of state. Once again, an intrastate end-of-divorce move may be permissible without court review if covered by one of the exclusions or exceptions. One intrastate move exclusion is based on the defendant's consent, which must be recorded with the court. The defendant could also agree to the custodial parent's moving out of state, and this also requires court review and approval. To obtain the defendant's consent, and get court approval when necessary, see "Change of Children's Residence Provisions" in Appendix H.

Child Support

No divorce issue is more controversial than child support. Child support recipients—women usually—and child support payers—ordinarily men—have organized into two opposing camps, and each feels victimized by the present system of child support.

Child support recipients have been faced with massive nonpayment of support. According to federal figures, in more than a half of child support cases nationally no child support is paid at all (other studies put this percentage even higher). And according to recent figures, Michigan child support recipients are owed a staggering $7 billion in overdue support.

What makes this payment record even more dismal is that it comes after decades of child support reform. For years, states were notoriously lax in collecting child support. Soaring welfare costs in the 1970s signaled that

---

*   This kind of maneuver may not possible if your residence has already been established by a prior family law case, such as a family support or paternity case.

More Information

About Michigan child support, ask for the booklet "Michigan Child Support Services and You!" from:

State Court Administrative Office
P.O. Box 30048
Lansing, MI 48909

The *Michigan Child Support Formula Manual* is included as part of Appendix H in this book.

About child support enforcement, contact:

Association for Children for Enforcement of Support (ACES)
2260 Upton Ave.
Toledo, OH 43606
(800) 738-2237
www.childsupport-aces.org

Contact the fathers' rights groups cited on page 12 for information about fathers and child support.

many payers were avoiding their child support obligations. In 1975, the federal government passed new laws encouraging states to enforce child support orders.

In 1985, yet another federal law was enacted to strengthen child support enforcement. The new law also expanded the definition of child support to include more than just payments for food, clothing and shelter. According to the new law, child support may include payment of the costs of children's medical, dental and other health care, as well as child care and educational expenses.

In spite of these efforts, child support payment is still spotty. Believe it or not, Michigan has a better-than-average enforcement system, with a "collection rate" (where at least one payment is received) of 60% in 2001. But that only looks good compared to the 44% national average.

Child support payers also have an ax to grind. One of their chief complaints has been that child support orders are unpredictable, varying almost at the whim of judges. Some studies agree. One in Denver found that the amount of child support depended on the skill of one's lawyer, the judge in the case and even the season of the year! In Michigan, state officials surveyed child support in the mid-1980s by sending two fictional child support cases to 69 Michigan counties, asking them to figure child support. To their shock, the surveyors got back almost as many different answers as they sent questionnaires.

The Michigan survey revealed that many counties figured child support as a flat percentage of the payer's income. Typically, 20% was charged for one child, 30% for two children and 40% for three or more. Other counties used a modified flat-rate method, while a few counties seemed to have no method at all.

Not only did those customary methods of figuring child support produce variable orders, they were actually contrary to Michigan law. The law says that child support must be based on three primary factors: 1) the noncustodial parent's income 2) the custodial parent's income 3) the needs of the children. The customary methods for figuring child support failed to account for all these factors. The flat-rate method, for example, considered the noncustodial parent's income only and ignored the resources of the custodial parent. And none of the customary methods took the needs of the children into account.

Child Support Formula

What this suggested was that Michigan needed a uniform child support formula, based on the three child support factors. A few Michigan counties had had these formulas for years. Nevertheless, many judges opposed any child support formulas or guidelines because they wished to preserve their right to set child support on a case-by-case basis.

Like it or not, Michigan was forced to adopt a uniform child support formula by the 1985 federal child support law. This law required states to adopt such guidelines by October 1, 1987, or risk losing valuable federal aid. Michigan dutifully complied and put its child support formula into effect in May 1987.

The child support formula assumes that the needs of children can be fixed as a percentage of a family's total income, which varies with the amount of family income and the number and ages of the children. According to the formula, these needs must be shared by the parents in proportion to their income. The child support recipient pays his/her share by direct spending on the children, while the payer-parent contributes in the form of child support. By using this method of figuring child support, the formula employs all three child support factors, as required by law.

At first, the Michigan child support formula was merely an optional guideline which judges could follow as they wished. But in 1991, the formula became mandatory, with a few exceptions. Now, all Michigan child support is supposed to be set by the formula.

Adjusting the Formula

Not every case fits neatly within the Michigan child support formula and its schedules. The authors of the formula anticipated many of these exceptional cases and provided for adjustments to the schedules.

When parents have no or low income, the formula adjusts so their modest income isn't consumed by child support. Conversely, an adjustment is made for high-income payers, capping child support at certain maximums.

There are also adjustments for parents with joint physical, split or mixed custody, and extended parenting time. In these special cases, the parents are providing considerable direct support when the children are living with them, justifying adjustment of their child support obligations.

Adjustments are also available for health care, child care and educational expenses. Extra amounts for these costs can be tacked onto the base child support amounts. These adjustments are explained in "Adjusting the Child Support Schedules" on page 245 in Appendix H.

Departing from the Formula

If simple adjustment isn't enough, it's possible to depart from the Michigan child support formula and set child support at a non-formula amount. You can depart by agreement with the defendant, or upon your request alone. Either way, you must have a good reason for departure and the court must approve. For more about departure, see "Departing from the Child Support Formula" on page 247 in Appendix H.

Payment of Child Support

Method of Payment

In 1991, Michigan also adopted a new method of collecting child support. Previously, child support was typically paid under the honor system, with payers voluntarily making support payments to the friend of the court. Only when payers got behind was an income withholding order issued directing their source of income (usually employers) to withhold money and pay it to the friend of the court.

As child support debts began piling up, it became apparent that the honor system of payment wasn't working. In 1991, this system was replaced by immediate income withholding. Under the new method, income withholding normally starts when a child support order goes into effect. At that time, the friend of the court contacts the payer's employer or other source of income and sets up withholding.

Immediate income withholding is designed for the bulk of cases. Courts and child support recipients prefer this method of payment because it's reliable. On the other hand, some child support payers dislike the payment method since it means extra paperwork for their employers.

In some cases, you can drop immediate income withholding and choose another method of payment. You can do this by opting out of the friend of the court system, either totally, partially or in a limited way. See Appendix C for more about the types of opt-outs and whether you qualify.

After opting out of immediate income withholding, the new method of payment continues as long the payer makes regular payments. But if the payer falls behind by a month's worth of payments, the friend of the court must act to put immediate income withholding back in effect. The friend of the court will schedule a hearing on the payment issue, and the court will decide which method of payment should be used.

Form and Frequency of Payment

Whichever method of payment is in force, child support usually takes the form of periodic cash payments. Until recently, child support was typically paid weekly. Since late 2002, child support must be computed and paid by the month.

Child support is normally paid through the friend of the court system to the state disbursement unit (SDU). In some cases, it's possible, with court permission, to opt out of this system, such as when immediate income withholding is avoided. Appendix C has more about opt-outs.

When child support recipients are getting Family Independence Program (FIP) payments (formerly AFDC), they must assign their child support to the state. After assignment, the child support is transferred to the Michigan Family Independence Agency (FIA) (formerly the Department of Social Services (DSS)), instead of the recipient, to offset the cost of the FIPs.

Duration of Child Support

When a divorce with minor children is filed, the court can order child support during the divorce as a form of preliminary relief (see "Do I Need 'Preliminary Relief'?" on page 59 for more about preliminary child support). With or without a preliminary child support order, the court normally orders final child support in the Judgment of Divorce at the end of the divorce.

The divorce judgment makes child support payable until the children are 18* or 19½ as long as they are 1) regularly attending high school on a full-time basis with a reasonable expectation of completing sufficient credits to graduate from high school 2) residing on a full-time basis with the recipient of the support or at an institution.

Michigan used to stop child support when children turned 18, even if they were still attending high school. But in 1990 the child support law was amended, and over-18 children became entitled to child support while attending high school as described above. What's more, child support payers can *voluntarily* agree to pay support for even longer periods. For example, they might agree to provide child support while their children attend college.

Cancellation of Child Support

One of the worst things about the old child support collection system was cancellation of unpaid child support. When delinquent payers were brought into court, judges often allowed them to pay just a percentage of the debt, canceling the rest.

This kind of cancellation, or retroactive modification, of child support is now forbidden by law. These days, each child support payment becomes a separate judgment when due, and cannot normally be modified or canceled.** Child support payers can ask for modification of their child support obligations, but this is possible only for future payments, effective the day the modification motion is served on the child support recipient.

Centralization of Child Support Services

For years, county friends of the court were the primary collectors and distributors of support (both child support and alimony). Today, a new state agency in Lansing, the state disbursement unit (SDU), has taken over these duties.

Under the new centralized system, support payers (employers deducting support under immediate income withholding or payers paying support themselves) will send all payments to the SDU. The SDU is supposed to distribute these payments to support recipients across the state within two days after arrival in Lansing.

The aim of the SDU is quicker payment, more accurate record-keeping and ultimately better enforcement. Right now, most enforcement stays with

---

*   Sometimes child support can end before age 18 if the minor child becomes emancipated by: 1) marriage 2) enlistment in the military 3) court order.

** There are two small exceptions to this rule: 1) a court-approved retroactive modification agreement between the parties 2) retroactive modification of a child support debt when one party hid income.

local friends of the court, but some enforcement responsibility is being transferred to the state.

Health Care, Child Care and Educational Expenses

In recent years, the concept of child support has been expanded to pay for more than the basic needs of children (food, clothing and shelter). Today, child support also covers children's health care, child care and educational expenses.

With its ever-increasing cost, health care is naturally the greatest concern. Court orders like divorce judgments require parents to continue health plan coverage reasonably available to them. Parents must also share uninsured health care expenses. See "Health Care" on page 249 in Appendix H for more about children's health care and suggestions for parents without access to coverage.

Similarly, parents can be ordered to pick up the cost of child care and educational expenses of their children. The Michigan child support formula provides for the addition of a child care supplement to the base child support amount. Educational expenses can be assigned to one or both parents. For more about these topics, see "Adding to Base Child Support" on page 244.

Court-Ordered Child Support

Child support can be ordered during a divorce, as a form of preliminary relief (see "Do I Need 'Preliminary Relief'?" on page 59 for more about preliminary child support), and/or at the end of the divorce in the judgment of divorce. Either way, the order will make the support payable until each child is 18 or 19½ if still attending high school.

When child support is contested, the court must set the support according to the Michigan child support formula, unless it's "unjust or inappropriate" to do so. In that exceptional case, the court can depart from the formula and order a different amount of child support. With the parents battling over child support, the court will almost certainly order payment by immediate income withholding.

Uncontested Child Support

Ordinarily, you use the Michigan child support formula to figure your child support. "Child Support Provisions" in Appendix H has information about setting support under the formula. But in exceptional cases, you and the defendant can agree to set child support outside the formula. See "Departing from the Child Support Formula" on page 247 for when and how to do this.

Your child support will probably be paid by immediate income withholding, since this is now the normal method of payment. Nevertheless, sometimes it's permissible to avoid immediate income withholding and choose another payment method. As Appendix C explains, you can do this by opting out of the friend of the court system totally, partially or in a limited way.

By law, child support must continue until each child is 18 or 19½ if still attending high school. Child support payers can voluntarily pay support even longer, such as while a child attends college. But this takes a special agreement between the parents, which is difficult to prepare. If you want to provide for long-term child support, contact a lawyer for help.

Property Division

Years ago, divorce property division was little more than divvying up pots, pans and clothing. But today a lot more may be at stake. *Forbes* magazine recently listed the women receiving the largest divorce property divisions. Topping the list were Anne Bass, ex-wife of real estate magnate Sid Bass ($200 million), Frances Lear, who divorced Norman Lear, producer of *All in the Family* and *Maude*, ($112 million), and actress Amy Irving, ex-wife of filmmaker Steven Spielberg ($100 million).

What all these divorces have in common is that they happened in either Texas or California, which are community property states. In these states, marriage is considered an equal financial partnership, so most property acquired during a marriage belongs to the spouses equally, regardless of which spouse earned or owned it. And when a marriage ends—by death or divorce—each spouse gets one-half of the marital property.

Only nine states, mostly in the South and West, have community property. The rest, including Michigan, have a different system of property ownership and division. At one time, Michigan divided property during divorce strictly according to ownership: Each spouse got whatever they owned. This system was simple and neat, but it discriminated against wives because husbands usually owned most property.

Accused of unfairness, Michigan adopted an equitable distribution system of property division in divorce cases. Like community property law, equitable distribution recognizes that marriage is a financial partnership, giving each spouse a share of the property regardless of ownership.

Despite that similarity, community property and equitable distribution divide property very differently. Spouses always get equal shares of community property. In equitable distribution, the shares can be equal or unequal. All the law asks is that the division be "just and reasonable" or "equitable" under the circumstances.

The flexibility of equitable distribution shows up in court decisions. For example, in Michigan divorces wives have gotten as much as 90% or as little as 10% of the property. Under equitable distribution, such lopsided divisions are permissible if justified by the facts of the case. Nevertheless, these are exceptional cases. In the vast majority of divorces, a 50-50 split, or something close to it, is the equitable division.

Court-Ordered Property Division

When spouses wrangle over property, the court must divide it for them during a trial. According to equitable distribution, the division must be "just and reasonable" or "equitable." But since these general principles don't give enough guidance, courts have developed nine specific factors for property division:

- duration of the marriage
- contribution of the parties to the marital estate
- age of the parties
- health of the parties
- life status of the parties
- necessities and circumstances of the parties
- earning abilities of the parties
- past relations and conduct of the parties
- general principles of equity

In many states, property divisions are based solely on economic factors. If fault is taken into account, it's only to the extent that fault has had an impact on the property. For example, California ignores fault in property divisions except when one spouse has squandered the community property. In that case of "economic fault," the other spouse gets a greater share of the property.

Most of Michigan's property division factors are also economic. But fault creeps into divorce when the property division is contested through the "past relations and conduct of the parties" factor. And in Michigan, this fault isn't confined to misuse of property. It can include almost any type of marital misconduct, no matter how embarrassing or lurid.

Since equitable distribution is designed to be flexible, courts can weigh the property division factors much as they wish. They can focus on the important factors in the case, while disregarding others that don't apply. Courts may also consider other things through the catch-all "general principles of equity" factor.

Courts can avoid all that if the parties have a prenuptial agreement, since the agreement will normally control the division of property. Prenuptial agreements (also called antenuptial agreements or marital contracts) are contracts between spouses-to-be spelling out how property shall be divided when the marriage ends by death or divorce.

Michigan courts weren't always willing to use prenuptial agreements during divorce. For years, they refused to enforce these agreements believing that they encouraged divorce. But in 1991, the Michigan Court of Appeals reversed that rule and decided that prenuptial agreements are enforceable when: 1) the agreement was fairly entered into before the marriage 2) the agreement itself was fair at the time it was signed 3) facts and circumstances haven't changed enough since the agreement was signed that would make it unfair to enforce the agreement.

Uncontested Property Division

Before you and your spouse agree on a property division, you must know the extent and value of your property. "Can I Get a Fair Property Division?"

on page 53 has important information about that. It tells which property is divisible in a divorce, and how to value it.

After you agree on a property division, the court should approve it because you have more control over property division than other divorce issues. If you happen to have a prenuptial agreement dealing with divorce, you should be able to use it to divide your property, unless the agreement is "unfair" (see above for the fairness requirements for prenuptial agreements). Whatever you decide about property division, see "Property Division Provisions" in Appendix H for information about providing for and carrying out the division.

Alimony

From the start, American courts awarded support in the form of alimony to wives. In 1641, just two years after the first American divorce, Massachusetts Bay Colony passed a law giving wives a right to alimony.

During this era, courts regarded alimony as wife-support, and husbands never got it. But in the 1960s, states revised their alimony laws to make it payable to either men or women. Michigan amended its alimony law in 1970 to permit alimony for men.

Since then, there have been some well-publicized cases of women paying alimony to men. Actresses Jane Seymour and Roseanne Barr reportedly paid their former husbands alimony. And even among the less famous, men are receiving alimony more often as women achieve financial parity with men. But typically, men are the alimony payers and women are the recipients.

Despite all the attention it gets, alimony has never been very common. At the beginning of this century, alimony was awarded in a scant 9.3% of divorces. Although exact figures are hard to come by, that percentage seems to have increased during the next 50 years. One study of California divorces in 1968 found that wives received alimony in 20% of divorces. But by 1975, only 14% of divorce cases included alimony.

As the number of alimony orders declined, the duration of alimony also shrank. Years ago, alimony was usually an open-ended award which continued indefinitely until the wife remarried or died. Nowadays, alimony is likely to be for a limited time—maybe a year or two—to help the recipient get back on his/her feet after divorce. This kind of short-term alimony is sometimes referred to as rehabilitative or transitional alimony.

In Michigan, alimony can be paid during a divorce or afterward. Alimony during a divorce is available as preliminary relief, but only through a temporary order issued after a motion and hearing. See "Do I Need 'Preliminary Relief'?" on page 59 for more about preliminary alimony.

Whether or not preliminary alimony has been ordered, alimony can be granted in the Judgment of Divorce at the end of the divorce. In most cases, alimony takes the form of cash payments payable periodically (weekly, monthly, etc.). These payments won't last forever because judgments usually make alimony subject to conditions ending it. These conditions are negotiable, but most judgments contain several of the following:

Death. Alimony is almost always terminated when the recipient dies (as explained below, there are sound tax reasons for making such a provision). Alimony doesn't automatically end when the payer dies, and it can survive and become a debt of his/her estate. Nevertheless, judgments often terminate alimony when payers die.

Remarriage. Alimony often ends when the recipient remarries, but seldom ends if the payer remarries.

Cohabitation. To prevent recipients from choosing cohabitation over remarriage as a way to keep alimony, the alimony may end if the recipient cohabitates with a member of the opposite sex.

Date. Alimony may end on a specific date.

Modification. In Michigan, true alimony has customarily been open to modification when there has been a change in the parties' circumstances. A modification could result in an increase, decrease or even termination of the alimony.

Michigan law does allow divorce parties to designate alimony as non-modifiable. However, this has to be done carefully in a negotiated divorce settlement; you can't do it in an uncontested divorce without input from the defendant. Thus, all alimony described in this book remains modifiable.

Types of Alimony

Alimony is a slippery word because Michigan divorce law, federal tax law and federal bankruptcy law all define alimony differently. Adding to complications, Michigan court rules use the phrase "spousal support" instead of alimony. Because of this, the forms in this book also use spousal support to mean alimony, although the text will continue to use the familiar term alimony.

Michigan divorce law regards as alimony any divorce-related payments of money or other property from one (ex)spouse to the other for purposes of support. As explained before, alimony usually takes the form of cash payments paid periodically (weekly, monthly, etc.). There is another kind of so-called alimony, alimony-in-gross, which is often paid in several lump-sum payments. Despite its name, alimony-in-gross is really division of a liquid asset: money. Thus, alimony-in-gross is really property division and not true alimony.

Federal law has its own rules for defining alimony. The federal tax law generally disregards what parties call their payments. Instead, it considers support payments as alimony if they are:

- paid in cash (including checks or money orders)
- made to a spouse or to someone on his/her behalf
- made in a divorce document (such as a divorce order or judgment)

- made when the spouses are living apart (subject to several exceptions, including payment of temporary alimony)
- end on the death of the recipient-spouse
- not provided as child support
- not designated as something other than alimony

These tax rules are important because payments that qualify as alimony get special tax treatment. The payments are deductible by the payer and counted as income for the recipient.

Federal bankruptcy law has yet another definition of alimony. According to bankruptcy law, support payments qualify as alimony if they are: 1) intended by the parties as alimony 2) actually used for support 3) a reasonable amount of support. When payments are treated as alimony under bankruptcy law, they're protected from elimination or discharge during bankruptcy of the payer. If the payments don't qualify as alimony, the payer can sometimes discharge them in bankruptcy.

Payment of Alimony

Like child support, alimony is normally paid by immediate income withholding to the state disbursement unit (SDU). But it's possible to set up other payment methods, and have alimony paid to the SDU without immediate income withholding or directly to the payee. See "Choosing an Alimony Payment Method" in Appendix H for more about these other payment options.

Court-Ordered Alimony

When spouses contest the issue of alimony, the court must decide the issue in a trial. To determine whether alimony is payable, the court considers the following factors:

- length of the marriage
- ability of the parties to work
- source of and amount of property awarded to the parties
- age of the parties
- ability of the parties to pay alimony
- present situation of the parties
- needs of the parties
- health of the parties
- prior standard of living of the parties and whether either is responsible for the support of others
- past relations and conduct of the parties
- general principles of equity

Like property division, the procedure for deciding alimony is flexible, so a court may apply these factors as it chooses. It can weigh the factors unequally, disregard ones that don't apply or add others that seem important through the catch-all "general principles of equity" factor.

Most of the alimony factors are economic. This makes sense because what alimony is really about is the need of one spouse for support and the ability of the other to pay it. But fault can creep in through the "past relations and conduct of the parties" factor. As with property division, fault in contested alimony cases may include almost any evidence of marital misconduct.

After a court decides that alimony is due, it must then determine the amount. In Michigan, there are no uniform alimony guidelines as there are for child support. So most judges set alimony on a case-by-case basis using the following factors:

- length of the marriage
- contributions of the parties to the joint estate
- age and health of the parties
- parties' stations in life
- necessities of the parties
- earning ability of the parties

In 1983, Washtenaw County rejected the case-by-case approach and adopted an alimony formula. It judges the strength of an alimony claim (length of the marriage, age, income and job skills are the most important factors), adjusts the claim for other factors and then provides for a mathematical computation of alimony. Recently, other counties have begun using Washtenaw's alimony formula or adaptations of it. This suggests a need for a uniform state-wide alimony formula, which may be developed in the future.

Uncontested Alimony

Since alimony isn't ordered in most divorces, divorce judgments usually waive (surrender) alimony. Sometimes it's possible to reserve alimony, allowing you to ask for it after the divorce. Or you and your spouse can agree to have alimony granted by including an alimony order in your divorce judgment.

"Alimony Provisions" in Appendix H has more information about all those methods of dealing with alimony. It also includes two basic alimony orders for short- and long-term alimony, which you can adapt to your situation.

Other Divorce Issues

Ending the marriage, custody, parenting time, residence of children, child support, property division, and alimony aren't the only divorce issues. But any other divorce issues are relatively minor and seldom contested.

Name Change

Name change for women and minor children is another minor divorce issue. After a divorce, women often want to drop their married names and resume maiden or former names. For them, Michigan law offers two name change methods: 1) common law name change by usage 2) court-ordered name change from: (a) the court when the divorce is granted (b) a separate name change case later.

The usage method is the easiest because all you do is choose a new name and begin using it regularly. No court order is necessary. The name change is legal as long as you're not adopting a new name for a fraudulent or improper purpose.

The trouble with the usage method is that it's no longer very effective. These days, with the general anxiety about security and special concern about identity theft, authorities want official proof of name changes; informal name changes aren't acceptable any more. As a result, most women choose formal court-ordered name changes.

It's easy for a woman to change her name during divorce. When the divorce is final, the court can allow the wife, whether she is plaintiff or defendant, to adopt a different surname (last name). She may resume a maiden or former married name, or choose any other surname. The only restriction is that the name change mustn't be sought with "any fraudulent or evil intent" (to avoid past debts, hide from law enforcement officers, etc.). The divorce papers in this book have provisions for women to ask for name changes (in the divorce complaint) and receive name changes (in the divorce judgment).

Some women who ultimately want to change their names aren't ready for name changes during divorce. They may want to keep their married names so they match the names of their young children. Then later, when the children are older, they may be ready to change their names.

Women seeking name changes postdivorce must file separate name change cases. Before filing, they must satisfy a one-year county residency requirement. They must be fingerprinted by the police and submit to a criminal background check. After publishing a legal notice in the newspaper, they must attend a court hearing to get the name change.

Needless to say, this procedure takes much more effort than a divorce name change. That's why most women, if they have a choice, choose a name change during divorce.

Michigan name change law doesn't say that children can change their names during divorce. Nevertheless, some courts have allowed name changes for minor children during divorce. If the parents disagree about the child's name change, the issue is decided by the court according to the same best interests test used in custody and parenting time disputes.

Name change at divorce is seldom an issue for men, because men don't customarily change their names at marriage. However, today some men add their wives' surnames to their own, by hyphenation, at marriage, and may then want to drop the addition at divorce.

Michigan divorce law isn't very helpful for men in this predicament. The law has no provision for male name changes during divorce. To change their names at divorce, men must do it by custom and usage under the common law method, of file a separate name change case, outside of divorce, to get a formal a court-ordered name change.

Dependency Exemptions

When parents do their income taxes, they can claim extra exemptions for dependent children. These exemptions are valuable because they act like deductions and reduce income tax.

After a divorce, the custodial parent is entitled to the dependency exemptions for the children. However, these exemptions can be assigned to the noncustodial parent by the agreement of the parties or by the court if they contest the issue. Either way, the divorce judgment must make the assignment. "Assigning Dependency Exemptions" in Appendix H has more about assignment and sample assignment provisions.

PART III: Doing an Uncontested Divorce Yourself

Most uncontested divorces go smoothly. But divorce remains a difficult legal procedure, and can sometimes get complicated. There may be a problem with jurisdiction, trouble serving the divorce papers, difficulty dividing the property or the danger of spouse abuse. All these problems and more can make your divorce—although it's uncontested—too difficult for you to do yourself.

Am I Married?

It may seem silly, but the first thing you should do before a divorce is make sure you are really married. If you discover that you aren't married, you won't need a divorce to split up.

The legality of a marriage is typically judged by the law of where it began, not where it ends. If you were married in Michigan, you look at Michigan marriage law. Those married out of state must consider the marriage law of that place.

Michigan authorizes two types of marriage: 1) ceremonial marriage, performed by most clergymen and some government officials 2) secret marriage, a rather obscure form of marriage before a probate judge for the benefit of: (a) people with a good reason to keep their marriage secret (b) children under the age of 16 in certain circumstances. Other states have different types of ceremonial marriage, which are valid in Michigan.

Most states have abolished common law marriage, in which couples informally agree to live together as husband and wife. However, many states had it in the past. Michigan recognized common law marriage until January

1, 1957. Today, only the District of Columbia and the following states permit common law marriage:

- Alabama
- Colorado
- Iowa
- Kansas
- Montana

- Pennsylvania
- Rhode Island
- South Carolina
- Texas
- Utah

If your common law marriage began in one of these states, it's legal in Michigan. Or if it began in Michigan before January 1, 1957, or in other states while they recognized the institution, it's also valid here.

If you doubt whether you are really married, check with the official of the office where you believe your marriage license is filed. In Michigan, that official is the county clerk who issued the license to you; in other states it might be someone else.

Another way to trace marriage records is through a state vital records office. Every state has an office that compiles records of marriages, divorces, births and deaths. By writing to the vital records office of the state in which you think you were married, you can get a copy of your marriage license, if one exists.

After you confirm that you are married, you should also make sure that your marriage hasn't already ended by a divorce or annulment. Unlike common law marriage, there is no such thing as informal "common law" divorce. So despite what some people think, tearing up your marriage license, giving back wedding rings, etc. will not make you divorced. Therefore, any divorce that your spouse may have gotten must have been court-ordered.

If you think that you may have been involved in a prior divorce, investigate and see whether a divorce judgment (also known as a decree or order in some states) was ever issued in the case. The court where the divorce was filed will have record of the judgment. If you don't have much information about the divorce, use the procedure described above to contact the vital records office of the state where the divorce was filed. It should have a record of the divorce judgment, if in fact one was issued.

Naturally, your spouse's death also ends your marriage. You might not know about this if you've separated from your spouse and remained out of touch. If you suspect that your spouse has died, you can confirm that by checking to see if a death certificate was filed. In Michigan, death certificates are filed with the county clerk of the place of death. If you don't know the county, use the state vital records office. A quicker way to check on the death of anyone is through the Social Security Administration's (SSA) death index.

More Information

To obtain Michigan marriage, divorce and death records, contact Michigan's vital records office:

Department of Community Health
Division for Vital Records and Health Studies
P.O. Box 30195
Lansing, MI 48909
(517) 335-8496

To find vital records offices in other states, order the booklet "Where to Write for Vital Records" (#107L), by sending a $4.25 check (payable to "Superintendent of Documents"), to:

R. Woods
CIC - 01A
P.O. Box 100
Pueblo, CO 81002

You can also order this booklet with a credit card by calling (888) 878-3256. Or you can read or print the booklet at www.pueblo.gsa.gov.

You can also find state vital records through www.vitalrec.com.

The SSA's death index lists deceased people whose survivors have received social security death benefits. Not everyone applies for or receives these benefits, so the index isn't 100% complete, but it's a good place to start.

To use the index, call the SSA at (800) 772-1213.

The index is also available at www.ancestry.com for a fee.

It's also possible to have your spouse legally declared dead after a long disappearance. Like most states, Michigan has an Enoch Arden law (so called after the shipwrecked sailor of the Tennyson poem who returned from ten years at sea to find his wife remarried), which allows a person to be declared dead after seven years of complete absence.

Do I Really Want to End My Marriage?

When you get a divorce, the marriage between you and your spouse is ended finally and irrevocably. This allows each of you to remarry, if you wish. As someone divorce-bound, you're probably well aware of these and other benefits of divorce.

But as you prepare to divorce, don't forget the many advantages of remaining married. Recently, when Vermont lawmakers were debating their controversial same-sex civil union law, legal experts there counted around 300 benefits of marriage offered by state law. Michigan law certainly provides as many or more. All in all, marriage offers many valuable rights, such as: 1) support 2) property rights 3) estate and will rights 4) private benefits 5) public benefits 6) miscellaneous rights.

To be sure, some of these rights can be continued or compensated after a divorce. You can sometimes get postdivorce support in the form of alimony, and your property rights, including rights in retirement plans, can be recovered in the property division of the divorce.

But many marital rights are lost forever by a divorce. After a divorce, you lose all rights to your spouse's estate, including: 1) the right to inherit a share of his/her estate if s/he dies without a will 2) the right to take a minimum share of the estate, if the will slights you 3) dower (an estate that widows have in their husbands' real property) 4) miscellaneous allowances from your deceased spouse's estate. Divorce also automatically revokes all distributions of property and some appointments in your spouse's will which benefit you.

You may also lose valuable private benefits, often provided by an employer, available through your spouse, such as retirement, fringe, life and health plan benefits. There are substitutes for some of these, such as COBRA-provided health care coverage (see "Coverage for Spouse" on page 142 for more about this coverage), but never completely and usually at a higher cost.

The death of your spouse after your divorce will leave you without public benefits, such as wrongful death claims or survivor's benefits from worker's compensation or no-fault automobile insurance, that you might have enjoyed had you remained married. What's worse, if you happen to divorce before the tenth anniversary of your marriage, you may lose the right to get social security benefits based on your spouse's earnings record.

Divorce also jeopardizes other miscellaneous marital rights that you may have never thought about. For example, aliens (noncitizens) can lose

---

More Information

On divorce and social security, get "A Woman's Guide to Social Security" from your local social security office.

See "Can I Get A Fair Property Division?" on page 53 for resources about retirement benefits.

Good information about these and other topics:

Divorce & Money, 4th ed., Violet Woodhouse and Dale Fetherling, Berkeley: Nolo Press, 2002

The Dollars and Sense of Divorce, Judith Briles, et al., Chicago: Dearborn Trade Publishing, 1998

More Information

Some non-profit counselors are listed in the yellow pages under "Social Service Organizations." For-profit counselors appear under the "Marriage, Family, Child & Individual Counselors" category.

See page 10 about obtaining a referral to a counselor from the **American Association for Marraige and Family Therapy**.

entrance or residence rights when they divorce U.S. citizens. After a divorce, you cannot file a joint income tax return, and may face a bigger tax bill. Marriage also entitles you to discounts on airplane tickets, hotels, etc., which single people don't always enjoy.

After considering all that marriage offers, you may decide that it isn't so bad after all. If you think that your marriage can be saved, you may find marriage counseling helpful. Many religious and human service organizations provide counseling, usually without charge. Private marriage and family counselors offer similar services. These private counselors charge fees for their services, but some health plans pay for the cost.

Is Divorce the Best Way to End My Marriage?

Divorce isn't the only cure for a bad marriage. By declaring a marriage nonexistent, an annulment also ends the marriage. A legal separation—known as separate maintenance in Michigan—ends a marital relationship, although the marriage itself is left intact. Like divorce, an annulment or separate maintenance allows the court to decide the issues of custody, parenting time, residence of children, child support, property division and alimony. Before you choose a divorce, consider whether an annulment or separate maintenance might be better for you.

Annulment

Many people don't really understand annulment. For one thing, they often confuse legal annulments with religious annulments. Legal annulments are granted by courts of law, and affect one's legal rights. Some religious denominations, notably the Roman Catholic Church, offer religious annulments. These end marriages in the eyes in the church, restoring various religious privileges. A religious annulment is obtained from the religious organization and has absolutely no effect on legal rights.

Another misunderstanding about annulments is that they are routinely available for spouses who have been married for a short time and simply want to "call the whole thing off." The fact is, the length of a marriage is often insignificant: A marriage of a few days may not be annullable, just as a marriage of many years can be annulled. The real distinction between divorce and annulment is that a divorce ends a valid marriage, while an annulment is a legal declaration that no marriage ever existed because of a serious legal defect in the marriage at the time it was performed.

Like most states, Michigan presumes that marriages are legally valid. As a result, minor legal defects in a marriage, such as irregularities in the marriage ceremony, lack of authority of the person who performed the ceremony, etc., are excusable. But if the legal defect is serious, the marriage is subject to annulment. In Michigan, the serious legal defects providing grounds for an annulment concern whether the spouses: 1) had the legal capacity to marry 2) properly consented to marriage.*

Legal capacity. One must satisfy several requirements to marry in Michigan. If a spouse failed to meet any of these requirements when the marriage was performed, the spouse lacked the legal capacity for marriage. This defect can provide grounds for annulment:

¶ *Bigamy.* A spouse marries while already married to someone else.

¶ *Incest.* The spouses are related too closely by blood (you cannot marry a parent, child, grandchild, grandparent, brother or sister, aunt or uncle, niece or nephew or first cousin) or marriage (a stepparent, stepchild, stepgrandchild, son- or daughter-in-law, father- or mother-in-law, spouse of a grandchild or grandparent-in-law are all not marriageable).

¶ *Same-sex marriage.* Michigan doesn't permit same-sex marriage, or recognize same-sex marriages from other states.

¶ *Underage.* Eighteen is the age of consent to marry in Michigan. Men and women 16-18 can marry if they obtain the proper parental consent. Under some circumstances, children under 16 can marry with parental consent in a secret marriage in probate court. Anyone who marries while underage and/or without the proper parental consent, lacks the legal capacity to marry.

¶ *Mental incompetency.* Mental incompetency of a spouse at the time of a marriage is an additional legal incapacity. Onset of mental incompetency after marriage doesn't affect the marriage.

¶ *Physical incapacity.* Sterility and some kinds of sexual dysfunction, which exist at the time of the marriage, are also recognized as incapacities.

DIVORCE IN HASTE; REPENT AT LEISURE.

Glossary

Divorce–legal procedure that ends a marriage.

Annulment–says that a marriage is legally defective and never really existed.

Separate maintenance–like a legal separation, allowing the spouses to live apart with the marriage still intact.

---

*   As mentioned before, the legality of a marriage is judged by the law of the state where it began. These annulment grounds apply to Michigan marriages only. There may be different annulment grounds for out-of-state marriages.

Consent. According to Michigan law, both spouses must give proper consent to their marriage. If a spouse's consent is absent or defective, for any of the reasons below, the marriage may be annulled:

¶ *Force.* A spouse's consent to the marriage is obtained forcibly. Ordinarily, the force must be the use or threat of physical force, but in some cases extreme psychological duress will qualify as force.

¶ *Intoxication.* A spouse's consent to the marriage might be defective if s/he is under the influence of alcohol or drugs when the marriage is performed.

¶ *Fraud.* Fraud is a misrepresentation that causes someone to do something. If fraud is used to obtain consent to a marriage, the fraud can invalidate the marriage. Michigan law is clear that the fraud must affect an essential part of the marriage. For example, a spouse's misrepresentation about his/her ability to have or want children, or about an intention to engage in cohabitation or sexual relations, may be important enough to annul the marriage. But misrepresentations by a spouse about character, wealth, family background or premarital life don't provide fraud grounds for an annulment.

¶ *Sham marriage.* Even when consent to a marriage is given voluntarily and knowingly, the consent might be defective if it wasn't seriously intended. Marriages based on such false consent are regarded as sham marriages, making them subject to annulment. An example of a sham marriage is a marriage by an alien (noncitizen) who marries a U.S. citizen solely to obtain permanent residence in this country. In that case, the alien's marriage may appear to be proper, but it is really nothing more than a ruse to obtain residence in this country.

If you possess any of these grounds for annulment, you may be able to end your marriage by annulment. Or you can disregard the annulment grounds, file for divorce and end your marriage that way. Which is the better choice?

There is no simple answer to this question because divorces closely resemble annulments. Both procedures end marriages and free spouses to remarry. They both settle custody, parenting time, residence of children, child support and property division. But alimony, especially long-term alimony, is difficult to get in an annulment.

An annulment may be quicker than a divorce. Annulments don't have waiting periods as divorces do (see "How Long Will My Divorce Take?" on page 48 for information about divorce waiting periods). And there are no state or county residence requirements for annulments as there are in divorce cases (see "Can I Get a Divorce in Michigan?" and "Can I File the Divorce in My County?" on pages 43-45 for more on state and county divorce residence requirements).

On the other hand, the grounds for annulment are harder to prove and easier to defend against than the no-fault divorce grounds. What's worse, most annulment grounds are based on fault. This means that an annulment can be messy, like divorce was under the old fault law.

If you believe that you have grounds for an annulment and cannot decide whether to file for divorce or annulment, talk with a lawyer about which procedure to use. Act quickly because it's possible to lose annulment grounds by waiting too long. If you decide to seek an annulment, have the lawyer represent you because this book doesn't have instructions or forms for annulment.

Separation

Unlike divorce or annulment, separation doesn't end a marriage. It merely ends the marital relationship between the spouses, leaving the marriage itself intact. Despite that fact, there may be sound reasons for choosing separation over divorce or annulment.

Years ago, people often separated to avoid the social stigma of divorce. With divorce more common now, this stigma has faded. Nevertheless, some people may still want to separate and remain married for social or religious reasons.

Some couples choose separation for more practical reasons. As explained before, spouses can lose valuable marital rights when their marriage ends. Since separation doesn't break the legal bond of marriage, it preserves these marital rights. With this in mind, spouses may decide to separate temporarily, and divorce later when losing these rights isn't so important. For example, spouses married eight or nine years might agree to separate for a few years, and then divorce, so they can qualify for social security benefits based on each other's earnings under the ten-year rule mentioned above. Or they may remain married to preserve benefits like health plan coverage.

Informal Separation

You don't need to go to court to separate. As a matter of fact, spouses can separate informally and live apart indefinitely. Separated spouses usually work out arrangements for custody, parenting time, residence of children, child support, property division and sometimes alimony. To avoid disputes, some estranged spouses enter into written separation or settlement agreements. These agreements spell out how custody, parenting time, residence of children, child support, property division and alimony are handled during the separation. In addition, the agreement can settle these issues for any divorce following the separation.

When separated spouses disagree about those issues, a court can step in to provide child support and alimony. Michigan's family support act allows a custodial spouse to get child support and/or alimony from the noncustodial spouse when s/he has failed to contribute any family support. For more information about family support, contact a support specialist at the FIA. In many cases, the FIA will file the family support claim for you.

An informal separation—even one with a written separation agreement—is difficult to maintain. If the spouses disagree about something, they

Michigan Divorce Jurisdiction

	Defendant is a Michigan resident (and has been for at least 180 days immediately before the divorce is filed)	Defendant once resided with plaintiff in Michigan during their marriage, then moved out of state	Defendant never resided with plaintiff in Michigan during their marriage
Plaintiff is a Michigan resident (and has been for at least 180 days immediately before the divorce is filed)	Full jurisdiction immediately*	Full jurisdiction immediately**	Limited jurisdiction immediately**
Plaintiff once resided with defendant in Michigan during their marriage, then moved out of state	Full jurisdiction immediately	No jurisdiction until plaintiff (or defendant) moves back to Michigan and has resided here at least 180 days immediately before the divorce is filed, then full jurisdiction**	
Plaintiff never resided with defendant in Michigan during their marriage	Full jurisdiction immediately		No jurisdiction until plaintiff (or defendant) moves to Michigan and has resided here at least 180 days immediately before the divorce is filed, then only limited jurisdiction**

* In fact, either plaintiff or defendant can satisfy the 180-day residence requirement by having resided in Michigan at least 180 days immediately before the divorce is filed.

** Full jurisdiction can also be obtained on a nonresident defendant by serving him/her while present in Michigan, such as during a visit to the state.

have no place to resolve their dispute. As a result, some separated spouses seek a formal, court-ordered separation, which is popularly known as a legal separation.

Legal Separation: Separate Maintenance

Michigan law provides for a special type of legal separation called separate maintenance. Separate maintenance doesn't end the marriage. But it settles the issues of custody, parenting time, residence of children, child support, property division and alimony, while the spouses live apart.

The procedure for getting a separate maintenance is like that for a divorce. Even the same no-fault grounds are used. Despite the resemblance, it's much harder to get a separate maintenance because Michigan law allows a defendant in a separate maintenance case to ask for a divorce instead. After the request, the court must grant a divorce if the marriage is broken. Therefore, it's impossible to get a separate maintenance without the approval of the other spouse. All this makes separate maintenance difficult, so see a lawyer if you want one.

Can I Get a Divorce in Michigan?

After deciding that a divorce is what you want, you must then determine whether you can get one in Michigan. Not everyone is entitled to divorce in Michigan. To get a divorce in this state, Michigan courts must have jurisdiction to hear your divorce case. Jurisdiction is based on the residences of you, your spouse and children.

Residence

Residence is important to your case as the basis for jurisdiction. But what is it really? Residence has several different legal meanings. For the purposes of divorce, residence means your permanent home, or the place where you intend to stay.

Long-time residents of Michigan don't have to worry about residence. But if you've moved to the state recently, you can establish residence by: 1) registering to vote here 2) getting a Michigan driver's license 3) owning property in the state (it's even better if you file for a homestead property tax exemption at your Michigan address) 4) working and filing income tax returns here.

Once established in Michigan, residence isn't lost by temporary absences out of state, such as vacations or business trips. Nor is it disturbed by leaving the state under military or government orders. For example, a resident of Michigan who enters U.S. military or foreign service remains a Michigan resident during active duty wherever assigned.

Residence may be important for the purposes of jurisdiction before you file for divorce, but it fades in significance afterward. After filing, you won't lose jurisdiction (or county venue, which is explained below) by changing your residence. Your ability to move post-divorce-filing may however be restricted by Michigan's residence-of-children law (see "Residence of Children" on page 17 for more about this law).

> ## Glossary
>
> *Plaintiff*–spouse who files for divorce.
>
> *Defendant*–spouse against whom divorce is filed.
>
> *Jurisdiction*–power of a court to decide a divorce case.
>
> *Venue*—in divorce cases, the correct county for divorce-filing.

Divorce Jurisdiction

Michigan divorce jurisdiction is based on the past and present residences of the spouses. These residences determine whether there is either full or limited jurisdiction for the case. A court can take full jurisdiction when at least the defendant-spouse is residing in Michigan (the plaintiff-spouse may be residing here as well), or when the spouses resided together in Michigan at some time during their marriage. Limited jurisdiction exists when only the plaintiff-spouse resides in Michigan and the defendant never resided here with him/her during their marriage.

Michigan Custody Jurisdiction

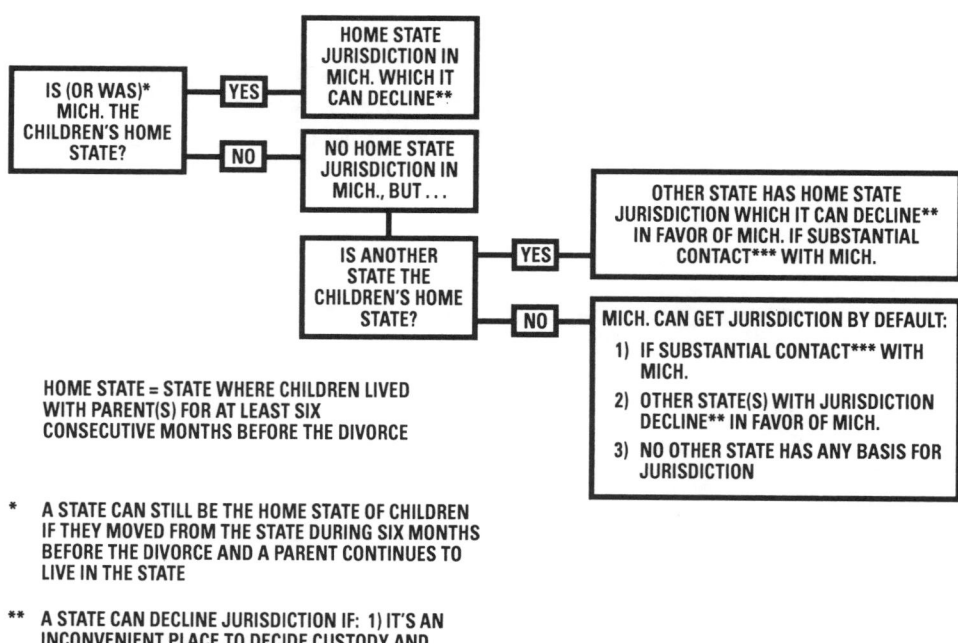

HOME STATE = STATE WHERE CHILDREN LIVED
WITH PARENT(S) FOR AT LEAST SIX
CONSECUTIVE MONTHS BEFORE THE DIVORCE

*   A STATE CAN STILL BE THE HOME STATE OF CHILDREN
    IF THEY MOVED FROM THE STATE DURING SIX MONTHS
    BEFORE THE DIVORCE AND A PARENT CONTINUES TO
    LIVE IN THE STATE

** A STATE CAN DECLINE JURISDICTION IF: 1) IT'S AN
    INCONVENIENT PLACE TO DECIDE CUSTODY AND
    ANOTHER STATE IS MORE CONVENIENT, OR 2) ITS
    JURISDICTION IS BASED ON MISCONDUCT OF A
    PARTY (SUCH AS KIDNAPPING)

*** SUBSTANTIAL CONTACT = 1) CHILDREN AND THE
    CHILDREN'S PARENT(S) HAVE A SIGNIFICANT
    CONNECTION TO THE STATE, AND 2) SUBSTANTIAL
    EVIDENCE ABOUT THE CHILDREN EXISTS IN THAT STATE

Like other states, Michigan also imposes a residence requirement on divorce to discourage migratory divorce. In Michigan, the residence period is 180 days. The chart on page 42 depicts Michigan divorce jurisdiction with the residence requirement added.

The concept of jurisdiction is difficult, but it's important because it determines how much of your case the court can decide. As explained in Part II, divorce is divisible into several issues: end of marriage, custody, parenting time, residence of children, child support, property division and alimony. For reasons that are too complicated to explain here, certain divorce issues may need a particular type of jurisdiction. For example, child support, property division and alimony require full jurisdiction. Ending a marriage can use either limited or full jurisdiction.

What about custody and the related issues of parenting time and residence of children? As it happens, these divorce issues have their own jurisdiction rules, imposed by the Uniform Child Custody Jurisdiction and Enforcement Act (UCCJEA). In essence, this law, which all states have adopted, says that custody jurisdiction should usually be in the "home state" of children. A home state is similar to residence, or a permanent home. The chart on the opposite page illustrates.

When a court has full jurisdiction, with proper custody jurisdiction, it can do a divorce completely. It can end the marriage, order child support and alimony, divide the property and award custody and parenting time.

But with only limited jurisdiction, without power over custody, a court can do little. It can always end the marriage, and may be able to decide custody and parenting time. But it cannot order child support, divide property or award alimony.

If you have only limited jurisdiction in your case, seek legal advice. The lawyer can advise whether you can get by with that. If not, the lawyer could tell you how to get full Michigan jurisdiction or file for divorce in your spouse's state.

Can I File the Divorce in My County?

Assuming Michigan courts have some type of jurisdiction for your divorce, you must then file in the Michigan county with proper venue. In divorce cases, venue exists in the county where either you or your spouse has resided at least 10 days immediately before the divorce is filed. Incidentally, residence for venue purposes is a place of permanent habitation, just as it is for jurisdiction.

Naturally, when you both reside in the same county, the divorce must be filed there. But when you reside in different Michigan counties, venue is proper in either county. For the sake of convenience, most people choose to file in their own counties.

If the defendant resides out of state, venue will be in the Michigan county where the plaintiff resides. In those rare cases with out-of-state plaintiffs, venue will be in the Michigan county where the defendant resides. There is also a special venue rule for plaintiffs married to foreign-born or alien defendants, when there is a reasonable fear that the defendant may take the parties' children outside the U.S. In that case, the plaintiff may file in any Michigan county without regard to the 10-day residence rule. These special circumstances must be alleged in the divorce complaint.

What If My Spouse and I File for Divorce At the Same Time?

This is the dueling divorces problem: You and your spouse file for divorce around the same time, perhaps even before the divorce papers are served on each other. If both cases were filed in Michigan, the one filed first has priority and the later one must be dismissed (to dismiss the second case, see Appendix G about voluntary dismissal of divorce cases).

When the divorces are filed in different states, the situation is more complicated. If both states really have full jurisdiction, the first case filed usually has priority. But typically, only one state will be the home state of the minor children, giving this state custody jurisdiction under the Uniform Child Custody Jurisdiction and Enforcement Act (UCCJEA) (see page "Can I Get a Divorce in Michigan?" on page 43 for more about using the children's home state as the basis for custody jurisdiction). As a result, the state qualifying as the children's home state will be the only one with full jurisdiction, and will have priority over the other state. The divorce case filed in the home state/full jurisdiction state will have priority even if it was filed second.

Can My Spouse Be Served with the Divorce Papers?

Regardless of the type of jurisdiction for a divorce, the defendant must get notice of the divorce. Like other lawsuits, notice in divorce cases is provided by serving the initial divorce papers on defendants. Service is explained in detail in Chapter 2.

At this point, you should know that service is easy and cheap if your spouse is available to receive the divorce papers. In that case, you can obtain service by any of three methods: 1) acknowledgment 2) mail 3) delivery. It doesn't matter where your spouse lives, because these service methods can be used anywhere in or outside Michigan.

Service can be difficult if a defendant is elusive (you know where the defendant is, but s/he is eluding or avoiding you). It's even more difficult if the defendant has disappeared (you don't know the whereabouts of the defendant). Luckily, the court rules provide for forms of alternate service to give hard-to-find defendants some type of notice (Appendix D has more about obtaining alternate service on elusive or disappeared defendants).

Thanks to this wide choice of service methods, you can be confident that when there is jurisdiction for your divorce there will be a way to serve the defendant.

What If My Spouse or I Am Imprisoned?

Incarceration of a spouse naturally puts a great strain on a marriage. If the marriage should break, the imprisonment also creates special problems for the divorce, whether the prisoner is plaintiff or defendant.

Divorce by an Imprisoned Plaintiff

Before filing, an imprisoned plaintiff must choose the correct county for filing. Choice of county is called venue and is controlled by the county residence of the divorce parties.

Prisoners are subject to special residence rules for venue. According to Michigan law, prisoners are presumed to remain residents of the county they resided in immediately before imprisonment. However, prisoners can become residents of the county of imprisonment if they can prove that they intend to reside there after release. Keep these residence rules in mind as you choose venue as directed in "Can I File the Divorce in My County?" on page 45.

Prisoners shouldn't have any difficulty serving their non-institutionalized spouses with divorce papers. The three regular methods of service (acknowledgment, mail, delivery), plus alternate service methods, are available to prisoners. Service by mail is probably easiest and cheapest. All these service methods and rules are explained in "Service" on page 99.

Plaintiff-prisoners do face a special problem at the end of divorce, during the final hearing. Ordinarily, divorce plaintiffs must appear personally in court and give some brief testimony for the Judgment of Divorce. To satisfy the court appearance requirement, some counties transport prisoners to court for final hearings in divorce. But transportation is expensive, especially for counties with large prison populations.

As an alternative, many counties allow and encourage prisoners to give their testimony in written or electronic form. The court rules permit this because they excuse court appearances in exceptional cases. Prisoners should contact prison legal services for help with giving final hearing testimony without a court appearance.

More Information
About divorce problems for prisoners, including giving final hearing testimony from prison, contact:
Prison Legal Services of Michigan SPSM 3855 Cooper St. Jackson, MI 49201 (517) 780-6639

Filing against a Defendant-Prisoner

There are some special rules for divorces against incarcerated defendants when minor children are involved. These rules try to make sure the inmate gets full due process (notice and opportunity to respond) during the divorce.

Before filing, the plaintiff must consider the choice-of-county, or venue, rules when choosing where to file (see "Can I File the Divorce in My County?" on page 45 for more about venue). Typically, plaintiffs file in their home counties, so the residence of a defendant-prisoner isn't an issue. But if you want to file where a defendant-prisoner resides, see the section above about how the residence of prisoners is determined.

You must know where the defendant is imprisoned and have his/her prisoner identification number. You may already know these things; if not, use a state or federal prison locator service to find out. After you have this information, you must take several special steps:

¶ In the caption of the Summons and Complaint (MC 01), add the following items in the defendant's box:

1) "Defendant is an inmate at [name of correctional facility] with prisoner identification number [prisoner identification number]."

2) "A telephone hearing with defendant must be held as provided by MCR 2.004"

¶ Later, after filing and service, the court will issue an order scheduling a hearing or conference with the defendant, by telephone, at his/her correctional facility.

During the telephone hearing, court officials must confirm that the defendant was served with the divorce papers, has access to a lawyer, if one is wanted, how s/he can communicate with the court and set any future hearings in the case.

¶ After the telephone hearing, the defendant will probably default and the case will proceed normally like other uncontested cases.

> ### More Information
>
> To locate a prison inmate for service and/or obtain the inmate's prisoner identification number, use a prison locator service.
>
> Michigan's locator service can be reached at (517) 335-7570.
>
> For prisoners in other state prisons, see the Johnson and Knox book cited on page 197. It lists all the states' prison locator services.
>
> The federal prison locator is (202) 307-3126.

The easiest way to serve a defendant in prison is by mail. Service by mail is described in "Service" on page 99, along with the other service methods. When your service-helper mails the service papers to the defendant, make sure the defendant's prisoner identification number appears next to his/her name in the address on the envelope. Many prisons require this number for delivery of mail to prisoners. If the defendant refuses to take and sign for the mailing, you can always use service by delivery, through the sheriff's office in the county where the prison is located.

What If My Spouse or I Am in the Military?

Military service adds both practical and legal problems to a divorce. As a practical matter, it may be difficult to find and serve papers on a defendant-servicemember stationed at a faraway military base. There are also state and federal military relief laws protecting active-duty servicemembers from hard-to-handle lawsuits. The federal law, the Soldiers' and Sailors' Civil Relief Act of 1940 (SSCRA), is an especially stiff challenge when the servicemember is a defendant who is uncooperative or unresponsive.

Appendix F has complete information about dealing with military servicemembers whether as divorce plaintiffs or defendants.

How Long Will My Divorce Take?

Uncontested divorces take longer to complete than most uncontested lawsuits because Michigan law imposes two statutory waiting periods on divorces:

- 60 days in cases without minor children
- six months in cases with minor children

The waiting periods serve to delay divorces. The reason for the delay is two-fold. It gives the parties a chance to cool off, and possibly reconcile, after the heat of the divorce filing has passed. And in divorces with minor children, the delay also gives the friend of the court time to investigate the case (more about this later).

In your case, the six-month statutory waiting period applies. This means that at least six months must elapse between the day you file your divorce and the day you finish it in court at the final hearing.

The law says that the waiting period can be shortened to no less than 60 days in cases of "unusual hardship or compelling necessity." These cases might include divorces in which there has been physical abuse or violence, or divorces between spouse who have been separated for a long time. The trouble is, you must file a motion and get the judge's permission to shorten the waiting period. Because this book lacks the instructions and forms for such a motion, see a lawyer if you want to do that.

In addition to the statutory waiting period, there may also be unpredictable court-caused delays. Some courts are very busy and may not be able to hear your divorce immediately after the statutory waiting period expires. As a result, your divorce will take at least six months, and maybe a while longer if the court is busy.

How Much Will My Divorce Cost?

Doing your own divorce saves you lawyer fees, but not the court fees of the case. These court fees are due in all divorces—with or without lawyers. The court fees for uncontested divorces with minor children include:

Filing fee. The fee for filing a divorce is $150.

Service fee. You can expect to pay $0-30 to have the divorce papers served. The amount of the service fee depends on the method of service you use. Service by acknowledgment is usually available for free. Service by mail is around $8. Service by delivery is usually $16-30. If you use a sheriff for service by delivery, the sheriff charges a $16 fee, plus mileage (billed at the current state government rate) to and from the defendant. Commercial process servers' fees for service by delivery may be slightly higher.

Motion fee. You must pay a $20 fee whenever you file a motion. You probably won't need to file any motions in your uncontested divorce case, unless you have to ask for something extraordinary, like alternate service.

Friend of the court fee. A $30-70 fee is charged to cover the cost of the friend of the court's services in your case. The amount of the friend of the court fee varies according to the friend of the court's involvement in a divorce:
- $30 in cases with no investigation or mediation by the friend of the court
- $50 in cases mediated by the friend of the court
- $70 in cases where there is an investigation and recommendation by the friend of the court

Divorce Children

	Children included in divorce	Comments/exceptions
Children born during plaintiff's and defendant's current marriage	Yes	But paternity of children born during a marriage can be disproved by strong evidence that the father is not really the father. If paternity is disproved, the child would usually not be included in the divorce.
Unborn children of the marriage	Yes	
Children born during a previous marriage of plaintiff and defendant	Yes	
Children born to plaintiff and defendant outside of their marriage	Yes, if...	Paternity has been established before the divorce or if it can be proved during the divorce.
Children legally adopted by plaintiff and defendant during their marriage	Yes	
Stepchildren of plaintiff or defendant	No	But if a stepchild was adopted by plaintiff or defendant in a stepparent adoption, it will be a legally adopted child of theirs.
Children given up for adoption, or children over whom both plaintiff and defendant have lost parental rights	No	But if only one parent has lost parental rights, include the children in the divorce and explain the circumstances of the parent's loss of parental rights.

The law seems to require payment of the friend of the court fee at the end of a divorce. But many counties charge $30 of this fee at the beginning, and collect any remainder at the end of the divorce.

Some counties don't require friend of the court investigations and recommendations in uncontested divorce cases (see "Friend of the Court Investigation" on page 121 for more about this). But since most counties do, you can expect to pay the full $70 friend of the court fee. In that case, your court fees, minus the service fee, should be $220 ($150 filing fee and $70 friend of the court fee). Add to that a service fee, which depends on the method of service used.

Thanks to a landmark U.S. Supreme Court decision, poor people don't have to pay these court fees. In *Boddie v. Connecticut,* the supreme court decided that states must give everyone access to divorce, since they alone have the power to grant divorces. This means that those who can't afford divorce court fees are entitled to exemptions from payment. After the *Boddie* decision in 1971, Michigan adopted fee exemption rules for all types of cases, including divorce. See Appendix A for information about qualifying and applying for a fee exemption.

Which Children Must Be Included in My Divorce?

The children of your divorce ("divorce children") must include all the minor children of you and your spouse. In some cases, your adult children must also be included in the divorce for the purpose of support only.

Minor Children

The minor divorce children are the children you and your spouse have had together who are minors (under age 18) on the day you file for divorce. These children must be listed in your divorce papers, and shall be the subject of the custody, parenting time, residence of children and child support orders in the divorce.

If you have a blended family, with children of you and your spouse and children from other marriages or relationships, include only the children of you and your spouse in the divorce; leave out the other children.

In most cases, the divorce children are simply the minor children born during the spouses' current marriage. But in some cases, the divorce children are defined differently, as the chart on the opposite page shows. Include minor children in these exceptional categories (adoptees, out-of-wedlocks after proof of paternity, etc.) as you would other minor children.

You ought to be able to handle some of the exceptional cases without much problem. If you adopted children during your marriage, just include them in your divorce as you would biological children. When the wife is pregnant, mention her pregnancy in paragraph #7 of your divorce complaint. Then at the end of the divorce, list the child in the divorce judgment as follows: 1) by name and the date of birth if born during the divorce 2) as "unborn child" with the due date as the date of birth if still unborn.

Things aren't as simple when the paternity of children is at stake. Paternity is a legal judgment that a suspected father of a child really fathered the child. These days, paternity can be proved or disproved with almost 100% accuracy by genetic testing of blood samples from the mother, child and suspected father.

Paternity can be decided as an extra issue during divorce. The trouble is, adding paternity to a divorce makes the case too complicated to do yourself. That's why you should consider dealing with paternity pre-divorce, in a separate paternity case. If you can do that, paternity will be settled before you file, keeping the divorce simple enough to do yourself.

According to Michigan paternity law, you can deal with paternity pre-divorce for children you and your spouse had together before marriage (out

---

To Obtain

Help with establishing paternity of out-of-wedlock children, mothers should contact the local Family Independence Agency (FIA), which has special proof-of-paternity services available for them.

of wedlock). If the husband's paternity is proved, include the out-of-wedlock children among your divorce children; exclude these children if paternity is disproved.

Children born during your marriage (in wedlock) are presumed to be the husband's children. Incredibly, this presumption applies even if you and your husband have been separated for years and have had no physical contact since separation. The law is apparently willing to tolerate this rather absurd conclusion to promote something more important: the legitimacy of children.

For technical reasons, the paternity law doesn't permit a pre-divorce paternity case challenging the paternity presumption of in-wedlock children, to disprove paternity. If you suspect that your husband isn't really the father of in-wedlock children, you should have the issue decided during your divorce. But as explained before, adding paternity to your case will make the divorce too difficult for you to do by yourself.

Whatever you do, don't ignore paternity until after the divorce. By waiting that long, you may lose the right to deal with the issue at all.

Adult Children

In some cases, you must include certain dependent adult children in your divorce case. According to Michigan law, adult children between the ages of 18 and 19½ are entitled to support if they are: 1) regularly attending high school on a full-time basis with a reasonable expectation of completing sufficient credits to graduate from high school 2) residing on a full-time basis with the recipient of the support or at an institution.

You must add these children to your divorce papers, if they qualify as divorce children in the chart. Paragraph #5b of the Complaint for Divorce (GRP 1a) has a special place for them. They will receive child support while they remain in high school. But adult children won't be covered by the custody, parenting time or residence orders, since these stop at age 18.

Must I Have the Friend of the Court in My Case?

Ordinarily, the friend of the court, which is a family court official, must participate in all divorces with minor children. The friend of the court performs a number of functions in divorce cases, including investigation and recommendation to the judge on divorce issues, refereeing, mediation, and review, modification and enforcement of orders (see "Friend of the Court" on page 72 for more about the friend of the court and its duties).

In most cases, the friend of the court's participation is beneficial. The friend of the court is a neutral third party who can help settle any disputes that break out. Its bookkeeping function for support is particularly helpful. Nevertheless, some divorces are completely amicable and the parties don't need or want friend of the court services.

According to a 2002 law, it's now possible to "opt out" of the friend of the court system—totally, partially or in a limited way—and manage the case yourself. This isn't always wise, and many cases are ineligible for opt-out. Appendix C has lots more about the pluses and minuses of opting out, the three types of opt-outs, opt-out restrictions and instructions and forms for opting out.

Can I Get a Fair Property Division?

As explained in "Property Division" on page 27, you are entitled to an equitable division of your property in a divorce. But exactly which property is subject to division?

Some states have rigid schemes for dividing property in divorces. They classify property as either marital-community property or nonmarital-separate property. In these states, only marital-community property is divisible during divorce.

In Michigan, by contrast, divorce property division is more flexible. Everything the spouses own is potentially subject to division. Despite what many people believe, this may include property the spouses brought into their marriage. It can also reach inheritances, will gifts or other gifts (including wedding gifts) received before or during the marriage.

Ordinarily, premarital property, inheritances and gifts are left out of divorce property division, and the spouse who owns this property keeps it. But the nonowner-spouse may claim a share of this property when: 1) s/he or the parties' children need the property for support 2) s/he has contributed to "acquisition, improvement or accumulation" of the property.

Saying that all property is potentially divisible in a divorce begs the question of what is property? Does it include everything the spouses possess, or only those things with a definite market value?

A generation ago, everyone agreed that divisible property was confined to real property (land and buildings) and personal property, such as cash, bank accounts, stocks, bonds, household goods, motor vehicles, tools, etc., with a definite market value. But during the last 20 years, the definition of property has steadily expanded to include almost anything of value, regardless of whether it has a market value. So besides the familiar old property that has always been divided in divorces, there are several types of "new property" that may also be divisible:

Retirement benefits. For years, courts refused to divide retirement benefits, such as pensions, despite the fact that these benefits are often the most valuable things spouses own. Ultimately, courts realized the unfairness of that position and now nearly all states permit the division of pensions and other retirement benefits.

Today, Michigan courts divide almost any type of retirement benefit provided by public- or private-sector employers, including pensions, 401(k), profit-sharing, employee stock ownership (ESOP) and saving/thrift plans. Also divisible are individual retirement benefits, such as individual retirement arrangement (IRA), simplified employee pension (SEP) and Keogh

---

More Information

About retirement benefits, send $24.95 for *Your Pension Rights at Divorce: What Women Need to Know* to:

Pension Rights Center
1140 19th St. NW
Suite 602
Washington, DC 20036

(HR-10) plans. The only type of retirement benefit immune from division is social security because it already has a built-in means of paying benefits to divorced spouses (see "Do I Really Want to End My Marriage?" on page 37 for more about obtaining social security off your spouse's earnings record).

Employee benefits. Employees are often eligible for valuable fringe benefits, such as health plan coverage, sick and vacation pay, expense accounts, club memberships, meal allowances, lodging, discounts, etc. Some of these benefits, such as banked sick and vacation pay, have been divided in divorce cases in Michigan.

Life insurance. Life insurance is often overlooked during property division, but it's divisible if it has a cash value. Whole life insurance policies usually have a cash value; term insurance policies ordinarily don't.

Businesses. Businesses, such as a sole proprietorship (one-person business) or an interest in a partnership or a small corporation whose stock is not traded publicly, are also divorce property.

Education. Michigan was one of the first states to include education in divorce property divisions. According to Michigan law, education leading to an advanced degree (graduate, law, medicine, etc.) is divisible when the degree was the result of a "concerted family effort." What this means is that the nondegree-spouse contributed financial or other support to the spouse earning the advanced degree. If so, the nondegree-spouse's contribution can be valued and awarded to him/her.

Legal claims. Some legal claims that a spouse has against third parties, such as personal injury or workers' compensation claims, are property that can be divided in divorces. For example, in one Michigan case a husband was awarded $700,000 for a libel claim, and the divorce court ruled that his wife was entitled to about half of the money.

Spouses may also have legal claims against each other that can be decided in a divorce. At one time, it was impossible for spouses to sue each other for personal injuries. This immunity has been abolished and spouses are adding personal injury claims to divorces more often.

Debts. Although it's hard to think of debts as property, they should be weighed during the property division because debts influence the overall fairness of the division.

Whether your property is old, new or a mixture of both, you must have a good grasp of the extent and value of your property. Otherwise, you and your spouse risk agreeing to an inequitable property division. In all, you should do three things before you agree to a property division: 1) *inventory* your property 2) *value* it 3) find a way to *divide* it.

Inventorying Property

Property division begins with a complete inventory of all the property you and your spouse own. Ordinarily, only property owned when the divorce is filed will be divided. Property transferred before the divorce* or acquired during the divorce is normally left out of the division. So take your inventory just before you file.

As you inventory your property, you may find that you don't know very much about it. In many marriages, one spouse handles the finances, leaving the other spouse in the dark. Luckily, there are several informal ways to get the financial information you need for the inventory.

Start with documents around the house, such as paycheck stubs, bank statements and retirement plan booklets. If you and your spouse have a joint safe deposit box, go through the box. You might find deeds, land contracts, stocks, bonds and life insurance policies hidden there.

Your recent joint personal tax returns, especially any schedules attached to these returns, can reveal valuable information about real property (schedules D and E), bank accounts (schedule B), and businesses (schedules C and F). Likewise, joint business income tax returns have important information about businesses. If you have discarded these returns, you can order copies by submitting Form 4506 to your IRS filing center.

Have you and your spouse applied for a loan recently? If so, you probably prepared a financial statement as part of the loan application. Since federal law makes it a crime to submit false information in the statement, it can be a reliable source of financial information.

If these informal methods fail to give you the financial information you need, there is a formal fact-finding device called discovery. Discovery comes in several forms, including depositions (oral interrogation out of court), interrogatories (written questions) and requests for documents. All these discovery methods are available during divorce to get you the financial information you need. The trouble is, discovery is difficult for nonlawyers to use. If you think you need it, contact a lawyer for help.

Valuing Property

There are many methods of valuing property. Michigan law doesn't say which method must be used, but fair market value seems to be the accepted measure of value.

Fair market value is usually defined as the price property would bring in a sale between a willing buyer and willing seller. When the property is subject to a debt, an adjustment may be necessary. For indebted property, the equity value of the property—its fair market value minus the debt against it—is often used instead of gross fair market value.

---

*   But see "Does My Property Need Protection?" on page 58 for how courts can stop a spouse from transferring property to keep it out of the divorce.

More Information

NADA has an online version of the bluebooks at www.nadaguides.com with values for automobiles (cars, trucks, vans etc.), classic cars, motorcycles, boats, recreational vehicles and manufactured homes. The similar Kelley Blue Book can be accessed at www.kbb.com.

Stock quotes are available at www.naq.com

The U.S. government savings bond Web site, www.savingsbond.gov, has a calculator to figure the redemption value of E/EE bonds.

Schroeder's Antiques Price Guide, 22nd ed., Sharon and Bob Huxford, Paducah, KY: Collector Books, 2003, is the best general price guide for antiques.

Davenport's Art Reference and Price Guide, Lisa Reinhardt, ed., Phoenix: Gordon's Art Reference, 2002, is a reliable price reference for fine art.

More Information

To find an appraiser, look in the yellow pages under "Appraisers."

Or contact one of the appraisal trade associations for a referral to a certified appraiser near you:

American Society of Appraisers at (800) 272-8258 or www.appraisers.org

International Society of Appraisers at (206) 241-0359 or www.isa-appraisers.org

Appraisers Association of America at (212) 889-5405 or www.appraisersassoc.org

To value real property, you can either: 1) compare your property to the sale prices of other similar property sold recently in your neighborhood 2) double the amount of your property's tax assessment, since assessments are usually around 50% of market value.

You should be able to establish the fair market value of most kinds of personal property informally without going to the trouble and expense of getting formal appraisals.

Cash or near-cash assets (bank accounts, certificates of deposit, money market funds, etc.) are worth their present account balances. The value of stocks, corporate bonds and other securities are listed daily in the *Wall Street Journal*. Use the current redemption value for series E/EE U.S. savings bonds. You can value whole life insurance by figuring the cash surrender value on the policy chart, or by asking the insurance company or your insurance agent for this value.

The value of motor vehicles can be obtained from National Automobile Dealer Association (NADA) bluebooks. There are also price guides for stamps, coins, jewelry and antiques. You can estimate the value of household goods and tools by comparing them to similar used items.

If these resources don't provide accurate valuations of your property, you can always get formal appraisals. There are appraisers who are competent to value many types of property and specialists who appraise one type of property. People who buy and sell property, such as automobile or antique dealers, can also give appraisals.

The valuation of some new property, such as retirement benefits and businesses, poses special problems. These things have value, but there is no marketplace in which their value can be fixed. After all, you can't very well sell your pension to someone else. You may be able to sell a small business, but the market is often faulty and you won't get what it's really worth. Despite these problems, there are ways to assign value to new property so it can be divided in divorce cases.

Before you can value retirement benefits, you must know what kind of benefit it is. There are two basic kinds of plans providing retirement benefits:

Defined benefit plan. In a defined benefit plan, or pension plan, the employer promises to pay stipulated benefits at retirement or death. These benefits are paid according to formulas which are usually based on a combination of the employee's age, years of service and earnings.

What an employee with a defined benefit plan has is the employer's promise of benefits; there is no retirement account reserved for the employee. Instead, the employer's retirement contributions (typically only the employer contributes) are pooled in a common fund, and retirement benefits are drawn from the fund as needed.

Most large private- and public-sector employers have defined benefit plans, although some are now discontinuing them in favor of defined contribution plans, especially the popular 401(k) plan.

Other employers have adopted a new kind of defined benefit plan, called a cash balance plan, which resembles a 401(k) plan. In cash balance plans, employers make hypothetical contributions to employees' retirement "accounts," like in defined contribution plans. But in reality, these accounts are merely bookkeeping entries, and all retirement benefits are drawn from a common fund. Thus, a cash balance plan remains a defined benefit plan.

Defined contribution plan. In some ways, a defined contribution plan is the opposite of a defined benefit plan. With a defined contribution plan, the employer's contributions, instead of the retirement benefits, are fixed. Each employee has a separate retirement account earmarked for him/her, to which s/he may contribute. The money in the employee's retirement account is invested (usually by the employer), and any investment income is added to the account. At retirement, benefits are paid from the account as the employee directs.

There are many types of defined contributions plans: 401(k), profit-sharing, ESOP and saving/thrift plans (provided by employers), and IRA, SEP and Keogh (HR-10) plans (individual plans). Typically, small businesses have defined contributions plans, although the giant TIAA-CREF (the Teachers Insurance and Annuity Account-College Retirement Equity Fund), which provides retirement benefits to public school teachers, is a defined contribution plan.

The value of a defined benefit plan lies in the benefits the plan will pay in the future. These future benefits can be reduced to a current lump-sum value, called present value. Figuring present value isn't easy, but an accountant or pension specialist can do it for you. To value a defined contribution plan, you simply take the current account balance. You can get this figure from a recent benefit statement or by requesting it from the retirement plan administrator.

Valuing a business is also difficult. If the business cannot be sold as a going concern, the book value of the business (tangible business assets minus business liabilities) may be used. But if the business is marketable, consider valuing the business by multiplying the average annual net earnings (before taxes) by a multiplier (1, 1½, 2, etc.) customary for that type of business. If you own a business jointly with others, you may have a buy-sell agreement with the co-owners fixing the value of your share, and you can use this value.

Dividing Property

All real property must be divided by separate property division provisions in the divorce judgment. Some personal property, including valuable things like motor vehicles and new property (retirement benefits, businesses, etc.) must also be divided individually. But you can divide most personal property, such as household goods, clothing, and personal items, by just splitting it up. "Property Division Provisions" in Appendix H has more information and sample provisions for all kinds of property divisions.

Does My Property Need Protection?

Divorce sometimes puts property at risk. Spouses may try to transfer property to others, before or during the divorce, to keep it out of the property division. If the divorce is bitter, spouses may take out their frustrations on the property. A while ago, a Macomb County woman got back at her husband by destroying his collection of rare Frank Sinatra records (when Sinatra read about the incident he graciously offered to replace some of the discs). But that's nothing compared to a Seattle husband who, to spite his wife, took a bulldozer and demolished their $90,000 house!

Michigan courts have the power to prevent this kind of mischief. They can issue orders protecting property from transfer or destruction. Regrettably, this book doesn't have the instructions and forms to get these orders, so see a lawyer if you need one.

Debts can also jeopardize property and wealth during divorce. Financial stability often breaks down amid a divorce, as spouses are tempted to run up debts on joint accounts. Both spouses are liable for these joint debts regardless of which spouse incurred them. Thus, it's a good idea to close or at least freeze all joint accounts (credit card, charge accounts, etc.), if possible, immediately after separation.

You can close a joint account quickly if no debts remain in the account. If debts exist, you can pay these off or sometimes transfer them to individual accounts. Another option is to freeze the account, so no new debt is added, followed by payment later.

Do I Need to Change My Estate Plan?

Married couples often have estate plans mirroring each other. The husband's will may give all his property to the wife, and name her as personal representative, with her will doing the same. Or they may have living (*inter vivos*) trusts with each other as trustee and beneficiary. Their financial and health care powers of attorney may appoint the other spouse as agent. Spouses may also be the beneficiaries of life insurance and retirement benefits.

Even without an estate plan, spouses are entitled, by law, to many estate rights. These include the right to a share of a spouse's estate, dower (an estate that widows have in their husbands' real property), and other allowances from the spouse's estate.

As explained in "After Your Divorce" on page 141, a divorce terminates all these estate rights. But there is always a risk that one spouse may die or become incapacitated *during* the divorce, giving the other control of the property. If you're in good health, this risk is small and probably not worth worrying about. But if you're in poor health, you may want to do some quick estate planning during the divorce.

There are a few things you can do yourself without a lawyer. You can revise your will or living trust naming a new personal representative in the will or a new trustee/beneficiaries in the trust. If you've appointed your spouse as agent under a financial or health care power of attorney, you can make a new one with another agent. And unless you and your spouse have agreed otherwise, you can change the designation of your spouse as beneficiary of your life insurance and retirement benefits.

To do more, you're going to need legal help. In Michigan, you normally cannot totally disinherit your spouse by will, since spouses are guaranteed a minimum share of the estate. However, a lawyer can prepare a will for you reducing your spouse's share to that legal minimum. In exceptional cases, spouses can lose their estate rights by marital misconduct (bigamy, absence, desertion, neglect for one year or more). A lawyer can tell you whether you qualify for this exception, and how to disinherit your spouse if you do.

A lawyer can also advise you about releasing estate rights. You may have already done that in a prenuptial agreement. The lawyer can tell you whether the release was effective. It's also possible to release estate rights in a postnuptial agreement (signed after marriage), especially during a separation leading to divorce. A lawyer should prepare that kind of agreement. After any release of estate rights, you are free to benefit whomever you like in your will.

With a lawyer's help, you could also convert any joint tenancy property (also known as tenancy by the entirety property) into tenancy in common ownership. Unlike other forms of joint property, tenancy in common doesn't have rights of survivorship. So when a spouse-owner dies, the surviving spouse doesn't get everything. Instead, the deceased spouse's estate and the surviving spouse split the property. This division makes tenancy in common ideal for estranged spouses who want to keep their shares of joint property separate.

Do I Need "Preliminary Relief"?

In most lawsuits, you don't get any relief (the things you're asking for in your lawsuit) unless and until you win the case. Divorce is different. In divorce cases it's often possible to get some relief before the end of the divorce.

As mentioned in Part II of this chapter, courts may temporarily decide the issues of custody, parenting time, residence of children, child support and alimony. And as pointed out previously in this part, courts can also do some preliminary property division/protection during divorces. If a court grants an order for preliminary relief, the issue is decided until the end of the case when the court makes a final decision.

Preliminary relief is important in contested cases, both for practical and tactical reasons. But this relief can be useful in uncontested cases as well. For example, a preliminary order can give one parent custody of the children and child support while the divorce is pending. Without a court order like this, both parents are entitled to share the children and the parental obligation to support the children cannot be legally enforced.

The trouble is, the legal procedures for getting preliminary relief are complicated. Before you seek the relief, decide whether it's really necessary.

Alternatives to Preliminary Relief

Preliminary relief is useful but it isn't required in divorce cases, and you can often get by without it. When you are self-sufficient, you may not need preliminary relief at all. Or if the defendant is unavailable, or impoverished and unable to provide any support, it may not be worth seeking.

If you believe preliminary relief is necessary, you may be able to improvise a substitute. You and the defendant can agree to have the equivalent of preliminary relief provided privately out of court. For example, you both might informally agree on custody, parenting time and payment of child support or alimony, without a court order, while your divorce is pending. In many ways, informal arrangements like this resemble what you might obtain in preliminary relief from the court, except that it won't be legally enforceable.*

Another option is to seek support *before* you file for divorce. As explained in "Separation" on page 41, you can obtain child support or alimony from a nonsupporting spouse under the family support laws Michigan and other states have. If you obtain a family support order, it will continue during the divorce and serve as a substitute for preliminary child support and/or alimony. But to get family support, you must ask for it before you file for divorce. Afterward, it's too late because the divorce law takes over and controls all requests for support.

If you meet income eligibility, you can also get support from the Family Independence Program (FIP). After FIP enrollment, county officials will typically seek family support from the noncustodial spouse, to get reimbursement for the FIP benefits. As with your own family support case, all this should be done *before* the divorce is filed. If you seek FIP payments after filing, then a preliminary order is necessary to get reimbursement.

If none of these substitutes works, and you believe you must have preliminary relief, see Appendix B, which has complete information, instructions and forms for seeking the interim kind of preliminary relief.

More Information

On adjusting to life during and after divorce:

Creative Divorce, Mel Krantzler, New York: M. Evans and Company, Inc., 1973

The Good Divorce, Constance Ahrons, New York: HarperCollins, 1994

About being a single parent, contact a local chapter of **Parents Without Partners**. Its Web site, www.parentswithout-partners.org, has a handy chapter finder.

---

*   Another problem with paying alimony informally out of court is that the payer won't be entitled to an income tax deduction for the payments, since they're not being paid in a divorce document.

Can I Socialize during the Divorce?

As couples split up, they often wonder whether they can start new social or sexual relationships. What you do during separation and divorce ought to be your own business. But regrettably, extramarital activity can be interpreted as marital fault, which could hurt you later.

In a contested divorce, marital fault from extramarital activity may influence custody, parenting time, property division and alimony. Marital fault shouldn't cause problems in uncontested cases since everything is agreeable. But the fault could be important later on, if custody or parenting time becomes contested in a post-divorce dispute.

As a result, use your common sense as you begin your single life. You don't have to live like a hermit. But as a parent, you should be discreet in your new social and sexual relationships. That will prevent any possible legal trouble now or later.

Can I Keep the Divorce Secret?

Although court files are public records, courts have the power to restrict access to the contents of files by sealing them. In fact, courts once routinely sealed divorce cases between wealthy or influential people.

In 1991, new court rules were adopted governing court secrecy. Now one must file a motion to seal a file and convince the court that there is "good cause" for sealing.* Because of these rules, it's difficult to have divorce files sealed. If you want to try to get your file sealed, contact a lawyer for help.

Some local newspapers cover legal news and publish lists of divorces granted by the courts in their area. There is really no way to keep that information out of the papers, since the completion of a divorce is a matter of public record even if the divorce file itself has been sealed.

Will I Have Tax Problems from the Divorce?

At one time, divorce was a tax nightmare. Not only were the tax rules for divorce complex, divorce itself had many negative tax consequences. These rules were changed by the Tax Reform Act of 1984 (TRA). The TRA is a rare example of a tax law that actually made the law simpler and fairer.

---

*   A related problem is editing papers, which the defendant must receive, to keep selected personal information out of the hands of a defendant-spouse abuser. See "Keeping Personal Information away from a Spouse-Abuser" on page 65 for more about this issue.

More Information

On taxes and divorce, obtain "Tax Information for Divorced or Separated Individuals" (Pub. 504).

About the EITC, see "Earned Income Tax Credit" (Pub. 596).

These booklets are available from any IRS office, by calling the agency at (800) 829-3676, or you can view these on the IRS Web site: www.irs.gov.

The TRA redefined which divorce-related payments qualify as alimony (see "Alimony" on page 29 for more about these alimony tax rules). But the TRA didn't alter how alimony is taxed. It's still income for the recipient and a deduction (technically an adjustment to gross income) for the payer.

The TRA treats child support as it was under the old law. It's neither income to the recipient nor a deduction for the payer. However, the TRA scrapped the complicated old rules for claiming exemptions for dependent children. The TRA says that the custodial parent* is normally entitled to the dependency exemptions. The custodial parent may assign the exemptions to the noncustodial parent by filing an IRS form, Release of Claim to Exemption for Child of Divorced or Separated Parents (Form 8332). Or the divorce court can assign the dependency exemptions to the noncustodial parent (see "Assigning Dependency Exemptions" in Appendix H for more about dependency exemptions).

For many low-income custodial parents, there's a tax benefit more valuable than dependency exemptions: earned income tax credit (EITC). The EITC, which has a maximum value of $4,140 in 2002, not only provides a credit against income tax owed, it can also be converted into a cash payment if you don't owe any income tax.

The EITC was originally designed for custodial parents living with and taking care of children. Since 1994, noncustodians can also qualify for the EITC, but the credit is reduced for them. Either way, there are complicated rules for qualifying for the EITC, which are explained in the IRS's EITC publication. If you need help claiming the credit, look for a local nonprofit tax clinic or program. Watch out for commercial tax preparation companies which charge a lot for tax return preparation, and which offer "advances" (loans really) against your EITC. These services can take a big bite (30% or more) out of your credit.

The most far-reaching change wrought by the TRA was to make all transfers of property between divorcing spouses nontaxable. Previously, spouses could gain or lose income from the property divisions of their divorces. Such gain or loss from a divorce is no longer possible under the new law, although income tax problems can still crop up later when a spouse sells property obtained in the divorce.

What If My Spouse Is Mentally Incompetent?

If your spouse has been declared mentally incompetent by a probate court, s/he must be specially represented in the divorce. After a declaration of mental incompetency, the probate court may appoint a conservator (a legal

---

*   For tax purposes, the custodial parent is the one with physical custody of the children. If parents have joint physical custody, the custodial parent is the one with physical custody the greater number of days per year.

representative like a guardian) to manage the incompetent's affairs. A conservator has the authority to represent the incompetent in a divorce.

If you have been appointed as your spouse's conservator, you won't be able to represent him/her in the divorce because of the obvious conflict of interest. But you can ask the probate court for appointment of another person as conservator, and the new conservator could handle the divorce.

An alternative is to have a *guardian ad litem* (GAL) appointed for your mentally incompetent spouse. While a conservator has broad powers to manage affairs, a GAL's authority is limited to representing the incompetent in a single lawsuit. In a divorce, the court handling the divorce, not a probate court, can appoint a GAL for a spouse after the divorce is filed.

Whatever arrangements are made for your incompetent spouse, they should be completed before or soon after you file your divorce. Then you can serve the spouse's conservator or GAL with the divorce papers, and the divorce can proceed normally.

What If I Need to File for Bankruptcy?

Divorce and bankruptcy seem to go together because financial problems often cause divorce. According to one study, divorced people file for bankruptcy at three times the rate of the nondivorced population. Despite this link, divorce and bankruptcy aren't as compatible as they ought to be. Each procedure requires a separate case, filed in different courts (divorce in state court; bankruptcy in federal court), using different laws and rules.

Because of these problems, if you're considering both a divorce and a bankruptcy, seek legal advice. The lawyer can advise you about the relationship between divorce and bankruptcy, which type of bankruptcy to file (there are several), and whether to file singly or jointly (even separated spouses are permitted to file joint bankruptcies).

Don't wait to get legal help, because the timing of a divorce and bankruptcy can be important. In some cases, it's better to file the bankruptcy before completion of the divorce to protect exempt marital property. In other cases, the divorce should be finished before the bankruptcy is started so that some debts and obligations—but never child support or alimony—can be wiped out. There are no firm rules about the sequence of cases; the timing will depend on the nature of your property and debts. Your lawyer should be able to explain what's best in your situation.

What If I Want to Dismiss the Divorce?

According to one estimate, 20-30% of all divorces are voluntarily withdrawn and dismissed. No one knows the exact reason for all these dismissals, but it's likely that most cases were dropped after the spouses reconciled.

There's no penalty for withdrawing your divorce after you start it. On the contrary, Michigan law encourages reconciliation and dismissal at every step of a divorce. In part, that's what the statutory waiting period is for. If you and your spouse decide to reconcile, see Appendix G for instructions and the form to dismiss your divorce.

What If My Spouse Abuses Me?

The physical abuse of one spouse by the other—usually, but not always, a wife at the hands of her husband—has been a constant problem with marriage and divorce. It's been estimated that spouse abuse is a problem in one out of three marriages. Sometimes this domestic violence becomes deadly. According to recent FBI figures, nearly a third of all female homicide victims are murdered by either their husbands or boyfriends.

For years, the legal system offered abused spouses little protection. It often seemed that family violence was a private matter into which the legal system wouldn't intervene. But that attitude has changed, and Michigan's spouse abuse laws have been toughened recently. Today it's possible to get personal protection orders (PPOs) preventing your spouse from:

> ## More Information
>
> About spouse abuse, get:
>
> *Getting Free: You Can End Abuse and Take Back Your Life*, Ginny Nicarthy, Seattle: The Seal Press, 1997
>
> On Michigan's spouse abuse laws, ask your state senator or representative for a *Survivor's Handbook for Battered Women*.
>
> Call the **National Spouse Abuse Hotline** at (800) 799-7233 for referral to a spouse abuse shelter in your area.

- assaulting, attacking, beating, wounding or molesting you or someone else
- threatening to kill or physically injure you or someone else any act or conduct interfering with personal liberty or causing a reasonable apprehension of violence, such as stalking, harassment or unwanted contact
- interfering with you at work or school
- having access to your personal records or those of your children to get information about you
- purchasing or possessing a firearm
- entering property (so that your spouse can be ordered away from your home, even when it's the joint marital home)
- interfering with your removal of personal property or children from your spouse's property
- removing minor children from the person with legal custody, except as allowed by a court order

You don't have to wait until a divorce to get a PPO. They're available anytime there's domestic abuse, even before you file. After filing, you can get a PPO while the divorce is pending. It's also possible to get a permanent PPO injunction in your divorce judgment, which can remain in effect for any specified period of time.

When a spouse violates a PPO, s/he can be immediately arrested by the police, even if they didn't see the offense. Violation of a PPO is both a civil and criminal contempt of court, punishable by a maximum fine of $500 and 93 days in jail.

For all the protection it offers, Michigan's PPO law is complicated, making it difficult for nonlawyers to use. That's why it's best to have a lawyer when you're facing spouse abuse. If you have a low income, contact legal aid. The legal aid offices are very busy, but they usually give priority to spouse abuse cases. Or you can rely on a private lawyer for help. If you're determined to represent yourself, you can obtain PPO forms and instructions from the clerk of your circuit or family court. Since 1994, all Michigan circuit and family courts must make these materials available.

Whatever you do, keep in mind that a PPO cannot guarantee your safety. A court order is only a piece of paper; it won't stop someone bent on violence. If you believe your spouse is determined to harm you, take whatever precautions are necessary to protect yourself—with or without a PPO. This may even mean moving to a safe place. You may be able to find refuge with a friend or relative. There are also special shelters for abused spouses (and their children). Michigan has around 50 shelters serving every part of the state.

Keeping Personal Information away from a Spouse-Abuser

Several divorce papers contain personal information about you, your children, employment and health care coverage. During the divorce, the defendant gets copies of these papers.

If there's a danger of spouse abuse from the defendant, and you're keeping a distance, you may not want to reveal your current address and employment to the defendant. In exceptional cases like this, you can receive permission to withhold personal information from the divorce papers, and provide it separately and confidentially to the court. Ask the friend of the court about withholding personal information this way.

Where Can I File If My Spouse or I Am Native American?

Did you know that Michigan has the largest Native American population in the Eastern United States? Michigan has 12 federally-recognized Indian tribes and 4 which are recognized by the state. These tribes keep tribal rolls listing all members of the tribe (persons not on these rolls aren't regarded as members). The tribes often have their own reservations with separate tribal court systems which can grant divorces.

Native Americans can always file for divorce in regular state courts. But if they live in "Indian country" (reservation land plus satellite communities), they may have the option of filing in a tribal court. A divorce they receive there will be according to tribal law, which can be very different from the law described in this book.

Another concern is a federal law, the Indian Child Welfare Act, protecting the custody of Native American children. But this act doesn't normally apply to divorce, except when the custody of Indian children is assigned to nonparent third parties.

> ### More Information
>
> About divorce in tribal courts, contact:
>
> **Michigan Indian Legal Services**
> 814 S. Garfield Ave.
> Suite A
> Traverse City, MI 49686
> (800) 968-6877

What If My Spouse or I Am an "Alien" (Noncitizen)?

If you or your spouse are aliens, your foreign nationality probably won't prevent you from getting a divorce in Michigan (see below about aliens and jurisdiction). But your alien status can have all kinds of hidden effects on the divorce, which are also explained below.

Can an Alien Get a Divorce in Michigan?

In the United States, divorce jurisdiction is based on residence. If you reside here you can get a divorce, regardless of your nationality. But in other countries, particularly civil law areas (basically the non-English speaking world), divorce jurisdiction is usually determined by nationality, not residence. In these countries, you must be a citizen to get a divorce. A few countries, such as Ireland, don't bother with divorce jurisdiction at all because they refuse to permit divorce.

If you're a citizen of one of those countries, a divorce you get in Michigan might not be recognized in your country. This won't be a problem if you have broken all ties with the country. But it could spell trouble if you intend to return to the country, or have children or property there. To find out how a Michigan divorce will be treated in your native country, check with your embassy or consulate.

Divorce by a Plaintiff-Alien

An alien living in Michigan can usually file for divorce here, and the divorce will go through. What an alien must consider is the impact the divorce will have on his/her residence rights. The impact is different for two types of aliens:

Glossary

Immigrant—an alien who intends to settle in the country permanently.

Nonimmigrant—an alien who is staying in the country temporarily.

Immigrant. Aliens married to U.S. citizens typically apply for permanent residence here as spouses of citizens, becoming "lawful permanent residents." Aliens married two years or more quickly gain permanent residence. But aliens in shorter marriages usually get conditional residence, because of a suspicion that the marriage might be a sham.

A divorce during the two-year conditional residence period can be a problem for an immigrant. The divorce itself doesn't prove that the marriage is a sham (that's judged by the parties' intentions when they got married). But a divorce makes it more difficult to prove the marriage is real, especially without the help of an estranged spouse.

Nonimmigrant. A divorce can jeopardize the residence rights of a nonimmigrant, particularly if admission status depends solely on marriage. After the marriage is terminated by the divorce, this status is gone and the nonimmigrant may face deportation (there are some exceptions if there has been spouse/child abuse or in cases of extreme hardship).

Plaintiff-Citizen Filing Divorce against a Defendant-Alien

As a U.S. citizen filing for divorce, your citizenship is secure, and won't be affected by the divorce. The divorce could have an impact on the defendant-alien's residence rights, as described above. Nevertheless, the divorce could have an unforeseen effect on you.

Typically, U.S. citizens marrying aliens seek residence rights for them by filing a support affidavit. The affidavit promises to support the alien-spouse or else reimburse the government for any public assistance the alien might receive until the alien: 1) becomes a U.S. citizen 2) establishes an earnings record in the U.S. This obligation to support, which is actually a contract, survives divorce. So if you divorce an alien, and the alien receives public assistance, you could be liable for reimbursement.

Do You Need Legal Help?

If your divorce looks too complicated for you to do yourself, you need legal help. How do you find a good lawyer? The best way is by recommendation from someone you trust. But if you can't find a lawyer by word of mouth, legal services and referrals are available from:

Legal aid. Those who meet federal poverty guidelines are eligible for legal aid from one of the legal aid organizations located throughout the state. The problem is, these programs are often so understaffed that they can help only a fraction of those eligible for their services. To find the legal aid office in your area, look under "Attorneys" or "Social Service Organizations" in the yellow pages.

Legal clinics and services. Newspapers often carry advertisements for low-cost uncontested divorce services. Some of these services are offered by local attorneys doing business as clinics, while others may be branches of national legal service companies.

Lawyers. These days lawyers aren't shy about advertising, and you can find their ads in newspapers and the yellow pages. County bar associations in several of the larger counties provide lawyer referral services. To obtain lawyer referrals in other counties, call the state bar referral service at (800) 968-0738.

On the other hand, you may have decided that your divorce isn't too complicated. If that's true, you're ready to move on to Chapter 2 and begin your divorce.

Chapter 2

Legal Basics

Overview of Divorce Procedure

PART I: Starting Your Divorce

PART II: Finishing Your Divorce

After Your Divorce

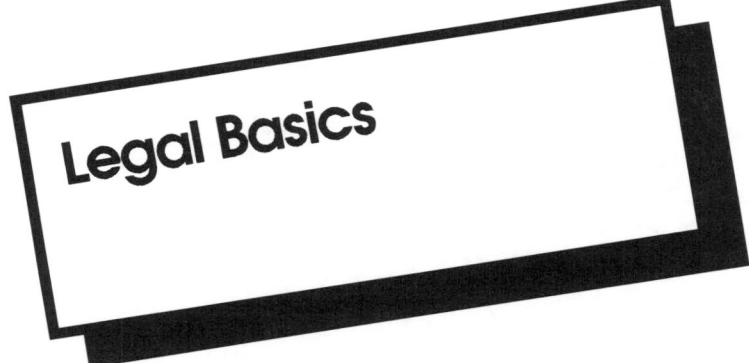

Legal Basics

For lawyers, an uncontested divorce isn't much more than a clerical task, which they usually assign to their secretaries. But nonlawyers are often stumped by the simplest things: How do I fill out the divorce papers? Where do I file them? When do I file them? How do I find the right court? This section deals with these legal basics and more, so you will be as well-prepared as any lawyer.

Court System

Before 1998, divorce cases were handled by the general circuit courts of Michigan. On January 1, 1998, Michigan's court system was reorganized and new family courts (which are technically divisions of the circuit courts) went into operation. Michigan family courts deal with all kinds of family-related cases: divorce (including after-judgment matters), annulment, separate maintenance, family support, custody, parenting time, paternity, domestic violence, child abuse and neglect, juvenile delinquency, guardianship/conservatorship, adoption, emancipation of minors and name change cases.

The philosophy of the family court system is to specialize in family law matters, unlike the general circuit courts which deal with all kinds of civil and criminal cases. Michigan family courts also have a "one-family, one-judge" policy, which brings all of a family's cases before the same judge, who is familiar with the family and its problems.

Family courts may be fairly new, but the court personnel haven't changed. The following people have responsibility for your divorce case:

Judge. Your divorce is handled by a family court judge, who is either a circuit court or probate court judge on assignment to the family court. You cannot choose the judge for your case. Ordinarily, when you file the clerk randomly assigns a judge to your case. But if you or members of your family have other family law cases pending in the court, the clerk will try to assign your divorce to the judge hearing the other case(s). With this assignment, the same judge will handle all the family's cases. If you dislike the judge, you cannot get another unless you can prove that the judge is actually biased or prejudiced against you.

Clerk. The family court clerk receives all your divorce papers and maintains a case file for them. Throughout this book, the family court clerk is simply called the clerk. In most counties, the county clerk is the clerk of the family court. But some counties have a special family court clerk, separate from the county clerk.

To find out who does the family court clerking in your county, call the county clerk and ask for information. Or simply look up the county government listing in the telephone book, and see if there is a separate listing for a clerk of the family division of the circuit court.

Prosecuting attorney. County prosecuting attorneys have the power to intervene in divorce cases to protect the interests of minor children and the "public good." Busy with criminal prosecutions, they seldom do that. Nevertheless, prosecuting attorneys (except in Kent, Macomb, Oakland and Wayne Counties) are entitled to notice of all divorces with minor children and must receive copies of the summons and divorce complaint.

Friend of the court. When it became apparent that prosecuting attorneys weren't bothering with divorces, the office of the friend of the court was created to provide better supervision of divorces with minor children or when alimony is sought.

Friends of the court play a number of roles during divorce. They conduct investigations and make recommendations to the judge about the issues of custody, parenting time, child support, and alimony. They may also review and approve judgments and other orders before they are submitted to the judge. The friend of the court was traditionally the collector, distributor and enforcer of child support and alimony. But many of these duties have now been transferred to the state disbursement unit. In contested cases, the friend of the court may act as a referee or mediator.

Until recently, the friend of the court participated in every divorce case with minor children. But under a 2002 law, it's sometimes possible to "opt out" of the friend of the court system. After an opt-out (there are several kinds), the friend of the court won't manage the case, and the parties must assume this responsibility. For more about opting out, see Appendix C.

State disbursement unit. The SDU is a new state agency, in Lansing, which has taken over collection and distribution of support (child support and alimony) from the local county friends of the court. See "Centralization of Child Support Services" on page 25 for more about this transfer of duties.

Family Independence Agency. The FIA is a state agency, formerly the Department of Social Services (DSS), in charge of public assistance like the Family Independence Progam (FIP), Medicaid and other benefits. The FIA also assists in establishing and enforcing child support orders, particularly when the family is receiving public assistance.

Courtroom clerk. The courtroom clerk sits in the courtroom next to the judge while the court is in session. During a trial, the courtroom clerk is responsible for marking and receiving exhibits. In an uncontested divorce case, the courtroom clerk has a smaller role, but in some counties s/he may receive and file papers during the final hearing.

Assignment clerk. Several of the larger counties use special assignment clerks to schedule court hearings. In these counties, final hearings in uncontested divorce cases may be scheduled through the assignment clerk.

Court reporter. The court reporter sits below the judge and records the court proceedings. In an uncontested divorce case, the court reporter makes a record of the final hearing, although it's unlikely that a transcript of the hearing will ever be needed.

Judge's secretary. Working in the judge's office, the judge's secretary may help in submitting papers to the judge for review.

Law clerk. Most judges have law clerks, who are often law students or new lawyers. Law clerks help judges with a number of tasks, including review of papers.

In many counties, these court personnel are conveniently located under one roof, usually in a courthouse or county building. But in other counties, whose court systems have outgrown their courthouses, court personnel may be scattered among several buildings. Before you begin your divorce, make sure you know where the court personnel are located.

The first person you want to find is the clerk, because you will begin your divorce in the clerk's office by filing the initial divorce papers there.

Papers

Many divorce-filers are surprised to find that courts won't do the divorce paperwork for you. Instead, it's your responsibility to prepare all the divorce papers. Don't try to do this all at once; prepare the papers as you need them, during each step of your divorce.

Preparing Papers

Whenever possible, type the divorce papers. But if you can't, it's permissible to print them by hand in ink. Either way, make sure the papers are neat and legible.

The divorce papers you file must also be accurate and honest. Judges can penalize those who intentionally or even carelessly file false legal papers. Ordinarily, these penalties are payments of money to opponents hurt by the false papers.

But for some false papers the penalties are severe. When you sign an affidavit, you swear to the notary public that the contents are true. You do much the same when you sign papers with a verification declaration ("I declare that the statements above are true to the best of my information, knowledge, and belief"). According to Michigan law, it's a crime to knowingly file a false affidavit, while the intentional falsification of a verified document is a contempt of court. Don't be alarmed by these penalties; just make sure that your papers are accurate and honest.

Among your divorce papers are several forms issued by the State Court Administrative Office (SCAO). These state forms include Michigan court forms and friend of the court forms, which are coded in the lower left corner by type (MC or FOC), number and date of release. Besides these state forms, a few counties, notably Wayne (number-coded), have local forms.

Added to the state forms are several Grand River Press forms (code: GRP/number/date). The Grand River Press forms include most of the important divorce papers, such as the complaint, default and judgment. The state used to publish these forms, but discontinued publication in 1989. The Grand River Press forms have been created to replace them.

You may notice a difference in the type-size of the papers. On Jan. 1, 2004, a new court rule went into effect requiring that all court papers, except the state-issued (SCAO) forms, must be in 12-point type. Thus, the printing on all the GRP forms was increased to 12-point size. Also, when you fill in the papers, try to print or type in a larger size (no fine print) matching the printing on these forms.

The new court rule also specifies that all court papers must be 8½ x 11." Previously, this was the maximum size, but papers could be a little smaller. Prior editions of this book were 8½ x 11," making the perforated forms .25" smaller after detachment from the book (perforation of the forms causes a .25" loss in the binding margin). Now, the book has been increased in overall width by .25" to make up this difference.

More Information

An affidavit is a legal paper stating facts that must be sworn to under oath before someone, such as a notary public, who can give oaths.

To obtain notary services, look in the yellow pages under "Notaries Public," or contact insurance agencies, banks or mailing/shipping stores, which often have notary services available.

Every form has a special purpose and each is prepared differently. Yet all the forms share similar captions which are filled in as follows:

STATE OF MICHIGAN Circuit Court - Family Division OJIBWAY COUNTY	JUDGMENT OF DIVORCE Page 1 of ____ pages	CASE NO. 89-00501-DM JUDGE TUBBS
Plaintiff (appearing *in propria persona*): DARLENE ANN LOVELACE 121 S. MAIN LAKE CITY, MI 48800 772-0000	v	**Defendant:** DUDLEY ERNEST LOVELACE 900 S. MAPLE LAKE CITY, MI 48800 773-3004

STATE OF MICHIGAN Circuit Court - Family Division OJIBWAY COUNTY	JUDGMENT OF DIVORCE Page 2 of ____ pages	CASE NO. 89-00501-DM
Plaintiff: DARLENE ANN LOVELACE	v	**Defendant:** DUDLEY ERNEST LOVELACE

As you can see, the papers have either a long or short caption. In a long caption, you must put the county where the divorce is filed in the upper left corner. The names, addresses and telephone numbers of you, as plaintiff, and your spouse, as defendant, go in the two large boxes. Some state-issued forms may ask for court or friend of the court addresses and telephone numbers. You can get this extra information from a telephone directory (look under the "County Government" listing in the blue (government) pages).

Incidentally, the italicized Latin phrase in the caption of many of the forms signals that this is a self-help divorce. *In propria persona* (sometimes abbreviated to *in pro per*) means "in your own person," indicating that you are doing the case yourself without a lawyer. Some of the state-issued forms, such as the Summons and Complaint (MC 01), have caption boxes for lawyer representatives. You can leave these boxes blank, or insert in them: "In Pro Per."

Your case number goes in the upper right corner. This number starts with a two-digit number for the year followed by several other numbers. It ends with a two-letter case-type code. All cases in Michigan have codes according to their type: A divorce with minor children bears a DM code and divorces without minor children have a DO code. Because a case number isn't assigned until filing, you won't have it for your initial divorce papers, so

To Obtain

Extra copies of Wayne County forms, call the Wayne County Friend of the Court's form fax line at (313) 967-3662. The line has a menu where you can select the form you want, which is then faxed to a fax number you specify.

The Wayne County circuit court system also has a Web site, www.3rdcc.org, from which you can view and/or download forms.

You should have enough caption labels for all your papers. But if you run out, you can get more in the clerk's office in room 201 of the Coleman A. Young Municipal Center (CAYMC) (formerly the City-County Bldg.) at 2 Woodward Ave. in Detroit.

leave the case number spaces blank on them. But include your case number in the captions of all your other papers.

If you're in a larger county that has more than one family court judge, write the name of your judge below the case numbers on all the papers you file after the initial divorce papers. This will help direct the papers to the correct case file and judge.

With a short caption, you can omit much of the above information. All you need for a short caption is the court, case number and your and your spouse's names as plaintiff and defendant.

Wayne County, which has the state's largest court system, has a caption-labeling system to prevent mishandling of court papers. When you file a divorce in Wayne County, the clerk prints strips of caption labels for both parties. Notice how the clerk takes several labels and affixes these to the captions of your initial divorce papers. As you file other papers, use labels from your strip to label them in the same way. Save the other strip of caption labels because you must have it served on the defendant later.

Copying Papers

As you prepare divorce papers, make some photocopies. Except for some of the initial papers, make three photocopies of each divorce paper. After copying, put "FOC" (an abbreviation for friend of the court) in the upper left corner of one photocopy of each paper. The friend of the court gets copies of all your papers through the clerk. By earmarking your papers with "FOC," you ensure that these copies are directed to the friend of the court. In all, you should have enough divorce papers and copies to distribute as follows:

- original - court (clerk)
- 1st copy - friend of the court
- 2nd copy - plaintiff
- 3rd copy - defendant

When you photocopy divorce papers, copy both sides of any two-sided forms because some papers have important information on the reverse. Most two-sided forms are tumble-printed, with their reverse sides upside down. This makes it possible to read the reverse sides while the papers are fastened to a file folder by simply lifting them up. When you photocopy these two-sided forms, you might not be able to run your copies through the photocopier again to make a tumble-printed form. If so, just make the paper into a two-page form and staple the pages together.

With all these papers and copies, it's easy to get disorganized. To keep track of everything, prepare a file for all your divorce papers. Not only will this file keep you organized during the divorce, it will give you a complete record of the case afterward.

When you file your divorce, the clerk will open a file for your case. As you file papers, the clerk will ordinarily use the following procedure:

- keep the original for your case file
- take the copy marked "FOC" and forward it to the friend of the court
- return a true copy* for the plaintiff
- return a true copy for the defendant

You can file papers with the clerk personally, by mail or sometimes even by facsimile (fax). Despite these options, it's usually best to file the initial divorce papers in person and the other papers this way whenever you can. By filing personally, you can pay any fees that are due and immediately get back copies of your papers for service on the other party.

For filing by mail, send your papers and any fees to the clerk along with a cover letter asking for filing and return of the copies you have enclosed. To get the copies back quickly, include a self-addressed envelope with postage.

Filing by fax isn't allowed when filing fees are due (unless you have paid in advance by depositing money with the clerk), because the clerk won't accept a filing without payment of the filing fee. Moreover, the clerk won't send or fax back copies of the papers you file, so there's no way to get copies. Thus, fax-filing should be used in emergency, when you have to file in a hurry to meet a filing deadline.

You must pay several fees to get a divorce (see "How Much Will My Divorce Cost?" on page 49 for a description of the fees). Except for the service fee, you pay these fees to the clerk. Clerks usually accept cash, personal checks and money orders as payment. After you pay, the clerk may give you a receipt, which you should keep as proof of payment.

The service fee is paid outside of court. As mentioned before, you can choose from among several methods of service: 1) acknowledgment 2) mail 3) delivery. You can usually obtain service by acknowledgment for free. When you use service by mail, you pay the post office for the mailing. If you

---

*   When a clerk returns a copy of a paper to you, it may have a stamp or seal indicating that it's a true copy. This says that the copy is real. Try to get true copies of all papers you file, especially court orders (ex parte order and the divorce judgment).

Courtroom Etiquette

During a court hearing, you should follow these rules of courtroom behavior:

- Dress neatly and be well-groomed.
- Be on time.
- Be courteous to the judge and others.
- Wait until called on to speak.
- Don't interrupt while the judge or others are talking; you will get your chance to speak.
- After the judge makes a decision, don't persist in arguing your view.

use service by delivery, you pay the server, who is usually a sheriff or commercial process server. Ordinarily, the server bills you for the service fee after service when s/he returns the proof of service to you. But if you use service by delivery out of town or out of state, it's a good idea to prepay the service fee. When you send the service papers to the server, include a check or money order for $30 or so, and a note asking the server to refund/bill you for the difference between your prepayment and his service fee.

If you qualify, you can get an exemption from payment of the court fees. You are exempt from payment if you are receiving public assistance or have a low income. Appendix A has more about qualifying for a fee exemption, and instructions and the affidavit to apply for the exemption.

If you've received a fee exemption, you won't have to pay any court fees during your divorce (although you might have to pay them at the end of the divorce). If the clerk tries to charge you a fee during your divorce, refer the clerk to the fee exemption affidavit, which will be in your case file.

Time

During your divorce, you must deal with several important time periods and deadlines, including: 1) 180-day state residence requirement 2) 10-day county residence requirement 3) answering period (usually 21 or 28 days) 4) statutory waiting period (six months for divorces with minor children) 5) filing deadlines for various papers.

The court rules have detailed provisions to figure periods of time. For a time period of days, the period begins on the day after the day of an act (filing, service, establishment of residence, etc.); the day of the act itself isn't counted. The last day of the period is counted, unless it falls on a Saturday, Sunday or legal holiday. In that case, the period extends to the next day that isn't a Saturday, Sunday or legal holiday.

Example: You serve a defendant by mail on May 1. The 28-day answering period after service by mail begins on May 2 (the day after the day of service) and ends on May 29 (which in this example is not a Saturday, Sunday or legal holiday). The defendant has until May 29 to answer.

Example: You serve a defendant by mail on May 1. The 28-day answering period after service by mail begins on May 2 (the day after the day of service) and ends on May 29. But this year May 29 is Memorial Day, a legal holiday, so the answering period extends to May 30. The defendant must answer by May 30.

Like a time period of days, a time period of months begins on the day after the day of an act. The last day of the period is the same day of the month on which the period began. If there is no such day, the last day of the period is whatever the last day of that month is. As with time periods of days, a time period of months that ends on a Saturday, Sunday or legal holiday extends to the next day that isn't a Saturday, Sunday or legal holiday.

> *Example:* You file your divorce complaint on May 1. The six-month statutory waiting period begins on May 2 (the day after the day of the complaint filing) and ends on November 2 (the same day of the month as the day on which the period began). Your final hearing could be scheduled anytime after November 2.

> *Example:* You file your divorce complaint on May 30. The six-month statutory waiting period begins on May 31 (the day after the day of the complaint filing) and ends on November 30. The waiting period ends on November 30 because there is no Nov. 31. Your final hearing could be scheduled anytime after November 30.

To avoid time problems, you can simply estimate the time period and then add a little more time for safety. For example, if you figure that a time period ends sometime during the first week of a month, you could wait until the middle of the month to take action, avoiding any danger of acting too quickly.

Courthouse Appearances

During your divorce, you must appear once or possibly twice in court before the judge. You may also have to make an informal appearance or two at the courthouse, outside the courtroom.

Court Hearings

All divorce plaintiffs are expected to attend a final hearing, in court before the judge, at the end of the case. During the hearing, you must give some brief testimony to get a Judgment of Divorce (GRP 4). Less often, a court hearing may also be necessary if you seek preliminary relief, the defendant objects to the relief and the friend of the court's efforts to settle the dispute fail.

For either type of court hearing, make sure you know the location of the hearing beforehand. Court hearings normally take place in the courtroom of the judge assigned to your case, which is usually in the county courthouse or similar county building.

Go to the place of the court hearing on the scheduled day and time. Try to arrive around 30 minutes before the hearing, to take care of any last-minute business. By arriving early, you can also observe other hearings. Be prepared to spend most of the morning or afternoon at the hearing, since it may not start on time.

When your case is called by the courtroom clerk, step forward and identify yourself. Mention that you are representing yourself. Take a seat at one of the tables inside the bar (the gate) of the court, and get ready to begin your presentation.

Other Courthouse Appearances

You may also attend a case conference (in some counties) or referee hearing (if preliminary relief is sought and contested) outside of the courtroom. These are informal sessions held by court personnel without the judge. As with a formal court hearing, know where the meeting is held, be on time and observe normal courtroom etiquette.

Special Arrangements for a Courthouse Appearance

If you have a handicap (mobility, visual, speech or hearing impairment), court personnel can make special accommodations for your courthouse appearance. For non-English-speakers, the court can appoint an interpreter to translate the proceedings into your language.

Handicapper Accommodations

Tell court personnel about the handicap by preparing a Request for Accommodations (MC 70) (see the sample MC 70 at the end of this section). File or send the form to the clerk well ahead of the scheduled appearance. Court personnel will contact you before the appearance, and discuss the accommodation you need.

In exceptional cases, special accommodations aren't enough and you may be excused from the court appearance. If so, you can give information, such as testimony for a final hearing, in written or electronic form (by telephone, for example). Persons with severe handicaps may qualify for this exception. Prisoners are also frequently excused from court attendance, and can give written or electronic testimony (see "What If My Spouse or I Am Imprisoned?" on page 46 for more about this procedure).

Foreign Language Interpreters

The court can appoint a foreign language interpreter if you can't speak English well enough to understand the court proceedings. Use the Motion and Order for Appointment of Foreign Language Interpreter (MC 81) (a sample MC 81 appears at the end of this section). The court may skip a hearing on this motion, and simply sign the order.

You could file the MC 81 any time during the divorce. Whenever you file, send a copy of the motion to the defendant, even if s/he has defaulted, at his or her last known address.

Incidentally, there are special foreign language Summons and Complaint (MC 01) forms available in Arabic, Chinese, Hmong, Korean, Russian and Spanish. You can get these from the friend of the court, and use the special forms if your spouse speaks one of these languages, but isn't fluent in English.

Local Rules and Forms

For years, there were variations in divorce procedures among Michigan's 83 counties. In 1993, the state tried to standardize procedures by abolishing all local divorce rules and forms. But little by little, several counties, Wayne in particular, have been permitted to re-adopt local rules and forms.

Don't panic if you encounter some local practices that aren't described in this book. Ask the local authorities what the local practice is and adapt to it. Luckily, variations tend to be minor. They typically concern scheduling the final hearing or dealing with the friend of the court.

New Laws, Rules, Forms and Fees

These days, divorce laws, rules, forms and fees change regularly. Congress and the Michigan Legislature are constantly passing new divorce laws. Added to this are the thousands of decisions courts issue each year, some of which affect divorce.

As a result of this activity, parts of this book may become outdated. To keep the book current, Grand River Press offers an update about recent changes in divorce law. See the order form in the front of this book for update information.

To Obtain

Laws, court rules and other legal information, visit a law library. Most county courthouses have law libraries which are open to the public. The divorce laws are in the MCLAs (Michigan Compiled Laws Annotated) and MSAs (Michigan Statutes Annotated); the court rules are published in *Michigan Rules of Court - State* by the West Group (this volume also includes all the local court rules).

Online, you can access Michigan law via www.michiganlegislature.org, using the search engine to search by section or subject. The basic divorce laws are MCL 552.1-552.1803 and 722.21-722.31 (Child Custody Act of 1970).

For court rules, go to www.courts.michigan.gov/supremecourt, scroll down and click on the "Court Rules Online" icon, and a table of contents will pop up with several choices: 1) under "Michigan Court Rules," select "Chapter 3 Special Proceedings and Actions" for the divorce court rules of MCR 3.201-3.219. 2) under "Local Court Rules," select "Circuit Courts" for local court rules arranged by county.

Approved, SCAO

REQUEST FOR ACCOMMODATIONS

Court name and location

OJIBWAY COUNTY CIRCUIT COURT-FAMILY DIVISION
200 N. MAIN
LAKE CITY, MI 48800

Today's date

4-10-89

Instructions for completing form: *Provide your name, address, and telephone number. Check the boxes which apply to you and provide any necessary details. When you have completed this request, please return it to the court at the above address.*

1. Name

DARLENE A. LOVELACE

Address

121 S. MAIN

City

LAKE CITY

State	Zip	Telephone no.
MI	48800	772-0000

2. Court activity you need accommodations for:

☒ Hearing   5-7-89
        Date

☐ Mediation meeting   Date

☐ Jury duty   Date(s)

☐ Other (specify):   include dates if relevant

3. What is the nature of your disability?

☒ Physical mobility impairment (wheelchair, walker, crutches, etc.)

☐ Speech impairment (specify): _____

☐ Visual impairment

☐ Hearing impairment (specify)   ☐ deaf   ☐ hard of hearing

☐ Other (specify): _____

4. What type of accommodation are you requesting?

☐ Interpreter for deaf (specify whether ASL, tactile, oral, etc.) _____

☐ Assistive listening device (specify type of device) _____

☒ Physical location accessible for persons with a physical mobility concern.

☐ Other (specify) _____

For court use only

MC 70 (10/97) **REQUEST FOR ACCOMMODATIONS**

Approved, SCAO

Original - Court file
1st copy - Assignment Clerk/Extra
2nd copy - Friend of the Court/Extra

3rd copy - Opposing party
4th copy - Moving party

STATE OF MICHIGAN		
JUDICIAL DISTRICT	**MOTION AND ORDER FOR APPOINTMENT**	
JUDICIAL CIRCUIT	**OF FOREIGN LANGUAGE INTERPRETER**	CASE NO.
COUNTY		

Court address

Court telephone no.

Plaintiff name(s)

☒ moving party

Plaintiff's attorney, bar no., address, and telephone no.

v

Defendant name(s)

☐ moving party

Defendant's attorney, bar no., address, and telephone no.

MOTION

1. I state that I am unable to speak English sufficiently to understand and participate in the proceedings in this case.
2. ☐ I am represented by an attorney.   ☒ I am not represented by an attorney.
3. I request the court to appoint a foreign language interpreter to interpret for me.
4. I request an interpreter who speaks the ___KOREAN___ language.
5. If required, place my request on the motion calendar.

___8-1-89___
Date

___Darlene A. Lovelace___
Signature

To be completed only if the court
requires a hearing on the motion

You are notified that a hearing has been scheduled on this matter for:

NOTICE OF HEARING

Judge		Bar no.	Date	
Hearing location				Time
☐ Court address above	☐			

THE CLERK WILL SCHEDULE A HEARING ON THE MOTION, IF NECESSARY.

If you require special accommodations to use the court because of disabilities, please contact the court immediately to make arrangements.

_____
Date

_____
Signature

CERTIFICATE OF MAILING

I certify that on this date I mailed a copy of this motion and notice of hearing (if applicable) to the other party at the last known address.

___8-1-89___
Date

___Darlene A. Lovelace___
Signature

IT IS ORDERED the above motion is

ORDER

___8-15-89___
Date

☒ granted.   ☐ denied.

___Lester Jubbs___
Judge

MC 81 (10/01) **MOTION AND ORDER FOR APPOINTMENT OF FOREIGN LANGUAGE INTERPRETER**

Overview of Divorce Procedure

At first, divorce procedure may seem forbidding. But it's really not so mysterious when you break it down into steps and understand the purpose of each step.

Like any lawsuit, a divorce starts when the plaintiff files a paper known as a complaint. Despite its rather alarming name, a complaint is simply the document that starts a lawsuit. A divorce complaint contains facts about the parties and their marriage, and then asks for relief on the divorce issues. At filing, the clerk issues a summons in the case notifying the defendant and others that a divorce has been filed.

In some cases, the plaintiff wants preliminary relief, and files special papers for an order settling custody, parenting time, residence of children and child support while the divorce is pending. Preliminary relief is optional, and there are alternatives to the relief described in Part III of Chapter 1.

The complaint, summons, preliminary relief papers (if preliminary relief is sought) and several other papers make up the initial divorce papers.

Because the friend of the court and prosecuting attorney have interests in divorces with minor children, they must receive notice of the divorce by getting copies of the initial divorce papers. The defendant must also get notice. This is provided by serving the initial divorce papers on the defendant. There are three regular methods of service, plus a couple of alternate service methods for elusive or disappeared defendants.

After service, the defendant may respond to the plaintiff's complaint within an answering period. The defendant's response can be either by filing: 1) an answer to the complaint or 2) a motion objecting to the complaint. If the plaintiff has asked for preliminary relief, the defendant can object to this request, and then the issue is decided by a friend of the court referee or the judge.

In the vast majority of cases, defendants don't bother to respond, putting them in default. The plaintiff can then go to the clerk and have the defendant's default declared. With this declaration, the case is officially an uncontested divorce, or what lawyers sometimes call a *pro confesso* or "pro con" divorce case.

But if the defendant responds to the complaint within the answering period, the divorce is contested. In that case, the plaintiff should seek a lawyer to take over the case because it's difficult to handle a contested case without a lawyer.

Meanwhile, the six-month statutory waiting period is running. This waiting period gives the friend of the court a chance to investigate the case and make recommendations to the judge about several divorce issues. The friend of the court puts these recommendations in a report which the plaintiff must use in preparing the divorce judgment.

The Judgment of Divorce settles all the divorce issues once and for all, replacing any preliminary orders on the issues. The judgment is issued by the court at the end of the divorce, during a final hearing. The plaintiff must appear at the hearing and give testimony or "proofs" in support of the judgment. This sounds scary, but the final hearing is usually very brief and easy to get through. After the final hearing, the plaintiff files the divorce judgment making the divorce final.

This book has organized the divorce procedure into two parts: "Starting Your Divorce" (Part I) and "Finishing Your Divorce" (Part II). Part I has two steps: "Filing" and "Service." Part II includes three steps: "Default," "Waiting for Final Hearing" and "Final Hearing." The flowchart below summarizes these steps and the time to perform them.

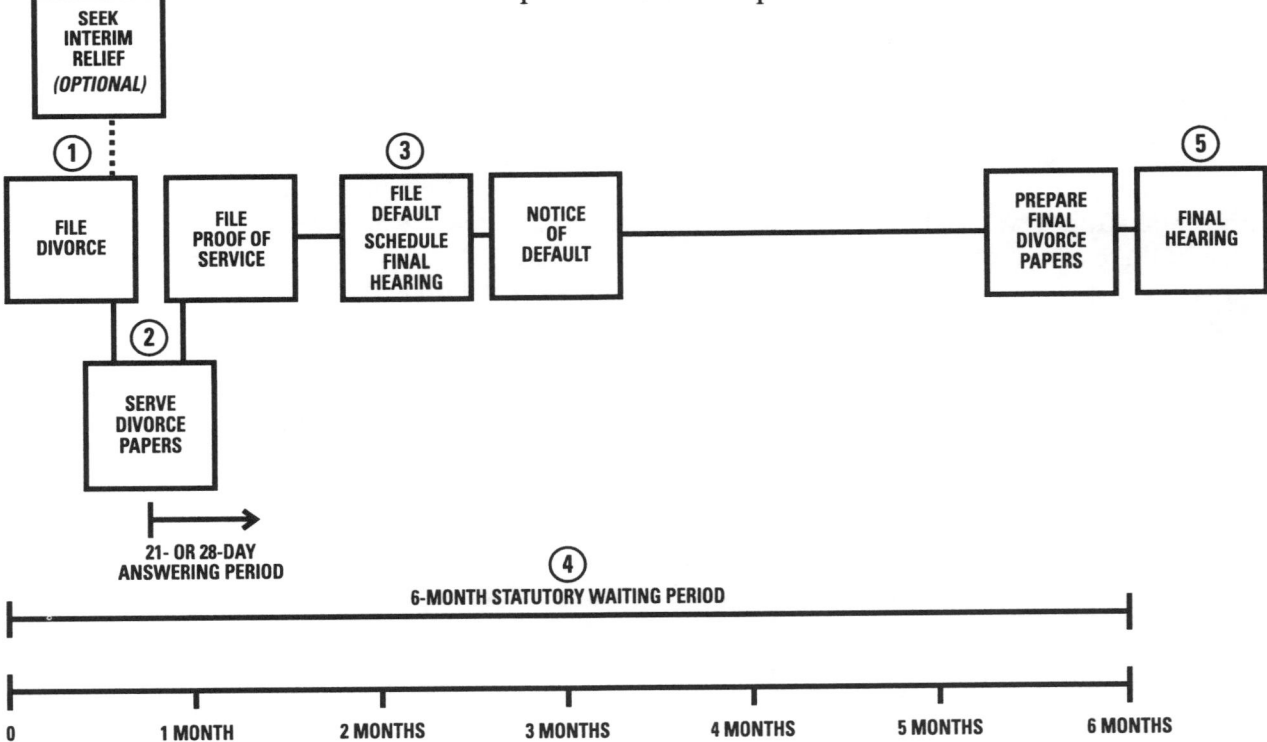

PART I:
Starting Your Divorce

1 Filing

Preparing Your Initial Divorce Papers

You begin your divorce by preparing the initial divorce papers. These papers include the complaint, summons and several related papers. The divorce complaint describes the basic facts of your marriage. It also tells the court that your marriage has broken down by citing the no-fault grounds for divorce. Finally, the complaint asks the court to decide the divorce issues. The purpose of the summons is to notify the defendant that you have filed a divorce complaint, and that s/he may respond to it.

The complaint and summons are contained in a set of forms: the Summons and Complaint (MC 01) and Complaint for Divorce (GRP 1). The Summons and Complaint (MC 01) includes the summons in the case along with the first part of the complaint. The Complaint for Divorce (GRP 1) is a continuation of this form and contains the main body of the complaint.

Although the complaint and summons provide a good deal of information about your marriage, the friend of the court needs more personal and financial information. The friend of the court gets that extra information in the Verified Statement (FOC 23). This paper must be given to the clerk along with your initial divorce papers when you file for divorce. Unlike the other divorce papers, the clerk doesn't place the Verified Statement (FOC 23) in your case file. Instead, the clerk forwards the statement to the friend of the court, without keeping a copy for the file.

Like all the other states, Michigan has adopted the Uniform Child Custody Jurisdiction and Enforcement Act (UCCJEA). Among other things, the act requires filing of the Uniform Child Custody Jurisdiction Enforcement Act Affidavit (MC 416) describing the past and present residences of your minor children. This information tells the court whether there is Michigan jurisdiction over the issues of custody, parenting time and residence of children when such jurisdiction is contested (see "Can I Get a Divorce in Michigan?" on page 43 for more about this).

Optional and Local Papers

Your initial divorce papers will include a few extra papers if you decide to seek preliminary relief (see "Do I Need 'Preliminary Relief'?" on page 59 for more about this option, and Appendix B for complete information, instructions and forms for seeking the interim kind of preliminary relief). For interim relief, you will need an Ex Parte Order (GRP 5), in Wayne County only, a Certificate of Conformity for Domestic Relations Order or Judgment (1225), and later on, maybe an Income Withholding Order (FOC 5).

If you want a fee exemption, you must also prepare the Affidavit and Order, Suspension of Fees/Costs (MC 20) (see Appendix A for the form and instructions).

In every Wayne County divorce with minor children, you must file a Certificate on Behalf of Plaintiff Regarding Ex Parte Interim Support Order to say whether or not you are seeking interim relief.

The blank forms for the initial divorce papers and all other divorce papers are located in the forms section in the back of the book. Optional forms like the Ex Parte Order (GRP 5) and Affidavit and Order, Suspension of Fees/Costs (MC 20), and local forms like the Certificate on Behalf of Plaintiff Regarding Ex Parte Interim Support Order, for Wayne County divorces, are located in a special section. All the forms are perforated so you can easily tear them out of the book.

There are filled-in samples of the initial divorce papers at the end of this section; other sample forms appear at the end of the sections they relate to by subject matter. For general information about form preparation, see "Papers" on page 74.

Ordinarily, you must make three photocopies of your divorce papers. The clerk gets the original, leaving copies for the friend of the court, defendant and you. But the initial divorce papers are distributed a little differently from the other divorce papers. The table below shows how many copies of the initial divorce papers you need:

<table>
<tr><td>●</td><td>Summons and Complaint</td><td>MC 01</td><td>5</td></tr>
<tr><td>●</td><td>Complaint for Divorce</td><td>GRP 1</td><td>4</td></tr>
<tr><td>●</td><td>Verified Statement</td><td>FOC 23</td><td>2</td></tr>
<tr><td>●</td><td>Uniform Child Custody Jurisdiction Enforcement Act Affidavit</td><td>MC 416</td><td>3</td></tr>
<tr><td>★</td><td>interim relief papers, if relief is sought (see Appendix B)</td><td></td><td></td></tr>
<tr><td>★</td><td>Affidavit and Order, Suspension of Fees/Costs</td><td>MC 20</td><td>3</td></tr>
</table>

Special Symbols

● regular paper

■ regular practice

★ optional paper or practice

◆ local paper or practice

+ Certificate on Behalf of Plaintiff Regard-   3
  ing Ex Parte Interim Support Order (in
  Wayne County only)

As explained in "Preparing Papers" on page 74, you must mark a copy of each paper with "FOC" in the upper left corner. This earmark reminds the clerk to forward the paper to the friend of the court.

Like the friend of the court, the prosecuting attorney (except in Kent, Macomb, Oakland and Wayne Counties) is also entitled to copies of the Summons and Complaint (MC 01) and Complaint for Divorce (GRP 1). Put "Pros. Atty." in the upper left corners of both papers so the clerk will forward them to the prosecuting attorney. Except for this pair of papers, the prosecuting attorney normally doesn't get any other papers during the divorce.

Filing Your Divorce

Start your divorce by filing it with the clerk (see "Court System" on page 71 for information about finding the clerk).

To file, you must have all your initial divorce papers and be ready to pay some of the court fees (see "How Much Will My Divorce Cost?" on page 49 for a description of these fees). Unless you obtain a fee exemption, you must pay the filing fee and probably a portion of the friend of the court fee. Most counties ask for payment of at least $30 of the friend of the court fee at filing. Others collect the friend of the court fee later, usually at the end of the divorce. Call the clerk before you file to find out the practice in your county, or just bring enough money to cover both the filing fee and $30 of the friend of the court fee.

Whatever you do, you should have the following items when you go to the clerk's office to file your divorce:

- Summons and Complaint   MC 01
  - original
  - 5 copies (one earmarked "FOC" and another "Pros. Atty.")

- Complaint for Divorce   GRP 1
  - original
  - 4 copies (one earmarked "FOC" and another "Pros. Atty.")

- Verified Statement   FOC 23
  - original

- Uniform Child Custody Jurisdiction Enforcement Act   MC 416
  Affidavit
  - original
  - 3 copies (one earmarked "FOC")

- money for the court fees

★   interim relief papers, if relief is sought (see Appendix
    B)

★   Affidavit and Order, Suspension of Fees/Costs   MC 20
    • original
    • 3 copies (one earmarked "FOC")

✦   Certificate on Behalf of Plaintiff Regarding Ex Parte
    Interim Support Order (in Wayne County only)
    • original
    • 3 copies (one earmarked "FOC")

When you arrive at the clerk's office, tell the clerk that you want to file
a divorce complaint. The clerk should then do the following to file your
divorce:

■   Take the Summons and Complaint (MC 01) and the five copies and: 1)
    assign a judge to the case and stamp his/her name on these papers 2)
    enter a case number on them 3) complete the summons boxes in the
    middle of the papers. File the Summons and Complaint (MC 01), take
    the friend of the court's and prosecuting attorney's copies and return
    three copies to you.

■   File the Complaint for Divorce (GRP 1), take the friend of the court's and
    prosecuting attorney's copies, and return two copies to you.

■   Take the Verified Statement (FOC 23) for the friend of the court.

■   File the Uniform Child Custody Jurisdiction Enforcement Act Affidavit
    (MC 416), take the friend of the court's copy and return two copies to
    you.

■   Take the money for the court fees.

★   File the Affidavit and Order, Suspension of Fees/Costs (MC 20), if used,
    to suspend the fees immediately; or submit the form to the judge for
    consideration. Take the friend of the court's copy and return two copies
    to you.

✦   In Wayne County only, file the Certificate on Behalf of Plaintiff Regard-
    ing Ex Parte Interim Support Order, take the friend of the court's copy
    and return two copies to you.

✦   In Wayne County only, prepare caption labels, label the captions of the
    initial divorce papers and give you two strips of caption labels.

If you are seeking interim relief, hold back the interim relief papers, such
as the Ex Parte Order (GRP 5), from filing at this time. See Appendix B about
when and how to present these to the judge, and if the relief is granted, how
to file the papers.

Before You Leave the Clerk's Office

Before you leave the clerk's office, ask for two items not provided in this book: 1) two friend of the court pamphlets 2) a Record of Divorce or Annulment (DCH-0838). You will use these later in the divorce, but it's convenient to pick them up now during filing.

The friend of the court pamphlet describes the office of the friend of the court and its role in divorces. Keep one pamphlet for yourself. The other pamphlet must be served on the defendant along with the other service papers, as described in the next section.

The Record of Divorce or Annulment (DCH-0838) asks for personal and marital information. You complete and file the form at the end of the divorce, when you get the judgment. After filing, the clerk sends the DCH-0838 to the Michigan Department of Community Health for addition to the state's vital records.

Are you seeking interim relief? If so, you might ask the clerk whether the county has a standard interim order form, and whether it's customary for the friend of the court to review interim orders before submission to the judge. In large counties, with many judges, you might also inquire whether the judge assigned to your case considers interim relief, or whether a specially designated judge considers these requests for all divorce cases.

To Obtain

If the clerk doesn't have friend of the court pamphlets, you can get these from the friend of the court's office.

Record of Divorce or Annulment (DCH-0838) forms are also available from:

Department of Community Health
Division for Vital Records and Health Studies
P.O. Box 30195
Lansing, MI 48909
(517) 335-8496

Getting Preliminary Relief

Before you leave the courthouse, it's a good time to ask for interim relief, if you have decided to seek it. You ask for an interim order directly from the judge, at the judge's office, using several papers filed shortly before and a few you held back. Appendix B has complete information, instructions and forms for seeking interim relief.

Original - Court
1st copy - Defendant

2nd copy - Plaintiff
3rd copy - Return

CASE NO.

Approved, SCAO

STATE OF MICHIGAN
JUDICIAL DISTRICT
JUDICIAL CIRCUIT
COUNTY PROBATE

SUMMONS AND COMPLAINT

Court tele

Court address

Plaintiff name(s), address(es), and telephone no(s)

v

Defendant name(s), address(es), and telephone no(s).

Plaintiff attorney, bar no., address, and telephone no.

FILL OUT CAPTION ON THIS AND ALL OTHER PAPERS AS SHOWN IN "PREPARING PAPERS"

In the name of the people of the State of Michigan you are notified:

SUMMONS   **NOTICE TO THE DEFENDANT:**
1. You are being sued.
2. **YOU HAVE 21 DAYS** after receiving this summons to file an answer with the court and serve a copy on the other party o take other lawful action (28 days if you were served by mail or you were served outside this state).
3. If you do not answer or take other action within the time allowed, judgment may be entered against you for the relief dem in the complaint.

CLERK WILL COMPLETE SUMMONS BOXES

Issued	This summons expires	Court clerk
3-1-89	5-31-89	Martha Gee

*This summons is invalid unless served on or before its expiration date.

COMPLAINT   *Instruction: The following is information that is required to be in the caption of every complaint and is to be completed by the plaintiff. Actual allegations and the claim for relief must be stated on additional complaint pages and attached to this form.*

Family Division Cases
☒ There is no other pending or resolved action within the jurisdiction of the family division of circuit court involving the family or family members of the parties.
☐ An action within the jurisdiction of the family division of the circuit court involving the family or family members of the parties has been previously filed in _____ Court.
The action ☐ remains ☐ is no longer pending. The docket number and the judge assigned to the action a

Docket no.

DESCRIBE ANY PRIOR FAMILY CASES INVOLVING YOU OR YOUR FAMILY, SO DIVORCE CAN BE DIRECTED TO FAMILY COURT JUDGE HANDLING PRIOR CASES

General Civil Cases
☒ There is no other pending or resolved civil action arising out of the same transaction or occurrence as alleged in
☐ A civil action between these parties or other parties arising out of the transaction or occurrence alleged in the been previously filed in _____ is no longer pending. The docket number and the judge assigned to the ac
The action ☐ remains ☐ is no longer pending. The docket number and the judge assigned to the ac

Docket no.

Judge

VENUE
Plaintiff(s) residence (include city, township, or village)   (SEE CAPTIONS ABOVE)
Defendant(s) residence (include city, township, or village)

Place where action arose or business conducted

Darlene A. Lovelace
Signature of attorney/plaintiff

2-28-89
Date

If you require special accommodations to use the court because of a disability or if you require a foreign language interpreter to help you to fully participate in court proceedings, please contact the court immediately to make arrangements.

MC 01 (5/03) **SUMMONS AND COMPLAINT**   MCR 2.102(B)(11), MCR 2.104, MCR 2.105, MCR 2.107, MCR 2.113(C)(2)(a), (b), MCR 3.206(A)

STATE OF MICHIGAN
Circuit Court - Family Division
_____ COUNTY

COMPLAINT FOR DIVORCE

CASE NO. _____

INCLUDE FULL NAMES

Plaintiff: ☐ Husband ☒ Wife

DARLENE ANN LOVELACE

Plaintiff's name before this marriage:

DARLENE ANN ALBRIGHT

v

Defendant:

DUDLEY ERNEST LOVELACE

Defendant's name before this marriage:

SAME

1. Plaintiff's residence: at least
   ☒ 180 days in Michigan
   ☒ 10 days in this county   immediately before filing of t...
   and/or
   Defendant's residence: at least
   ☒ 180 days in Michigan
   ☒ 10 days in this county   immediately before filing of this com...

SEE "CAN I GET A DIVORCE IN MICHIGAN?" FOR MORE ON RESIDENCE

CHECK BOXES AS THEY APPLY

2. Date of marriage _9-1-85_   Place of marriage _LAKE CITY, MICHIGAN_

3. The parties stopped living together as husband and wife on or about _1-15-89_

4. There has been a breakdown of the marriage relationship to the extent that the objects of matrimony have been destroyed and there remains no reasonable likelihood that the marriage can be preserved.

5. Children of the parties or born during the marriage:
   a. Minor (under-18) children:

   DUANE WESLEY LOVELACE   _6-1-86_
   DARRYL WENDELL LOVELACE   _7-1-87_

SEE "WHICH CHILDREN MUST BE INCLUDED IN MY DIVORCE?" FOR MORE ABOUT CHILDREN

   b. Adult children age 18-19½ entitled to support:

6. There ☐ is ☒ is not ... dren. The court with this ju... ith prior continuing jurisdiction of minor children. ... case # _____

CHECK IF YOU HAVE ALREADY DIVIDED ALL PROPERTY

7. The wife ☒ is not ...egnan... and the estimated date of birth is _____

8. There ☒ is ☐ is no property to be divided; ☐ division of property is controlled by the parties' prenuptial agreement attached as exhibit 1.

GRP 1a (1/04)   **COMPLAINT FOR DIVORCE, 1st extension page to MC 01**

IF YOU HAVE A PRENUPTIAL AGREEMENT CHECK BOX IN PARAGRAPH 8, MAKE PHOTOCOPIES OF THE AGREEMENT, WRITE EXHIBIT 1 AT TOP OF EACH, AND ATTACH COPIES TO ORIGINAL GRP1 AND ALL COPIES

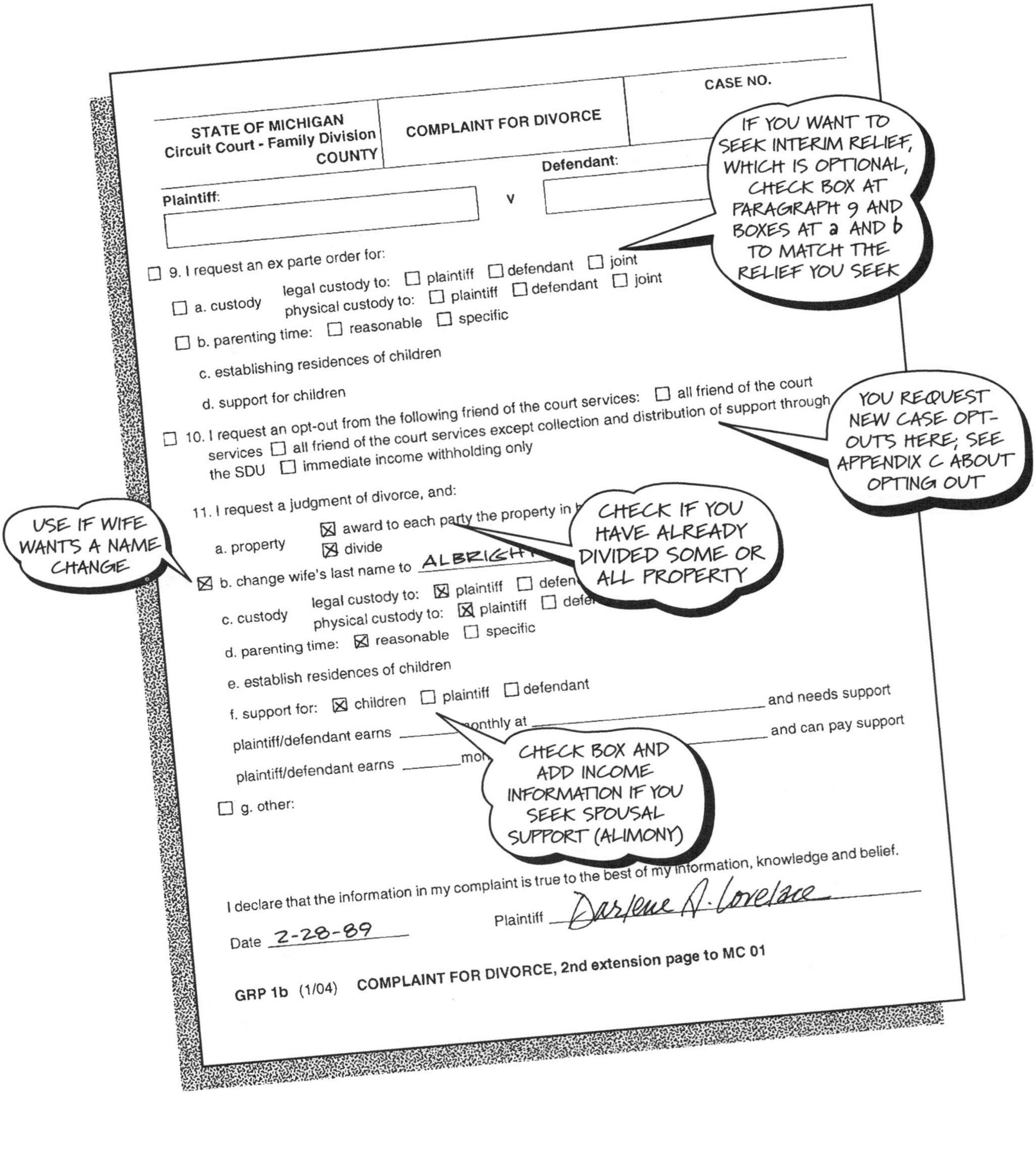

STATE OF MICHIGAN
Circuit Court - Family Division
COUNTY

COMPLAINT FOR DIVORCE

CASE NO.

Plaintiff: v Defendant:

☐ 9. I request an ex parte order for:

☐ a. custody legal custody to: ☐ plaintiff ☐ defendant ☐ joint
physical custody to: ☐ plaintiff ☐ defendant ☐ joint

☐ b. parenting time: ☐ reasonable ☐ specific

c. establishing residences of children

d. support for children

☐ 10. I request an opt-out from the following friend of the court services: ☐ all friend of the court services ☐ all friend of the court services except collection and distribution of support through the SDU ☐ immediate income withholding only

11. I request a judgment of divorce, and:

a. property ☒ award to each party the property in h
☒ divide

☒ b. change wife's last name to ALBRIGH

c. custody legal custody to: ☒ plaintiff ☐ defen
physical custody to: ☒ plaintiff ☐ defe

d. parenting time: ☒ reasonable ☐ specific

e. establish residences of children

f. support for: ☒ children ☐ plaintiff ☐ defendant

plaintiff/defendant earns ______ monthly at ______ and needs support

plaintiff/defendant earns ______ mo ______ and can pay support

☐ g. other:

I declare that the information in my complaint is true to the best of my information, knowledge and belief.

Date 2-28-89 Plaintiff Darlene A. Lovelace

GRP 1b (1/04) COMPLAINT FOR DIVORCE, 2nd extension page to MC 01

Original - Friend of the Court
1st copy - Plaintiff/Attorney
2nd copy - Defendant/Attorney

	CASE NO.

Approved, SCAO

STATE OF MICHIGAN
JUDICIAL CIRCUIT
COUNTY

VERIFIED STATEMENT

1. Mother's last name	First name	Middle name	2. Any other names by which wife is or has been known
LOVELACE	DARLENE	ANN	

	4. Social security number	5. Driver license number and state
	380-16-1010	M 650 603 440 886 MICH.

3. Date of birth
5-1-65

6. Mailing address and residence address (if different)
121 S. MAIN, LAKE CITY, MI 48800

12. Scars, tattoos, etc.

7. Eye color	8. Hair color	9. Height	10. Weight	11. Race	15. Maiden name	16. Occupation
BLUE	BLONDE	5'6"	120	WHITE	ALBRIGHT	WAITRESS

13. Home telephone no.	14. Work telephone no.			18. Gross weekly income
772-0000	772-0011			$250

17. Business/Employer's name and address
10,000 PANCAKES, 111 M-78, LAKE CITY, MI 48800

19. Has wife applied for or does she receive public assistance? If yes, please specify kind.	20. AFDC and recipient identification numbers
☐ Yes ☒ No	

21. Father's last name	First name	Middle name	22. Any other names by which husband is or has been known
LOVELACE	DUDLEY	ERNEST	

	24. Social security number	25. Driver license number and state
	379-10-5567	M 649 601 402 701 MICH.

23. Date of birth
6-15-64

26. Mailing address and residence address (if different)
900 S. MAPLE, LAKE CITY, MI 48800

32. Scars, tattoos, etc.

27. Eye color	28. Hair color	29. Height	30. Weight	31. Race	35. Occupation
BROWN	BLACK	6'	170	WHITE	SALESMAN

33. Home telephone no.	34. Work telephone no.			37. Gross weekly income
773-3004	773-0011			$375

36. Business/Employer's name and address
WATERBED WORLD, 1000 SERVICE RD., LAKE CITY, MI 48800

38. Has husband applied for or does he receive public assistance? If yes, please specify kind.	39. AFDC and recipient identification numbers
☐ Yes ☒ No	

40. a. Name of Minor Child Involved in Case	b. Birth Date	c. Age	d. Soc. Sec. No.	e. Residential Address
DUANE WESLEY LOVELACE	6-1-86	2	466-10-1001	121 S. MAIN, LAKE CITY, MI 48800
DARRYL WENDELL LOVELACE	7-1-87	1	469-00-4411	" " "

41. a. Name of Other Minor Child of Either Party	b. Birth Date	c. Age	d. Soc. Sec. No.	e. Residential Address

42. Health care coverage available for each minor child			
a. Name of Minor Child	b. Name of Policy Holder	c. Name of Insurance Co./HMO	d. Policy/Certificate/Contract No.
DUANE WESLEY LOVELACE	DUDLEY E. LOVELACE	LAKEVIEW HMO	226-8978-24
DARRYL WENDELL LOVELACE	"	"	

43. Names and addresses of person(s) other than parties, if any, who may have custody of child(ren) during pendency of this case

• If any of the public assistance information above changes before your judgment is entered, you are required to give the Friend of the Court written notice of the change.

I declare that the statements above are true to the best of my information, knowledge, and belief.

Darlene A. Lovelace
Signature

MCR 3.206(B)

2-28-89
Date
FOC 23 (5/93) **VERIFIED STATEMENT**

Approved, SCAO

Original - Court
1st copy - FOC (if applicable)
2nd copy - Defendant/Respondent
3rd copy - Plaintiff/Petitioner

STATE OF MICHIGAN
JUDICIAL CIRCUIT
PROBATE COURT
COUNTY

Court address

UNIFORM CHILD CUSTODY JURISDICTION ENFORCEMENT ACT AFFIDAVIT

CASE NO.

Court telephone no.

CASE NAME: LOVELACE V. LOVELACE

1. The name and present address of each child (under 18) in this case is:

DUANE WESLEY LOVELACE 121 S. MAIN, LAKE CITY, MI 48800
DARRYL WENDELL LOVELACE   "   "

2. The addresses where the child(ren) has/have lived within the last 5 years are:

SAME AS ABOVE

3. The name(s) and present address(es) of custodians with whom the child(ren) has/have lived within the last 5 years are:

DARLENE A. LOVELACE 121 S. MAIN, LAKE CITY, MI 48800
DUDLEY E. LOVELACE   900 S MAPLE,   "

4. I do not know of, and have not participated (as a party, witness, or in any other capacity) in any other court proceeding (including divorce, separate maintenance, separation, neglect, abuse, dependency, guardianship, termination of parental rights, and protection from domestic violence) concerning the custody or parenting of in this state or any other state, **except:** specify case name and number, court name and address, and date of child custody determination, if one

5. I do not know of any pending proceeding that could affect the current child custody proceeding, including a proceeding for enforcement or a proceeding relating to domestic violence, a protective order, termination of parental rights, or adoption, in this state or any other state, **except:** specify case name and number, court name and address, and nature of the proceeding

That proceeding ☐ is continuing.   ☐ has been stayed by the court.
☐ Temporary action by this court is necessary to protect the child(ren) because the child(ren) has/have been subjected to or threatened with mistreatment or abuse or is/are otherwise neglected or dependent. Attach explanation

6. I do not know of any person who is not already a party to this proceeding who has physical custody or, or who claims rights of legal or physical custody of, or parenting time with, the child(ren), **except:** state name(s) and address(es) of each person

7. The child(ren)'s "home state" is MICHIGAN

☐ 8. I state that a party's or child's health, safety, or liberty would be put at risk by the disclosure of this identifying . See back for definition

I have filled this form out completely, and I acknowledge a continuing duty to advise this court of any proceeding in any other state that could affect the current child-custody proceeding.

Signature of affiant _Darlene A. Lovelace_

DARLENE A. LOVELACE
Name of affiant (type or print)

121 S. MAIN, LAKE CITY, MI
Address of affiant

Subscribed and sworn to before me on 2-28-89 , OJIBWAY
                                        Date
My commission expires: 1-1-90   Signature: Loretta Smiley   County, Michigan.
                        Date

MC 416 (3/02) **UNIFORM CHILD CUSTODY JURISDICTION ENFORCEMENT ACT AFFIDAVIT**   MCL 722.1206, MCL 722...

IF YOU HAVE TO ANSWER EITHER OF THESE PARAGRAPHS, SEE "SPECIAL NOTICE TO A PRIOR COURT" IN APPENDIX E

IF YOU HAVE TO ANSWER THIS PARAGRAPH, SEE "SPECIAL NOTICE TO A THIRD PARTY WITH CUSTODY" IN APPENDIX E

NOTARY PUBLIC WILL COMPLETE THIS SECTION

CASE NO.

CERTIFICATE ON BEHALF OF PLAINTIFF

STATE OF MICHIGAN
THIRD JUDICIAL CIRCUIT
WAYNE COUNTY

PLAINTIFF

REVIEW BOTH SIDES
IF YOU ARE PRESENTING
IF YOU ARE NOT PRESEN
PLEASE PUT A LARGE 'X'

I AM PRESENTIN
FOLLOWING PRO

CUSTODY (with N

SOLE LE

JOINT LE

JOINT LE

ADDRESSES (

CHILD'S

PARTIE

EMPLO

DOMICILE MO

PARENTING T

SUPPORT M

PAYAB

IF MO

IMME

STAT

HEALTH CA

NOTICE RE

I CERTIFY THAT I A
GUIDELINES.
DATE

Address

City

A. Please che
or petition)
the Court,
THE RIE
VERIF

B. Provide
document

STATE OF MICHIGAN
THIRD JUDICIAL CIRCUIT
WAYNE COUNTY

CERTIFICATE ON BEHALF OF PLAINTIFF
REGARDING EX PARTE
INTERIM SUPPORT ORDER

CASE NO.

PLAINTIFF'S NAME

REVIEW BOTH SIDES OF THIS FORM BEFORE
IF YOU ARE NOT PRESENTING AN EX PARTE ORDER, C
IF YOU ARE PRESENTING AN EX PARTE ORDER, COMP
PLEASE PUT A LARGE 'X' ACROSS THE SIDE YO

X I AM NOT PRESENTING AN EX PARTE INTERIM SUP
THE FOLLOWING REASON(S): (CHECK THE REASO

___1. A prior order for support of the minor child/children is

Name of County _____ Case Number _____

___2. The non-custodial party is not the parent of the c /children named in the complaint and the complaint so states.

___3. The Court lacks personal jurisdiction over the endant because the whereabouts of the Defendant are unknown. Service will be by publication.

___4. The parties are presently residing together nd the child/children are being adequately supported and there is no public assistance or applica for public assistance pending.

X 5. I am the custodial parent and the other party is providing appropriate support for the child/children and there is no public assistance or pending application for public assistance pending.

___6. The child/children are receiving Social Security Dependant Benefits as support.

___7. The non-custodial parent is unemployed, receives Public Assistance or Supplemental Security Income (SSI) and has no other source of income. A request for a Friend of the Court child support investigation has been made.

___8. The ability of the non-custodial parent to provide support for the minor child/children has not been determined. A motion for a temporary child support order has been filed.

___9. Other _____

I CERTIFY THAT THE ABOVE INFORMATION IS CORRECT TO THE BEST OF MY KNOWLEDGE.

DATE **2-28-89** **DARLENE LOVELACE** , _Darlene Lovelace_ P_____
Attorney's or Party's Printed Name/Signature

Address **121 S MAIN**

City **LAKE CITY** State **MI** Zip Code **48800** Telephone **(517) 772-0000**

ate item(s), sign and serve the original of this certificate, the complaint (or counter-claim
MCL 600.659 custody affidavit upon the Court, the County Clerk, the Friend of
ERIFIED STATEMENT- FRIEND OF THE COURT' MUST
THE OTHER PARTY. DO NOT GIVE THE COUNTY CLE

Court with a copy of the PROOF OF SERVICE setting fo
ave been served upon the other party.

2 Service

Your divorce affects more than just you, so others are entitled to know about it. In a divorce with minor children, the following persons must get notice of the divorce:

- friend of the court
- prosecuting attorney
- defendant

Whether you realize it or not, the friend of the court and prosecuting have already received notice when you earmarked copies of the initial divorce papers with "FOC" and "Pros. Atty." and filed them with the clerk. If you somehow neglected to do that, you should go back to the clerk's office and file the missing papers.

Serving the Defendant

Due process requires that the defendant receive notice of the divorce so s/he can respond to it. Notice to defendants is provided by serving copies of the initial divorce papers on them. You should begin service as soon as possible, within a few days after filing.

Although the purpose of service is notice, don't assume that you can skip it when the defendant already knows about the divorce. And don't try to serve the defendant by simply giving the divorce papers to him/her. No doubt your spouse would get informal notice of the divorce these ways. But the law requires that the defendant receive *official* notice of the divorce by service.

Official notice can only be accomplished by one of the service methods described below. With these methods, the court knows for sure that the defendant got notice of the divorce. For this reason, service is absolutely necessary. The service rules may seem artificial and even rather silly at times, but they must be followed carefully. If you omit service, or violate the service rules, there's a chance your whole divorce will be invalid.

There are three methods of serving defendants who are available to be served: 1) acknowledgment 2) mail 3) delivery. Each method can be used anywhere in the state of Michigan. These service methods can also be used outside the state (including foreign countries), as long as there is Michigan jurisdiction over the nonresident defendant (see "Can I Get a Divorce in Michigan?" on page 43 for more about jurisdiction).

Despite service's wide reach, there are a few restrictions on serving papers. You, as a party to the case, are disqualified from serving the initial divorce papers yourself. Instead, you must have a neutral third party serve the papers for you. For service by delivery, a professional server, such as a sheriff or commercial process server, can serve for you. But when you choose service by acknowledgment or service by mail, you must enlist a helper (who can be any mentally competent adult), such as a friend, to help with service. The helper acts as a straw man through whose hands the divorce papers pass to the defendant.

Whichever service method you choose, you mustn't have the divorce papers served on a Sunday, an election day, or on the defendant while s/he is at, en route or returning from a court appearance. Michigan law provides immunity from service in all these situations.

Special Symbols

● regular paper

■ regular practice

★ optional paper or practice

✦ local paper or practice

Preparing for Service

The defendant must be served with papers listed below, which shall be referred to collectively as the "service papers:"

●	Summons and Complaint	MC 01
●	Complaint for Divorce	GRP 1
●	Verified Statement	FOC 23
●	Uniform Child Custody Jurisdiction Enforcement Act Affidavit	MC 416
●	friend of the court pamphlet	
★	interim relief papers, if relief has been obtained already (see Appendix B)	
★	Affidavit and Order, Suspension of Fees/Costs	MC 20

✦ Certificate on Behalf of Plaintiff Regarding Ex Parte Interim
Support Order (in Wayne County only)

✦ a strip of caption labels (in Wayne County only)

After the defendant is served with these papers, service must be proved in a proof of service. Each method of service (acknowledgment, mail, delivery) is proved differently. But all are proved in the Proof of Service on the reverse of your extra copy of the Summons and Complaint (MC 01). This paper will be referred to as the "proof of service copy of the Summons and Complaint (MC 01)." After service, you file it with the clerk so that your case file shows that the defendant was served.

Service by Acknowledgment

Service by acknowledgment is the simplest method of service. To use this method, you need the cooperation of the defendant and the assistance of a helper. If the defendant is in another county or state, you must find someone there to act as your helper.

Service is accomplished by having the helper hand the service papers to the defendant. You may be present during the transfer, but the helper, not you, must be the one who actually hands the service papers to the defendant. The day of service is the day the defendant receives the service papers from the helper.

Proving Service by Acknowledgment

Immediately after service, the helper should have the defendant date (with time and day) and sign the Acknowledgment of Service, which is at the bottom of the reverse of your proof of service copy of the Summons and Complaint (MC 01). Make three copies of this paper, earmark one "FOC" and save another for filing later as your proof of service.

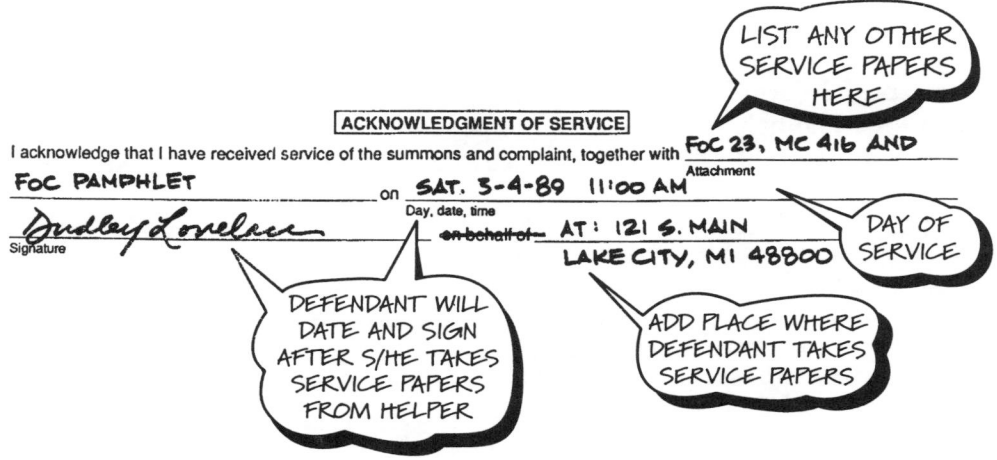

Service by Mail

Service by mail is a little more expensive than service by acknowledgment. But it's a very effective method of service because it goes anywhere U.S. mail is delivered—even overseas.* The court rules permit service by mail through either registered or certified mail. Because certified mail is cheaper than registered mail, certified mail is the best choice.

When you serve by mail, you need the assistance of a helper and the U.S. Postal Service. Your helper mails the service papers to the defendant and the postal service delivers these to him/her by certified mail.

To prove service, you need several special services available with certified mail: 1) restricted delivery 2) return receipt service. By restricting delivery, the service papers are delivered only to the defendant personally or someone s/he has designated in writing to receive mail. The return receipt provides proof of who received the papers, the date of delivery and the address of delivery only if this is different from the address on the envelope. This receipt becomes a key part of the proof of service.

Before you have the service papers mailed, prepare the mailing by placing your service papers in an envelope addressed to the defendant with your helper's name and address as the return address. In addition, you or your helper must prepare two certified mail forms: 1) Certified Mail Receipt (PS Form 3800) 2) Domestic Return Receipt (PS Form 3811), which are available at any post office.

On the PS Form 3800, fill in the defendant's name and address at the bottom of the form. For the PS Form 3811, write your helper's name and address on the front of the card, and on the reverse complete boxes #1-4. In section #2, transfer the article number from the PS Form 3800. In section #3, check the certified mail box, and ask for restricted delivery in #4.

After you complete the PS Form 3800 and 3811, peel off the plastic strips on the ends of the PS 3811 and attach the card to the envelope (there probably won't be room on the front of the envelope, so attach it to the reverse side). On the front of the envelope, to the left of the defendant's address and below your helper's return address, write "Restricted Delivery" and "Return Receipt Requested" on the envelope. By making these notations (the PS Form 3800 calls this "endorsement"), you will remind the letter carrier to restrict delivery and get a receipt.

Have your helper take the envelope containing the service papers, with the Domestic Return Receipt (PS Form 3811) attached, the Certified Mail Receipt (PS Form 3800) and money to pay for the mailing to a post office window. The helper should ask the postal clerk to mail the envelope by certified mail with the special services you have written on the envelope.

---

*   The service by mail described above deals with mail sent inside the United States and to military mail overseas. For service by mail in foreign countries, ask the post office about recorded delivery, which is similar to domestic certified mail and offers restricted delivery and return receipt service. The Recorded Delivery Receipt (PS Form 8099) explains this type of delivery.

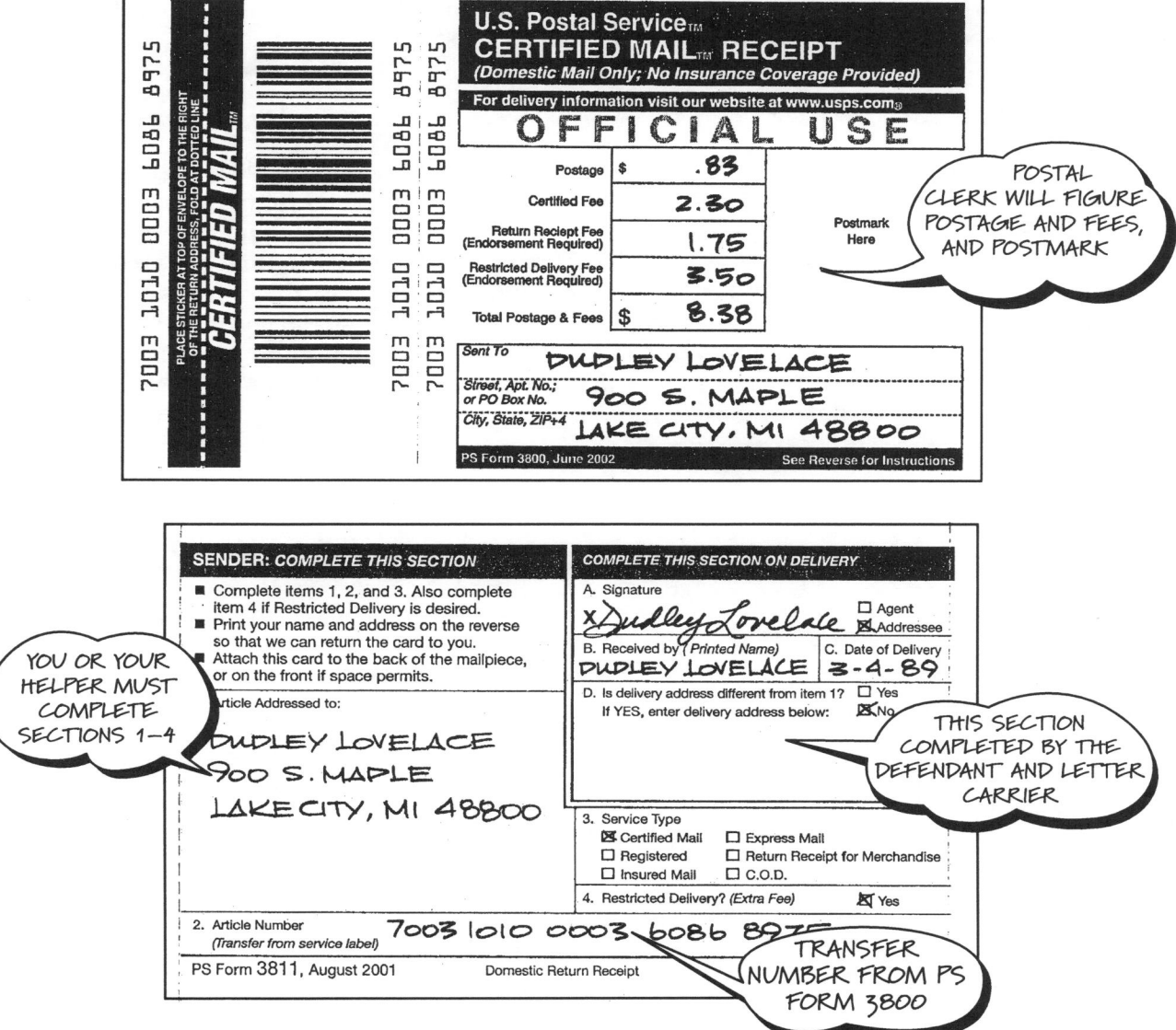

The clerk will prepare the certified mailing and return a postmarked Certified Mail Receipt (PS Form 3800) to your helper. Keep this receipt for your records.

Later, a letter carrier will deliver the mailing to the defendant, get his/her name (printed), signature and other delivery information on the reverse of the Domestic Return Receipt (PS Form 3811). Within a few days, your helper should get the PS Form 3811 back in the mail. You can then have your helper prove the service as described below. The day of service is the day the defendant receives the mailing from the letter carrier.

If your helper gets the whole envelope back, instead of the Domestic Return Receipt (PS Form 3811) alone, service by mail has failed. The defendant may have refused to accept the mailing, wasn't home or has moved without leaving a current forwarding order. Whatever the case, you will have to abandon service by mail because it only works when the defendant is ready and willing to take the certified mailing from the letter carrier. If service by mail fails, try service by delivery instead.

Proving Service by Mail

After your helper gets the Domestic Return Receipt (PS Form 3811) back in the mail, have him/her prove service on the reverse of your proof of service copy of the Summons and Complaint (MC 01). Complete the information about the service by mail under the Affidavit of Process Server, and have the helper sign the form before a notary public. As proof of the defendant's receipt of the mailing, staple the Domestic Return Receipt (PS Form 3811) to the reverse of your proof of service copy of the Summons and Complaint (MC 01). Make three copies of this paper, earmark one "FOC" and save another for filing later as your proof of service.

PROOF OF SERVICE	SUMMONS AND COMPLAINT Case No.

TO PROCESS SERVER: You are to serve the summons and complaint not later than 91 days from the date of filing or the date of expiration on the order for second summons. You must make and file your return with the court clerk. If you are unable to complete service you must return this original and all copies to the court clerk.

CERTIFICATE / AFFIDAVIT OF SERVICE / NON-SERVICE

☐ OFFICER CERTIFICATE	**OR**	☒ AFFIDAVIT OF PROCESS SERVER
I certify that I am a sheriff, deputy sheriff, bailiff, appointed court officer, or attorney for a party [MCR 2.104(A)(2)], and that: (notarization not required)		Being first duly sworn, I state that I am a legally competent adult who is not a p... ...e party, and that: (notarizati...

☐ I served personally a copy of the summons and complaint,
☒ I served by registered or certified mail (copy of return receipt attached) a copy of t...

[speech bubble: LIST ANY OTHER SERVICE PAPERS HERE]

together with FOC 23, MC416 AND FOC PAMPHLET
                    List all documents served with the Summons and Complaint

_____ on the defendant(s):

Defendant's name	Complete address(es) of service	Day, date, time
DUDLEY LOVELACE	900 S. MAPLE, LAKE CITY, MI 48800	SAT. 3-4-89

[speech bubble: GET DATE FROM PS FORM 3811] *[speech bubble: DAY OF SERVICE]*

☐ I have personally attempted to serve the summons and complaint, together with any attachments on the following defendant(s) and have been unable to complete service.

Defendant's name	Complete address(es) of service	Day, date, time

Service fee $	Miles traveled	Mileage fee $	Total fee $	Signature *Ruth Darling*

Subscribed and sworn to before me on **3-7-89**
                                                         Date

Title OJIBWAY _____ County, Michigan.

My commission expires: **1-1-90**   Signature: *Loretta Smiley*
                                    Date   Deputy court clerk/Notary public

Service by Delivery

You can also obtain service by having someone deliver the service papers to the defendant. Any mentally competent adult except you can do that. If the defendant is cooperative, you could have a helper perform service by delivery for you. But in that case it would be much easier to have the defendant simply acknowledge delivery of the service papers from your helper and get service by acknowledgment. Therefore, it's likely that you will use service by delivery for defendants who live out of town or state, or are otherwise hard to serve.

Service by delivery is usually carried out by a professional server, such as a sheriff or commercial process server. Whatever other service options you have, county sheriff departments will always serve papers for you. They often have a separate division or deputy in charge of service. In small towns or rural areas, the sheriff may be the only choice for service. Larger cities usually have commercial process servers as an alternative to the sheriff.

Both types of servers charge fees for service. By law, sheriffs charge a basic service fee of $16 plus mileage (billed at the current state government rate) for travel to and from the defendant. However, a sheriff's service fee can be suspended if you get a fee exemption (see Appendix A for details). Even if you have to pay, sheriffs' service fees are normally cheaper than those of commercial process servers, who often charge upward of $30 for service. On the other hand, commercial process servers may be more persistent in finding and serving defendants.

Whomever you choose, you can often reduce the service fees by having the defendant pick up the service papers at the server's office. This saves the server's mileage fee. It also spares the defendant the possible embarrassment of being served with legal papers at home or work. If the defendant is willing, tell the server that the defendant will pick up the papers, and then have the defendant call the server to arrange for pick-up.

To obtain service by delivery in your area, take the service papers along with your proof of service copy of the Summons and Complaint (MC 01) to the server and ask for service on the defendant. The server will serve the defendant at the address in the captions of your papers. If the defendant can be found at another place, tell the server about the other address.

When the defendant lives in another county or state, you must find a server nearby. After you find one, mail the service papers and your proof of service copy of the Summons and Complaint (MC 01) to the server. Enclose a note asking for service and return of a proof of service (see also "Fees" on page 77 about prepaying an out-of-town server's service fee).

When you're seeking service outside the state of Michigan, you should mention in your note that the server must prove service in the Affidavit of

---

More Information

To find sheriffs, look under the county government section for the sheriff department in a telephone directory. For commercial process servers, use a telephone directory for the defendant's area and search under "Process Servers" in the yellow pages.

Or you can find both kinds of process servers through process server trade associations, which provide referrals:

Court Officers, Deputy Sheriffs & Process Servers of Michigan (CODSA) at (989) 831-7644 or www.codsa.com

National Association of Professional Process Servers (NAPPS) at (800) 477-8211 or www.napps.com

United States Process Servers Association (USPSA) at (217) 787-5966 or www.usprocessservers.com

Process server, on the reverse of the proof of service copy of the Summons and Complaint (MC 01). An out-of-state process server must use the affidavit, instead of the Officer Certificate, because only Michigan court officers (such as Michigan sheriffs and their deputies) may use the certificate. In addition, ask the process server to have the notary public affix a seal on the affidavit, since documents with out-of-state notarizations must be sealed.

If all goes as planned, the server will find the defendant and deliver the service papers to him/her. The day of service is the day the server delivers the service papers to the defendant.

Proving Service by Delivery

After service, the server will prove service on the reverse of the proof of service copy of the Summons and Complaint (MC 01) that you gave the server. For service by Michigan court officers, the proof of service will appear in the Officer Certificate; all other servers must use the Affidavit of Process Server.

After service is proved, the server will return your proof of service copy of the Summons and Complaint (MC 01) to you. Make three copies of this paper, earmark one "FOC" and save another for filing later as your proof of service.

Service Problems

In most cases, service by any of the three regular service methods goes smoothly. But certain service methods are best for particular defendants, such as prisoners and military servicemembers. And sometimes you may even have to use alternate service if a defendant is difficult to serve.

Serving Prisoners and Military Servicemembers

Service by mail seems to work best on incarcerated defendants. See "What If My Spouse or I Am Imprisoned?" on page 46 for tips on serving prisoners by mail. Service by mail is also the most effective way to serve military servicemembers, for reasons explained in "What If My Spouse or I Am in the Military?" on page 48.

Alternate Service

The regular methods of service work only if the defendant is available for service. But if the defendant is elusive (avoiding service) or has disappeared, you must resort to some form of alternate service. Appendix D has complete instructions and forms for serving elusive or disappeared defendants.

If you're convinced you need alternate service, don't wait too long to seek it. The summons in the Summons and Complaint (MC 01) lasts for 91 days after it's issued (this expiration date should have been inserted by the clerk on the front of the summons). If you fail to complete service within that time, the summons will expire and the clerk will dismiss your case (see below for more about the danger of dismissal).

There is a way to ask the judge for a new summons before the old one expires, but it's a lot of bother. The better way is to use alternate service as soon as it becomes apparent that regular service methods aren't working.

Filing the Proof of Service

Whatever method of service you use, be sure to file the proof of service soon after service is completed. This is important because delay in filing the proof of service can result in dismissal of your divorce.

As mentioned above, a summons expires after 91 days. When there's no proof of service on file after 91 days, the clerk will assume that service has failed and begin dismissal of the case for "no progress." (The clerk should give advance warning of dismissal by sending you a Notice of Intent to

Dismiss for No Progress (MC 26).) After dismissal for no progress, you can file a motion asking the judge to reinstate the case. But reinstatement isn't guaranteed, and the judge may deny the motion. In that case, you would have to refile your divorce and start over.

To avoid that trap, make sure that you file the proof of service quickly, well before the 91-day summons expiration period elapses. Take/send the proof of service, which is on the reverse of your proof of service copy of the Summons and Complaint (MC 01),* plus three copies to the clerk. The clerk will file the original, take the friend of the court copy and return two copies to you.

Special Notice of Your Divorce

In the vast majority of divorces with minor children, the friend of the court, prosecuting attorney and defendant are the only ones entitled to notice of the divorce. But sometimes others may be entitled to special notice of the divorce. These include situations in which: 1) someone other than you or your spouse (a third party) has physical custody of your minor children 2) your minor child is subject to an ongoing case concerning the child's custody and/or parenting time. See Appendix E for more about these situations, and instructions and the form for giving special notice.

---

*   If alternate service was used, the proof of service is on the reverse of either the MC 304 or MC 307.

1 Filing

Filed with the clerk during filing:

☐ Summons and Complaint   MC 01

☐ Complaint for Divorce   GRP 1

☐ Verified Statement   FOC 23

☐ Uniform Child Custody Jurisdiction Enforcement Act
   Affidavit   MC 416

☆ Affidavit and Order, Suspension of Fees/Costs   MC 20

◆ Certificate on Behalf of Plaintiff Regarding Ex Parte Interim
   Support Order (in Wayne County only)

Requested from the clerk during filing (for use later):

☐ two friend of the court pamphlets

☐ Record of Divorce or Annulment   DCH-0838

◆ two strips of caption labels (in Wayne County only)

Filed with the clerk later, if interim relief has been obtained:

                                                                                    GRP 5

☆ Ex Parte Order

◆ Certificate of Conformity for Domestic Relations Order or   1225
   Judgment (in Wayne County only)

**Filed with the clerk even later, if interim relief has been obtained, unless
the friend of the court does everything to start immediate income withholding:**

                                                                                    FOC 5

☆ Income Withholding Order

Symbols
   ▫ regular paper
   ☆ optional paper
   ◆ local paper

2 Service

Service papers served on the defendant:

☐ Summons and Complaint

MC 01

☐ Complaint for Divorce

GRP 1

☐ Verified Statement

FOC 23

☐ Uniform Child Custody Jurisdiction Enforcement Act Affidavit

MC 416

☐ a friend of the court pamphlet

☆ if interim relief has been obtained already, Ex Parte Order and Certificate of Conformity for Domestic Relations Order or Judgment (in Wayne County only)

GRP 5/1225

☆ Affidavit and Order, Suspension of Fees/Costs

MC 20

◇ a strip of caption labels (in Wayne County only)

◇ Certificate on Behalf of Plaintiff Regarding Ex Parte Interim Support Order (in Wayne County only)

The friend of the court must also receive copies of the service papers (and all other divorce papers), from the extra copies of papers you give the clerk earmarked "FOC."

Except in Kent, Macomb, Oakland and Wayne Counties, the county prosecuting attorney must receive copies of two service papers: Summons and Complaint (MC 01) and Complaint for Divorce (GRP 1).

Filed with the clerk soon after service:

☐ proof of service

MC 01

☆ proof of service of interim relief papers, if these were served separately from the service papers

GRP 5

PART II:
Finishing Your Divorce

3 Default

You've filed the divorce and served notice of the case. After several weeks, you're ready for the final part of your divorce, which begins with the default.

A default is important because it means that the defendant isn't contesting the divorce. Until then, you're relying on the defendant's word that the divorce is agreeable. But with the default, your divorce becomes *officially* uncontested, making it impossible for the defendant to re-enter and contest the case without special permission from the court.

Although you may be anxious to get the default, you must wait and see if the defendant responds to your divorce complaint. S/he can respond by filing with the court and sending you either: 1) an Answer to your complaint 2) a motion objecting to the complaint. If the defendant does neither, you can go ahead and apply for a default from the clerk.

To avoid default, the defendant must respond in one of those two ways within the applicable answering period. All answering periods begin the day after the day of service (see "Time" on page 78 for more about computing time periods). The length of answering periods depends on the method of service. The chart on the next page depicts this.

Your copy of the proof of service, which you should have filed earlier, shows the day of service. Use that and the chart to figure the answering period in your case. If the defendant hasn't responded by the end of that answering period, you're ready to get the default.

Scheduling the Final Hearing

Although your divorce may only be a month or two old when you apply for the default, it's not too early to schedule the final hearing for your case. As

Answering Periods

Method of service	Day of service	Answering period
Service by acknowledgment	Day defendant takes the service papers from helper	21 days in Michigan or 28 days out of state
Service by mail	Day defendant takes the mailing of the service papers from letter carrier	28 days
Service by delivery	Day server delivers the service papers to defendant	21 days in Michigan or 28 days out of state
Alternate service:		
mailing	Day the service papers are sent	28 days
tacking	Day the service papers are tacked to door	28 days
household delivery	Day the service papers are delivered to person in defendant's household	28 days
publication	Day of final publication of advertisement	Set by judge in MC 307 (a minimum of 28 days after final publication date)
posting	Last day of posting period	Set by judge in MC 307 (a minimum of 28 days after last day of posting period)

required by law, you must appear in court at a final hearing to receive your divorce judgment. Final hearings in divorce cases are usually heard on special days, called motion days, which courts set aside each week or month. During these motion days, judges may hear many final hearings, often at 10- or 15-minute intervals. Nevertheless, judges' motion day schedules fill up quickly, so it's a good idea to schedule your final hearing at the time of the default. If you wait, you risk delaying the conclusion of your divorce.

As previously mentioned, Michigan imposes a six-month waiting period on divorce cases with minor children (see "How Long Will My Divorce Take?" on page 48 for more on statutory waiting periods). This means that at least six months must elapse between the day you filed your divorce (this date is stamped on your Summons and Complaint (MC 01)) and the day of your final hearing.

Although you may want to get your divorce over with sooner, you must observe the waiting period. So when you schedule your final hearing, set it for a day at least six months after the day you filed your divorce (see "Time" on page 78 for more about figuring time in months).

Courts use several methods to schedule final hearings in uncontested divorce cases. In many counties, you can schedule a final hearing orally. When you get the default, ask the clerk to schedule a final hearing sometime after the statutory waiting period has expired. The clerk will reserve a time for you on the judge's motion day schedule or calendar (make sure that you make a note of the time and date).

In other counties, you must file a written request for a final hearing. In Wayne County, for example, you must request a final hearing on a special request form known as a praecipe. Wayne County's praecipe is a yellow slip of paper called the At Issue Praecipe for Default Judgment in Domestic Relations Action (#1121), which is available from the clerk in room 201 of the Coleman A. Young Municipal Center (CAYMC) (formerly the City-County Bldg.) at 2 Woodward Ave. in Detroit. You file the praecipe with the docket management office in room 770 of the CAYMC. Docket management will have the final hearing scheduled and mail a notice of the time and date to you. Several other counties also use praecipes or similar written forms. If your county is among them, ask the clerk for the particular form and use it as directed.

In some counties, such as Oakland, the clerk will schedule the final hearing for you. These counties typically have computerized case management systems that set final hearings automatically. After the hearing is set, a notice of the time and date will be sent to you.

As you can see, there is a great deal of variation when it comes to scheduling final hearings. In fact, there is probably more variation here than in any other part of divorce procedure. To find out the practice in your county, ask the clerk when you get the default.

Getting the Default

When the defendant has failed to respond to your complaint within the applicable answering period, s/he has defaulted, allowing you to apply to the clerk for a default. The clerk declares or enters the default, but you must prepare the Default (GRP 2) form.

Default and the Military Relief Laws

Glancing at the Default (GRP 2) you'll see some business in the Affidavit section about the defendant's possible service in the military. Why do you have to concern yourself with this issue when you get an uncontested divorce? It's necessary because of a pair of military relief laws (one federal and one state) which protect active-duty servicemembers from hard-to-handle lawsuits, including divorces.

Appendix F has lots more about the military relief laws and their legal impact. In general, the laws provide lawsuit protection to *active-duty* servicemembers, whether as plaintiff or defendant, in the five branches (Army, Navy, Marine Corps, Air Force and Coast Guard) of the U.S. military, and the two branches of the Michigan National Guard (Army National Guard and Air National Guard). See "Military Relief Laws" on page 213 for more about the scope of these laws.

In uncontested divorces, the military relief laws typically become an issue that must be dealt with in several situations:

Defendant isn't in active-duty military service. By observing the defendant recently, you know that s/he isn't an active-duty servicemember. As a result, you can check the first outdented box in paragraph #4 of the Default (GRP 2), saying that the defendant isn't in active-duty U.S. military service. In addition, check the box that this information is based on your personal knowledge. This will let the court know that the military relief laws don't apply to the defendant.

Defendant is in active-duty military service. You must check the second outdented box in paragraph #4 saying that the defendant is in active-duty military service. See "Divorcing a Defendant-Servicemember" on page 217 for more about dealing with an active-duty defendant-servicemember and the military relief laws protecting them.

More Information

When you don't know whether or not the defendant is in active-duty military service, you may have to use the military locators to find out. All five service branches have these which provide information about their servicemembers.

Ask for this information in the Request for Certification of Military Status form included in this book. You may have to make requests to all the locators, so fill out the form once and photocopy the form several times. The Request for Certification of Military Status form includes the addresses of the five locator services and the fees they charge for a request.

One problem with any military locator request is that the locators won't give detailed information about troops in deployed units or overseas. But the locators should be able to confirm or deny active-duty status (omitting exact location information), which is all you need for your default application.

One easy way to satisfy these laws is to obtain a waiver of the laws' protections from the defendant. You can get a waiver in the Waiver of Military Relief Rights (GRP 6). Then in paragraph #4 of the Default (GRP 2), check the box indicating that the defendant has waived all lawsuit relief rights, and attach the waiver to the form. See "Waiver of Military Relief Law Rights by the Defendant" on page 218 for more about waiver.

If the defendant-servicemember won't waive, you'll have to deal with the stay remedy of the Soldiers' and Sailors' Civil Relief Act of 1940 (SSCRA). See "Divorcing a Defendant-Servicemember" on page 217 for more about this law. In paragraph #4 of the GRP 2, check the "other" box, and in the space provided say whether or not the defendant has requested a SSCRA stay.

Defendant's (non)military status unknown. The defendant may be elusive or has disappeared, so you don't know personally (hearsay (second-hand information) must be disregarded) whether s/he is in active-duty military service. Or maybe you know that the defendant is in the military, but aren't sure whether s/he is in active or inactive service (reservists frequently change status, especially during a call-up).

Either way, see the sidebox about how to determine the defendant's (non)military status through a military locator service. After you discover the defendant's (non)military status, check the correct boxes in paragraph #4 of the Default (GRP 2) as described above.

Applying for the Default from the Clerk

You can apply to the clerk for the default by mail or personally. Applying in person is best because you can also schedule the final hearing orally or by written request during the visit. Either way, when you apply for the default you should have:

- Default   GRP 2
  - original
  - 3 copies (one earmarked "FOC")

★ special papers for dealing with a defendant-military servicemember, such as the Waiver of Military Relief Law Rights (GRP 6) (see Appendix F)

✦ praecipe (if needed to schedule the final hearing)

Tell the clerk you want to file a default. The clerk should do the following:

■ Take the Default (GRP 2) and the three copies and complete the Entry section of these papers. File the original Default (GRP 2), take the friend of the court's copy and return two copies to you.

★ File any special papers for dealing with a defendant-servicemember, take the friend of the court's copy and return two copies to you.

✦ After your oral or written request (by praecipe), schedule a final hearing for your case (unless you do it elsewhere or later).

After the Default

Despite the fact that the defendant is removed from the case when you get a default, s/he is due a final notice about the default and upcoming final hearing. By giving this notice, the defendant can't complain later that s/he didn't know about the default and the divorce judgment.

After you get the default, prepare the Notice section of the Notice of Entry of Default and Request for Default Judgment of Divorce (GRP 3). Make a photocopy of the paper and attach a copy of the Default (GRP 2). Send the two papers to the defendant by ordinary first-class mail. If the defendant has disappeared, send the papers to his/her last known address.

If possible, send the Notice of Entry of Default and Request for Default Judgment of Divorce (GRP 3) with attached Default (GRP 2) to the defendant within a few days or weeks after the default. But if you haven't gotten a final hearing date by then (because in some counties the court will schedule it and mail you a notice), you must wait until the final hearing is scheduled. This might be anytime during the statutory waiting period. But don't wait too long, since the court rules say that the Notice of Entry of Default and Request for Default Judgment of Divorce

---

Special Symbols

- ● regular paper
- ■ regular practice
- ★ optional paper or practice
- ✦ local paper or practice

(GRP 3) must be sent to the defendant *no later than seven days before your final hearing.*

After you send the Notice of Entry of Default and Request for Default Judgment of Divorce (GRP 3) with attached Default (GRP 2) to the defendant, complete the Proof of Mailing section on the original GRP 3. Make two photocopies of the form and earmark one "FOC." File/send the Notice of Entry of Default and Request for Default Judgment of Divorce (GRP 3) and the friend of the court's copy to the clerk.

STATE OF MICHIGAN Circuit Court - Family Division COUNTY	DEFAULT Application, Affidavit and Entry	CASE NO.

Plaintiff (appearing *in propria persona*):		Defendant:
	v	

APPLICATION

(annotation: INSERT DAY OF SERVICE)

1. As shown by the proof ~~on~~ file, defendant was served with a summons and complaint on 3-4-89

2. Defendant did not respond to the complaint within 21 days (28 days if served by mail or out of state).

I request the clerk to enter the default of defendant for failure to plead or otherwise defend as provided by law.

Date 5-15-89   Plaintiff *Darlene A. Lovelace*

AFFIDAVIT

Plaintiff, being sworn, says:

3. Defendant is not a minor or an incompetent person.

4. Defendant
☒ is not in active-duty service of the U.S. military. This information is based on ☒ personal knowledge. ☐ attached responses from military locator services

☐ is in active-duty service of the U.S. military, and ☐ has waived all lawsuit relief rights under the Soldiers' and Sailors' Civil Relief Act of 1940 and/or MCL 32.517 or a similar military relief law from another state in the attached waiver form.
☐ other: _____

(annotation: CHECK THIS BOX IF THE DEFENDANT IS IN THE MILITARY, AND THEN SEE APPENDIX F ABOUT HOW TO DEAL WITH A DEFENDANT-SERVICE MEMBER)

Date 5-15-89   Plaintiff *Darlene A. Lovelace*

Subscribed and sworn to before me on 5-15-89 , OJIBWAY County, Michigan

Notary public *Loretta Smiley*

My commission expires 1-1-90

ENTRY

The default of defendant is entered for failure to plead or otherwise defend.

Date 5-16-89   Court clerk *Martha Gee*

(annotation: CLERK WILL DATE AND SIGN)

GRP 2 (1/04)   DEFAULT, Application, Affidavit and Entry

STATE OF MICHIGAN
Circuit Court - Family Division
_____ COUNTY

NOTICE OF ENTRY OF DEFAULT AND REQUEST FOR DEFAULT JUDGMENT OF DIVORCE

CASE NO.

Plaintiff (appearing *in propria persona*):

v

Defendant:

NOTICE

TO THE DEFENDANT:

1. Your default was entered on ___5-16-89___, as sh_____ ____ult.

2. I will be requesting a default Judgment of Divorce, a___ _ hearing on this request is scheduled for ___9-7-89___ at ___9:00 A.M.___ in the courtroom of the judge in this case.

> INSERT DATE AND TIME OF HEARING

3. At the hearing, the judge may enter a Judgment of Divorce granting the relief I requested in my Complaint for Divorce and/or grant other relief.

Date ___5-17-89___

Plaintiff ___Darlene A. Lovelace___

PROOF OF MAILING

On the date below, I sent copies of this notice and the Default entered in this case to defendant at his/her address in the caption above by ordinary first-class mail.

I declare that the statement above is true to the best of my information, knowledge and belief.

Date ___5-17-89___

Plaintiff ___Darlene A. Lovelace___

GRP 3   (1/04)   NOTICE OF/ DEFAULT/ REQUEST FOR DEFAULT JUDGMENT OF DIVORCE

Request for Certification of Military Status

TO:

Army Worldwide Locator
U.S. Army Enlisted Records and Evaluation Center
8899 E. 56th St.
Indianapolis, IN 46249-5301
Fee: $3.50 payable by check or money to "Finance Officer"

World Wide Locator
Bureau of Naval Personnel
Pers-324D
2 Navy Annex
Washington, DC 20370-3240
Fee: $3.50 payable by check or money to "U.S. Treasurer"

Headquarters U.S. Marine Corps
Personnel Management Support Branch (MMSB-17)
2008 Elliot Rd.
Quantico, VA 22134-5030
Fee: $3.50 payable by check or money to "U.S. Treasurer"

HQ AFPC/MSIMD
550 C St. West, Suite 50
Randolph AFB, TX 78150-4752
Fee: $3.50 payable by check or money order to "DAO-DE RAFB"

Coast Guard Locator Service
Commanding Officer (RAS)
444 SE Quincy St.
Topeka, KS 66683-3591
Fee: $3.50 payable by check or money order to "U.S. Treasurer"

RE:

Case name _LOVELACE v. LOVELACE_

Case number _89-00501-DM_

Full name of defendant _DUDLEY ERNEST LOVELACE_

Defendant's date of birth _6-15-64_

Defendant's social security number _379-10-5567_

Defendant's rank and service number (if known) _____

Defendant's last duty assignment (if known) _____

Defendant's last military address (if known) _____

I am the plaintiff in the above divorce case seeking a default judgment of divorce against the defendant. I must know whether or not the defendant is currently in the active duty of your branch of the U.S. military service, to comply with the Soldiers' and Sailors' Civil Relief Act of 1940 and/or Michigan Compiled Law 32.517 or a similar military relief law from another state.

Please respond with a certificate of the defendant's (non)military status, unit of assignment and military address, if any, as soon as possible. If the defendant is overseas or in a deployed unit, please certify whether the defendant is or is not in active-duty service and omit the other requested information from your response.

A self-addressed stamped envelope is enclosed for your response. A certification fee is also enclosed, but if I qualify for a fee waiver (as spouse), please refund my payment.

Date _3-15-89_

Signature _Darlene A. Lovelace_

Name _DARLENE A. LOVELACE_

Address _121. S. MAIN_

LAKE CITY, MI 48800

Telephone: _(517)772-0000_

4 Waiting for Final Hearing

After filing, service and default, you must wait for your final hearing during the six-month statutory waiting period. You won't have to do much during the waiting period, but several important things can happen to you during the wait.

Friend of the Court Investigation

As mentioned in "Court System" on page 71, the friend of the court does several things during a divorce. One of the friend of the court's jobs is to investigate divorce cases and make recommendations about custody, parenting time, residence of children, child support and alimony. Judges may use these recommendations to decide divorce issues. The friend of the court's recommendations aren't binding on judges, but they're influential and often followed.

Friend of the court investigations and recommendations are required in all contested divorce cases. In uncontested cases, they're optional. Nevertheless, many counties routinely use them in uncontested cases.

Ordinarily, the friend of the court will start the investigation. But in some counties, you must request it. If you haven't been contacted by the friend of the court within two or three months after filing your divorce, call and see if you must request an investigation.

The friend of the court is already familiar with your case because the clerk has given it copies of all your divorce papers. Even so, friends of the court need extra information for their investigations. To get more information, some friends of the court personally interview the parties. But since most don't have enough staff to hold interviews in every case, they often send questionnaires to the parties. Many use the Friend of the Court Case Questionnaire (FOC 39). This four-page questionnaire has questions about personal history, income, health care coverage and child care expenses. Your answers should give the friend of the court enough information to make recommendations about all the divorce issues.

After the investigation, the friend of the court prepares a recommendation on the divorce issues in a report. The report may be the Friend of the Court Support Recommendation (FOC 33), or it may be an informal letter on the friend of the court's letterhead. The friend of the court submits this report to the judge and sends copies to the parties.

Examine the friend of the court's report to see if it coincides with your and the defendant's position on the divorce issues. In most uncontested cases, the recommendations in the report should resemble your views on custody, parenting time, residence of children, child support and alimony. If they don't, you must be prepared to justify your position to the judge at the final hearing. If the difference between you and the friend of the court is small, you should be able to work out the difference. But if the difference is great, you might need a lawyer to get your view across.

Case Conference

The friend of the court may not be the only one to intervene in your divorce during the waiting period. The clerk may send a notice asking you to attend a pretrial, scheduling or other conference about your case. These case conferences give the clerk a chance to find out more about the progress of cases. They also provide you with practical information about the court's final hearing and judgment procedures. Case conferences are designed for contested cases, but some counties also hold them for uncontested divorce cases.

If the clerk schedules a case conference for you, make sure you go because the court can dismiss your case if you don't attend. Case conferences are usually held in a conference room at the courthouse, not in a courtroom. The defendant probably won't show up, and this should add to the relaxed and informal atmosphere. Nevertheless, court personnel might use the conference to ask you about the case or have you complete a case questionnaire about the progress of your case.

Prosecuting Attorney

Like the friend of the court, the prosecuting attorney knows about your divorce from the copies of the summons and complaint received during filing. Most prosecuting attorneys don't bother to intervene in divorces. But in some counties, the prosecuting attorney may file a paper, called an appearance, to show that s/he is aware of your divorce. In a few counties, the prosecuting attorney may also want to review your final divorce papers, particularly when the custodial parent is receiving FIP payments. Check with the friend of the court to see if this extra review is necessary in your county.

5 Final Hearing

The final hearing comes at the end of your divorce. This hearing is held in court before the judge assigned to your case. You must attend the hearing and give some brief testimony to get a Judgment of Divorce (GPR 4), which decides all the divorce issues. Your divorce becomes final immediately after the hearing, when the judgment is filed.

Final Divorce Papers

The final hearing requires some preparation. About a week before the hearing, you should prepare the final divorce papers. These include the Judgment of Divorce (GRP 4), Income Withholding Order (FOC 5) and several other papers.

The Judgment of Divorce (GRP 4) is by far the most important divorce paper. The judgment ends the marriage, awards custody, arranges parenting time, establishes children's residence, orders child support, divides property and deals with alimony. But the judgment doesn't stop there. The custody, parenting time, residence of children and child support provisions continue until the youngest child becomes an adult. Hence, the Judgment of Divorce (GRP 4) may govern the lives of you, the defendant and your children far into the future.

The Income Withholding Order (FOC 5) is also important because it sets up automatic collection of child support. As explained in "Payment of Child Support" on page 23, child support is normally paid by immediate withholding of money from the payer's source of income (usually an employer).

The Income Withholding Order (FOC 5) provides for immediate income withholding. After the order is filed, the friend of the court sends a copy of the order along with an income withholding notice to the payer's employer or other source of income. The employer then begins to withhold the child support and sends it to the SDU.

Although the Judgment of Divorce (GRP 4) and Income Withholding Order (FOC 5) are court orders, you must prepare them for the court.* The Judgment of Divorce (GRP 4) should reflect your and the defendant's informal agreement on the divorce issues. At the same time, the judgment should comply with the friend of the court's report on those issues.**

Besides the Judgment of Divorce (GRP 4) and Income Withholding Order (FOC 5), your final divorce papers include the Record of Divorce or Annulment (DCH-0838). You probably got this form from the clerk when you filed the divorce. If not, you can obtain it from the clerk any time. To prepare the Record of Divorce or Annulment (DCH-0838) for filing, answer questions #1-16 and #19-20.

In Wayne County only, you must prepare two extra papers: Certificate of Conformity for Domestic Relations Order or Judgment (1225) and Order Data Form-Support (FD/FOC 4002). The certification tells the judge that your divorce judgment satisfies all legal requirements and agrees with the friend of the court's report. The data form paves the way for collection of support.

Approval of Final Divorce Papers

Some counties want the friend of the court to review your final papers to make sure everything is in order. If that's necessary in your county, submit your Judgment of Divorce (GRP 4) and Income Withholding Order (FOC 5) to the friend of the court a week or so before your final hearing. If the papers are satisfactory, the friend of the court will approve them orally or by signing the papers. If they're unsatisfactory, the friend of the court should suggest corrections.

In Wayne County only, you don't need the friend of the court's approval if you can truthfully say in the Certificate of Conformity for Domestic Relations Order or Judgment (1225) that your judgment complies with the friend of the court's report. If it doesn't, you must get the Wayne County Friend of the Court's approval of the judgment.

---

*   If income withholding is already in effect (from a pre-divorce family support case or an ex parte order issued during the divorce), you won't have to prepare another Income Withholding Order (FOC 5). In some counties, the friend of the court will prepare the Income Withholding Order (FOC 5) for you; in others you must do this. Check with the friend of the court to find out the local policy.

**   See "Friend of the Court Investigation" on page 121 for what to do when the friend of the court's report conflicts with your views.

Preparing for the Final Hearing

Before you appear in court for your final hearing, you may want to prepare the testimony for the hearing. Since you don't have a lawyer to question you during the hearing, you must give your testimony straight through, in a monologue. This is a little more difficult than testifying by answering questions. Therefore, you might find it helpful to plan your testimony beforehand.

One way you can do that is by using a script to organize your testimony. By preparing a testimony script, you should be able to memorize the bulk of your testimony. You can also take your testimony script with you to the final hearing and rely on it a bit if your memory fails while you're on the witness stand (using written materials to jog a witness' memory is called "refreshing the recollection," and is permitted by the rules of evidence).

Luckily, the testimony you give during a final hearing is usually quite brief; in most cases it's simply a repetition of the information contained in the divorce complaint. Some courts even skip the testimony entirely, and merely have you swear that the contents of the complaint are true.

You give all the testimony for your hearing; you don't need any testimony from the defendant or other witnesses. In fact, the defendant will probably be absent. Defendants have the right to attend final hearings, but they cannot directly participate because of their default. As a result, defendants seldom attend final hearings in uncontested divorce cases.

On the other hand, having the defendant at the final hearing can be helpful to the judge. With the defendant present, the judge can ask him/her about special or complicated arrangements, such as:

- complicated property division, with the sale of a home or division of new property, such as retirement benefits
- elaborate joint physical custody schedules
- change of the children's residence soon after the divorce
- opting out of the friend of the court system
- military issues, such as satisfaction of the military relief laws
- wife's name change

Special Symbols
● regular paper
■ regular practice
★ optional paper or practice
✦ local paper or practice

Before the Final Hearing

When you attend the final hearing, you must pay any remainder of the friend of the court fee. As mentioned in "Filing Your Divorce" on page 89, many counties collect $30 of the $70 friend of the court fee at filing and the rest at the end of the divorce. If you paid only $30 up front, and the friend of the court did an investigation and recommendation in your case, the remainder of $40 is due at your final hearing.

Besides money for the friend of the court fee, it's a good idea to bring your file with all your divorce papers to the final hearing. If you haven't kept a file, at least bring the following items:

- Judgment of Divorce   GRP 4
  - original
  - 3 copies (one earmarked "FOC")

- Income Withholding Order   FOC 5
  - original
  - 3 copies (one earmarked "FOC")

- Record of Divorce or Annulment   DCH-0838

- money for the friend of the court fee

- testimony script

- ✦ Certificate of Conformity for Domestic Relations   1225
  Order or Judgment (in Wayne County only)
  - original
  - 3 copies (one earmarked "FOC")

- ✦ Order Data Form-Support (in Wayne County only)   FD/FOC 4002
  - original

Attending the Final Hearing

When you go to the courthouse for the final hearing, arrive early so you can take care of any final details. This is a good time to pay any remainder of the friend of the court fee you owe. Clerks often want you to check in with them to let them know that you are present and ready for the final hearing. In some counties, the clerk will give your case file to you to take to the courtroom. But in most counties the clerk will send the file to the courtroom ahead of time.

You should go to your judge's courtroom before the final hearing is scheduled to begin and wait in the visitor's section in back (see "Court Appearances" on page 79 for more about how courts conduct hearings, and how you should conduct yourself during a hearing in court). As your case is called, identify yourself, step forward and take a place at one of the tables. When the judge tells you to proceed, offer your Judgment of Divorce (GRP 4) and Income Withholding Order (FOC 5) to the judge, and say you're ready to give the testimony.

After you take the witness stand and are sworn in, give the testimony as you have planned it. If you omit something important, the judge may question you briefly to complete the testimony. When your testimony is finished, ask the judge to enter your Judgment of Divorce (GRP 4). If the judgment is satisfactory, the judge will sign the original Judgment of Divorce (GRP 4), Income Withholding Order (FOC 5) and maybe some copies.

If the judge objects to your judgment, s/he should tell you what the problem is. It may be something you can fix on the spot. If not, ask the judge for an opportunity to correct the judgment later. The court rules permit you to submit a corrected judgment to the judge within 14 days after the final hearing. If you get that chance, make any necessary modifications of your Judgment of Divorce (GRP 4) and take it to the judge's office. S/he should sign it there and you won't need another final hearing.

But if something really goes wrong during your final hearing, ask the judge for an adjournment. Find out what the problem is and, after you fix it, reschedule another final hearing. If you reschedule the final hearing, you must also give the defendant notice of the new final hearing in the Notice of Entry of Default and Request for Default Judgment of Divorce (GRP 3). This notice must be given at least seven days before the new final hearing takes place (see "After the Default" on page 115 for more about giving this notice).

Filing the Final Divorce Papers

After the final hearing, file your final divorce papers with the clerk and pay the final court fees (unless you paid these before the hearing). Filing the papers quickly is important because, according to paragraph #12 of the Judgment of Divorce (GRP 4a), your divorce only becomes final when you file the judgment. At that time, your marriage is ended and all the other provisions of the judgment take effect.

In a few counties, you can file your final divorce papers (and pay any final court fees) with the courtroom clerk during the final hearing. But in most counties, you must return to the clerk's office, where the clerk will:

■ File the Judgment of Divorce (GRP 4), take the friend of the court's copy and return two copies to you.

■ File the Income Withholding Order (FOC 5), take the friend of the court's copy and return two copies to you.

■ Take the Record of Divorce or Annulment (DCH-0838).

■ Take the money for any remainder of the friend of the court fee you owe (unless you paid the fee before your final hearing began).

✦ In Wayne County only, 1) file the Certificate of Conformity for Domestic Relations Order or Judgment (1225), take the friend of the court's copy and return two copies to you 2) take the Order Data Form-Support (FD/FOC 4002) for delivery to the Wayne County Friend of the Court along with the friend of the court's copy of the judgment.

Before you leave the clerk's office, you may want to obtain several *certified* copies of the Judgment of Divorce (GRP 4). These copies can be helpful in carrying out the judgment's property division or verifying a name change. See "After Your Divorce" on page 141 for more about these issues. Bring extra money for certified copies because the clerk charges $10 for issuing a certified copy plus $1 for each page of the document.

After the Final Hearing

Naturally, the defendant must know what the Judgment of Divorce (GRP 4) says because its provisions affect him/her. After the final hearing, the clerk should send the defendant a brief notice that a judgment was issued. However, the clerk doesn't send a copy of the Judgment of Divorce (GRP 4) itself to the defendant along with this notice. That's your responsibility.

You must send the judgment to the defendant within seven days of the final hearing. To do that, send true copies of the Judgment of Divorce (GRP 4) and Income Withholding Order (FOC 5) to the defendant by ordinary first-class mail. If the defendant has disappeared, send these to his/her last known address. After the mailing, prepare the Proof of Mailing (MC 302). Make two copies and earmark one "FOC." Then file/send the original and the friend of the court's copy to the clerk.

STATE OF MICHIGAN Circuit Court - Family Division _____ COUNTY	JUDGMENT OF DIVORCE Page 1 of 5 pages	CASE NO.

Plaintiff (appearing *in propria persona*):

v

Defendant:

Date of hearing __9-7-89__   Judge __LESTER TUBBS__

USE FOR WIFE'S NAME CHANGE

After the defendant's default, **IT IS ORDERED:**

1. **DIVORCE:** The parties are divorced.
2. **CHILDREN:** There ☒ are ☐ are not children of the parties or born during the
   are under 18 or adult and entitled to support.
☒ 3. **NAME CHANGE:** Wife's last name is changed to __ALBRIGHT__
4. **SPOUSAL SUPPORT:** Spousal support is

☒ not granted for   ☒ wife. ☒ husband.
☐ reserved for   ☐ wife. ☐ husband.
☐ granted later in the judgment for ☐ wife. ☐ husband.

SEE "ALIMONY PROVISIONS" IN APPENDIX H FOR MORE ON SPOUSAL SUPPORT (ALIMONY)

5. **PROPERTY DIVISION:**
   A. **Real property:** (Land and buildings)
      ☐ The parties do not own any real property.
      ☒ Real property is divided elsewhere in this judgment.
   All real property owned by the parties in joint tenancy or tenancy by the entirety is converted to te
   cy in common, unless this judgment provides otherwise.
   B. **Personal property:** (All other property)
      ☒ Each party is awarded the personal property in his or her posses
      ☒ Personal property is divided elsewhere in this judgment.

SEE "PROPERTY DIVISION PROVISIONS" IN APPENDIX H FOR MORE ON PROPERTY DIVISIONS

CHECK BOXES AS THEY APPLY

6. **STATUTORY RIGHTS:** All interests of the parties in the property of the other, now owned or later acquired, under MCL 700.2201-700.2405, are extinguish[ed] including those known as dower under MCL 558.1-558.29.
7. **BENEFICIARY RIGHTS:** The rights each party has to the pro[ceeds of life?] insurance, endowments or annuities upon the life of the other as a[re?] ment during or in anticipation of marriage, are ☒ extinguished.
8. **RETIREMENT BENEFITS:** Any rights of either party in any pens[ion] benefit of the other, whether these rights are vested or unvested, a[re?] ☒ extinguished. ☐ awarded later in the judgment.

SEE "PROPERTY DIVISION PROVISIONS" IN APPENDIX H FOR MORE ON DIVIDING RETIREMENT BENEFITS

9. **DOCUMENTATION:** Each party shall promptly and properly execute and de[liver] documents to carry out the terms of this judgment. A certified copy of this ju[dgment] recorded with the register of deeds in any county of this state where property [is?]
10. **PRIOR ORDERS:** Except as otherwise provided in this judgment, any nonfinal orders or injunc-tions entered in this action are terminated.
☐ 11. **SUSPENDED FEES AND COSTS:** The previously suspended fees and costs in this case of _____ shall be ☐ paid by ☐ plaintiff ☐ defendant to the clerk. ☐ waived finally.
12. **EFFECTIVE DATE OF JUDGMENT:** This judgment shall become effective immediately after it is signed by the judge and filed with the clerk.

GRP 4a (1/04)   JUDGMENT OF DIVORCE, page 1

STATE OF MICHIGAN
Circuit Court - Family Division
COUNTY

JUDGMENT OF DIVORCE
Page 2 of 5 pages

CASE NO.

Plaintiff:

Defendant:

v

IT IS ALSO ORDERED:

13. INALIENABLE RIGHTS OF CHILDREN: The children have the right to the love and affection of both parents. The parties shall cooperate during child-rearing to promote the well-being of the children and maintain strong parent-child relationships. The parties must also cooperate in carrying out the child-related provisions of this judgment.

14. CUSTODY: Custody of the minor children is granted as follows:

PL = Plaintiff   DF = Defendant   JT = Joint   3rd = Third party, named here:

CHILD'S NAME	DATE Of BIRTH	LEGAL CUSTODY	PHYSICAL CUSTODY
DUANE WESLEY LOVELACE	6-1-86	PL	PL
DARRYL WENDELL LOVELACE	7-1-87	PL	PL

THIS IS SOLE CUSTODY; SEE "CUSTODY PROVISIONS" IN APPENDIX H FOR OTHER TYPES OF CUSTODY

IF YOU WANT SPECIFIC PARENTING TIME, CHECK BOX AND SEE "PARENTING TIME PROVISIONS" IN APPENDIX H

15. PARENTING TIME: Any parent without physical custody shall have parenting time as follows:
☒ reasonable ☐ specific (describe specific parenting time later in this judgment)

16. RESIDENCE OF CHILDREN:

a. **Local residences.** A parent whose custody or parenting time of a child is governed by this order shall not change the legal residence of the child except in compliance with section 11 of the Custody Act of 1970," 1970 PA 91, MCL 722.31; or: ☐ After an agreement of the par effective _____, the residence of the following minor children:

Names _____

shall be changed from their current residence with ☐ plaintiff ☐ defendant

at _____

to _____

YOU CAN CHANGE THE RESIDENCE OF CHILDREN HERE WITH THE AGREEMENT OF THE DEFENDANT

b. **State residence (domicile).** The minor children's residences (domicile) shall not be moved from the state of Michigan without the prior approval of the court.

c. **Notice of change of residence.** The person awarded custody shall promptly notify the friend of the court in writing when the minor is moved to another address.

GRP 4b (1/04)   JUDGMENT OF DIVORCE, page 2

STATE OF MICHIGAN Circuit Court - Family Division COUNTY	JUDGMENT OF DIVORCE Page 3 of 5 pages	CASE NO.

Plaintiff: v   Defendant:

IT IS ALSO ORDERED:

17. CHILD SUPPORT:

a. **Amount.** Child support shall be paid monthly, in advance on the first day of the month, as follows:

Support payer: DUDLEY E. LOVELACE   Support payee: DARLENE A. LOVELACE

Children supported:	One	Two	Three	Four	Five or more
Base support:	$ 333	$ 512	$	$	$
Child care:	$	$	$	$	$
Total:	$ 333	$ 512	$		

☒ Base support shall abate 50% after 6 consecutive overni~~...~~ MCSF.
☐ Support based on shared economic responsibility ~~...~~ obligation of
$ _____ and _____ overnights of parenting ~~...~~

These support provisions ☒ do ☐ do not follow th~~...~~ pro-

> SEE "CHILD SUPPORT PROVISIONS" IN APPENDIX H FOR HOW TO FIGURE CHILD SUPPORT

b. **Duration.** Child support shall last until each child is age ~~...~~ whichever is later, but no longer than age ~~...~~ vided in MCL 552.605b.

c. **Redirection, assignment and abatement.** Subject to the procedures described in MCL 552.605d: 1) support may be redirected to the person who is legally responsible for the actual care, support and maintenance of a child when that person is different from the payee of support, 2) support for a child in foster care shall be assigned to the Family Independence Agency 3) support shall abate for a child who resides on a full-time basis with the payer of support.

18. HEALTH CARE FOR CHILDREN:

a. **Health care coverage.** ☐ Plaintiff ☒ Defendant shall carry insurance (as the term "insurer" is defined in MCL 552.602(o) covering hospital, dental, optical and other health care expenses) when coverage is available at a reasonable cost through an employer or under an existing individual policy.

b. **Uninsured health care expenses:**

1. **Ordinary expenses.** Uninsured health care expenses defined as ordinary by sec. IV-D(2) of the MCSF are paid through the base support amount in paragraph #17.

2. **Extraordinary expenses.** Plaintiff shall pay 38 % and defendant shall pay 62 % of the uninsured health care expenses defined as extraordinary under MCSF IV-D(3). These expenses must be paid within 28 days of a written payment request or the obligation may be enforced as provided by law.

c. **Qualified medical support order.** This order is a qualified medical support order under 29 USC 1169. To qualify this order, a notice to enroll may be issued to the child support payer under MCL 552.626b. A parent may contest the notice by requesting a review or hearing concerning availability of health care at a reasonable cost.

GRP 4c (1/04)   JUDGMENT OF DIVORCE, page 3

STATE OF MICHIGAN Circuit Court - Family Division COUNTY	JUDGMENT OF DIVORCE Page 4 of 5 pages	CASE NO.

Plaintiff:

Defendant:

v

IT IS ALSO ORDERED:

19. PAYMENT OF SUPPORT:

a. Child support shall be paid

by ☒ immediate income withholding ☐ without income withholding until past-due support equals or exceeds the monthly amount of support

to ☒ state disbursement unit (SDU). ☐ directly to the payee. ☐ other:

b. Any spousal support shall be paid

by ☐ immediate income withholding ☐ without income withholding until past-due support equals or exceeds the monthly amount of support

to ☐ state disbursement unit (SDU). ☐ directly to the payee. ☐ other:

20. PAST-DUE SUPPORT:

a. **Retroactive modification.** Support is an order the date it is due and shall not be modified retroactively except as allowed by MCL 552.603 and 552.603b.

b. **Lien and surcharge.** Unpaid support is a lien on the payer's property by operation of law and the payer's property can be encumbered or seized if past-due support exceeds two times the monthly amount of periodic support payments. In a friend of the court case, a surcharge will be added to past-due support as provided by MCL 552.603a.

c. **Current arrearage.** Past-due support owed from a nonfinal order in this case, including amounts owed to the state of Michigan, is preserved and shall be paid as stated later in this judgment.

21. FRIEND OF THE COURT SERVICES AND FEES:

☐ a. **Friend of the court opt-out.** The friend of the court shall be removed from this case as follows:

☐ The previously ordered opt-out from these friend of the court services: ☐ all friend of the services ☐ all friend of the court services except collection and distribution of support th the SDU ☐ immediate income withholding only ☐ shall remain in effect. ☐ sh

☐ This case shall be opted out of these friend of the court services: ☐ all friend of the cou vices ☐ all friend of the court services except collection and distribution of support throug SDU ☐ immediate income withholding only

b. **Friend of the court fees.** While a friend of the court case, the support payer shall pay friend o the court service fees and other statutory fees.

22. PERSONAL INFORMATION: The parties' current residence addresses and telephone nos. appear in the main caption of this judgment. Their current sources of income are listed below:

Source of income:

Address:

Telephone no:

Plaintiff
10,000 PANCAKES
111 M-78
LAKE CITY, MI 48800
772-0011

Defendant
WATERBED WORLD
1000 SERVICE RD.
LAKE CITY MI 48800
773-0011

The parties have previously provided information about their health care coverage, social security nos., driver's and occupational licenses. In a friend of the court case, they must inform the friend of the court of any changes or additions to the personal information cited in this section, reporting changes in their residence information in writing within 21 days of a change.

GRP 4d (1/04)   JUDGMENT OF DIVORCE, page 4

(speech bubble:) YOU CAN EXTEND A PREVIOUS OPT-OUT, OR BEGIN ONE, IN THIS PARAGRAPH; SEE APPENDIX C

STATE OF MICHIGAN Circuit Court - Family Division _____ COUNTY	JUDGMENT OF DIVORCE Final of 5 pages	CASE NO.

Plaintiff:

v

Defendant:

IT IS ALSO ORDERED:

23.

24.

ETC.

INCLUDE ADDITIONAL JUDGMENT PROVISIONS HERE AS NEEDED

CHECK THESE BOXES TO CLOSE THE CASE

JUDGE WILL DATE AND SIGN AT FINAL HEARING

judgment ☒ resolves ☐ does not resolve the pending claim in this case, and ☒ closes ☐ does close the case, except to the extent jurisdiction is retained by law.

Reviewed by FOC _____

Date 9-7-89 _____   Judge *Lester Tubbs* _____

GRP 4e (1/04)   JUDGMENT OF DIVORCE, final page

Approved, SCAO

	Original - Court	2nd copy - Plaintiff
STATE OF MICHIGAN	1st copy - Friend of the Court	3rd copy - Defendant
JUDICIAL CIRCUIT		Additional copies to all sources of income
COUNTY	INCOME WITHHOLDING ORDER	CASE NO.

Friend of the Court address

INCOME WITHHOLDING ORDER
☒ Court ordered   ☐ Consent

CASE NO.

Plaintiff's name and address

Court telephone no.

v

Defendant's name and address

Regarding: **DUDLEY E. LOVELACE**
Payer

379-10-5567
Social security number

Date of order: **9-7-89**

Judge: **LESTER TUBBS**

1. The court finds that the above payer owes current support, statutory fees, and/or arrearages in the above case, and notice has been given as required by law.

2. Income is defined as: commissions, earnings, salaries, wages, and other income due now or in the future from an employer and successor employers; any payment due now or in the future from a profit-sharing plan, pension plan, insurance contract, annuity, unemployment compensation, supplemental unemployment benefits, and worker's compensation; any amount of money due the payer under a support order as a debt of any other individual, partnership, association, private or public corporation, the United States or any Federal agency, any state or political subdivision of any state, or any other legal entity indebted to the payer.

IT IS ORDERED:

3. The source of income shall withhold payer's income as specified in the attached notice of income withholding and in any subsequent notices.

4. The State Disbursement Unit shall receive and disburse these funds for the purpose of collecting support, statutory fees, and the payment of all arrearages.

5. Any income withheld under this order shall be paid to the State Disbursement Unit within 3 days after the date of withholding.

6. If the payer's existing support order is modified by an order of the court, the office of the friend of the court shall send a notice of modification to the source of income by ordinary mail. The amount assigned or withheld shall be changed to conform with the court modification within 7 days after receipt of the notice of modification.

Darlene A. Lovelace
Signature of preparer

Judge _Lester Tubbs_

☐ I consent to the terms of this order.
Payer's signature

Bar no.

CERTIFICATE OF MAILING

I certify that on this date I mailed a copy of this order to the parties and sources of income by ordinary mail addressed to their last known addresses.

Date _____

Signature _____

FOC 5 (4/01) INCOME WITHHOLDING ORDER

MCL 552.601 et seq.; MSA 25.164(1) et seq

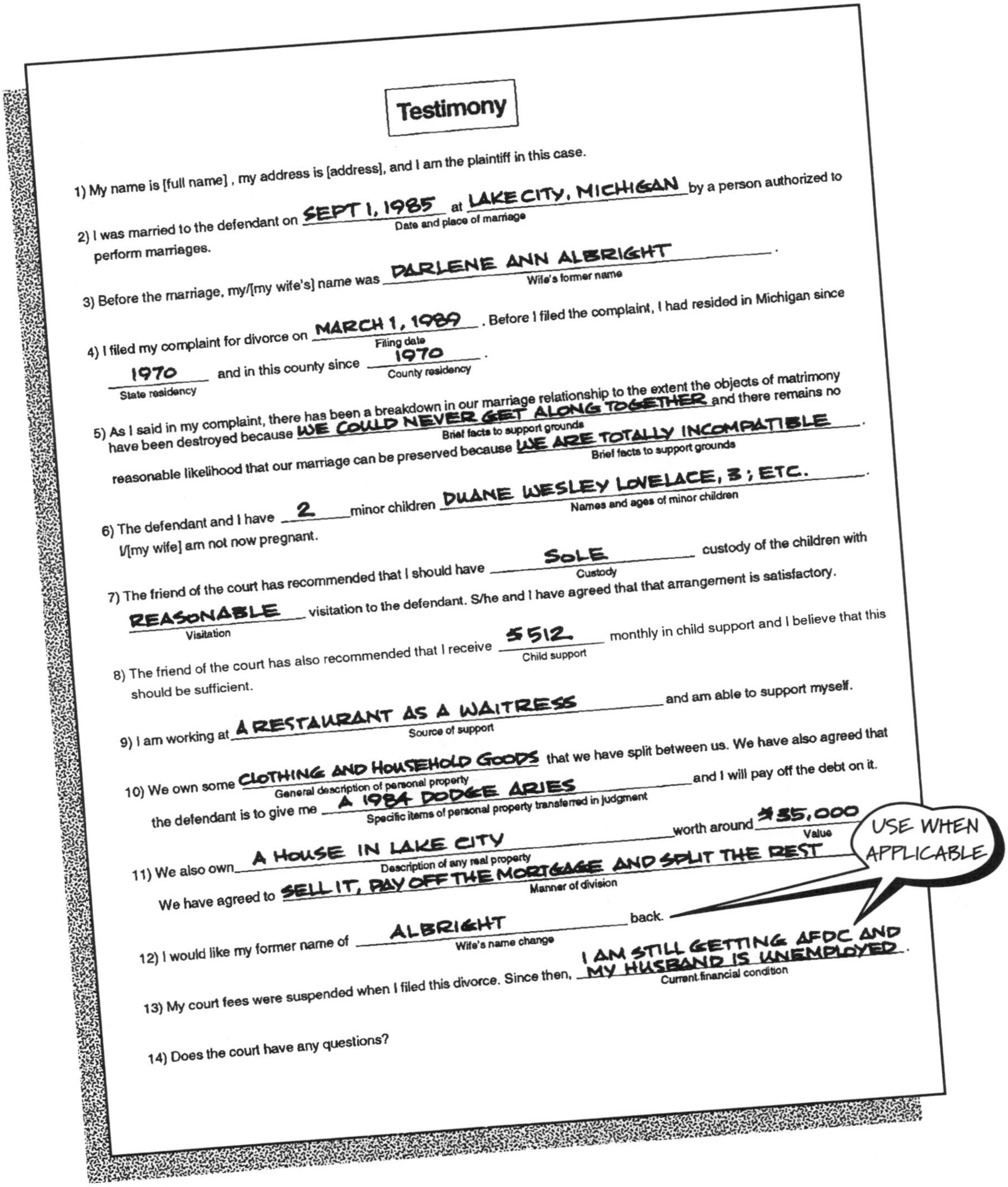

Testimony

1) My name is [full name] , my address is [address], and I am the plaintiff in this case.

2) I was married to the defendant on **SEPT 1, 1985** at **LAKE CITY, MICHIGAN** by a person authorized to
perform marriages.
_{Date and place of marriage}

3) Before the marriage, my/[my wife's] name was **DARLENE ANN ALBRIGHT** .
_{Wife's former name}

4) I filed my complaint for divorce on **MARCH 1, 1989** . Before I filed the complaint, I had resided in Michigan since
_{Filing date}
1970 and in this county since **1970**
_{State residency}   _{County residency}

5) As I said in my complaint, there has been a breakdown in our marriage relationship to the extent the objects of matrimony
have been destroyed because **WE COULD NEVER GET ALONG TOGETHER** and there remains no
_{Brief facts to support grounds}
reasonable likelihood that our marriage can be preserved because **WE ARE TOTALLY INCOMPATIBLE** .
_{Brief facts to support grounds}

6) The defendant and I have **2** minor children **DUANE WESLEY LOVELACE, 3 ; ETC.** .
_{Names and ages of minor children}
I/[my wife] am not now pregnant.

7) The friend of the court has recommended that I should have **SOLE** custody of the children with
_{Custody}
REASONABLE visitation to the defendant. S/he and I have agreed that that arrangement is satisfactory.
_{Visitation}

8) The friend of the court has also recommended that I receive **$512.** monthly in child support and I believe that this
_{Child support}
should be sufficient.

9) I am working at **A RESTAURANT AS A WAITRESS** and am able to support myself.
_{Source of support}

10) We own some **CLOTHING AND HOUSEHOLD GOODS** that we have split between us. We have also agreed that
_{General description of personal property}
the defendant is to give me **A 1984 DODGE ARIES** and I will pay off the debt on it.
_{Specific items of personal property transferred in judgment}

11) We also own **A HOUSE IN LAKE CITY** worth around **$35,000**
_{Description of any real property}   _{Value}
We have agreed to **SELL IT, PAY OFF THE MORTGAGE AND SPLIT THE REST**
_{Manner of division}

12) I would like my former name of **ALBRIGHT** back.
_{Wife's name change}

13) My court fees were suspended when I filed this divorce. Since then, **I AM STILL GETTING AFDC AND MY HUSBAND IS UNEMPLOYED** .
_{Current financial condition}

14) Does the court have any questions?

(handwritten note with arrow: USE WHEN APPLICABLE)

STATE OF MICHIGAN
THIRD JUDICIAL CIRCUIT
WAYNE COUNTY
Penobscot Bldg. 645 Griswold Ave. Detroit, MI 48226

CERTIFICATE OF CONFORMITY
FOR DOMESTIC RELATIONS
ORDER OR JUDGMENT

CASE NO.

313-224-5372

PLAINTIFF'S NAME	V.	DEFENDANT'S NAME

I certify the attached Order or Judgment as presented for entry to be in full conformity with the requirements set forth by statute, INCLUDING A PROVISION FOR IMMEDIATE INCOME WITHHOLDING (WHICH SHALL BE IMPLEMENTED BY THE FRIEND OF THE COURT), THE PAYER'S SOCIAL SECURITY NUMBER AND THE NAME AND ADDRESS OF HIS/HER SOURCE OF INCOME IF KNOWN , UNLESS OTHERWISE ORDERED BY THE COURT, and with Michigan Court Rules 3.201 and following, and if applicable, includes all provisions of the Friend of the Court recommendation or is in conformity with the decision of

_____ rendered on the _____ day of

_____ , 19 _____.

9-5-89
Date

Darlene A. Lovelace
Attorney / Bar No.
PLAINTIFF

Instructions : Please sign and present this Certificate to the Court Clerk when the Order or Judgment is presented for entry. If an ex parte interim order is being presented to the Judge, please complete the "Certificate on Behalf of Plaintiff regarding Ex Parte Interim Support Order" and follow Local Court Rule 3.206.

USE THIS FORM
IN WAYNE
COUNTY ONLY.

#1225 (7/95) CERTIFICATE OF CONFORMITY FOR DOMESTIC RELATIONS ORDER OR JUDGMENT

PAGE 1 OF 2

ORDER DETAILS

STATE OF MICHIGAN
COUNTY OF WAYNE
THIRD JUDICIAL CIRCUIT COURT
FAMILY DIVISION

ORDER DATA FORM-SUPPORT
Re: SUBMISSION FOR LOADING
ATTACHED SUPPORT ORDER INTO
MiCSES ON FOC COMPUTER SYSTEM

THE ORDER WAS ENTERED ON:
9-7-89
(DATE ON ORDER STAMPED BY JUDGE'S CLERK)

> USE THIS FORM IN WAYNE COUNTY ONLY. SEE THE BLANK FORM WHICH HAS A TWO-PAGE PREFACE WITH MORE INSTRUCTIONS

*INDICATES REQUIRED INFORMATION
CHECK ONLY THE BOXES WHICH APPLY TO PROVISIONS IN THE SUBMITTED ORDER

* PLAINTIFF NAME:
DARLENE ANN LOVELACE

* DEFENDANT NAME:
DUDLEY ERNEST LOVELACE

*THIS ORDER IS: ☐ TEMPORARY ☒ JUDGMENT ☐ MODIFICATION
☐ EX PARTE (PROOF OF SERVICE REQUIRED)
*WERE CHILD SUPPORT GUIDELINES FOLLOWED? ☒ YES ☐ NO ☐ NOT APPLICABLE.

*THE CHILD SUPPORT PAYER IS ☐ PLAINTIFF ☒ DEFENDANT ☐ PAY DIRECT, NOT THROUGH FOC.

☐ CHILD SUPPORT. COMMENCEMENT DATE IS 9-7-89

* 5 CHILDREN PER WEEK CHILD SUPPORT AMOUNT	* 4 CHILDREN PER WEEK CHILD SUPPORT AMOUNT	* 3 CHILDREN PER WEEK CHILD SUPPORT AMOUNT	* 2 CHILDREN PER WEEK CHILD SUPPORT AMOUNT	* 1 CHILD PER WEEK CHILD SUPPORT AMOUNT
$	$	$	$ 512/MONTH	$ 333/MONTH PER WEEK

☒ INCOME WITHHOLDING: ☒ PROCESS AT GUIDELINE AMOUNT ☐ PROCESS AT $ _____ PER WEEK

☒ CHILD SUPPORT ARREARAGE: ☐ SET AT $ _____ AS OF DATE: _____
☒ PRESERVED ☐ CANCELED AS OF DATE: _____ PER WEEK, COMMENCEMENT DATE IS _____ :

☐ CHILD CARE EXPENSES: $ _____
END DATE IS ☐ GUIDELINE DATE OR ☐ DATE: _____
☐ CHILD CARE ARREARAGE: ☐ SET AT $ _____ AS OF DATE: _____
☐ PRESERVED ☐ CANCELED AS OF DATE: _____

☐ ARREARAGE ADJUSTMENT: ☐ ADD ADDITIONAL OBLIGATION IN AMOUNT OF $ _____
☐ DIRECT CREDIT IN AMOUNT OF $ _____

☒ MEDICAL INSURANCE IN ORDER.
☒ CHILD SUPPORT PAYER RESPONSIBLE FOR 66 % OF UNINSURED MEDICAL EXPENSES.

☒ PARENTING TIME ABATEMENT: 50 % PARENTING TIME CREDIT AFTER 6 CONSECUTIVE OVERNIGHTS.
☒ PARENTING TIME ORDERED: (CHECK ONE):
☒ REASONABLE ☐ SPECIFIC ☐ SUPERVISED ☐ RESERVED ☐ REFER TO FAMILY COUNSELING/OTHER

*THE SPOUSAL SUPPORT PAYER IS ☐ PLAINTIFF ☐ DEFENDANT ☒ NOT APPLICABLE.
☐ SPOUSAL SUPPORT: ☐ $ _____ PER WEEK, COMMENCEMENT DATE: _____
☐ PERMANENT ☐ END DATE _____ ☐ PAY DIRECT, NOT THROUGH FOC
☐ SPOUSAL SUPPORT ARREARAGE: ☐ SET AT $ _____ AS OF DATE: _____
☐ PRESERVED ☐ CANCELED AS OF DATE: _____

☐ ORDER REFERS MATTERS TO DIVORCE INVESTIGATION/MODIFICATION FOR FURTHER INVESTIGATION.

I CERTIFY THAT THE ABOVE INFORMATION IS TRUE TO THE BEST OF MY KNOWLEDGE, INFORMATION AND BELIEF, AND IS IN FULL CONFORMITY WITH THE REQUIREMENTS SET FORTH BY STATUTE AND COURT RULE AND THE DECISION OF THE COURT. (NOTE: FOC WILL NOT READ THE ORDER WHEN ENTERING IT ON MiCSES.)

9-5-89
DATE:

Darlene Lovelace
SIGNATURE OF ~~ATTORNEY~~ PLAINTIFF

BAR NO.

PLEASE PRINT:
ATTORNEY NAME
121 S. MAIN
ADDRESS
LAKE CITY, MI 48800
CITY/STATE/ZIP

772-0000
TELEPHONE NO.

FD/FOC 4002 (11/06/02) ORDER DATA FORM-SUPPORT

PAGE 2 OF 2

DEMOGRAPHICS

STATE OF MICHIGAN
COUNTY OF WAYNE
THIRD JUDICIAL CIRCUIT
COURT
FAMILY DIVISION

ORDER DATA FORM-SUPPORT
Re: SUBMISSION FOR LOADING
ATTACHED SUPPORT ORDER INTO
MiCSES ON FOC COMPUTER SYSTEM

THE ORDER WAS ENTERED ON:
9-7-89
(DATE ON ORDER STAMPED BY JUDGE'S CLERK)

USE THIS FORM
IN WAYNE
COUNTY ONLY.

CASE #: _____

JUDGE _____

*INDICATES REQUIRED INFORMATION

CHECK ONLY THE BOXES WHICH APPLY TO PROVISIONS IN THE SUBMITTED ORDER

* PLAINTIFF NAME:
DARLENE ANN LOVELACE

* DEFENDANT NAME:
DUDLEY ERNEST LOVELACE

* NAME(S) OF CHILDREN (OLDEST TO YOUNGEST)	* DATE(S) OF BIRTH	* SOCIAL SECURITY NUMBER(S)
DUANE WESLEY LOVELACE	6-1-86	466-10-1001
DARRYL WENDELL LOVELACE	7-1-87	469-00 4411

(ADD ADDITIONAL CHILDREN ON SEPARATE SHEET)

NON-CUSTODIAL PARENT (OR FATHER IF JOINT CUSTODY)

* NAME: DUDLEY E. LOVELACE
* DATE OF BIRTH: 6-15-64
* SOC. SEC. NO. 379-10-5567
☐ PLAINTIFF ☒ DEFENDANT

* RESIDENTIAL ADDRESS: 900 S. MAPLE
* CITY, STATE, ZIP: LAKE CITY, MI 48800
OTHER TELEPHONE NUMBERS:
☒ WORK ☐ MOBILE 773-0011
HOME TELEPHONE NO.: 773-3004

* EMPLOYER: WATERBED WORLD
* EMPLOYER ADDRESS: 1000 SERVICE RD. LAKE CITY, MI 48800
EMPLOYER TELEPHONE NO.: 773-0011
FIA/TANF NO.:
NOW ACTIVE: ☐ YES ☐ NO
EMPLOYER FED I.D. NO.: 38-0017760

CUSTODIAL PERSON (OR MOTHER IF JOINT CUSTODY)

* NAME: DARLENE A. LOVELACE
* DATE OF BIRTH: 5-1-65
* SOC. SEC. NO. 380-16-1010
☒ PLAINTIFF ☐ DEFENDANT

* RESIDENTIAL ADDRESS: 121 S. MAIN
* CITY, STATE, ZIP: LAKE CITY, MI 48800
OTHER TELEPHONE NUMBERS:
☒ WORK ☐ MOBILE 772-0011
HOME TELEPHONE NO.: 772-0000

* EMPLOYER: 10,000 PANCAKES
* EMPLOYER ADDRESS: 111 M-78 LAKE CITY, MI 48800
EMPLOYER TELEPHONE NO.: 772-0011
FIA/TANF NO.:
NOW ACTIVE: ☐ YES ☐ NO
EMPLOYER FED I.D. NO.: 38-1111707

I CERTIFY THAT THE ABOVE INFORMATION IS TRUE TO THE BEST OF MY KNOWLEDGE, INFORMATION AND BELIEF, AND IS IN FULL CONFORMITY WITH THE REQUIREMENTS SET FORTH BY STATUTE AND COURT RULE AND THE DECISION OF THE COURT. (NOTE: FOC WILL NOT READ THE ORDER WHEN ENTERING IT ON MiCSES.)

DATE: 9-5-89

SIGNATURE OF ~~ATTORNEY~~ PLAINTIFF: *Darlene Lovelace*

PLEASE PRINT: _____
ATTORNEY NAME

BAR NO. _____

FD/FOC 4002 (11/06/02) ORDER DATA FORM-SUPPORT

Approved, SCAO

STATE OF MICHIGAN JUDICIAL DISTRICT JUDICIAL CIRCUIT	PROOF OF MAILING	CASE NO.
		Court telephone no.

Court address

Plaintiff(s)		Defendant(s)
	v	

On the date below I sent by first class mail a copy of _____ JUDGMENT OF DIVORCE AND INCOME WITHHOLDING ORDER

to: Names and addresses

DUDLEY LOVELACE
900 S. MAPLE
LAKE CITY, MI 48800

I declare that the statements above are true to the best of my information, knowledge and belief.

DARLENE A. LOVELACE

9-8-89
Date

Name (typed)

Darlene A. Lovelace
Signature

MC 302 (5/88) PROOF OF MAILING

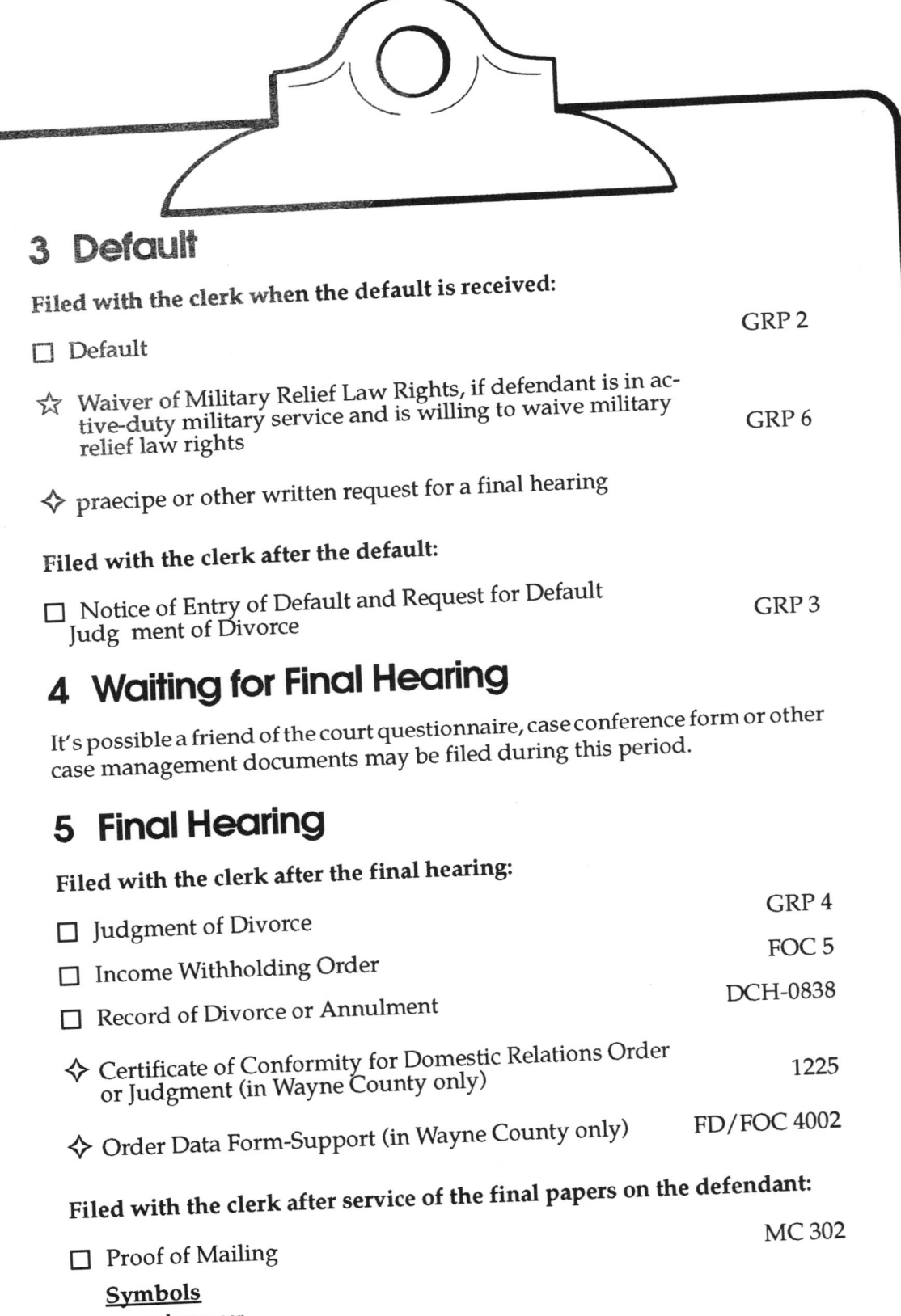

3 Default

Filed with the clerk when the default is received:

☐ Default   GRP 2

☆ Waiver of Military Relief Law Rights, if defendant is in active-duty military service and is willing to waive military relief law rights   GRP 6

◇ praecipe or other written request for a final hearing

Filed with the clerk after the default:

☐ Notice of Entry of Default and Request for Default Judg ment of Divorce   GRP 3

4 Waiting for Final Hearing

It's possible a friend of the court questionnaire, case conference form or other case management documents may be filed during this period.

5 Final Hearing

Filed with the clerk after the final hearing:

☐ Judgment of Divorce   GRP 4

☐ Income Withholding Order   FOC 5

☐ Record of Divorce or Annulment   DCH-0838

◇ Certificate of Conformity for Domestic Relations Order or Judgment (in Wayne County only)   1225

◇ Order Data Form-Support (in Wayne County only)   FD/FOC 4002

Filed with the clerk after service of the final papers on the defendant:

☐ Proof of Mailing   MC 302

Symbols
◻ regular paper
☆ optional paper
◇ local paper

After Your Divorce

Although your divorce is over, there's still some work to do. The Judgment of Divorce (GRP 4) takes legal effect at filing, but you must carry out several judgment provisions. What's more, the end of your marriage may require changes in your will, powers of attorney, insurance, retirement benefits, etc.

Transferring Property

The Judgment of Divorce (GRP 4) divided your property, but it's your responsibility to transfer ownership of the property.

Ownership of real property must be transferred by deed. For transfers between ex-spouses, a simple form of deed called a quit claim deed is customarily used. Lawyers or real estate brokers can prepare these for a small fee.

If your ex-spouse is uncooperative or unavailable for transfer, you can sometimes use the divorce judgment to transfer ownership of real property yourself. To use the judgment this way, it must describe the property in detail (see "Property Division Provisions" in Appendix H for more about describing property using legal descriptions or identification numbers). You must also have an official certified copy of the judgment for the transfer. These are available from the clerk for a small fee.

You can transfer Michigan real property by recording a certified copy of the divorce judgment with the register of deeds for the county where the property is located. This transfer method isn't available for out-of-state real property.

Personal property without titles (clothing, household goods, etc.) can be transferred by simply changing possession of the items. But both possession and title must be transferred for personal property with titles (stocks, bonds, motor vehicles, etc.).

To Obtain

A certified copy of your divorce judgment, go to the clerk of the court that granted your divorce.

There is a $10 fee for issuing a certified copy, plus $1 for each page of the document.

Stocks and bonds can be transferred through the designated transfer agent (usually a bank but sometimes the issuing company itself).

Transfer titles to motor vehicles through a secretary of state office by applying for a new title after the current owner has signed off on the back of the old certificate of title.

If the owner refuses to cooperate, you can use a certified copy of the divorce judgment for transfer of title. When you apply for a new title, submit a certified copy of the judgment, and you won't need your ex's signature on the old certificate of title.

Debts

You may have already closed or frozen joint accounts (see "Does My Property Need Protection?" on page 58 for more about handling joint accounts during divorce). If you haven't, do this at once. Otherwise, your ex can add new joint debt after the divorce for which you may be liable.

Health Care Coverage

With the high cost of health care these days, health care coverage is a necessity. Your children need this coverage, and maybe you need coverage for yourself.

Coverage for Children

Divorce judgments typically require one or both parents to continue (or obtain) health care plans covering the children, if available at a reasonable cost. Even with coverage, there are bound to be small (ordinary) or large (extraordinary) uninsured expenses created by deductibles, co-payments or gaps in coverage.

"Health Care" on page 249 explains how to handle health care coverage, and has suggestions if no coverage is available. This section also explains absorbing ordinary and extraordinary health care expenses of children.

If you choose COBRA-coverage through your ex-spouse's employer, as described on page 248, contact his/her employee benefits office within 60 days after your divorce judgment is granted. Wait longer and you can lose the right to obtain health care through the COBRA law.

Coverage for Spouse

Some of the health care plans and programs, such as MIChild and Healthy Kids, are designed for children and don't apply to adults. But others do. Parents of children receiving Medicaid through the Healthy Kids program can qualify for Medicaid themselves. Ex-spouses are also eligible for COBRA-coverage, county health plans, the Hill-Burton program or coverage through individual policies. All these options are described on page 248.

Estate Planning

Paragraphs #7 and #8 of the Judgment of Divorce (GRP 4a) end all claims you and your ex-spouse have against each other's life insurance and retirement benefits (unless you preserved these rights in the judgment).

Despite these provisions, you should contact your insurance agent and/or retirement plan administrator and revoke any designations of your spouse as beneficiary. Because of a legal peculiarity, a divorce judgment's revocations aren't always effective, making individual revocation necessary. As you make the revocations, it's a good time to designate new beneficiaries.

Paragraph #6 of the Judgment of Divorce (GRP 4a) cuts off all rights that spouses have in their partners' estates (see "Do I Really Want to End My Marriage?" on page 37 for a description of these rights). And although the judgment doesn't mention it, Michigan law says that divorce automatically revokes: 1) all rights that spouses have been given in each other's will 2) a will appointment of a spouse as personal representative.

But besides those selected will provisions, divorce doesn't touch any other parts of a will. The will, minus the provisions benefiting an ex-spouse, remains in force. All the same, you should carefully review your will after divorce. The removal of your ex-spouse from the will may have upset your scheme of property distribution and appointments. After review, you may decide that your will needs revision or even replacement.

These days, some people have living (*inter vivos*) trusts instead of wills. If you have one, with your ex as trustee and/or beneficiary, you'll probably want to amend the trust and remove your ex.

You might have already revoked your durable power of attorney for financial affairs naming your ex-spouse as agent. If not, you may want to revoke it now. Simply give or send a written notice telling your ex that you are revoking the power of attorney and his/her powers under it. Make sure you keep a copy of the revocation.

In 1990, Michigan created a special health care power of attorney allowing you to designate an agent, called a patient advocate, to make health care decisions, including the termination of life-sustaining treatment, on your behalf. Like durable powers of attorney, spouses who make these arrangements often name each other as patient advocates.

The health care power of attorney law helpfully provides that a designation of a spouse as patient advocate is suspended while a divorce is pending. Then, when the divorce judgment is filed, the health care power of attorney is automatically revoked, unless you named a successor patient advocate. In that case, the power of attorney remains in effect with the successor as patient advocate.

More Information

About estate planning, including tips for single parents about naming guardians for minor children after divorce, order *The Michigan Estate Planning Book: A Complete Do-It-Yourself Guide to Planning an Estate in Michigan*, using the order form at the front of this book.

Name Change

If you changed your name during the divorce, you must report the name change to the following agencies and offices, so documents issued by them can be revised:

- Michigan Secretary of State (driver's license and voter registration)
- Social Security Administration (social security card)
- passport acceptance agency (U.S. Post Office, county clerk, etc.) (passport)
- financial institutions (bank accounts, credit cards, etc.)
- insurance companies (life, disability and health insurance policies and documents)
- heath care providers (health care files and documents at doctor, dentist, etc.)

- utilities (accounts with utilities, telephone companies, cable television, etc.)
- employer (employee benefits documents)
- schools and alumni associations (school records, alumni directories, etc.)
- airlines (frequent flier programs)

Typically, you must visit many of these offices and agencies in person to change your name; it's difficult to make the change over the telephone or Internet. Many of these agencies and offices also require evidence of your name change. For proof, bring certified copies of the Judgment of Divorce (GRP 4).

Credit Problems

Today, in our consumer economy credit is more important than ever. As always, lenders look at credit reports (tracking a person's borrowing and payment habits) when making lending decisions. But more and more, auto and homeowner insurance companies are using credit histories to determine insurability and premiums, and mortgage companies base interest rates on creditworthiness.

After divorce, many women suddenly discover that they can't get credit because they have no credit history. A woman may lose credit if her credit was reported in her previous married name. Even women who don't change their names may suffer a loss of credit it they got credit through their husbands' credit reports.

The solution to these credit woes is building a credit history in your own name. If you had credit under your former married name, you can add this

---

More Information

About enforcement or modification of the custody, parenting time, residence of children, child support or alimony provision of a divorce judgment, plus information about post-divorce name change, tax problems, debt and credit issues, order *After the Divorce: A Do-It-Yourself Guide to Enforcing or Modifying a Divorce Judgment in Michigan,* using the order form at the front of this book.

information to your credit file. Joint accounts with your husband may have been reported in your husband's name only (all joint accounts opened after June 1, 1977, are supposed to reported in both spouses' names). If so, you can sometimes persuade credit reporting agencies to add these credit references to your file.

In addition, you can apply for new credit from banks, retailers and other creditors to build a credit history. A federal law, the Equal Credit Opportunity Act (ECOA), bars creditors from canceling old credit accounts you had during marriage if you still meet their lending standards (you may have to submit new information to prove your creditworthiness). The ECOA also guarantees creditworthy persons access to credit regardless of sex or marital status, and outlaws various discriminatory credit practices.

As you build a credit history, make sure you pay your bills on time, because this factor has the biggest impact on credit. It's also smart to have a good mix of credit, with both revolving (credit cards, charge accounts) and installment (mortgages, loans) debt.

One thing to avoid are credit repair services. These firms often charge a lot for meager results. Even worse, they can sometimes commit illegal practices for which you can be liable.

More Information

Credit agencies receive credit information from lenders and merchants, compile this information into credit reports and sell these to lenders and others. To check on your credit status, get copies of your credit reports from the three main credit reporting agencies:

Equifax: P.O. Box 105873, Atlanta, GA 30348, (800) 685-1111 or www.equifax.com

Experian: P.O. Box 2104, Allen, TX 75013, (888) 397-3742 or www.experian.com

TransUnion: TransUnion LLC, Consumer Disclosure Center, P.O. Box 1000, Chester, PA 19022, (800) 888-4213 or www.transunion.com

Each report is around $10, but consumers are entitled to one free report per year from each company.

Each agency's report has different credit information. To compare them all, you can get a combined three-in-one report. TrueCredit.com offers a combined report for around $35. TransUnion also provides referrals to TrueCredit.

Be careful about ordering seemingly free credit reports on the Internet. Many of these offers appear to be free, but have hidden fees and costs.

Ask for the brochures "Women and Credit Histories" and "Equal Credit Opportunity" from:

Federal Trade Commission
Attn: Ed Bush
6th & Pennsylvania Ave. N.W.
Washington, D.C. 20580

Appendices

Appendix A: Fee Exemption

Appendix B: Preliminary Relief

Appendix C: Opting Out of the Friend of the Court System

Appendix D: Alternate Service

Appendix E: Giving Special Notice of Your Divorce

Appendix F: Divorce and the Military

Appendix G: Dismissing Your Divorce

Appendix H: Additional Judgment Provisions

Michigan Child Support Formula Manual

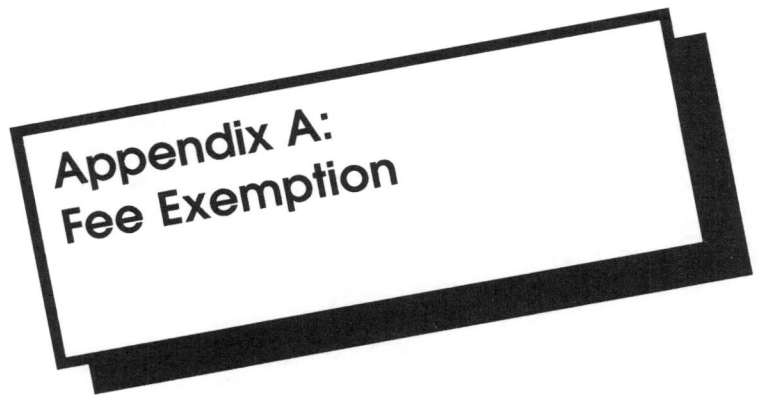

Appendix A: Fee Exemption

Michigan law exempts some poor people from payment of the court fees of their divorces (see "How Much Will My Divorce Cost?" on page 49 for a description of these fees). If you qualify, you can get an exemption from payment of the: 1) filing fee 2) any motion fee 3) friend of the court fee. You can also get an exemption from the service fee when you must use: 1) an official server (such as a sheriff for service by delivery; or a sheriff, policeman, or court officer for alternate service by posting) 2) publication for alternate service. Otherwise, you must pay the service fee yourself for service by mail or service by delivery using a commercial process server.

Who can qualify for a fee exemption? The court rules say that persons receiving "any form of public assistance" are automatically entitled to a fee exemption. The rules don't define public assistance, but presumably it includes the main public welfare programs: 1) Family Independence Program (FIP) payments (formerly AFDC) 2) Temporary Assistance for Needy Families (TANF) 3) Supplemental Security Income (SSI) 4) food stamps 5) Medicaid.

In addition, the court rules say that indigent persons may qualify for fee exemptions. Indigent is just another word for poor. In Michigan, judges determine indigency on a case-by-case basis after they have reviewed applicants' financial information (income and assets versus obligations).

The fee exemption rules apply to all types of lawsuits, but there is a special rule for divorce cases. Although you and your spouse may be separated and financially independent, you're still treated as a family unit for fee exemption purposes. If you cannot pay the fees, but your spouse can, s/he may be ordered to pay them for you. If neither of you can pay the fees, because of: 1) receipt of public assistance 2) indigency, both of you are exempt from payment.

Obtaining a Fee Exemption

Obtaining a fee exemption is a two-step procedure: 1) initial suspension of fees when a divorce is filed 2) final exemption (or payment) of the fees at the end of the divorce. To get fees suspended initially, prepare the Affidavit section of the Affidavit and Order, Suspension of Fees/Costs (MC 20), and submit it to the clerk when you file your initial divorce papers.

A fee exemption request itself is a kind of motion for which a motion fee would normally be paid. However, the court rules say that no motion fee is due for fee exemption requests.

The clerk gives automatic fee exemptions to plaintiffs receiving public assistance. If you claim indigency, the clerk will pass the Affidavit and Order, Suspension of Fees/Costs (MC 20) onto the judge for review. If the judge agrees that you're indigent, s/he will order a fee suspension on the reverse of the Affidavit and Order, Suspension of Fees/Costs (MC 20). A denial of your application would be indicated in the same place.

If your application is successful, you won't have to pay any fees during your divorce. However, the court will review your fee exemption at the end of the divorce. At that time, it will take another look at your financial condition and make a final decision about the fees.

During your testimony at the final hearing, you must mention that your fees were suspended at the beginning of the divorce. The judge will then re-examine your financial condition and either: 1) order you or your spouse to pay the fees 2) give you and your spouse a final waiver from payment of the fees. The same standards apply then as before; those on public assistance get an automatic exemption, while those claiming indigency must cite facts to prove it. To prove indigency, you should give extra testimony about your present financial condition.

Whatever the judge decides, you can provide for payment of the suspended fees (by you or the defendant) or a final fee waiver in paragraph #11 of the Judgment of Divorce (GRP 4a). Insert the amount of the suspended fees and check the correct box.

	Original - Court 1st copy - Applicant	2nd copy - Opposing party PROBATE OSM CODE: OSF
Approved, SCAO **STATE OF MICHIGAN** JUDICIAL DISTRICT JUDICIAL CIRCUIT COUNTY PROBATE	**AFFIDAVIT AND ORDER SUSPENSION OF FEES/COSTS**	**CASE NO.** Court telephone no.

Court address

Plaintiff/Petitioner name, address, and telephone no.		Defendant/Respondent name, address, and telephone no.
	v	
Plaintiff's/Petitioner's attorney, bar no., address, and telephone no.		Defendant's/Respondent's attorney, bar no., address, and telephone no.

☐ Probate   In the matter of _____

NOTE: Requests for waiver/suspension of transcript costs must be made separately by motion.   ☐ **AFFIDAVIT**

1. The attached pleading is to be filed with the court by or on behalf of   DARLENE A. LOVELACE ,
Name

applicant, who is ☒ plaintiff/petitioner.   ☐ defendant/respondent.

2. The applicant is entitled to and asks the court for suspension of fees and costs in the action for the following reason:

☒ a. S/he is currently receiving public assistance: $ ___400___ per MONTH Case No.: V1336092 B

☒ b. S/he is unable to pay those fees and costs because of indigency, based on the following facts:

INCOME: 10,000 PANCAKES, 111 M-78, LAKE CITY, MI 48800
Employer name and address

1 YR. $250 $225   per ☒ week. ☐ month. ☐ two we
Length of employment   Average gross pay   Average net pay

ASSETS: State value of car, home, bank deposits, bonds, stocks, etc.
HOUSEHOLD GOODS $1,000
CAR $1,000

OBLIGATIONS: Itemize monthly rent, installment payments, mortgage payments, child support, etc.
CAR PAYMENT $75   FOOD $200
RENT $250

☐ 3. (in domestic relations cases only) The applicant is entitled to an order requiring his/her spouse to pay attorney

REIMBURSEMENT: It is understood that the court may order the applicant to pay the fees and costs when the reason
waiver or suspension no longer exists.

Darlene A. Lovelace
Affiant signature

Subscribed and sworn to before me on   2-28-89 ,   OJIBWAY _____ County, Michigan.
Date

My commission expires: 1-1-90   Signature: Loretta Smiley
Date   Deputy clerk/Register/Notary public

(SEE REVERSE SIDE FOR ORDER)

MC 20 (6/03) **AFFIDAVIT AND ORDER, SUSPENSION OF FEES/COSTS**

Callout annotations:

COMPLETE 2a. IF YOU ARE RECEIVING PUBLIC ASSISTANCE

COMPLETE 2b. INSTEAD IF YOU ARE CLAIMING INDIGENCY

PRISONERS CLAIMING INDIGENCY SHOULD CHECK BOX 2b., SKIP REST OF THE SECTION, AND ATTACH CERTIFIED COPY OF THEIR INSTITUTIONAL ACCOUNT FOR PRIOR YEAR

IF YOU MUST USE AN OFFICIAL SERVER, OR MUST GET ALTERNATE SERVICE BY PUBLICATION, EXPLAIN THAT ON A SHEET ATTACHED TO THIS FORM

CERTIFICATION OF ATTORNEY

1. I have reviewed the affidavit of indigency, and I certify that its contents are true to the best of my information, knowledge, and belief.

2. I will bring to the court's attention the matter of suspended costs and fees and the availability of funds to pay them before any disposition is entered. I will report at that time any changes in the information contained in the affidavit of indigency or any other information regarding the affiant's financial status or alterations of the fee arrangement.

Date _____

Attorney signature _____

Attorney name (type or print) _____

Bar no. _____

CERTIFICATION BY PERSON OTHER THAN PARTY

1. I have personal knowledge of the facts appearing in the affidavit.

2. The person in whose behalf the petition is filed is unable to sign it because of

☐ minority: _____
Date of birth

Relationship: _____   ☐ other disability: _____
Nature of disability

LEAVE CERTIFICATIONS BLANK

Date _____

Affiant signature _____

Affiant name (type or print) _____

Address _____

City, state, zip _____

Telephone no. _____

JUDGE WILL SUSPEND FEES OR DENY FEE SUSPENSION BELOW

ORDER

IT IS ORDERED:

☒ 1. Fees and costs in this action required by law or court rule are waived/suspended until further order of the court. Before any final disposition or discontinuance is entered, the moving party shall bring the fee and costs suspension to the attention of the judge for final disposition.

☐ 2. The applicant's spouse shall pay the fees and costs required by law or court rule.

☐ 3. This application is denied.

3-1-89
Date _____

Lester Jubbs
Judge _____

Bar no. _____

JUDGE WILL DATE AND SIGN

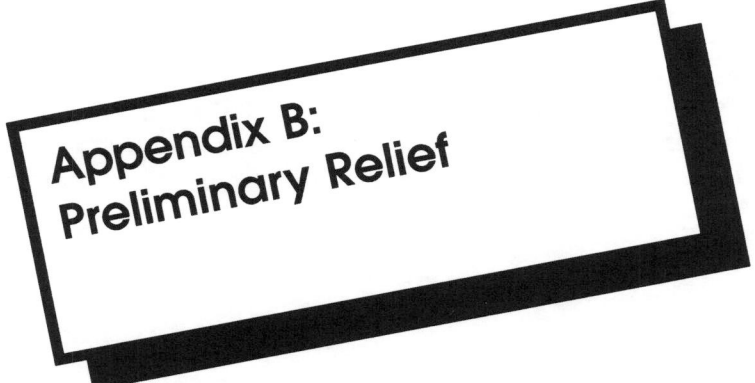

Appendix B: Preliminary Relief

As explained in "Do I Need 'Preliminary Relief'?" on page 59, you can ask for preliminary relief deciding custody, parenting time, residence of children, child support and alimony, while the divorce is pending. If the request succeeds, the order granting preliminary relief settles these issues until final decision in the Judgment of Divorce (GRP 4).

Courts provide preliminary relief in two forms: 1) quick interim relief, without prior notice to the defendant, followed by an interim order 2) temporary relief, after input from both parties, issued in a temporary order.

Plaintiffs typically seek interim relief right after they file for divorce. The judge considers the request informally, and either denies interim relief or grants it by signing a so-called ex parte order. The defendant must receive a copy of this order, and afterward has a chance to object to the order. If the defendant doesn't object, the ex parte order goes into effect, and governs custody, parenting time, residence of children and child support, until the end of the divorce.

To object, the defendant must file a written objection to the ex parte order within 14 days. After an objection, the friend of the court must intervene and try to settle the dispute. If this effort fails, a hearing must be held before the judge, with both sides in court, to decide interim relief.

Temporary relief begins and ends as a two-sided procedure. The plaintiff starts by filing a motion asking for temporary relief. The friend of the court usually intervenes to investigate, referee or mediate the request. If this fails,

---

Glossary

Ex parte order–(pronounced "X-par-tay") is an order granting interim relief. The "ex parte" phrase means "from a part," denoting that the order is obtained by the plaintiff alone, without input from the defendant.

Temporary order–is an order granting temporary relief after a hearing with both sides present.

the motion goes to the judge, who decides the issue during a court hearing with both sides present.

By the time requests for interim and temporary relief reach the judge, there is hardly any difference between them. As a result, the relief the judge grants at a court hearing on interim relief is in the form of a temporary order. A temporary order is also issued after a hearing on a request for temporary relief.

Interim vs. Temporary Relief

In many ways, interim and temporary relief are similar, and actually merge during a court hearing on disputed relief. Which type of relief is the better choice?

To be sure, there are a few differences in what can be obtained from each type of relief. You can get custody, parenting time, residence of children and child support, but never alimony, with interim relief; temporary relief can decide all five issues. In addition, interim relief may only confirm the status quo, not change it. For example, if your husband has moved out and left you with control of the children, an ex parte order can give you sole or joint custody. Reversing the scenario, the husband cannot move out, file for divorce and get an ex parte order transferring custody of the children to him, since this would upset the custody status quo. A temporary order, by contrast, can either confirm or change the status quo existing at the beginning of the divorce.

On the other hand, interim relief is usually much easier to obtain. A plaintiff can receive the relief directly from the judge, without a hearing, and then the burden is on the defendant to oppose it. With temporary relief, you must file a motion and schedule and attend a hearing on the motion. In fact, you may have to do this twice, if the motion is first refereed by the friend of the court and then heard by the judge in court later.

All in all, from a plaintiff's point of view, it usually makes more sense to start with interim relief, and hope the defendant doesn't object (many defendants don't). If an objection is filed, the plaintiff must deal with the friend of the court and attend a court hearing later. But both of these steps are also necessary for temporary relief, so a plaintiff isn't much worse off by having tried interim relief first.

Preparing a Request for Interim Relief

If you want to seek interim relief, it's easy to make the request right after you file for divorce. So while you're preparing your initial divorce papers, as described in "Filing" on page 87, you will have to make some special preparations for interim relief.

You must first request interim relief in your Complaint for Divorce (GRP 1b), by checking boxes a and/or b, in paragraph #9, for the type of relief you want. The facts to support this request are embedded in the complaint and other initial divorce papers; normally you don't have to add more information in affidavits or other supporting documents, as was once necessary.

Counties handle interim relief orders in different ways. Some counties have a standard ex parte order form, whose use is encouraged or even required. In other counties, it's your responsibility to prepare an ex parte order before submitting it to the judge.

If you must do an interim order yourself, use the Ex Parte Order (GRP 5). For guidance, see the sample order at the end of this appendix. The bulk of the GRP 5 is what lawyers call "boilerplate," or standard provisions required by law. But key paragraphs #1, 2, 3 and 4, deal with custody, parenting time, residence of children and child support.

In paragraph #1, you can assign custody of minor children. There are several custody options, including sole, joint, split and mixed custody (see "Custody" on page 9 and "Custody Provisions" on page 236 for more about custody choices and how to provide for these in the custody box in paragraph #1). As you choose custody, remember that an ex parte order may only confirm existing custody, not re-assign it.

For simplicity, paragraph #2 provides for reasonable parenting time only. This choice avoids devising a complicated specific parenting time schedule for a fairly brief time until the end of the divorce.

Similarly, paragraph #3 confirms the dual local residences of the children established at divorce-filing. If you want to move early in the divorce, consider moving before you file since residence isn't normally fixed until filing (see "Residence of Children" on page 17 for more about residence of children).

Except in special cases, child support is determined by the *Michigan Child Support Formula Manual* and the child support schedules in the manual (see "Child Support" on page 21 and "Child Support Provisions" on page 242 for more about child support, the child support schedules and how to provide for child support in the box in paragraph #4a in the required "tiered" format (amount for three children, amount for two children, amount for one child, etc.).

For several special situations, such as joint physical, split or mixed custody, the Michigan child support formula has adjustments covering the special situation (see "Adjusting the Child Support Schedules" on page 245 for more about these special cases). In truly exceptional situations, you can receive permission to depart from the formula, and set support outside the guidelines (see "Departing from the Child Support Formula" on page 247 for more information about departure).

Cohabitation

One particularly difficult situation is cohabitation during divorce. Parties seldom live together after a divorce, but sometimes stay together temporarily while a divorce is pending. Cohabitation is difficult for the Michigan child support formula to cope with because the formula assumes that the parties have divided into separate households. When parents are living together with the children, this assumption is invalid and the formula doesn't really fit.

Despite this problem, cohabitation periods during divorce tend to be brief, and can usually be worked around. For example, you might live with the defendant after filing for divorce, while s/he looks for another place to live. If you get an ex parte order for child support during the period of cohabitation, you can write "reserved until further order of this court" in the blank space above the child support box in paragraph #4a. Then, when the defendant moves out, you can go back to the judge and modify the ex parte order, by adding child support. The friend of the court can help with the modification, using the Order Modifying Ex Parte Order (FOC 62).

In every Wayne County divorce with minor children, you must file a Certificate on Behalf of Plaintiff Regarding Ex Parte Interim Support Order. The sample certificate on page 97 is for a case without interim relief, with an explanation of why the relief isn't being sought on the reverse of the form. But when you are requesting interim relief, describe this relief on the front side, as shown in the sample form.

Wayne County plaintiffs must also complete a Certificate of Conformity for Domestic Relations Order or Judgment (1225), saying that the ex parte order satisfies court requirements (this form would be identical to the sample one on page 136). The certificate must be submitted to the judge with the Ex Parte Order (GRP 5), and then filed with the clerk and served on the defendant with the GRP 5.

And finally, Wayne County requires an Order Data Form-Support (FD/FOC 4002) for support processing. There is a sample of this form on page 137, for the divorce judgment. You also must prepare one for an Ex Parte Order (GRP 5), and send or deliver it to the Wayne County Friend of the Court. The instructions with the form explains this procedure.

Paragraph #4b of the Ex Parte Order (GRP 5) allows for payment of child support by immediate income withholding. But because of a legal peculiarity, this provision doesn't go into effect until later. See "After You Get Interim Relief" on page 169 for more about setting up immediate income withholding through an Income Withholding Order (FOC 5), after an ex parte order takes effect.

After you prepare an Ex Parte Order (GRP 5), and the extra forms in Wayne County only, make three copies of each form and mark one copy of each as the friend of the court's copy. See "Papers" on page 74 for more about preparing forms like these.

Getting an Interim Order

You can seek interim relief right after you file for divorce, or return to the courthouse and ask for the relief later. It's usually convenient to ask for the relief immediately after filing—you're at the courthouse anyway—so that's the procedure described below.

To seek interim relief right away, bring the Ex Parte Order (GRP 5) with you as you file for divorce. But hold the order back from filing then. The judge must approve your request for interim relief before you file the order; if the request is denied, the order is withdrawn and never filed.

After the divorce is filed, you may want to ask the clerk about interim relief procedures before you leave. See "Before You Leave the Clerk's Office" on page 91 about which information you need to know. Remember: The clerk can only give general information about divorce procedures, and cannot give specific legal advice.

Friend of the Court Review

Some counties want the friend of the court to review the Ex Parte Order (GRP 5) before submission to the judge. In Wayne County, you can skip friend of the court review if you can say in the Certificate of Conformity for Domestic Relations Order or Judgment (1225) that the ex parte order has all the required provisions (the GRP 5 was designed to meet Wayne County requirements).

When review by the friend of the court is necessary, take copies of the initial divorce papers you have filed and the unfiled ex parte order to the friend of the court's office. A staff member there may be able to review the order while you wait. If satisfactory, the staff member may sign the GRP 5c, showing approval. Or the staff member may suggest modification of the order, which you might be able to do on the spot. Afterward, the friend of the court will return all the papers to you.

Requesting Interim Relief from the Judge

In most counties, you must seek interim relief from the judge assigned to your case at filing. In a few large counties, there may be a specially designated judge who reviews interim relief requests from all divorce cases.

Whoever handles your request, go to that judge's office. Judges consider requests for interim relief informally, in their offices. For the request, the judge must review the unfiled Ex Parte Order (GRP 5) and copies of your already-filed initial divorce papers. If you're trying to opt out of the friend of the court system, this is also a good time to submit your opt-out papers to the judge (see Appendix C for more about opt-out papers and procedures). The judge may have quick access to your case file with the filed papers, or you can leave your own copies with the judge temporarily.

Ask the judge's secretary or law clerk to have the judge review your interim relief request, and ask when you can return for a decision on the request. If you're lucky, the judge may be able to review your papers while you wait, or within a short time later.

On return, ask the judge's secretary or law clerk about the judge's decision. If the request was denied, the judge will note the denial on the case file-copy of your Complaint for Divorce (GRP 1). If the problem was small, you might be able to correct the order then or later, and resubmit the ex parte order to the judge. But after a complete denial of relief, you must withdraw the ex parte order. If you want to seek preliminary relief again, you must file a motion for temporary relief.

If the judge grants interim relief as submitted, s/he will sign the Ex Parte Order (GRP 5) and maybe some copies. Return to the clerk's office and file the original order and the friend of the court's copy. You will get back two true copies of the GRP 5, which you should keep for your records and for service on the defendant.

Serving the Ex Parte Order on the Defendant

For service, just include a true copy of the Ex Parte Order (GRP 5) among the service papers served on the defendant (see "Service" on page 99 for more about service and proving service). After service, when you prove service on the reverse of the Summons and Complaint (MC 01), list the GRP 5 as an additional service paper.

If interim relief was delayed, and you already have had the service papers served, you can serve the ex parte order separately. Make an extra copy of the Ex Parte Order (GRP 5) and send a true copy of the order to the defendant by ordinary first-class mail. Afterward, prove service in the Proof of Mailing at the bottom of the extra copy of the GRP 5. Make two copies of this form, keep one copy and send the filled-in form and a friend of the court's copy to the clerk for filing.

Whichever service method you choose, don't delay service, or making and filing a proof of service. The ex parte order is enforceable only after service, and the friend of the court needs a proof of service of the order to start income withholding.

The Defendant's Response to the Ex Parte Order

After receiving an ex parte order, the defendant has a choice: do nothing and let the order go into effect or object to the order. Each choice has important consequences for what happens next in the case. These are depicted in the chart on the opposite page, and described in the following sections.

The defendant has 14 days to object after receiving service of the ex parte order. If the order was added to the service papers, service is made when the service papers are served on the defendant by acknowledgment, mail or delivery, as described in "Service" on page 99. If the order was served separately by mail as described above, service is complete when sent (not received). See "Time" on page 78 for more about figuring time periods like the 14-day objection deadline.

No Objection

If the defendant doesn't file an objection within the 14-day objection period, the Ex Parte Order (GRP 5) goes into effect, and becomes a temporary order. The order is effective at entry (when the judge-signed order is filed with the clerk) and legally enforceable after service on the defendant, with one exception.

All the ex parte order's provisions take effect when the order is entered except the income withholding order in paragraph #4b of the GRP 5b. Immediate income withholding is delayed another week after the 14-day objection period (or longer if the defendant objects to the order; in that case the delay continues until after a court hearing on the ex parte order has been held). As a result, the defendant owes child support from the day when the

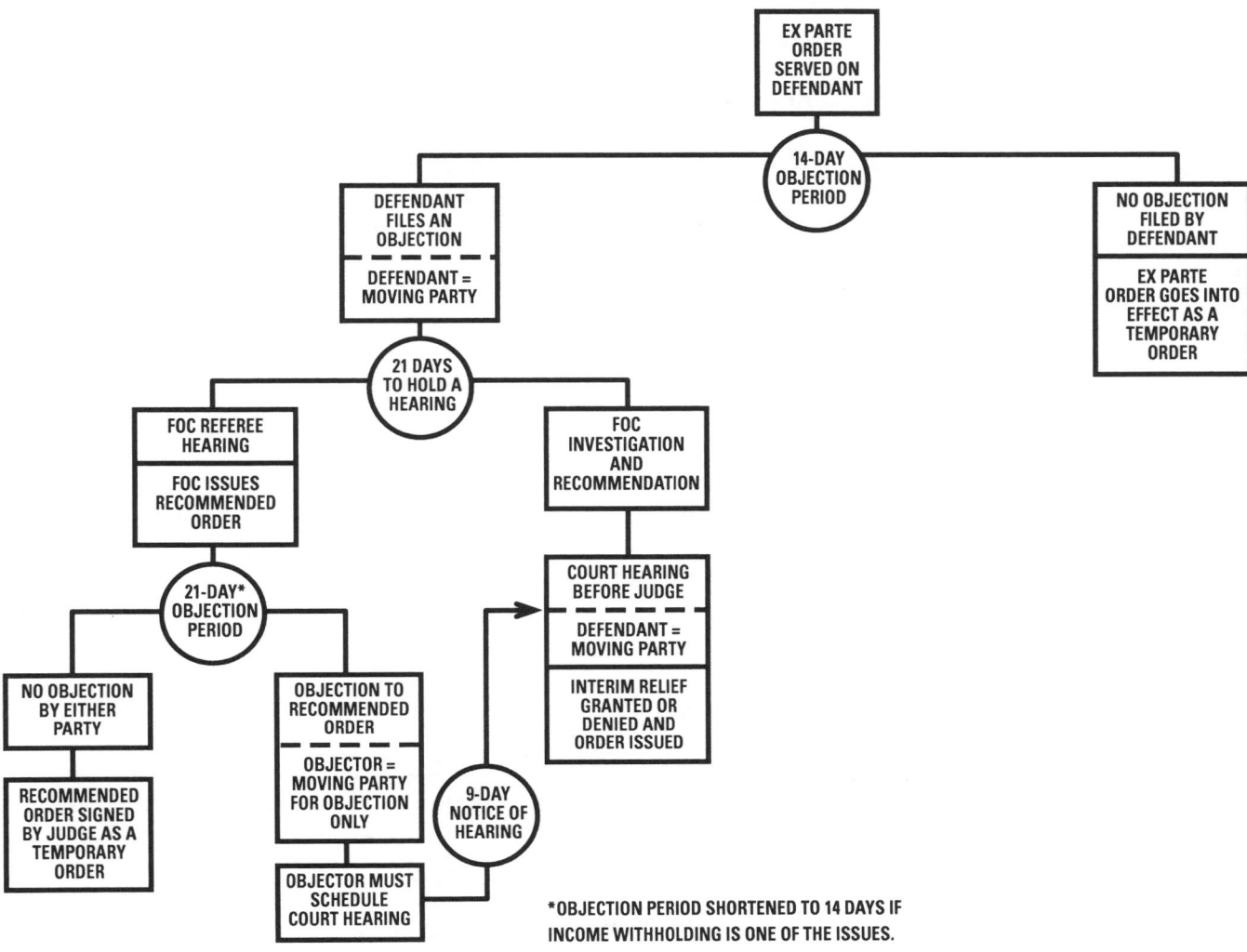

ex parte order was entered, but the support isn't payable by income withholding until at least 21 days later.

See "After You Get Interim Relief" on page 169 about how to set up immediate income withholding after it goes into effect.

Objection

During the 14-day objection period, the defendant can object to the Ex Parte Order (GRP 5) in several ways. The defendant can file an objection to the order, move to rescind (cancel) the order or combine an objection and motion to rescind in one form, which is often the Objection to Ex Parte Order and Motion to Rescind or Modify (FOC 61). In the objection, the defendant should cite the provisions of the order s/he objects to, removing the agreed-to provisions from the dispute. The defendant may object to provisions outright or object by suggesting modifications in the order.

Any kind of objection must be written, and filed with the clerk within 14 days after the defendant receives service of the ex parte order. The defendant must also send you a copy of the objection at or around that time.

After the defendant's objection, the friend of the court must schedule a hearing on the disputed order. The hearing must take place 21 days after the defendant's objection. The matter could be set for a court hearing directly before the judge. But often the friend of the court will schedule a hearing before one of its referees, in an effort to settle the dispute. The notice of hearing sent by the friend of the court will say which kind of hearing (referee or court) has been scheduled.

Friend of the Court

As explained in "Court System" on page 71, the friend of the court plays several roles during divorce, including investigation and refereeing. In a dispute over interim relief, the friend of the court may do either an investigation (summed up in a report and recommendation to the judge) or refereeing, but probably not both.

Investigation

Before the case is heard in court, the friend of the court may investigate your request for interim relief, and make a report and recommendation to the judge. During an investigation, the friend of the court investigator may contact the parties, their children and others to gather facts about the dispute. Or if you want input, you can request an interview during the investigation.

The investigator summarizes the facts in a report which also contains a recommendation to the judge about deciding the request. The investigator's report is sent to the parties and put in the case file for the benefit of the judge. The judge may consider the report and recommendations, but isn't bound by either. The report cannot be submitted as evidence later at a court hearing (it usually contains lots of hearsay), unless both parties agree to admission of the report.

Refereeing

Refereeing is a more direct way to settle contested interim relief. The friend of the court, as referee, assumes a semi-judicial role, hears the request in a simulated court hearing, and then issues a recommended decision. Either party can reject the recommendation, sending the case onto the judge.

Any kind of request for interim relief can be refereed. The parties can agree to refereeing, one party can ask for it or the judge can order it. But typically, family court judges in a county decide which kinds of issues are suitable for refereeing, and all these requests are routinely refereed. Some counties use refereeing selectively, while other counties, such as Wayne, require refereeing for every dispute over interim relief.

In many ways, a referee hearing resembles a court hearing. Each side can have a lawyer, testimony may be taken, the rules of evidence apply and the proceedings are recorded. The difference is informality. A referee hearing is typically held in a conference room at the friend of the court's office or a similar informal setting, instead of a courtroom.

During a referee hearing, the defendant presents his/her case against interim relief. Then, it's your turn to support the relief. Both sides may offer limited evidence, usually their own testimony (seldom from other witnesses), or documents like paycheck stubs or W-2 forms.

Afterward, the friend of the court referee must make findings in the case, and must read these into the record of the hearing or put them in a written report. The referee must also issue a recommended order deciding the interim relief request. The parties may be satisfied with the recommendation, and then the recommended order will be signed by the judge as a temporary order.

Either party can object to the friend of the court's recommended order because of a perceived factual or legal error in the recommendation. An objector who objects merely to harass or delay can be assessed costs by the court. The instructions below explain how to object.

Objecting to the Friend of the Court's Recommendation

There are two deadlines for objecting to a referee's recommended order: 1) 14 days if at least one of the issues is whether child support should be paid by immediate income withholding 2) 21 days for all other issues. These objection periods begin when you receive the recommended order, and the deadlines are satisfied by filing the objection with the clerk (see "Time" on page 78 for more about figuring time periods of days).

Fill out the objection form

Use the Objection to Referee's Recommended Order (FOC 68) for your objection. Fill out the objection as shown in the sample form at the end of this appendix. Incidentally, the objector becomes the moving party for the purposes of the objection only.

Schedule a court hearing

After an objection to a referee's recommended order, the dispute moves onto a court hearing before a judge. It's up to the objector to schedule this hearing.

Contact the clerk or friend of the court office to find out who schedules court hearings in the county. Typically, court hearings are arranged by the (court) clerk or a special assignment clerk, with a simple request.

But in some counties, you must file a written request for a hearing in a special request form known as a praecipe. In Wayne County, for example, you ask for a hearing by filing a Request for Hearing on a Motion (Praecipe) Order/Judgment (FD/FOC 4021). Ask the Wayne County Clerk for a copy of this form as part of a larger Miscellaneous Motion Packet (FD/FOC 4037), which includes instructions and related material.

Before scheduling the court hearing, the objector should estimate how much time the court will need to hear the matter. The type of court hearing—whether it's evidentiary or nonevidentiary—dictates the amount of time necessary for the hearing (see "Court Hearing" below for an explanation of the difference, and which issues require each type of hearing).

A nonevidentiary hearing normally takes 15-30 minutes. Short hearings like this are often scheduled on the motion days that judges hold each week. An evidentiary hearing requires a bigger chunk of time, since it takes more time to receive evidence. You should be able to obtain a bigger block of time on the judge's motion day or during a non-motion day.

In scheduling a court hearing, the objector must set it far enough in advance to give the opponent enough notice, so s/he can prepare for the hearing. For an objection served by mail, nine days notice is necessary. Thus, there must be at least a nine-day interval between service of the objection by mail (which is complete upon mailing) and the court hearing. See "Time" on page 78 for information about figuring time periods of days.

After the objector gets the information about the date, time and place of the hearing, s/he must insert this information in the Notice of Hearing section of the Objection to Referee's Recommended Order (FOC 68), and make three copies of the form.

File the objection

The objector must take the Objection to Referee's Recommended Order (FOC 68) and copies to the clerk. The clerk will file the original objection, keep a copy for the friend of the court and return two copies to the objector.

Serve the objection

The objector must serve the objection on the other party by sending a copy to him/her by ordinary first-class mail. Afterward, the objector must prove service in the Certificate of Mailing at the bottom of the FOC 68. The objector should make an extra copy of the FOC 68, fill out the certificate and make two copies of this form. The objector must send the filled-in form and a friend of the court's copy to the clerk, and also keep a copy.

Court Hearing

If the friend of the court's investigation or refereeing didn't settle the matter, your request for interim relief will be decided by the judge during a court hearing. The judge considers the disputed interim relief anew (or "de novo" as the FOC 68 says), without regard to any referee findings. If there was a referee hearing, it's as if it never happened.

There are two kinds of court hearings: 1) nonevidentiary, where little or no evidence is introduced and the parties merely make legal arguments to the judge 2) evidentiary, where evidence, such as testimony, is presented. Which type of court hearing do you need? The test is whether you and the defendant agree on the facts surrounding the interim relief request. If these facts aren't in dispute, a nonevidentiary hearing will do; disputed facts spell the need for a full evidentiary hearing.

There are four possible issues at stake in an interim order: custody, parenting time, residence of children and child support. Parenting time is unlikely to be disputed because the reasonable parenting time the ex parte order provides for is noncontroversial. The residence of children is also a nonissue because the ex parte order merely confirms the current residences.

Custody, on the other hand, almost always involves factual issues, and will probably require an evidentiary hearing. Disputes over child support usually concern the amount of the child support or the method of payment. With either issue, the facts are often known or easily proved, calling for either a very limited evidentiary hearing or a nonevidentiary one.

Preparing for a Court Hearing

Regardless of which issues are at stake, you must plan all parts of your case carefully. Your legal arguments must be well-organized, with convincing evidence to support them.

Securing evidence is by far the most important part of pre-hearing preparation. If you want testimony from witnesses, you must have them attend the hearing. Any documents or other things you want to introduce at the hearing must also be obtained beforehand.

Sometimes, witnesses volunteer to testify and important documents are readily available. But other times, you must obtain this evidence by subpoena.

Subpoenas

For an evidentiary court hearing, you may need the testimony of witnesses and/or portable items (documents, photographs, etc.), which witnesses have in their control. If they won't provide these to you voluntarily, you may have to get them by subpoena.

Who Can Be Subpoenaed?

Not everyone can be subpoenaed. Michigan's court rules say that subpoenas may only be issued to people who are present inside the state of Michigan; out-of-state individuals are immune from Michigan subpoenas.

Subpoena Costs

Courts issue subpoenas without charge. But to encourage attendance, a subpoenaed witness is entitled to a daily court attendance fee of the greater of: 1) $12, or 2) the witness' daily lost wages or salary up to a maximum of $15 per day (unless unemployed, most witnesses will qualify for an attendance fee of $15 per day). The witness must also receive mileage at the current state government mileage rate for travel to and from the courthouse for each day at court.

In most cases, these court attendance fees (daily attendance fee and mileage fee) must be offered to the witness, in the form of cash, money order or cashier's check, when the subpoena is served on the subpoenaed witness. There may also be costs for serving subpoenas, which are described in "Serving Subpoenas" below.

Time for Subpoena

You must obtain subpoenas in advance of a court hearing and have them served before the hearing. The extra time gives the subpoenaed witness the chance to make arrangements to attend court and/or obtain requested items. According to the court rules, subpoenaed witnesses are entitled to a minimum of two days notice. As a result, make sure your subpoenas are served on the witnesses at least two days before the hearing. See "Time" on page 78 for help with figuring time periods of days.

Obtaining a Subpoena

Lawyers, who are officers of the court, can issue their own subpoenas. As a nonlawyer, you will have to get your subpoenas from the clerk.

Some clerks have automated systems for issuing subpoenas, and will make them for you at their office. But in most counties, you must prepare a Subpoena (MC 11), and then submit it to the clerk for issuing.

Complete the Subpoena (MC 11) as shown in the sample at the end of this section. Make four copies. Go to the clerk and have the clerk issue the subpoena by signing and sealing the original and all copies.

Set aside one copy of the Subpoena (MC 11) for proof of service. After service, you must have proof that the Subpoena (MC 11) was served on the witness. You prove service on the reverse of the extra copy of the MC 11, which will be referred to as the proof of service copy of the Subpoena (MC 11).

Serving Subpoenas

There are three ways to serve subpoenas: acknowledgment, mail and delivery. Service by acknowledgment is easiest and cheapest, followed by mail and then delivery.

Service by Acknowledgment

Service by acknowledgment is by far the simplest method of service. There are actually two ways to acknowledge service: personally and by mail. Both are easy to use.

Personal Acknowledgment

For personal acknowledgment, you simply hand the Subpoena (MC 11) and the court attendance fees to the witness. If the witness is in another Michigan county, you can arrange to have someone give the Subpoena (MC 11) and fees to the witness there. Service by personal acknowledgment is complete when the witness receives the Subpoena (MC 11) from you or your helper.

Proving Service by Personal Acknowledgment

Immediately after service, you or your helper should have the witness date (with both time and day) and sign the Acknowledgment of Service, which is at the bottom of the reverse of your proof of service copy of the Subpoena (MC 11). Afterward, make three copies of this paper, earmark one "FOC" and save for filing later as your proof of service.

Acknowledgment by Mail

A subpoenaed witness can also acknowledge service through the mail. You simply send the Subpoena (MC 11), your proof of service copy of the Subpoena (MC 11), and the court attendance fees to the witness by ordinary first-class mail. Service by acknowledgment by mail is complete when the subpoenaed witness receives the mailing.

Proving Service by Acknowledgment by Mail

Immediately after service, the witness should date (with both time and day) and sign the Acknowledgment of Service, which is at the bottom of the reverse of your proof of service copy of the Subpoena (MC 11). The witness must then give or mail the proof of service copy of the Subpoena (MC 11) to you. Afterward, make three copies of this paper, earmark one "FOC" and save for filing later as your proof of service.

Service by Mail

Service by mail is a little more expensive than service by acknowledgment. But it's a very effective method of service because it goes anywhere U.S. mail is delivered. The court rules permit service by mail through either registered or certified mail. Use certified mail because it's cheaper than registered mail.

Cheaper (and easier) yet is service by acknowledgment by mail, since you can obtain acknowledgment by ordinary mail. Thus, you will probably want to use the acknowledgment method for witnesses who are friendly and willing to acknowledge service by mail. Service by mail, on the other hand, is better suited for witnesses you don't know or whom you suspect are uncooperative.

Serving a subpoena by mail is much like serving the service papers by mail. So see "Service by Mail" on page 102 for complete instructions for service by mail and proving service. Just substitute the MC 11 for any reference to the MC 01 in that section.

Service by Delivery

You can also serve a Subpoena (MC 11) by delivering it to the witness. You or any mentally competent adult can deliver a Subpoena (MC 11).

If the witness is friendly and cooperative, consider service by personal acknowledgment instead of service by delivery* Therefore, it's likely that you will serve by delivery when the witness is unfriendly, lives faraway or is otherwise difficult to serve. Moreover, service by delivery will probably be carried out by a professional process server, such as a commercial process server or a sheriff.

The procedure for serving a subpoena or the service papers by delivery is about the same. So see "Service by Delivery" on page 105 for instructions for service by delivery and proving service. Just substitute the MC 11 for any reference to the MC 01 in that section.

Witness in Court

If the witness obeys the subpoena, s/he will appear at the court hearing and give the testimony or produce the things you seek. But if the witness doesn't show up, you can ask for adjournment of the hearing. The court should grant your request for more time. The court can also force the uncooperative witness to appear for the next hearing by threatening to hold him/her in contempt of court.

Making Your Case in Court

At the court hearing, the defendant is the moving party, because s/he made interim relief the issue by objecting to the relief. This is true even if you were the objector-moving party against the referee's recommended order. If so, you re-assume the role of non-moving party at the court hearing.

During the court hearing, the judge will listen to both sides: the defendant's objection to the interim relief and your reasons for it. Your case for the relief is really two things: the facts (evidence) and legal rules (law) supporting relief.

Custody

Custody is decided according to the best interests of the children and the two custody presumptions (custodial and parental), when these presumptions apply to the case.

The best interests of the children are determined by the 12 or 13 factors in the child custody act of 1970 (see "Custody" on page 9 for a complete list). During the custody hearing, the judge must make factual findings on *all* the best interest factors. Consequently, both parties must deal with each factor as they present evidence and make legal arguments. Some factors may not apply to the case, yet even these must be considered and rejected.

---

*   Service by personal acknowledgment and delivery are similar. The only difference is the proof of service. With an acknowledgment, the witness assists in proving service; for delivery, the server proves service without help from the witness.

The custody presumptions may not be factors in the case. If the parents have been living together with the children just before the divorce, there probably hasn't been enough time for establishment of a custodial environment. But if one parent has been absent during that period, it may apply and be important.

The parental presumption isn't likely to be an issue because it's usually parents who battle for custody during a divorce. But third parties can sometimes intervene in ongoing custody disputes, such as divorces, and seek custody. If this happens, the parental presumption is important in defeating the third party's custody claim.

When a presumption applies, "clear and convincing" evidence must be introduced to overcome the presumption. For example, in a custody dispute between a noncustodial parent and a custodial parent invoking the custodial presumption, the noncustodian might show physical abuse of the children by the custodian. This kind of evidence would probably qualify as clear and convincing evidence that the best interests of the children are for transferring custody from one parent to the other.

Since a custody hearing is likely to be evidentiary, with important issues at stake, you must make careful preparations for the hearing. Sometimes, it may even be necessary to subpoena witnesses, such as teachers, counselors, social workers or neighbors. See "Preparing for a Court Hearing" above for more information about pre-hearing preparations.

> ## Glossary
>
> *Clear and convincing evidence*–is evidence that makes something highly probable.
>
> Or you could look at it this way: On an imaginary evidence scale, clear and convincing evidence falls somewhere between a preponderance of evidence (factual assertions are "more likely than not") standard used in ordinary civil cases, but less than the beyond-a-reasonable-doubt test in criminal cases.

Child Support

When child support is contested, the issues usually boil down to two things: 1) amount of child support (not only monetary child support, but also non-cash forms of child support: payment of health care, child care and educational expenses) 2) method of payment.

As explained in "Child Support" on page 21, the amount of child support is determined by the income of both parents and the needs of the children. These factors are embodied in the Michigan child support formula and the child support schedules, which set child support in most cases.

There are frequently disputes over the amount of income a parent receives, but this issue can be resolved with documentary evidence like paycheck stubs, W-2 forms and income tax returns. Health care, child care and educational expenses can be proved with medical bills, child care provider statements, etc. After the facts are established, the Michigan child support formula provides detailed rules about which parent should pay and how much.

In exceptional cases, departure from the Michigan child support formula is permissible. To depart from the formula, you must show that the formula amount is somehow "unjust or inappropriate" in your case. See "Departing from the Child Support Formula" on page 247 for more information about departure.

As for the method of payment, immediate income withholding is the normal way of paying child support. You can avoid immediate income withholding by opting out of the friend of the court system. Appendix C explains the various opt-out options.

Court Hearing Itself

See "Courthouse Appearances" on page 79 for information about appearing in court, including finding the courtroom, arrival there and how to conduct yourself during the hearing.

When your case is called by the courtroom clerk, step forward and identify yourself. Mention that you are representing yourself. Take a seat at one of the tables inside the bar (the gate) of the court, and get ready to present your case. The format of the hearing hinges on whether the defendant shows up for the hearing. If s/he is absent, the hearing should be brief, with you winning by default. A full hearing with arguments from both sides is necessary when the defendant appears at the hearing. Expect to have the defendant at hearing, then you'll be prepared if s/he attends and relieved if s/he doesn't.

The Defendant Doesn't Attend the Hearing

The defendant, as the moving party, must appear to argue against your request for interim relief. Thus, the defendant's absence should result in dismissal of the defendant's objection, and confirmation of the ex parte order as a temporary order granting relief.

The Defendant Attends the Hearing

Things won't be so easy when your ex is present at the hearing. Facing opposition, you must present your case forcefully to counter the defendant's objections to your interim relief.

The judge will probably start the hearing with some informal questioning of both parties. For a nonevidentiary hearing, the judge will go right to the legal arguments, since evidence isn't necessary. Each side gets to present their legal arguments for or against interim relief, with the defendant arguing first as the moving party. After the first round of arguments, the judge may ask each side for rebuttal arguments, to respond to what has already been said. After arguments, the judge decides whether to sustain defendant's objection to the ex parte order.

At an evidentiary hearing, evidence precedes legal argument. The judge will ask the defendant, as the moving party, to go first. S/he must take the witness stand, be sworn and give testimony. The defendant may also introduce documents during the testimony, or call other witnesses, who may also have documents. You and the judge may ask questions during the defendant's testimony or that given by the witnesses.

Then the reverse happens: You give testimony and the defendant and the judge can question you. Witnesses or documentary evidence you present are also subject to questioning and examination.

After all the evidence is received, the judge gives both parties the opportunity to present their legal arguments. The judge may then ask for another round of arguments, in rebuttal, allowing each party one last word.

When the arguments are finished, the judge decides the objection. The judge may rule immediately, "from the bench," or take the case "under submission," and rule later, perhaps in writing. The judge will probably rule right away on simple issues, like child support, after a nonevidentiary hearing; more complicated issues, like custody, presented in a full evidentiary hearing may require more time for decision.

After the judge rules, the decision must be put into a court order. Since the defendant is the moving party, it's his/her responsibility to prepare the order granting or denying your request for interim relief.

An order denying interim relief might be very brief, just a one-paragraph order rejecting relief. If relief is granted completely, the Ex Parte Order (GRP 5) can simply be confirmed as a temporary order. But if the judge's decision was mixed, with relief granted in part and denied in part, the defendant must prepare a proposed order following the judge's decision.

You have the right to review any proposed order the defendant makes, and can agree to it, if you believe the order follows the judge's decision. If not, you can object to the proposed order, and the correct wording of the order (but not the legal issues in the order) must be decided during another court hearing. The friend of the court distributes a form for objecting, Objection to Proposed Order (FOC 78), which comes with an instruction booklet.

After You Get Interim Relief

If your request for interim relief is ultimately successful (from the defendant's failure to object to the ex parte order initially, or after a referee or court hearing), you must put the ex parte/temporary order into effect. The main concern is starting immediate income withholding for collection of child support.

In most counties, the friend of the court sets up income withholding after receiving copies of the ex parte/temporary order and proof of service of the order. The friend of the court will get an Income Withholding Order (FOC 5) from the judge, and issue an income withholding notice to the payer's source of income (an employer usually). After this, income withholding may begin.

But in some counties, you must start this process by preparing and submitting an Income Withholding Order (FOC 5) to the judge for signing, and provide copies to the defendant and friend of the court. The FOC 5 for collection of support from an ex parte/temporary order would be identical to the sample one on page 134.

Modification or Termination of the Order

An ex parte/temporary order remains in force until the end of the divorce. But during this time, either party can file a motion to modify the order. The motion must be decided at a referee or court hearing, and may be granted for "good cause." Or the parties can agree to a modification, which the friend of the court and judge must review and approve.

Ordinarily, an ex parte order/temporary order terminates at the end of the divorce, when the divorce judgment decides all issues. However, it's permissible to carry over a provision from a preliminary order into the judgment, and sometimes it makes sense to do so. For example, unpaid child support due from a preliminary order must be preserved or else it's canceled. Paragraph #20c of the Judgment of Divorce (GRP 4d) preserves such unpaid child support. To preserve other things, you must add these separately in extra provisions in the GRP 4e.

STATE OF MICHIGAN Circuit Court - Family Division COUNTY	EX PARTE ORDER for Custody, Parenting Time, Residence of Children and Support	CASE NO.

Plaintiff (appearing *in propria persona*):		Defendant:
	V	

Date of order _3-1-89_   Judge _LESTER TUBBS_

While this case is pending, **IT IS ORDERED**:

1. **CUSTODY**: Custody of the minor children is granted as follows:

PL = Plaintiff   DF = Defendant   JT = Joint   3rd = Third party, named here:

CHILD'S NAME	DATE Of BIRTH	LEGAL CUSTODY	PHYSICAL CUSTODY
DUANE WESLEY LOVELACE	6-1-86	PL	PL
DARRYL WENDELL LOVELACE	7-1-87	PL	PL

2. **PARENTING TIME**: Any parent without physical custody shall have reasonable parenting time.

3. **RESIDENCE OF CHILDREN**:

   a. **Local residences.** A parent whose custody or parenting time of a child is governed by this order shall not change the legal residence of the child except in compliance with section 11 of the "Child Custody Act of 1970," 1970 PA 91, MCL 722.31.

   b. **State residence (domicile)**. The minor children's residences (domicile) shall not be moved from the state of Michigan without the prior approval of the court.

   c. **Notice of change of residence**. The person awarded custody shall promptly notify the friend of the court in writing when the minor is moved to another address.

GRP 5a (1/04)   **EX PARTE ORDER, page 1**

STATE OF MICHIGAN Circuit Court - Family Division COUNTY	EX PARTE ORDER for Custody, Parenting Time, Residence of Children and Support	CASE NO.
Plaintiff:	v Defendant:	

IT IS ALSO ORDERED:

4. CHILD SUPPORT:

a. **Amount.** Child support shall be paid monthly, in advance on the first day of the month, as follows:

Support payer: DUDLEY E. LOVELACE   Support payee: DARLENE A. LOVELACE

Children supported:	One	Two	Three	Four	Five or more
Base support:	$ 333	$ 512	$	$	$
Child care:	$	$	$	$	$
Total:	$ 333	$ 512	$	$	$

☒ Base support shall abate 50% after 6 consecutive overnights under sec. IV-C of the MCSF.

☐ Support based on shared economic responsibility was set using payer's general support obligation of $_____ and _____ overnights of parenting.

These support provisions ☒ do ☐ do not follow the child support formula.

b. **Method of payment.** Child support shall be paid

by ☒ immediate income withholding ☐ without income withholding until past-due support equals or exceeds the monthly amount of support

to ☒ state disbursement unit (SDU). ☐ directly to the payee. ☐ other:

c. **Duration.** Child support shall last until each child is age 18 or graduates from high school as provided in MCL 552.605b, whichever is later, but no longer than age 19½.

d. **Redirection, assignment and abatement.** Subject to the procedures described in MCL 552.605d: 1) support may be redirected to the person who is legally responsible for the actual care, support and maintenance of a child when that person is different from the payee of support 2) support for a child in foster care shall be assigned to the Family Independence Agency 3) support shall abate for a child who resides on a full-time basis with the payer of support.

5. HEALTH CARE FOR CHILDREN:

a. **Health care coverage.** ☐ Plaintiff ☒ Defendant shall carry insurance (as the term "insurer" is defined in MCL 552.602(o) covering hospital, dental, optical and other health care expenses) when coverage is available at a reasonable cost through an employer or under an existing individual policy.

b. **Uninsured health care expenses.** Uninsured health care expenses defined as ordinary by sec. IV-D(2) of the MCSF are paid through the base support amount in paragraph #4. Plaintiff shall pay ___38___ % and defendant shall pay ___62___ % of the uninsured health care expenses defined as extraordinary under MCSF IV-D(3). These expenses must be paid within 28 days of a written payment request or the obligation may be enforced as provided by law.

c. **Qualified medical support order.** This order is a qualified medical support order under 29 USC 1169. To qualify this order, a notice to enroll may be issued to the child support payer under MCL 552.626b. A parent may contest the notice by requesting a review or hearing concerning availability of health care at a reasonable cost.

GRP 5b (1/04)   EX PARTE ORDER, page 2

STATE OF MICHIGAN Circuit Court - Family Division COUNTY	EX PARTE ORDER for Custody, Parenting Time, Residence of Children and Support	CASE NO.

Plaintiff:	v	Defendant:

IT IS ALSO ORDERED:

6. **FRIEND OF THE COURT SERVICES AND FEES:**
   ☐ a. **Friend of the court opt-out.** This case shall be opted out of the following friend of the court services: ☐ all friend of the court services ☐ all friend of the court services except collection and distribution of child support through the SDU ☐ immediate income withholding only
   b. **Friend of the court fees.** While a friend of the court case, the child support payer shall pay friend of the court service fees and other statutory fees.

7. **PERSONAL INFORMATION:** The parties' current residence information appears in the main caption of this order. In a friend of the court case, the parties shall keep the friend of the court informed of residence changes or changes in their sources of income or available health care coverage (including the health care provider, coverage identification no. and persons covered).

8. **EFFECTIVENESS AND ENFORCEABILITY:** This order is effective when entered with the clerk and enforceable after service on defendant.

NOTICE

TO THE DEFENDANT:

9. You may file a written objection to this order or a motion to modify or rescind this order. You must file the written objection or motion with the clerk of the court within 14 days after you were served with this order. You must serve a true copy of the objection or motion on the friend of the court and the party who obtained the order.

10. If you file a written objection, the friend of the court must try to resolve the dispute. If the friend of the court cannot resolve the dispute and if you wish to bring the matter before the court without the assistance of counsel, ... court must provide you with form pleadings and written instructions and mus... ... the court.

11. The ex parte or... ... a temporary order if you do not file a written objection or motion to... ...order and a request for a hearing. Even if an objection is filed, the ... ...ct and must be obeyed unless changed by a later court order.

JUDGE WILL DATE AND SIGN IF S/HE APPROVES THE ORDER

Reviewed by FOC: _____

Date **3-1-89** _____ Judge *Lester Dubos*

USE PROOF OF MAILING ONLY IF YOU SEND THE ORDER TO DEFENDANT SEPARATELY FROM THE SERVICE PAPERS

PROOF OF MAILING

On the date below, I sent a true copy of this order to defendant at his/her address in the ... by ordinary first-class mail.

I declare that the statement above is true to the best of my information, knowledge and belief.

Date _____ Plaintiff _____

GRP 5c (1/04) EX PARTE ORDER, page 3

Approved, SCAO

	Original - Court 1st copy - Moving Party 2nd copy - Objecting Party	3rd copy - Friend of the Court 4th copy - Proof of Service 5th copy - Proof of Service
		CASE NO.
STATE OF MICHIGAN JUDICIAL CIRCUIT COUNTY	OBJECTION TO REFEREE'S RECOMMENDED ORDER	
		Court telephone no.

Court address

Plaintiff's name, address, and telephone no. [X] Moving party	Defendant's name, address, and telephone no. [ ] Moving party
Third party's name, address, and telephone no. [ ] Movin	

PARTY WHO OBJECTS TO ORDER IS MOVING PARTY HERE

I object to the entry of the referee's recommended order dated _____3-30-89_____ and request a de novo hearing by the court. My objection is based on the following reason(s):

IN DECIDING CUSTODY, REFEREE DIDN'T CONSIDER ALL THE BEST INTEREST FACTORS. THE REFEREE OMITTED THE DOMESTIC VIOLENCE FACTOR, ALTHOUGH THERE WAS EVIDENCE OF SUCH ABUSE BY DEFENDANT.

SAY WHY YOU BELIEVE REFEREE ERRED IN ITS DECISION

I declare that the statements above are true to the best of my information, knowledge, and belief.

_____4-15-89_____
Date

Darlene Lovelace
Signature of objecting party
DARLENE LOVELACE
Name (type or print)

NOTICE OF HEARING

A hearing will be held on this objection before Hon. _LESTER TUBBS_
Name of judge

on _____5-15-89_____ at _9:00 AM_ at _OJIBWAY COUNTY COURTHOUSE_
Date   Time   Place

If you require special accommodations to use the court because of a disability, please contact the court immediately to make arrangements.

CERTIFICATE OF MAILING

I certify that on this date I mailed a copy of this objection and notice of hearing on the other party(ies) by ordinary mail at the above address(es).

_____4-15-89_____
Date

Darlene Lovelace
Signature of objecting party

MCR 3.215(E)

FOC 68 (6/98) OBJECTION TO REFEREE'S RECOMMENDED ORDER

Approved, SCAO

Original - Return
1st copy - Witness
2nd copy - File
3rd copy - Extra

STATE OF MICHIGAN
JUDICIAL DISTRICT
JUDICIAL CIRCUIT
COUNTY PROBATE

Court address

SUBPOENA
Order to Appear and/or Produce

CASE NO.

Police Report No. (if applicable)

Court telephone no.

Plaintiff(s)/Petitioner(s)

☐ People of the State of Michigan
☒ DARLENE LOVELACE

☒ Civil
☐ Criminal

☐ Probate In the matter of

v

Defendant(s)/Respondent(s)

DUDLEY LOVELACE

Charge

> CHECK BOX #2 TO OBTAIN WITNESS' TESTIMONY AND/OR BOX #3 TO OBTAIN DOCUMENTS OR OTHER THINGS THE WITNESS HAS.

In the Name of the People of the State of Michigan. TO: JOHN QUICK, LAKESIDE FAMILY COUNSELING CENTER, 100 S. FRONT, LAKE CITY, MI 48800

If you require special accommodations to use the court because of disabilities, please contact the court immediately to make arrangements.

YOU ARE ORDERED:

☒ 1. to appear personally at the time and place stated below: You may be required to appear from time to time and day to day until excused.

☒ The court address above ☐ Other:

Day	Date	Time
TUESDAY	5-15-89	9:00 AM

☒ 2. Testify at trial / examination / hearing.

☒ 3. Produce/permit inspection or copying of the following items: ALL DOCUMENTS, RECORDS AND FILES REGARDING PSYCHOLOGICAL TESTING AND/OR EVALUATION OF DUANE W. LOVELACE AND DARRYL W. LOVELACE

☐ 4. Testify as to your assets, and bring with you the items listed in line 3 above.

☐ 5. Testify at deposition.

☐ 6. MCL 600.6104(2), 600.6116, or 600.6119 prohibition against transferring or disposing of property is attached.

☐ 7. Other: _____

☒ 8. Person requesting subpoena
DARLENE LOVELACE

Telephone no.
772-0000

Address
121 S. MAIN

City
LAKE CITY

State
MI

Zip
48800

NOTE: If requesting a debtor's examination under MCL 600.6110, or an injunction under item 6. this subpoena must be issued by a judge. For a debtor examination, the affidavit of debtor examination under item 6. this form must also be completed. Debtor's assets can also be discovered through MCR 2.305 without the need for an affidavit of debtor examination or issuance of this subpoena by a judge.

FAILURE TO OBEY THE COMMANDS OF THE SUBPOENA OR APPEAR AT THE STATED TIME AND PLACE MAY SUBJECT YOU TO PENALTY FOR CONTEMPT OF COURT.

Date
5-1-89

Judge/Clerk/Attorney
Martha Gee

Bar no.

Court use only
☐ Served ☐ Not served

MC 11 (6/99) SUBPOENA, Order to Appear and/or Produce

MCL 600.1455, 600.1701, 600.6110, 600.6119;
MSA 27A.1455, 27A.1701, 27A.6110, 27A.6119, MCR 2.506

USE OFFICER CERTIFICATE OR AFFIDAVIT OF PROCESS SERVER TO PROVE SERVICE BY DELIVERY OR SERVICE BY MAIL.

SUBPOENA

Case No. 90-00501-DM

PROOF OF SERVICE

...ER: You must make and file your return with the court clerk. If you are unable to complete service, you must
...and all copies to the court clerk.

CERTIFICATE / AFFIDAVIT OF SERVICE / NON-SERVICE

☐ **OFFICER CERTIFICATE**	OR	☐ **AFFIDAVIT OF PROCESS SERVER**

I certify that I am a sheriff, deputy sheriff, bailiff, appointed court officer, or attorney for a party [MCR 2.104(A)(2)], and that: (notary not required)

Being first duly sworn, I state that I am a legally competent adult who is not a party or an officer of a corporate party, and that: (notary required)

☐ I served a copy of the subpoena, together with _____ Attachment

☐ personally (including required fees, if any)
☐ by registered or certified mail (copy of return receipt attached) on:

Name(s)	Complete address(es) of service	Day, date, time

☐ After diligent search and inquiry, I have been unable to find and serve the following person(s): _____

I have made the following efforts in attempting to serve process: _____

☐ I have personally attempted to serve the subpoena and required fees, if any, together with _____ Attachment

on _____ Name

_____ and have been unable to complete service because

at _____
the address was incorrect at the time of filing.

Service fee $	Miles traveled	Mileage fee $	Total fee $

Signature _____

Title _____

_____ County, Michigan.

Subscribed and sworn to before me on _____ Date

My commission expires: _____ Date   Signature: _____ Deputy court clerk/Notary public

ACKNOWLEDGMENT OF SERVICE

I acknowledge that I have received service of the subpoena and required fees, if any, together with _____ Attachment

on MON. 5-5-89 9:00 AM
Day, date, time

John Quick
Signature

~~on behalf of~~ AT: 100 S. FRONT
LAKE CITY, MI 48800

THIS IS A PROOF OF SERVICE BY ACKNOWLEDGMENT.

AFFIDAVIT FOR JUDGMENT DEBTOR EXAMINATION

I request that the court issue a subpoena which orders the party named on this form to be examined under oath before a judge concerning the money or property of:
for the following reasons:

Under penalty of contempt of court, I declare that the above statements are true to the best of my information, knowledge, and belief.

_____
Date

Signature _____

MCR 2.105

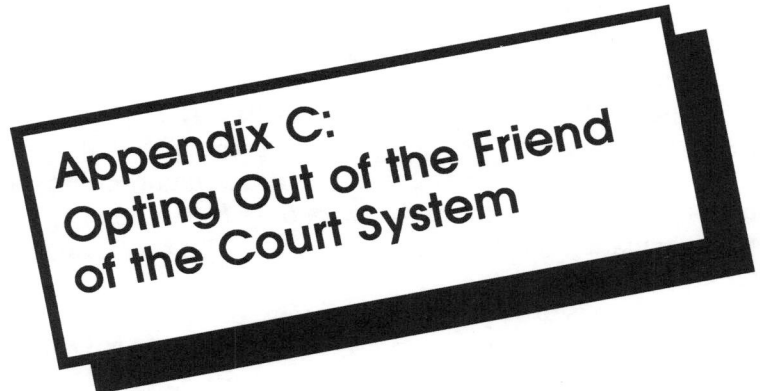

Appendix C:
Opting Out of the Friend
of the Court System

The friend of the court has been a part of Michigan family law since 1919. The friend of the court provides a number of services in divorce cases, including investigation and recommendation to the judge on divorce issues, refereeing and mediation of disputes, and review, modification and enforcement of orders. All in all, the friend of the court has served the state and divorce families well over the years.

But recently, cracks in the friend of the court system have developed. In 2001, a major *Detroit News* investigation found that many county friends of the court were struggling with a backlog of cases and provided poor service. The next year, Michigan lawmakers tried to improve the system, passing a package of laws reforming friend of the court operations.

In the biggest break from the past, a new law allows divorce parties to "opt out" of the friend of the court system. Lawmakers had found that more than a half of divorce cases were problem-free, with parents meeting all obligations. They decided to remove some of these cases from the system, letting the friend of the court concentrate on tough cases.

In fact, the opt-out law, which is explained below, is a good deal more complicated than that. There are several types of opt-outs. And there are many restrictions on opting out, and automatic triggers for bringing cases back under friend of the court control.

Is it worth considering an opt-out? Supporters of the opt-out law say that friend of the court intervention in a divorce isn't necessary if the spouses are cooperative. Opponents of the law argue that threat of friend of the court enforcement makes parents more agreeable, and without this leverage there will be more disputes during divorce and judgment violations afterward.

There is such a thing as an amicable divorce, and parents often cooperate during and after divorce. However, the friend of the court performs several valuable functions, which shouldn't be underestimated. More than anything, the friend of the court is supposed to be an honest broker amid divorce. If there's a dispute over something it has record of what went wrong; otherwise, it's one parent's word against the other. In particular, the friend of the court performs an important bookkeeping function, keeping track of support payments (support and parenting time are the source of most divorce judgment violations).

Maybe the best approach is to stay within the friend of the court system for a while, at the beginning of the divorce, and see if you like it. If you don't, you can then see about opting out. Or if you decide to opt out, consider either a partial or limited opt-out, instead of a total one.

Types of Opt-Outs

The 2002 opt-out law allows several kinds of opt-outs from the friend of the court system:

- total opt-out from all friend of the court services
- partial opt-out from all friend of the court services except collection and distribution of support through the state disbursement unit (SDU) (with or without immediate income withholding as the method of payment)
- limited opt-out from immediate income withholding only, but receipt of all other friend of the court services

Total Opt-Out

In some cases, you can opt out of the friend of the court system completely, giving up all friend of the court services in your divorce. Afterward, you are responsible for all future management of your case, including payment of support (you lose SDU-payment of support with a total opt-out). You must have the consent of the defendant to get (and keep) a total opt-out. And the judge must review and approve your opt-out request.

The timing of an opt-out is important. You can get a total opt-out at the beginning of a divorce (new case) or later while the case is pending (open case). The procedures for new- and open-case opt-outs are a little different, and these are described below.

Total Opt-Out in a New Case

You can opt out of a new-filed case, so the friend of the court never enters the case and never opens a file for the case. Not every case is eligible for this kind of opt-out. The opt-out law bars opting out of a new case when:

- a party is eligible for FIA services (also known as title IV-D services) because of past or current receipt of public assistance
- a party is applying for FIA services
- a party requests friend of the court services
- there is evidence of 1) domestic violence, or 2) uneven bargaining position between the parties, and evidence that a party hasn't applied for FIA services against the best interests of that party or the children

If your case is eligible for opting out, you must request an opt-out at the start of your divorce, when you file. As you prepare your initial divorce papers (see "Filing" on page 87 for more about preparing these papers), make additions to two of these papers:

- Complaint for Divorce (GRP 1b), check the outdented box for paragraph #10 to show you want to opt out, and then check the first box inside that paragraph to opt out of "all friend of the court services" (total opt-out).
- Ex Parte Order (GRP 5c), check the box at paragraph #6a to show you want to opt out, and then check the first box inside that paragraph to opt out of "all friend of the court services" (total opt-out). Also, in paragraph #4b of the GRP 5b, select payment of support without immediate income withholding and directly to the payee.

You must also prepare three extra papers, which will be referred to as the "opt-out papers:"

• Advice of Rights Regarding Use of Friend of the Court Services	FOC 101	2
• Supplemental Notice to Advice of Rights Regarding Use of Friend of the Court Services	FOC 101a	2
• Order Exempting Case from Friend of the Court Services	FOC 102	2

The FOC 101 and 101a warn you which services you lose by opting out. You and the defendant must receive separate copies of these forms, and both of you must date and sign the original forms, which will be filed with court. This tells the court that both parties consent to the opt-out.

The FOC 102 is the actual opt-out order. You select a total opt-out by leaving the boxes in paragraph #13a and b unchecked. The sample form shows you how to make the correct choice. Afterward, paperclip the signed FOC 101 and 101a to the FOC 102.

After you file your divorce, you must bring the opt-out request to the judge right away. By acting quickly, you can keep the friend of the court out of the case before it opens a file. A good time for opting out is when you seek interim relief, if you are asking for this form of preliminary relief (see Appendix B for more about interim relief). When you apply to the judge for the relief, just add your (unfiled) opt-out papers to the (unfiled) interim relief papers. This procedure is described in "Requesting Interim Relief from the Judge" on page 157.

Not everyone seeks interim relief. If you're not, you must apply to the to the judge separately for an opt-out. Again, see "Requesting Interim Relief from the Judge" on page 157, and use the same procedure to request an opt-out from the judge in his/her office.

If the judge approves an opt-out, file the opt-out papers with the clerk (the friend of the court won't get copies since it has dropped out of the case), and serve another set of copies on the defendant with the service papers (see "Service" on page 99 for more about service). After receiving a denial, you must withdraw your opt-out papers and the judge will note the denial on the Complaint for Divorce (GRP 1) or in the case file.

After an opt-out, the friend of the court won't participate in your case. As a result, disregard all references in Chapter 2 to the friend of the court's receiving papers, investigating, recommending, refereeing, mediating or reviewing orders. Despite the opt-out, don't be surprised if the friend of the court reappears in your case. Some judges will have the friend of the court step back in a case, even after a total opt-out, for limited purposes, such as refereeing.

As the divorce continues, you may change your mind and want the friend of the court back in your case. All you have to do is submit a simple written request to the friend of the court; no motion is necessary. You can use the Request to Reopen Friend of the Court Case (FOC 104) for this purpose. The friend of the court will also intervene on its own when: 1) either party requests friend of the court services 2) a party applies for public assistance.

At the end of the divorce, you must decide whether you want the friend of the court in or out of your case during the post-divorce (called the post-judgment) period. During this time, which can last for years (until the youngest child turns 18), the friend of the court provides services for modification and enforcement of the divorce judgment (the FOC 101 has a good summary of these post-judgment duties).

If you still want the friend of the court out of the case, you must say so in the Judgment of Divorce (GRP 4). Ordinarily, the opt-out order would expire according to paragraph #10 of the Judgment of Divorce (GRP 4a), as a nonfinal order. But you can extend the opt-out order in paragraph #21 of the divorce judgment. Check the outdented box at #21a, the outdented box below that, the first box inside the paragraph describing your total opt-out and the second-to-last box indicating that this opt-out shall remain in effect.

Since you're having support paid from payer directly to payee, without immediate income withholding through the SDU, you must provide for this in paragraph #19 of the Judgment of Divorce (GRP 4d). Check the correct boxes in paragraph #19. Omit the Income Withholding Order (FOC 5) from your final divorce papers, because this is unnecessary. Also, describe the opt-out to the judge during your testimony at the final hearing.

If you want the friend of the court back in your case post-judgment, you could file a Request to Reopen Friend of the Court Case (FOC 104) before the hearing. Or you can check the outdented box at paragraph #21a of the

Judgment of Divorce (GRP 4d), the outdented box below that, the first box inside that paragraph and then check the last box inside that paragraph to say that the previously ordered opt-out shall terminate. Don't forget the correct method of support payment in paragraph #19, adding the Income Withholding Order (FOC 5) as needed.

There's yet another choice: You want to change your opt-out, switching from a total opt-out to a partial or limited one. For a partial opt-out, see "Partial Opt-Out" for general information and "Partial Opt-Out in an Open Case" below about the steps for opting out at the end of a divorce. Likewise, see "Limited Opt-Out" and "Limited Opt-Out in an Open Case" below about limited opt-outs.

To switch opt-outs, terminate the previously ordered opt-out in the first part of paragraph #21a of the Judgment of Divorce (GRP 4d). Then, inside the second part of that paragraph, choose the new opt-out you want by checking the second box (for a partial opt-out) or the third box (for a limited one). Explain the switch to the judge at the final hearing.

Total Opt-Out in an Open Case

The friend of the court may have participated in your case while it was pending. But now you want to opt out totally from the friend of the court system for the post-divorce (called the post-judgment) period. It's possible to have the friend of the court withdraw from the case and close its file that way with the consent of the defendant and approval of the court.

Not every open divorce case is eligible for total opt out. Like a new case, there are several restrictions which are similar but not the same as the ones for a new case:

- a party objects to opting out
- a party is eligible to receive FIA services (also known as title IV-D services) because the party receives public assistance
- a party is eligible to receive FIA services because the party received public assistance and an arrearage is owed to the state
- no support arrearage or custody or parenting time order violation has occurred in the last 12 months
- neither party has reopened a friend of the court case during the last 12 months
- there is evidence of 1) domestic violence, or 2) uneven bargaining position between the parties, and evidence that a party is opting out against the best interests of that party or the children

If you want to opt out late in your case, the final hearing, when the divorce judgment is granted, is a convenient time. Otherwise, you must file a separate motion and schedule a hearing on your request. Before the final hearing, prepare three extra "opt-out papers:"

- Advice of Rights Regarding Use of   FOC 101   2
  Friend of the Court Services

• Supplemental Notice to Advice of Rights Regarding Use of Friend of the Court Services	FOC 101a	2
• Order Exempting Case from Friend of the Court Services	FOC 102	2

The FOC 101 and 101a warn you which services you lose by opting out. You and the defendant must receive separate copies of these forms, and both of you must date and sign the original forms which will be filed with the court. This tells the court that both parties consent to the opt-out.

The FOC 102 is the actual opt-out order. You select a total opt-out by leaving the boxes in paragraph #13a and b unchecked. The sample form shows you how to make the correct choice. Afterward, paperclip the signed FOC 101 and 101a to the FOC 102.

You must also prepare your Judgment of Divorce (GRP 4) to provide for a total opt-out. In paragraph #21 of the Judgment of Divorce (GPR 4d), check the first outdented box to show that you are opting out, and the third outdented box indicating that this is a new opt-out. Inside the second part of paragraph #21a, check the first box opting out of all friend of the court services. In paragraph #19, choose your new method of support payment, without income withholding and probably with direct payment to the payee. Also, omit the FOC 5 from your final divorce papers.

During the final hearing, include the FOC 101, 101a and 102 among your final divorce papers (see "Final Hearing" on page 123 for more about preparing, filing and sending the final divorce papers to the defendant after the divorce). In your testimony, say that you want to opt out. It's also helpful to have the defendant on hand to confirm the opt-out; but the defendant's signing the FOC 101 and 101a is sufficient to show consent.

If the judge denies your opt-out request, just correct the Judgment of Divorce (GRP 4) by removing all the opt-out provisions described above, and choose payment of support by immediate income withholding to the SDU in paragraph #19 of the GRP 4d.

After opting out, the friend of the court won't help with any judgment modification or enforcement during the post-judgment period. But if you want the friend of the court back in your case, just file the Request to Reopen Friend of the Court Case (FOC 104). The friend of the court will also re-enter the case automatically if: 1) either party requests friend of the court services 2) a party applies for public assistance.

Partial Opt-Out

Ordinarily, when you opt-out totally from the friend of the court system you give up all friend of the court services, including payment of support (child support and/or alimony) through the SDU. See "Court System" on page 71 for more about SDU operations. SDU-payment is an efficient means of collecting and distributing support, and not everyone opting out wants to lose this.

Luckily, the 2002 opt-out law allows partial opt-outs: You give up all friend of the court services except payment of support to the SDU. If you choose this option, you also have two subchoices: 1) SDU-payment by immediate income withholding 2) SDU-payment without immediate income withholding, and payment from the payer directly to the SDU.

A partial opt-out is a lot like a total opt-out (they're really just different choices on the Order Exempting Case from Friend of the Court Services (FOC 102), and they share similar procedures. And as with a total opt-out, the steps for opting out of new cases (before the friend of the court's entry into the case) are a little different from open-case opt-outs (after the friend of the court has entered the case).

Partial Opt-Out in a New Case

The procedures (form preparation, submission of papers to the judge, etc.) for a partial opt-out in a new case are almost identical to those in a new-case total opt-out. And the same four restrictions apply (eligibility for FIA services, application for FIA services, etc.). For information about these procedures and restrictions, see "Total Opt-Out in a New Case" on page 178.

Where a total and partial opt-out diverge is in the paperwork. When you prepare the FOC 102, pay special attention to paragraph #13 (untouched in a total opt-out). This is where a partial opt-out occurs. Having opted out of the friend of the court system, you, in essence, opt back in for SDU payment.

More Information
About paying support to the state disbursement unit (SDU), call the unit at (866) 540-0008 or use its Web site: www.mi-sdu.com.

After you bring the SDU back, you have a further choice: Do you want the SDU to collect the support by immediate income withholding or by direct payment from the payer? By checking the first box, #13a, you get SDU-payment by immediate income withholding. You have to set this up (or continue it), the friend of the court (which is out of the case) won't do this for you. With choice #13b, you get SDU-help without immediate income withholding. Instead, the payer must pay the support directly to the SDU. You must make arrangements for this method of payment.

Your Ex Parte Order (GRP 5) must mirror the choices you have made. In paragraph #4b of the GRP 5b, you want to check payment to the SDU. But in the line above, choose the immediate income withholding box for payment by income withholding (matches #13a on the FOC 102) or the without income witholding box (matches #13b on the FOC 102) for direct payment to the SDU. If you skip immediate income withholding, omit the Income Withholding Order (FOC 5) from your interim relief papers.

After an opt-out, the friend of the court won't participate in your case. As a result, disregard all references in Chapter 2 to the friend of the court's receiving copies of papers, investigating, recommending, refereeing, mediating or reviewing orders. The only friend of the court involvement will be the SDU. Despite the opt-out, don't be surprised if the friend of the court re-appears in your case. Some judges will have the friend of the court step back in a case, even after a partial opt-out, for limited purposes, such as refereeing.

As the divorce continues, you may change your mind and want the friend of the court back in your case. Or you may want a total or limited opt-out for the post-divorce period. See "Total Opt-Out in an Open Case" on page 181 about reopening a friend of the court case or switching the opt-out at the end of the divorce.

Partial Opt-Out in an Open Case

Partially opting out from an open case resembles an open-case total opt-out. And the same six restrictions (objection, eligibility for FIA services, etc.) apply. See "Total Opt-Out in an Open Case" on page 181 for more about these procedures and restrictions.

There is a difference in the paperwork. When you prepare the Order Exempting Case from Friend of the Court Services (FOC 102), pay close attention to paragraph #13 (unused in a total opt-out). This is where a partial opt-out occurs. Having opted out of the friend of the court system, you, in essence, opt back in for SDU-payment.

After you opt back for SDU collection, you have a choice: Do you want the SDU to collect the support by immediate income withholding or by direct payment from the payer? By checking the first box, #13a, you get SDU-payment by immediate income withholding. You have to set up the withholding yourself (or continue it), the friend of the court won't do this for you. With choice #13b, you elect payment from the payer to the SDU, without immediate income withholding.

Your Judgment of Divorce must also follow the choices you have made. In paragraph #19 of the GRP 4d, you want to check payment to the SDU. But in the line above, choose the immediate income withholding box for payment by income withholding (matches #13a on the FOC 102) or without income withholding (matches #13b on the FOC 102) for direct payment to the SDU. If you skip immediate income withholding, omit the Income Withholding Order (FOC 5) from your final divorce papers.

Limited Opt-Out

You may be happy with the friend of the court's services for custody, parenting time and support; all you want is a different method of support (child support and/or alimony) payment. The law allows you to opt out of immediate income withholding only, which is the normal means of paying support, and choose another payment method. Other payment options include: 1) payment to the SDU directly 2) direct payment to the support payee/recipient.

After a limited opt-out, you will have access to the usual friend of the court services. You may or may not have SDU collection and distribution of support. But either way, the friend of the court will monitor payments and enforce support obligations, including health care.

There are two ways to avoid immediate income withholding through a limited opt-out: 1) with the consent of the defendant 2) for "good cause," without the consent of the defendant. Either kind requires court approval.

As with total and partial opt-outs, there are some restrictions, although fewer ones, on limited opt-outs. You can't opt out for good cause if: 1) support is already past due 2) it's in the best interests of the children to have immediate income withholding.

Limited Opt-Out in a New Case

You can get a limited opt out at the beginning of your divorce, if* and when you seek interim relief. That way, none of the interim child support will be paid by income withholding, and you can choose another method of payment.

As you prepare your initial divorce papers (see "Filing" on page 87 for more about preparing these papers), make additions to two of these papers:

- Complaint for Divorce (GRP 1b), check the outdented box in paragraph #10 to show you want to opt out, and then the third box inside that paragraph to opt out of "immediate income withholding only" (limited opt-out).
- Ex Parte Order (GRP 5c), check the box at paragraph #6a to show you want to opt-out, and then check the third box inside that paragraph to opt out of "immediate income withholding only." Also, in paragraph #4b of the GRP 5b, select payment of support without income withholding and payment to the SDU or directly to the payee.

You must also prepare one or two extra papers, which will be referred to in this section as the "opt-out papers." To opt out with the agreement of the defendant you need both forms; opt-outs for cause use the order only:

• Agreement Suspending Immediate Income Withholding	FOC 63	2
• Order Suspending Immediate Income Withholding	FOC 64	2

In an agreed-to opt-out, both you and the defendant must sign the FOC 63. Indicate the alternate method of payment you want in paragraph #2. The FOC 64 is used in both agreed-to and for-cause opt-outs. See the sample forms at the end of this appendix for help with both forms.

For convenience, you can seek the opt-out when you ask for interim relief (see Appendix B for more about this form of preliminary relief). When you apply to the judge for interim relief, just add your (unfiled) opt-out papers to the (unfiled) interim relief papers. This procedure is described in "Requesting Interim Relief from the Judge" on page 157.

---

* If you aren't seeking interim relief, there's no court-ordered support and no need for a limited opt-out at this point.

Not everyone seeks interim relief. If you're not, you must apply to the to the judge separately for an opt-out. Again, see "Requesting Interim Relief from the Judge" on page 157, and use the same procedure to request an opt-out from the judge in his/her office.

If the judge approves an opt-out, file the opt-out paper(s) and friend of the court copies with the clerk, and serve another set of copies on the defendant with the service papers (see "Service" on page 99 for more about service). After a denial, you must withdraw your opt-out papers and the judge will note the denial on the Complaint for Divorce (GRP 1) or in the case file. With a denial, any interim child support will be paid by immediate income withholding.

After a limited opt-out, the friend of the court will participate in your case, as in other divorces. The only difference is that interim child support won't be paid by immediate income withholding. The friend of the court should help you set up the other method of payment.

During the divorce, immediate income withholding will resume if past-due support equals or exceeds one month of support. You can also ask for resumption of immediate income withholding, but this takes a separate motion and hearing.

At the end of the divorce, you must decide how you want support paid during the post-divorce (called the post-judgment) period. Do you want to continue the limited opt-out, do you want payment by immediate income withholding or do you want another type of opt-out?

To continue without immediate income withholding, you must extend the FOC 64, which would normally expire as a nonfinal order. In paragraph #21 of the Judgment of Divorce (4d), check the first outdented box at a, the outdented box below that and the third and fourth boxes inside the paragraph indicating that the previously ordered limited opt-out shall remain in effect. Also, omit the Income Withholding Order (FOC 5) from your final divorce papers.

If you want to reinstate immediate income withholding, repeat the procedure above, but say that the previously ordered opt-out shall terminate. And don't forget to select the correct method of support payment in paragraph #19, adding the FOC 5 as needed.

There's another possibility: You want to change your opt-out, switching from a limited opt-out to a partial or total one. For a partial opt-out, see "Total Opt-Out" for general information and "Total Opt-Out in an Open Case" above about the steps for opting out at the end of a divorce. Likewise, see "Partial Opt-Out" and "Partial Opt-Out in an Open Case" above about partial opt-outs.

Limited Opt-Out in an Open Case

You may have had interim support paid by immediate income withholding, or skipped interim relief completely. But now, at the end of the divorce, you want a limited opt-out of immediate income withholding for the post-divorce period.

The final hearing is a good time to ask for an opt-out because you're going before the judge anyway. Prior to the final hearing, prepare one or two extra "opt-out papers." To opt out with the agreement of the defendant, you need both forms; opt-outs for cause use the order only:

- Agreement Suspending Immediate Income Withholding   FOC 63   3

- Order Suspending Immediate Income Withholding   FOC 64   3

You must obtain the consent of the defendant for an agreed-to opt-out. At a minimum, the defendant must sign the FOC 63. It's also helpful if the defendant can attend the final hearing and confirm that s/he agrees to payment without immediate income withholding. But the defendant's signing the FOC 63 should be sufficient to show consent.

You must also prepare your Judgment of Divorce (GRP 4) to account for the opt-out. In paragraph #21 of the GRP 4d, check the first and third outdented boxes, and the last box in the second paragraph indicating that the opt-out is from immediate income withholding only. Then in paragraph #19, check the box showing that support is being paid without immediate income withholding, and choose payment to either the SDU or the payee directly. Also, omit the Income Withholding Order (FOC 5), since this goes with immediate income withholding.

During the final hearing, include the FOC 63 and/or 64 among your final divorce papers (see "Final Hearing" on page 123 for more about preparing, filing and sending final divorce papers to the defendant). In your testimony, say that you want to avoid immediate income withholding and describe your alternate method of payment.

If the judge denies your opt-out request, just correct the Judgment of Divorce (GRP 4) to provide for immediate income withholding and add back the FOC 5.

If the judge approves your opt-out request, the support will be paid without immediate income withholding. If you want it back, you must file a motion. The friend of the court will also take steps to reimpose immediate income withholding when past-due support equals or exceeds one month of support.

Original - Court (to be filed with motion)

continued from page 1

Approved, SCAO

STATE OF MIC
JUDIC

Friend of the Court addre

1. Right to Refuse F

a. You have the rig
court involveme
services not be
provided both pa

1) Neither of y
2) There is no
3) The court fir

b. If you already ha
parties agree, a

1) Neither of y
2) There is no
3) The court fir
4) No money i
5) No arrearag
6) Neither of y

2. Friend of the Cou

The friend of the c
you choose to refu

a. **Accounting S**

Friends of the
1) friend of the
and 3) annual

b. **Support Enfor**

The friend of th
child support e

- Paying supp
- Asking the c
- Having unpa
- Reporting s
- Collecting s

If you choose
of the court is
changing inc

c. **Medical Supp**

The friend of t
the amounts t
authorized to

d. **Support Revi**

Once every tw
After completi
recommends
modified.

FOC 101 (6/03) AD

Advice of Rights Rega

e. **Custody and Pare**

For friend of the co
it is violated. Child

- Asking the cou
order.
- Suspending the
- Awarding make
- Joint meetings

f. **Custody and Pa**

For disputes abou
and provide repo

g. **Mediation Servi**

Friend of the cou
parenting time di

3. State Disburseme

a. **State Disburser**

If you choose no
through, the stat
cannot provide y

All payments ma
more than one c
friend of the cc
in the same ma
to use the SDU

b. **Your Rights U**

Title IV-D of the
funding to be us
of the court. If

Check below only i
must be attached t

I have read this adv

☒ I acknowledge th
this choice can ta
approval. I also
rights.

Signature

If you did not che
court services, yo

I request IV-D serv

Date

Original - Court (to be filed with motion)
1st copy - Plaintiff
2nd copy - Defendant

Approved, SCAO

| STATE OF MICHIGAN JUDICIAL CIRCUIT COUNTY | SUPPLEMENTAL NOTICE TO ADVICE OF RIGHTS REGARDING USE OF FRIEND OF THE COURT SERVICES | CASE NO. |

Friend of the Court address   Telephone no.

1. State Disbursement Unit Payments

a. **State Disbursement Unit (SDU)**

If you opt out of the friend of the court, you may continue to make payments through the State Disbursement Unit (SDU). The SDU uses the friend of the court for most accounting functions and cannot provide you with all of the accounting functions the friend of the court provides.

For friend of the court cases, payments are made through the SDU and distributed to the amounts due as required by federal law. When a payer has more than one case, federal law determines how a payment is divided between the cases. **Even if parties opt out of the friend of the court, payments through the SDU must be divided between all payer's cases and distributed in the same manner as payments on friend of the court cases.**

b. **SDU Limitations**

The SDU relies on the friend of the court records to determine the amount of income withholding. The SDU also requires the friend of the court to set up any income withholding or change in income withholding. If you choose not to accept friend of the court services, the SDU will not be able to process payments through income withholding if the person paying support changes jobs or the amount withheld changes.

Under federal law, the state of Michigan is converting its friend of the court to a new single child support enforcement computer system. County friend of the court offices will be converted under a schedule that begins in March, 2003 and continues until September 30, 2003. Until the conversion is completed, only the friend of the court can process checks. If you choose not to accept friend of the court services, you will not be able to use the SDU until all of your cases are converted to MiCSES version 2.4 or greater.

2. Your Acknowledgment of System Limitations on Your Right to Opt Out of Friend of the Court Services

Please sign and return this form to the friend of the court.

I have read this form and I want to opt out of the friend of the court. I understand that I cannot opt out of the friend of the court with SDU services until this case is converted to MiCSES version 2.4 or greater.

2-28-89
Date

DATE: 2-28-89

Darlene Lovelace
Signature

Dudley Lovelace

FOC 101a (6/03) SUPPLEMENTAL NOTICE TO ADVICE OF RIGHTS REGARDING USE OF FRIEND OF THE COURT SERVICES

Approved, SCAO

Original - Court
1st copy - Plaintiff

2nd copy - Defendant
3rd copy - Friend of the Court

STATE OF MICHIGAN
JUDICIAL CIRCUIT
COUNTY

Friend of the Court address

**ORDER EXEMPTING CASE FROM
FRIEND OF THE COURT SERVICES**

CASE NO.

Plaintiff's name and address

FAX no.

Telephone no.

Defendant's name and address

Attorney:

v

Attorney:

Bar no.

Date of hearing: 3-1-89

THE COURT FINDS:
1. There is no evidence of domestic
2. Granting the parties the relief the
3. The parties have filed execut
4. Neither party receives publi
5. No money is due the state
6. No arrearage or custody
7. Neither party has reopen
8. The parties do not wa ☒
   checked unless exceptiona

IT IS ORDERED:
9. Subject to the provisions
10. This case is not a title ☒
11. The friend of the court shall
    time, or support in this case.
12. The parties are responsible for
13. Except as indicated below, there is n
    and the friend of the court shall terminate a
    the payer must keep the friend of the court
    care coverage that is available to the pay
    insurance company, health care organiz
    and the names and birth dates of the
    ☐ a. Support shall be paid through t
       extent allowed by statutes an
       The friend of the court shall notify
       concerning income withholding will be
    ☐ b. Support shall be paid through the SDU.
       If support payments are to be made through the SDU by income withholding or otherwise, the friend of the court shall not close
       the friend of the court case until the SDU notifies the friend of the court that it has been provided with the information necessary
       to process the child support payments. There will be no accounting for support that is not paid through the SDU.
14. The friend of the court shall open a friend of the court case if a party applies for public assistance relating to a child of the parties
    or either party submits to the friend of the court a written request to reopen the friend of the court case. If this case becomes
    a friend of the court case for any reason, the provisions on the other side of this order shall apply.

THIS ORDER IS FOR A TOTAL OPT-OUT.

CHECK THE BOX AT #13a FOR A PARTIAL OPT-OUT WITH SDU-PAYMENT BY IMMEDIATE INCOME WITHHOLDING; CHECK THE BOX AT #13b FOR A PARTIAL OPT-OUT WITH SDU-PAYMENT BUT WITHOUT IMMEDIATE INCOME WITHHOLDING.

3-1-89
Date

See provisions on back.

Judge

I certify that on this date I mailed a copy of this order to the other party by ordinary mail addressed to the last known address.

CERTIFICATE OF MAILING

Date

Signature

FOC 102 (6/03) ORDER EXEMPTING CASE FROM FRIEND OF THE COURT SERVICES

MCL 552.505, MCL 552.505a

Approved, SCAO

Original - Court
1st copy - Friend of the Court

2nd copy - Plaintiff
3rd copy - Defendant

STATE OF MICHIGAN
JUDICIAL CIRCUIT
COUNTY

REQUEST TO REOPEN
FRIEND OF THE COURT CASE

CASE NO.

Telephone no.

Friend of the Court address

Plaintiff's name and address

Defendant's name and address

Attorney:

Attorney:

1. On **3-1-89** _____ an order was entered exempting this case from friend of the court services.
   Date

I REQUEST that the friend of the court case be reopened upon filing of this request with the friend of the court office.

CERTIFICATE OF MAILING

I certify that on this date I mailed a copy of this request to the other party by ordinary mail addressed to the last known address.

7-1-89 _____
Date

Darlene Lovelace
Signature

MCL 552.505, MCL 552.505a

FOC 104 (6/03) **REQUEST TO REOPEN FRIEND OF THE COURT CASE**

Original - Court
2nd copy - Friend of the Court
3rd copy - Plaintiff
4th copy - Defendant

CASE NO.

Court telephone no.

Approved, SCAO

STATE OF MICHIGAN
JUDICIAL CIRCUIT
COUNTY

**AGREEMENT SUSPENDING
IMMEDIATE INCOME WITHHOLDING**

Friend of the Court address

Plaintiff's name and address

NOTE: MCL 552.604(3); MSA 25.164(4)(3)
requires that all new and modified support orders after
December 31, 1990 include a provision for immediate
income withholding and that income withholding take
effect immediately unless the parties enter into a written
agreement that the income withholding order shall not
take effect immediately.

v

Defendant's name and address

We understand that by law an order of income withholding in a support order shall take ef... agree to the following:

1. The order of income withholding shall not take effect immediately.

2. An alternative payment arrangement shall be made as follows:

THE DEFENDANT SHALL PAY THE SUPPORT DIRECTLY TO THE SDU.

DESCRIBE OTHER METHOD OF PAYMENT

3. Both the payer and the recipient of support shall keep the friend of the court informed of the following:
   a. the name, address, and telephone number of his/her current source of income;
   b. any health care coverage that is available to him/her as a benefit of employment or that is maintained by him/her; the name of the insurance company, health care organization, or health maintenance organization; the policy, certificate or contract number; and the name(s) and birth date(s) of the person(s) for whose benefit s/he maintains health care coverage under the policy, certificate, or contract; and
   c. his/her current residence and mailing address.

4. We further understand that proceedings to implement income withholding shall commence if the payer of support falls one month behind in his/her support payments.

5. We recognize that the court may order withholding of income to take effect immediately for cause or at the request of the payer.

9-5-89
Date
Darlene Lovelace
Plaintiff's signature

9-5-89
Date
Dudley Lovelace
Defendant's signature

MCL 552.604; MSA 25.164(4)

FOC 63 (4/01) AGREEMENT SUSPENDING IMMEDIATE INCOME WITHHOLDING

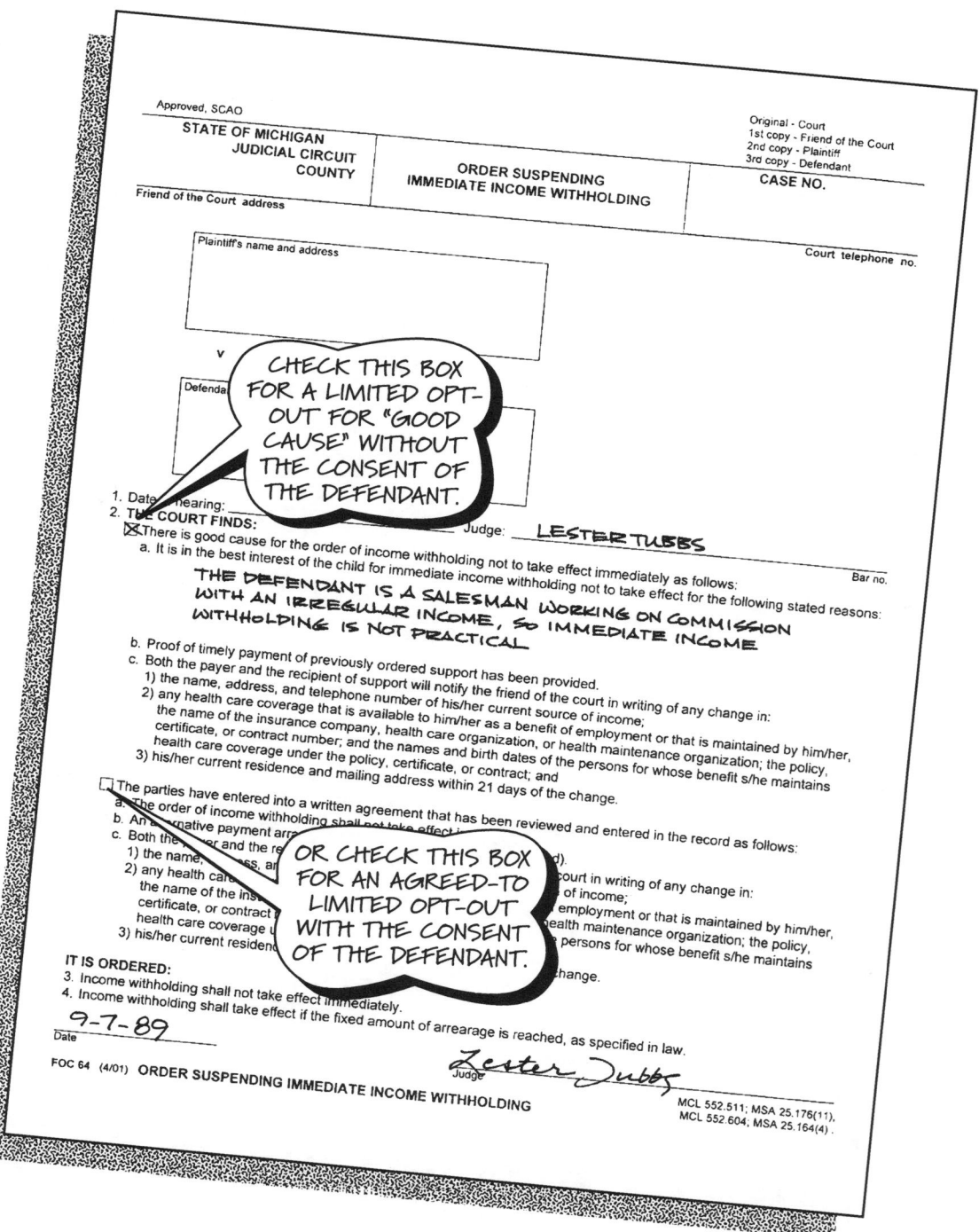

Appendix D:
Alternate Service

The regular service methods of service by acknowledgment, mail and delivery are very effective when defendants are available for service. But if the defendant is hiding from service (an elusive defendant), or has disappeared entirely (a disappeared defendant), you must use another method of service.

Luckily, the court rules authorize alternate service on elusive and disappeared defendants. By using alternate service, your divorce can go ahead normally, just as if you had served the defendant by one of the regular service methods.

Forms of Alternate Service

Alternate service can take several forms including: 1) mailing 2) tacking (attaching papers to a door) 3) household delivery (delivering papers to an adult in the defendant's household) 4) publication (with or without an accompanying registered mailing) 5) posting (with or without an accompanying registered mailing) 6) any combination of #1-5 7) something completely different (by itself or in combination with any of #1-5).

The judge picks from among these options to devise a method of alternate service for the defendant. The method is designed to give the defendant actual notice of the divorce. But if the alternate service doesn't give actual notice, that's all right. Elusive and disappeared defendants are legally entitled to whatever notice alternate service provides, even if this means no actual notice.

When the defendant is elusive, the judge will probably order either mailing, tacking, household delivery or a combination of these. But these things won't work on disappeared defendants whose whereabouts are unknown. For them, judges normally order publication or posting. With either method, judges can order registered mailing of the service papers to the defendant's last known address. If that address appears to be outdated, the judge can skip the mailing and order publication or posting alone.

Whatever form alternate service takes, keep in mind that you cannot perform it yourself because you're disqualified from serving as a party to the divorce. Like regular service, you must have a server—a helper or professional server—to carry out alternate service. You can apply for and help with the alternate service, but the helper or server must serve the service papers for you (see "Preparing for Service" on page 100 for which papers make up your service papers).

Alternate Service for an Elusive Defendant

With an elusive defendant, you know his/her home and/or business address. Before you apply for alternate service, you must try service by delivery on the defendant at those or other places. For service by delivery, use the procedure described in "Service by Delivery" on page 105. Since the service will probably be difficult, use a professional server, such as a sheriff or commercial process server. Tell the server to attempt delivery not once but three or four times.

You must also ask the server to describe each attempt in the Verification of Process Server section of the Motion and Verification for Alternate Service (MC 303), which you should give to the server along with the service papers. The server's description of each delivery attempt must include specific information about the date, place and result of the attempt, as shown in the sample form at the end of this appendix.

If the server succeeds in serving the defendant during those attempts, you have obtained service on the defendant by delivery, and don't need alternate service. But if service by delivery fails, the server will return the service papers to you and you can apply for alternate service.

Make sure that the server has completed the Verification of Process Server section in the Motion and Verification for Alternate Service (MC 303), and then pay the server for the attempted service. You must complete the top portion of the Motion and Verification for Alternate Service (MC 303), above the verification section. Because you are trying to serve an elusive defendant, complete paragraph #2a of the motion showing that you know the defendant's current home and/or business address. You should also complete the caption and paragraph #1 of the Order for Alternate Service (MC 304), and return to the clerk with:

- Motion and Verification for Alternate Service   MC 303
  - original
  - two copies (one earmarked "FOC")

- Order for Alternate Service   MC 304
  - original

- $20 motion fee

File the Motion and Verification for Alternate Service (MC 303) and the friend of the court's copy with the clerk. After filing, go to your judge's office and submit a copy of the Motion and Verification for Alternate Service (MC 303) and the original Order for Alternate Service (MC 304) to the judge's secretary. The judge will review your motion in his/her office (although probably not while you wait), so a court hearing on the motion won't be necessary. If the judge grants your motion for alternate service, get the papers back from the judge's office, make four photocopies of the Order for Alternate Service (MC 304) and earmark one "FOC." Return to the clerk and file the original and the friend of the court's copy.

Examine the Order for Alternate Service (MC 304) to see which method of alternate service the judge has designed for the defendant. It will probably be either mailing, tacking, household delivery or a combination of these. (If the judge has ordered several things, prepare multiple sets of the service papers and the Order for Alternate Service (MC 304) because you will need separate sets of these papers for each form of alternate service ordered.) However, the judge could order another method of alternate service, which would be described in paragraph #2d. If the judge orders publication or posting, see the sections on these below.

Mailing

For this type of mailing, ordinary first-class mailing is permissible. Have your helper or server mail the service papers and a copy of the Order for Alternate Service (MC 304) to the person named by the judge in paragraph #2a of the order. The recipient might be the defendant personally or a friend or relative of the defendant. The day of service is the day the mailing is sent, not received. After the mailing is sent, have the helper or server complete paragraph #1 in the Proof of Service section on the reverse of one of your copies of the Order for Alternate Service (MC 304).

Tacking

When tacking has been ordered, have your helper or server take the service papers and a copy of the Order for Alternate Service (MC 304) to the address indicated at paragraph #2b of the order, and attach them to the front door at this address. The day of service is the day the papers are tacked to the door. After tacking, the helper or server must complete paragraph #2 in the Proof of Service section on the reverse of the copy of the Order for Alternate Service (MC 304) that you're using to prove service.

Household Delivery

To use this service method, your helper or server takes the service papers and a copy of the Order for Alternate Service (MC 304) to the defendant's house and delivers them to any adult living there. The helper or server must also tell that person to give the papers to the defendant. The day of service is the day the papers are delivered to the person in defendant's household. After delivery, the helper or server must prove service on the reverse of your proof of service copy of the Order for Alternate Service (MC 304). In this case, proof of the household delivery is made in paragraph #3 in the Proof of Service section of that paper.

Proof of Service by Mailing, Tacking or Household Delivery

After service by mailing, tacking or household delivery has been proved on the reverse of a copy of the Order for Alternate Service (MC 304), make three copies of this paper, earmark one "FOC" and save another for filing later as your proof of service.

Alternate Service for a Disappeared Defendant

If you don't know the current home or business address of the defendant, you might be able to convince the court that the defendant has disappeared and obtain alternate service by publication or posting. But before you ask for that, you must prove the defendant's disappearance by searching for his/her current home and business addresses.

Your search will be shaped by the information you have about the defendant. If you don't know much, start with one of the general sources of information listed below, moving to specific sources as you find out more.

¶ *Telephone directory.*

- *Telephone books.* If you know the city where the defendant lives, look in the telephone book for that city. Many libraries keep large collections of telephone books.

- *CD-ROMs.* Libraries often have CD-ROMs with all the listed telephone numbers and addresses in the U.S. The two main ones are PhoneDisc and SelectPhone.

- *Internet search/telephone directories.* Many Web browsers have search functions, such as AOL's PeopleConnection, Yahoo's PeopleSearch or MSN's FindPeople. These are basically just compilations of all U.S. telephone directories (minus unlisted numbers). These Web browsers also offer more powerful searches for people, but at a steep price, which isn't always a good value.

You can often find this same information at a telephone directory Web site, such as:

- SwitchBoard.com
- AnyWho.com
- WhitePages.com

¶ *City/suburban directories* Libraries frequently have these "reverse" directories, such as Polk's and Bresser's, which cross-index names, addresses and telephone numbers in various ways (Polk: names, addresses and telephone numbers; Bresser: addresses and telephone numbers). So for example, if you have someone's telephone number, Polk's will give you that person's name and street address. Polk's is also online at www.mrpolk.com.

¶ *Internet search engine.* You can go to an Internet search engine, such as Google, AltaVista, AskJeeves or AlltheWeb, and type in the defendant's name. (If s/he has a common name, put the name inside quotation marks or you'll get too much unsorted information. Also, try variations in the first name.) Your search may reveal information about the defendant from newspaper articles, press releases, etc. Search via several search engines because they have different data.

¶ *News database.* The defendant may have been in the news recently. Check the Web site of the newspaper(s) in the defendant's area. Nexis (also available through Lexis) compiles a lot of this material. Nexis is expensive to subscribe to, but many libraries offer free access. Factiva is another service with similar data.

¶ *Motor vehicle records.* Like most states, Michigan provides information about licensed drivers and vehicle registration/ownership (title). This information isn't given as freely as it used to be (you once could get it over the telephone). Now you have to submit an application and have a good reason to receive the information.

In Michigan, driver's license and motor vehicle registration/ownership information is available from the Secretary of State's record lookup service. Call (517) 322-1624 and ask for a record lookup request form. Information is also available at www.michigan.gov/sos, under the "Services to Businesses" icon. In sec. 4D of the request form, say that you are making the request in connection with a civil proceeding. The fee for the request is $7.

In other states, these requests are typically handled by department of motor vehicles (DMV) offices. The Johnson and Knox book lists all these offices.

¶ *Voter registration.* If the defendant is registered to vote, you can obtain address information from the voting registrar, which is the city or township clerk in Michigan.

Obtain

Find Anyone Fast, 3rd ed., Richard Johnson and Debra Knox, Spartanburg, SC: MIE Publishing, 2001.

This book is loaded with helpful information about finding people, including a list of all 50 state vital records offices, prison locator services, DMV departments and tips for deciphering e-mail addresses.

¶ *Real property records*. The defendant may have been involved in a real property transaction as a seller, buyer, mortgagor (mortgage-borrower), etc. You can get this information from:

- *County register of deeds*. At the register of deeds office there are indexes listing sellers or mortgagors (grantors) and buyers (grantees) of property. Some counties have put this information online; try the Web site of the county where you think the defendant's real property is located.

- Several private Internet companies provide real property information nationwide:
  Public Records Online at www.netronline.com/public_records.htm
  Search Systems at www.searchsystems.net

  Note: Most searches are free, but some require payment; not all counties have put their property records online.

¶ *Association memberships*. If you know or believe the defendant belongs to a trade, professional or social organization, contact the organization for information.

- *Association directories*. These directories list associations which may have directories of members:
  Directories in Print, Detroit: Gale Group, 2004
  Encyclopedia of Associations, Detroit: Gale Group, 2004
  National Trade and Professional Associations of the United States, Buck Downs, et al., eds., Washington, DC: Columbia Books, 2004

- *State licensing bureau*. In Michigan, many trades and professions are regulated by the Bureau of Commercial Services. You can find out if someone is licensed to practice a trade or profession in the state by calling the bureau's licensing verification unit at (517) 241-9427 or go to www.michigan.gov/cis, and select the "Online Services" icon.

¶ *School directories*. If the defendant is a student or faculty member at a school, get the school directory.

Has the defendant graduated from a school? Schools, especially colleges and universities, keep extensive data on their alumni. Contact the school directly for information or try www.alumni.net

¶ *Contact friends, relatives, etc*. Contact the defendant's friends, relatives, former neighbors, landlords and employers to see if they know where s/he is now.

¶ *Parent locator*. Michigan and the federal government have parent locator services which have special access to public records to find missing parents. Contact the friend of the court or the FIA to use these services. You may have to pay a small fee for these services unless you're receiving FIP payments.

¶ *Postal search.* The U.S. Postal Service discontinued the release of change-of-address information. But you can get the equivalent by:

1) Sending a first-class letter to the defendant's last known address. On the envelope, put your return address and just below that write: "Do not forward—Address correction requested"

2) If the defendant has an active change-of-address card on file (they last for one year), the letter will come back to you with the defendant's new address.

The defendant may have special characteristics or circumstances which will influence the search.

¶ *Military servicemember.* If the defendant is an active-duty servicemember, reservist, or veteran, there are special ways to search for the defendant. See "Divorcing a Defendant-Servicemember" on page 217 for more about locating active-duty servicemembers. The Johnson and Knox book on locating military personnel cited on page 216 also has tips on locating reservists and veterans.

¶ *Prisoner.* Do you know or suspect the defendant is an inmate at a state or federal prison? If you do, see "What If My Spouse or I Am Imprisoned?" on page 46 for more about finding prisoners through state and federal prison locator services.

¶ *Homeless person.* As transients, homeless people are naturally difficult to find. But the Salvation Army maintains a list, organized by region, of homeless people. You can request a search after paying a search fee. The Johnson and Knox book cited in this section lists the four regional centers; the Midwest center covering Michigan is:

>The Salvation Army
>Missing Persons Services
>10 W. Algonquin Rd.
>Des Plaines, IL 60016
>(847) 294-2000

¶ *Overseas resident.* If the defendant is overseas, you may be able to find him/her through the U.S. Department of State:

1) Contact the state department's Passport Services Office and see if the defendant's passport contains an overseas destination and maybe even an address. Write the passport services at:

>Passport Services
>Research and Liaison Branch
>111 19th St. NW
>Suite 200
>Washington, DC 20522

2) After you locate the country where the defendant is living, contact the U.S. embassy in that country. The embassy can often request the foreign country to provide the defendant's current address there. For help with these embassy requests, contact the U.S. Department of State at (202) 647-4000. Or you can try locating the defendant yourself in the foreign country using Infobel.com, an international telephone directory.

¶ *Professional search.* If you can afford it, hire a private investigator to find the defendant. They have access to special databases which are very effective. The cost is around $30-200 to do a basic search of five databases. For a PI in your area, look in the yellow pages or ask for a referral from:

Michigan Council of Private Investigators
(800) 266-6274
www.mcpihome.com

National Association of Investigative Specialists
(512) 719-3595
www.pimail.com/nais

During your search for the defendant, keep a written record of when and what you did. For example, if you contact relatives or friends of the defendant, record the date, person with whom you spoke and what s/he said. Keep any written evidence of your attempts to find the defendant, such as return-to-sender letters to him/her or correspondence with others about the defendant's disappearance. All this information is valuable because you will use it later when you apply for alternate service.

If you find the defendant's home and/or business address during your search, attempt service on him/her using one of the regular service methods.* But if you cannot locate the defendant, the failure will show that the defendant has disappeared, allowing you to apply for alternate service by publication or posting.

Complete the top portion of the Motion and Verification for Alternate Service (MC 303) above the Verification of Process Server section, which you can leave blank. Since you're trying to serve a disappeared defendant, complete paragraph #2b of the motion saying that you don't know the defendant's current home and business addresses.

After you complete the Motion and Verification for Alternate Service (MC 303), attach any written materials (undelivered letters, correspondence with the defendant's friends and relatives, etc.) showing that you failed to discover the defendant's whereabouts. Then complete the caption and first two lines of the Order for Service by Publication/Posting and Notice of Action (MC 307). After you prepare these papers, return to the clerk with:

---

*   If you discover the defendant's current home or business address, but fail to have him/her served there, see above on serving an elusive defendant.

- Motion and Verification for Alternate Service   MC 303
  - original
  - two copies (one earmarked "FOC")

- Order for Service by Publication/Posting and Notice of Ac-   MC 307
  tion
  - original

- $20 motion fee

File the Motion and Verification for Alternate Service (MC 303) and the friend of the court's copy with the clerk. After filing, go to your judge's office and submit a copy of the Motion and Verification for Alternate Service (MC 303) and the original Order for Service by Publication/Posting and Notice of Action (MC 307) to the judge's secretary. The judge will review your motion in his/her office (although probably not while you wait), so a court hearing on the motion won't be necessary. If the judge grants your motion for alternate service, get the papers back from the judge's office, make three photocopies of the Order for Service by Publication/Posting and Notice of Action (MC 307) and earmark one "FOC." Return to the clerk and file the original and the friend of the court's copy.

Examine the Order for Service by Publication/Posting and Notice of Action (MC 307) to see which method of alternate service the judge has devised for the defendant. It's probably either publication (paragraph #2) or posting (paragraph #3), and possibly a registered mailing (paragraph #4). If registered mailing has been ordered, make an extra photocopy of the Order for Service by Publication/Posting and Notice of Action (MC 307).

Publication

If the judge has ordered publication as the alternate service in your case, you must publish a legal advertisement in a newspaper. Maybe you have seen fine-print legal advertisements in your local newspaper. This is the kind of ad you must have published.

The court rules say that the legal advertisement must be published in a newspaper in the county where the defendant resides when you know the defendant's residence. If you don't know where the defendant is residing, the court rules permit advertisement in the county where the case is filed. Since your defendant has disappeared, you can advertise in the county where you filed for divorce, which is probably your county.

See which newspaper the judge has chosen as the publisher of your advertisement in paragraph #2 of the Order for Service by Publication/Posting and Notice of Action (MC 307). Take/send a copy of the MC 307 to that newspaper and ask it to prepare a legal advertisement for you. The newspaper will create an advertisement using the caption and paragraph #1 of the Order for Service by Publication/Posting and Notice of Action (MC 307). It will publish the advertisement as instructed in paragraph #2 of the order. Ordinarily, publication must be once a week for three consecutive weeks.

Once the advertisement has been published the required number of times, the newspaper will bill you for the cost of publication.* After you pay the bill, the newspaper will complete the Affidavit of Publishing on the reverse of the copy of the Order for Service by Publication/Posting and Notice of Action (MC 307) that you gave it and return this paper to you.

If the defendant's last known address is out of date, the judge will probably omit registered mailing of the service papers to the defendant. But if the defendant's last known address is fairly recent, mailing may be required.

If the judge has ordered registered mailing, have a helper mail the service papers and a copy of the Order for Service by Publication/Posting and Notice of Action (MC 307) to the defendant at his/her last known address. This mailing must be by registered (not certified) mail, return receipt requested. The mailing must be sent sometime before the date of the last publication of the legal advertisement.

Afterward, have your helper complete the Affidavit of Mailing on the reverse of a copy of the Order for Service by Publication/Posting and Notice of Action (MC 307), and attach both the Receipt for Registered Mail (PS Form 3806) and the Domestic Return Receipt (PS Form 3811), signed or unsigned by the defendant, to it. Your helper can use the Affidavit of Mailing on the same copy of the Order for Service by Publication/Posting and Notice of Action (MC 307) that the newspaper used to prove publication, or you can use another copy. Either way, make three copies of the reverse of the order(s), mark "FOC" on one copy and save another for filing later as your proof of service.

Posting

Judges seem to prefer publication as the method of alternate service for disappeared defendants, and posting is seldom ordered. But if posting was ordered in your Order for Service by Publication/Posting and Notice of Action (MC 307), look at paragraph #3 to see who was designated as the poster. That person might be a sheriff, policeman or court official, such as a bailiff. Take four copies of the Order for Service by Publication/Posting and Notice of Action (MC 307) to the person designated as the poster and request posting of the order.

The poster will post the order in the courthouse and the two other public places the court has specified in paragraph #3. Ordinarily, the order will

---

*   The cost of your advertisement depends on its size and the frequency of publication. Since you really only need to publish the caption and paragraph #1 of the Order for Service by Publication/Posting and Notice of Action (MC 307), your advertisement should not be very large. The newspaper may want to print the entire order, but that is unnecessary and will cost you more. Your advertisement will probably be published three times. In that case, there is a minimum charge of around $45, but the cost will probably be slightly more, perhaps $50-100.

remain posted for three consecutive weeks. After the posting period expires, the poster will bill you for posting services and prove the posting in the Affidavit of Posting on the reverse of the extra copy of the Order for Service by Publication/Posting and Notice of Action (MC 307).

Like alternate service by publication, alternate service by posting can be with or without registered mailing of the service papers to the defendant. If the judge has ordered registered mailing in paragraph #4 of the Order for Service by Publication/Posting and Notice of Action (MC 307), have your helper mail the service papers and a copy of the MC 307 to the defendant at his/her last known address. This mailing should be made by registered (not certified) mail, return receipt requested. The mailing must be sent sometime before the last week of the posting.

Afterward, have your helper complete the Affidavit of Mailing on the reverse of a copy of the Order for Service by Publication/Posting and Notice of Action (MC 307), and attach both the Receipt for Registered Mail (PS Form 3806) and the Domestic Return Receipt (PS Form 3811), signed or unsigned by the defendant, to it. Your helper can complete the Affidavit of Mailing on the same copy of the Order for Service by Publication/Posting and Notice of Action (MC 307) that the poster used to prove posting, or you can use another copy. Either way, make three copies of the reverse of the order(s), mark "FOC" on one copy and save another for filing later as your proof of service.

Original · Court
1st copy · Serving party
2nd copy · Extra

Approved, SCAO

STATE OF MICHIGAN JUDICIAL DISTRICT JUDICIAL CIRCUIT	MOTION AND VERIFICATION FOR ALTERNATE SERVICE	CASE NO.
		Court telephone no.

Court address

Plaintiff name(s), address(es), and telephone number(s)		Defendant name(s), address(es), and telephone number(s)
	v	

1. Service of process upon __DUDLEY E. LOVELACE__ cannot reasonably be made as otherwise provided in MCR 2.105, as shown in the following verification of process server.

2. Defendant's last known home and business addresses are:

__900 S. MAPLE__   __LAKE CITY__   __MI__   __48800__
Home address   City   State   Zip

__1000 SERVICE RD.__   "   "   "
Business address   City   State   Zip

a. I believe the ☒ home / ☒ business address shown above is current.

> COMPLETE 2a.
> FOR AN
> ELUSIVE
> DEFENDANT

> COMPLETE 2b.
> INSTEAD FOR A
> DISAPPEARED
> DEFENDANT

b. I do not know defendant's current ☒ home / ☒ business address. I have made the following efforts to ascertain the current address: __3-4-89 SEARCHED TELEPHONE AND CITY DIRECTORIES/__ __3-7-89 REQUESTED ADDRESS CORRECTION FROM USPS/3-7-89 DID RECORD LOOKUP AT MICHIGAN SECRETARY OF STATE/3-7-89 WROTE TO MABEL LOVELACE (MOTHER)(SEE ATTACHED LETTER); ALL WITHOUT RESULTS.__

3. I request the court order service by alternate means.

I declare that the statements above are true to the best of my information, knowledge and belief.

__3-15-89__   __Darlene A. Lovelace__
Date   Attorney signature

Address   Attorney name (type or print)   Bar no.

City, state, zip   Telephone no.

VERIFICATION OF PROCESS SERVER

1. I have tried to serve process on this defendant as described: State date, place, and what occurred on each occasion

__3-4-89__ TRIED TO SERVE DEFENDANT AT 900 S. MAPLE, LAKE CITY, MI, BUT A WOMAN THERE TOLD ME DEFENDANT WAS NOT AT HOME WHEN IT APPEARED HE WAS.

__3-5-89__ "   "

__3-7-89__ TRIED TO SERVE DEFENDANT AT 1000 SERVICE RD, LAKE CITY, MI, BUT HIS EMPLOYER PREVENTED SERVICE.

__3-8-89__ TRIED TO SERVE DEFENDANT AT 1000 SERVICE RD, LAKE CITY, MI, BUT HE SPED AWAY IN HIS CAR.

I declare that the statements above are true to the best of my information, knowledge and belief.

__3-14-89__   __Chester Gunn__
Date   Signature

                                                              CHESTER GUNN
                                                              Process Server (type or print)

> SERVER MUST
> COMPLETE VERIFICATION
> OF PROCESS SERVER FOR
> ATTEMPTED SERVICE ON
> AN ELUSIVE DEFENDANT

TION FOR ALTERNATE SERVICE   MCR 2.105

Approved, SCAO

STATE OF MICHIGAN		Original - Court
JUDICIAL DISTRICT	ORDER FOR ALTERNATE SERVICE	1st copy - Defendant
JUDICIAL CIRCUIT		2nd copy - Plaintiff
		3rd copy - Return

Court address   CASE NO.

Plaintiff name(s), address(es), and telephone no.(s)   Court telephone no.

Defendant name(s), address(es), and telephone no.(s)

v

Plaintiff's attorney, bar no., address, and telephone no.

THE COURT FINDS:

1. Service of process upon defendant ___DUDLEY E. LOVELACE___

cannot reasonably be made as provided in MCR 2.105, and service of process may be made in a manner which is reasonably calculated to give defendant actual notice of the proceedings and an opportunity to be heard.

IT IS ORDERED:

2. Service of the summons and complaint and a copy of this order may be made by the following method(s):

a. ☒ First class mail to ___900 S. MAPLE, LAKE CITY, MI___

b. ☒ Tacking or firmly affixing to the door at ___"___

c. ☒ Delivering at ___"___

to a member of defendant's household who is of suitable age and discretion to receive process, with instructions to deliver it promptly to defendant.

d. ☐ Other: ___

JUDGE WILL CHOOSE ONE OR MORE OF THESE METHODS

3. For each method used, proof of service must be filed promptly with the court.

___3-17-89___
Date

___Lester Jubbs___
Judge   Bar no.

MC 304 (3/00) ORDER FOR ALTERNATE SERVICE

MCR 2.103, MCR 2.105

PROOF OF SERVICE

I served a copy of the summons and complaint and a copy of the order for alternate service upon

DUDLEY E. LOVELACE _____ , on SAT. 3-18-89
                                                                Date

1. First class mail to _900 S. MAPLE, LAKE CITY, MI_____ , on SAT. 3-18-89
                                                                Date

2. Tacking or firmly affixing to the door at _____ " _____ , on MON. 3-20-89
                                                                Date

3. Delivering at _____ suitable age and discretion to receive process, with instructions to deliver

   to a member of _____

   it prompt_ly to defe_____

4. Other: _____ , on _____
                                                                Date

_3-21-89_   _Ruth Darling_____
Date   Signature

Service fee	Miles traveled	Mileage fee	Total fee
$		$	$

                                                    Title

Subscribed and sworn to before me on _3-21-89_   _OJIBWAY_____ County, Michigan.
                                      Date

My commission expires: _1-1-90_   Signature: _Loretta Smiley_____
                        Date   Deputy court clerk/Notary public

DAY OF SERVICE

HELPER/SERVER MUST PROVE EVERY SERVICE METHOD ORDERED AND USED

IF SEVERAL SERVICE METHODS WERE USED ON DIFFERENT DAYS, USE LAST DAY AS DAY OF SERVICE (3-20-89 IN THIS CASE)

Approved, SCAO

STATE OF MICHIGAN JUDICIAL DISTRICT JUDICIAL CIRCUIT	ORDER FOR SERVICE BY PUBLICATION/POSTING AND NOTICE OF ACTION	Original - Court 2nd copy - Moving party 1st copy - Defendant 3rd copy - Return CASE NO.

Court address

Plaintiff name(s) and address(es)

v

Defendant name(s) and address(es)

Court telephone no.

Plaintiff's attorney, bar no., address, and telephone no.

TO: _DUDLEY E. LOVELACE_

COMPLETE THIS LINE

JUDGE WILL COMPLETE REST OF ORDER

IT IS ORDERED:

1. You are being sued by plaintiff in this court to _OBTAIN A JUDGMENT OF DIVORCE_

permitted by law in this court at the court address above on or before _6-1-89_ . You must file your answer or take other action
Date
so, a default judgment may be entered against you for the relief demanded in the complaint filed in this case. If you

JUDGE WILL CHOOSE EITHER PUBLICATION OR POSTING

2. A copy of this order shall be published once each week in _OJIBWAY NEWS_
☒ three consecutive weeks,   Name of publication
for ☐ _____ , and proof of publication shall be filed in this court.

3. _CHESTER GUNN_
Name
at _100 S. MAIN, LAKE CITY, MI_ shall post a copy of this order in the courthouse, and
Location
at _201 W. LAKE, LAKE CITY, MI_ and
Location
☒ three continuous weeks,
for ☐ _____ , and shall file proof of posting in this court.

4. A copy of this order shall be sent to _DUDLEY E. LOVELACE_
Name

MAILING MAY OR MAY NOT BE ORDERED TO GO ALONG WITH PUBLICATION OR POSTING

__ receipt requested, before the ☒ date of the last publication,   at the last known address
☒ last week of posting,   and the affidavit of mailing shall be

_3-17-89_
Date

Lester Tubbs
Judge   Bar no.

MC 307 (8/88) ORDER FOR SERVICE BY PUBLICATION/POSTING AND NOTICE OF ACTION

MCR 2.106

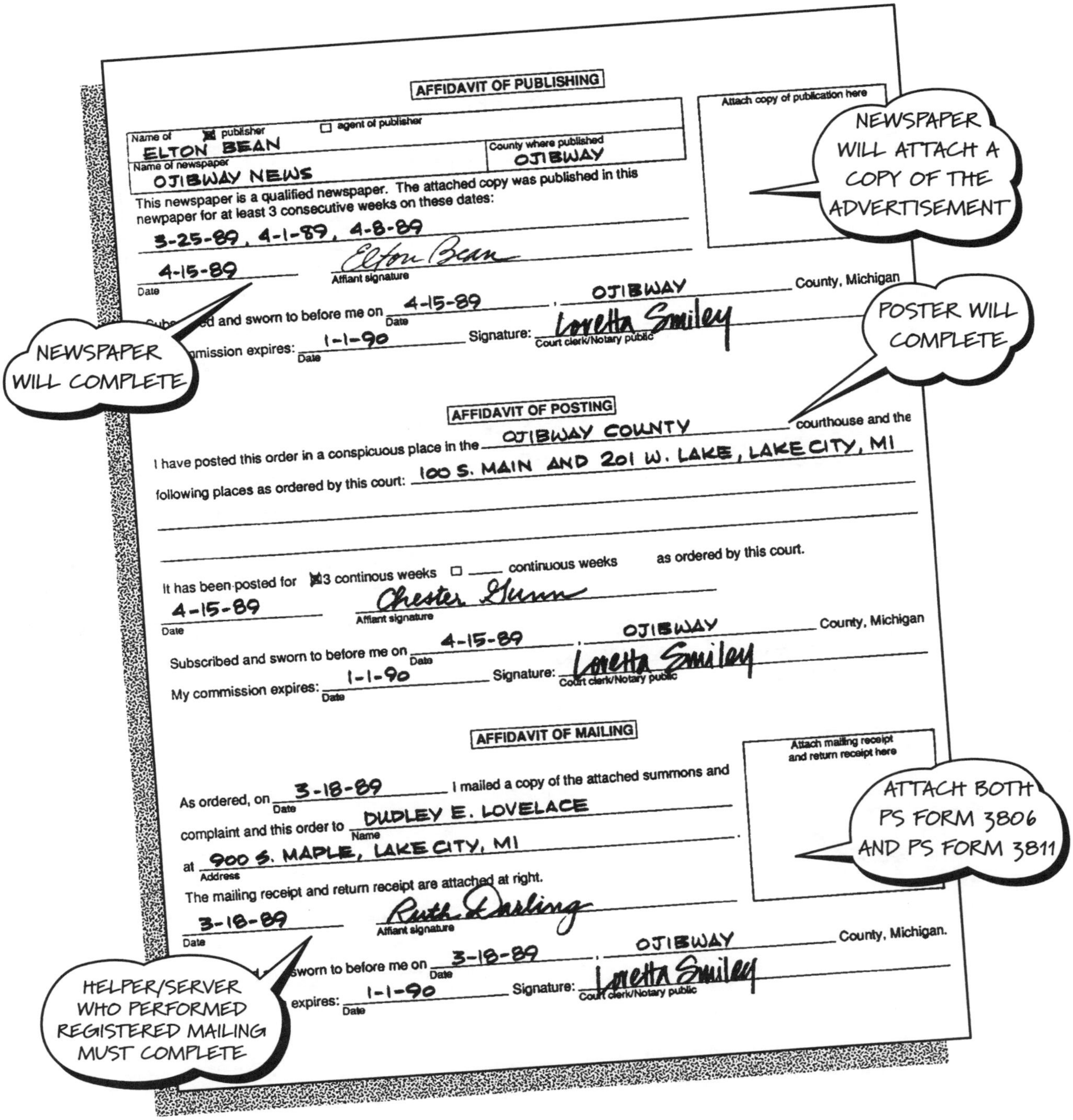

AFFIDAVIT OF PUBLISHING

Name of ☒ publisher ☐ agent of publisher
ELTON BEAN
County where published
OJIBWAY
Name of newspaper
OJIBWAY NEWS

This newspaper is a qualified newspaper. The attached copy was published in this newpaper for at least 3 consecutive weeks on these dates:
3-25-89, 4-1-89, 4-8-89

4-15-89 — Date
Elton Bean — Affiant signature

Attach copy of publication here

OJIBWAY County, Michigan
...ed and sworn to before me on 4-15-89 (Date)
...mission expires: 1-1-90 (Date)
Signature: Loretta Smiley — Court clerk/Notary public

AFFIDAVIT OF POSTING

I have posted this order in a conspicuous place in the OJIBWAY COUNTY courthouse and the following places as ordered by this court: 100 S. MAIN AND 201 W. LAKE, LAKE CITY, MI

It has been posted for ☒ 3 continous weeks ☐ ____ continuous weeks as ordered by this court.

4-15-89 — Date
Chester Gunn — Affiant signature

OJIBWAY County, Michigan
Subscribed and sworn to before me on 4-15-89 (Date)
My commission expires: 1-1-90 (Date)
Signature: Loretta Smiley — Court clerk/Notary public

AFFIDAVIT OF MAILING

Attach mailing receipt and return receipt here

As ordered, on 3-18-89 (Date) I mailed a copy of the attached summons and complaint and this order to DUDLEY E. LOVELACE (Name)
at 900 S. MAPLE, LAKE CITY, MI (Address).
The mailing receipt and return receipt are attached at right.

3-18-89 — Date
Ruth Darling — Affiant signature

OJIBWAY County, Michigan.
...sworn to before me on 3-18-89 (Date)
...expires: 1-1-90 (Date)
Signature: Loretta Smiley — Court clerk/Notary public

Appendix E: Giving Special Notice of Your Divorce

In most divorce cases with minor children, only the friend of the court, prosecuting attorney and defendant are entitled to notice of the divorce. However, you must give special notice of your divorce in two special situations: 1) when someone other than you or the defendant (a non-parent third party) has physical custody of your minor children 2) when a minor child of yours is subject to a continuing prior custody and/or parenting time case in Michigan.*

Special Notice to a Third Party with Custody

Sometimes parents informally give physical custody of their minor children to family or friends. In other cases, parents may lose physical custody of their minor children by court order during independent third-party custody, paternity, juvenile delinquency, protective (abuse/neglect or dependency), guardianship, mental commitment or adoption cases.** If any of these things has happened to you, so that a third party has physical custody of your

---

* When your minor child(ren) is involved in a continuing prior custody and/or parenting time case in a court outside of Michigan, there could be a lack of Michigan jurisdiction for the custody and parenting time issues of your divorce (see the footnote in "Can I Get a Divorce in Michigan?" on page 43 for more about this possibility).

** If one of these cases has resulted in full termination of your parental rights, the children may no longer be yours (see "Which Children Must Be Included in My Divorce?" on page 51). On the other hand, it's possible to lose custody of children without losing full parental rights.

children (this fact should have been noted in paragraph #6 of your Uniform Child Custody Jurisdiction Enforcement Act Affidavit (MC 416)), the third-party custodian is entitled to special notice of your divorce.

The purpose of the notice is to let the third party know that a divorce has been filed which might result in a return of custody to you or the defendant. Recent court decisions have curtailed third-party custody rights, and to prevail in a custody dispute a third party must prove parental unfitness. As a result, the third party's odds of gaining custody are small, but they must be notified anyway.

When special notice is due, you should give it during the "Service" step of your divorce. To give this notice, prepare an extra set of service papers and have them served on the third party by service by mail or delivery, as described in "Service" on page 99. Have that service proved on the reverse of an extra copy of the Summons and Complaint (MC 01), and file it and a friend of the court's copy with the clerk. Finally, if the third party received custody of your children during a prior court proceeding, you might also have to give special notice to the court and court officials, as described below.

Special Notice to a Prior Court

The divorce court will almost always determine the issues of custody, parenting time and residence of children in divorce cases with minor children. When another court has already decided these issues in a prior case, the divorce court's decision could possibly upset the prior court's decision. The divorce court is permitted to make a new custody, parenting time and residence order—it isn't bound by the prior court's decision—but special notice of the divorce must sometimes be given to the prior court letting it know that its order is being replaced.

You don't need to give special notice to a prior court in every case. Notice is due only when the prior court is: 1) a Michigan court, which 2) made a custody, parenting time and/or residence of children order about minor children 3) in a case that is "continuing." Examples of these cases include independent third-party custody or parenting time, paternity, juvenile delinquency, protective (abuse/neglect or dependency), guardianship, mental commitment or adoption cases. Your affirmative response to paragraph #4 or 5 of the Uniform Child Custody Jurisdiction Enforcement Act Affidavit (MC 416) is a tip-off that a prior court has made the kind of order triggering special notice.

Nevertheless, the prior court is only entitled to notice if the case is continuing; if the prior case is over, no notice is due. For example, let's assume that while you were living in another Michigan county your 14-year-old child committed a crime and was returned to you for two-year home probation after a juvenile delinquency proceeding in family court. In this instance, the family court and several officials must get special notice of your divorce during the two-year probationary period since the case is continuing. But after expiration of the two-year probation, the family court in the other county wouldn't be due notice because the juvenile delinquency case is no longer continuing.

When you're in doubt about the status of a prior case involving your minor children, call the court and ask. If you're still confused, send the special notice anyway since it's usually better to give an unnecessary notice than fail to give one that's required.

If you must give special notice of your divorce to a prior court, do it in the middle of your divorce, after your schedule your final hearing. Don't wait too long because the notice must be sent *at least 21 days before the final hearing*.

To give the special notice, prepare the Notice to Prior Court of Proceedings Affecting Minor(s) (MC 28), and make four photocopies. Send copies of the notice to the: 1) clerk or register of the prior court 2) the friend of the court, juvenile officer and/or prosecuting attorney involved in the prior case.

Afterward, file the Notice to Prior Court of Proceedings Affecting Minor(s) (MC 28) and the friend of the court copy with the clerk of the court where your divorce is filed. In addition, if the prior court gave physical custody of the children to someone other than you or the defendant, you might also have to give special notice to that third-party custodian, as described above.

At the end of the divorce, the clerk is supposed to send the prior court a copy of the Judgment of Divorce (GRP 4). You may want to check with the clerk to make sure the judgment is sent.

Original - Originating court
Copies as needed
OSM CODE: NPC

Approved, SCAO

STATE OF MICHIGAN JUDICIAL CIRCUIT PROBATE COURT COUNTY	NOTICE TO PRIOR COURT OF PROCEEDINGS AFFECTING MINOR(S)	CASE NO.
		Court telephone no.

Court address

Name(s) of parent(s)/guardian(s)/plaintiff/defendant	Name(s), alias(es), and dates of birth of minor(s)
DARLENE A. LOVELACE DUDLEY E. LOVELACE	DUANE WESLEY LOVELACE 6-1-86

Case no. of other court

TO: County of _SUPERIOR CIRCUIT COURT - FAMILY DIVISION_
  ☒ Court Clerk or Register
  ☐ Friend of the Court
  ☒ Prosecuting Attorney
  ☒ Juvenile Officer

NOTICE:

1. ☒ a. A complaint/petition/motion was filed with this court that affects the ~~...~~ nuing

   jurisdiction of your court. A hearing on the complaint/petition/moti~~on~~

   _9-7-89_
   Date
   _9:00 A.M._
   Time
   COURTROOM OF JUDGE TUBBS
   Location

   ☐ b. The attached order was entered on _____
                                          Date

2. The actions of the court in this matter may supersede part or all of the order(s) previously entered by your court as the best interests of the minor(s) require.

(INSERT DATE, TIME AND PLACE OF THE FINAL HEARING)

CERTIFICATE OF MAILING

I certify that on this date I mailed a copy of this notice to the prior court by first class mail.

_6-15-89_   _Darlene A. Lovelace_
Date   Signature

Note: If item 1. a. is checked, this notice must be mailed at least 21 days prior to hearing.

Do not write below this line - For court use only

MCL 712A.2(b)(2), MCL 712A.3a, MCR 3.205, MCR 5.112, MCR 3.92

MC 28 (9/03) NOTICE TO PRIOR COURT OF PROCEEDINGS AFFECTING MINOR(S)

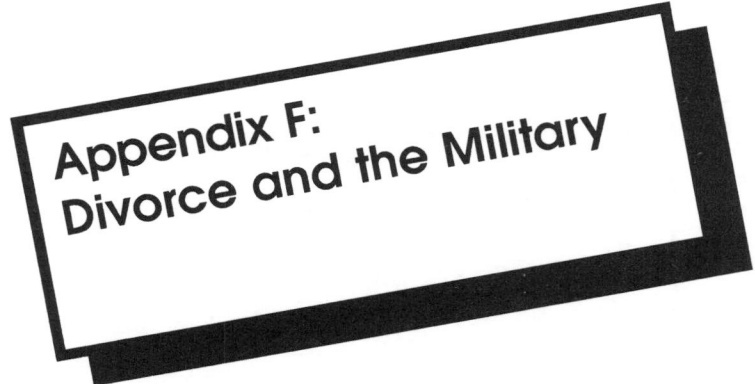

Appendix F: Divorce and the Military

Divorce by or against a spouse in active-duty military service creates several special problems. Right away, there can be practical problems with locating and serving papers on the servicemember who may be stationed at a distant military base. The military has its own retirement plan and health care system which are unlike civilian ones and are often difficult to navigate. The military also has special benefits, like PX and commissary, that can be divided during divorce.

Military Relief Laws

By far the biggest problem posed by a divorce with a military spouse are the state and federal military relief laws protecting active-duty servicemembers. These relief laws protect both plaintiffs and defendants serving in the military. But they're a bigger problem for plaintiffs filing against defendant-servicemembers, as the following sections explain.

Federal Soldiers' and Sailors' Civil Relief Act of 1940 (SSCRA)

The federal SSCRA, which has the widest scope, covers servicemembers in the active duty of the U.S. military (see the sidebox for which personnel are covered by the SSCRA). The act offers several forms of relief to servicemembers protecting them from some kinds of debts, taxes, installment contracts, lawsuits, etc. The intent of the SSCRA is to protect servicemembers from these obligations so they can focus on their military duties.

More Information

The SSCRA covers all five service branches of the U. S. military:

- **Army**
- **Navy**
- **Marine Corps**
- **Air Force**
- **Coast Guard**

The act also covers officers of the Public Health Service assigned to duty with the Army and Navy.

The SSCRA protects servicemembers in the *active duty* of the U.S. military which are made up of two components:

Active component. Members of regular units (Regular Army, Regular Navy, etc.).

Reserve component. Servicemembers *activated* from the two segments of the military reserve:

- *Reserves*. Each service branch has its own reserve units (Army Reserve (Army), Naval Reserve (Navy), etc.).
- *National Guard*. State Army National Guard (attached to the Army) and Air National Guard (attached to the Air Force) units, including Michigan's army and air units.

Reservists are ordered to active duty selectively (call-up) for training, discipline or operations. Reservists can also be activated (mobilized), usually in unit strength, by the president in various ways (selective, partial, full or total mobilization) for a national emergency, such as war.

The SSCRA protects servicemembers lawfully away from active duty, such as during a period of leave or hospitalization.

The act covers military inductees (after receiving induction orders) and even pre-inductees who are receiving training or education preparing them for induction.

The SSCRA sometimes covers servicemembers' dependents, but not from lawsuits which is the focus here.

The act doesn't apply to civilians working for the military.

It's the lawsuit relief protections of the SSCRA that have an impact divorce. In essence, these protections shield servicemembers from hard-to-handle lawsuits, including divorces. There are two main lawsuit relief remedies:

Stay. During a lawsuit, a servicemember can ask for a stay or freezing of the case if s/he is serving outside the state where the lawsuit was filed. The court must grant the stay unless the member's ability to participate in the case isn't "materially affected" by military service. The length of the stay is up to the court, but it can last no more than 90 days beyond the end of military service. Typically, a stay will last only until the servicemember can get leave so s/he can deal with the lawsuit.

Reopening a default judgment. If a servicemember doesn't participate in the lawsuit, and a default judgment is ultimately issued, s/he can ask for reopening of the case. The request must be made no later than 90 days after the servicemember leaves military service. Reopening isn't guaranteed; the member must have a good defense and show that military service impaired his/her ability to take part in the case.

The SSCRA's lawsuit relief remedies are really designed for different situations. But sometimes a servicemember can use both remedies; other times using one means loss of the other. The SSCRA also allows a servicemember to waive (give up) these relief protections. The chart on the opposite page explains how these remedies fit together.

During peacetime, the SSCRA's lawsuit relief protections seldom totally bar a divorce against a servicemember. At a minimum, the act requires a little extra paperwork and the divorce can go through as smoothly as one against a civilian. At most, the divorce will be frozen until the servicemember can respond, either by obtaining leave or by separation from the service.

In a war, the SSCRA's stay remedy may be extended. For example, during the Persian Gulf War in 1990-91, SSCRA stays were expanded effectively freezing all lawsuits against active-duty servicemembers until after the war. This kind of total-but-temporary freeze could be used again in a future war or crisis.

SSCRA Lawsuit Relief Rights

	Right to request stay	**Right to request reopening of default judgment**
Defendant signs a waiver of SSCRA rights	No	No
Defendant asks court for a stay or other relief	Yes	No
Defendant doesn't respond:		
open case	Court may appoint a GAL,* who can ask for a stay or other relief	Yes
closed case	(2) Yes, if case is reopened	(1) Yes, then may ask for a stay

* GAL = *guardian ad litem*

Michigan Military Relief Law

Many people don't know it, but Michigan has a military relief law similar to the SSCRA. The state law covers Michigan National Guardmembers in active duty (see the sidebox for the extent of the law's coverage). Like the federal law, Michigan's law offers protection from some debt collection, foreclosures, utility shutoffs and lawsuits.

Unlike the SSCRA, Michigan's relief law offers absolute protection from lawsuits, without regard to hardship for the servicemember. After activation of guardmembers, Michigan's law effectively freezes lawsuits against them until termination of their active-duty service for the state.

More Information

Michigan's military relief law covers members in Michigan's two National Guard units:

- **Army National Guard**
- **Air National Guard**

The law protects guardmembers in *active duty* for more than seven days after activation by the governor: 1) to support civilian authority (such as during a riot, flood, etc.) 2) for a war or emergency of the state or nation.

The protections of the law extend beyond the period of active duty for some things, but not for lawsuit relief which is the focus here.

Note: Other states have similar military relief laws protecting their National Guardmembers which could be an issue if a party is in the active duty of an out-of-state unit.

Divorce by a Plaintiff-Servicemember

More Information

It can be difficult to find the address of active-duty servicemembers. But there are several resources that can help. For good general information, get:

How to Locate Anyone Who Is or Has Been in the Military: Armed Forces Locator Guide, 8th ed., Richard Johnson and Debra Knox, Spartanburg, SC: MIE Publishing, 1999, available from the publisher at (800) 937-2133 or through www.militaryusa.com.

If you know where the defendant is stationed, call the base locator (often just the information operator at the base). The Johnson and Knox book has a list of base locators telephone numbers for all military installations in the U.S. and worldwide. Besides finding the defendant, the base locator can also provide information about contacting the defendant's commanding officer for carrying out service.

When you know the defendant's service branch, contact the locator service for that branch. If you don't know which branch the defendant is serving in, contact all the military locators.

To make a location request, you need the defendant's full name and date of birth or social security number; other information like rank, service number and last duty assignment is helpful. The locators charge fees for requests, but these are sometimes waived for family member-requesters.

For convenience, a locator request form is included in this book: the Military Locator Request. This form addresses the five military locators and lists the fees they charge. If you're making multiple requests, photocopy extras as needed.

Send your locator requests to the military locators with the fees and a self-addressed stamped envelope. You will typically receive a response within a few weeks.

One problem with all the military locators is that they typically won't release current military addresses or duty assignments of troops overseas, aboard ships or in combat, for security reasons. You may be able to get around this problem if you know the overseas base or ship with the defendant. The Johnson and Knox book cited above has lists of all overseas military installations and Navy and Coast Guard ships and home ports. The book has suggestions about improvising addresses to servicemembers overseas or at sea using APO (American post office) and FPO (foreign post office) addresses.

You might get lucky and contact the defendant that way. If not, you will have to use a form of alternate service (see Appendix D for more about alternate service). Be sure to attach the (failed) locator response(s) to your motion for alternate service. The alternate service may involve service on the defendant's relatives who probably have his/her address.

Before filing, a plaintiff-servicemember must decide where to file. Choosing the correct state is known as jurisdiction (see "Can I Get a Divorce in Michigan?" on page 43 about jurisdiction), while choice of county inside Michigan is called venue (venue rules are covered in "Can I File the Divorce in My County?" on page 45). Both jurisdiction and venue are based on residence, or one's permanent home.

Special residence rules apply to military servicemembers. Ordinarily, servicemembers keep their pre-enlistment state and county residence. So if you were a Michigan resident before enlistment, you're still a resident of Michigan and your home county regardless of where you are stationed now. You may then file either in your old home county or the Michigan county where the defendant is residing now. If you have lost your Michigan residence, you must file in the Michigan county where the defendant lives.

Wherever you file, you can file by mail and have the divorce papers served by any of the service methods. Later on, other papers can be filed by mail and the divorce conducted long-distance.

The SSCRA protects whichever party—plaintiff or defendant—is in active-duty military service. A military plaintiff wouldn't invoke the act to block his/her own divorce, so the SSCRA seldom becomes an issue when the plaintiff is the servicemember.

There is one instance in which a plaintiff-servicemember might use the stay remedy of the act. At the end of the divorce, you must attend a final hearing in court and give brief testimony for the Judgment of Divorce. To make this appearance, you may need to obtain leave to return home. If leave can be arranged, the SSCRA will be satisfied and the divorce can be completed normally. But if you can't coordinate your leave with the court's hearing schedule, you could invoke the act's stay remedy and ask for rescheduling of the final hearing to coincide with your leave.

Divorcing a Defendant-Servicemember

Before you begin the divorce, choose the correct state (this choice is known as jurisdiction, and is covered in "Can I Get a Divorce in Michigan?" on page 43) and county (choice of county is known as venue; see "Can I File the Divorce in My County?" on page 45 for venue rules) for filing. Both jurisdiction and venue are based on residence, or one's permanent home.

There are special residence rules for servicemembers which can affect jurisdiction and venue. Ordinarily, servicemembers keep their pre-enlistment state and county residence, no matter how far away they are stationed now. So if the defendant resided in Michigan with you during your marriage just before entry into the service, there should be full Michigan jurisdiction.

For convenience, you will probably file in the Michigan county where you live now. But you may have another choice: defendant's pre-enlistment home county, since his/her residence continues there during the period of military service.

Before you can have the divorce papers served, you must know where the defendant is stationed. If you've lost touch, there are ways to find military personnel through a military locator service. The sidebox explains how to contact a base locator (when you know where the defendant is stationed) or a service branch locator (when you lack specific information).

The best way to serve a military spouse is by mail, since the U.S. Postal Service delivers mail (including certified mail necessary for service) to military bases all over the world. Military mail overseas can be a little slow, so allow extra time for service outside the country. See "Service" on page 99 for more about serving by mail and by the other service methods.

If a defendant is stationed at a stateside military base and refuses to accept mailed service, contact the sheriff or a commercial process server in the county and arrange for service by delivery. Military personnel living off base can be served at home without a problem. But except for the Air Force, most service branches don't allow process servers to enter military bases and serve servicemembers there directly. Instead, the defendant-servicemember's commanding officer sets up a time and place for service, if the member agrees to accept the papers; if s/he refuses service, the commanding officer notifies the server of the refusal. Sheriffs and commercial process servers in areas with military bases should be familiar with these service procedures.

Oddly, service can be easier at a military base in a foreign country. Overseas, commanding officers can carry out service, but are discouraged from acting as actual process servers. As a compromise, you can contact the

---

More Information

About military retirement benefits, health care coverage and other benefits (such as PX and commissary) available to a divorced non-military spouse, order for $10 the booklet "A Guide for Military Separation or Divorce" from:

Ex-Partners of Servicemembers for Equality (Ex-Pose)
P.O. Box 11191
Alexandria, VA 22312
(703) 941-5844

About division of military retirement pay from a servicemember's point of view, get:

Divorce and the Military II: A Comprehensive Guide for Service Members, Spouses, and Attorneys, 2nd ed., Marsha L. Thole and Frank W. Ault, Redlands, CA: The American Retirees Association, 2001

defendant's commander and suggest service by acknowledgment (see "Service by Acknowledgment" on page 101 for instructions). The commander can hand the service papers to the defendant, and ask for acknowledgment of service. If the defendant refuses service, the commanding officer cannot force service, and will notify you of the refusal.

Satisfying the Military Relief Laws

After service, you must come to grips with the military relief laws. If the defendant is protected by Michigan's military relief law, or if the SSCRA has put a temporary ban on all lawsuits, you can only proceed with a waiver from the defendant (see below on getting a waiver).

But typically, the defendant will be protected by the SSCRA's lawsuit relief remedies (stay and default judgment reopening). As explained before, these are flexible remedies which often allow divorces to go through. Here are several typical scenarios where the SSCRA is satisfied and the divorce can be completed.

Waiver of Military Relief Laws by the Defendant

As with other legal rights, a defendant-servicemember can voluntarily waive (give up) his/her lawsuit relief rights provided by the military relief laws. The waiver cuts off these rights, allowing the divorce to go through normally.

Waiver is the only way to satisfy Michigan's military relief law and the SSCRA when it has imposed a temporary wartime freeze on lawsuits. But even if the SSCRA applies in its normal peacetime form, waiver always makes it easier for the divorce to proceed.

If the defendant is willing to waive, send the Waiver of Military Relief Law Rights (GRP 6) to the defendant and have him/her sign the form. After you get the GRP 6 back, attach the form to the Default (GRP 2) as described in "Default and the Military Relief Laws" on page 113.

The Defendant Seeks a SSCRA Stay

After receiving the divorce papers, the defendant may contact the court and ask for a stay or other relief under the SSCRA. The defendant may ask for this personally, with the help of a legal assistance lawyer, which the military provides, or through a privately-retained lawyer. A stay request may be informal, such as a letter from the servicemember to the court, or a formal motion filed by the defendant's lawyer. In some cases, the court can even issue a stay on its own.

In considering a request for a stay, the judge must determine if the defendant's military service has a material effect on the servicemember's ability to participate in the case. Courts have defined material effect in terms of two main factors:

Financial hardship. Courts want to know if military service has caused a financial hardship for the servicemember, which has impaired the ability to respond. Military service often means a loss of income and extra financial obligations. On the other hand, some large employers make up the difference in pay and offer extra benefits to activated employees, resulting in no net loss of income. Under- or unemployed servicemembers may actually see an increase in income from military service.

Geographical distance. This is probably the most important factor. If the defendant-servicemember is at sea or stationed overseas, a good argument can be made that military service is hampering the defendant in the case. On the other hand, leave can cancel distance, since the servicemember can often use the leave to return home and participate in the case. Thus, the availability of leave is often the deciding issue for a stay request. It's also important for determining the length of the stay, if one is issued.

Sometimes, the defendant or his/her lawyer will include facts about financial hardship and distance (including availability of leave) in the stay request. Other times, the stay request may be brief, with few facts. If facts are sketchy, the court may not have enough information to rule on the request. You can step in and ask the defendant for the necessary information, including:

- When does your present enlistment expire?
- When do you expect to be released from active duty?
- When are you due to be transferred from you present duty station?
- Do you know where you will be assigned after you complete your current tour of duty?
- What ordinary or emergency leave do you have available?
- Describe any efforts you have made to obtain leave to participate in this case.
- If you joined active-duty service during the prior two years, what is the difference between your pre-service and in-service annual income?

You can ask for this information in an informal letter to the defendant or his/her lawyer. If the defendant won't respond, you can ask for this information from the defendant's commanding officers. It's customary to start with the defendant's immediate commander, and then work up the chain of command until you get a response. Any response received should be filed with the clerk, and brought to the attention of the judge if a stay becomes an issue.

If the court grants the defendant's stay request, the stay will merely delay the divorce, not end it. The court should grant the stay only until the defendant has time to deal with the divorce. This could be until the next period of leave, or when the defendant leaves the service, when separation is imminent. You can wait until the stay expires, and then resume the divorce where you left off.

If the stay is long, the clerk may try to dismiss the case for no progress. You can prevent dismissal by pointing out the stay to the clerk, and explain that this is the reason for delay in the case.

Whether a stay is granted or denied, the fact that the defendant (personally or through a lawyer) made the stay request is important. The stay request is regarded as the defendant's chief SSCRA remedy, and results in loss of the right to request reopening of any default judgment of divorce entered later.

As a result, when you the file the Default (GRP 2), check the second outdented box and the "other" box in paragraph #4, and then mention in the blank line that the defendant has requested a SSCRA stay. Bring this to the judge's attention also during your testimony at the final hearing.

The Defendant Doesn't Respond

It's more difficult dealing with an unresponsive defendant-servicemember. Your checking the second outdented box only in paragraph #4 of the Default (GRP 2) signals to the court that the defendant is in the military, but hasn't given up SSCRA protection by waiver or by requesting a stay. The court must then decide whether and how to protect the defendant under the act.

For an unresponsive defendant, the court can appoint a *guardian ad litem* (GAL), usually a local lawyer, to protect the defendant. Despite the appointment, a GAL doesn't directly represent the servicemember, who probably wasn't consulted about the appointment and may not know the GAL even exists (the member may not know about the GAL's appointment if s/he is cut off from normal communications, such as during combat or a tour of duty at sea).

Typically, a GAL will ask for a stay, but could seek other relief. A GAL's stay request is judged the same way as one from the defendant: A stay will be issued unless the defendant's military service doesn't materially affect his/her ability to participate in the case. If the court grants the GAL's stay request, you must wait for the stay to expire before resuming the case.

When a defendant-servicemember asks for a stay (personally or through a non-GAL lawyer), the member gives up the right to request for reopening a default judgment later. This rule doesn't apply to a GAL-requested stay, because of the peculiar relationship between the GAL and servicemember described above. An unresponsive defendant will also retain the right to ask for reopening if the court declined to appoint a GAL.

If an unstayed case goes forward to a default judgment, the defendant can request reopening the judgment. The defendant can make the request anytime while in military service and even within 90 days after leaving the service. Reopening of the case isn't automatic. The defendant must show both a good defense and some prejudice from military service to get back in the case.

If the case is reopened, the defendant may be able to participate right away. But if the defendant is still serving in the military, or just recently left the service, s/he can ask for a stay, to get extra time to defend. As with pre-judgment stays, the defendant must prove a material effect from military service on his/her ability to participate in the case to obtain a stay.

STATE OF MICHIGAN Circuit Court - Family Division COUNTY	WAIVER OF MILITARY RELIEF LAW RIGHTS	CASE NO.

Plaintiff (appearing *in propria persona*):

v

Defendant:

Defendant says:

1. I am in the active duty of the following unit of the U.S. military:

THE 333RD MILITARY POLICE COMPANY, MICHIGAN ARMY NATIONAL GUARD

2. I waive all lawsuit relief rights provided to me in this case by the Soldiers' and Sailors' Civil Relief Act of 1940 and/or Michigan's military relief law (MCL 32.517) or a similar military relief law from another state.

Date 4-1-89   Defendant *Dudley E. Lovelace*

GRP 6   (1/04)   WAIVER OF MILITARY RELIEF LAW RIGHTS

Military Locator Request

TO:

Army Worldwide Locator
U.S. Army Enlisted Records and Evaluation Center
8899 E. 56th St.
Indianapolis, IN 46249-5301
Fee: $3.50 payable by check or money to "Finance Officer"

HQ AFPC/MSIMD
550 C St. West, Suite 50
Randolph AFB, TX 78150-4752
Fee: $3.50 payable by check or money order to "DAO-DE
RAFB"

World Wide Locator
Bureau of Naval Personnel
Pers-324D
2 Navy Annex
Washington, DC 20370-3240
Fee: $3.50 payable by check or money to "U.S. Treasurer"

Coast Guard Locator Service
Commanding Officer (RAS)
444 SE Quincy St.
Topeka, KS 66683-3591
Fee: $3.50 payable by check or money order to "U.S.
Treasurer"

Headquarters U.S. Marine Corps
Personnel Management Support Branch (MMSB-17)
2008 Elliot Rd.
Quantico, VA 22134-5030
Fee: $3.50 payable by check or money to "U.S. Treasurer"

RE:

Case name ___LOVELACE v. LOVELACE___

Case number ___89-00501-DM___

Full name of defendant ___DUDLEY ERNEST LOVELACE___

Defendant's date of birth ___6-15-64___

Defendant's social security number ___379-10-5567___

Defendant's rank and service number (if known) ___—___

Defendant's last duty assignment (if known) ___—___

Defendant's last military address (if known) ___—___

I am the plaintiff in the above case seeking a divorce against the defendant. I request information about the defendant's current rank, service number, unit of assignment and military address. I need this information for service of process, to satisfy the military relief laws and other reasons related to this divorce case.

A self-addressed stamped envelope is enclosed for your response. A locator fee is also enclosed, but if I qualify for a fee waiver (as spouse), please refund my payment.

Date ___3-15-89___

Signature ___Darlene A. Lovelace___

Name ___DARLENE A. LOVELACE___

Address ___121 S. MAIN___

___LAKE CITY, MI 48800___

Telephone: ___(517) 772-0000___

Appendix G: Dismissing Your Divorce

If you and your spouse reconcile during the divorce, you may be anxious to dismiss the divorce immediately. But this may not always be wise. It takes a lot of work to file a divorce, so why jeopardize all your effort with a hasty dismissal? Wait a while and see if the reconciliation lasts. If it does, go ahead and dismiss your divorce as described below. But if your reconciliation fails, pick up the divorce where you left off and finish it.

At one time, it was possible to let a divorce remain in court for months or even years while the parties attempted reconciliation. These days, courts are under pressure to move cases along quickly, so they won't tolerate very much delay. Nevertheless, you probably could let your divorce sit for a few months. Just make sure that your proof of service is on file with the clerk or else the clerk may dismiss the case for no progress after the 91-day summons expiration period (see "Filing the Proof of Service" on page 107 for more about this danger).

After you decide that your reconciliation is going to last, go ahead and dismiss your divorce. To dismiss your uncontested divorce, fill out the Notice of Dismissal by Plaintiff section of the Dismissal (MC 09). Choose dismissal "without prejudice" because this makes it easier to file another divorce later should your marriage break down again. After you prepare the Dismissal (MC 09), file it and the friend of the court's copy with the clerk. You should also send a copy to the defendant.

Incidentally, if your fees were suspended at the beginning of the divorce, you must deal with the fees again before you file the Dismissal (MC 09). At that time, the court can order a final fee exemption or require payment of the fees (see Appendix A for more about the fee exemption procedure).

Original - Court
1st copy - Applicant
Other copies - All appearing parties

Approved, SCAO

STATE OF MICHIGAN	DISMISSAL	CASE NO.
JUDICIAL DISTRICT		
JUDICIAL CIRCUIT		
COUNTY PROBATE		Court telephone no.

Court address

Plaintiff name(s) and address(es)

v

Defendant name(s) and address(es)

Plaintiff's attorney, bar no., address, and telephone no.

Defendant's attorney, bar no., address, and telephone no.

☒ **NOTICE OF DISMISSAL BY PLAINTIFF**

☐ with
☒ without   prejudice as to:

1. Plaintiff/Attorney for plaintiff files this notice of dismissal of this case
   ☒ all defendants.
   ☐ the following defendant(s): _____

2. I certify, under penalty of contempt, that:
   a. This notice is the first dismissal filed by the plaintiff based upon or including the same claim against the defendant.
   b. All costs of filing and service have been paid.
   c. **No answer or motion has been served upon the plaintiff by the defendant** as of the date of this notice.
   d. A copy of this notice has been provided to the appearing defendant/attorney by ☒ mail   ☐ personal service.

7-1-89   _Darlene A. Lovelace_
Date   Plaintiff/Attorney signature

☐ **STIPULATION TO DISMISS**

☐ with
☐ without   prejudice as to:

I stipulate to the dismissal of this case
   ☐ all parties.
   ☐ the following parties: _____

_____   _____
Date   Plaintiff/Attorney signature

_____   _____
Date   Defendant/Attorney signature

☐ **ORDER TO DISMISS**

☐ with
☐ without   prejudice. Conditions, if any: _____

IT IS ORDERED this case is dismissed

_____

_____

_____   _____   Bar no.
Date   Judge

MC 09 (6/97) **DISMISSAL**   MCR 2.504

Appendix H:
Additional Judgment
Provisions

The first four pages of the Judgment of Divorce (GRP 4a, b, c and d) contain standard judgment provisions that should take care of most divorce cases with minor children. But in special cases, these standard provisions might not be enough.

Luckily, the judgment form is open-ended and expandable allowing you to add extra judgment provisions. If have you just a few additions, insert these in the blank space on the Judgment of Divorce (GRP 4e). When you need more room, use the Judgment of Divorce (GRP 4x). Among your judgment papers, sandwich the GRP 4x between the GRP 4d and 4e as a fifth page of the judgment, with the GRP 4e becoming the sixth page. If you need even more space, make photocopies of the GRP 4x and add several of these expansion pages. As you expand the judgment this way, remember to number the judgment pages consecutively in the captions of the forms.

The sections below deal with special situations in which you might need additional judgment provisions. Sample judgment provisions are also included which you can use or adapt to your case.

Property Division Provisions

Before you can provide for a property division in your judgment, you must do a complete inventory and valuation of your property (see "Can I Get a Fair Property Division?" on page 53 for more about inventorying and valuing property). You and the defendant should also agree to an overall division of your property. If you have a prenuptial agreement dealing with divorce, this document will normally control the division. Otherwise, you must decide the shares each of you is to receive. Are you going to divide your property equally, 55-45, 60-40, etc.? After you do all those things, you're ready to begin the actual division of property.

Dividing Real Property

All real property must be divided specifically in your divorce judgment. This rule applies both to real property owned by spouses jointly (joint real property) and real property that a spouse owns alone (solely-owned real property). The provisions below divide joint and solely-owned real property in three ways: 1) trade-off 2) buy-out (by one spouse from the other) 3) sale (to third parties). There are several other ways to divide real property, but these are far too complicated to do by yourself.

More Information
The court rules specify a judgment style which you must follow in adding provisions to your judgment: • There must be only one subject or topic per judgment provision. • All provisions must be numbered consecutively. • All provisions must have a descriptive introductory heading, which is normally in bold on printed forms. However, you can underline introductory headings as a substitute for bold-face type.

If you and your spouse don't own any real property, check the first box in paragraph #5A of the Judgment of Divorce (GRP 4a). If you are property-owners, check the second box and then divide the property in the Judgment of Divorce (GRP 4e).

As you divide real property, include the street address and legal description. Adding the legal description is important because this permits you to use the judgment as a substitute deed if one spouse refuses to sign a deed for the property (see "Transferring Property" on page 141 for more about using a judgment to transfer property this way). You can find the legal description in a deed, land contract, mortgage, abstract of title or title insurance policy for the property.

Joint Real Property

If you do nothing with joint real property in your divorce judgment, the property automatically converts to tenancy in common ownership. This might be acceptable for a while. As tenants in common, you and the defendant would each get an equal share of the property. If either of you were to die, your share would pass to your heirs/will beneficiaries, not your ex-spouse, because tenancy in common property doesn't have rights of survivorship.

But in the long run, tenancy in common ownership isn't practical for divorced persons. A tenancy in common is really like a partnership. Both tenants in common have an equal right to possess and use the property, and each has a duty to maintain it. This kind of close-knit arrangement is seldom suitable for ex-spouses.

Consequently, you should divide your joint real property in another way. The provisions below suggest several division options, some of which you may be able to handle yourself.

Trade-Off

If enough property is available, one spouse can trade his/her share of the joint property for an equivalent amount of other property. For example, let's say that spouses jointly own a house worth $50,000 and have $50,000 of miscellaneous property. If the spouses agree to an equal property division, the defendant could trade his/her one-half share of the house for the plaintiff's half-interest in the miscellaneous property. After giving all the miscellaneous property to the defendant elsewhere in the property division, the spouses might use a provision like the one below to give the jointly-owned house to the plaintiff:

23. <u>Real Property</u>. Plaintiff is awarded the property located at 121 S. Main, Lake City, Michigan, and described below, free of any claims of defendant:

Lot 2 of Assessor's Plat, Lake City, Ojibway County, Michigan

Plaintiff shall be responsible for any indebtedness against the property and hold defendant harmless from liability for this debt.

Buy-Out

Instead of a trade-off, one spouse could purchase the other's share of the joint real property. The provision below provides for a buy-out of the defendant's share by the plaintiff for cash:

23. <u>Real Property</u>. Plaintiff shall be awarded the property located at 121 S. Main, Lake City, Michigan, and described below, free of any claims of defendant, upon the payment of $25,000 to defendant:

Lot 2 of Assessor's Plat, Lake City, Ojibway County, Michigan

Plaintiff shall be responsible for any indebtedness against the property and hold defendant harmless from liability for this debt.

This provision lets the plaintiff buy out the defendant with a single cash payment. If the buyer-spouse can't afford to pay cash, s/he could make installment payments. But to provide for that type of buy-out, one must know about installment sales, how to secure them and their tax consequences. All these things are quite complicated, so seek legal help if you want to provide for a buy-out on an installment basis.

Sale

The sale of joint property to third parties is another way to handle joint property. You can arrange for an immediate sale at the time of your divorce or delay the sale until later. Either way, the sale provision will usually convert the joint property into a tenancy in common until the sale. Then, the provision will typically require: 1) pay-off of any mortgage or land contract against the property 2) payment of all selling costs (broker's commission, closing costs, etc.) 3) division of any remaining proceeds. A good sale provision should also say who shall possess and maintain the property before the sale. All these things are included in the immediate sale provision below:

23. <u>Real Property</u>. The property located at 121 S. Main, Lake City, Michigan, and described below, shall be owned by plaintiff and defendant as tenants in common:

Lot 2 of Assessor's Plat, Lake City, Ojibway County, Michigan

This property shall be sold as soon as possible at a price and terms the parties shall agree upon. After the property is sold, the proceeds of the sale shall be applied first to satisfy any indebtedness against the property, then against all the costs of sale (including any broker's commission and closing costs). Any remainder shall be divided [equally] between the parties.

Until the closing of the sale, plaintiff shall have sole possession of the property. Plaintiff shall be responsible for any mortgage or land contract payments, taxes, insurance and other expenses of maintaining the property during this time until the day of closing.

An immediate sale is simple and provides for a clean break between the spouses. There may also be sound tax reasons for selling real property around the time of a divorce, especially when the property is the former marital home. However, an immediate sale may displace a parent and children living at the home.

A delayed sale can solve that problem. It can permit the in-home parent to live in the former marital home for a while, yet will eventually allow the other parent to receive his/her share of the property when the delayed sale occurs. The trouble is, a delayed sale is difficult to provide for in a judgment. The events triggering the delayed sale (remarriage of the in-home parent, maturity of children, etc.) must be anticipated and carefully described in the provision. The other parent may want interest on his/her share of the property, and have it protected by a mortgage or other security. Finally, the income tax consequences from a delayed sale can be unfavorable. For all these reasons, if you want a delayed sale, go to a lawyer for help.

Solely-Owned Real Property

If you fail to deal with solely-owned real property in your judgment, the owner-spouse retains ownership of the property free of any claim or interest of the other spouse (in part, that's what paragraph #6 of the Judgment of Divorce (GRP 4a) is about). But you shouldn't leave it at that. Even if you want the owner-spouse to keep his/her solely-owned property (presumably because of a trade-off or buy-out), you should say so in your judgment. When you want another disposition of the property, such as a sale to a third party, you must provide for that as well.

Trade-Off

In this case, the nonowner is trading off his/her hypothetical share in the owner-spouse's solely-owned real property for equivalent property elsewhere in the property division. The owner-spouse keeps ownership of the property:

23. <u>Real Property</u>. Plaintiff is awarded the property located at 121 S. Main, Lake City, Michigan, and described below, free of any claims of defendant:

Lot 2 of Assessor's Plat, Lake City, Ojibway County, Michigan

Plaintiff shall be responsible for any indebtedness against the property and hold defendant harmless from liability for this debt.

Buy-Out

The owner-spouse buys out the nonowner's "share" in his/her solely-owned real property for cash:*

23. <u>Real Property</u>. Plaintiff shall be awarded the property located at 121 S. Main, Lake City, Michigan, and described below, free of any claims of defendant, upon the payment of $25,000 to defendant:

Lot 2 of Assessor's Plat, Lake City, Ojibway County, Michigan

Plaintiff shall be responsible for any indebtedness against the property and hold defendant harmless from liability for this debt.

Sale

In this scenario, the solely-owned property must be sold as soon as possible to a third party followed by a division of the proceeds:**

23. <u>Real Property</u>. The property located at 121 S. Main, Lake City, Michigan, and described below, shall be owned by plaintiff and defendant as tenants in common:

Lot 2 of Assessor's Plat, Lake City, Ojibway County, Michigan

This property shall be sold as soon as possible at a price and terms the parties shall agree upon. After the property is sold, the proceeds of the sale shall be applied first to satisfy any indebtedness against the property, then against all the costs of sale (including any broker's commission and closing costs). Any remainder shall be divided [equally] between the parties.

Until the closing of the sale, plaintiff shall have sole possession of the property. Plaintiff shall be responsible for any mortgage or land contract payments, taxes, insurance and other expenses of maintaining the property during that time until the day of closing.

---

*   As an alternative, you can provide for an installment sale. But as explained above, that's probably too difficult for you to arrange yourself.

**   Instead of an immediate sale, you could choose a delayed sale. Yet, as mentioned above, you will probably need legal help to provide for that arrangement.

Dividing Personal Property

You may have already divided the bulk of your personal property, such as clothing, household goods, bank accounts and motor vehicles, during or even before your divorce. Courts usually permit informal divisions of personal property because they know that you cannot wait until the end of your divorce to divide essential items. If you have already divided some or all of your personal property that way, confirm the division by checking the first box in paragraph #5B of the Judgment of Divorce (GRP 4a).

On the other hand, you should specifically mention personal property that hasn't yet been transferred to the intended recipient at the time of your final hearing. This avoids confusion about ownership later. For example, if you and the defendant have agreed that the defendant must give you an automobile, a dinette set and a $1,000 bank account, you should say so in your judgment. Check the second box in paragraph #5B of the Judgment of Divorce (GRP 4a), and include this provision in the Judgment of Divorce (GRP 4e):

> 23. <u>Personal Property</u>. Plaintiff is awarded the following personal property free of any claims of defendant:
>
> 1984 Dodge Aries automobile VIN VL29C4B266259
>
> Five-piece (table and four chairs) Contemporary dinette set
>
> Ojibway State Bank savings account #00012400-001, with a current balance of $1,000
>
> Plaintiff shall be responsible for any indebtedness against this property and hold defendant harmless from liability for this debt.

You can adapt this provision to divide almost any type of personal property. But use it only for the distribution of important items of personal property. Don't clutter up your judgment by mentioning every piece of furniture or article of clothing.

Whenever you use such a provision, include a complete description of the property since this aids transfer of the item later (see "After Your Divorce" on page 141 for more information about transferring property). Describe the property fully and mention any identification numbers (account numbers for financial accounts, vehicle identification numbers (VINs) for automobiles, hull numbers for boats, etc.), as in the example above.

Dividing Retirement Benefits, Businesses and Other New Property

A divorce property division isn't complete without considering so-called new property (retirement benefits, businesses, etc.). The problem is, new property is often difficult to divide. Unlike a house or an automobile, you can't put retirement benefits on the market, sell them and divide the proceeds (most retirement plans prohibit this kind of sale or transfer even if you could find a buyer).

A business can also be hard to liquidate. Some one-person businesses depend on the skill of their owner-operators and may be impossible to sell as going concerns. And even when a small business can be sold, it must often be sold as a piece because few people will buy a share of a small business.

Despite these problems, the law has devised ways to divide new property, often without actually distributing it.

Dividing Retirement Benefits

Michigan courts have approved two methods for dividing retirement benefits: 1) trade-off 2) division of payments.

In a trade-off, the nonemployee-spouse trades his/her interest in the retirement benefits for a like share of other property. As an example, let's assume that a couple owns an automobile worth $10,000 and the husband has retirement benefits with a present value of $10,000. If the spouses agree to an equal property division, the wife might trade her one-half interest in the retirement benefits for the husband's half-interest in the automobile. Thus, the retirement benefits stay with the husband, but the wife gets the automobile. By this means, the retirement benefits have been divided, but without actually distributing them.

The other method of division—division of payments—results in the actual distribution of the retirement benefits to both spouses. With this method, the retirement benefits are divided fractionally between the spouses as payments are made. For example, if the husband is receiving monthly payments, and the parties want an equal division of property, they could assign one-half of the payments to each spouse monthly.

Each of these methods has pluses and minuses. Trade-off is nice because it gives the nonemployee-spouse value immediately, without waiting for the retirement plan to mature (pay benefits). But it requires an estimation of the present value of the benefits, which is complicated (see "Can I Get a Fair Property Division?" on page 53 for more about the valuation of retirement plans). Trade-off also places the risk that the employee-spouse will never collect the benefits (because of premature death, early retirement, discharge, bankruptcy of the employer, etc.) on the employee-spouse alone. If the employee-spouse never gets benefits, s/he has traded off other property for nothing. And finally, a trade-off may not be possible if the value of the retirement benefits is great and there is no other property that can be traded for them.

It's simpler to just divide the retirement benefits. Unlike a trade-off, you normally won't have to estimate the total value of the benefits, since your dividing the payments, not the total benefits package. This avoids making a difficult present value calculation. Dividing payments also spreads the risks associated with the retirement benefits to both spouses. If the retirement plan fails, both spouses share the loss; if benefits increase in the future, each spouse shares in the gain.

But unless the retirement plan is mature (paying benefits), dividing payments often won't give the nonemployee-spouse any property immediately after the divorce. What's more, a division-of-payments order is difficult to provide for in a divorce judgment. You must use precise language or it won't be legally effective. For this reason, if you want to divide retirement benefits during divorce yourself, you will have to use the trade-off method. To do that, simply check the first box in paragraph #8 of your Judgment of Divorce (GRP 4a), and then give or get equivalent property elsewhere in the property division. If you want to use the division-of-payments method, see a lawyer.

Individual retirement arrangements (IRAs), which are individual retirement plans, can be divided in several ways, including: 1) transfer from the owner-spouse to the other spouse 2) trade-off 3) withdrawal and division of the proceeds.

To transfer an IRA, describe the account and provide for transfer in a judgment provision, like the bank account example on page 230. This kind of divorce-related transfer isn't considered a withdrawal, so no tax or early withdrawal penalty is imposed. But tax and an early withdrawal penalty may be due if the new owner of the account withdraws money from it prematurely. If you want to trade off an IRA for other property, make sure that you have checked the first box in paragraph #8 of your Judgment of Divorce (GRP 4a), and give the nonowner-spouse equivalent property elsewhere in the judgment. You can also withdraw the money in an IRA and divide it. But if the IRA-owner is younger than 59½, that's a premature withdrawal and a penalty will be imposed.

Keogh (HR-10) plans are another type of individual retirement plan. Like IRAs, these plans can be transferred, traded or withdrawn and divided. But transferring or withdrawing Keoghs can have bad tax consequences, leaving trade-off as the best method of division in most cases.

Dividing Businesses and Other New Property

Business interests can be transferred between spouses or liquidated and divided. In many cases, trade-off is the best method of division. To trade off a business, create a judgment provision like the one below, assigning the business to the business-owner, and then give the nonbusiness-owner equivalent property elsewhere in the property division.

23. <u>Personal Property</u>. Defendant is awarded all the assets, including inventory, supplies, fixtures, equipment, accounts and goodwill, in

the House of Waterbeds, Lake City, Michigan, free of any claims of plaintiff. Defendant shall hold plaintiff harmless from any liability in connection with this business.

Division of Debts

As you end your marriage, who is responsible for debts you leave behind? If you do nothing, the following general rules govern liability for sole debts (debts incurred by a spouse alone) and joint debts (debts taken on by spouses together):

Sole debt. The spouse who incurred the debt (debtor-spouse) remains liable for it after the divorce. The nondebtor-spouse generally won't be liable for the debt unless s/he gave the debtor-spouse authority, as an agent, to incur debts of the nondebtor-spouse's behalf. The agent's authority can be express, implied or even given after the fact, by ratification of what the debtor-spouse did.

Joint debt. Because both spouses incurred joint debts, each remains liable for these after divorce.

By dividing debts in your divorce judgment, you can modify this liability to an extent. A debt provision can shift the liability for a sole debt from the debtor-spouse to the other spouse. It could also have one spouse assume liability for a joint debt or a sole debt for which both spouses are liable under the agent exception described above.

Not all debts may be reassigned that way. Educational and personal loans are better left with those incurring them, since they have a bigger incentive to pay them. Likewise, debts secured by property (mortgages, land contracts and other liens) are customarily transferred to the recipients of the secured property. (For this reason, all the sample property division provisions in this appendix transfer secured debts together with the property securing them.) On the other hand, general unsecured debts, such as credit card or charge account debts, are good choices for division.

Whatever you decide, any debt provision you insert in your judgment must describe the debt and say who is responsible for paying it, as in the following provision:

23. <u>Debts</u>. Defendant is responsible for, and must hold plaintiff harmless from, the following debts:

    Lake City Department Store charge account #22224445 with a current balance of $540

    Mastercredit account #5215 0200 3400 6529 with a current balance of $1,233.33

Debt Division and Creditors' Rights

Although you and the defendant can rearrange debts in your judgment, your arrangements won't affect the rights of the creditors holding the debts. Your creditors will have the same rights after your divorce as they had before.*

Example: A couple got a joint car loan from a bank (creditor). In their divorce, the wife received ownership of the car and the car loan was assigned to her by a debt provision in the divorce judgment. She falls behind on the car payments. The bank could sue the husband because the debt division didn't affect his liability to the bank.

If a debt division doesn't change creditors' rights, why go to the trouble of dividing debts in your divorce judgment? The advantage to debt division is that it provides a legal claim, known as indemnity, against the spouse assuming the debt. The indemnity can then be used as a defense or as a direct claim.

Glossary

Indemnity–legal claim making someone else answerable for your obligation to a third person.

Example: A couple gets a joint car loan from a bank (creditor). In their divorce, the wife gets the car and agrees to pay the loan off in a debt division provision. After she falls behind in car payments, the bank sues both spouses. The husband could cite the indemnity from the debt division and shift liability to the wife. Had the bank sued the husband alone, he could add the wife to the case and raise the indemnity against her this way.

Alimony Provisions

Every divorce judgment must deal with alimony** and settle the issue for *both* spouses by either: 1) waiving (giving up) 2) reserving 3) or granting alimony.

When you want to waive alimony for you or the defendant, indicate in paragraph #4 of your Judgment of Divorce (GRP 4a) that alimony is "not granted for" that particular party. By making that choice, you permanently waive alimony for the party whose box you have checked, and s/he won't be permitted to seek alimony later.

---

*   A creditor can agree to release a spouse from liability for a joint debt. In that case, the released spouse would no longer be liable to the creditor for the debt. Nevertheless, most creditors won't consent to such releases because they prefer to have two debtors rather than one.

**   In the judgment, alimony is called by its real name: spousal support.

If you want to leave the issue of alimony open for a party, check the box indicating that alimony is "reserved for" that party. You cannot reserve alimony merely because you find the issue of alimony bothersome and don't want to deal with it now. To reserve alimony, you must have a good reason for the reservation, such as: 1) there is only limited jurisdiction in the case (see "Can I Get a Divorce in Michigan?" on page 43 about why limited jurisdiction isn't enough for alimony) 2) the payer is elusive or has disappeared and you cannot determine his/her ability to pay alimony 3) the would-be recipient of the alimony is making a personal or career change and isn't sure of his/her financial needs now. When alimony is reserved for a party, s/he can come back to court later and ask for alimony. At that time, the court will decide whether it should be paid.

If you and the defendant have agreed on some type of alimony, check the box in paragraph #4 of the GRP 4a that says alimony is "granted elsewhere in this judgment for" the recipient. You must then include an alimony provision in your Judgment of Divorce (GRP 4e) (see below for sample alimony provisions).

When you're dealing with alimony in your judgment, make sure that you settle it for both parties in one of the three ways described above. If you fail to settle alimony for a party, the failure automatically reserves alimony for that party, allowing him/her to ask for it later.

The alimony provisions below are for short- and long-term alimony. Both provisions make the alimony subject to several conditions. You can omit any of these or add others. But keep in mind that the death-of-the-recipient condition is necessary to qualify the payments as alimony for federal tax purposes. Without that condition, the payments won't be deductible by the payer.

Short-Term Alimony

23. <u>Spousal Support</u>.   Defendant shall pay to plaintiff $200 monthly in advance on the first day of the month. This spousal support shall be modifiable. Payment of the support shall begin on September 7, 1989, and end immediately on the happening of any of the following events:

(a) [September 7, 1991]

(b) death of plaintiff

(c) death of defendant

(d) remarriage of plaintiff

(e) cohabitation by plaintiff with a member of the opposite sex

After plaintiff's spousal support ends, it shall be forever barred to her.

Long-Term Alimony

23. <u>Spousal Support</u>. Defendant shall pay to plaintiff $200 monthly in advance on the first day of the month. This spousal support shall be modifiable. Payment of the support shall begin on September 7, 1989, and end immediately on the happening of any of the following events:

(a) death of plaintiff

(b) death of defendant

(c) remarriage of plaintiff

(d) cohabitation by plaintiff with a member of the opposite sex

After plaintiff's spousal support ends, it shall be forever barred to her.

Choosing an Alimony Payment Method

When you provide for alimony, you must also arrange for a method of payment. As with the other kind of support, child support, the normal way of paying alimony is by immediate income withholding through the friend of the court system to the state disbursement unit (SDU). With this method, the alimony payer's source of income (usually an employer) deducts the alimony from the payer's wages or salary and sends the money to the state disbursement unit (SDU), which forwards it to the alimony recipient. The friend of the court monitors payment, so it can enforce the obligation.

If you want payment of alimony by immediate income withholding to the SDU, select this method of payment in paragraph #19 of the Judgment of Divorce (GRP 4d). In subparagraph b, check payment by immediate income withholding and to the SDU.

Or you can choose another method of paying alimony. You could skip immediate income withholding and provide for payment directly to the SDU or directly to the payee. Simply select the correct boxes in paragraph #19b of the GRP 4d.

Incidentally, the method for paying alimony doesn't have to match the child support method, and you can mix methods in paragraph #19. For example, you could have child support paid by immediate income withholding to the SDU, and then bypass income withholding and have alimony paid directly to the payee.

Custody Provisions

Parents have a number of custody choices: sole custody, several forms of joint custody, split custody, mixed custody and third-party custody.

The sample judgment on page 130 contains sole custody provisions for the children. The custody provisions below depict two types of joint custody; joint legal custody for Duane and joint physical custody for Darryl:

14. **CUSTODY:** Custody of the minor children is granted as follows:

PL = Plaintiff   DF = Defendant   JT = Joint   3rd = Third party, named here:

CHILD'S NAME	DATE Of BIRTH	LEGAL CUSTODY	PHYSICAL CUSTODY
DUANE WESLEY LOVELACE	6-1-86	JT	PL
DARRYL WENDELL LOVELACE	7-1-87	JT	JT

Joint Physical Custody

Whenever you choose joint physical custody, you must decide whether to provide for a specific physical custody schedule or leave it open and flexible. It's permissible to leave joint physical custody open, allowing you and the defendant to exchange custody as you go and at your convenience. If you want this arrangement, you needn't do any more than choose the joint physical custody option, as shown above.

But joint physical custody is difficult to manage. If you anticipate problems, you should specify in advance how you and the defendant will share physical custody. To provide for joint physical custody with a specific custody schedule, choose joint physical custody in paragraph #14 of the Judgment of Divorce (GRP 4b), as described above. Then add a specific joint physical custody provision in the Judgment of Divorce (GRP 4e). The provisions below are examples of split-time, block-time, and bird's nest joint physical custody provisions which you can adapt to your situation.

Split-Time Custody

23. <u>Joint Physical Custody</u>. The parties shall have joint physical custody of their minor children as follows: Plaintiff shall have physical custody during weekdays from 8:30 a.m. Monday until 6:00 p.m. Friday. Defendant shall have physical custody during weekends from 6:00 p.m. Friday until 8:30 a.m. Monday.

You can arrange for split-time custody in many ways. The sample provision above provides for weekday/weekend split-time custody, but you could substitute another schedule listed below, or any other schedule:

- day/day
- 3½ days/3½ days
- 3 days/4 days
- weekdays/weekend
- one week/one week
- two weeks/two weeks
- one week/three weeks

- month/month
- two months/two months
- etc.

Block-Time Custody: school year/summer vacation

23. <u>Joint Physical Custody</u>. The parties shall have joint physical custody of their minor children as follows: Plaintiff shall have physical custody from [seven] days before the first day of school in the fall until [seven] days after the last day of school in the spring. Defendant shall have physical custody of the children during the remaining summer school vacation period.

"Bird's Nest" Custody

23. <u>Joint Physical Custody</u>. The parties shall have joint physical custody of their minor children as follows: The parties will alternate residence in the family home [monthly]. Each party shall exercise physical custody while residing with the children at the family home.

When you select joint physical custody, don't about forget parenting time. Some types of joint physical custody, such as frequent split-time or bird's nest custody, might not require any or much parenting time (except perhaps during holidays). But parenting time may be necessary for infrequent split-time or block-time custody. In that case, you should include a parenting time provision in your judgment as described below.

Split Custody

You can split sole, joint legal or even joint physical custody of children. Split sole or joint legal custody by assigning physical custody to different parents (legal custody stays with each custodial parent in split sole custody; it's shared with split joint legal custody). The custody provision below depicts split sole custody:

14. **CUSTODY:** Custody of the minor children is granted as follows:

PL = Plaintiff   DF = Defendant   JT = Joint   3rd = Third party, named here:

CHILD'S NAME	DATE Of BIRTH	LEGAL CUSTODY	PHYSICAL CUSTODY
DUANE WESLEY LOVELACE	6-1-86	PL	PL
DARRYL WENDELL LOVELACE	7-1-87	DF	DF

It's possible to split joint physical custody by putting the children on different custody schedules, so they don't move in sync between the parents. The custody provisions below specify split block-time joint physical custody:

14. **CUSTODY:** Custody of the minor children is granted as follows:

PL = Plaintiff   DF = Defendant   JT = Joint   3rd = Third party, named here:

CHILD'S NAME	DATE Of BIRTH	LEGAL CUSTODY	PHYSICAL CUSTODY
DUANE WESLEY LOVELACE	6-1-86	JT	JT
DARRYL WENDELL LOVELACE	7-1-87	JT	JT

23. <u>Split Joint Physical Custody</u>.   The parties shall have custody of their minor children as follows:

(a) Plaintiff shall have physical custody of Duane Wesley Lovelace from [seven] days before the first day of school in the fall until [seven] days after the last day of school in the spring. Defendant shall have physical custody of Duane Wesley Lovelace during the remaining summer school vacation period.

(b) Defendant shall have physical custody of Darryl Wendell Lovelace from [seven] days before the first day of school in the fall until [seven] days after the last day of school in the spring. Plaintiff shall have physical custody of Darryl Wendell Lovelace during the remaining summer school vacation period.

Mixed Custody

You can mix custody by choosing different types of custody for the children within a family. The custody provision below mixes sole custody and joint physical custody:

14. **CUSTODY:** Custody of the minor children is granted as follows:

PL = Plaintiff   DF = Defendant   JT = Joint   3rd = Third party, named here:

CHILD'S NAME	DATE Of BIRTH	LEGAL CUSTODY	PHYSICAL CUSTODY
DUANE WESLEY LOVELACE	6-1-86	PL	PL
DARRYL WENDELL LOVELACE	7-1-87	JT	JT

[A specific joint physical custody provision for Darryl is optional here.]

Third-Party Custody

To assign custody to a nonparent "third party," name the nonparent in the space near the third party notation. Then, insert 3rd in the legal and physical custody columns as you would PL, DF or JT.

Parenting Time Provisions

If you want the flexible type of parenting time known as reasonable parenting time, check the "reasonable" box in paragraph #15 of the Judgment of Divorce (GRP 4b), as in the sample judgment on page 130. By selecting that option, you and the defendant can arrange parenting time as you like.

To fix parenting time according to a specific schedule, check the "specific" box in paragraph #15 of the Judgment of Divorce (GRP 4b). Then add a specific parenting time provision in the GRP 4e or 4x later in the judgment. In this provision, you can specify the time, terms, and conditions of the parenting time. Naturally, the provision must suit you and your children, but you should be able to adapt one of the following examples to your situation:

23. <u>Specific Parenting Time</u>. Defendant shall have parenting time during:

(a) alternate weekends from 6:00 p.m. Friday until 6:00 p.m. Sunday. If a state holiday falls on a Monday following a weekend visitation, the visitation shall extend to 6:00 p.m. on that Monday holiday

(b) in even-numbered years, from 6:00 p.m. on the last day before Christmas school vacation until noon on Christmas Day

(c) in odd-numbered years, from noon on Christmas Day until 6:00 p.m. on the day before school resumes

(d) in odd-numbered years, from 6:00 p.m. on the Wednesday before Thanksgiving Day until 6:00 p.m. on the following Sunday

(e) Easter Sunday in even-numbered years

(f) in even-numbered years, from 6:00 p.m. on the last day before spring school vacation until 6:00 p.m. on the day before school resumes

(g) in even-numbered years, the children's birthdays

(h) [Two] weeks during the children's summer school vacation, beginning not less than 30 days after written notice to plaintiff and ending at least seven days before school resumes.

(i) other times as the parties may agree upon

At the beginning of any period of parenting time, plaintiff shall have the children ready at the time specified and defendant shall return them promptly at the end of the parenting time. Plaintiff shall be responsible for transporting the children to begin parenting time and defendant shall be responsible for returning them from parenting time.

This parenting time provision is suitable for parents who live close to each other after their divorce. For parents living far apart, parenting time on alternating weekends and split holidays is impractical. In these cases, parents should choose infrequent parenting time, where the noncustodial parent has extended periods of parenting time instead of more frequent access. The provision below is designed for parents who live a considerable distance from each other, requiring airplane travel for the parenting time:

23. <u>Specific Parenting Time</u>. Defendant shall have parenting time during:

   (a) in even-numbered years, Christmas school vacation

   (b) in odd-numbered years, Thanksgiving school vacation

   (c) in odd-numbered years, spring school vacation

   (d) [Four] weeks during the children's summer school vacation, beginning not less than 30 days after written notice to plaintiff and ending at least seven days before school resumes.

   (e) other times as the parties may agree upon

   At the beginning of any period of parenting time, plaintiff shall have the children ready at the time specified and defendant shall return them promptly at the end of the parenting time. [The parties shall share equally] the cost of transporting the children to and from the parenting time.

Change of Children's Residence Provisions

As explained in "Residence of Children" on page 17, at divorce-filing local residences of minor children are established with each parent. The divorce also has the effect of fixing residence in the state of Michigan.

It's possible that the children's local residences have changed during the divorce. Many intrastate moves are permissible without court review, under one of the exclusions and exceptions allowed by Michigan's residence law. Out-of-state moves during this period seldom happen.

Wherever the residences of the children are at the end of the divorce, the divorce judgment re-affirms these in paragraph #16 of the Judgment of Divorce (GRP 4b). With this provision, the residences are set for the post-judgment period.

On the other hand, some parents may want to move around the end of the divorce or soon afterward. If court approval of the move is required (only some intrastate moves need court review; all interstate moves do), the defendant must consent and the court must approve the move. After defaulting, the defendant is out of the case so it's difficult for him/her to give consent for the moveaway. The best way is for the defendant to appear at the final hearing and give oral consent. See "Preparing for the Final Hearing" on page 125 for more about having the defendant attend the final hearing.

In reviewing an agreed-to moveaway, courts are concerned about the impact of the move on the stay-behind parents' custody and parenting time. You can avoid this problem by shaping your joint custody and parenting time to fit the proposed move. So, you might choose both with less frequent exchanges of the children. And if long-distance travel is necessary, you should specify how and who pays. By looking ahead this way, the court should be satisfied that the move won't upset the custody and parenting time arrangements in your judgment.

You also need to authorize the moveaway in paragraph #16 of the Judgment of Divorce (GRP 4b). Check the box inside paragraph #16a that there has been an agreement about change of residence. Include the effective date of the move, the names of the children moving, which parent is relocating and their old and new residences.

After the move takes place, you must notify the friend of the court of the new address of you and the children, as required by paragraph #16c and 22 of the judgment.

Child Support Provisions

As mentioned in "Child Support" on page 21, the amount of child support is normally set by the Michigan child support formula since it controls most cases. In fact, the friend of the court often gives you child support figures based on the formula when it makes a recommendation on the issue. If so, you can simply plug these numbers into your divorce judgment.

On the other hand, some counties don't require friend of the court recommendations in uncontested divorces. In that case, you must use the formula to figure child support yourself. The formula is explained in the *Michigan Child Support Formula Manual* issued by the state. The manual is included at the end of this appendix (the manual's original pagination is retained, so all page references are to the manual's own pagination).

In exceptional cases, you may be able to depart from the child support formula and set child support at a different amount. "Departing from the Child Support Formula" on page 247 explains when and how to do that. But even if you depart from the formula, you must still figure child support under the formula to show the court how and why your amount is different.

Providing for Child Support

Using the Formula and Child Support Schedules

The *Michigan Child Support Formula Manual* has a set of tables or schedules that you can use to figure child support. But before you can do that, you must determine the gross and net income of you and the defendant.

Simply put, gross income includes wages, salary, commissions and most other types of gain. However, the following items are not regarded as income: 1) gifts 2) inheritances 3) many public benefits, such as FIP payments, TANF, SSI and food stamps. Pages 3-7 of the manual explain the concept of income (including a chart listing 33 types of income), and pages 10-14 describe items excluded from income.

After establishing your gross income, you must deduct allowable deductions from gross monthly income to find your net monthly income. The formula permits the following deductions from gross income:

- FICA
- federal, state and local taxes
- alimony paid to other parent
- mandatory deductions from income (most union dues and some retirement plan contributions)
- health or life insurance premiums for children
- pre-existing support obligations (such as child support) from a previous marriage or relationship (but not payments on child support arrearages)

The formula manual recommends that income be determined from actual tax returns whenever possible. This shouldn't be very difficult for wage- and salary-earners. They can take annual gross wages/salary from their W-2 forms, subtract the annual amount of deductions from income listed above, and derive net annual income. Divide this figure by 12 to get net monthly income.

When people receive income from other sources (such as commissions, interest, dividends and self-employment), determining net income is much harder. Nevertheless, you can use that person's most recent federal income tax return to estimate his/her net income. Take the adjusted gross income from the return and subtract the total annual amount of deductions listed above. Divide the remainder by 12 to find net monthly income.

More Information

The state used to revise the *Michigan Child Support Formual Manual* annually, usually in January, making small cost-of-living adjustments to some of the child support schedules. Less frequently, the child support guidelines and rules (such as the definition of income, allowable deductions from gross income, adjustments to the schedules, etc.) are revised. The state reviews the manual every four years for major revisions.

The manual reproduced in this book is the 2001 edition revised for 2003-04. Recently, publication of the manual has become more irregular, so it's difficult to say when a new one will be issued. But if you're doing your divorce in late 2004 or later, check and see if a new manual is in effect.

The state used to print and sell the manual. In 2002, the state discontinued sales of the manual. The state provides a limited number of printed copies of the manual to friends of the court and libraries, including most law libraries. You may be able to examine a copy there.

The state's Friend of the Court Bureau also provides the manual online for free. It's available there to view, or you can download a file and print your own copy. The bureau's Web site is: www.courts.michigan.gov/scao/services/focb/focb.htm

The bureau's Web site also has a handy child support calculator program, called GUIDELIN, which you can download from the site.

Figuring Base Child Support

After you establish the net monthly income of both you and the defendant, use the child support schedules to figure your child support in a three-step procedure:

1) Take the net monthly income of you and the defendant and round the amounts off to the nearest increment of $50 (so, for example, 265 becomes 250 and 285 becomes 300).

2) Locate the correct schedule according to the number of minor children you have. Using that schedule, find the custodial parent's income along the top row and the noncustodial parent's income in the left column. The number where the row and column intersect is the current child support amount.

3) Besides current child support, you must also show how the child support will decrease in the future as each child becomes independent. Go back to the child support schedules and figure the child support with one less child, two less children, etc., down to one child. Insert all these child support amounts as the base support in the child support box in paragraph #17 of your Judgment of Divorce (GRP 4c), as shown on page 131.

Adding to Base Child Support

As explained before, child support pays for more than the cost of feeding, clothing and sheltering children; it also covers health care, child care and educational expenses. Extra amounts can be added to the base child support amount to pay for these other costs.

Uninsured Health Care Expenses: Ordinary Expenses

If health plan coverage is available, one or both parents must provide coverage for the children. (The health care coverage obligations of parents are explained in "Health Care Coverage" on page 249.) But these days, not everyone has coverage. And even when coverage is available, it often leaves gaps, such as deductibles, co-payments and other uninsured expenses.

The child support formula attempts to cover uninsured expenses in several ways. The big or extraordinary expenses are divided between the parents (see "Uninsured Health Care Expenses" on page 249 for more about this sharing). That leaves ordinary uninsured expenses. These include small out-of-pocket costs for things like nonprescription drugs, vitamins, cough syrup, etc. The child support formula has estimated the monthly costs of these items per child for the child support payer (see the chart on page 31 of the manual). It has built these amounts, invisibly, into the child support schedules. So when the payer pays base child support, s/he is also paying his/her share of the ordinary uninsured health care expenses.

Child Care

The formula also allows a supplement for child care, which can be added to the base child support amount derived from the child support schedules. To qualify for the supplement, a parent must obtain child care services from a babysitter or day care center because of: 1) work 2) an opportunity to look for work 3) education to prepare for work. Ordinarily, custodial parents use child care the most. But noncustodial parents may also need it during parenting time. Both parents can qualify to receive the supplement.

If you plan to obtain child care, but haven't done so yet, the friend of the court can help you get a contingent child care supplement. This contingent supplement is based on estimated child care expenses. The supplement goes into effect if and when you obtain child care and begin paying child care expenses.

The child care supplement is available to take care of children up to the start of the school year following their 12th birthdays. The supplement can sometimes be obtained for older children when they need supervision for health or safety reasons.

Pages 29-33 of the formula manual explain the child care supplement and how to figure it. Generally, you take the actual child care expenses, deduct any federal income tax credit obtained for them and divide the remainder between the parents in proportion to their income. This amount is then added to the base child support amount in the child support box in paragraph #17 of the Judgment of Divorce (GRP 4c).

Educational Expenses

The children themselves may have educational expenses, and these can be paid as another form of child support. For example, there may be private school tuition, or fees for music lessons, athletic instruction, summer camps, scouting, and social activities. These expenses can be assigned to the parents in percentages you choose.

23. Educational Expenses. In addition to base child support, plaintiff shall pay [20%] and defendant shall pay [80%] of the [annual tuition at St. Francis Elementary School, Lake City, Michigan,] for the parties' children.

Reserving Child Support

As explained before, child support is based on the needs of the children and the income of *both* parents. When the defendant withholds financial information or has disappeared, you won't know his/her income, making child support difficult to figure. If this happened in your case, contact your FIA caseworker, if you have one, or the agency. The FIA has special means for determining parental income and assets.

If all fails and you cannot figure child support, put "reserved until further order of this court" in the space above paragraph #17a of your Judgment of Divorce (GRP 4c), and leave the child support box empty. By reserving child support, you will be able to reopen the issue later when you catch up with the defendant. You must also reserve child support when there is only limited jurisdiction in your case.

Adjusting the Child Support Schedules

Not every case fits neatly within the Michigan child support formula and child support schedules. The formula anticipated many of these exceptional cases and provided for adjustments to the schedules. The sections below describe several special cases, with the necessary adjustments.

Parents with Low or High Income

The Michigan child support formula believes that low-income parents shouldn't be discouraged from continuing or seeking work by imposing burdensome child support obligations upon them. The formula considers a parent with a net monthly income of $696 or less as a low-income parent.

For low-income noncustodial parents, the formula generally recommends that they pay around 10% of their net monthly income (but not less than $25 per month) as child support, regardless of the number of children. Low-income custodial parents get a break by having the bulk of their income disregarded when child support is figured. Pages 21-23 of the formula manual explain in detail these low-income adjustments.

Needless to say, low-income adjustments could be abused by parents. Noncustodial parents might quit working or reduce their income to avoid paying child support. Custodial parents might give up income to get more child support.

The formula recognizes this problem and provides that income can be imputed (assigned) to parents who have voluntarily and unjustifiably reduced their income. A judge decides whether income must be imputed to a parent. If so, parents can have income imputed to them according to what they could earn, rather than what they do earn. To determine parents' unused earning ability, judges must consider their prior employment experience, education, special skills and training, the local employment market, and several other factors.

Another type of adjustment must also be made when the parents' two (total family) incomes exceed the amounts in the child support schedules. The formula believes that children shouldn't share fully in parents' great wealth, so it limits support for children of affluent parents to a reasonable amount. Page 24 of the manual explains the adjustment for high earners.

Joint Parenting and the Shared Economic Responsbility Formula (SERF)

The Michigan child support formula is based on the idea that custodial parents support their children with direct spending on food, clothing, shelter, etc., while noncustodial parents provide support indirectly by paying child support. This arrangement breaks down when noncustodial parents share physical custody with the other parent or have long periods of parenting time. When noncustodial parents are also taking care of the children, it's unfair to make them provide support by both direct spending and paying child support. With this in mind, the formula adjusts child support for parents with extended joint physical custody or parenting time.

The formula manual provides a joint parenting adjustment, called a shared economic responsibility formula (SERF), when the payer has physical custody, parenting time or a combination of both, for 128 overnights or more during a year.

128 overnights might seem like a lot of time. But a joint physical custody schedule with generous parenting time can quickly reach the SERF threshold. What's more, the state is studying reducing that threshold to fewer overnights, although the issue has been controversial and a final decision has yet to be made.

Pages 27-29 of the formula manual describe the SERF adjustment in detail. If an adjustment is necessary, check the second small box inside the large child support box in paragraph #17 of the Judgment of Divorce (GRP 4c), showing that support is "based on shared economic responsibility." The base amount of support (before adjustment under the shared economic responsibility formula) and the number of overnights with the payer must be taken out of the shared economic responsibility formula and plugged into the two lines in this section.

The formula manual also recommends an abatement (decrease) of child support during extended parenting time. The formula regards extended parenting time as parenting time for six or more consecutive nights with the noncustodial parent. In that case, the formula suggests a 50% abatement during the extended parenting time (except in shared economic responsibility cases, since it already accounts for extended parenting time). You can select the recommended 50% abatement by checking the first small box inside the large child support box in paragraph #17 of the GRP 4c.

Split, Mixed and Third-Party Custody

The normal assumptions about child support also don't apply to special types of custody such as split, mixed or third-party custody.

With split or mixed custody, both parents have custody of one or more children. Since the parents are simultaneously custodial and noncustodial parents, each might owe and be owed child support. In that case, the formula provides a way to set off the parents' child support obligations and arrive at a net amount due one parent. This set-off is explained on pages 26-27 of the manual.

Sometimes custody of children is assigned to one or more nonparent third parties. In these cases, the manual, on page 34, recommends that both parents pay child support to the third-party custodians. With third-party custody, the parents will be the (joint) payers of support and the third-party custodian will be the payee.

Departing from the Child Support Formula

As explained in "Child Support" on page 21, in some cases it's permissible to depart from the Michigan child support formula and set child support at a different amount. Sometimes you and the defendant can agree to the departure. Or you might be able to depart when you can show the court that it is "unjust or inappropriate" to apply the formula. The first page of the manual explains departure.

Either way, you need the court's approval of the departure. The formula is designed to fit most cases, so courts are hesitant to allow departure. In fact, you must be able to show all of the following things before the court can approve departure:

- the child support specified by the formula for your case
- how your child support departs from the formula

More Information

As explained here, the child support formula has ways to cover small (ordinary) and large (extraordinary) uninsured health care expenses. But you want to obtain health care coverage and avoid uninsured expenses whenever possible. Look into some of these coverage options:

Medicaid (Healthy Kids). Children in low-income families should qualify for Medicaid (called the Healthy Kids program in Michigan), which provides full health care coverage. Children receiving Family Independence Program (FIP) payments automatically qualify for Medicaid. In Michigan the family income ceilings for Medicaid are higher than those for the FIP, allowing children to get Medicaid even if they don't qualify for the FIP.

Children's Health Insurance Program (MIChild). All states now have special health care coverage for children from families without employer-provided coverage but who make too much to qualify for Medicaid. Michigan's program is called MIChild (pronounced "my child.")

COBRA coverage. A 1985 law, the Consolidated Omnibus Budget Reconciliation Act, or COBRA for short, can provide health care coverage. Immediately after divorce, COBRA allows you to obtain health care coverage for you and/or dependent children from your ex's employer-provided group plan (if the employer has 20 or more employees), which can last for a maximum of three years. What's more, you don't have to show medical insurability to get COBRA-coverage, so for example, you can get coverage immediately when you have high medical risks or pre-existing conditions.

One drawback to COBRA: You may have to pay the plan premiums (both the employer and employee shares) yourself. But fortunately, the premiums must be charged at group rates, which are usually lower than individual rates.

County health plans. Ingham County has devised a health plan for those without health care coverage. It provides coverage for doctor's visits and prescription drugs, but not hospitalization. Other counties have signed on to Ingham's plan extending it all over the state.

Hill-Burton program. Years ago, the federal government provided loans and grants to many hospitals for construction and modernization under the Hill-Burton Act. In return, these Hill-Burton hospitals promised to provide a certain amount of reduced-cost or free care to low-income patients. Many hospitals have fulfilled their Hill-Burton obligations, and don't have to provide this care any more; others still must (as of 2001, there were still around 50 Hill-Burton health care facilities in Michigan). If you are hospitalized at a Hill-Burton hospital you may qualify for uncompensated care.

Individual policy. You can go into the open market and obtain an individual health plan. This type of care can be expensive, but you can limit the cost by choosing higher deductibles and co-payments.

- the reason for the departure
- the value of any property or other concessions made in lieu of support

To satisfy these requirements, prepare the Judgment of Divorce (GRP 4) as described in "Final Divorce Papers" on page 123. Insert your non-formula child support in the box in paragraph #17, and check the last small box indicating that the provisions do not follow the child support formula. Then add the following provision to your Judgment of Divorce (GRP 4e):

23. <u>Departure from Child Support Formula</u>. The child support in paragraph #17 departs from the amount specified in the child support formula. Nevertheless, the court approves the departure because it is unjust or inappropriate to order child support according to the formula. The court also finds that:

(a) the monthly child support specified in the formula is [$400]

(b) the amount ordered is [$500] per month, which is [$100 more] than the formula amount

(c) the reason for the departure is [the parties' daughter Deborah is visually impaired and needs extra support]

(d) the child support recipient received [no property or alimony] in lieu of child support

Using the child support schedules, figure what the child support is under the formula. Insert this amount in subparagraph (a). Place your non-formula amount in (b), and state the extent of the departure. You must also describe the reason for departure from the formula. One possible reason is that the child support recipient is getting alimony or property instead of more child support. State whether or not that's true in (d). If it is, use that as your reason in (c). But you may have another reason for departure, such as:

Personal debts. Many people emerge from divorce saddled with business or consumer debts. The formula takes business debts into account (business-owners can deduct them to figure net income), while it ignores consumer debts. But if consumer debts have diminished income and the ability to pay child support, these debts can be grounds for departure.

Special needs of children. The formula provides for the needs of healthy children, but it doesn't take care of the needs of handicapped children or those with extraordinary needs.

Extraordinary income of children. The formula says that the incidental income of children should be disregarded when child support is figured. But in some cases a child may have extraordinary income from a professional activity, trust or other source. The formula doesn't apply when children have extraordinary income of their own.

Health Care

Years ago, when medical costs were less, divorce judgments paid little attention to health care coverage for children. But these days, health care coverage is vital, and there are several ways judgments provide it.

Health Care Coverage

According to paragraph #18a of the Judgment of Divorce (GRP 4c), one or both parents are required to continue, or obtain, health care coverage when available at a reasonable cost. Employees can often get coverage for their children as a benefit of employment. Self-employed parents must provide coverage if the insurance is affordable; self-employeds don't have to provide coverage they can't afford.

More Information
About the Healthy Kids or MIChild programs, contact your local county health department, the FIA or the Michigan Department of Community Health at (888) 988-6300.
About COBRA, send a self-addressed stamped envelope to:
Insurance Continuation **Older Women's League (OWL)** 666 11th St. NW Washington, DC 20001
For information about local county health programs like Ingham's, call your local county health department.
About the Hill-Burton program, ask the hospital administration if the hospital is a Hill-Burton facility.
To look into individual coverage, go to Quotesmith.com for lists of health plan providers with premium estimates, without having to submit personal data.
After you find a possible provider, make sure the company is reliable and licensed by checking with Michigan's **Office of Financial and Insurance Services** at: P.O. Box 30004 Lansing, MI 48909 (517) 373-0220

Uninsured Health Care Expenses

Even the best health care coverage is bound to leave a few gaps: deductibles, co-payments and other uninsured expenses. With inferior coverage or none at all, gaps turn into gaping holes, creating a big liability for uninsured expenses.

As described above, the child support formula tries to cover small uninsured health care expenses, called ordinary expenses, by building a small supplement into the monthly child support amounts. See "Uninsured Health Care Expenses: Ordinary Expenses" on page 244 for more about these supplements.

Large or extraordinary uninsured health care expenses must also be assigned to the parents. On page 31, the formula manual recommends dividing extraordinary health care expenses between the parents according to the ratio of their incomes. So if the defendant-father earns 75% of the total family income, he would pay 75% of the expenses and the plaintiff-mother

25%. You can specify other sharing percentages (but parents cannot be assigned more than 90% or less than 10% of the extraordinary expenses). Whatever you choose, you must insert the percentage shares in paragraph #18b(2) of the Judgment of Divorce (GRP 4c).

Payment of Child Support

As explained in "Payment of Child Support" on page 23, child support is usually withheld immediately from the payer's source of income (typically wages or salary from an employer), and sent to the state disbursement unit (SDU) for transfer to the payee.

Immediate income withholding is popular with child support recipients and courts because it makes child support easier to collect. On the other hand, some child support payers dislike it because it creates more paperwork for their employers. They may want to avoid immediate income withholding and set up a different method of payment.

In some cases, it's possible to avoid immediate income withholding of child support and choose another method of payment. You can do this by opting out of the friend of the court system, either totally, partially or in a limited way. See Appendix C for complete opt-out information and forms.

Assigning Dependency Exemptions

As mentioned before, a custodial parent may claim dependent children as dependency exemptions on his/her income tax returns. However, the custodial parent can agree to assign these exemptions to the noncustodial parent. In a contested case, the divorce court can assign them to either parent.

For assignment, you need a special provision in your Judgment of Divorce (GRP 4). The assignment provision must order the custodial parent to release the dependency exemptions on the IRS's own assignment form, Release of Claim to Exemption for Child of Divorced or Separated Parents (Form 8332). After release, the noncustodial parent attaches this form to his/her income tax returns to claim the exemptions.

Form 8332 permits assignment of dependency exemptions annually, for several years, or permanently. From an assigning custodial parent's point of view, it's best to assign annually. That way, the assignment can be tied to payment of child support. And if the child support isn't fully paid by the end of the year, the custodial parent can withhold the assignment.

You must also decide whether the assignment can be modified after the divorce if circumstances change. A custodial parent will normally favor modifiability (because s/he can ask for cancellation of the assignment after nonpayment of child support); the noncustodial parent won't (because s/he wants assignment without linkage to support). Michigan law isn't clear about the modifiability of dependency exemption assignments. But generally, assignments tied to child support (an issue which is always subject to review and modification after divorce) are more modifiable than assignments which are part of property division (property division is usually nonmodifiable).

The assignment provisions below are identical except that the first example is part of child support and more apt to be modifiable, while the second is linked to property division and tends to be nonmodifiable:

23. <u>Dependency Exemptions</u>. In addition to regular child support, defendant may claim the parties' children as dependency exemptions on city, state and federal income tax returns, beginning with the tax year [1989] and continuing afterward, under the following conditions:

(a) as long as defendant has paid child support ordered in this judgment in full by the end of the year, defendant may claim the parties' children as dependency exemptions for this year

(b) after full payment of child support, plaintiff shall release the dependency exemptions for this year by executing IRS Form 8332 (or similar documents) and delivering it to defendant

(c) if defendant has not paid child support in full by the end of the year, plaintiff shall not release the dependency exemptions for this year and may claim the exemptions for this year

23. <u>Dependency Exemptions</u>. In addition to the regular property division, defendant may claim the parties' children as dependency exemptions on city, state and federal income tax returns, beginning with the tax year [1989] and continuing afterward, under the following conditions:

(a) as long as defendant has paid child support ordered in this judgment in full by the end of the year, defendant may claim the parties' children as dependency exemptions for this year

(b) after full payment of child support, plaintiff shall release the dependency exemptions for this year by executing IRS Form 8332 (or similar documents) and delivering it to defendant

(c) if defendant has not paid child support in full by the end of the year, plaintiff shall not release the dependency exemptions for this year and may claim the exemptions for this year

Michigan
Child Support Formula
Manual

2001

Friend of the Court Bureau
State Court Administrative Office
P.O. Box 30048
Lansing, Michigan 48909

Michigan
Child Support Formula
Manual

2001
Thirteenth Revision

John D. Ferry, Jr.
State Court Administrator
State Court Administrative Office
P.O. Box 30048
Lansing, Michigan 48909

TABLE OF CONTENTS

Changes to the Child Support Formula Manual   ii

Preface   iii

Purpose of this Formula   iv

I. Statutory Requirements   1
- A.   Application of and Deviation from the Formula 1
- B.   Requirement to Investigate and to Petition for Modification 1
- C.   Minimum Threshold Amount 2

II. Determining Net Income   3
- A.   Sources and Variations in Income 3
- B.   Children's Income 4
- C.   Overtime and Second Jobs 5
- D.   Social Security Retirement/Disability Benefits 5
- E.   Deferred Compensation/Individual Retirement Account (IRA) 6
- F.   Inheritances, One-Time Gifts 6
- G.   Means Tested Sources of Income 7
- H.   Identifying Net Income 7
- I.   Imputation of Income 8
- J.   Non-Income Producing and Low-Income Producing Assets 9
- K.   Allowable Deductions from Gross Income 10
- L.   Existing Support Orders 11
- M.   Other Minor Children 11
- N.   Stepchildren 12
- O.   Special Considerations in Determining Income 14

III. Calculating Child Support Amounts   17
- A.   Calculating Child Support Using Table III 17
- B.   Calculating Child Support Using Support Schedules 21
- C.   Calculation of Child Support in Low/No Income Cases 21
- D.   Calculation of Child Support in High Income Cases 24

IV. Miscellaneous Provisions   25
- A.   Different Custody Arrangements For Different Children 25
- B.   Shared Economic Responsibility 26
- C.   Parenting Time Abatement 27
- D.   Health Care Expenses 28
- E.   Child Care Expenses 29
- F.   Third Party Custodians 32
- G.   Arrearage Guidelines 32
- H.   Stipulated Agreements 35
- I.   Ex Parte and Temporary Orders 36
- J.   Child Support Recommendations in Contested Custody Cases 38

**Appendix A: Statutory Requirements
for Support Investigations**   39

**Appendix B: Reasonable Cost of
Maintaining Health Insurance Coverage**   45

Appendix C: Support Schedules   49
- One Child Support Schedule 51
- Two Children Support Schedule 59
- Three Children Support Schedule 67
- Four Children Support Schedule 75
- Five or More Children Support Schedule 83

Changes to the Child Support Formula Manual

	2001 Formula Manual Changes
Page No.	**Change**
1	Clarified deviation language, and <u>Burba</u> v <u>Burba</u> [461 Mich 637 (2000)] added as a reference for deviation.
5	Clarified social security language that no "additional" support is to be paid when the grant is greater than the calculated support amount.
17-19	Updated Table III with the August 2000 CPI-U Detroit figure.
21-23	Updated low income amount with the 2000 DHHS Poverty Guideline figure in the Low/No Income section.
26	Added note regarding deviation to Shared Economic Responsibility section.
27-28	Clarified Parenting Time Abatement section for when less than all of the children visit.
47	Updated Reasonable Cost of Health Insurance Coverage Table with August 2000 CPI-U Detroit and new low income figures; modified table format.
Appendix C	Support Schedules updated based on changes to Table III and the poverty guideline.

Preface

The Michigan Friend of the Court Act of 1982 and the Federal Child Support Enforcement Amendments of 1984 require the State Court Administrative Office's Friend of the Court Bureau to develop "a formula to be used in establishing and modifying as a guideline in recommending a child support amount. The formula shall be based upon the needs of the child and the actual resources of each parent." MCL 552.519(3)(a)(vi); MSA 25.176(19)(3)(a)(vi), 42 USC 667(467)(a). "The child support formula developed by the bureau . . . shall be used as a guideline in recommending child support" by the Friend of the Court offices (emphasis added). MCL 552.505(e); MSA 25.176(5)(e). In 1998, the Friend of the Court Act was amended to also provide "the formula shall include guidelines for setting and administratively adjusting the amount of periodic payments on overdue support..."

A subcommittee of the Friend of the Court Advisory Committee began work on this guideline in 1983. The subcommittee, popularly known as the Child Support Guideline Committee, extensively reviewed methodologies currently in use for determining child support in Michigan and nationwide, held public hearings, conducted original research and received input from professional economists and other researchers. A final report was submitted to the Friend of the Court Advisory Committee in May of 1986.

The Friend of the Court Advisory Committee, after receiving public comment, first adopted the guideline in December of 1986, effective May, 1987. The Advisory Committee established a standing Subcommittee to review comments and to make recommendations for the periodic update of the child support guideline.

The formula will be reviewed at least every four years as required by federal legislation, more commonly referred to as the Family Support Act of 1988. Comments should be made in writing to:

Friend of the Court Advisory Committee
c/o State Court Administrative Office
P.O. Box 30048
Lansing, MI 48909

Additional copies of this document are available:

on the internet at   http://www.supremecourt.state.mi.us/courtdata/friend.htm;

at Depository Libraries for the State of Michigan Documents (to see a list please see the Library of Michigan web page http://www.libofmich.lib.mi.us/services/midoclibs.html; or

for prepaid purchase for $5.00. Make check or money order payable to the State of Michigan and send a request to:

Department of Management and Budget
Office Services Division
Materials Management
P.O. Box 30026
Lansing, Michigan 48909

Purpose of this Formula

The formula is based on common factors which are appropriate for use in the determination of child support obligations. The factors include parental income, family size and ages of children. Based on these factors, the formula provides for appropriate support amounts in divorce judgments, paternity orders, family support orders and other cases involving the support of children.

Use of the formula is required in establishing child support recommendations in domestic relations cases. The formula will insure greater uniformity by those who make recommendations and increase predictability for those who require child support orders.

There may be special cases where the formula cannot be relied on exclusively. For these cases, the formula will provide the court and friend of the court with points of reference from which a support determination can be made. In addition, it is anticipated that this document will assist parents in reaching agreements on the appropriate level of child support at the time of a divorce or other domestic relations proceeding, or upon modification of a previous order.

I. Statutory Requirements

A. Application of and Deviation from the Formula

The court must follow the Formula, whether or not the parties agree on the amount of support, except where it has an "unjust or inappropriate" result. The same standard applies to the friend of the court office when making support recommendations. Each of the enabling statutes state:

"(2)   Except as otherwise provided in this section, the court shall order support in an amount determined by application of the child support formula developed by the state friend of the court bureau. The court may enter an order that deviates from the formula if the court determines from the facts of the case that application of the child support formula would be unjust or inappropriate and sets forth in writing or on the record all of the following:

    (a)   The support amount determined by application of the child support formula.

    (b)   How the support order deviates from the child support formula.

    (c)   The value of property or other support awarded in lieu of the payment of child support, if applicable.

    (d)   The reasons why application of the child support formula would be unjust or inappropriate in the case.

(3)   Subsection (2) does not prohibit the court from entering a support order that is agreed to by the parties and that deviates from the child support formula, if the requirements of subsection (2) are met."

See: MCL 552.15; MSA 25.95, MCL 552.16; MSA 25.96, MCL 552.17; MSA 25.97, MCL 552.452; MSA 25.222(2), MCL 552.517; MSA 25.176(17), MCL 722.27; MSA 25.312(7), MCL 722.3; MSA 25.244(3), MCL 722.717; MSA 25.497, MCL 780.164; MSA 25.225(14), Ghidotti v Barber 459 Mich 189 (1998), and Burba v Burba 461 Mich 637 (2000).

The Michigan Supreme Court has held that the statutory deviation factors must be recorded. "While a trial court may enter an order of support that deviates from the formula, it may not do so without setting forth in writing or on the record why following the formula would be unjust or inappropriate." Ghidotti v Barber 459 Mich 189 (1998). The criteria for deviating from the formula are mandatory, and to fulfill its statutory duty, a court must carefully articulate these factors to memorialize and explain its holding. Burba v Burba 461 Mich 637, 644-45 (2000).

B. Requirement to Investigate and to Petition for Modification

Under Section 17 of the Friend of the Court Act [MCL 552.517; MSA 25.176(17)], included in Appendix A), after a final judgment or order has been entered, the friend of the court office is required to periodically review support orders under the criteria outlined in the Act. The Act also requires the friend of the court office to petition the court if there is a determination that a modification is necessary, unless:

(a) the difference between the existing support order and the proposed support amount is within the minimum threshold amount or (b) the court had previously determined that application of the formula was unjust or inappropriate, and the office determines that the facts of the case, the reason for the deviation, and amount of the prior ordered deviation all remain unchanged.

C.   Minimum Threshold Amount

The "minimum threshold amount" requires that the friend of the court office petition for a modification if the proposed change is ten-percent (10%) or more of the existing order or $5 per week (or the equivalent for orders based on other time periods other than weekly), whichever is less.

For the actual language and requirements of the Friend of the Court Act on child support review and modification process, please see MCL 552.517; MSA 25.176 et seq. in Appendix A.

Example:

The friend of the court office conducts a support review as required by statute and the current support order is $70. The proposed change is to $76. The friend of the court office must petition the court to modify the order, since the change is greater than the $5.00 threshold.

The friend of the court office conducts a support review as required by statute and the current support order is $20. The proposed change is to $17. The friend of the court office must petition the court to modify the order, since the $3.00 change is greater than the 10% threshold.

The friend of the court office conducts a support review as required by statute and the current support order is $30. The proposed change is to $32. The office is not required to petition to modify the order since the change is less than the 10% threshold and less than the $5.00 threshold.

II. Determining Net Income

The term "net income" refers to gross income minus all of the deductions allowed for the purpose of calculating child support. "Net income" many times will not be equivalent to an individual's net pay, net taxable income, or other similar terms used by other governmental agencies.

A.   Sources and Variations in Income

Where there is evidence of considerable year-to-year variation in income due to things like overtime, second jobs, bonuses, or profit sharing, information from at least the preceding twelve months should be used in calculating net income. This will minimize seasonal effects or other variations in income. Certain occupations and self-employed persons may have considerable variation in income from year to year. The use of three years income information is recommended where such variation exists.

"Income" means any of the following:

(i)   Commissions, earnings, salaries, wages, and other income due or to be due in the future to an individual from his or her employer and successor employers.

(ii)   A payment due or to be due in the future to an individual from a profit-sharing plan, a pension plan, an insurance contract, an annuity, social security, unemployment compensation, supplemental unemployment benefits, or worker's compensation.

(iii)   An amount of money that is due to an individual as a debt of another individual, partnership, association, or private or public corporation, the United States or a federal agency, this state or a political subdivision of this state, another state or a political subdivision of another state, or another legal entity that is indebted to the individual. (MCL 552.602(i); MSA 25.164(2))

"Source of income" means an employer or successor employer or any other individual or entity that owes or will owe income to the payer. (MCL 552.602(v); MSA 25.164(2))

The following list outlines types of income from which custodial and noncustodial parents' incomes should be determined. Although the list includes the most common forms of income, it is not an exhaustive list, and other sources may be considered. These sources of income are for the purpose of establishing child support and may not correspond to the sources of taxable income as set forth by the Internal Revenue Service (IRS).

Types of Income:

1.   Salaries and Wages
2.   Cost of Living Allowance (COLA)
3.   Shift Premium
4.   Overtime (see instructions on page 5)
5.   Second Job (see instructions on page 5)
6.   Commissions
7.   All Bonuses

Types of Income (Continued):

8.   Profit Sharing
9.   Interest
10. Dividends
11. Annuities
12. Pensions/Longevity
13. Deferred Compensation/Individual Retirement Account(IRA)(see instructions on page 6)
14. Trust Fund Payments
15. Unemployment Benefits
16. Strike Pay
17. Supplemental Unemployment Benefits (SUB) Pay
18. Sick Benefits
19. Worker's Compensation
20. Social Security Retirement/Disability Benefits (see instructions on page 5)
21. Veteran Administration Benefits
22. Disability Insurance
23. G.I. Benefits - excluding education allotment
24. National Guard and Reserves Drill Pay
25. Armed Services - Base pay plus allowance for quarters, rations and specialty pay
26. Dividends Earned from Life Insurance Policies
27. Allowance for Rent (when provided by the employer as a fringe benefit)
28. Rental Income
29. Alimony/Spousal Support
30. Net Gambling Winnings

31. Tax-exempt income, such as the interest and dividends paid on municipal bonds and other government securities.

32. Insurance or other similar payments received as compensation for lost earnings (but not payments to compensate for medical bills or for property loss or damage).

33. Adoption Subsidy - standard/basic needs portion for child(ren) in case under consideration (see Section B. Children's Income, for exceptions).

See Section O on Page 14 below, for special considerations to keep in mind when determining the income of self-employed persons, business owners, and business executives.

B.   Children's Income

A minor child's benefits from a Supplemental Security Income (SSI) program or income from employment received prior to attaining eighteen (18) years of age and/or prior to graduation from high school, while attending school on a full time basis, should not ordinarily be considered as income. There may be cases, however, where a child is a professional and/or is involved in some activity and earns a large sum of money. In these cases, discretion must be exercised.

The medical needs and intensive rate portion of the Adoption Subsidy and all of the Family Support Subsidy shall not be considered as income. These subsidies are excluded as public policy has identified them as necessary for meeting special emotional and physical needs of children and families.

C.   Overtime and Second Jobs

All of overtime and second job income should be considered in the determination of child support payments. Any evidence produced that overtime or second job hours will be changed in the future should be taken into consideration when determining net income.

D.   Social Security Retirement/Disability Benefits

When children receive dependent benefits from a Social Security Retirement, Survivor's or Disability Insurance Program based on the earnings record of the noncustodial parent, those benefits should <u>not</u> be considered as income to the custodial parent. However, those benefits should be considered, for the purpose of making a child support recommendation, according to the following instructions:

Step 1:   Determine the noncustodial and the custodial parents' net weekly incomes.

Step 2:   Determine the normal support amount from the appropriate schedule.

Step 3:   Determine the weekly amount of Social Security benefits attributable to the noncustodial parent received for the child(ren).

Step 4:   Subtract the attributable weekly amount from the appropriate amount of support calculated based on the parents' incomes.

If the grant received by the child(ren) from Social Security is <u>greater than</u> the normal support recommendation, no additional support should be recommended. If the grant received by the child(ren) from Social Security is <u>less than</u> the normal support recommendation, the difference between the grant amount and the support recommendation should be made up by the support recommendation.

Example: Adjust support for noncustodial social security benefits paid for minor children.

Step 1:   Determine the noncustodial and the custodial parents' net weekly incomes.

The noncustodial parent earns $400 net per week.

The custodial parent earns $200 net per week.

Step 2: For five minor children, determine the normal support amount from the five or more children schedule.

Support is $216.00   per week for five children

Step 3: Determine the weekly amount of Social Security benefits attributable to the noncustodial parent received for the child(ren).

$430.00 children's monthly benefit attributable to the noncustodial parent.

$430.00   (per month) ÷   4.345   (weeks per month) = $99.00 (per week)

Step 4: Subtract the attributable weekly amount from the appropriate amount of support calculated based on the parents' incomes.

$216.00   (weekly support) - $99.00   (weekly benefit) = $117.00 (per week)

All other Social Security Retirement, Survivor's or Disability Insurance Benefits received by the children shall be considered income of the custodial parent. (For Supplemental Security Income (SSI), see Means Tested Sources of Income on page 7)

The following cases offer information regarding consideration of social security benefits: Frens v Frens, 191 MichApp 654 (1990); and Jenerou v Jenerou, 200 MichApp 265 (1993).

E.   Deferred Compensation/Individual Retirement Account (IRA)

If a payer retires and receives payment from an IRA, defined contribution, or deferred compensation plan, income from contributions to the plan which were previously assessed for child support should be excluded on a prorated basis.

Example:
A payer's IRA account totals $200,000 at the time of retirement, but $15,000 in contributions to the account were made while the payer was under an obligation to pay child support, and were included as income at that time. Therefore, 15/200 of the benefit payments should be excluded from consideration when computing child support from those payments.

F.   Inheritances, One-Time Gifts

Interest earned from inheritances and gifts should be considered as income. Property and principal should not be considered as income.

G. **Means Tested Sources of Income**

Means tested sources of income such as Temporary Assistance to Needy Families (TANF), Family Independence Payments (FIP)(formerly AFDC), Food Stamps, Earned Income Credit (Federal Taxes), Supplemental Security Income (SSI), etc. should <u>not</u> be considered as income to either parent for the purpose of determining child support (Exception: Other Minor Children, see page 11).

H. **Identifying Net Income**

Net income should be determined from actual tax returns whenever possible. When tax returns cannot be obtained, the following is recommended:

1. Employer Tax Guides for federal, state and local taxes may be used to determine net income by subtracting the appropriate number of exemptions and their associated deductions from gross earnings.

2. When determining parties' net incomes for the purpose of establishing <u>temporary</u> child support recommendations, use the parties' current filing status.

3. When determining the parties' net incomes for the purpose of modifying an existing child support order, it is beneficial for both parents to produce their actual tax returns because it will provide more accuracy in the determination of actual taxes paid. In the event that tax returns are not made available, taxes should be estimated based on the best available information such as W-2 forms, employer's statements, employer tax guides, pay vouchers, testimony, etc.

If parents and their new spouses file joint tax returns, <u>and that return is made available</u>, it will be necessary to ascertain each spouse's income. The new spouse's income is deducted from the total joint income and joint taxes are prorated between the spouses. <u>When prorating the joint taxes between the spouses, use the fraction obtained by dividing the employment income (salary, wages, tips, commissions, bonuses, profit sharing, etc.) of the parent by the total employment income of the parent and the new spouse</u>.

Example:			
Step 1:	Parent's employment income:		$20,000
	New spouse's employment income:		+$40,000
	Total employment income:		$60,000
Step 2:	Parent's employment income divided by total employment income:		$20,000/$60,000
	Resulting fraction/percentage:		1/3 or 33.3%
Step 3:	Total joint tax obligation* (as stated on the tax return)		$15,000

        *Including taxes on non-employment income such as
interest, dividends, capital gains, etc.

Multiply fraction/percentage by total joint tax obligation:	1/3 x $15,000
Parent's share of joint tax obligation:	$5,000

When the joint tax return of the parent and the new spouse is <u>not</u> made available, assume that the parent's income is the total family income and determine the joint tax obligation using the parent's income. Also assume that the parent is entitled to each dependency tax exemption claimed by the parent and the new spouse.

Note: This approach may have the effect of understating the parent's tax liability and, therefore, overstating his/her net income. Parents with new spouses who file joint income tax returns should be advised that the failure to make the joint return available may result in a financial penalty to them in the form of a higher or lower support recommendation based on the above assumptions.

I.   Imputation of Income

Imputation of income is treating a party as having income or resources that the party does not actually have. This usually occurs in cases where a party voluntarily reduces his/her income.

The determination as to the appropriateness of imputation in a particular case is a judicial one. In all cases in which the friend of the court investigation shows voluntary reduction of income or where there is voluntary unexercised ability to earn, the friend of the court <u>shall</u> make two recommendations: one is based on actual income and the other is based on actual plus imputed income. The recommendation should also take into account the possible inclusion of a child care recommendation where imputation would make that issue relevant. The recommendation shall include the basis for imputation and the basis of the amount imputed.

In considering a party's unexercised ability to earn, the friend of the court shall consider among other equitable factors the following criteria:

1. Prior employment experience;
2. Educational level;
3. Physical and mental disabilities;
4. The presence of children of the marriage in the party's home and its impact on the earnings of the parties;
5. Availability of employment in the local geographical area;
6. The prevailing wage rates in the local geographical area;
7. Special skills and training; or
8. Whether there is any evidence that the party in question is able to earn the imputed income.

This imputation provision must be applied equally to payers and payees and to men and women. Imputation is <u>not</u> appropriate where:

1.   A payee/payer source of income is a means tested income such as Temporary Assistance to Needy Families (TANF), Family Independence Payments (FIP)(formerly AFDC), Food Stamps, Supplemental Security Income (SSI), etc.;

2.   There has not been a significant reduction in income compared to the period preceding the filing of the complaint (or the motion for modification, in a modification proceeding); or

3.   The party is employed full time (35 or more hours per week), but is in a situation where employment income has been reduced through reduced hours (such as leaving a second job or refusing overtime).

In cases in which income is imputed, the amount imputed should be sufficient to bring total income up to the level it would have been if there had been no reduction in income, <u>provided</u> that the imputation computation shall not be based on any hours beyond 40 per week nor any overtime or shift premiums.

The following cases offer guidance in determining whether imputation of income is appropriate; <u>Travis</u> v <u>Travis</u>, 19 Mich App 128 (1969); <u>Moncada</u> v <u>Moncada</u>, 81 Mich App 26 (1978); <u>Dunn</u> v <u>Dunn</u>, 105 Mich App 793 (1981); <u>Heilman</u> v <u>Heilman</u>, 95 Mich App 728 (1980); <u>Joslin</u> v <u>LaVance</u>, 154 Mich App 501 (1986); <u>Rohloff</u> v <u>Rohloff</u>, 161 Mich App 766 (1987); <u>Daniels</u> v <u>Daniels</u>, 165 Mich App 726 (1988); <u>Olson</u> v <u>Olson</u>, 189 Mich App 620 (1991) (aff'd in lieu of lv gtd, 439 Mich 986); and <u>Ghidotti</u> v <u>Barber</u> [459 Mich 189 (1998)].

J.   Non-Income Producing and Low-Income Producing Assets

Non-income or low-income producing assets should be evaluated to establish a reasonable rate of expected return depending on the type and nature of the asset. The expected income should be used when determining child support. The intent of this section is to prohibit a parent from placing investments into non-income and low-income producing assets during the time child support is due, and to insure that child support is based upon appropriate or expected asset value/income relationships; it is not to require or deny certain types of investments.

Non-income producing assets such as cash, cash surrender value of insurance policies, loans to or stock in a controlled or family owned corporation, loans to third parties, real estate, jewelry, antiques, collections, inventories, vehicles, pension and profit sharing plans, etc., that are owned by custodial and noncustodial parents, after the property is distributed pursuant to the judgment of divorce or at the time child support recommendations are made, may be used to determine expected income. Expected income may be attributed to those assets by using current average interest rates for passbook savings accounts, treasury bills, treasury bonds, certificates of deposit, etc.

Certain non-income producing assets such as a home and its reasonable furnishings, an automobile, and other small non-income assets should be excluded from consideration.

K.   Allowable Deductions from Gross Income

1.   Alimony/Spousal Support

Any alimony/spousal support orders should be deducted prior to the calculation and deduction of federal, state and local income taxes. The calculation of Social Security taxes (FICA) is based on gross income before deduction of the alimony/spousal support order.

2.   Federal, State, and Local Taxes

3.   F.I.C.A.

In the absence of an explicit written agreement or judicial order to the contrary, allocation of tax exemptions must be based on the actual residence of the child. That is, the person with whom the child resides the greater number of days during the calendar year should be presumed to be entitled to the dependent exemption for that child.

In determining filing status (Single or Married) presume the status that is most consistent with the situation of the parties as of the date of the order based on this recommendation.

> ***Example:***
> If a party is currently single, presume they will stay single and will have a single filing status. If and when a party's actual filing status changes, they can request a support modification based on that actual change of circumstance.

4.   Any mandatory withholdings when they are required as a condition of employment (for example, most union dues and some retirement plans).

5.   The determinable portion of health insurance premiums for the child(ren).

When a determinable portion of the health insurance co-pay/premiums, being paid by either parent, can specifically be attributed to the child(ren), that portion should be subtracted dollar for dollar from that parent's gross income. If a party has a health insurance policy that covers family members other than the minor children, the "determinable portion" would be the average cost per person covered by the policy.

6.   Premiums for term equivalent insurance policies when the child(ren) are the beneficiaries.

When term life insurance premiums are being paid by either parent and the child(ren) is (are), by order or judgment, the beneficiaries of the policy, that premium should be deducted dollar for dollar from gross income. In the case of whole life insurance policies, where the child(ren) is (are) the beneficiaries, a premium amount should be calculated for the term insurance equivalent and then subtracted dollar for dollar from gross income.

7. Employer contributions to private qualified pension plans, to the extent that such contributions are less than 5.5% of the employee's gross income.

L. Existing Support Orders

Existing support orders, which are orders for children other than those in the case specifically under consideration, require an adjustment to the parents' net incomes in order to determine the net income on which child support for the case under consideration should be based. Determine each parent's prior and subsequent support orders which are for children other than those in the case specifically under consideration and subtract that amount, dollar for dollar, from their net incomes. In determining the amount of an existing support order that should be deducted, subtract only the actual amount of the order, <u>including court-ordered child care expenses</u>. Payments on an arrearage should <u>not</u> be deducted.

If there is reliable information that the existing order has not been complied with for a significant period of time, two recommendations shall be prepared, one with and one without the existing order adjustment.

Example:
The noncustodial parent earns $300 net per week and pays child support of $61 per week for one child in another case.

$$\$300 - 61 = \$239$$

The noncustodial parent's support obligation for the case under consideration would be based on a weekly net income of $239.

M. Other Minor Children

The following method should be used for determining the net incomes of parents who currently have biological or legally adopted children from other relationships living in their households.

Step 1: Determine the net weekly income of the custodial and the noncustodial parents. (For purposes of an other children adjustment only, include the other biological/adoptive child(ren) income, other than from employment, as part of the parents' income. Do not include income of the parties' stepchildren or court ordered child support).

Step 2: Determine the number of biological/legally adopted children living in the custodial and/or the noncustodial parents' households.

Step 3: Adjust each parent's net income by subtracting the dollar amount of an existing support order (if applicable). Adjust each parent's net income according to the number of biological/legally adopted children in their household by multiplying their net incomes by the appropriate percentage found in Table I.

When parents have other children, the applicable percentages are derived from the <u>average</u> percentages calculated by using Table III (see page 17). When there is 1 biological/legally adopted child in the custodial or the noncustodial parent's household, multiply net income by .896 (see Table I, page 12). The factor of .896 is derived by dividing the average base support percentage for 1 child (20.8%) by 2 and then subtracting that number (10.4) from 100. When there are 2 biological/legally adopted children, multiply by .841, when there are 3 biological/legally adopted children, multiply by .798, when there are 4 biological/legally adopted children, multiply by .773, and when there are 5 biological/legally adopted children, multiply by .752.

> Step 4:   Apply each parent's income, as determined in Step 3 to the schedule with the correct number of children for whom this modification is being sought. This results in the appropriate amount of support to be paid by the noncustodial parent.

Table I
Percentages Applied to Net Income
when Parents have Other Children

Number of Children	Adjustment Percentage
1	89.6%
2	84.1%
3	79.8%
4	77.3%
5 or more	75.2%

Example:

The noncustodial parent earns $400 net per week. The custodial parent, who earns $220 net per week, requests a modification of the support order for the three children. In considering this modification request, the two biological children currently living in the noncustodial parent's household should be taken into account.

> Step 1:   Noncustodial parent earns $400 net per week. Custodial parent earns $220 net per week.

> Step 2:   There are two biological/legally adopted children living in the noncustodial parent's household.

> Step 3: $ 400 x .841 = $336   is the net income figure used to calculate support for the noncustodial parent.

> Step 4:   Determine the amount of support for the three children from the prior marriage based on the noncustodial parent's income of $336 and custodial parent's income of $220.

N.   Stepchildren

In general, stepchildren should not be considered when determining the appropriateness of a child support modification for a stepparent. In Michigan, children are the responsibility of their natural/adoptive parents. However, there may be cases in which support is unavailable from <u>both</u> natural/adoptive parents <u>and</u> stepparents are required to make substantial contributions to their stepchildren's support.

Both of the following conditions **<u>must</u>** be satisfied before stepchildren may be considered:

<u>Condition One:</u>
It may be appropriate to consider stepchildren when their noncustodial parent earns no income and does not have the ability to earn income; **and**

<u>Condition Two:</u>
It may be appropriate to consider stepchildren when their custodial parent earns no income and does not have the ability to earn income.

After it is established that **both** of these conditions exist, the following method should be used for determining the net incomes of parents who currently have stepchildren living in their households.

<u>Step 1:</u>   Determine the net weekly incomes of the parties in the case under review.

<u>Step 2:</u>   Determine the number of stepchildren living in the party-stepparent's household for whom the party-stepparent is the sole source of income.

<u>Step 3:</u>   Adjust the stepparent's income, according to the number of stepchildren in the current household, by multiplying the stepparent's income by the appropriate adjustment percentage from Table II.

The applicable percentages when parents have stepchildren are derived from the average percentages calculated by using Table III (see page 17). When there is one stepchild in the stepparent's household, multiply by .948 (see Table II). The factor of .948 is derived by dividing the average support percentage for one child (20.8%) by 4 and then subtracting that number (5.2) from 100. When there are 2 stepchildren, multiply by .921, when there are 3 stepchildren, multiply by .899, when there are 4 stepchildren, multiply by .886, when there are 5 stepchildren, multiply by .876.

<u>Step 4:</u>   Apply the stepparent's adjusted income, as determined in Step 3, and their former spouse's income to the schedule with the correct number of children for whom this modification is being sought.

Table II
Percentages Applied to Net Income
when Parents have Stepchildren

Number of Children	Adjustment Percentage
1	94.8%
2	92.1%

13

3	89.9%
4	88.6%
5 or more	87.6%

O.   Special Considerations in Determining Income of Self-Employed Persons, Business Owners, and Business Executives

There are special difficulties in determining the income of self-employed persons and business owners. This is due to at least four related causes. First, self-employed persons and business owners often have types of income and expenses not frequently encountered in determining the income of wage- and salary-earning employees. Second, the tax rules and tax forms associated with self-employment income are not only quite different from those associated with ordinary income from employment, but are designed with many additional purposes unrelated to child support determination and may therefore be difficult to translate into child support terms. Third, business balance sheets and other records also have purposes unrelated to child support determination, and are similarly difficult to translate into child support terms. Finally, there are potential difficulties because persons who have significant control over the form and manner of their own compensation may be able to arrange that compensation so as to be able to minimize the amount visible to friends of the court and others. To a somewhat lesser extent, all these considerations also apply to business executives who may have little or no ownership interest in the business.

The objective of determining income for purposes of this formula is to estimate as accurately as possible the amount of income actually available for support of children. Because tax rules and forms, and business balance sheets, as noted above, have quite different purposes, it is necessary to examine such documents carefully, with an emphasis on what is not available from those documents and what needs translation into child support terms.

These considerations apply to **all** forms of self-employment and business ownership, regardless of whether the business is organized as a corporation, a partnership, a sole proprietorship, or is a completely informal operation (of course, the form of organization will make a major difference in the sort of tax documents and business records available). As noted, many of them will also apply to business executives, again without regard to the form of legal organization of the business.

Special attention should be given to the following factors:

1. **Unusual forms of income**:

The employment income of self-employed persons, business owners, and business executives may come in many forms other than wages and salaries. These might include distributed profits of the business (including under a profit-sharing plan), officers' fees and other compensation, management or consulting fees, commissions, and bonuses.

2. **In-kind income**:

14

Income might be received in a form other than cash. Among the most common forms of such income are use of a company car, free admission to entertainment provided by the business to its clients, and purchases of stock or other goods and services. All such in-kind income should be priced at it's market value (the price that a person not affiliated with the business would have had to pay); the amount (if any) that was paid by the party for the goods or services out of his or her pocket should be subtracted; and the remaining amount counted as income (note that part or all of the items added to income in this section may be allowable as deductions under Section 6 on Page 15).

3. **Re-directed income**:

In some cases, income to the owner or executive might be treated by the company as if it were something else. One example would be personal loans to the owner or executive which will not be paid back. These can later be "forgiven" by the company, or otherwise converted into income to the individual, once the time of child support determination is past. Although it should be presumed that such loans are in fact income, the presumption may be overcome if there is a history of such past loans being made and being repaid in a timely manner with market interest rates, and the current loan is at market interest rates and is fully paid up in accordance with a commercially reasonable time schedule. The amount by which a commercially reasonable repayment amount exceeds the amount actually repaid should be treated as income.

Another form of redirected income is payments by the business (in the form of wages, salaries, or payments for services) made to friends or relatives of the individual. If the individual cannot demonstrate that there is a history of such payments preceding the separation (or motion for redetermination of child support) by several months or that the payments are a fair market value payment for services actually performed, then the payments shall be treated as income to the individual.

4. **Deferred income**:

It is possible for business owners and executives to reduce their income for the period of child support determination by temporarily lowering their own salaries, fees, distributed profits, etc. Past practices should be examined with care to determine whether the most recent information on such incomes is in line with historical patterns. For example, if it has been normal for a business to distribute a certain percentage of profits to owners, but the most recent year's distribution was substantially below that percentage, income for child support determination should be based on the historical average. Recent reductions in salary, bonuses, management fees, etc., as a percentage of gross income of the business should be treated similarly.

5. **Fringe benefits**

Certain fringe benefits paid by the business should be counted as income to the individual for child support determination purposes, even though such payments are not considered income for tax purposes. These include contributions to pension or other retirement plans, except for the employer share of social security and medicare (FICA) taxes and contributions to qualified private retirement plans of up to 5.5% of the individual's gross income. Contributions in excess of these exceptions are to be counted as income.

6. **Deductions**:

For a wide variety of historical and policy reasons, there are a considerable number of deductions allowed for taxation of business and individuals that are irrelevant to, and therefore **not** allowed as deductions from income for purposes of, child support determination <u>except for expenses which are consistent with the nature of the business</u>. These include the following:

a. Rent paid by the business to the individual (unless the rent is otherwise counted as income to the individual);

b. Certain depreciation allowances. (Depreciation is an allowance for the presumed declining market value of assets used by the business. For tax purposes, depreciation allowances serve the function of spreading the deduction that would be associated with the expense of a purchase over several tax years; because the depreciation periods typically understate the useful life of many assets, depreciation allowances also provide some incentive to purchase new assets.) The **only** depreciation allowances that are permitted to be used as deductions from income for child support purposes are those that: 1) involve the property of the individual (not a corporation or partnership); **and** 2) involve tangible personal property (thus not financial assets or realty) other than automobiles or home offices; **and** 3) are based on straight-line (and not accelerated) tax depreciation. (Straight-line depreciation is when equal dollar amounts are claimed as depreciation allowances on a given asset in each of several tax years. Individuals who used accelerated depreciation on their tax returns can claim a deduction for the straight-line amount, provided the deduction meets the other criteria, if they can prove through an affidavit from an independent CPA what the straight-line amounts would have been).

c. Home office expenses, including rent, hazard insurance, utilities, repairs, and maintenance;

d. Business entertainment expenses on themselves (expenses on customers are allowable as deductions);

e. Travel expenses, except where such expenses are inherent in the nature of the business or occupation (e.g., For a traveling salesperson), and in no case in excess of rates allowed by the state of Michigan for travel by it's employees (such as automobile mileage rates, airplane coach rates, etc.);

f. Automobile repair and maintenance expenses.

Note: Some items listed above appear in more than one section. This is because they may appear on both individual and employer tax returns, in somewhat different guises.

III. Calculating Child Support Amounts

This section describes the methods of calculating support. One is by using various percentages of total family income and calculating support based on a ratio of incomes. In cases where parties have no or low income, a poverty level or low income calculation method is used. Another method is to use the child support schedules.

A.   Calculating Child Support Using Table III

Various percentages of net income are used to determine child support in this formula. The percentages are based on the number of children and the level of total net family income. The percentages are displayed in Table III shown below. The total net family income levels against which the percentages are applied are adjusted on an annual basis, using the Consumer Price Index for Metropolitan Detroit, with December, 1985 as the base.

Table III
Total Child Support at Various Income Levels

Table III		ONE CHILD				
Monthly Family Net Income	Percentage Allocated [1]	Base Support	+	Marginal Percentage	over	Income Level
$999	25.5%	$254.75	+	24.17%	over	$999
$1,604	25.0%	$401.00	+	17.50%	over	$1,604
$2,187	23.0%	$503.01	+	16.66%	over	$2,187
$2,807	21.6%	$606.31	+	14.64%	over	$2,807
$3,645	20.0%	$729.00	+	13.91%	over	$3,645
$5,176	18.2%	$942.03	+	12.37%	over	$5,176
$6,379	17.1%	$1,090.81	+	11.23%	over	$6,379
$8,019	15.9%	$1,275.02	+	10.00%	over	$8,019

[1] *NOTE: Due to the Low/No Income adjustment, these figures may not be applied if a parent earns a minimal income. See Item C in this section.*

17

Table III (Continued)
Total Child Support at Various Income Levels

Table III		TWO CHILDREN				
Monthly Family Net Income	Percentage Allocated [1]	Base Support	+	Marginal Percentage	over	Income Level
$999	39.4%	$393.61	+	36.22%	over	$999
$1,604	38.2%	$612.73	+	26.20%	over	$1,604
$2,187	35.0%	$765.45	+	23.68%	over	$2,187
$2,807	32.5%	$912.28	+	22.50%	over	$2,807
$3,645	30.2%	$1,100.79	+	21.75%	over	$3,645
$5,176	27.7%	$1,433.75	+	20.28%	over	$5,176
$6,379	26.3%	$1,677.68	+	17.01%	over	$6,379
$8,019	24.4%	$1,956.64	+	15.00%	over	$8,019

Table III		THREE CHILDREN				
Monthly Family Net Income	Percentage Allocated [1]	Base Support	+	Marginal Percentage	over	Income Level
$999	49.4%	$493.51	+	47.28%	over	$999
$1,604	48.6%	$779.54	+	35.10%	over	$1,604
$2,187	45.0%	$984.15	+	30.51%	over	$2,187
$2,807	41.8%	$1,173.33	+	28.75%	over	$2,807
$3,645	38.8%	$1,414.26	+	27.98%	over	$3,645
$5,176	35.6%	$1,842.66	+	23.40%	over	$5,176
$6,379	33.3%	$2,124.21	+	19.61%	over	$6,379
$8,019	30.5%	$2,445.80	+	19.00%	over	$8,019

[1] *NOTE: Due to the Low/No Income adjustment, these figures may not be applied if a parent earns a minimal income. See Item C in this section.*

Effective July 1, 2003

Table III (Continued)
Total Child Support at Various Income Levels

Table III	FOUR CHILDREN					
Monthly Family Net Income	Percentage Allocated [1]	Base Support	+	Marginal Percentage	over	Income Level
$999	55.6%	$555.44	+	52.68%	over	$999
$1,604	54.5%	$874.18	+	39.87%	over	$1,604
$2,187	50.6%	$1,106.62	+	34.30%	over	$2,187
$2,807	47.0%	$1,319.29	+	33.08%	over	$2,807
$3,645	43.8%	$1,596.51	+	31.97%	over	$3,645
$5,176	40.3%	$2,085.93	+	24.92%	over	$5,176
$6,379	37.4%	$2,385.75	+	23.22%	over	$6,379
$8,019	34.5%	$2,766.56	+	22.00%	over	$8,019

Table III	FIVE OR MORE CHILDREN					
Monthly Family Net Income	Percentage Allocated [1]	Base Support	+	Marginal Percentage	over	Income Level
$999	60.8%	$607.39	+	57.35%	over	$999
$1,604	59.5%	$954.38	+	42.62%	over	$1,604
$2,187	55.0%	$1,202.85	+	37.80%	over	$2,187
$2,807	51.2%	$1,437.18	+	37.28%	over	$2,807
$3,645	48.0%	$1,749.60	+	35.83%	over	$3,645
$5,176	44.4%	$2,298.14	+	24.78%	over	$5,176
$6,379	40.7%	$2,596.25	+	24.08%	over	$6,379
$8,019	37.3%	$2,991.09	+	23.00%	over	$8,019

[1] *NOTE: Due to the Low/No Income adjustment, these figures may not be applied if a parent earns a minimal income. See Item C in this section.*

19

The first step in determining each parent's child support obligation is to calculate total net family income per month. If either parent's income is near or below the poverty level, see Section III C on page 21. Second, apply the appropriate child support percentage from Table III from pages 17 to 19 the net income determination to calculate the actual child support amount. The third step is to apportion the support amount between both parents based on the ratio of their incomes. The final step in determining child support is to add a health care supplement to the calculated support amount (see page 29).

The Table III calculation formula is:

$$\{A + [B \times (C-D)]\} \times (E \div C) + F = G$$

[note: if E> P and C < I then support is calculated (C x J) (E ÷ C)+F = G]

For the purposes of this formula:

A	=	Base Support for Family Income (Table III, column 3)
B	=	Marginal Percentage (Table III, column 4)
C	=	Actual Total Net Family Income (add net incomes of parties, rounded to nearest whole dollar)
D	=	Table Family Income Amount (Table III,, column 5)
E	=	Noncustodial Parent Allowable Net Income (round to nearest whole dollar)
F	=	Health Care Supplement (Section IV D 2)
G	=	Noncustodial General Care Support-using Table III calculation (round to nearest whole dollar)
P	=	Poverty Level Income (Section III C)
I	=	Table Family Income Amount lowest level
J	=	Base Percentage (Table III, column 2)

Example: Using Table III, calculate the total monthly ly support amount for the five children in this family.

Step 1:   Calculate Family net monthly income.

Noncustodial parent earns $1,750 net per month.
Custodial parent earns $950 net per month.

Add the parents' net monthly incomes to determine the total net family income per month:
$1,750 + $950 = $2,700

Step 2: Calculate the total monthly support amount

{$1202.85 + [37.80% x ($2700 -$2187)} x ($1750 ÷ 2700) + $45.68 = G Child Support

{$1202.85 + [.3780 x ($513)]} x (.6481) + $45.68 = G Child Support

{$1202.85 + [$193.91]} x (.6481) + $45.68 = G Child Support

{$1396.76} x (.6481) + $45.68 = G Child Support

$905.24 + $45.68 = $951 Child Support per month

20

B.   **Calculating Child Support Using Support Schedules**

The schedules provided at **www.courts.michigan.gov/scao/services/focb/focb.htm** make the child support calculations automatically. The schedules include the amount required for the health care supplement. To use the schedules, apply the following steps, illustrated by the hypothetical example used in Section III A, above:

Step 1: Determine each parent's net monthly income.

Step 2: Determine the noncustodial parent's monthly support obligation by using the support schedule for five children. Find the noncustodial parent's net monthly income of $1,750 on the vertical column and the custodial parent's net monthly income of $950 on the horizontal row. Follow the horizontal line to the right from the noncustodial income amount to the axis where it intersects with the vertical line from the custodial income amount. The $951 amount shown at the intersection of the lines is the noncustodial parent's monthly support obligation. The health care supplement is included.

Note: Support amounts in the schedules may vary slightly from the actual longhand calculations due to rounding.

To comply with MCR 3.211(E)(1), and to avoid recalculating support each time a child is added to or deleted from an order, all support orders must include the amount for each child in multi-children families. For example, for this family of five children the order would state:

$951 per month for 5 children,
$870 per month for 4 children,
$772 per month for 3 children,
$601 per month for 2 children,
$394 per month for 1 child.

C.   **Calculation of Child Support in Low/No Income Cases**

For the purpose of this formula, low income is defined as $738 or less per month, in a single person household (2002 United States HHS Poverty Guideline). The formula described in Section III A, does not apply when parents earn low incomes. When either the noncustodial or custodial parent earns no or low income, the support amount will be determined according to the following procedure.

1.   In cases where noncustodial parents earn $738 or less per month, they will pay 10% of their incomes for child support plus the health care supplement found in Section IV D 2 on page 29, irrespective of the number of children. The percentage adjustment (10%) should be decreased by 1% for every additional $450 that the custodial parent earns. (see Table IV, page 22)

21

Table IV Poverty Level Income Percentage Adjustment Table			
Custodial Net Income	% Adjust	Custodial Net Income	% Adjust
$0 - $738	10%	$2,250 - $2,699	5%
$739 - $899	9%	$2,700 - $3,149	4%
$900 - $1,349	8%	$3,150 - $3,599	3%
$1,350 - $1,799	7%	$3,600 - $4,049	2%
$1,800 - $2,249	6%	$4,050 or more	1%

The non-custodial parent <u>poverty level income calculation</u> formula is:

(E x K (or $25 whichever is more, see Section III C 3, below)) + F = L

For the purposes of this formula:

E = Non-custodial Parent Net Income of $738 or less (round to nearest whole dollar)
K = Percentage Adjustment (percentage income factor from Table IV, (Section III C 1))
F = Health Care Supplement (Section IV D)
L = Support Amount (Round to nearest whole dollar amount)

Example: Using the non-custodial parent poverty level income calculation, figure the total support amount for three children in this family.

Step 1: Calculate Family net monthly income.

Noncustodial parent earns $600 net per month
Custodial parent earns $1,400 net per month.

Step 2: Calculate the total monthly support amount

($600 x 7% (or $25 whichever is more, see number 3, below)) + $32.63 = L

($42.00) + $32.63 = $75

2.   In low income cases where non-custodial parents earn more than $738 per month, **the support amount is** <u>the apportioned support amount (calculated using the formula in Section III A)</u>, **or is** <u>the difference between the noncustodial parents' net monthly income and the poverty level ($738) plus the support amount that they would pay at $738 (using the non-custodial parent poverty level income calculation, above)</u>, **whichever is less.** This allows the non-custodial parent to retain approximately 90-100% of the poverty level amount.

22

The non-custodial parent <u>low income calculation</u> formula is:

[($738 x K (or $25 whichever is more see number 3, below)) + F] + (E -$738) = M
$$\text{if M} < \text{G then M} = \mathbf{L}$$
$$\text{if M} \geq \text{G then G} = \mathbf{L}$$

For the purposes of this formula:

P	=	Poverty Level Income (Section III(C))
K	=	Percentage Adjustment (percentage income factor from Table IV (Section III C 1))
F	=	Health Care Supplement (Section IV D)
E	=	Non-custodial Parent Net Income (round to nearest whole dollar)
M	=	Non-custodial Support-using Low Income Adjustment calculation
G	=	Non-Custodial Support-using Table III calculation
L	=	Support Amount (Round to nearest whole dollar amount)

> ***Example:*** Using the non-custodial parent low income calculation, figure the total monthly support amount for four children in this family.

Step 1: Calculate net income.

Noncustodial parent earns $900 net per month.
Custodial parent earns $1,200 net per month.

Step 2: Calculate the total monthly support amount

[($738 x 8% (or $25)+ $39.15] + (900 -738) = M

[($59.04 (or $25)) + $39.15] + (162) = M

[$98.19] + ($162) = $260

Step 3: The support amount is the lesser of the results from the low income calculation formula and from the Table III calculation formula:

M = $260
G = $498 = {$874.18 + [39.87% x ($2100 - $1604)]} x ($900 ÷ $2100) + $39.15
Therefore, the support amount in this example is $260.

3. Support should not be recommended in amounts of less than $25 per month (plus the health care supplement), unless support is reserved by the court order.

4. When custodial parents earn $738 or less per month, their incomes will not be used in calculating support. In this way parents retain enough to meet their basic necessities, while contributing as much as possible to the support of their children.

Note: This adjustment is built into the schedules in Appendix C, and need not be separately calculated when using those tables.

23

D.   Calculation of Child Support in High Income Cases

In high income cases, where total family income exceeds the income categories listed on the schedules in Appendix C, the support amount should be calculated according to Table III.

For example, using Table III for one child, at a combined net income of $8,019 per month, the support recommendation would be $1956.64 plus 10% of the amount over $8,019. Total support would then be apportioned between both parents, and have the $13.05 health care supplement added.

Example: Using Table III, calculate the total support amount for the two children in this family.

Step 1:   Calculate Family net monthly income.

Noncustodial parent earns $6,000 net per month.
Custodial parent earns $3,000 net per month.

Add the parent's net monthly incomes to determine the total net family income:
$6,000 + $3,000 =$9,000

Step 2: Calculate the total monthly support amount

{$1956.64 + [15.00% x ($9,000 -$8,019]} x ($6,000 ÷ $9,000) + $26.10 = G Child Support

{$1956.64 + [.1500 x ($980} x (.6667) + $26.10 = G Child Support

{$1956.64 + [$147.00]} x (.6667) + $26.10 = G Child Support

{$2,1063.64} x (.6667) + $26.10 = G Child Support

$1,402.50 + $26.10 = $1,429 Child Support per month

24

IV. Miscellaneous Provisions

A. Different Custody Arrangements For Different Children

It is not unusual for the court to order different custody arrangements for different children. The most obvious arrangement is for one parent to have sole custody of some children and the other parent to have sole custody of other children; this type of arrangement is usually called "split custody". However, it is also possible for some children to be in the sole custody of a parent and other children to be part of a shared custody arrangement, or for shared custody arrangements to vary from child to child. All this real-life complexity can make child support computations equally complex. The following method of computation is intended to apply in all such complex arrangements:

Step 1: Determine **each custody arrangement** involved in the present case (e.g., sole custody of one child with Parent A and sole custody of a second child with Parent B; shared custody of two children 60-40 with Parent A and B respectively and sole custody of a third child with Parent B; etc.).

Step 2: For **each custody arrangement** involved, compute what the child support would be for **the child(ren) in that custody arrangement** as if there were no other children.
(Note: In order to keep distinct the amounts that would be paid from one parent to the other, record the computed support payments from Parent B to Parent A as positive numbers and those from Parent A to Parent B as negative numbers.

Step 3: **Add** the amounts obtained in Step 2. Remember to subtract the negative numbers from positive numbers. The sum of all amounts is the support amount. (Note: If it is negative, it is a payment from Parent A to Parent B; if it is positive, it is a payment from Parent B to Parent A.)

Example 1:

Step 1:   There are two children, one each in sole custody of Parent A and Parent B. Parent B has net income of $300 per week, and Parent A has net income of $250 per week.

Step 2:   A) Custody Arrangement #1: Parent A has sole custody of one child, the support amount would be $69 per week. This is recorded as +$69 since it is the amount to be a paid from Parent B to Parent A.

B) Custody Arrangement #2: If Parent B had sole custody of one child, the support amount would be $58 per week. This is recorded as -$58 since it is the amount to be a paid from Parent A to Parent B.

Step 3:   Add +$69 and -$58 for a support amount of +$11. (Note: the positive number indicates the payment is to be made by Parent B to Parent A.

26

Example 2:

Step 1: There are three children. Two are in the sole custody of Parent A, but the third is in a shared custody arrangement with 60% of the time spent with Parent B and 40% spent with Parent A. Parent B has net income of $350 per week, and Parent A has net income of $280 per week.

Step 2: A) Custody Arrangement #1: two children are in the sole custody of Parent A, the support amount is $118 per week. This is recorded as +$118 since it is the amount to be paid from Parent B to Parent A.

B) Custody Arrangement #2: one child is in a shared custody arrangement, the support amount (computed according to the procedure and formula in shared economic responsibility subsection below) would be $20. It should be recorded as -$20 per week as payment from Parent A to Parent B.

Step 3: Add +$118 and -$20 for a for a total support payment of +$98 from Parent B to Parent A.

B. Shared Economic Responsibility

When children share substantial amounts of time with each parent, <u>whether or not there is a joint physical custody order</u>, child support must be calculated by offsetting the parties' support obligations. Substantial shared time with children translates into economic sharing beginning when the parent with the lesser amount of time with the children has the children in his/her care for a minimum of 128 overnights annually. The formula should only be used if it can be determined from the specific terms of the custody/parenting time order that the children will be with that parent for at least the 128 overnight threshold. The economic sharing formula should only be applied to support orders entered concurrent with an initial custody/parenting time determination or to modifications of custody/parenting time based upon changed circumstances. It shall <u>not</u> be retroactively applied to existing orders. The economic sharing formula is:

$$\frac{(P^A_d)^2\,(P^B_s) - (P^B_d)^2\,(P^A_s)}{(P^A_d)^2 + (P^B_d)^2} = \text{Support}$$

For the purposes of this formula:

P^A_d	=	The number of overnights the children spend with Parent A.
P^B_d	=	The number of overnights the children spend with Parent B.
P^A_s	=	Parent A's normal support obligation determined from the schedule. (This is accomplished by applying one parent's income along one axis and the other parent's income along the other axis on the appropriate schedule).
P^B_s	=	Parent B's normal support obligation determined from the schedule.

Notes: Parenting time abatement should <u>never</u> be used in conjunction with the economic sharing formula, as the economic sharing adjustment inherently reflects substantial economic sharing.

27

If application of this section has an unjust or inappropriate result, a deviation should be considered.

Example:

Parent[A] has the child 209 days. Parent[A] earns $200 net per week.
Parent[B] has the child 156 days. Parent[B] earns $300 net per week.

Support would be determined by using the one child schedule at one income of $300 and the other income of $200.

The normal support amount which Parent[A] would pay is $48 per week.
The normal support amount which Parent[B] would pay is $71 per week.

$$\frac{(209)^2 \ (\$71) - (156)^2 \ (\$48)}{(209)^2 + (156)^2} \qquad = \qquad \text{Weekly Support}$$

$$\frac{\$3,101,351 - \$1,168,128}{43,681 + 24,336} \qquad = \qquad \text{Weekly Support}$$

$$\frac{\$1,933,223}{68,017} \qquad = \qquad \$28.42$$

Parent[B] should pay $28.00 <u>each week</u> for child support.

C.   Parenting Time Abatement

Every child support order should address the issue of parenting time abatement. In the absence of such a provision, no abatement should occur except by consent of the parties. Parenting time abatement should <u>not</u> be used in conjunction with the shared economic responsibility formula since that formula contemplates substantial economic sharing, and since the formula has already accounted for time spent by the child(ren) in both households. Likewise, since the calculation of child care expenses contains an adjustment for child care costs incurred by each parent during the time the child(ren) are in their care, the parenting time abatement should <u>not</u> be applied to the child care portion of a support order.

A 50% retroactive abatement in a child's weekly support is to occur after a child spends six (6) <u>consecutive</u> overnight periods with the noncustodial parent. The parenting time abatement should be calculated for each day of the parenting time period.

Example:

The noncustodial parent picks up three children at 9:00 p.m. Thursday, June 14, and returns one child at 11:00 a.m. Sunday, June 24, and the other children at 3:00 p.m. Saturday, June 30. One child spent ten(10) consecutive overnights in the noncustodial parent's household, while the other two were there for seventeen (17) consecutive overnights. The noncustodial parent is entitled to ten (10) days parenting time abatement for one child and seventeen (17) days parenting time abatement for two children. If child support was $105 per week, the ordered 50% abatement would be determined as follows:

Step 1   Determine the daily support amount per child

$105.00	÷	7	days	=	$15.00	Per day
$15.00	÷	3	children	=	$5.00	Per child per day

29

Step 2   Based on the number of overnights, daily support, and participating children, figure the support for each period of parenting time

($5.00   x   1   child) x   10   days   = $50.00

($5.00   x   2   children) x   17   days   = $170.00

Step 3   Figure the 50% abatement

$50.00   x   50%   = $25.00   For the 10 days with one child

$170.00   x   50%   = $85.00   For the 17 days with two children

Total abatement for period $110.00

D.   Health Care Expenses

1.   According to several Michigan statutes regarding domestic relations matters, "[t]he court shall require that one or both parents shall obtain or maintain any health care coverage that is available to them at a reasonable cost, as a benefit of employment. If a parent is self-employed and maintains health care coverage, the court shall require the parent to obtain or maintain dependent coverage for the benefit of the child, if available at a reasonable cost." MCL 552.452; MSA 25.222(2), MCL 722.3; MSA 25.244(3), MCL 722.717; MSA 25.497 and MCL 552.16; MSA 25.96.

"Health care" means the products or services provided or prescribed by a person or organization licensed or legally authorized to provide or prescribe human health care products or services, including, but not limited to, the following professionals: chiropractors, dentists, oral surgeons, orthodontists, prosthedontists, periodontists, endodontists, pedodontists, dental hygienists, dental assistants, medical doctors, physician's assistants, registered professional nurses, licensed practical nurses, nurse midwifes, nurse anesthetists, nurse practitioners, trained attendants, optometrists, osteopaths, pharmacists, physical therapists, physiotherapists, physical therapy technicians, chiropodists, podiatrists, foot specialists, psychologists, psychological assistants, psychological examiners, clinical social workers and providers of prosthetic devices. It also includes the following health facilities or agencies (even when located in a correctional institution or a university, college, or other educational institution): ambulances, advanced mobile emergency care services, clinical laboratories, county medical care facilities, freestanding surgical outpatient facilities, health maintenance organizations, homes for the aged, hospitals, and nursing homes.

2.   A defined amount for ordinary expenditures on health care, which need not be documented, is added into the total support amount in the schedules found in Appendix C. The amounts added are found in Table V.

Table V:
Health Care Support Supplement

Number of Children	Monthly Health Care Amount
1	$13.05
2	$26.10
3	$32.63
4	$39.15
5	$45.68

Ordinary expenditures on health care include such remedial items as nonprescription medications, vitamins, and bandages purchased by the household on a routine basis in anticipation of minor illnesses and injuries. It is presumed that the custodial parent will contribute similar amounts and no proof of these ordinary health care expenditures need be provided by the custodial parent.

3. All uninsured health care expenses, other than ordinary expenditures on health care, should be apportioned between parents based on the ratio of their incomes, provided that the proportion paid by either party shall not be less than 10% nor more than 90%.

E. Child Care Expenses

When the custodian and/or non-custodial parent incurs work-related child care expenses, an additional child care adjustment is required. Work-related child care expenses include those net expenses which allow the parent to look for employment, retain paid employment, or to enroll in and attend an educational program which will improve employment opportunities.

1. When custodians have an established pattern of child care and can verify that they have actual, predictable and reasonable child care expenses on behalf of the children in the case under consideration, the total net expenses to each should be apportioned between the parents according to the ratio of their incomes.

2. In calculating child care expenses to be apportioned between the parents, the net cost to the parent or custodian must be used. The net cost of child care is figured by deducting any child care subsidies, credits (including federal tax credit), or reimbursements from any public or private source from the gross cost of child care.

The non-custodial parent's portion of the custodian's child care costs minus the custodian's portion of the non-custodial parent's child care shall be added to the amount of support in the appropriate Child Support Formula table.

29

The non-custodial parent's portion of the custodian's child care costs minus the custodian's portion of the non-custodial parent's child care shall be added to the amount of support in the appropriate Child Support Formula table.

3.   When custodian's do not have an established pattern of child care expenses, they may request that the friend of the court place a contingent child care provision in the child support recommendation. The recommendation will provide a specific amount for child support and a projected amount for child care. The projected determination should be based on information regarding average child care costs in the community as provided by the local friend of the court or on three written quotations for child care as provided to the friend of the court by the custodial parent. The net cost of child care shall be computed in the same manner as when there is an established pattern of child care. This contingent provision will become effective upon the following:

Step 1:   Proof provided by the custodian of employment or enrollment in an educational or training program which will improve employment opportunities.

Step 2:   Proof provided by the custodian of actual out-of-pocket child care expenses.

Step 3:   The friend of the court notifying the non-custodial parent of the activation of the contingent recommendation and providing that parent with a copy of the verifying documents.

Note: The implementation of the contingent provision may constitute a change of circumstances which would warrant a review and recommendation by the friend of the court.

4.   Child care shall be recommended up to the start of the school year immediately following the 12th birthday of the child but only to the extent thereafter that the health and safety needs of the child require continued child care.

5.   In calculating annual child care costs, it shall be assumed that the court's specific parenting time and custody orders are followed. If a child care provider requires payment to retain an available slot for a child without regard to whether the child attends during parenting times, vacations, illness or other temporary absences, the required payment shall be used in computing child care costs.

6.   Prior to making a recommendation, documentation of a parent's child care costs shall be provided by the custodian to the friend of the court on the State Court Administrative Office Approved Child Care Verification Form, or its equivalent.

Example:
The parents have two minor children. The custodian has a gross weekly income of $245 with gross child care costs of $75 per week. The custodian's net weekly income per the Child Support Formula is $203. The non-custodial parent has a gross weekly income of $500 with gross child care costs of

$85 for four of the six weeks extended summer parenting time specified in the court order. The non-custodial parent's net weekly income per the Child Support Formula is $350. Neither parent contractually guarantees his or her child care provider payment of specific child care costs.

Step	Custodian	Non-custodial Parent
Step I: Calculate each parent's gross annual child care costs.	52 weeks minus 6 weeks parenting time equals 46 weeks multiplied by $75 per week equals $3,450 annually.	4 weeks multiplied by $85 per week equals $340 annually.
Step II: Subtract the appropriate subsidy, credit, or reimbursement deductions.	$3,450 annual costs minus $966 credit equals $2,484.	$340 annual costs minus $0 credit equals $340.
Step III: Divide annual net child care costs by 52 to obtain average weekly child care costs.	$2,484 divided by 52 weeks equals $48 per week.	$340 divided by 52 weeks equals $7 per week.
Step IV: Prorate each parent's share of the other parent's average net weekly child care cost based on the net income of the parents per the Child Support Formula.	Non-custodial parent's prorated share of the parties' net income is 63% (Total net income of parties divided by the non-custodial parent's net income) $48 multiplied by 63% equals $31 per week.	Custodian's prorated share of the parties' net income is 37% (Total net income of parties divided by the custodian's net income) $7 multiplied by 37% equals $3 per week.
Step V: Subtract the higher child care prorated share from the lower child care prorated share.	$31 non-custodial share of custodian's child care minus $3 custodial parent share of non-custodial's child care equals net child care of $28.	
Step VI: Add the net child care amount to the Formula tables if non-custodial prorated share is higher. Subtract the net child care amount from the Formula tables if the custodian's share is higher.	Add the $28 in child care to the child support amount from the schedules to determine the total support recommendation.	

F. Third Party Custodians

When a child is in the physical custody of a third party, <u>both</u> of the natural parents should be required to pay support. The level of support should be determined and apportioned according to the incomes of both parents.

Example 1:
Use this method when the parents of the child(ren) live in the same household:

Step 1:   Both noncustodial parents live in the same household. The first parent earns $300 net per week. The second parent earns $200 net per week. There are two children living with the third party custodian.

Step 2:   Total family income is $500 net per week. Apply $500 to the noncustodial axis and $0 to the custodial axis on the two children schedule. The total family support amount is $178.

Step 3:   Calculate each parent's individual support obligations by apportioning the total family support between the incomes of both parents.

First Parent:	$178 x ($300 ÷ $500) = $107
Second Parent:	$178 x ($200 ÷ $500) = $71

Example 2:
Use this method when the parents of the child(ren) live in separate households.

Step 1:   Both noncustodial parents live in separate households. The first parent earns $500 net per week. The second parent earns $300 net per week. There are three children living with the third party custodian.

Step 2:   Apply the $500 to the noncustodial axis and $0 to the custodial axis on the three children schedule. The first parent should pay $229.

Apply $300 to the noncustodial axis and $0 to the custodial axis on the three children schedule. The second parent should pay $154.

G. Arrearage Guidelines

The Arrearage Guideline is for use by friends of the court, referees, and judges in making arrearage payment determinations to ensure statewide consistency by trial courts and friend of the court offices. Federal law requires states to have procedures to increase the amount of payments to include amounts for arrearages (42 U.S.C. 666(c)(1)(H)). State statute requires that the formula contain guidelines for setting and administratively adjusting the amount of periodic payments for overdue support (MCL 552.519(3)(a)(vi)).

1. Application

Support arrearages should be repaid as quickly as possible. If all, or a substantial portion of the arrearage cannot be paid immediately the Arrearage Guideline should be used when setting arrearage payment amounts where support or fees are owed. This guideline is not intended to interfere with the enforcement of past-due support and its collection through concurrent means and as quickly as is allowed by law, and does not apply to payments set for writs of garnishment and other lump sum collections. Each case is decided on its own merits. The Arrearage Guideline is not intended to interfere with judicial discretion in setting fair and equitable payment amounts, and thus may establish payment amounts that deviate from the Guideline.

In order to repay arrearages as quickly as possible, the total-payment-amount used for determining the arrearage payment amount for collection must be the higher of: the most recent total-payment-amount, or the total-payment-amount presently figured using the arrearage payment calculation and current support charge. If the support charge has been reduced since the most recent total-payment-amount was set for reasons other than a reduction in payer's income, the amount of that reduction is added to that total-payment-amount's arrearage payment amount and it automatically becomes the new arrearage payment amount. If the most recent total-payment-amount is the payment amount chosen, the aggregate amount remains the same, but consists of a reduced support and an increased arrearage payment amount, the total-payment-amount collected remains in effect until the arrearage has been paid in full or until modified or adjusted by the court or friend of the court.

Statute requires the friend of the court office to use the Arrearage Guideline in setting arrearage payment amounts. Further, when making administrative adjustments to arrearage payment amounts, the office shall follow procedures "to afford the payer due process including at least notice, an opportunity for an administrative hearing, and an opportunity for an appeal on the record to an independent administrative or judicial tribunal."(MCL 552.517e)

When applying the guideline, any monies held or retained by the friend of the court office or state disbursement unit as payment of past due child support, when applying the Guideline, should be subtracted from the amount of arrearage used to calculate the repayment amount.

The friend of the court office may utilize its discretion and deviate from the Guideline to increase the arrearage repayment amount if there has been no other significant change in circumstances (e.g. different source of income, higher income, etc.), and 1) if the payer has made all of the payments for the entire period since the repayment amount was set, and 2) arrearages have increased by an amount greater than one month's support solely because of accumulation of child support surcharge.

2. Arrearage Payment Calculation

When applying the guideline, the weekly arrearage payment is one percent (1%) of the total support arrearage at the time of the review, but not less than $20.00 nor more than the weekly current support amount (if no current support charge use the last ordered charge amount). Payments set by this Guideline should be rounded to the nearest whole dollar amount.

Note: 1.0% per week will eliminate most arrearages and surcharge in approximately two years. (0.1549% approximates the minimum weekly amount needed to stay current with surcharge)

When figuring a confinement expense repayment amount, the weekly total-payment-amount should be based on the total amount owed at the time of the review. To calculate the total arrearage payment, add confinement expenses to other support arrearages and apply the calculation in the preceding paragraph (i.e. 1%, $20.00, or current order amount). A portion of the weekly total-payment-amount must be designated by the court as a confinement expense repayment amount. The weekly confinement expense repayment amount should not be less than $5.00, nor more than the confinement expenses pro-rata share of the total amount owed. Laws, regulations, and other policy determine how these amounts will be distributed on a specific case.

3.   Adjustment of Payment Amounts When Current Support Obligations Terminate

If arrearages exist when a current support obligation terminates or is reduced for reasons other than a reduction in the payer's income, there shall be no automatic reduction in the weekly total-payment-amount unless ordered by the court. The amount of the reduction in the current support amount is added to the current arrearage payment amount and automatically becomes the new arrearage payment amount. The total-payment-amount collected remains in effect until the arrearage has been paid in full or until modified or adjusted by the court or friend of the court.

Example:
> If a payer is required to pay $50.00 per week, $30.00 as current support plus $20.00 toward arrears, and the current support order expires, the payer would continue to pay $50.00 per week, all to be applied on the arrearage.

4.   Guideline Deviation

When application of this Guideline creates an unjust or inappropriate result, deviation may occur and alternate arrearage payment amount established.

5.   Exceptions to Applying Guideline

This Guideline should not be applied when its application creates an unjust or inappropriate result.

The friend of the court should not routinely apply the Guideline to administratively change repayment amounts in cases where:

- the court has set a specific periodic arrearage payment amount in a support, enforcement, or arrearage repayment order, and since entry of that order the arrearages have not

36

increased by an amount equivalent to one month's support based on the current support amount (if no current support charge use the last ordered charge amount);

- the total amount of arrearage has been reduced, but has not been paid in full since the repayment amount was set (applying the guideline when arrears have decreased since the repayment amount was set, subsequent adjustments extend the repayment period);

- the court previously ordered, or the friend of the court implemented a repayment amount that deviates from the Guideline based either upon an unjust or inappropriate result or a formal agreement between the parties, and circumstances have not significantly changed since entry of that order or implementation of the repayment amount; or

- In interstate cases where Michigan and another state's tribunal have entered an order regarding the same payer and child, and the support order and arrears accumulated under the Michigan order are being enforced by another jurisdiction.

6. Administrative Adjustment Records

Information should be maintained to record: administrative adjustments by offices, arrearage repayment amounts deviating from the Guideline, and the reasons for deviation.

7. Definitions

For the purposes of this Guideline, the underlined words mean:

Administrative Adjustment means a change in an amount not ordered by the court.

Arrearage Payment Amount means periodic amounts in addition to current support which are specifically designated to reduce the arrearage owed, but are not arrearage payments set for writs of garnishment and lump sum orders.

Confinement Expense means an amount of money ordered by the circuit court under the paternity act for the necessary expenses incurred by or for the mother in connection with her confinement or of other expenses incurred in connection with the pregnancy of the mother.

One Month's Support means an amount of support equivalent to the sum of the periodic charges that would occur in one month under the current support order, or absent a current support charge the amount using the last ordered periodic amount.

Total-payment-amount means the sum of regular periodic current and past-due support, fee, and other amounts set by court order (support, enforcement, repayment, etc.) or by administrative adjustment by the friend of the court office to collect support by income withholding or other means.

H. Stipulated Agreements

When parents combine property settlement with child support provisions, the provisions must be clearly stated in the Judgment of Divorce to be given continued effect.

I.   Ex Parte and Temporary Orders

According to Michigan Court Rule 3.207(B) and (C), the following rules apply to ex parte and temporary support orders:

"(B)   Ex Parte Orders.

(1)   Pending the entry of a temporary order, the court may enter an ex parte order if the court is satisfied by specific facts set forth in an affidavit or verified pleading that irreparable injury, loss, or damage will result from the delay required to effect notice, or that notice itself will precipitate adverse action before an order can be issued.

(2)   The moving party must arrange for the service of true copies of the ex parte order on the friend of the court and the other party.

(3)   An ex parte order is effective upon entry and enforceable upon service.

(4)   An ex parte order remains in effect until modified or superseded by a temporary or final order.

(5)   An ex parte order providing for child support, custody, or visitation pursuant to MCL 722.27a; MSA 25.312(7a), must include the following notice:

"NOTICE:

1. You may file a written objection to this order or a motion to modify or rescind this order. You must file the written objection or motion with the clerk of the court within 14 days after you were served with this order. You must serve a true copy of the objection or motion on the friend of the court and the party who obtained the order.

2. If you file a written objection, the friend of the court must try to resolve the dispute. If the friend of the court cannot resolve the dispute and if you wish to bring the matter before the court without the assistance of counsel, the friend of the court must provide you with form pleadings and written instructions and must schedule a hearing with the court.

3. The ex parte order will automatically become a temporary order if you do not file a written objection or motion to modify or rescind the ex parte order and a request for a

38

hearing. Even if an objection is filed, the ex parte order will remain in effect and must be obeyed unless changed by a later court order."

(6)   In all other cases, the ex parte order must state that it will automatically become a temporary order if the other party does not file a written objection or motion to modify or rescind the ex parte order and a request for a hearing. The written objection or motion and the request for a hearing must be filed with the clerk of the court, and a true copy provided to the friend of the court and the other party, within 14 days after the order is served.

> (a)   If there is a timely objection or motion and a request for a hearing, the hearing must be held within 21 days after the objection or motion and request are filed.

> (b)   A change that occurs after the hearing may be made retroactive to the date the ex parte order was entered.

(7)   The provisions of MCR 3.310 apply to temporary restraining orders in domestic relations cases.

(C)   Temporary Orders.

(1)   A request for a temporary order may be made at any time during the pendency of the case by filing a verified motion that sets forth facts sufficient to support the relief requested.

(2)   A temporary order may not be issued without a hearing, unless the parties agree otherwise or fail to file a written objection or motion as provided in subrules (B)(5) and (6).

(3)   A temporary order may be modified at any time during the pendency of the case, following a hearing and upon a showing of good cause.

(4)   A temporary order must state its effective date and whether its provisions may be modified retroactively by a subsequent order.

(5)   A temporary order remains in effect until modified or until the entry of the final judgment or order.

(6)   A temporary order not yet satisfied is vacated by the entry of the final judgment or order, unless specifically continued or preserved. This does not apply to support arrearages that have been assigned to the state, which are preserved unless specifically waived or reduced by the final judgment or order."

In cases in which the court orders a support amount pending the final judgment, the following procedure is recommended:

If a party is ordered to pay taxes, mortgage, home insurance, telephone or utilities in an ex parte or temporary order, the child support amount should be adjusted in consideration of these payments. The expenses for which either party is ordered responsible should be subtracted dollar for dollar from that parent's net weekly income for the purposes of determining that parent's child support obligation.

Example:
It is determined the noncustodial parent's net income per week is $350. This parent has been ordered to pay weekly shelter expenses for the family which amount to $105 per week.

$350	Net weekly income
-$105	Weekly shelter expense
$245	Adjusted weekly income

The child support amount should be based on the custodial parent's weekly net income and the noncustodial parent's weekly <u>adjusted</u> income of $245.

J.   Child Support Recommendations in Contested Custody Cases

In cases where custody is contested, a child support recommendation should be made for each proposed custodial arrangement. Each recommendation shall be provided to the court and to the parties.

NOTE:

When determining a child support recommendation from the schedules in this Formula, careful consideration should be given not only to the schedules themselves but to all recommendations provided. Use of select portions of the Formula may result in an improper support recommendation.

Appendix A: Statutory Requirements for Support Investigations

MCL 552.517 **Child support order, review after final judgment; notices; conduct of review; modification order; certain determinations requiring report; contents of report; petition for modification; scheduling of hearing; objection to determination of no change in order; petition to require dependent health care coverage; costs.**

Sec. 17.

(1)   After a final judgment containing a child support order has been entered in a domestic relations matter, the office shall periodically review the order, as follows:

(a)   If a child is being supported in whole or in part by public assistance, not less than once each 24 months unless both of the following apply:

(i) The office receives notice from the family independence agency that good cause exists not to proceed with support action.

(ii) Neither party has requested a review.

(b)   At the initiative of the office, if there are reasonable grounds to believe that the amount of child support awarded in the judgment should be modified or that dependent health care coverage is available and the support order should be modified to include an order for health care coverage. Reasonable grounds to review an order pursuant to this subdivision include temporary or permanent changes in the physical custody of a child that the court has not ordered, increased or decreased need of the child, probable access by an employed parent to dependent health care coverage, or changed financial conditions of a recipient or a payer of child support including, but not limited to, application for or receipt of public assistance, unemployment compensation, or worker's compensation.

(c)   Upon receipt of a written request from either party. Within 15 days after receipt of the review request, the office shall determine whether the order is due for review. The office is not required to investigate more than 1 request received from a party each 24 months.

(d)   If a child is receiving medical assistance, not less than once each 24 months unless either of the following applies:

(i) The order requires provision of health care coverage for the child and neither party has requested a review.

(ii) The office receives notice from the family independence agency that good cause exists not to proceed with support action and neither party has requested a review.

(e)   If requested by the initiating state for a recipient of services in that state under Part D of title IV of the social security act, 42 U.S.C. 651 to 669, not less than once each 24 months. Within 15 days after receipt of a review request, the office shall determine whether an order is due for review.

(2)   Within 180 days after determining that a review is required under subsection (1), the office shall send notices as provided in section 17b(2) and (3), conduct a review, and obtain a modification of the order if appropriate.

(3)   The office shall use the child support formula developed by the bureau under section 19 in calculating the child support award. If the office determines from the facts of the case that application of the child support formula would be unjust or inappropriate, or that income should not be based on actual income earned by the parties, the office shall prepare a written report that includes all of the following:

    (a)   The support amount, based on actual income earned by the parties, determined by application of the child support formula and all factual assumptions upon which that support amount is based.

    (b)   An alternative support recommendation and all factual assumptions upon which the alternative support recommendation is based.

    (c)   How the alternative support recommendation deviates from the child support formula.

    (d)   The reasons for the alternative support recommendation.

    (e)   All evidence known to the friend of the court that the individual is or is not able to earn the income imputed to him or her.

(4)   The office shall petition the court if modification is determined to be necessary under subsection (3) unless either of the following applies:

    (a)   The difference between the existing and projected child support award is within the minimum threshold for modification of a child support amount as established by the formula.

    (b)   The court previously determined that application of the formula was unjust or inappropriate and the office determines under subsection (3) that the facts of the case and the reasons and amount of the prior deviation remain unchanged.

(5)   A petition for modification may be made at the same time the parties are provided with notice under section 17b(3). A hearing held on a proposed modification shall be scheduled no earlier than 30 days after the date of the notice provided for in section 17b(3).

(6)   If the office determines there should be no change in the order and a party objects to the determination in writing to the office within 30 days after the date of the notice provided for in section 17b(3), the office shall schedule a hearing before the court.

(7)   If a support order lacks provisions for health care coverage, the office shall petition the court for a modification to require that 1 or both parents obtain or maintain health care coverage for the benefit of each child who is subject to the support order if either of the following is true:

    (a)   Either parent has health care coverage available, as a benefit of employment, for the benefit of the child at a reasonable cost.

    (b)   Either parent is self-employed, maintains health care coverage for himself or herself, and can obtain health care coverage for the benefit of the child at a reasonable cost.

(8)   The office shall determine the costs to each parent for dependent health care coverage and child care costs and shall disclose those costs in the report under section 17b(4).

MCL 552.517a **Provision of form motions, responses and orders to payers and payees.**

Sec. 17a.   The office shall make available to an individual form motions, responses, and orders for in requesting the court to modify the individual's child support order, or in responding to a motion for support modification without the assistance of legal counsel. The office shall make available instructions on preparing and filing the forms, instructions on service of process, and instructions on scheduling a modification hearing.

MCL 552.517b **Review of order; notice of right to request; notice of review; notice of increase or decrease in amount of child support, modification to order health care, or determination of no change in order; availability of documents.**

Sec. 17b.

(1)   Each party subject to a child support order shall be notified of the right to request a review of the order as provided in section 17, and the place and manner in which to make the request. For a domestic relations matter initiated on or after 90 days after the effective date of this section, the notice shall be provided by the office or, pursuant to court rule, by the plaintiff, using the informational pamphlet required under section 5. Unless notice is provided to the party in the informational pamphlet, no later than 180 days after the effective date of this section, the office in each judicial circuit shall send a notice to each party subject to a child support order informing the party of the right to request a review of the order. The notice shall be sent to the party's last known address.

(2)   The office shall notify each party of a review of a child support order under section 17 at least 30 days before the review is conducted. The notice shall request income, expense, or other information as needed from the party to conduct the review and shall specify the date by which that information is due. The notice shall be sent to each party to his or her last known address.

(3)   After a review of a child support order has been conducted, the office shall notify each party of a proposed increase or decrease in the amount of child support, a proposed modification to order health care coverage, or a determination that there should be no change in the order. Notice of an increase or decrease in child support or a modification to order health care coverage can be provided by or with a copy of the petition for modification. The notice shall also inform the parties of both of the following:

    (a)   That the party may object to the proposed modification or determination that there should be no change in the order at a hearing before a referee or the court.

    (b)   The time, place, and manner in which to raise objections.

(4)   The office shall make available to each party and his or her attorney a copy of the written report, transcript, recommendation, and supporting documents or a summary of supporting documents prepared or used by the office under section 17 before the court modifies a support order.

MCL 552.517c Review of support order in another state; procedures.

Sec. 17c.

(1)   If Michigan is the initiating state in an interstate domestic relations matter involving child support, the office shall determine whether a review of a support order in another state is appropriate in accordance with section 17 and is appropriate based upon the residence and jurisdiction of the parties.

(2)   If the office determines that a review of a support order in another state is appropriate, the office shall obtain income, expense, and other information needed to conduct the review from the requesting party or recipient of public assistance or medical assistance.

(3)   The office shall initiate a request for a review within 20 calendar days after receipt of the information requested under subsection (2).

(4)   The office shall forward to a party who resides in Michigan a copy of each notice issued by the responding state in conjunction with the review and modification of a support order, which notice is sent to the office for distribution.

Appendix B: Reasonable Cost of Maintaining Health Insurance Coverage

Appendix B: Reasonable Cost of Maintaining Health Insurance Coverage

Michigan Statutes [MCL 552.15; MCL 552.517(7)(a)] require the friend of the court, when a support order lacks provisions for health care coverage, to petition, and the court to order in any event, one or both parties to obtain and maintain health care coverage for the benefit of each child who is subject to the support order if:

(a)   Either parent has health care coverage available, as a benefit of employment, for the benefit of the child at a reasonable cost, or

(b)   Either parent is self-employed, maintains health care coverage, and can obtain health care coverage for the benefit of the child at a reasonable cost.

Federal Regulations [45 CFR 306.51] specify that cost of maintaining health insurance is considered reasonable if it is employment-related or other group health insurance.

The following table and text addressing the reasonable cost of maintaining health insurance coverage is provided to assist friends of the court, referees and judges in making determinations of the reasonable cost of maintaining health insurance coverage.

1.   The following table should be used for 2003:

Reasonable Cost of Health Insurance Coverage				
Net Monthly Earnings of Parent		Maximum (Monthly) Reasonable Cost of Maintaining Health Insurance Coverage		
$738.00 or less		$0.00		
$738.01 to $1,521.87		$0 + 6%	over	$738.01
$1,521.88 to $2,391.51		$47 + 10%	over	$1,521.88
$2,391.52 to $3,261.15		$134 + 14%	over	$2,391.52
$3,261.16 to $4,130.79		$256 + 18%	over	$3,261.16
$4,130.80 to $5,000.43		$413 + 22%	over	$4,130.80
$5,000.44 and above		$604		

2.   For the sole purpose of determining the reasonable cost of maintaining health care coverage, the cost of providing child support, child care, and health care insurance, not including arrearages, should not exceed 50% of a parent's net income as defined in the Michigan Child Support Formula Manual.

Effective July 1, 2003

3.   The cost of providing health care insurance coverage pertains only to the cost of providing it for the children, which may or may not include the costs associated with insuring the parent providing the coverage.

4.   The Reasonable Cost of Health Insurance Coverage Table will be annually updated with the Michigan Child Support Formula Manual.

a.   The table will be annually adjusted for changes in the United States HHS Poverty Guideline. The figure used will be the amount released in the preceding year.

b. The earnings levels in the table will be adjusted annually for inflation using the consumer price index (CPI-U Detroit, August). The amounts in the original Reasonable Cost of Health Insurance Coverage Table serve as a baseline figure established, based upon the CPI-U for Detroit as of August 1996.

Appendix C: Support Schedules

One Child Monthly Support Schedule

CUSTODIAL PARENT INCOME

NONCUSTODIAL PARENT INCOME	0	250	300	350	400	450	500	550	600	650	700	750	800	850	900	950	1000
250]	38	38	38	38	38	38	38	38	38	38	38	38	38	38	38	38	38
300]	43	43	43	43	43	43	43	43	43	43	43	40	40	40	38	38	38
350]	48	48	48	48	48	48	48	48	48	48	48	45	45	45	41	41	41
400]	53	53	53	53	53	53	53	53	53	53	53	49	49	49	45	45	45
450]	58	58	58	58	58	58	58	58	58	58	58	54	54	54	49	49	49
500]	63	63	63	63	63	63	63	63	63	63	63	58	58	58	53	53	53
550]	68	68	68	68	68	68	68	68	68	68	68	63	63	63	57	57	57
600]	73	73	73	73	73	73	73	73	73	73	73	67	67	67	61	61	61
650]	78	78	78	78	78	78	78	78	78	78	78	72	72	72	65	65	65
700]	83	83	83	83	83	83	83	83	83	83	83	76	76	76	69	69	69
750]	99	99	99	99	99	99	99	99	99	99	99	91	91	91	84	84	84
800]	149	149	149	149	149	149	149	149	149	149	149	141	141	141	134	134	134
850]	199	199	199	199	199	199	199	199	199	199	199	191	191	191	184	184	184
900]	243	243	243	243	243	243	243	243	243	243	243	236	234	232	231	229	228
950]	255	255	255	255	255	255	255	255	255	255	255	247	245	243	241	239	238
1000]	268	268	268	268	268	268	268	268	268	268	268	257	255	253	251	250	248
1050]	280	280	280	280	280	280	280	280	280	280	280	267	265	263	262	260	258
1100]	292	292	292	292	292	292	292	292	292	292	292	277	275	273	272	270	269
1150]	304	304	304	304	304	304	304	304	304	304	304	287	285	283	282	280	279
1200]	316	316	316	316	316	316	316	316	316	316	316	297	295	293	292	290	289
1250]	328	328	328	328	328	328	328	328	328	328	328	307	305	303	302	300	298
1300]	341	341	341	341	341	341	341	341	341	341	341	317	315	313	312	310	308
1350]	353	353	353	353	353	353	353	353	353	353	353	327	325	323	321	319	318
1400]	365	365	365	365	365	365	365	365	365	365	365	336	335	333	331	329	327
1450]	377	377	377	377	377	377	377	377	377	377	377	346	344	342	340	338	337
1500]	389	389	389	389	389	389	389	389	389	389	389	355	353	351	350	348	346
1550]	401	401	401	401	401	401	401	401	401	401	401	365	363	361	359	357	356
1600]	413	413	413	413	413	413	413	413	413	413	413	374	372	370	368	367	365
1650]	422	422	422	422	422	422	422	422	422	422	422	383	381	379	378	376	374
1700]	431	431	431	431	431	431	431	431	431	431	431	392	391	389	387	385	384
1750]	440	440	440	440	440	440	440	440	440	440	440	402	400	398	396	394	393
1800]	448	448	448	448	448	448	448	448	448	448	448	411	409	407	405	404	402
1850]	457	457	457	457	457	457	457	457	457	457	457	420	418	416	415	413	411
1900]	466	466	466	466	466	466	466	466	466	466	466	429	427	425	424	421	419
1950]	475	475	475	475	475	475	475	475	475	475	475	438	436	434	432	430	428
2000]	483	483	483	483	483	483	483	483	483	483	483	447	445	443	441	438	436
2050]	492	492	492	492	492	492	492	492	492	492	492	456	454	451	449	447	444
2100]	501	501	501	501	501	501	501	501	501	501	501	464	462	460	457	455	453
2150]	510	510	510	510	510	510	510	510	510	510	510	473	470	468	466	463	461
2200]	518	518	518	518	518	518	518	518	518	518	518	481	478	476	474	472	469
2250]	527	527	527	527	527	527	527	527	527	527	527	489	487	484	482	480	478
2300]	535	535	535	535	535	535	535	535	535	535	535	497	495	492	490	488	486
2350]	543	543	543	543	543	543	543	543	543	543	543	505	503	501	498	496	494
2400]	552	552	552	552	552	552	552	552	552	552	552	513	511	509	506	504	502
2450]	560	560	560	560	560	560	560	560	560	560	560	521	519	517	515	513	510
2500]	568	568	568	568	568	568	568	568	568	568	568	529	527	525	523	521	519

One Child Monthly Support Schedule

CUSTODIAL PARENT INCOME

NONCUSTODIAL PARENT INCOME

	0	250	300	350	400	450	500	550	600	650	700	750	800	850	900	950	1000
2550]	577	577	577	577	577	577	577	577	577	577	577	537	535	533	531	529	527
2600]	585	585	585	585	585	585	585	585	585	585	585	545	543	541	539	537	535
2650]	593	593	593	593	593	593	593	593	593	593	593	553	551	549	547	545	543
2700]	602	602	602	602	602	602	602	602	602	602	602	561	559	557	555	553	551
2750]	610	610	610	610	610	610	610	610	610	610	610	569	567	565	563	561	558
2800]	618	618	618	618	618	618	618	618	618	618	618	577	575	573	571	568	566
2850]	626	626	626	626	626	626	626	626	626	626	626	585	583	580	578	576	574
2900]	633	633	633	633	633	633	633	633	633	633	633	593	590	588	586	584	582
2950]	640	640	640	640	640	640	640	640	640	640	640	600	598	596	593	591	589
3000]	648	648	648	648	648	648	648	648	648	648	648	608	606	603	601	599	597
3050]	655	655	655	655	655	655	655	655	655	655	655	615	613	611	609	607	604
3100]	662	662	662	662	662	662	662	662	662	662	662	623	621	618	616	614	612
3150]	670	670	670	670	670	670	670	670	670	670	670	631	628	626	624	622	620
3200]	677	677	677	677	677	677	677	677	677	677	677	638	636	634	631	629	627
3250]	684	684	684	684	684	684	684	684	684	684	684	645	643	641	639	637	635
3300]	692	692	692	692	692	692	692	692	692	692	692	653	651	649	646	644	642
3350]	699	699	699	699	699	699	699	699	699	699	699	660	658	656	654	652	650
3400]	706	706	706	706	706	706	706	706	706	706	706	668	666	664	662	659	658
3450]	713	713	713	713	713	713	713	713	713	713	713	675	673	671	669	667	665
3500]	721	721	721	721	721	721	721	721	721	721	721	683	681	679	676	674	673
3550]	728	728	728	728	728	728	728	728	728	728	728	690	688	686	684	682	680
3600]	735	735	735	735	735	735	735	735	735	735	735	698	695	693	691	689	688
3650]	743	743	743	743	743	743	743	743	743	743	743	705	703	701	699	697	695
3700]	750	750	750	750	750	750	750	750	750	750	750	712	710	708	706	704	702
3750]	757	757	757	757	757	757	757	757	757	757	757	720	718	716	714	712	710
3800]	764	764	764	764	764	764	764	764	764	764	764	727	725	723	721	719	717
3850]	771	771	771	771	771	771	771	771	771	771	771	734	732	730	729	727	725
3900]	778	778	778	778	778	778	778	778	778	778	778	742	740	738	736	734	732
3950]	784	784	784	784	784	784	784	784	784	784	784	749	747	745	743	741	740
4000]	791	791	791	791	791	791	791	791	791	791	791	756	754	753	751	749	747
4050]	798	798	798	798	798	798	798	798	798	798	798	764	762	760	758	756	754
4100]	805	805	805	805	805	805	805	805	805	805	805	771	769	767	765	764	762
4150]	812	812	812	812	812	812	812	812	812	812	812	778	776	775	773	771	769
4200]	819	819	819	819	819	819	819	819	819	819	819	786	784	782	780	778	776
4250]	826	826	826	826	826	826	826	826	826	826	826	793	791	789	787	785	783
4300]	833	833	833	833	833	833	833	833	833	833	833	800	798	797	794	792	790
4350]	840	840	840	840	840	840	840	840	840	840	840	807	806	804	801	799	797
4400]	847	847	847	847	847	847	847	847	847	847	847	815	813	810	808	806	803
4450]	854	854	854	854	854	854	854	854	854	854	854	822	819	817	815	812	810
4500]	861	861	861	861	861	861	861	861	861	861	861	828	826	824	821	819	817
4550]	868	868	868	868	868	868	868	868	868	868	868	835	833	830	828	826	823
4600]	875	875	875	875	875	875	875	875	875	875	875	842	839	837	834	832	830
4650]	882	882	882	882	882	882	882	882	882	882	882	848	846	843	841	839	837
4700]	889	889	889	889	889	889	889	889	889	889	889	855	852	850	848	845	843
4750]	896	896	896	896	896	896	896	896	896	896	896	861	859	857	854	852	850
4800]	903	903	903	903	903	903	903	903	903	903	903	868	865	863	861	859	857
4850]	910	910	910	910	910	910	910	910	910	910	910	874	872	870	868	865	863
4900]	917	917	917	917	917	917	917	917	917	917	917	881	879	876	874	872	870
4950]	924	924	924	924	924	924	924	924	924	924	924	887	885	883	881	879	876
5000]	931	931	931	931	931	931	931	931	931	931	931	894	892	889	887	885	883

One Child Monthly Support Schedule

CUSTODIAL PARENT INCOME

	1050	1100	1150	1200	1250	1300	1350	1400	1450	1500	1550	1600	1650	1700	1750	1800
250]	38	38	38	38	38	38	38	38	38	38	38	38	38	38	38	38
300]	38	38	38	38	38	38	38	38	38	38	38	38	38	38	38	38
350]	41	41	41	41	41	41	38	38	38	38	38	38	38	38	38	38
400]	45	45	45	45	45	45	41	41	41	41	41	41	41	41	41	38
450]	49	49	49	49	49	49	45	45	45	45	45	45	45	45	45	40
500]	53	53	53	53	53	53	48	48	48	48	48	48	48	48	48	43
550]	57	57	57	57	57	57	52	52	52	52	52	52	52	52	52	46
600]	61	61	61	61	61	61	55	55	55	55	55	55	55	55	55	49
650]	65	65	65	65	65	65	59	59	59	59	59	59	59	59	59	52
700]	69	69	69	69	69	69	62	62	62	62	62	62	62	62	62	55
750]	84	84	84	84	84	84	77	77	77	77	77	77	77	77	77	69
800]	134	134	134	134	134	134	127	127	127	127	127	127	127	127	127	119
850]	184	184	184	184	184	184	177	177	177	177	177	177	177	177	177	169
900]	226	225	223	222	221	220	218	217	216	215	214	213	212	211	210	209
950]	236	235	234	232	231	230	229	227	226	225	224	223	222	221	220	219
1000]	247	245	244	243	241	240	239	237	236	235	234	233	232	231	230	229
1050]	257	256	254	253	251	250	249	247	246	245	244	243	242	241	240	239
1100]	267	266	264	263	261	260	259	257	256	255	254	253	252	251	249	248
1150]	277	276	274	272	271	270	268	267	266	265	264	263	262	260	259	258
1200]	287	285	284	282	281	280	278	277	276	275	273	272	271	270	268	267
1250]	297	295	294	292	291	289	288	287	285	284	283	282	280	279	277	276
1300]	306	305	303	302	300	299	298	296	295	294	292	291	289	288	287	285
1350]	316	314	313	311	310	309	307	306	305	303	302	300	299	297	296	294
1400]	326	324	322	321	320	318	317	316	314	312	311	309	308	306	305	303
1450]	335	333	332	330	329	328	326	325	323	321	320	318	317	315	314	312
1500]	345	343	341	340	339	337	335	334	332	330	329	327	326	324	323	321
1550]	354	352	351	349	348	346	344	343	341	339	338	336	335	333	332	330
1600]	363	362	360	359	357	355	353	351	350	348	347	345	343	342	341	339
1650]	373	371	370	368	366	364	362	360	359	357	355	354	352	351	349	348
1700]	382	380	378	376	375	373	371	369	367	366	364	363	361	360	358	357
1750]	391	389	387	385	383	381	380	378	376	374	373	371	370	368	367	366
1800]	400	398	396	394	392	390	388	386	385	383	382	380	378	377	376	374
1850]	409	406	404	402	400	399	397	395	393	392	390	389	387	386	384	383
1900]	417	415	413	411	409	407	405	404	402	400	399	397	396	394	393	391
1950]	426	423	421	419	418	416	414	412	411	409	407	406	404	403	401	400
2000]	434	432	430	428	426	424	422	421	419	417	416	414	413	411	410	408
2050]	442	440	438	436	435	433	431	429	428	426	424	423	421	420	418	416
2100]	451	449	447	445	443	441	439	438	436	434	433	431	429	428	426	425
2150]	459	457	455	453	451	450	448	446	444	443	441	439	438	436	434	433
2200]	467	465	463	462	460	458	456	455	453	451	449	448	446	444	443	441
2250]	476	474	472	470	468	466	465	463	461	459	457	456	454	452	451	449
2300]	484	482	480	478	476	475	473	471	469	467	466	464	462	461	459	458
2350]	492	490	488	486	485	483	481	479	477	475	474	472	470	469	467	466
2400]	500	498	496	495	493	491	489	487	485	483	482	480	478	477	475	474
2450]	508	507	505	503	501	499	497	495	493	492	490	488	486	485	483	482
2500]	517	515	513	511	509	507	505	503	501	500	498	496	495	493	491	490

NONCUSTODIAL PARENT INCOME

One Child Monthly Support Schedule

CUSTODIAL PARENT INCOME

	1050	1100	1150	1200	1250	1300	1350	1400	1450	1500	1550	1600	1650	1700	1750	1800
2550]	525	523	521	519	517	515	513	511	509	508	506	504	503	501	499	498
2600]	533	531	529	527	525	523	521	519	517	515	514	512	511	509	507	506
2650]	541	539	536	534	532	531	529	527	525	523	522	520	518	517	515	514
2700]	548	546	544	542	540	538	537	535	533	531	530	528	526	525	523	522
2750]	556	554	552	550	548	546	544	543	541	539	538	536	534	533	531	530
2800]	564	562	560	558	556	554	552	551	549	547	545	544	542	541	539	538
2850]	572	570	568	566	564	562	560	558	557	555	553	552	550	549	547	546
2900]	579	577	575	573	572	570	568	566	564	563	561	559	558	556	555	553
2950]	587	585	583	581	579	577	576	574	572	571	569	567	566	564	563	561
3000]	595	593	591	589	587	585	583	582	580	578	577	575	574	572	571	569
3050]	602	600	599	597	595	593	591	589	588	586	584	583	581	580	578	577
3100]	610	608	606	604	602	601	599	597	595	594	592	591	589	588	586	585
3150]	618	616	614	612	610	608	607	605	603	602	600	598	597	595	594	592
3200]	625	623	621	620	618	616	614	613	611	609	608	606	605	603	602	600
3250]	633	631	629	627	625	624	622	620	619	617	615	614	612	611	609	608
3300]	640	639	637	635	633	631	630	628	626	625	623	622	620	619	617	616
3350]	648	646	644	642	641	639	637	636	634	632	631	629	628	626	625	623
3400]	656	654	652	650	648	647	645	643	642	640	638	637	635	634	633	631
3450]	663	661	659	658	656	654	652	651	649	648	646	645	643	642	640	638
3500]	671	669	667	665	663	662	660	658	657	655	654	652	651	649	647	645
3550]	678	676	675	673	671	669	668	666	664	663	661	660	658	656	654	652
3600]	686	684	682	680	679	677	675	674	672	671	669	667	665	663	661	660
3650]	693	691	690	688	686	684	683	681	680	678	676	674	672	670	669	667
3700]	701	699	697	695	694	692	690	689	687	685	683	681	679	678	676	674
3750]	708	706	705	703	701	700	698	696	695	692	690	688	686	685	683	681
3800]	716	714	712	710	709	707	705	704	702	699	697	695	694	692	690	688
3850]	723	721	720	718	716	715	713	711	708	706	704	702	701	699	697	695
3900]	730	729	727	725	724	722	720	718	715	713	711	709	708	706	704	702
3950]	738	736	734	733	731	729	727	724	722	720	718	716	715	713	711	709
4000]	745	744	742	740	738	736	733	731	729	727	725	723	721	720	718	716
4050]	753	751	749	747	745	742	740	738	736	734	732	730	728	727	725	723
4100]	760	758	756	754	751	749	747	745	743	741	739	737	735	734	732	730
4150]	767	765	763	760	758	756	754	752	750	748	746	744	742	740	739	737
4200]	774	772	769	767	765	763	761	759	757	755	753	751	749	747	746	744
4250]	781	778	776	774	772	770	768	766	764	762	760	758	756	754	753	751
4300]	787	785	783	781	779	777	775	773	771	769	767	765	763	761	759	758
4350]	794	792	790	788	786	783	781	779	777	776	774	772	770	768	766	765
4400]	801	799	797	794	792	790	788	786	784	782	780	779	777	775	773	771
4450]	808	805	803	801	799	797	795	793	791	789	787	785	784	782	780	778
4500]	814	812	810	808	806	804	802	800	798	796	794	792	790	789	787	785
4550]	821	819	817	815	813	811	809	807	805	803	801	799	797	796	794	792
4600]	828	826	823	821	819	817	815	813	812	810	808	806	804	802	801	799
4650]	834	832	830	828	826	824	822	820	818	816	815	813	811	809	807	805
4700]	841	839	837	835	833	831	829	827	825	823	821	820	818	816	814	812
4750]	848	846	844	842	840	838	836	834	832	830	828	826	824	822	820	818
4800]	854	852	850	848	846	844	842	840	839	837	835	833	831	829	826	824
4850]	861	859	857	855	853	851	849	847	845	843	841	839	837	835	833	831
4900]	868	866	864	862	860	858	856	854	852	850	848	846	843	841	839	837
4950]	874	872	870	868	866	864	862	861	859	856	854	852	850	848	846	844
5000]	881	879	877	875	873	871	869	867	865	863	860	858	856	854	852	850

(Left margin, vertical text: NONCUSTODIAL PARENT INCOME)

One Child Monthly Support Schedule

CUSTODIAL PARENT INCOME

	1850	1900	1950	2000	2050	2100	2150	2200	2250	2300	2350	2400	2450	2500	2550	2600
250]	38	38	38	38	38	38	38	38	38	38	38	38	38	38	38	38
300]	38	38	38	38	38	38	38	38	38	38	38	38	38	38	38	38
350]	38	38	38	38	38	38	38	38	38	38	38	38	38	38	38	38
400]	38	38	38	38	38	38	38	38	38	38	38	38	38	38	38	38
450]	40	40	40	40	40	40	40	40	38	38	38	38	38	38	38	38
500]	43	43	43	43	43	43	43	43	38	38	38	38	38	38	38	38
550]	46	46	46	46	46	46	46	46	41	41	41	41	41	41	41	41
600]	49	49	49	49	49	49	49	49	43	43	43	43	43	43	43	43
650]	52	52	52	52	52	52	52	52	46	46	46	46	46	46	46	46
700]	55	55	55	55	55	55	55	55	48	48	48	48	48	48	48	48
750]	69	69	69	69	69	69	69	69	62	62	62	62	62	62	62	62
800]	119	119	119	119	119	119	119	119	112	112	112	112	112	112	112	112
850]	169	169	169	169	169	169	169	169	162	162	162	162	162	162	162	162
900]	208	208	207	205	204	203	202	202	201	200	199	198	197	197	196	195
950]	218	217	216	215	214	213	212	211	210	209	208	208	207	206	205	204
1000]	228	227	226	225	224	222	221	221	220	219	218	217	216	215	214	214
1050]	238	236	235	234	233	232	231	230	229	228	227	226	225	225	224	223
1100]	247	246	245	243	242	241	240	239	238	237	236	235	235	234	233	232
1150]	256	255	254	253	252	251	249	248	247	247	246	245	244	243	242	241
1200]	266	264	263	262	261	260	259	258	257	256	255	254	253	252	251	250
1250]	275	274	272	271	270	269	268	267	266	265	264	263	262	261	260	259
1300]	284	283	282	280	279	278	277	276	275	274	273	272	271	270	269	268
1350]	293	292	291	289	288	287	286	285	284	283	282	281	280	279	278	277
1400]	302	301	300	298	297	296	295	294	293	292	291	290	289	287	286	285
1450]	311	310	309	307	306	305	304	303	302	301	299	298	297	296	295	294
1500]	320	319	318	316	315	314	313	312	310	309	308	307	306	305	304	303
1550]	329	328	326	325	324	323	322	320	319	318	317	316	315	314	313	312
1600]	338	337	335	334	333	332	330	329	328	327	326	324	323	322	321	320
1650]	347	345	344	343	342	340	339	338	336	335	334	333	332	331	330	329
1700]	355	354	353	352	350	349	348	346	345	344	343	342	340	339	338	337
1750]	364	363	361	360	359	357	356	355	354	352	351	350	349	348	347	346
1800]	373	371	370	369	367	366	365	363	362	361	360	359	357	356	355	354
1850]	381	380	378	377	376	374	373	372	371	369	368	367	366	365	364	363
1900]	390	388	387	385	384	383	381	380	379	378	377	375	374	373	372	371
1950]	398	397	395	394	393	391	390	389	387	386	385	384	383	382	380	379
2000]	407	405	404	402	401	400	398	397	396	394	393	392	391	390	389	388
2050]	415	413	412	411	409	408	407	405	404	403	402	400	399	398	397	396
2100]	423	422	420	419	417	416	415	414	412	411	410	409	408	406	405	404
2150]	431	430	429	427	426	424	423	422	421	419	418	417	416	415	414	413
2200]	440	438	437	435	434	433	431	430	429	428	426	425	424	423	422	421
2250]	448	446	445	444	442	441	440	438	437	436	435	433	432	431	430	429
2300]	456	455	453	452	450	449	448	446	445	444	443	442	440	439	438	437
2350]	464	463	461	460	458	457	456	455	453	452	451	450	449	447	446	445
2400]	472	471	469	468	467	465	464	463	461	460	459	458	457	456	455	453
2450]	480	479	477	476	475	473	472	471	470	468	467	466	465	464	463	462
2500]	488	487	486	484	483	481	480	479	478	476	475	474	473	472	471	470

NONCUSTODIAL PARENT INCOME

One Child Monthly Support Schedule

CUSTODIAL PARENT INCOME

	1850	1900	1950	2000	2050	2100	2150	2200	2250	2300	2350	2400	2450	2500	2550	2600
2550]	496	495	494	492	491	489	488	487	486	484	483	482	481	480	479	478
2600]	504	503	502	500	499	498	496	495	494	492	491	490	489	488	487	486
2650]	512	511	510	508	507	506	504	503	502	501	499	498	497	496	495	493
2700]	520	519	518	516	515	513	512	511	510	508	507	506	505	504	502	501
2750]	528	527	525	524	523	521	520	519	518	516	515	514	513	511	510	508
2800]	536	535	533	532	531	529	528	527	526	524	523	522	520	519	517	516
2850]	544	543	541	540	539	537	536	535	534	532	531	529	528	526	525	523
2900]	552	551	549	548	546	545	544	543	541	540	538	537	535	534	532	531
2950]	560	558	557	556	554	553	552	551	549	548	546	544	543	541	540	538
3000]	568	566	565	564	562	561	560	558	557	555	553	552	550	549	547	546
3050]	575	574	573	571	570	569	567	566	564	562	561	559	558	556	555	553
3100]	583	582	581	579	578	576	575	573	571	570	568	567	565	564	562	561
3150]	591	590	588	587	586	584	582	580	579	577	576	574	572	571	569	568
3200]	599	597	596	595	593	591	589	588	586	584	583	581	580	578	577	575
3250]	607	605	604	602	600	598	597	595	593	592	590	589	587	586	584	583
3300]	614	613	611	609	607	606	604	602	601	599	598	596	594	593	591	590
3350]	622	620	618	616	615	613	611	610	608	606	605	603	602	600	599	597
3400]	629	627	625	624	622	620	618	617	615	614	612	611	609	608	606	605
3450]	636	634	633	631	629	627	626	624	622	621	619	618	616	615	613	612
3500]	643	642	640	638	636	635	633	631	630	628	627	625	624	622	621	619
3550]	651	649	647	645	643	642	640	638	637	635	634	632	631	629	628	626
3600]	658	656	654	652	651	649	647	646	644	642	641	639	638	636	635	634
3650]	665	663	661	659	658	656	654	653	651	650	648	647	645	644	642	641
3700]	672	670	668	667	665	663	662	660	658	657	655	654	652	651	649	648
3750]	679	677	675	674	672	670	669	667	666	664	662	661	659	658	657	655
3800]	686	684	683	681	679	677	676	674	673	671	670	668	667	665	664	662
3850]	693	691	690	688	686	685	683	681	680	678	677	675	674	672	671	669
3900]	700	698	697	695	693	692	690	688	687	685	684	682	681	679	677	676
3950]	707	705	704	702	700	699	697	695	694	692	691	689	688	686	684	682
4000]	714	712	711	709	707	706	704	703	701	699	698	696	694	693	691	689
4050]	721	719	718	716	714	713	711	710	708	706	705	703	701	699	698	696
4100]	728	726	725	723	721	720	718	717	715	713	712	710	708	706	704	703
4150]	735	733	732	730	728	727	725	724	722	720	718	716	715	713	711	709
4200]	742	740	739	737	735	734	732	730	729	727	725	723	721	719	718	716
4250]	749	747	746	744	742	741	739	737	735	733	731	730	728	726	724	723
4300]	756	754	753	751	749	748	746	744	742	740	738	736	734	733	731	729
4350]	763	761	760	758	756	754	752	750	748	746	745	743	741	739	738	736
4400]	770	768	766	765	763	761	759	757	755	753	751	749	748	746	744	743
4450]	777	775	773	771	769	767	765	763	761	760	758	756	754	753	751	749
4500]	784	782	780	778	776	774	772	770	768	766	764	763	761	759	757	756
4550]	790	788	786	784	782	780	778	776	775	773	771	769	767	766	764	762
4600]	797	795	793	791	789	787	785	783	781	779	777	776	774	772	771	769
4650]	803	801	799	797	795	793	791	789	788	786	784	782	780	779	777	775
4700]	810	808	806	804	802	800	798	796	794	792	790	789	787	785	784	782
4750]	816	814	812	810	808	806	804	802	801	799	797	795	794	792	790	788
4800]	822	820	818	816	814	813	811	809	807	805	803	802	800	798	797	795
4850]	829	827	825	823	821	819	817	815	813	812	810	808	806	805	803	801
4900]	835	833	831	829	827	825	824	822	820	818	816	815	813	811	810	808
4950]	842	840	838	836	834	832	830	828	826	825	823	821	819	818	816	814
5000]	848	846	844	842	840	838	836	835	833	831	829	828	826	824	823	821

(Left margin, reading vertically: NONCUSTODIAL PARENT INCOME)

Effective July 1, 2003

One Child Monthly Support Schedule

CUSTODIAL PARENT INCOME

	2650	2700	2750	2800	2850	2900	2950	3000	3050	3100	3150	3200	3250	3300	3350	3400
250]	38	38	38	38	38	38	38	38	38	38	38	38	38	38	38	38
300]	38	38	38	38	38	38	38	38	38	38	38	38	38	38	38	38
350]	38	38	38	38	38	38	38	38	38	38	38	38	38	38	38	38
400]	38	38	38	38	38	38	38	38	38	38	38	38	38	38	38	38
450]	38	38	38	38	38	38	38	38	38	38	38	38	38	38	38	38
500]	38	38	38	38	38	38	38	38	38	38	38	38	38	38	38	38
550]	41	38	38	38	38	38	38	38	38	38	38	38	38	38	38	38
600]	43	38	38	38	38	38	38	38	38	38	38	38	38	38	38	38
650]	46	39	39	39	39	39	39	39	39	39	38	38	38	38	38	38
700]	48	41	41	41	41	41	41	41	41	41	38	38	38	38	38	38
750]	62	55	55	55	55	55	55	55	55	55	50	50	50	50	50	50
800]	112	105	105	105	105	105	105	105	105	105	100	100	100	100	100	100
850]	162	155	155	155	155	155	155	155	155	155	150	150	150	150	150	150
900]	194	194	193	192	192	191	190	189	189	188	188	187	186	186	185	185
950]	204	203	202	201	201	200	199	199	198	197	197	196	195	195	194	194
1000]	213	212	211	211	210	209	208	208	207	206	206	205	204	204	203	203
1050]	222	221	220	220	219	218	217	217	216	215	215	214	213	213	212	211
1100]	231	230	229	229	228	227	226	226	225	224	224	223	222	222	221	220
1150]	240	239	238	238	237	236	235	235	234	233	232	232	231	230	230	229
1200]	249	248	247	247	246	245	244	243	243	242	241	241	240	239	239	238
1250]	258	257	256	255	255	254	253	252	251	251	250	249	249	248	247	247
1300]	267	266	265	264	263	263	262	261	260	259	259	258	257	257	256	255
1350]	276	275	274	273	272	271	271	270	269	268	267	267	266	265	265	264
1400]	285	284	283	282	281	280	279	278	278	277	276	275	275	274	273	273
1450]	293	292	291	290	290	289	288	287	286	285	285	284	283	283	282	281
1500]	302	301	300	299	298	297	297	296	295	294	293	293	292	291	290	290
1550]	311	310	309	308	307	306	305	304	303	303	302	301	300	300	299	298
1600]	319	318	317	316	315	315	314	313	312	311	310	310	309	308	307	307
1650]	328	327	326	325	324	323	322	321	320	320	319	318	317	317	316	315
1700]	336	335	334	333	332	332	331	330	329	328	327	327	326	325	324	324
1750]	345	344	343	342	341	340	339	338	337	337	336	335	334	333	333	332
1800]	353	352	351	350	349	348	348	347	346	345	344	343	343	342	341	340
1850]	362	361	360	359	358	357	356	355	354	353	353	352	351	350	349	348
1900]	370	369	368	367	366	365	364	363	363	362	361	360	359	358	357	356
1950]	378	377	376	375	374	374	373	372	371	370	369	368	367	366	365	364
2000]	387	386	385	384	383	382	381	380	379	378	377	377	375	374	373	372
2050]	395	394	393	392	391	390	389	388	387	387	386	384	383	382	381	380
2100]	403	402	401	400	399	398	397	397	396	395	394	392	391	390	389	388
2150]	412	411	410	409	408	407	406	405	404	403	401	400	399	398	397	396
2200]	420	419	418	417	416	415	414	413	412	410	409	408	407	406	405	404
2250]	428	427	426	425	424	423	422	421	419	418	417	416	415	414	413	412
2300]	436	435	434	433	432	431	430	429	427	426	425	424	423	421	420	419
2350]	444	443	442	441	440	439	438	436	435	434	433	432	430	429	428	427
2400]	452	451	450	449	448	447	445	444	443	442	440	439	438	437	436	435
2450]	460	459	458	457	456	454	453	452	451	449	448	447	446	445	444	442
2500]	469	467	466	465	463	462	461	459	458	457	456	455	453	452	451	450

NONCUSTODIAL PARENT INCOME

One Child Monthly Support Schedule

CUSTODIAL PARENT INCOME

	2650	2700	2750	2800	2850	2900	2950	3000	3050	3100	3150	3200	3250	3300	3350	3400
2550]	476	475	474	472	471	470	468	467	466	465	463	462	461	460	459	458
2600]	484	483	481	480	479	477	476	475	474	472	471	470	469	468	467	465
2650]	492	490	489	488	486	485	484	482	481	480	479	478	476	475	474	473
2700]	499	498	497	495	494	493	491	490	489	488	486	485	484	483	482	481
2750]	507	505	504	503	501	500	499	498	496	495	494	493	492	490	489	488
2800]	514	513	512	510	509	508	506	505	504	503	501	500	499	498	497	496
2850]	522	521	519	518	516	515	514	513	511	510	509	508	507	505	504	503
2900]	529	528	527	525	524	523	521	520	519	518	516	515	514	513	512	511
2950]	537	536	534	533	531	530	529	528	526	525	524	523	522	520	519	518
N 3000]	544	543	542	540	539	538	536	535	534	533	531	530	529	528	527	525
O 3050]	552	550	549	548	546	545	544	542	541	540	539	538	536	535	534	533
N 3100]	559	558	556	555	554	552	551	550	549	547	546	545	544	543	541	540
C 3150]	567	565	564	562	561	560	559	557	556	555	554	552	551	550	548	547
U 3200]	574	573	571	570	568	567	566	565	563	562	561	560	558	557	555	554
S 3250]	581	580	579	577	576	575	573	572	571	570	568	567	565	564	562	561
T 3300]	589	587	586	585	583	582	581	579	578	577	575	574	572	571	569	568
O 3350]	596	595	593	592	590	589	588	587	585	584	582	581	579	578	576	575
D 3400]	603	602	600	599	598	596	595	594	592	591	589	588	586	585	583	582
I 3450]	610	609	608	606	605	604	602	601	599	598	596	595	593	592	590	589
A L 3500]	618	616	615	614	612	611	609	608	606	605	603	602	600	599	597	596
3550]	625	624	622	621	619	618	616	615	613	612	610	609	607	606	604	603
P 3600]	632	631	629	628	626	625	623	622	620	619	617	616	614	613	611	610
A 3650]	639	638	636	635	633	632	630	628	627	625	624	622	621	620	618	617
R 3700]	647	645	643	642	640	638	637	635	634	632	631	629	628	626	625	624
E 3750]	654	652	650	649	647	645	644	642	641	639	638	636	635	633	632	631
N 3800]	660	659	657	655	654	652	651	649	648	646	645	643	642	640	639	637
T 3850]	667	666	664	662	661	659	657	656	654	653	651	650	648	647	646	644
3900]	674	672	671	669	667	666	664	663	661	660	658	657	655	654	652	651
I 3950]	681	679	677	676	674	673	671	669	668	666	665	663	662	661	659	658
N C 4000]	687	686	684	683	681	679	678	676	675	673	672	670	669	667	666	665
O 4050]	694	693	691	689	688	686	685	683	681	680	678	677	676	674	673	671
M 4100]	701	699	698	696	694	693	691	690	688	687	685	684	682	681	680	678
E 4150]	708	706	704	703	701	700	698	696	695	693	692	691	689	688	686	685
4200]	714	713	711	709	708	706	705	703	702	700	699	697	696	694	693	692
4250]	721	719	718	716	714	713	711	710	708	707	705	704	703	701	700	698
4300]	728	726	724	723	721	720	718	717	715	714	712	711	709	708	706	705
4350]	734	733	731	729	728	726	725	723	722	720	719	717	716	714	713	712
4400]	741	739	738	736	734	733	731	730	728	727	725	724	723	721	720	718
4450]	747	746	744	743	741	739	738	736	735	733	732	731	729	728	726	725
4500]	754	752	751	749	748	746	745	743	742	740	739	737	736	734	733	732
4550]	761	759	757	756	754	753	751	750	748	747	745	744	742	741	740	738
4600]	767	766	764	762	761	759	758	756	755	753	752	750	749	748	746	745
4650]	774	772	771	769	767	766	764	763	761	760	758	757	756	754	753	751
4700]	780	779	777	776	774	772	771	769	768	766	765	764	762	761	759	758
4750]	787	785	784	782	781	779	777	776	775	773	772	770	769	767	765	764
4800]	793	792	790	789	787	786	784	783	781	780	778	777	775	773	772	770
4850]	800	798	797	795	794	792	791	789	788	786	785	783	781	780	778	776
4900]	806	805	803	802	800	799	797	796	794	793	791	789	788	786	784	782
4950]	813	811	810	808	807	805	804	802	801	799	797	795	794	792	790	789
5000]	819	818	816	815	813	812	810	809	807	805	803	802	800	798	796	795

One Child Monthly Support Schedule

NONCUSTODIAL PARENT INCOME	CUSTODIAL PARENT INCOME															
	3450	3500	3550	3600	3650	3700	3750	3800	3850	3900	3950	4000	4050	4100	4150	4200
250]	38	38	38	38	38	38	38	38	38	38	38	38	38	38	38	38
300]	38	38	38	38	38	38	38	38	38	38	38	38	38	38	38	38
350]	38	38	38	38	38	38	38	38	38	38	38	38	38	38	38	38
400]	38	38	38	38	38	38	38	38	38	38	38	38	38	38	38	38
450]	38	38	38	38	38	38	38	38	38	38	38	38	38	38	38	38
500]	38	38	38	38	38	38	38	38	38	38	38	38	38	38	38	38
550]	38	38	38	38	38	38	38	38	38	38	38	38	38	38	38	38
600]	38	38	38	38	38	38	38	38	38	38	38	38	38	38	38	38
650]	38	38	38	38	38	38	38	38	38	38	38	38	38	38	38	38
700]	38	38	38	38	38	38	38	38	38	38	38	38	38	38	38	38
750]	50	50	50	50	50	50	50	50	50	50	50	50	50	50	50	50
800]	100	100	100	100	100	100	100	100	100	100	100	100	100	100	100	100
850]	150	150	150	150	150	150	150	150	150	150	150	150	150	150	150	150
900]	184	184	183	183	182	182	181	181	180	180	179	179	179	178	178	177
950]	193	193	192	192	191	191	190	190	189	189	188	188	187	187	187	186
1000]	202	201	201	200	200	199	199	198	198	197	197	197	196	196	195	195
1050]	211	210	210	209	209	208	208	207	207	206	206	205	205	204	204	203
1100]	220	219	219	218	217	217	216	216	215	215	214	214	213	213	212	212
1150]	229	228	227	227	226	226	225	225	224	224	223	223	222	221	221	220
1200]	237	237	236	235	235	234	234	233	233	232	232	231	230	230	229	229
1250]	246	245	245	244	244	243	242	242	241	241	240	240	239	238	238	237
1300]	255	254	253	253	252	252	251	250	250	249	249	248	247	247	246	245
1350]	263	263	262	261	261	260	260	259	258	258	257	256	255	255	254	253
1400]	272	271	271	270	269	269	268	267	267	266	265	264	264	263	262	262
1450]	280	280	279	278	278	277	277	276	275	274	273	273	272	271	271	270
1500]	289	288	288	287	286	286	285	284	283	282	282	281	280	279	279	278
1550]	297	297	296	295	295	294	293	292	291	291	290	289	288	288	287	286
1600]	306	305	305	304	303	302	301	300	300	299	298	297	296	296	295	294
1650]	314	314	313	312	311	310	309	309	308	307	306	305	305	304	303	302
1700]	323	322	321	320	319	318	317	317	316	315	314	313	313	312	311	310
1750]	331	330	329	328	327	326	326	325	324	323	322	321	321	320	319	318
1800]	339	338	337	336	335	334	334	333	332	331	330	329	329	328	327	326
1850]	347	346	345	344	343	342	342	341	340	339	338	337	337	336	335	334
1900]	355	354	353	352	351	350	350	349	348	347	346	345	344	344	343	342
1950]	363	362	361	360	359	358	357	357	356	355	354	353	352	352	351	350
2000]	371	370	369	368	367	366	365	365	364	363	362	361	360	359	359	358
2050]	379	378	377	376	375	374	373	372	371	371	370	369	368	367	366	366
2100]	387	386	385	384	383	382	381	380	379	378	378	377	376	375	374	373
2150]	395	394	393	392	391	390	389	388	387	386	385	384	384	383	382	381
2200]	403	402	401	400	399	398	397	396	395	394	393	392	391	391	390	389
2250]	410	409	408	407	406	405	405	404	403	402	401	400	399	398	397	396
2300]	418	417	416	415	414	413	412	411	410	410	409	408	407	406	405	404
2350]	426	425	424	423	422	421	420	419	418	417	416	415	414	413	412	411
2400]	434	433	432	431	430	429	428	427	426	425	424	423	422	421	420	419
2450]	441	440	439	438	437	436	435	434	433	433	432	430	429	428	427	426
2500]	449	448	447	446	445	444	443	442	441	440	439	438	437	436	435	434

One Child Monthly Support Schedule

CUSTODIAL PARENT INCOME

	3450	3500	3550	3600	3650	3700	3750	3800	3850	3900	3950	4000	4050	4100	4150	4200
2550]	457	456	455	454	453	452	451	450	449	447	446	445	444	443	442	441
2600]	464	463	462	461	460	459	458	457	456	455	454	453	451	450	449	448
2650]	472	471	470	469	468	467	466	464	463	462	461	460	459	458	457	456
2700]	480	478	477	476	475	474	473	472	471	469	468	467	466	465	464	463
2750]	487	486	485	484	483	482	480	479	478	477	476	474	473	472	471	470
2800]	495	494	492	491	490	489	488	486	485	484	483	482	481	479	478	477
2850]	502	501	500	499	497	496	495	494	492	491	490	489	488	487	486	484
2900]	510	508	507	506	505	503	502	501	500	498	497	496	495	494	493	492
2950]	517	516	514	513	512	510	509	508	507	506	504	503	502	501	500	499
3000]	524	523	521	520	519	518	516	515	514	513	512	510	509	508	507	506
3050]	531	530	529	527	526	525	524	522	521	520	519	518	516	515	514	513
3100]	538	537	536	534	533	532	531	529	528	527	526	525	524	522	521	520
3150]	546	544	543	542	540	539	538	537	535	534	533	532	531	529	528	527
3200]	553	551	550	549	547	546	545	544	542	541	540	539	538	537	535	534
3250]	560	558	557	556	554	553	552	551	549	548	547	546	545	544	542	541
3300]	567	565	564	563	561	560	559	558	556	555	554	553	552	551	550	548
3350]	574	572	571	570	568	567	566	565	563	562	561	560	559	558	557	555
3400]	581	579	578	577	575	574	573	572	570	569	568	567	566	565	563	562
3450]	588	586	585	584	582	581	580	579	577	576	575	574	573	572	570	569
3500]	595	593	592	591	589	588	587	586	584	583	582	581	580	579	577	576
3550]	602	600	599	598	596	595	594	593	591	590	589	588	587	585	584	583
3600]	609	607	606	605	603	602	601	599	598	597	596	595	594	592	591	590
3650]	615	614	613	611	610	609	608	606	605	604	603	602	600	599	598	597
3700]	622	621	620	618	617	616	615	613	612	611	610	608	607	606	605	604
3750]	629	628	627	625	624	623	621	620	619	618	617	615	614	613	612	611
3800]	636	635	633	632	631	630	628	627	626	625	623	622	621	620	619	618
3850]	643	642	640	639	638	636	635	634	633	631	630	629	628	627	626	624
3900]	650	648	647	646	644	643	642	641	639	638	637	636	635	634	632	631
3950]	657	655	654	653	651	650	649	647	646	645	644	643	642	640	639	637
4000]	663	662	661	659	658	657	656	654	653	652	651	649	648	647	645	644
4050]	670	669	667	666	665	664	662	661	660	659	657	656	655	653	652	650
4100]	677	675	674	673	672	670	669	668	667	665	664	663	661	660	658	657
4150]	684	682	681	680	678	677	676	675	673	672	670	669	667	666	665	663
4200]	690	689	688	686	685	684	683	681	680	678	677	675	674	672	671	670
4250]	697	696	694	693	692	691	689	688	686	685	683	682	680	679	677	676
4300]	704	702	701	700	698	697	696	694	693	691	690	688	687	685	684	682
4350]	710	709	708	706	705	704	702	701	699	698	696	695	693	692	690	689
4400]	717	716	714	713	712	710	708	707	705	704	702	701	699	698	697	695
4450]	724	722	721	720	718	716	715	713	712	710	709	707	706	704	703	701
4500]	730	729	728	726	724	723	721	720	718	717	715	714	712	711	709	708
4550]	737	735	734	732	731	729	727	726	724	723	721	720	718	717	715	714
4600]	743	742	740	738	737	735	734	732	731	729	728	726	725	723	722	720
4650]	750	748	746	745	743	742	740	738	737	735	734	732	731	729	728	727
4700]	756	754	753	751	749	748	746	745	743	742	740	739	737	736	734	733
4750]	762	760	759	757	756	754	752	751	749	748	746	745	743	742	741	739
4800]	768	767	765	763	762	760	759	757	756	754	753	751	750	748	747	745
4850]	775	773	771	770	768	766	765	763	762	760	759	757	756	754	753	752
4900]	781	779	777	776	774	773	771	770	768	766	765	764	762	761	759	758
4950]	787	785	784	782	780	779	777	776	774	773	771	770	768	767	765	764
5000]	793	791	790	788	787	785	783	782	780	779	777	776	774	773	772	770

NONCUSTODIAL PARENT INCOME

One Child Monthly Support Schedule

CUSTODIAL PARENT INCOME

	4250	4300	4350	4400	4450	4500	4550	4600	4650	4700	4750	4800	4850	4900	4950	5000
250]	38	38	38	38	38	38	38	38	38	38	38	38	38	38	38	38
300]	38	38	38	38	38	38	38	38	38	38	38	38	38	38	38	38
350]	38	38	38	38	38	38	38	38	38	38	38	38	38	38	38	38
400]	38	38	38	38	38	38	38	38	38	38	38	38	38	38	38	38
450]	38	38	38	38	38	38	38	38	38	38	38	38	38	38	38	38
500]	38	38	38	38	38	38	38	38	38	38	38	38	38	38	38	38
550]	38	38	38	38	38	38	38	38	38	38	38	38	38	38	38	38
600]	38	38	38	38	38	38	38	38	38	38	38	38	38	38	38	38
650]	38	38	38	38	38	38	38	38	38	38	38	38	38	38	38	38
700]	38	38	38	38	38	38	38	38	38	38	38	38	38	38	38	38
750]	50	50	50	50	50	50	50	50	50	50	50	50	50	50	50	50
800]	100	100	100	100	100	100	100	100	100	100	100	100	100	100	100	100
850]	150	150	150	150	150	150	150	150	150	150	150	150	150	150	150	150
900]	177	177	176	176	175	175	174	174	173	173	172	172	172	171	171	170
950]	186	185	185	184	184	183	183	182	182	181	181	180	180	180	179	179
1000]	194	194	193	193	192	192	191	191	190	190	189	189	188	188	187	187
1050]	203	202	202	201	201	200	200	199	199	198	198	197	197	196	196	195
1100]	211	211	210	209	209	208	208	207	207	206	206	205	205	204	204	204
1150]	220	219	218	218	217	217	216	216	215	215	214	214	213	213	212	212
1200]	228	227	227	226	226	225	224	224	223	223	222	222	221	221	220	220
1250]	236	236	235	234	234	233	233	232	232	231	231	230	230	229	229	228
1300]	245	244	243	243	242	241	241	240	240	239	239	238	238	237	237	236
1350]	253	252	252	251	250	250	249	249	248	247	247	246	246	245	245	244
1400]	261	260	260	259	258	258	257	257	256	255	255	254	254	253	253	252
1450]	269	269	268	267	267	266	265	265	264	264	263	262	262	261	261	260
1500]	277	277	276	275	275	274	273	273	272	272	271	270	270	269	269	268
1550]	285	285	284	283	283	282	281	281	280	280	279	278	278	277	276	276
1600]	294	293	292	291	291	290	289	289	288	288	287	286	286	285	284	284
1650]	302	301	300	299	299	298	297	297	296	296	295	294	293	293	292	291
1700]	310	309	308	307	307	306	305	305	304	303	303	302	301	300	300	299
1750]	318	317	316	315	315	314	313	313	312	311	310	310	309	308	307	307
1800]	325	325	324	323	323	322	321	321	320	319	318	317	317	316	315	314
1850]	333	333	332	331	331	330	329	328	327	327	326	325	324	323	323	322
1900]	341	341	340	339	338	338	337	336	335	334	333	333	332	331	330	330
1950]	349	348	348	347	346	345	344	344	343	342	341	340	339	339	338	337
2000]	357	356	355	355	354	353	352	351	350	349	349	348	347	346	345	345
2050]	365	364	363	362	361	360	360	359	358	357	356	355	355	354	353	352
2100]	373	372	371	370	369	368	367	366	365	365	364	363	362	361	360	360
2150]	380	379	378	377	376	376	375	374	373	372	371	370	370	369	368	367
2200]	388	387	386	385	384	383	382	381	380	379	379	378	377	376	375	375
2250]	395	394	393	392	391	391	390	389	388	387	386	385	384	384	383	382
2300]	403	402	401	400	399	398	397	396	395	394	394	393	392	391	390	389
2350]	410	409	408	407	406	405	404	404	403	402	401	400	399	398	397	397
2400]	418	417	416	415	414	413	412	411	410	409	408	407	407	406	405	404
2450]	425	424	423	422	421	420	419	418	417	416	416	415	414	413	412	411
2500]	432	431	430	429	428	428	427	426	425	424	423	422	421	420	419	419

NONCUSTODIAL PARENT INCOME

One Child Monthly Support Schedule

CUSTODIAL PARENT INCOME

	4250	4300	4350	4400	4450	4500	4550	4600	4650	4700	4750	4800	4850	4900	4950	5000
2550]	440	439	438	437	436	435	434	433	432	431	430	429	428	428	427	426
2600]	447	446	445	444	443	442	441	440	439	438	437	437	436	435	434	433
2650]	454	453	452	451	450	449	448	448	447	446	445	444	443	442	441	440
2700]	462	461	460	459	458	457	456	455	454	453	452	451	450	449	448	448
2750]	469	468	467	466	465	464	463	462	461	460	459	458	457	456	456	455
2800]	476	475	474	473	472	471	470	469	468	467	466	465	465	464	463	462
2850]	483	482	481	480	479	478	477	476	475	474	474	473	472	471	470	469
2900]	491	490	488	487	486	485	484	484	483	482	481	480	479	478	477	476
2950]	498	497	496	495	494	493	492	491	490	489	488	487	486	485	484	483
3000]	505	504	503	502	501	500	499	498	497	496	495	494	493	492	491	490
3050]	512	511	510	509	508	507	506	505	504	503	502	501	500	499	498	497
3100]	519	518	517	516	515	514	513	512	511	510	509	508	507	506	505	504
3150]	526	525	524	523	522	521	520	519	518	517	516	515	514	513	512	511
3200]	533	532	531	530	529	528	527	526	525	524	523	522	521	520	519	518
3250]	540	539	538	537	536	535	534	533	532	531	530	529	528	527	526	524
3300]	547	546	545	544	543	542	541	540	539	538	537	536	535	533	532	531
3350]	554	553	552	551	550	549	548	547	546	545	544	543	541	540	539	538
3400]	561	560	559	558	557	556	555	554	553	552	550	549	548	547	546	545
3450]	568	567	566	565	564	563	562	561	560	558	557	556	555	554	552	551
3500]	575	574	573	572	571	570	569	567	566	565	564	563	561	560	559	558
3550]	582	581	580	579	578	577	575	574	573	572	570	569	568	567	566	564
3600]	589	588	587	586	585	583	582	581	580	578	577	576	575	573	572	571
3650]	596	595	594	593	591	590	589	587	586	585	584	582	581	580	579	578
3700]	603	602	601	599	598	597	595	594	593	591	590	589	588	587	585	584
3750]	610	608	607	606	604	603	602	601	599	598	597	596	594	593	592	591
3800]	616	615	614	612	611	610	608	607	606	605	603	602	601	600	599	597
3850]	623	622	620	619	618	616	615	614	612	611	610	609	607	606	605	604
3900]	629	628	627	625	624	623	621	620	619	618	616	615	614	613	612	610
3950]	636	635	633	632	631	629	628	627	625	624	623	622	620	619	618	617
4000]	642	641	640	638	637	636	634	633	632	631	629	628	627	626	625	623
4050]	649	648	646	645	643	642	641	640	638	637	636	635	633	632	631	630
4100]	655	654	653	651	650	649	647	646	645	643	642	641	640	639	637	636
4150]	662	660	659	658	656	655	654	652	651	650	649	647	646	645	644	643
4200]	668	667	665	664	663	661	660	659	658	656	655	654	653	651	650	649
4250]	675	673	672	671	669	668	667	665	664	663	661	660	659	658	657	655
4300]	681	680	678	677	676	674	673	672	670	669	668	667	665	664	663	662
4350]	687	686	685	683	682	681	679	678	677	675	674	673	672	671	669	668
4400]	694	692	691	690	688	687	686	684	683	682	681	679	678	677	676	675
4450]	700	699	697	696	695	693	692	691	689	688	687	686	684	683	682	681
4500]	706	705	704	702	701	700	698	697	696	694	693	692	691	690	688	687
4550]	713	711	710	709	707	706	705	703	702	701	700	698	697	696	695	693
4600]	719	718	716	715	714	712	711	710	708	707	706	705	703	702	701	700
4650]	725	724	722	721	720	718	717	716	715	713	712	711	710	708	707	706
4700]	732	730	729	727	726	725	723	722	721	720	718	717	716	715	713	712
4750]	738	736	735	734	732	731	730	728	727	726	725	723	722	721	720	719
4800]	744	743	741	740	739	737	736	735	733	732	731	730	728	727	726	725
4850]	750	749	747	746	745	743	742	741	740	738	737	736	735	733	732	731
4900]	756	755	754	752	751	750	748	747	746	745	743	742	741	740	738	737
4950]	763	761	760	759	757	756	755	753	752	751	749	748	747	746	745	743
5000]	769	767	766	765	763	762	761	759	758	757	756	754	753	752	751	750

NONCUSTODIAL PARENT INCOME

Effective July 1, 2003

Two Children Monthly Support Schedule

CUSTODIAL PARENT INCOME

NONCUSTODIAL PARENT INCOME

	0	250	300	350	400	450	500	550	600	650	700	750	800	850	900	950	1000
250]	51	51	51	51	51	51	51	51	51	51	51	51	51	51	51	51	51
300]	56	56	56	56	56	56	56	56	56	56	56	53	53	53	51	51	51
350]	61	61	61	61	61	61	61	61	61	61	61	58	58	58	54	54	54
400]	66	66	66	66	66	66	66	66	66	66	66	62	62	62	58	58	58
450]	71	71	71	71	71	71	71	71	71	71	71	67	67	67	62	62	62
500]	76	76	76	76	76	76	76	76	76	76	76	71	71	71	66	66	66
550]	81	81	81	81	81	81	81	81	81	81	81	76	76	76	70	70	70
600]	86	86	86	86	86	86	86	86	86	86	86	80	80	80	74	74	74
650]	91	91	91	91	91	91	91	91	91	91	91	85	85	85	78	78	78
700]	96	96	96	96	96	96	96	96	96	96	96	89	89	89	82	82	82
750]	112	112	112	112	112	112	112	112	112	112	112	105	105	105	97	97	97
800]	162	162	162	162	162	162	162	162	162	162	162	155	155	155	147	147	147
850]	212	212	212	212	212	212	212	212	212	212	212	205	205	205	197	197	197
900]	262	262	262	262	262	262	262	262	262	262	262	255	255	255	247	247	247
950]	312	312	312	312	312	312	312	312	312	312	312	305	305	305	297	297	297
1000]	362	362	362	362	362	362	362	362	362	362	362	355	355	355	347	347	347
1050]	412	412	412	412	412	412	412	412	412	412	412	405	405	405	397	397	397
1100]	456	456	456	456	456	456	456	456	456	456	456	429	426	423	420	418	415
1150]	474	474	474	474	474	474	474	474	474	474	474	444	441	438	435	433	430
1200]	493	493	493	493	493	493	493	493	493	493	493	459	456	453	450	448	445
1250]	511	511	511	511	511	511	511	511	511	511	511	474	471	468	466	463	460
1300]	529	529	529	529	529	529	529	529	529	529	529	489	486	483	480	477	474
1350]	547	547	547	547	547	547	547	547	547	547	547	504	501	498	494	491	488
1400]	565	565	565	565	565	565	565	565	565	565	565	518	515	512	508	505	502
1450]	583	583	583	583	583	583	583	583	583	583	583	533	529	526	522	519	516
1500]	601	601	601	601	601	601	601	601	601	601	601	546	543	539	536	533	530
1550]	619	619	619	619	619	619	619	619	619	619	619	560	556	553	550	547	544
1600]	637	637	637	637	637	637	637	637	637	637	637	574	570	567	563	560	557
1650]	651	651	651	651	651	651	651	651	651	651	651	587	584	580	577	574	571
1700]	664	664	664	664	664	664	664	664	664	664	664	600	597	594	591	587	585
1750]	677	677	677	677	677	677	677	677	677	677	677	614	610	607	604	601	598
1800]	690	690	690	690	690	690	690	690	690	690	690	627	624	620	617	614	611
1850]	703	703	703	703	703	703	703	703	703	703	703	640	637	634	631	628	625
1900]	716	716	716	716	716	716	716	716	716	716	716	654	650	647	644	641	638
1950]	729	729	729	729	729	729	729	729	729	729	729	667	663	660	657	654	650
2000]	743	743	743	743	743	743	743	743	743	743	743	680	677	673	670	666	663
2050]	756	756	756	756	756	756	756	756	756	756	756	693	689	686	682	679	676
2100]	769	769	769	769	769	769	769	769	769	769	769	705	702	698	695	692	689
2150]	782	782	782	782	782	782	782	782	782	782	782	718	714	711	708	705	701
2200]	795	795	795	795	795	795	795	795	795	795	795	730	727	724	720	717	714
2250]	806	806	806	806	806	806	806	806	806	806	806	743	739	736	733	730	727
2300]	818	818	818	818	818	818	818	818	818	818	818	755	752	749	745	742	739
2350]	830	830	830	830	830	830	830	830	830	830	830	768	764	761	758	755	752
2400]	842	842	842	842	842	842	842	842	842	842	842	780	777	773	770	767	764
2450]	854	854	854	854	854	854	854	854	854	854	854	792	789	786	783	780	777
2500]	866	866	866	866	866	866	866	866	866	866	866	805	801	798	795	792	789

Two Children Monthly Support Schedule

CUSTODIAL PARENT INCOME

NONCUSTODIAL PARENT INCOME	0	250	300	350	400	450	500	550	600	650	700	750	800	850	900	950	1000
2550]	878	878	878	878	878	878	878	878	878	878	878	817	814	810	807	804	801
2600]	889	889	889	889	889	889	889	889	889	889	889	829	826	823	820	817	814
2650]	901	901	901	901	901	901	901	901	901	901	901	841	838	835	832	829	826
2700]	913	913	913	913	913	913	913	913	913	913	913	853	850	847	844	841	838
2750]	925	925	925	925	925	925	925	925	925	925	925	865	862	859	856	853	850
2800]	937	937	937	937	937	937	937	937	937	937	937	878	874	871	868	865	862
2850]	948	948	948	948	948	948	948	948	948	948	948	890	886	883	880	877	874
2900]	959	959	959	959	959	959	959	959	959	959	959	902	898	895	892	889	886
2950]	971	971	971	971	971	971	971	971	971	971	971	913	910	907	904	901	898
3000]	982	982	982	982	982	982	982	982	982	982	982	925	922	919	916	913	910
3050]	993	993	993	993	993	993	993	993	993	993	993	937	933	930	927	924	921
3100]	1004	1004	1004	1004	1004	1004	1004	1004	1004	1004	1004	948	945	942	939	936	933
3150]	1016	1016	1016	1016	1016	1016	1016	1016	1016	1016	1016	960	957	954	951	948	945
3200]	1027	1027	1027	1027	1027	1027	1027	1027	1027	1027	1027	972	969	965	962	960	957
3250]	1038	1038	1038	1038	1038	1038	1038	1038	1038	1038	1038	983	980	977	974	971	969
3300]	1049	1049	1049	1049	1049	1049	1049	1049	1049	1049	1049	995	992	989	986	983	980
3350]	1061	1061	1061	1061	1061	1061	1061	1061	1061	1061	1061	1006	1003	1000	998	995	992
3400]	1072	1072	1072	1072	1072	1072	1072	1072	1072	1072	1072	1018	1015	1012	1009	1006	1004
3450]	1083	1083	1083	1083	1083	1083	1083	1083	1083	1083	1083	1029	1027	1024	1021	1018	1015
3500]	1094	1094	1094	1094	1094	1094	1094	1094	1094	1094	1094	1041	1038	1035	1032	1030	1027
3550]	1106	1106	1106	1106	1106	1106	1106	1106	1106	1106	1106	1053	1050	1047	1044	1041	1039
3600]	1117	1117	1117	1117	1117	1117	1117	1117	1117	1117	1117	1064	1061	1058	1056	1053	1050
3650]	1128	1128	1128	1128	1128	1128	1128	1128	1128	1128	1128	1075	1073	1070	1067	1064	1062
3700]	1139	1139	1139	1139	1139	1139	1139	1139	1139	1139	1139	1087	1084	1081	1079	1076	1073
3750]	1150	1150	1150	1150	1150	1150	1150	1150	1150	1150	1150	1098	1096	1093	1090	1087	1085
3800]	1161	1161	1161	1161	1161	1161	1161	1161	1161	1161	1161	1110	1107	1104	1102	1099	1096
3850]	1171	1171	1171	1171	1171	1171	1171	1171	1171	1171	1171	1121	1118	1116	1113	1111	1108
3900]	1182	1182	1182	1182	1182	1182	1182	1182	1182	1182	1182	1133	1130	1127	1125	1122	1119
3950]	1193	1193	1193	1193	1193	1193	1193	1193	1193	1193	1193	1144	1141	1139	1136	1134	1131
4000]	1204	1204	1204	1204	1204	1204	1204	1204	1204	1204	1204	1155	1153	1150	1148	1145	1143
4050]	1215	1215	1215	1215	1215	1215	1215	1215	1215	1215	1215	1167	1164	1162	1159	1156	1154
4100]	1226	1226	1226	1226	1226	1226	1226	1226	1226	1226	1226	1178	1176	1173	1170	1168	1165
4150]	1237	1237	1237	1237	1237	1237	1237	1237	1237	1237	1237	1190	1187	1184	1182	1179	1177
4200]	1248	1248	1248	1248	1248	1248	1248	1248	1248	1248	1248	1201	1198	1196	1193	1191	1188
4250]	1258	1258	1258	1258	1258	1258	1258	1258	1258	1258	1258	1212	1210	1207	1205	1202	1199
4300]	1269	1269	1269	1269	1269	1269	1269	1269	1269	1269	1269	1224	1221	1219	1216	1213	1210
4350]	1280	1280	1280	1280	1280	1280	1280	1280	1280	1280	1280	1235	1232	1230	1226	1223	1221
4400]	1291	1291	1291	1291	1291	1291	1291	1291	1291	1291	1291	1246	1243	1240	1237	1234	1231
4450]	1302	1302	1302	1302	1302	1302	1302	1302	1302	1302	1302	1257	1254	1251	1248	1245	1242
4500]	1313	1313	1313	1313	1313	1313	1313	1313	1313	1313	1313	1268	1265	1262	1259	1256	1253
4550]	1324	1324	1324	1324	1324	1324	1324	1324	1324	1324	1324	1279	1275	1272	1269	1267	1264
4600]	1335	1335	1335	1335	1335	1335	1335	1335	1335	1335	1335	1289	1286	1283	1280	1277	1274
4650]	1345	1345	1345	1345	1345	1345	1345	1345	1345	1345	1345	1300	1297	1294	1291	1288	1285
4700]	1356	1356	1356	1356	1356	1356	1356	1356	1356	1356	1356	1310	1307	1304	1302	1299	1296
4750]	1367	1367	1367	1367	1367	1367	1367	1367	1367	1367	1367	1321	1318	1315	1312	1309	1307
4800]	1378	1378	1378	1378	1378	1378	1378	1378	1378	1378	1378	1332	1329	1326	1323	1320	1317
4850]	1389	1389	1389	1389	1389	1389	1389	1389	1389	1389	1389	1342	1339	1336	1334	1331	1328
4900]	1400	1400	1400	1400	1400	1400	1400	1400	1400	1400	1400	1353	1350	1347	1344	1342	1339
4950]	1411	1411	1411	1411	1411	1411	1411	1411	1411	1411	1411	1363	1361	1358	1355	1352	1349
5000]	1422	1422	1422	1422	1422	1422	1422	1422	1422	1422	1422	1374	1371	1368	1366	1363	1360

Two Children Monthly Support Schedule

CUSTODIAL PARENT INCOME

	1050	1100	1150	1200	1250	1300	1350	1400	1450	1500	1550	1600	1650	1700	1750	1800
250]	51	51	51	51	51	51	51	51	51	51	51	51	51	51	51	51
300]	51	51	51	51	51	51	51	51	51	51	51	51	51	51	51	51
350]	54	54	54	54	54	54	51	51	51	51	51	51	51	51	51	51
400]	58	58	58	58	58	58	54	54	54	54	54	54	54	54	54	51
450]	62	62	62	62	62	62	58	58	58	58	58	58	58	58	58	53
500]	66	66	66	66	66	66	61	61	61	61	61	61	61	61	61	56
550]	70	70	70	70	70	70	65	65	65	65	65	65	65	65	65	59
600]	74	74	74	74	74	74	68	68	68	68	68	68	68	68	68	62
650]	78	78	78	78	78	78	72	72	72	72	72	72	72	72	72	65
700]	82	82	82	82	82	82	75	75	75	75	75	75	75	75	75	68
750]	97	97	97	97	97	97	90	90	90	90	90	90	90	90	90	82
800]	147	147	147	147	147	147	140	140	140	140	140	140	140	140	140	132
850]	197	197	197	197	197	197	190	190	190	190	190	190	190	190	190	182
900]	247	247	247	247	247	247	240	240	240	240	240	240	240	240	240	232
950]	297	297	297	297	297	297	290	290	290	290	290	290	290	290	290	282
1000]	347	347	347	347	347	347	340	340	340	340	340	340	340	340	340	332
1050]	397	395	393	390	388	385	383	381	379	377	375	373	371	369	368	366
1100]	413	410	408	405	402	400	398	396	393	391	389	387	386	384	382	380
1150]	428	425	422	420	417	415	412	410	408	406	404	402	400	398	396	394
1200]	442	439	437	434	432	429	427	425	422	420	418	416	414	412	410	408
1250]	457	454	451	448	446	443	441	439	437	435	433	430	428	426	424	422
1300]	471	468	465	463	460	458	455	453	451	449	447	444	442	440	438	436
1350]	485	482	479	477	474	472	470	467	465	463	461	458	456	454	452	450
1400]	499	496	494	491	488	486	484	481	479	477	474	472	470	468	466	464
1450]	513	510	508	505	502	500	498	495	493	490	488	486	484	482	480	478
1500]	527	524	521	519	516	514	511	509	506	504	502	499	497	495	493	491
1550]	541	538	535	533	530	528	525	522	520	518	515	513	511	509	507	505
1600]	554	552	549	546	544	541	538	536	533	531	529	526	524	522	520	518
1650]	568	565	563	560	557	554	552	549	547	544	542	540	538	536	534	532
1700]	582	579	576	573	570	568	565	563	560	558	555	553	551	549	547	545
1750]	595	592	589	586	584	581	578	576	573	571	569	566	564	562	560	558
1800]	608	605	602	600	597	594	592	589	587	584	582	580	578	575	573	571
1850]	621	618	615	613	610	607	605	602	600	597	595	593	591	589	587	585
1900]	634	631	628	626	623	620	618	615	613	610	608	606	604	602	600	598
1950]	647	644	641	639	636	633	631	628	626	624	621	619	617	615	613	610
2000]	660	657	654	652	649	646	644	641	639	637	634	632	630	628	625	623
2050]	673	670	667	664	662	659	657	654	652	649	647	645	643	640	638	636
2100]	686	683	680	677	675	672	669	667	665	662	660	658	655	653	651	649
2150]	698	696	693	690	687	685	682	680	677	675	673	670	668	666	664	661
2200]	711	708	705	703	700	698	695	693	690	688	685	683	681	678	676	674
2250]	724	721	718	715	713	710	708	705	703	700	698	695	693	691	689	687
2300]	736	733	731	728	725	723	720	718	715	713	710	708	706	703	701	699
2350]	749	746	743	741	738	736	733	730	728	725	723	720	718	716	714	712
2400]	761	759	756	753	751	748	745	743	740	738	735	733	731	728	726	724
2450]	774	771	768	766	763	760	758	755	752	750	748	745	743	741	739	737
2500]	786	784	781	778	775	772	770	767	765	762	760	758	755	753	751	749

NONCUSTODIAL PARENT INCOME

Two Children Monthly Support Schedule

CUSTODIAL PARENT INCOME

	1050	1100	1150	1200	1250	1300	1350	1400	1450	1500	1550	1600	1650	1700	1750	1800
2550]	799	796	793	790	787	785	782	780	777	775	772	770	768	766	763	761
2600]	811	808	805	802	800	797	794	792	789	787	785	782	780	778	776	774
2650]	823	820	817	814	812	809	807	804	802	799	797	795	792	790	788	786
2700]	835	832	829	827	824	821	819	816	814	811	809	807	805	802	800	798
2750]	847	844	841	839	836	833	831	828	826	824	821	819	817	815	812	810
2800]	859	856	853	851	848	845	843	840	838	836	833	831	829	827	825	823
2850]	871	868	865	863	860	857	855	853	850	848	845	843	841	839	837	835
2900]	883	880	877	875	872	870	867	865	862	860	858	855	853	851	849	847
2950]	895	892	889	887	884	882	879	877	874	872	870	867	865	863	861	859
3000]	907	904	901	899	896	893	891	889	886	884	882	879	877	875	873	871
3050]	919	916	913	911	908	905	903	901	898	896	894	891	889	887	885	883
3100]	930	928	925	922	920	917	915	913	910	908	906	904	901	899	897	895
3150]	942	940	937	934	932	929	927	924	922	920	918	915	913	911	909	907
3200]	954	951	949	946	944	941	939	936	934	932	930	927	925	923	921	919
3250]	966	963	960	958	955	953	951	948	946	944	942	939	937	935	933	931
3300]	978	975	972	970	967	965	962	960	958	956	953	951	949	947	945	943
3350]	989	987	984	981	979	977	974	972	970	967	965	963	961	959	957	955
3400]	1001	998	996	993	991	988	986	984	982	979	977	975	973	971	969	967
3450]	1013	1010	1007	1005	1003	1000	998	996	993	991	989	987	985	983	981	978
3500]	1024	1022	1019	1017	1014	1012	1010	1007	1005	1003	1001	999	997	994	992	990
3550]	1036	1033	1031	1028	1026	1024	1021	1019	1017	1015	1013	1011	1008	1006	1003	1001
3600]	1048	1045	1043	1040	1038	1035	1033	1031	1029	1027	1024	1022	1020	1017	1015	1012
3650]	1059	1057	1054	1052	1049	1047	1045	1043	1040	1038	1036	1033	1031	1028	1026	1024
3700]	1071	1068	1066	1063	1061	1059	1057	1054	1052	1050	1047	1045	1042	1040	1037	1035
3750]	1082	1080	1077	1075	1073	1070	1068	1066	1064	1061	1058	1056	1053	1051	1048	1046
3800]	1094	1091	1089	1087	1084	1082	1080	1077	1075	1072	1070	1067	1065	1062	1060	1057
3850]	1105	1103	1101	1098	1096	1094	1091	1089	1086	1083	1081	1078	1076	1073	1071	1069
3900]	1117	1115	1112	1110	1108	1105	1102	1100	1097	1094	1092	1089	1087	1084	1082	1080
3950]	1129	1126	1124	1121	1119	1116	1113	1111	1108	1106	1103	1100	1098	1096	1093	1091
4000]	1140	1138	1135	1133	1130	1127	1124	1122	1119	1117	1114	1112	1109	1107	1104	1102
4050]	1152	1149	1147	1144	1141	1138	1135	1133	1130	1128	1125	1123	1120	1118	1116	1113
4100]	1163	1160	1158	1155	1152	1149	1147	1144	1141	1139	1136	1134	1131	1129	1127	1124
4150]	1174	1171	1168	1166	1163	1160	1158	1155	1152	1150	1147	1145	1143	1140	1138	1136
4200]	1185	1182	1179	1177	1174	1171	1168	1166	1163	1161	1158	1156	1154	1151	1149	1147
4250]	1196	1193	1190	1187	1185	1182	1179	1177	1174	1172	1169	1167	1165	1162	1160	1158
4300]	1207	1204	1201	1198	1196	1193	1190	1188	1185	1183	1180	1178	1176	1173	1171	1169
4350]	1218	1215	1212	1209	1207	1204	1201	1199	1196	1194	1191	1189	1187	1184	1182	1180
4400]	1228	1226	1223	1220	1218	1215	1212	1210	1207	1205	1202	1200	1198	1195	1193	1191
4450]	1239	1236	1234	1231	1228	1226	1223	1221	1218	1216	1213	1211	1209	1206	1204	1202
4500]	1250	1247	1245	1242	1239	1237	1234	1232	1229	1227	1224	1222	1220	1217	1215	1213
4550]	1261	1258	1255	1253	1250	1248	1245	1243	1240	1238	1235	1233	1231	1228	1226	1224
4600]	1272	1269	1266	1264	1261	1258	1256	1253	1251	1249	1246	1244	1242	1239	1237	1234
4650]	1282	1280	1277	1274	1272	1269	1267	1264	1262	1260	1257	1255	1253	1250	1248	1244
4700]	1293	1290	1288	1285	1283	1280	1278	1275	1273	1270	1268	1266	1264	1261	1257	1254
4750]	1304	1301	1299	1296	1293	1291	1288	1286	1284	1281	1279	1277	1274	1270	1267	1264
4800]	1315	1312	1309	1307	1304	1302	1299	1297	1294	1292	1290	1287	1284	1280	1277	1274
4850]	1325	1323	1320	1318	1315	1313	1310	1308	1305	1303	1300	1297	1293	1290	1287	1283
4900]	1336	1333	1331	1328	1326	1323	1321	1319	1316	1313	1310	1306	1303	1300	1296	1293
4950]	1347	1344	1342	1339	1337	1334	1332	1329	1326	1323	1319	1316	1313	1309	1306	1303
5000]	1358	1355	1352	1350	1347	1345	1343	1340	1336	1332	1329	1326	1322	1319	1316	1312

Row label (reading vertically at left): NONCUSTODIAL PARENT INCOME

Two Children Monthly Support Schedule

CUSTODIAL PARENT INCOME

	1850	1900	1950	2000	2050	2100	2150	2200	2250	2300	2350	2400	2450	2500	2550	2600
250]	51	51	51	51	51	51	51	51	51	51	51	51	51	51	51	51
300]	51	51	51	51	51	51	51	51	51	51	51	51	51	51	51	51
350]	51	51	51	51	51	51	51	51	51	51	51	51	51	51	51	51
400]	51	51	51	51	51	51	51	51	51	51	51	51	51	51	51	51
450]	53	53	53	53	53	53	53	53	51	51	51	51	51	51	51	51
500]	56	56	56	56	56	56	56	56	51	51	51	51	51	51	51	51
550]	59	59	59	59	59	59	59	59	54	54	54	54	54	54	54	54
600]	62	62	62	62	62	62	62	62	56	56	56	56	56	56	56	56
650]	65	65	65	65	65	65	65	65	59	59	59	59	59	59	59	59
700]	68	68	68	68	68	68	68	68	61	61	61	61	61	61	61	61
750]	82	82	82	82	82	82	82	82	75	75	75	75	75	75	75	75
800]	132	132	132	132	132	132	132	132	125	125	125	125	125	125	125	125
850]	182	182	182	182	182	182	182	182	175	175	175	175	175	175	175	175
900]	232	232	232	232	232	232	232	232	225	225	225	225	225	225	225	225
950]	282	282	282	282	282	282	282	282	275	275	275	275	275	275	275	275
1000]	332	332	332	332	332	332	332	332	325	325	325	325	325	325	325	325
1050]	364	362	361	359	357	356	354	353	352	350	349	348	347	345	344	343
1100]	378	377	375	373	372	370	369	367	366	364	363	362	361	359	358	357
1150]	392	391	389	387	386	384	383	381	380	378	377	376	375	373	372	371
1200]	407	405	403	401	400	398	397	395	394	392	391	390	388	387	386	384
1250]	421	419	417	415	414	412	411	409	408	406	405	403	402	401	399	398
1300]	434	433	431	429	428	426	424	423	421	420	419	417	416	414	413	412
1350]	448	446	445	443	441	440	438	437	435	434	432	431	429	428	426	425
1400]	462	460	458	457	455	453	452	450	449	447	446	444	443	441	440	438
1450]	476	474	472	470	469	467	465	464	462	461	459	457	456	455	453	452
1500]	489	487	486	484	482	481	479	477	476	474	472	471	469	468	466	465
1550]	503	501	499	497	496	494	492	491	489	487	486	484	483	481	480	478
1600]	516	514	513	511	509	507	506	504	502	500	499	497	496	494	493	491
1650]	530	528	526	524	522	520	519	517	515	514	512	510	509	507	506	505
1700]	543	541	539	537	535	534	532	530	528	527	525	524	522	521	519	518
1750]	556	554	552	550	549	547	545	543	541	540	538	537	535	534	532	531
1800]	569	567	565	563	562	560	558	556	554	553	551	550	548	547	545	544
1850]	582	580	578	576	575	573	571	569	567	566	564	563	561	559	558	557
1900]	595	593	591	589	588	586	584	582	580	579	577	575	574	572	571	569
1950]	608	606	604	602	600	599	597	595	593	592	590	588	587	585	584	582
2000]	621	619	617	615	613	611	610	608	606	604	603	601	600	598	596	595
2050]	634	632	630	628	626	624	622	621	619	617	615	614	612	611	609	608
2100]	647	645	643	641	639	637	635	633	632	630	628	627	625	623	622	620
2150]	659	657	655	653	651	650	648	646	644	643	641	639	638	636	635	633
2200]	672	670	668	666	664	662	660	659	657	655	654	652	650	649	647	646
2250]	685	682	680	679	677	675	673	671	669	668	666	665	663	661	660	658
2300]	697	695	693	691	689	687	686	684	682	680	679	677	675	674	672	671
2350]	710	708	706	704	702	700	698	696	695	693	691	690	688	686	685	683
2400]	722	720	718	716	714	712	711	709	707	705	704	702	701	699	697	696
2450]	734	732	730	729	727	725	723	721	720	718	716	715	713	711	710	708
2500]	747	745	743	741	739	737	735	734	732	730	729	727	725	724	722	721

NONCUSTODIAL PARENT INCOME

Two Children Monthly Support Schedule

CUSTODIAL PARENT INCOME

	1850	1900	1950	2000	2050	2100	2150	2200	2250	2300	2350	2400	2450	2500	2550	2600
2550]	759	757	755	753	751	750	748	746	744	743	741	739	738	736	735	733
2600]	772	770	768	766	764	762	760	758	757	755	753	752	750	749	747	745
2650]	784	782	780	778	776	774	773	771	769	767	766	764	763	761	759	757
2700]	796	794	792	790	788	787	785	783	781	780	778	776	775	773	771	769
2750]	808	806	804	803	801	799	797	795	794	792	790	789	787	785	783	781
2800]	821	819	817	815	813	811	809	808	806	804	803	801	799	797	795	793
2850]	833	831	829	827	825	823	822	820	818	816	815	813	811	809	807	805
2900]	845	843	841	839	837	835	834	832	830	828	826	824	822	820	819	817
2950]	857	855	853	851	849	848	846	844	842	840	838	836	834	832	830	828
3000]	869	867	865	863	862	860	858	856	854	852	850	848	846	844	842	840
3050]	881	879	877	875	874	872	870	868	866	864	862	860	858	856	854	852
3100]	893	891	889	888	886	884	882	879	877	875	873	871	869	867	866	864
3150]	905	903	901	900	898	895	893	891	889	887	885	883	881	879	877	875
3200]	917	915	913	911	909	907	905	903	901	899	896	895	893	891	889	887
3250]	929	927	925	923	921	919	916	914	912	910	908	906	904	902	900	899
3300]	941	939	937	934	932	930	928	926	924	922	920	918	916	914	912	910
3350]	953	951	948	946	944	942	939	937	935	933	931	929	927	925	924	922
3400]	964	962	960	957	955	953	951	949	947	945	943	941	939	937	935	933
3450]	976	973	971	969	967	964	962	960	958	956	954	952	950	948	947	945
3500]	987	985	983	980	978	976	974	972	970	968	966	964	962	960	958	956
3550]	999	996	994	992	990	987	985	983	981	979	977	975	973	971	970	968
3600]	1010	1008	1005	1003	1001	999	997	995	993	991	989	987	985	983	981	979
3650]	1021	1019	1017	1014	1012	1010	1008	1006	1004	1002	1000	998	996	994	992	991
3700]	1032	1030	1028	1026	1024	1021	1019	1017	1015	1013	1011	1009	1008	1006	1004	1002
3750]	1044	1042	1039	1037	1035	1033	1031	1029	1027	1025	1023	1021	1019	1017	1015	1013
3800]	1055	1053	1051	1048	1046	1044	1042	1040	1038	1036	1034	1032	1030	1028	1027	1024
3850]	1066	1064	1062	1060	1057	1055	1053	1051	1049	1047	1045	1043	1042	1040	1037	1035
3900]	1078	1075	1073	1071	1069	1067	1065	1063	1061	1059	1057	1055	1053	1051	1048	1045
3950]	1089	1086	1084	1082	1080	1078	1076	1074	1072	1070	1068	1066	1064	1061	1058	1055
4000]	1100	1098	1095	1093	1091	1089	1087	1085	1083	1081	1079	1077	1074	1071	1068	1066
4050]	1111	1109	1107	1105	1102	1100	1098	1096	1094	1092	1090	1087	1084	1081	1079	1076
4100]	1122	1120	1118	1116	1114	1112	1110	1108	1106	1103	1100	1097	1094	1092	1089	1086
4150]	1133	1131	1129	1127	1125	1123	1121	1119	1116	1113	1110	1107	1105	1102	1099	1096
4200]	1144	1142	1140	1138	1136	1134	1132	1129	1126	1123	1121	1118	1115	1112	1109	1107
4250]	1156	1153	1151	1149	1147	1145	1143	1140	1137	1134	1131	1128	1125	1122	1119	1117
4300]	1167	1165	1162	1160	1158	1156	1153	1150	1147	1144	1141	1138	1135	1132	1130	1127
4350]	1178	1176	1173	1171	1169	1166	1163	1160	1157	1154	1151	1148	1145	1142	1140	1137
4400]	1189	1187	1185	1182	1179	1176	1173	1170	1167	1164	1161	1158	1155	1152	1150	1147
4450]	1200	1198	1195	1192	1189	1186	1183	1180	1177	1174	1171	1168	1165	1162	1160	1157
4500]	1211	1208	1205	1202	1199	1196	1193	1190	1187	1184	1181	1178	1175	1173	1170	1167
4550]	1221	1218	1215	1212	1209	1206	1203	1200	1197	1194	1191	1188	1185	1183	1180	1177
4600]	1231	1228	1225	1222	1218	1215	1212	1209	1207	1204	1201	1198	1195	1193	1190	1187
4650]	1241	1238	1235	1231	1228	1225	1222	1219	1216	1214	1211	1208	1205	1202	1200	1197
4700]	1251	1248	1244	1241	1238	1235	1232	1229	1226	1223	1221	1218	1215	1212	1210	1207
4750]	1261	1257	1254	1251	1248	1245	1242	1239	1236	1233	1231	1228	1225	1222	1220	1217
4800]	1270	1267	1264	1261	1258	1255	1252	1249	1246	1243	1240	1238	1235	1232	1230	1227
4850]	1280	1277	1274	1271	1268	1265	1262	1259	1256	1253	1250	1248	1245	1242	1239	1237
4900]	1290	1287	1284	1280	1277	1274	1271	1269	1266	1263	1260	1257	1255	1252	1249	1247
4950]	1299	1296	1293	1290	1287	1284	1281	1278	1276	1273	1270	1267	1265	1262	1259	1257
5000]	1309	1306	1303	1300	1297	1294	1291	1288	1285	1282	1280	1277	1274	1272	1269	1266

The left margin reads vertically: NONCUSTODIAL PARENT INCOME

Two Children Monthly Support Schedule

CUSTODIAL PARENT INCOME

	2650	2700	2750	2800	2850	2900	2950	3000	3050	3100	3150	3200	3250	3300	3350	3400
250]	51	51	51	51	51	51	51	51	51	51	51	51	51	51	51	51
300]	51	51	51	51	51	51	51	51	51	51	51	51	51	51	51	51
350]	51	51	51	51	51	51	51	51	51	51	51	51	51	51	51	51
400]	51	51	51	51	51	51	51	51	51	51	51	51	51	51	51	51
450]	51	51	51	51	51	51	51	51	51	51	51	51	51	51	51	51
500]	51	51	51	51	51	51	51	51	51	51	51	51	51	51	51	51
550]	54	51	51	51	51	51	51	51	51	51	51	51	51	51	51	51
600]	56	51	51	51	51	51	51	51	51	51	51	51	51	51	51	51
650]	59	52	52	52	52	52	52	52	52	52	51	51	51	51	51	51
700]	61	54	54	54	54	54	54	54	54	54	51	51	51	51	51	51
750]	75	68	68	68	68	68	68	68	68	68	63	63	63	63	63	63
800]	125	118	118	118	118	118	118	118	118	118	113	113	113	113	113	113
850]	175	168	168	168	168	168	168	168	168	168	163	163	163	163	163	163
900]	225	218	218	218	218	218	218	218	218	218	213	213	213	213	213	213
950]	275	268	268	268	268	268	268	268	268	268	263	263	263	263	263	263
1000]	325	318	318	318	318	318	318	318	318	318	313	313	313	313	313	313
1050]	342	341	340	338	337	336	335	334	333	332	331	331	330	329	328	327
1100]	356	355	353	352	351	350	349	348	347	346	345	344	343	342	341	341
1150]	369	368	367	366	365	364	363	362	361	360	359	358	357	356	355	354
1200]	383	382	381	380	378	377	376	375	374	373	372	371	370	369	368	367
1250]	397	395	394	393	392	391	390	389	388	386	385	384	384	383	382	381
1300]	410	409	408	407	405	404	403	402	401	400	399	398	397	396	395	394
1350]	424	422	421	420	419	418	416	415	414	413	412	411	410	409	408	407
1400]	437	436	435	433	432	431	430	429	427	426	425	424	423	422	421	420
1450]	450	449	448	447	445	444	443	442	441	440	439	438	436	435	435	434
1500]	464	462	461	460	459	457	456	455	454	453	452	451	450	449	448	447
1550]	477	476	474	473	472	471	469	468	467	466	465	464	463	462	461	460
1600]	490	489	487	486	485	484	482	481	480	479	478	477	476	475	474	473
1650]	503	502	500	499	498	497	495	494	493	492	491	490	489	488	487	486
1700]	516	515	514	512	511	510	508	507	506	505	504	503	502	501	500	499
1750]	529	528	527	525	524	523	521	520	519	518	517	516	515	513	512	511
1800]	542	541	539	538	537	536	534	533	532	531	530	528	527	526	525	524
1850]	555	554	552	551	550	548	547	546	545	544	542	541	540	539	538	537
1900]	568	567	565	564	563	561	560	559	558	556	555	554	553	552	550	549
1950]	581	579	578	577	575	574	573	572	570	569	568	567	566	564	563	562
2000]	594	592	591	589	588	587	586	584	583	582	581	579	578	577	575	574
2050]	606	605	604	602	601	600	598	597	596	595	593	592	590	589	588	586
2100]	619	618	616	615	614	612	611	610	608	607	606	604	603	601	600	599
2150]	632	630	629	628	626	625	624	622	621	619	618	616	615	614	612	611
2200]	644	643	641	640	639	637	636	635	633	632	630	629	627	626	624	623
2250]	657	655	654	653	651	650	649	647	645	644	642	641	640	638	637	635
2300]	669	668	667	665	664	662	661	659	658	656	655	653	652	650	649	648
2350]	682	681	679	678	676	675	673	671	670	668	667	665	664	662	661	660
2400]	694	693	692	690	688	687	685	684	682	680	679	677	676	675	673	672
2450]	707	706	704	702	700	699	697	696	694	692	691	689	688	687	685	684
2500]	719	718	716	714	713	711	709	708	706	705	703	702	700	699	697	696

N O N C U S T O D I A L P A R E N T I N C O M E

Two Children Monthly Support Schedule

CUSTODIAL PARENT INCOME

NONCUSTODIAL PARENT INCOME	2650	2700	2750	2800	2850	2900	2950	3000	3050	3100	3150	3200	3250	3300	3350	3400
2550]	732	730	728	726	725	723	721	720	718	717	715	714	712	711	709	708
2600]	744	742	740	738	737	735	733	732	730	729	727	726	724	723	721	720
2650]	756	754	752	750	749	747	745	744	742	741	739	737	736	735	733	732
2700]	767	766	764	762	760	759	757	756	754	752	751	749	748	746	745	744
2750]	779	778	776	774	772	771	769	767	766	764	763	761	760	758	757	756
2800]	791	789	788	786	784	783	781	779	778	776	775	773	772	770	769	767
2850]	803	801	800	798	796	794	793	791	790	788	787	785	784	782	781	779
2900]	815	813	811	810	808	806	805	803	801	800	798	797	795	794	792	791
2950]	827	825	823	821	820	818	816	815	813	812	810	809	807	806	804	803
3000]	838	837	835	833	831	830	828	827	825	823	822	820	819	817	816	814
3050]	850	848	847	845	843	842	840	838	837	835	834	832	831	829	827	825
3100]	862	860	858	857	855	853	852	850	848	847	845	844	842	840	838	836
3150]	874	872	870	868	867	865	863	862	860	858	857	855	854	851	849	847
3200]	885	883	882	880	878	877	875	873	872	870	869	867	864	862	860	858
3250]	897	895	893	892	890	888	887	885	883	882	880	878	875	873	871	869
3300]	908	907	905	903	901	900	898	897	895	893	891	888	886	884	882	879
3350]	920	918	916	915	913	911	910	908	906	904	901	899	897	894	892	890
3400]	931	930	928	926	925	923	921	919	917	914	912	910	907	905	903	901
3450]	943	941	939	938	936	934	932	930	927	925	923	920	918	916	914	911
3500]	954	953	951	949	948	946	943	941	938	936	933	931	929	926	924	922
3550]	966	964	962	961	959	956	954	951	949	946	944	942	939	937	935	933
3600]	977	976	974	972	969	967	964	962	959	957	955	952	950	948	945	943
3650]	989	987	985	982	980	977	975	972	970	967	965	963	960	958	956	954
3700]	1000	998	995	993	990	988	985	983	980	978	976	973	971	969	966	964
3750]	1011	1009	1006	1003	1001	998	996	993	991	988	986	984	981	979	977	975
3800]	1022	1019	1016	1014	1011	1009	1006	1004	1001	999	996	994	992	990	987	985
3850]	1032	1029	1027	1024	1022	1019	1017	1014	1012	1009	1007	1005	1002	1000	998	996
3900]	1042	1040	1037	1034	1032	1029	1027	1024	1022	1020	1017	1015	1013	1010	1008	1006
3950]	1053	1050	1047	1045	1042	1040	1037	1035	1032	1030	1028	1025	1023	1021	1019	1016
4000]	1063	1060	1058	1055	1053	1050	1048	1045	1043	1040	1038	1036	1033	1031	1029	1027
4050]	1073	1071	1068	1065	1063	1060	1058	1055	1053	1051	1048	1046	1044	1042	1039	1037
4100]	1083	1081	1078	1076	1073	1071	1068	1066	1063	1061	1059	1056	1054	1052	1050	1047
4150]	1094	1091	1088	1086	1083	1081	1078	1076	1074	1071	1069	1067	1064	1062	1060	1058
4200]	1104	1101	1099	1096	1094	1091	1089	1086	1084	1081	1079	1077	1075	1072	1070	1068
4250]	1114	1111	1109	1106	1104	1101	1099	1096	1094	1092	1089	1087	1085	1083	1080	1078
4300]	1124	1122	1119	1116	1114	1111	1109	1107	1104	1102	1100	1097	1095	1093	1091	1088
4350]	1134	1132	1129	1127	1124	1122	1119	1117	1114	1112	1110	1107	1105	1103	1101	1099
4400]	1144	1142	1139	1137	1134	1132	1129	1127	1125	1122	1120	1118	1115	1113	1111	1109
4450]	1154	1152	1149	1147	1144	1142	1139	1137	1135	1132	1130	1128	1126	1123	1121	1119
4500]	1165	1162	1159	1157	1154	1152	1150	1147	1145	1142	1140	1138	1136	1133	1131	1129
4550]	1175	1172	1169	1167	1164	1162	1160	1157	1155	1153	1150	1148	1146	1144	1141	1139
4600]	1185	1182	1179	1177	1174	1172	1170	1167	1165	1163	1160	1158	1156	1154	1151	1149
4650]	1195	1192	1189	1187	1184	1182	1180	1177	1175	1173	1170	1168	1166	1164	1162	1159
4700]	1205	1202	1199	1197	1194	1192	1190	1187	1185	1183	1180	1178	1176	1174	1171	1168
4750]	1214	1212	1209	1207	1204	1202	1200	1197	1195	1193	1190	1188	1186	1183	1181	1178
4800]	1224	1222	1219	1217	1214	1212	1210	1207	1205	1203	1200	1198	1196	1193	1190	1187
4850]	1234	1232	1229	1227	1224	1222	1220	1217	1215	1213	1210	1208	1205	1202	1199	1197
4900]	1244	1242	1239	1237	1234	1232	1230	1227	1225	1223	1220	1217	1214	1212	1209	1206
4950]	1254	1252	1249	1247	1244	1242	1239	1237	1235	1232	1229	1226	1224	1221	1218	1215
5000]	1264	1261	1259	1256	1254	1252	1249	1247	1244	1241	1239	1236	1233	1230	1227	1225

Two Children Monthly Support Schedule

CUSTODIAL PARENT INCOME

		3450	3500	3550	3600	3650	3700	3750	3800	3850	3900	3950	4000	4050	4100	4150	4200
	250]	51	51	51	51	51	51	51	51	51	51	51	51	51	51	51	51
	300]	51	51	51	51	51	51	51	51	51	51	51	51	51	51	51	51
	350]	51	51	51	51	51	51	51	51	51	51	51	51	51	51	51	51
	400]	51	51	51	51	51	51	51	51	51	51	51	51	51	51	51	51
	450]	51	51	51	51	51	51	51	51	51	51	51	51	51	51	51	51
	500]	51	51	51	51	51	51	51	51	51	51	51	51	51	51	51	51
	550]	51	51	51	51	51	51	51	51	51	51	51	51	51	51	51	51
	600]	51	51	51	51	51	51	51	51	51	51	51	51	51	51	51	51
	650]	51	51	51	51	51	51	51	51	51	51	51	51	51	51	51	51
N	700]	51	51	51	51	51	51	51	51	51	51	51	51	51	51	51	51
O	750]	63	63	63	63	63	63	63	63	63	63	63	63	63	63	63	63
N	800]	113	113	113	113	113	113	113	113	113	113	113	113	113	113	113	113
C	850]	163	163	163	163	163	163	163	163	163	163	163	163	163	163	163	163
U	900]	213	213	213	213	213	213	213	213	213	213	213	213	213	213	213	213
S	950]	263	263	263	263	263	263	263	263	263	263	263	263	263	263	263	263
T																	
O	1000]	313	312	311	311	310	309	308	308	307	306	306	305	305	304	303	303
D	1050]	326	326	325	324	323	323	322	321	320	320	319	319	318	317	317	316
I	1100]	340	339	338	337	337	336	335	334	334	333	332	332	331	330	330	329
A	1150]	353	352	352	351	350	349	349	348	347	346	346	345	344	343	343	342
L	1200]	367	366	365	364	363	363	362	361	360	360	359	358	357	356	356	355
	1250]	380	379	378	377	377	376	375	374	373	373	372	371	370	369	369	368
P	1300]	393	392	391	391	390	389	388	387	387	386	385	384	383	382	381	381
A	1350]	406	405	405	404	403	402	401	400	400	399	398	397	396	395	394	393
R	1400]	420	419	418	417	416	415	414	413	412	411	411	410	409	408	407	406
E	1450]	433	432	431	430	429	428	427	426	425	424	423	422	421	420	420	419
N																	
T	1500]	446	445	444	443	442	441	440	439	438	437	436	435	434	433	432	431
	1550]	459	458	457	456	455	454	453	452	451	450	449	448	447	446	445	444
I	1600]	472	471	470	469	468	467	465	464	463	462	461	460	459	458	457	457
N	1650]	485	484	483	481	480	479	478	477	476	475	474	473	472	471	470	469
C	1700]	498	496	495	494	493	492	491	490	488	487	486	485	484	483	482	482
O	1750]	510	509	508	507	505	504	503	502	501	500	499	498	497	496	495	494
M	1800]	523	522	520	519	518	517	516	515	513	512	511	510	509	508	507	506
E	1850]	535	534	533	532	530	529	528	527	526	525	524	523	522	521	520	519
	1900]	548	547	545	544	543	542	541	539	538	537	536	535	534	533	532	531
	1950]	560	559	558	556	555	554	553	552	551	550	548	547	546	545	544	543
	2000]	573	571	570	569	568	566	565	564	563	562	561	560	559	558	557	556
	2050]	585	584	582	581	580	579	578	576	575	574	573	572	571	570	569	568
	2100]	597	596	595	593	592	591	590	589	588	586	585	584	583	582	581	580
	2150]	610	608	607	606	604	603	602	601	600	599	597	596	595	594	593	592
	2200]	622	620	619	618	617	615	614	613	612	611	610	609	607	606	605	604
	2250]	634	633	631	630	629	628	626	625	624	623	622	621	620	618	617	616
	2300]	646	645	644	642	641	640	639	637	636	635	634	633	632	630	629	627
	2350]	658	657	656	654	653	652	651	649	648	647	646	645	643	642	640	638
	2400]	670	669	668	666	665	664	663	661	660	659	658	657	655	653	651	650
	2450]	682	681	680	678	677	676	675	674	672	671	670	668	666	665	663	661
	2500]	694	693	692	691	689	688	687	686	684	683	681	679	678	676	674	672

Two Children Monthly Support Schedule

CUSTODIAL PARENT INCOME

	3450	3500	3550	3600	3650	3700	3750	3800	3850	3900	3950	4000	4050	4100	4150	4200
2550]	706	705	704	702	701	700	699	697	696	694	692	691	689	687	685	684
2600]	718	717	716	714	713	712	711	709	707	705	704	702	700	698	697	695
2650]	730	729	728	726	725	724	722	720	718	717	715	713	711	710	708	706
2700]	742	741	740	738	737	735	733	732	730	728	726	724	722	721	719	717
2750]	754	753	751	750	749	747	745	743	741	739	737	735	734	732	730	728
2800]	766	765	763	762	760	758	756	754	752	750	748	746	745	743	741	739
2850]	778	776	775	773	771	769	767	765	763	761	759	757	756	754	752	750
2900]	790	788	786	784	782	780	778	776	774	772	770	768	767	765	763	761
2950]	801	799	797	795	793	791	789	787	785	783	781	779	778	776	774	772
3000]	812	810	808	806	804	802	800	798	796	794	792	790	789	787	785	783
3050]	823	821	819	817	815	813	811	809	807	805	803	801	799	798	796	794
3100]	834	832	830	828	826	824	822	820	818	816	814	812	810	809	807	805
3150]	845	843	841	838	836	834	832	831	829	827	825	823	821	819	818	816
3200]	856	853	851	849	847	845	843	841	839	838	836	834	832	830	828	827
3250]	866	864	862	860	858	856	854	852	850	848	846	845	843	841	839	837
3300]	877	875	873	871	869	867	865	863	861	859	857	855	854	852	850	848
3350]	888	886	884	882	880	878	876	874	872	870	868	866	864	862	861	859
3400]	899	896	894	892	890	888	886	884	882	880	879	877	875	873	871	870
3450]	909	907	905	903	901	899	897	895	893	891	889	887	886	884	882	880
3500]	920	918	916	914	912	910	908	906	904	902	900	898	896	894	893	891
3550]	930	928	926	924	922	920	918	916	914	912	910	909	907	905	903	901
3600]	941	939	937	935	933	931	929	927	925	923	921	919	917	916	914	912
3650]	952	949	947	945	943	941	939	937	935	933	932	930	928	926	924	923
3700]	962	960	958	956	954	952	950	948	946	944	942	940	938	937	935	933
3750]	973	970	968	966	964	962	960	958	956	954	953	951	949	947	945	944
3800]	983	981	979	977	975	973	971	969	967	965	963	961	959	958	956	954
3850]	994	991	989	987	985	983	981	979	977	975	973	972	970	968	966	964
3900]	1004	1002	1000	998	996	994	992	990	988	986	984	982	980	978	976	974
3950]	1014	1012	1010	1008	1006	1004	1002	1000	998	996	994	992	991	988	986	984
4000]	1025	1023	1020	1018	1016	1014	1012	1010	1008	1007	1005	1003	1001	998	996	994
4050]	1035	1033	1031	1029	1027	1025	1023	1021	1019	1017	1015	1013	1010	1008	1006	1004
4100]	1045	1043	1041	1039	1037	1035	1033	1031	1029	1027	1025	1023	1020	1018	1016	1013
4150]	1056	1053	1051	1049	1047	1045	1043	1041	1039	1037	1035	1032	1030	1028	1025	1023
4200]	1066	1064	1062	1060	1058	1056	1054	1052	1049	1047	1045	1042	1040	1038	1035	1033
4250]	1076	1074	1072	1070	1068	1066	1064	1062	1059	1057	1054	1052	1050	1047	1045	1043
4300]	1086	1084	1082	1080	1078	1076	1074	1071	1069	1066	1064	1062	1059	1057	1055	1052
4350]	1097	1094	1092	1090	1088	1086	1083	1081	1078	1076	1074	1071	1069	1067	1064	1062
4400]	1107	1105	1103	1100	1098	1096	1093	1091	1088	1086	1083	1081	1079	1076	1074	1072
4450]	1117	1115	1113	1110	1108	1105	1103	1100	1098	1095	1093	1091	1088	1086	1084	1081
4500]	1127	1125	1122	1120	1117	1115	1112	1110	1107	1105	1103	1100	1098	1096	1093	1091
4550]	1137	1135	1132	1129	1127	1124	1122	1119	1117	1114	1112	1110	1107	1105	1103	1101
4600]	1147	1144	1142	1139	1136	1134	1131	1129	1126	1124	1122	1119	1117	1115	1112	1110
4650]	1156	1154	1151	1148	1146	1143	1141	1138	1136	1134	1131	1129	1126	1124	1122	1120
4700]	1166	1163	1161	1158	1155	1153	1150	1148	1145	1143	1141	1138	1136	1134	1131	1129
4750]	1175	1173	1170	1167	1165	1162	1160	1157	1155	1153	1150	1148	1145	1143	1141	1139
4800]	1185	1182	1179	1177	1174	1172	1169	1167	1164	1162	1160	1157	1155	1153	1150	1148
4850]	1194	1191	1189	1186	1184	1181	1179	1176	1174	1171	1169	1167	1164	1162	1160	1158
4900]	1203	1201	1198	1196	1193	1191	1188	1186	1183	1181	1178	1176	1174	1171	1169	1167
4950]	1213	1210	1208	1205	1202	1200	1197	1195	1193	1190	1188	1186	1183	1181	1179	1176
5000]	1222	1220	1217	1214	1212	1209	1207	1204	1202	1200	1197	1195	1193	1190	1188	1186

(Row labels on left margin, read vertically: NONCUSTODIAL PARENT INCOME)

Effective July 1, 2003

Two Children Monthly Support Schedule

CUSTODIAL PARENT INCOME

	4250	4300	4350	4400	4450	4500	4550	4600	4650	4700	4750	4800	4850	4900	4950	5000
250]	51	51	51	51	51	51	51	51	51	51	51	51	51	51	51	51
300]	51	51	51	51	51	51	51	51	51	51	51	51	51	51	51	51
350]	51	51	51	51	51	51	51	51	51	51	51	51	51	51	51	51
400]	51	51	51	51	51	51	51	51	51	51	51	51	51	51	51	51
450]	51	51	51	51	51	51	51	51	51	51	51	51	51	51	51	51
500]	51	51	51	51	51	51	51	51	51	51	51	51	51	51	51	51
550]	51	51	51	51	51	51	51	51	51	51	51	51	51	51	51	51
600]	51	51	51	51	51	51	51	51	51	51	51	51	51	51	51	51
650]	51	51	51	51	51	51	51	51	51	51	51	51	51	51	51	51
700]	51	51	51	51	51	51	51	51	51	51	51	63	63	63	63	63
750]	63	63	63	63	63	63	63	63	63	63	63	63	63	63	63	63
800]	113	113	113	113	113	113	113	113	113	113	113	113	113	113	113	113
850]	163	163	163	163	163	163	163	163	163	163	163	163	163	163	163	163
900]	213	213	213	213	213	213	213	213	213	213	213	213	213	213	213	213
950]	263	263	263	263	263	263	263	263	263	263	263	263	263	263	263	263
1000]	302	301	301	300	299	299	298	297	297	296	296	295	295	294	293	293
1050]	315	314	314	313	312	312	311	310	310	309	309	308	307	307	306	306
1100]	328	327	327	326	325	325	324	323	323	322	321	321	320	320	319	318
1150]	341	340	340	339	338	337	337	336	335	335	334	334	333	332	332	331
1200]	354	353	352	352	351	350	350	349	348	348	347	346	346	345	344	344
1250]	367	366	365	365	364	363	362	362	361	360	360	359	358	358	357	356
1300]	380	379	378	377	377	376	375	374	374	373	372	372	371	370	370	369
1350]	392	392	391	390	389	389	388	387	386	386	385	384	384	383	382	382
1400]	405	404	404	403	402	401	400	400	399	398	397	397	396	395	395	394
1450]	418	417	416	415	415	414	413	412	411	411	410	409	409	408	407	406
1500]	430	430	429	428	427	426	426	425	424	423	422	422	421	420	419	418
1550]	443	442	441	440	440	439	438	437	436	436	435	434	433	432	431	430
1600]	456	455	454	453	452	451	450	450	449	448	447	446	445	444	443	442
1650]	468	467	466	465	465	464	463	462	461	461	460	458	457	456	455	454
1700]	481	480	479	478	477	476	475	474	474	473	471	470	469	468	467	466
1750]	493	492	491	490	489	489	488	487	486	485	483	482	481	480	479	477
1800]	505	504	504	503	502	501	500	499	498	496	495	494	493	491	490	489
1850]	518	517	516	515	514	513	512	511	509	508	507	506	504	503	502	501
1900]	530	529	528	527	526	525	524	523	521	520	519	517	516	515	514	512
1950]	542	541	540	539	538	537	536	534	533	532	530	529	528	526	525	524
2000]	555	554	553	551	550	549	547	546	545	543	542	541	539	538	537	536
2050]	567	566	565	563	562	560	559	557	556	555	553	552	551	550	548	547
2100]	579	578	576	575	573	572	570	569	568	566	565	564	562	561	560	559
2150]	591	589	588	586	585	583	582	581	579	578	576	575	574	573	571	570
2200]	602	601	599	598	596	595	593	592	591	589	588	587	585	584	583	581
2250]	614	612	611	609	608	606	605	603	602	601	599	598	597	595	594	593
2300]	625	624	622	621	619	618	616	615	613	612	611	609	608	607	605	604
2350]	637	635	634	632	631	629	628	626	625	623	622	621	619	618	617	615
2400]	648	647	645	643	642	640	639	638	636	635	633	632	631	629	628	627
2450]	660	658	656	655	653	652	650	649	647	646	644	643	642	640	639	638
2500]	671	669	668	666	665	663	661	660	659	657	656	654	653	652	650	649

The left vertical label reads: NONCUSTODIAL PARENT INCOME

Two Children Monthly Support Schedule

CUSTODIAL PARENT INCOME

	4250	4300	4350	4400	4450	4500	4550	4600	4650	4700	4750	4800	4850	4900	4950	5000
2550]	682	680	679	677	676	674	673	671	670	668	667	665	664	663	661	660
2600]	693	692	690	688	687	685	684	682	681	679	678	677	675	674	672	671
2650]	704	703	701	700	698	697	695	693	692	691	689	688	686	685	683	682
2700]	716	714	712	711	709	708	706	705	703	702	700	699	697	696	695	693
2750]	727	725	723	722	720	719	717	716	714	713	711	710	708	707	706	704
2800]	738	736	734	733	731	730	728	727	725	724	722	721	719	718	716	715
2850]	749	747	745	744	742	741	739	738	736	735	733	732	730	729	727	726
2900]	760	758	756	755	753	752	750	749	747	746	744	743	741	740	738	737
2950]	771	769	767	766	764	763	761	759	758	756	755	753	752	751	749	748
3000]	782	780	778	777	775	773	772	770	769	767	766	764	763	761	760	759
3050]	793	791	789	788	786	784	783	781	780	778	777	775	774	772	771	769
3100]	803	802	800	798	797	795	794	792	790	789	787	786	784	783	781	780
3150]	814	812	811	809	808	806	804	803	801	800	798	797	795	794	792	790
3200]	825	823	822	820	818	817	815	814	812	810	809	807	806	804	802	800
3250]	836	834	832	831	829	827	826	824	823	821	820	818	816	814	812	811
3300]	846	845	843	841	840	838	837	835	833	832	830	828	826	824	823	821
3350]	857	855	854	852	850	849	847	846	844	842	840	838	837	835	833	831
3400]	868	866	864	863	861	859	858	856	854	853	851	849	847	845	843	841
3450]	878	877	875	873	872	870	869	867	865	863	861	859	857	855	853	851
3500]	889	887	886	884	882	881	879	877	875	873	871	869	867	865	863	861
3550]	900	898	896	895	893	891	889	887	885	883	881	879	877	875	873	872
3600]	910	909	907	905	903	901	899	897	895	893	891	889	887	885	883	882
3650]	921	919	917	915	913	911	909	907	905	903	901	899	897	895	894	892
3700]	931	930	928	925	923	921	919	917	915	913	911	909	907	905	904	902
3750]	942	940	938	935	933	931	929	927	925	923	921	919	917	915	914	912
3800]	952	950	948	945	943	941	939	937	935	933	931	929	927	925	923	922
3850]	962	960	958	955	953	951	949	947	945	943	941	939	937	935	933	932
3900]	972	970	967	965	963	961	959	957	955	953	951	949	947	945	943	941
3950]	982	980	977	975	973	971	969	967	965	963	961	959	957	955	953	951
4000]	992	989	987	985	983	981	979	977	975	973	971	969	967	965	963	961
4050]	1001	999	997	995	993	991	989	987	985	982	981	979	977	975	973	971
4100]	1011	1009	1007	1005	1003	1000	998	996	994	992	990	988	986	984	983	981
4150]	1021	1019	1017	1014	1012	1010	1008	1006	1004	1002	1000	998	996	994	992	990
4200]	1031	1029	1026	1024	1022	1020	1018	1016	1014	1012	1010	1008	1006	1004	1002	1000
4250]	1040	1038	1036	1034	1032	1030	1028	1026	1024	1022	1020	1018	1016	1014	1012	1010
4300]	1050	1048	1046	1044	1042	1039	1037	1035	1033	1031	1029	1027	1025	1023	1022	1020
4350]	1060	1058	1055	1053	1051	1049	1047	1045	1043	1041	1039	1037	1035	1033	1031	1029
4400]	1070	1067	1065	1063	1061	1059	1057	1055	1053	1051	1049	1047	1045	1043	1041	1039
4450]	1079	1077	1075	1073	1070	1068	1066	1064	1062	1060	1058	1056	1054	1052	1050	1049
4500]	1089	1087	1084	1082	1080	1078	1076	1074	1072	1070	1068	1066	1064	1062	1060	1058
4550]	1098	1096	1094	1092	1090	1088	1085	1083	1081	1079	1077	1075	1073	1072	1070	1068
4600]	1108	1106	1104	1101	1099	1097	1095	1093	1091	1089	1087	1085	1083	1081	1079	1077
4650]	1117	1115	1113	1111	1109	1107	1105	1103	1100	1098	1096	1095	1093	1091	1089	1087
4700]	1127	1125	1123	1120	1118	1116	1114	1112	1110	1108	1106	1104	1102	1100	1098	1096
4750]	1136	1134	1132	1130	1128	1126	1124	1122	1120	1117	1115	1114	1112	1110	1108	1106
4800]	1146	1144	1142	1139	1137	1135	1133	1131	1129	1127	1125	1123	1121	1119	1117	1115
4850]	1155	1153	1151	1149	1147	1145	1143	1140	1138	1136	1134	1132	1130	1129	1127	1125
4900]	1165	1163	1160	1158	1156	1154	1152	1150	1148	1146	1144	1142	1140	1138	1136	1134
4950]	1174	1172	1170	1168	1166	1163	1161	1159	1157	1155	1153	1151	1149	1147	1145	1144
5000]	1184	1181	1179	1177	1175	1173	1171	1169	1167	1165	1163	1161	1159	1157	1155	1153

NONCUSTODIAL PARENT INCOME

Three Children Monthly Support Schedule

CUSTODIAL PARENT INCOME

NONCUSTODIAL PARENT INCOME	0	250	300	350	400	450	500	550	600	650	700	750	800	850	900	950	1000
250]	58	58	58	58	58	58	58	58	58	58	58	58	58	58	58	58	58
300]	63	63	63	63	63	63	63	63	63	63	63	60	60	60	58	58	58
350]	68	68	68	68	68	68	68	68	68	68	68	64	64	64	61	61	61
400]	73	73	73	73	73	73	73	73	73	73	73	69	69	69	65	65	65
450]	78	78	78	78	78	78	78	78	78	78	78	73	73	73	69	69	69
500]	83	83	83	83	83	83	83	83	83	83	83	78	78	78	73	73	73
550]	88	88	88	88	88	88	88	88	88	88	88	82	82	82	77	77	77
600]	93	93	93	93	93	93	93	93	93	93	93	87	87	87	81	81	81
650]	98	98	98	98	98	98	98	98	98	98	98	91	91	91	85	85	85
700]	103	103	103	103	103	103	103	103	103	103	103	96	96	96	89	89	89
750]	118	118	118	118	118	118	118	118	118	118	118	111	111	111	104	104	104
800]	168	168	168	168	168	168	168	168	168	168	168	161	161	161	154	154	154
850]	218	218	218	218	218	218	218	218	218	218	218	211	211	211	204	204	204
900]	268	268	268	268	268	268	268	268	268	268	268	261	261	261	254	254	254
950]	318	318	318	318	318	318	318	318	318	318	318	311	311	311	304	304	304
1000]	368	368	368	368	368	368	368	368	368	368	368	361	361	361	354	354	354
1050]	418	418	418	418	418	418	418	418	418	418	418	411	411	411	404	404	404
1100]	468	468	468	468	468	468	468	468	468	468	468	461	461	461	454	454	454
1150]	518	518	518	518	518	518	518	518	518	518	518	511	511	511	504	504	504
1200]	568	568	568	568	568	568	568	568	568	568	568	561	561	561	554	554	554
1250]	618	618	618	618	618	618	618	618	618	618	618	607	603	600	597	594	590
1300]	668	668	668	668	668	668	668	668	668	668	668	626	623	620	617	612	608
1350]	692	692	692	692	692	692	692	692	692	692	692	646	642	639	635	631	627
1400]	716	716	716	716	716	716	716	716	716	716	716	665	661	657	653	649	645
1450]	739	739	739	739	739	739	739	739	739	739	739	684	679	675	671	666	663
1500]	763	763	763	763	763	763	763	763	763	763	763	702	697	693	688	684	680
1550]	787	787	787	787	787	787	787	787	787	787	787	719	715	710	706	702	698
1600]	810	810	810	810	810	810	810	810	810	810	810	737	732	728	724	720	716
1650]	828	828	828	828	828	828	828	828	828	828	828	754	749	745	741	737	733
1700]	846	846	846	846	846	846	846	846	846	846	846	771	767	763	759	755	751
1750]	863	863	863	863	863	863	863	863	863	863	863	788	784	780	776	772	768
1800]	881	881	881	881	881	881	881	881	881	881	881	806	801	797	793	789	786
1850]	899	899	899	899	899	899	899	899	899	899	899	823	818	814	810	806	802
1900]	916	916	916	916	916	916	916	916	916	916	916	840	835	831	827	823	819
1950]	934	934	934	934	934	934	934	934	934	934	934	856	852	848	844	840	835
2000]	951	951	951	951	951	951	951	951	951	951	951	873	869	865	860	856	852
2050]	969	969	969	969	969	969	969	969	969	969	969	890	885	881	877	872	868
2100]	986	986	986	986	986	986	986	986	986	986	986	906	902	897	893	889	885
2150]	1004	1004	1004	1004	1004	1004	1004	1004	1004	1004	1004	922	918	913	909	905	901
2200]	1021	1021	1021	1021	1021	1021	1021	1021	1021	1021	1021	938	934	929	925	921	917
2250]	1036	1036	1036	1036	1036	1036	1036	1036	1036	1036	1036	954	950	945	941	937	933
2300]	1051	1051	1051	1051	1051	1051	1051	1051	1051	1051	1051	970	966	961	957	953	949
2350]	1067	1067	1067	1067	1067	1067	1067	1067	1067	1067	1067	986	982	977	973	969	965
2400]	1082	1082	1082	1082	1082	1082	1082	1082	1082	1082	1082	1002	997	993	989	985	981
2450]	1097	1097	1097	1097	1097	1097	1097	1097	1097	1097	1097	1017	1013	1009	1005	1001	997
2500]	1112	1112	1112	1112	1112	1112	1112	1112	1112	1112	1112	1033	1029	1025	1021	1017	1013

Three Children Monthly Support Schedule

CUSTODIAL PARENT INCOME

	0	250	300	350	400	450	500	550	600	650	700	750	800	850	900	950	1000
2550]	1128	1128	1128	1128	1128	1128	1128	1128	1128	1128	1128	1049	1045	1040	1037	1033	1029
2600]	1143	1143	1143	1143	1143	1143	1143	1143	1143	1143	1143	1064	1060	1056	1052	1048	1045
2650]	1158	1158	1158	1158	1158	1158	1158	1158	1158	1158	1158	1080	1076	1072	1068	1064	1060
2700]	1173	1173	1173	1173	1173	1173	1173	1173	1173	1173	1173	1096	1091	1087	1084	1080	1076
2750]	1189	1189	1189	1189	1189	1189	1189	1189	1189	1189	1189	1111	1107	1103	1099	1095	1091
2800]	1204	1204	1204	1204	1204	1204	1204	1204	1204	1204	1204	1127	1123	1119	1115	1111	1107
2850]	1218	1218	1218	1218	1218	1218	1218	1218	1218	1218	1218	1142	1138	1134	1130	1126	1122
2900]	1233	1233	1233	1233	1233	1233	1233	1233	1233	1233	1233	1157	1153	1149	1145	1141	1137
2950]	1247	1247	1247	1247	1247	1247	1247	1247	1247	1247	1247	1172	1168	1164	1160	1156	1153
3000]	1261	1261	1261	1261	1261	1261	1261	1261	1261	1261	1261	1188	1183	1179	1175	1172	1168
3050]	1276	1276	1276	1276	1276	1276	1276	1276	1276	1276	1276	1203	1198	1194	1191	1187	1183
3100]	1290	1290	1290	1290	1290	1290	1290	1290	1290	1290	1290	1218	1213	1210	1206	1202	1198
3150]	1305	1305	1305	1305	1305	1305	1305	1305	1305	1305	1305	1233	1229	1225	1221	1217	1213
3200]	1319	1319	1319	1319	1319	1319	1319	1319	1319	1319	1319	1247	1244	1240	1236	1232	1228
3250]	1333	1333	1333	1333	1333	1333	1333	1333	1333	1333	1333	1262	1258	1255	1251	1247	1244
3300]	1348	1348	1348	1348	1348	1348	1348	1348	1348	1348	1348	1277	1273	1270	1266	1262	1259
3350]	1362	1362	1362	1362	1362	1362	1362	1362	1362	1362	1362	1292	1288	1285	1281	1277	1274
3400]	1376	1376	1376	1376	1376	1376	1376	1376	1376	1376	1376	1307	1303	1299	1296	1292	1289
3450]	1391	1391	1391	1391	1391	1391	1391	1391	1391	1391	1391	1322	1318	1314	1311	1307	1304
3500]	1405	1405	1405	1405	1405	1405	1405	1405	1405	1405	1405	1337	1333	1329	1326	1322	1319
3550]	1420	1420	1420	1420	1420	1420	1420	1420	1420	1420	1420	1352	1348	1344	1341	1337	1334
3600]	1434	1434	1434	1434	1434	1434	1434	1434	1434	1434	1434	1366	1363	1359	1355	1352	1349
3650]	1448	1448	1448	1448	1448	1448	1448	1448	1448	1448	1448	1381	1377	1374	1370	1367	1363
3700]	1462	1462	1462	1462	1462	1462	1462	1462	1462	1462	1462	1396	1392	1389	1385	1382	1378
3750]	1476	1476	1476	1476	1476	1476	1476	1476	1476	1476	1476	1411	1407	1403	1400	1397	1393
3800]	1490	1490	1490	1490	1490	1490	1490	1490	1490	1490	1490	1425	1422	1418	1415	1411	1408
3850]	1504	1504	1504	1504	1504	1504	1504	1504	1504	1504	1504	1440	1436	1433	1430	1426	1423
3900]	1518	1518	1518	1518	1518	1518	1518	1518	1518	1518	1518	1455	1451	1448	1444	1441	1438
3950]	1532	1532	1532	1532	1532	1532	1532	1532	1532	1532	1532	1469	1466	1462	1459	1456	1453
4000]	1546	1546	1546	1546	1546	1546	1546	1546	1546	1546	1546	1484	1480	1477	1474	1471	1467
4050]	1560	1560	1560	1560	1560	1560	1560	1560	1560	1560	1560	1499	1495	1492	1489	1485	1482
4100]	1574	1574	1574	1574	1574	1574	1574	1574	1574	1574	1574	1513	1510	1506	1503	1500	1497
4150]	1588	1588	1588	1588	1588	1588	1588	1588	1588	1588	1588	1528	1524	1521	1518	1515	1512
4200]	1602	1602	1602	1602	1602	1602	1602	1602	1602	1602	1602	1542	1539	1536	1533	1529	1525
4250]	1616	1616	1616	1616	1616	1616	1616	1616	1616	1616	1616	1557	1554	1550	1547	1543	1538
4300]	1630	1630	1630	1630	1630	1630	1630	1630	1630	1630	1630	1572	1568	1565	1561	1556	1551
4350]	1644	1644	1644	1644	1644	1644	1644	1644	1644	1644	1644	1586	1583	1579	1574	1569	1564
4400]	1658	1658	1658	1658	1658	1658	1658	1658	1658	1658	1658	1601	1597	1591	1586	1582	1577
4450]	1672	1672	1672	1672	1672	1672	1672	1672	1672	1672	1672	1614	1609	1604	1599	1594	1590
4500]	1686	1686	1686	1686	1686	1686	1686	1686	1686	1686	1686	1627	1622	1617	1612	1607	1602
4550]	1700	1700	1700	1700	1700	1700	1700	1700	1700	1700	1700	1639	1634	1629	1625	1620	1615
4600]	1714	1714	1714	1714	1714	1714	1714	1714	1714	1714	1714	1652	1647	1642	1637	1632	1628
4650]	1728	1728	1728	1728	1728	1728	1728	1728	1728	1728	1728	1665	1660	1655	1650	1645	1640
4700]	1742	1742	1742	1742	1742	1742	1742	1742	1742	1742	1742	1677	1672	1667	1662	1658	1653
4750]	1756	1756	1756	1756	1756	1756	1756	1756	1756	1756	1756	1689	1685	1680	1675	1670	1666
4800]	1770	1770	1770	1770	1770	1770	1770	1770	1770	1770	1770	1702	1697	1692	1688	1683	1678
4850]	1784	1784	1784	1784	1784	1784	1784	1784	1784	1784	1784	1714	1710	1705	1700	1696	1691
4900]	1798	1798	1798	1798	1798	1798	1798	1798	1798	1798	1798	1727	1722	1717	1713	1708	1704
4950]	1812	1812	1812	1812	1812	1812	1812	1812	1812	1812	1812	1739	1735	1730	1725	1721	1716
5000]	1826	1826	1826	1826	1826	1826	1826	1826	1826	1826	1826	1752	1747	1742	1738	1733	1729

Left vertical label: NONCUSTODIAL PARENT INCOME

Three Children Monthly Support Schedule

CUSTODIAL PARENT INCOME

	1050	1100	1150	1200	1250	1300	1350	1400	1450	1500	1550	1600	1650	1700	1750	1800
250]	58	58	58	58	58	58	58	58	58	58	58	58	58	58	58	58
300]	58	58	58	58	58	58	58	58	58	58	58	58	58	58	58	58
350]	61	61	61	61	61	61	58	58	58	58	58	58	58	58	58	58
400]	65	65	65	65	65	65	61	61	61	61	61	61	61	61	61	58
450]	69	69	69	69	69	69	64	64	64	64	64	64	64	64	64	60
500]	73	73	73	73	73	73	68	68	68	68	68	68	68	68	68	63
550]	77	77	77	77	77	77	71	71	71	71	71	71	71	71	71	66
600]	81	81	81	81	81	81	75	75	75	75	75	75	75	75	75	69
650]	85	85	85	85	85	85	78	78	78	78	78	78	78	78	78	72
700]	89	89	89	89	89	89	82	82	82	82	82	82	82	82	82	75
750]	104	104	104	104	104	104	96	96	96	96	96	96	96	96	96	89
800]	154	154	154	154	154	154	146	146	146	146	146	146	146	146	146	139
850]	204	204	204	204	204	204	196	196	196	196	196	196	196	196	196	189
900]	254	254	254	254	254	254	246	246	246	246	246	246	246	246	246	239
950]	304	304	304	304	304	304	296	296	296	296	296	296	296	296	296	289
1000]	354	354	354	354	354	354	346	346	346	346	346	346	346	346	346	339
1050]	404	404	404	404	404	404	396	396	396	396	396	396	396	396	396	389
1100]	454	454	454	454	454	454	446	446	446	446	446	446	446	446	446	439
1150]	504	504	504	504	504	504	496	496	496	496	496	496	496	496	496	489
1200]	554	554	554	554	554	551	546	545	542	540	537	535	532	529	527	524
1250]	586	583	579	576	572	569	566	563	561	558	555	553	550	547	545	542
1300]	605	601	597	594	591	588	585	582	579	576	573	571	568	565	563	560
1350]	623	619	616	612	609	606	603	600	597	594	591	588	586	583	580	578
1400]	641	637	634	630	627	624	621	618	615	612	609	606	603	601	598	595
1450]	659	655	652	648	645	642	639	636	633	630	627	624	621	618	615	613
1500]	677	673	670	666	663	660	657	653	650	647	644	641	638	636	633	630
1550]	694	691	687	684	681	677	674	671	668	664	661	659	656	653	650	648
1600]	712	709	705	702	698	695	691	688	685	682	679	676	673	670	668	665
1650]	730	726	723	719	715	712	708	705	702	699	696	693	690	687	685	682
1700]	747	744	740	736	732	729	726	722	719	716	713	710	707	705	702	699
1750]	765	761	757	753	749	746	743	739	736	733	730	727	724	722	719	716
1800]	781	777	774	770	766	763	759	756	753	750	747	744	741	739	736	733
1850]	798	794	790	787	783	780	776	773	770	767	764	761	758	755	753	750
1900]	815	811	807	803	800	796	793	790	787	784	781	778	775	772	770	767
1950]	831	827	824	820	816	813	810	806	803	800	797	794	792	789	786	783
2000]	848	844	840	837	833	830	826	823	820	817	814	811	808	805	803	800
2050]	864	860	857	853	850	846	843	840	837	834	831	828	825	822	819	816
2100]	881	877	873	869	866	863	859	856	853	850	847	844	841	838	835	833
2150]	897	893	889	886	882	879	876	873	870	867	863	860	857	854	852	849
2200]	913	909	906	902	899	895	892	889	886	883	880	877	874	871	868	865
2250]	929	926	922	918	915	912	908	905	902	899	896	893	890	887	884	881
2300]	945	942	938	935	931	928	925	921	918	915	912	909	906	903	900	897
2350]	961	958	954	951	947	944	941	937	934	931	928	925	922	919	916	913
2400]	977	974	970	967	963	960	957	953	950	947	944	941	938	935	932	930
2450]	993	990	986	983	979	976	972	969	966	963	960	957	954	951	948	945
2500]	1009	1006	1002	999	995	992	988	985	982	979	976	973	970	967	964	961

NONCUSTODIAL PARENT INCOME

Three Children Monthly Support Schedule

NONCUSTODIAL PARENT INCOME	CUSTODIAL PARENT INCOME															
	1050	1100	1150	1200	1250	1300	1350	1400	1450	1500	1550	1600	1650	1700	1750	1800
2550]	1025	1022	1018	1014	1011	1007	1004	1001	998	994	991	988	986	983	980	977
2600]	1041	1037	1034	1030	1026	1023	1020	1016	1013	1010	1007	1004	1001	999	996	993
2650]	1057	1053	1049	1046	1042	1039	1035	1032	1029	1026	1023	1020	1017	1014	1012	1009
2700]	1072	1068	1065	1061	1058	1054	1051	1048	1045	1042	1039	1036	1033	1030	1027	1025
2750]	1087	1084	1080	1077	1073	1070	1067	1063	1060	1057	1054	1051	1049	1046	1043	1040
2800]	1103	1099	1096	1092	1089	1085	1082	1079	1076	1073	1070	1067	1064	1061	1059	1056
2850]	1118	1115	1111	1108	1104	1101	1098	1095	1091	1088	1086	1083	1080	1077	1074	1072
2900]	1134	1130	1126	1123	1120	1116	1113	1110	1107	1104	1101	1098	1095	1093	1090	1087
2950]	1149	1145	1142	1138	1135	1132	1129	1125	1122	1119	1117	1114	1111	1108	1106	1103
3000]	1164	1161	1157	1154	1150	1147	1144	1141	1138	1135	1132	1129	1126	1124	1121	1119
3050]	1179	1176	1172	1169	1166	1163	1159	1156	1153	1150	1148	1145	1142	1139	1137	1134
3100]	1195	1191	1188	1184	1181	1178	1175	1172	1169	1166	1163	1160	1157	1155	1152	1150
3150]	1210	1206	1203	1200	1196	1193	1190	1187	1184	1181	1178	1176	1173	1170	1168	1165
3200]	1225	1221	1218	1215	1212	1208	1205	1202	1199	1197	1194	1191	1188	1186	1183	1180
3250]	1240	1237	1233	1230	1227	1224	1221	1218	1215	1212	1209	1206	1204	1201	1198	1196
3300]	1255	1252	1248	1245	1242	1239	1236	1233	1230	1227	1224	1222	1219	1216	1214	1211
3350]	1270	1267	1264	1260	1257	1254	1251	1248	1245	1242	1240	1237	1234	1232	1229	1227
3400]	1285	1282	1279	1275	1272	1269	1266	1263	1260	1258	1255	1252	1249	1247	1244	1241
3450]	1300	1297	1294	1291	1287	1284	1281	1278	1276	1273	1270	1267	1265	1262	1259	1255
3500]	1315	1312	1309	1306	1303	1300	1297	1294	1291	1288	1285	1283	1280	1277	1273	1269
3550]	1330	1327	1324	1321	1318	1315	1312	1309	1306	1303	1300	1298	1294	1290	1286	1282
3600]	1345	1342	1339	1336	1333	1330	1327	1324	1321	1318	1316	1312	1308	1304	1300	1296
3650]	1360	1357	1354	1351	1348	1345	1342	1339	1336	1333	1330	1326	1322	1318	1314	1310
3700]	1375	1372	1369	1366	1363	1360	1357	1354	1351	1348	1343	1339	1335	1331	1327	1323
3750]	1390	1387	1384	1381	1378	1375	1372	1369	1366	1361	1357	1353	1349	1345	1341	1337
3800]	1405	1402	1399	1396	1393	1390	1387	1383	1379	1375	1370	1366	1362	1358	1354	1350
3850]	1420	1417	1414	1411	1408	1405	1401	1397	1392	1388	1384	1380	1376	1372	1368	1364
3900]	1435	1431	1428	1425	1423	1419	1414	1410	1406	1401	1397	1393	1389	1385	1381	1377
3950]	1449	1446	1443	1440	1437	1432	1428	1423	1419	1415	1410	1406	1402	1398	1395	1391
4000]	1464	1461	1458	1454	1450	1445	1441	1436	1432	1428	1424	1420	1416	1412	1408	1404
4050]	1479	1476	1472	1467	1463	1458	1454	1450	1445	1441	1437	1433	1429	1425	1421	1418
4100]	1494	1490	1485	1481	1476	1471	1467	1463	1459	1454	1450	1446	1442	1438	1435	1431
4150]	1508	1503	1498	1494	1489	1485	1480	1476	1472	1468	1463	1459	1456	1452	1448	1444
4200]	1521	1516	1511	1507	1502	1498	1493	1489	1485	1481	1477	1473	1469	1465	1461	1457
4250]	1534	1529	1524	1520	1515	1511	1506	1502	1498	1494	1490	1486	1482	1478	1474	1471
4300]	1546	1542	1537	1533	1528	1524	1519	1515	1511	1507	1503	1499	1495	1491	1488	1484
4350]	1559	1555	1550	1545	1541	1537	1532	1528	1524	1520	1516	1512	1508	1505	1501	1497
4400]	1572	1567	1563	1558	1554	1550	1545	1541	1537	1533	1529	1525	1521	1518	1514	1510
4450]	1585	1580	1576	1571	1567	1563	1558	1554	1550	1546	1542	1538	1535	1531	1527	1524
4500]	1598	1593	1589	1584	1580	1576	1571	1567	1563	1559	1555	1551	1548	1544	1540	1537
4550]	1610	1606	1601	1597	1593	1588	1584	1580	1576	1572	1568	1565	1561	1557	1553	1550
4600]	1623	1619	1614	1610	1606	1601	1597	1593	1589	1585	1581	1578	1574	1570	1566	1562
4650]	1636	1631	1627	1623	1618	1614	1610	1606	1602	1598	1594	1591	1587	1583	1579	1574
4700]	1649	1644	1640	1635	1631	1627	1623	1619	1615	1611	1607	1604	1600	1596	1591	1586
4750]	1661	1657	1653	1648	1644	1640	1636	1632	1628	1624	1620	1616	1612	1607	1602	1597
4800]	1674	1670	1665	1661	1657	1653	1649	1645	1641	1637	1633	1629	1624	1619	1614	1609
4850]	1687	1682	1678	1674	1670	1666	1662	1658	1654	1650	1646	1640	1635	1630	1625	1621
4900]	1699	1695	1691	1686	1682	1678	1674	1670	1667	1662	1657	1652	1647	1642	1637	1632
4950]	1712	1708	1703	1699	1695	1691	1687	1683	1679	1674	1668	1663	1658	1653	1649	1644
5000]	1725	1720	1716	1712	1708	1704	1700	1695	1690	1685	1680	1675	1670	1665	1660	1655

Three Children Monthly Support Schedule

CUSTODIAL PARENT INCOME

		1850	1900	1950	2000	2050	2100	2150	2200	2250	2300	2350	2400	2450	2500	2550	2600
	250]	58	58	58	58	58	58	58	58	58	58	58	58	58	58	58	58
	300]	58	58	58	58	58	58	58	58	58	58	58	58	58	58	58	58
	350]	58	58	58	58	58	58	58	58	58	58	58	58	58	58	58	58
	400]	58	58	58	58	58	58	58	58	58	58	58	58	58	58	58	58
	450]	60	60	60	60	60	60	60	60	58	58	58	58	58	58	58	58
	500]	63	63	63	63	63	63	63	63	58	58	58	58	58	58	58	58
	550]	66	66	66	66	66	66	66	66	60	60	60	60	60	60	60	60
	600]	69	69	69	69	69	69	69	69	63	63	63	63	63	63	63	63
	650]	72	72	72	72	72	72	72	72	65	65	65	65	65	65	65	65
N	700]	75	75	75	75	75	75	75	75	68	68	68	68	68	68	68	68
O	750]	89	89	89	89	89	89	89	89	82	82	82	82	82	82	82	82
N	800]	139	139	139	139	139	139	139	139	132	132	132	132	132	132	132	132
C	850]	189	189	189	189	189	189	189	189	182	182	182	182	182	182	182	182
U	900]	239	239	239	239	239	239	239	239	232	232	232	232	232	232	232	232
S	950]	289	289	289	289	289	289	289	289	282	282	282	282	282	282	282	282
T																	
O	1000]	339	339	339	339	339	339	339	339	332	332	332	332	332	332	332	332
D	1050]	389	389	389	389	389	389	389	389	382	382	382	382	382	382	382	382
I	1100]	439	439	439	439	439	439	439	439	432	432	432	432	432	432	432	432
A	1150]	489	489	489	489	489	489	489	489	482	482	482	482	480	479	477	475
L	1200]	522	519	517	515	513	511	509	507	505	503	501	500	498	496	495	493
	1250]	540	537	535	533	531	529	527	525	523	521	519	517	516	514	512	510
P	1300]	558	555	553	551	549	546	544	542	541	539	537	535	533	531	530	528
A	1350]	575	573	571	568	566	564	562	560	558	556	554	552	550	549	547	545
R	1400]	593	591	588	586	584	582	580	578	576	574	572	570	568	566	564	562
E	1450]	610	608	606	603	601	599	597	595	593	591	589	587	585	583	581	580
N																	
T	1500]	628	625	623	621	619	617	614	612	610	608	606	604	602	600	598	597
	1550]	645	643	640	638	636	634	632	629	627	625	623	621	619	617	615	614
I	1600]	663	660	658	655	653	651	649	646	644	642	640	638	636	634	632	631
N	1650]	680	677	675	673	670	668	666	663	661	659	657	655	653	651	649	647
C	1700]	697	694	692	689	687	685	682	680	678	676	674	672	670	668	666	664
O	1750]	714	711	709	706	704	702	699	697	695	693	691	689	687	685	683	681
M	1800]	731	728	726	723	721	718	716	714	712	709	707	705	703	701	699	698
E	1850]	747	745	742	740	737	735	733	730	728	726	724	722	720	718	716	714
	1900]	764	761	759	756	754	752	749	747	745	743	741	739	737	735	733	731
	1950]	781	778	775	773	771	768	766	764	761	759	757	755	753	751	749	747
	2000]	797	794	792	789	787	785	782	780	778	776	774	771	769	768	766	764
	2050]	814	811	808	806	803	801	799	796	794	792	790	788	786	784	782	780
	2100]	830	827	825	822	820	817	815	813	811	808	806	804	802	800	798	796
	2150]	846	844	841	839	836	834	831	829	827	825	823	821	819	817	815	813
	2200]	862	860	857	855	852	850	848	845	843	841	839	837	835	833	831	829
	2250]	879	876	873	871	869	866	864	862	859	857	855	853	851	849	847	845
	2300]	895	892	890	887	885	882	880	878	876	873	871	869	867	865	863	861
	2350]	911	908	906	903	901	898	896	894	892	889	887	885	883	881	879	877
	2400]	927	924	922	919	917	914	912	910	908	906	903	901	899	897	895	893
	2450]	943	940	938	935	933	931	928	926	924	922	919	917	915	913	911	909
	2500]	959	956	954	951	949	946	944	942	940	938	935	933	931	929	927	925

Three Children Monthly Support Schedule

CUSTODIAL PARENT INCOME

	1850	1900	1950	2000	2050	2100	2150	2200	2250	2300	2350	2400	2450	2500	2550	2600
2550]	975	972	970	967	965	962	960	958	956	953	951	949	947	945	943	941
2600]	991	988	985	983	981	978	976	974	972	969	967	965	963	961	959	957
2650]	1006	1004	1001	999	996	994	992	990	987	985	983	981	979	977	975	971
2700]	1022	1020	1017	1015	1012	1010	1008	1005	1003	1001	999	997	995	992	989	986
2750]	1038	1035	1033	1030	1028	1026	1023	1021	1019	1017	1015	1013	1010	1007	1004	1001
2800]	1054	1051	1049	1046	1044	1041	1039	1037	1035	1033	1030	1028	1025	1021	1018	1015
2850]	1069	1067	1064	1062	1059	1057	1055	1053	1050	1048	1046	1042	1039	1036	1033	1030
2900]	1085	1082	1080	1077	1075	1073	1071	1068	1066	1063	1060	1057	1054	1050	1047	1044
2950]	1100	1098	1095	1093	1091	1088	1086	1084	1081	1078	1074	1071	1068	1065	1062	1059
3000]	1116	1113	1111	1109	1106	1104	1102	1099	1095	1092	1089	1085	1082	1079	1076	1073
3050]	1132	1129	1127	1124	1122	1120	1117	1113	1110	1106	1103	1100	1097	1093	1090	1087
3100]	1147	1145	1142	1140	1137	1134	1131	1127	1124	1121	1117	1114	1111	1108	1105	1101
3150]	1162	1160	1158	1155	1152	1149	1145	1142	1138	1135	1131	1128	1125	1122	1119	1116
3200]	1178	1175	1173	1170	1166	1163	1159	1156	1152	1149	1146	1142	1139	1136	1133	1130
3250]	1193	1191	1188	1184	1180	1177	1173	1170	1166	1163	1160	1156	1153	1150	1147	1144
3300]	1209	1206	1202	1198	1194	1191	1187	1184	1180	1177	1174	1170	1167	1164	1161	1158
3350]	1223	1219	1216	1212	1208	1205	1201	1198	1194	1191	1188	1184	1181	1178	1175	1172
3400]	1237	1233	1230	1226	1222	1219	1215	1212	1208	1205	1202	1198	1195	1192	1189	1186
3450]	1251	1247	1243	1240	1236	1232	1229	1226	1222	1219	1216	1212	1209	1206	1203	1200
3500]	1265	1261	1257	1253	1250	1246	1243	1239	1236	1233	1229	1226	1223	1220	1217	1214
3550]	1278	1275	1271	1267	1264	1260	1257	1253	1250	1247	1243	1240	1237	1234	1231	1228
3600]	1292	1288	1285	1281	1277	1274	1270	1267	1264	1260	1257	1254	1251	1248	1245	1242
3650]	1306	1302	1298	1295	1291	1288	1284	1281	1277	1274	1271	1268	1265	1262	1258	1256
3700]	1319	1316	1312	1308	1305	1301	1298	1294	1291	1288	1285	1281	1278	1275	1272	1269
3750]	1333	1329	1326	1322	1318	1315	1311	1308	1305	1302	1298	1295	1292	1289	1286	1283
3800]	1347	1343	1339	1336	1332	1329	1325	1322	1318	1315	1312	1309	1306	1303	1300	1296
3850]	1360	1356	1353	1349	1346	1342	1339	1335	1332	1329	1326	1323	1319	1316	1313	1309
3900]	1374	1370	1366	1363	1359	1356	1352	1349	1346	1342	1339	1336	1333	1330	1325	1321
3950]	1387	1383	1380	1376	1373	1369	1366	1363	1359	1356	1353	1350	1346	1342	1338	1334
4000]	1400	1397	1393	1390	1386	1383	1379	1376	1373	1370	1366	1363	1359	1354	1350	1346
4050]	1414	1410	1407	1403	1400	1396	1393	1390	1386	1383	1379	1375	1371	1367	1363	1359
4100]	1427	1424	1420	1416	1413	1410	1406	1403	1400	1396	1392	1387	1383	1379	1375	1371
4150]	1441	1437	1433	1430	1426	1423	1420	1416	1413	1408	1404	1400	1396	1391	1387	1383
4200]	1454	1450	1447	1443	1440	1436	1433	1429	1425	1421	1416	1412	1408	1404	1400	1396
4250]	1467	1464	1460	1457	1453	1450	1446	1441	1437	1433	1428	1424	1420	1416	1412	1408
4300]	1480	1477	1473	1470	1466	1463	1458	1454	1449	1445	1441	1436	1432	1428	1424	1420
4350]	1494	1490	1487	1483	1479	1475	1470	1466	1461	1457	1453	1448	1444	1440	1436	1432
4400]	1507	1503	1500	1496	1491	1487	1482	1478	1473	1469	1465	1461	1456	1452	1448	1444
4450]	1520	1516	1512	1508	1503	1499	1494	1490	1485	1481	1477	1473	1468	1464	1460	1456
4500]	1533	1529	1524	1520	1515	1511	1506	1502	1497	1493	1489	1485	1481	1476	1472	1469
4550]	1546	1541	1536	1532	1527	1522	1518	1514	1509	1505	1501	1497	1493	1488	1485	1481
4600]	1558	1553	1548	1543	1539	1534	1530	1525	1521	1517	1513	1509	1504	1500	1497	1493
4650]	1569	1564	1560	1555	1551	1546	1542	1537	1533	1529	1525	1520	1516	1512	1508	1505
4700]	1581	1576	1572	1567	1562	1558	1553	1549	1545	1541	1536	1532	1528	1524	1520	1517
4750]	1593	1588	1583	1579	1574	1570	1565	1561	1557	1552	1548	1544	1540	1536	1532	1528
4800]	1604	1600	1595	1590	1586	1581	1577	1573	1568	1564	1560	1556	1552	1548	1544	1540
4850]	1616	1611	1607	1602	1598	1593	1589	1584	1580	1576	1572	1568	1564	1560	1556	1552
4900]	1627	1623	1618	1614	1609	1605	1600	1596	1592	1588	1584	1580	1576	1572	1568	1564
4950]	1639	1634	1630	1625	1621	1616	1612	1608	1604	1600	1595	1591	1587	1584	1580	1576
5000]	1651	1646	1641	1637	1632	1628	1624	1620	1615	1611	1607	1603	1599	1595	1591	1588

NONCUSTODIAL PARENT INCOME

Three Children Monthly Support Schedule

CUSTODIAL PARENT INCOME

	2650	2700	2750	2800	2850	2900	2950	3000	3050	3100	3150	3200	3250	3300	3350	3400
250]	58	58	58	58	58	58	58	58	58	58	58	58	58	58	58	58
300]	58	58	58	58	58	58	58	58	58	58	58	58	58	58	58	58
350]	58	58	58	58	58	58	58	58	58	58	58	58	58	58	58	58
400]	58	58	58	58	58	58	58	58	58	58	58	58	58	58	58	58
450]	58	58	58	58	58	58	58	58	58	58	58	58	58	58	58	58
500]	58	58	58	58	58	58	58	58	58	58	58	58	58	58	58	58
550]	60	58	58	58	58	58	58	58	58	58	58	58	58	58	58	58
600]	63	58	58	58	58	58	58	58	58	58	58	58	58	58	58	58
650]	65	59	59	59	59	59	59	59	59	59	58	58	58	58	58	58
700]	68	61	61	61	61	61	61	61	61	61	58	58	58	58	58	58
750]	82	74	74	74	74	74	74	74	74	74	70	70	70	70	70	70
800]	132	124	124	124	124	124	124	124	124	124	120	120	120	120	120	120
850]	182	174	174	174	174	174	174	174	174	174	170	170	170	170	170	170
900]	232	224	224	224	224	224	224	224	224	224	220	220	220	220	220	220
950]	282	274	274	274	274	274	274	274	274	274	270	270	270	270	270	270
1000]	332	324	324	324	324	324	324	324	324	324	320	320	320	320	320	320
1050]	382	374	374	374	374	374	374	374	374	374	370	370	370	370	370	370
1100]	432	424	424	424	424	424	424	424	424	424	420	420	420	420	420	420
1150]	474	472	471	469	468	466	465	464	462	461	460	459	457	456	455	454
1200]	491	490	488	487	485	484	482	481	480	478	477	476	475	474	472	471
1250]	509	507	506	504	503	501	500	498	497	496	494	493	492	491	490	488
1300]	526	525	523	521	520	518	517	516	514	513	512	510	509	508	507	505
1350]	543	542	540	539	537	536	534	533	531	530	529	527	526	525	524	522
1400]	561	559	557	556	554	553	551	550	548	547	546	544	543	542	541	539
1450]	578	576	574	573	571	570	568	567	565	564	563	561	560	559	557	556
1500]	595	593	592	590	588	587	585	584	582	581	580	578	577	576	574	573
1550]	612	610	608	607	605	604	602	601	599	598	596	595	594	592	591	590
1600]	629	627	625	624	622	621	619	617	616	615	613	612	610	609	608	607
1650]	646	644	642	641	639	637	636	634	633	631	630	628	627	626	624	623
1700]	662	661	659	657	656	654	652	651	649	648	647	645	644	642	641	640
1750]	679	677	676	674	672	671	669	668	666	665	663	662	660	659	658	656
1800]	696	694	692	691	689	687	686	684	683	681	680	678	677	675	674	672
1850]	712	711	709	707	705	704	702	701	699	698	696	695	693	692	690	688
1900]	729	727	725	724	722	720	719	717	716	714	713	711	710	708	706	704
1950]	745	744	742	740	738	737	735	734	732	731	729	728	726	723	721	719
2000]	762	760	758	757	755	753	752	750	748	747	745	744	741	739	737	735
2050]	778	776	775	773	771	770	768	766	765	763	761	759	757	754	752	750
2100]	795	793	791	789	788	786	784	783	781	779	777	774	772	770	767	765
2150]	811	809	807	806	804	802	800	799	797	794	792	790	787	785	783	780
2200]	827	825	823	822	820	818	817	815	812	810	807	805	802	800	798	796
2250]	843	841	840	838	836	834	832	830	827	825	822	820	817	815	813	811
2300]	859	858	856	854	852	850	847	845	842	840	837	835	833	830	828	826
2350]	876	874	872	870	868	865	863	860	857	855	852	850	848	845	843	841
2400]	892	890	888	886	883	880	878	875	872	870	867	865	862	860	858	856
2450]	908	906	903	901	898	895	892	890	887	885	882	880	877	875	873	870
2500]	924	921	918	915	913	910	907	905	902	900	897	895	892	890	887	885

NONCUSTODIAL PARENT INCOME

Three Children Monthly Support Schedule

CUSTODIAL PARENT INCOME

	2650	2700	2750	2800	2850	2900	2950	3000	3050	3100	3150	3200	3250	3300	3350	3400
2550]	939	936	933	930	928	925	922	919	917	914	912	909	907	905	902	900
2600]	954	951	948	945	942	940	937	934	932	929	927	924	922	919	917	915
2650]	968	966	963	960	957	954	952	949	946	944	941	939	936	934	932	929
2700]	983	980	977	974	972	969	966	964	961	958	956	953	951	949	946	944
2750]	998	995	992	989	986	983	981	978	976	973	970	968	966	963	961	958
2800]	1012	1009	1006	1004	1001	998	995	993	990	988	985	983	980	978	975	973
2850]	1027	1024	1021	1018	1015	1013	1010	1007	1005	1002	999	997	995	992	990	987
2900]	1041	1038	1035	1033	1030	1027	1024	1022	1019	1016	1014	1011	1009	1007	1004	1002
2950]	1056	1053	1050	1047	1044	1041	1039	1036	1033	1031	1028	1026	1023	1021	1019	1016
3000]	1070	1067	1064	1061	1058	1056	1053	1050	1048	1045	1043	1040	1038	1035	1033	1030
3050]	1084	1081	1078	1076	1073	1070	1067	1065	1062	1060	1057	1054	1052	1050	1047	1044
3100]	1098	1096	1093	1090	1087	1084	1082	1079	1076	1074	1071	1069	1066	1064	1060	1057
3150]	1113	1110	1107	1104	1101	1099	1096	1093	1091	1088	1085	1083	1080	1077	1074	1070
3200]	1127	1124	1121	1118	1115	1113	1110	1107	1105	1102	1100	1097	1093	1090	1087	1084
3250]	1141	1138	1135	1132	1130	1127	1124	1121	1119	1116	1113	1110	1107	1103	1100	1097
3300]	1155	1152	1149	1146	1144	1141	1138	1136	1133	1130	1127	1123	1120	1116	1113	1110
3350]	1169	1166	1163	1161	1158	1155	1152	1150	1147	1143	1140	1136	1133	1129	1126	1123
3400]	1183	1180	1177	1175	1172	1169	1166	1163	1160	1156	1153	1149	1146	1143	1139	1136
3450]	1197	1194	1191	1189	1186	1183	1180	1176	1173	1169	1166	1162	1159	1156	1152	1149
3500]	1211	1208	1205	1202	1200	1197	1193	1189	1186	1182	1179	1175	1172	1168	1165	1162
3550]	1225	1222	1219	1216	1213	1209	1206	1202	1199	1195	1191	1188	1185	1181	1178	1175
3600]	1239	1236	1233	1230	1226	1222	1219	1215	1211	1208	1204	1201	1198	1194	1191	1188
3650]	1253	1250	1246	1243	1239	1235	1231	1228	1224	1221	1217	1214	1210	1207	1204	1201
3700]	1266	1263	1259	1255	1252	1248	1244	1240	1237	1233	1230	1226	1223	1220	1217	1213
3750]	1280	1276	1272	1268	1264	1260	1257	1253	1250	1246	1243	1239	1236	1233	1229	1226
3800]	1292	1288	1284	1281	1277	1273	1269	1266	1262	1259	1255	1252	1249	1245	1242	1239
3850]	1305	1301	1297	1293	1289	1286	1282	1278	1275	1271	1268	1265	1261	1258	1255	1251
3900]	1317	1313	1310	1306	1302	1298	1295	1291	1287	1284	1281	1277	1274	1270	1267	1264
3950]	1330	1326	1322	1318	1315	1311	1307	1304	1300	1297	1293	1290	1286	1283	1280	1277
4000]	1342	1338	1335	1331	1327	1323	1320	1316	1313	1309	1306	1302	1299	1296	1292	1289
4050]	1355	1351	1347	1343	1339	1336	1332	1329	1325	1321	1318	1315	1311	1308	1305	1302
4100]	1367	1363	1359	1356	1352	1348	1345	1341	1337	1334	1330	1327	1324	1320	1317	1314
4150]	1379	1376	1372	1368	1364	1361	1357	1353	1350	1346	1343	1340	1336	1333	1330	1326
4200]	1392	1388	1384	1380	1377	1373	1369	1366	1362	1359	1355	1352	1349	1345	1342	1339
4250]	1404	1400	1396	1393	1389	1385	1382	1378	1374	1371	1368	1364	1361	1358	1354	1351
4300]	1416	1412	1409	1405	1401	1397	1394	1390	1387	1383	1380	1377	1373	1370	1367	1364
4350]	1428	1425	1421	1417	1413	1410	1406	1403	1399	1396	1392	1389	1386	1382	1379	1376
4400]	1441	1437	1433	1429	1425	1422	1418	1415	1411	1408	1404	1401	1398	1394	1391	1388
4450]	1453	1449	1445	1441	1438	1434	1430	1427	1423	1420	1417	1413	1410	1407	1403	1400
4500]	1465	1461	1457	1453	1450	1446	1443	1439	1436	1432	1429	1425	1422	1419	1416	1413
4550]	1477	1473	1469	1465	1462	1458	1455	1451	1448	1444	1441	1438	1434	1431	1428	1425
4600]	1489	1485	1481	1478	1474	1470	1467	1463	1460	1456	1453	1450	1446	1443	1440	1437
4650]	1501	1497	1493	1490	1486	1482	1479	1475	1472	1468	1465	1462	1459	1455	1452	1449
4700]	1513	1509	1505	1502	1498	1494	1491	1487	1484	1481	1477	1474	1471	1467	1464	1461
4750]	1525	1521	1517	1514	1510	1506	1503	1499	1496	1493	1489	1486	1483	1479	1476	1473
4800]	1537	1533	1529	1525	1522	1518	1515	1511	1508	1505	1501	1498	1495	1491	1488	1484
4850]	1548	1545	1541	1537	1534	1530	1527	1523	1520	1516	1513	1510	1506	1503	1500	1496
4900]	1560	1557	1553	1549	1546	1542	1539	1535	1532	1528	1525	1521	1518	1515	1511	1508
4950]	1572	1568	1565	1561	1558	1554	1551	1547	1544	1540	1537	1533	1530	1526	1523	1520
5000]	1584	1580	1577	1573	1569	1566	1562	1559	1555	1552	1548	1545	1542	1538	1535	1532

(Left margin label: NONCUSTODIAL PARENT INCOME)

Effective July 1, 2003

Three Children Monthly Support Schedule

CUSTODIAL PARENT INCOME

	3450	3500	3550	3600	3650	3700	3750	3800	3850	3900	3950	4000	4050	4100	4150	4200
250]	58	58	58	58	58	58	58	58	58	58	58	58	58	58	58	58
300]	58	58	58	58	58	58	58	58	58	58	58	58	58	58	58	58
350]	58	58	58	58	58	58	58	58	58	58	58	58	58	58	58	58
400]	58	58	58	58	58	58	58	58	58	58	58	58	58	58	58	58
450]	58	58	58	58	58	58	58	58	58	58	58	58	58	58	58	58
500]	58	58	58	58	58	58	58	58	58	58	58	58	58	58	58	58
550]	58	58	58	58	58	58	58	58	58	58	58	58	58	58	58	58
600]	58	58	58	58	58	58	58	58	58	58	58	58	58	58	58	58
650]	58	58	58	58	58	58	58	58	58	58	58	58	58	58	58	58
700]	58	58	58	58	58	58	58	58	58	58	58	58	58	58	58	58
750]	70	70	70	70	70	70	70	70	70	70	70	70	70	70	70	70
800]	120	120	120	120	120	120	120	120	120	120	120	120	120	120	120	120
850]	170	170	170	170	170	170	170	170	170	170	170	170	170	170	170	170
900]	220	220	220	220	220	220	220	220	220	220	220	220	220	220	220	220
950]	270	270	270	270	270	270	270	270	270	270	270	270	270	270	270	270
1000]	320	320	320	320	320	320	320	320	320	320	320	320	320	320	320	320
1050]	370	370	370	370	370	370	370	370	370	370	370	370	370	370	370	370
1100]	420	420	420	420	420	420	420	420	420	420	420	420	420	420	420	420
1150]	453	452	451	450	449	448	447	446	445	444	443	442	441	440	439	437
1200]	470	469	468	467	466	465	464	463	462	461	460	459	458	456	455	454
1250]	487	486	485	484	483	482	481	480	479	478	477	475	474	473	471	470
1300]	504	503	502	501	500	499	498	497	496	495	493	492	490	489	487	486
1350]	521	520	519	518	517	516	515	514	512	511	509	508	506	505	504	502
1400]	538	537	536	535	534	533	532	530	529	527	525	524	522	521	520	518
1450]	555	554	553	552	550	549	548	546	545	543	541	540	538	537	535	534
1500]	572	571	569	568	567	566	564	562	561	559	557	556	554	553	551	550
1550]	589	587	586	585	584	582	580	578	577	575	573	572	570	569	567	566
1600]	605	604	603	601	599	598	596	594	592	591	589	587	586	584	583	581
1650]	622	621	619	617	615	613	612	610	608	606	605	603	602	600	598	597
1700]	638	637	635	633	631	629	627	626	624	622	620	619	617	616	614	612
1750]	655	653	651	649	647	645	643	641	639	638	636	634	633	631	629	628
1800]	670	668	666	664	662	660	659	657	655	653	652	650	648	646	645	643
1850]	686	684	682	680	678	676	674	672	670	669	667	665	664	662	660	659
1900]	701	699	697	695	693	691	690	688	686	684	682	681	679	677	676	674
1950]	717	715	713	711	709	707	705	703	701	699	698	696	694	692	691	689
2000]	732	730	728	726	724	722	720	718	717	715	713	711	709	708	706	704
2050]	748	746	743	741	739	737	736	734	732	730	728	726	725	723	721	719
2100]	763	761	759	757	755	753	751	749	747	745	743	741	740	738	736	735
2150]	778	776	774	772	770	768	766	764	762	760	758	756	755	753	751	750
2200]	793	791	789	787	785	783	781	779	777	775	773	772	770	768	766	764
2250]	808	806	804	802	800	798	796	794	792	790	788	786	785	783	781	778
2300]	823	821	819	817	815	813	811	809	807	805	803	801	800	797	795	793
2350]	838	836	834	832	830	828	826	824	822	820	818	816	814	812	809	807
2400]	853	851	849	847	845	843	841	839	837	835	833	831	828	826	823	821
2450]	868	866	864	862	860	857	855	853	852	850	847	845	842	840	837	835
2500]	883	881	879	876	874	872	870	868	866	864	861	859	856	854	851	849

(Left vertical axis label: NONCUSTODIAL PARENT INCOME)

Three Children Monthly Support Schedule

CUSTODIAL PARENT INCOME

	3450	3500	3550	3600	3650	3700	3750	3800	3850	3900	3950	4000	4050	4100	4150	4200
2550]	898	895	893	891	889	887	885	883	881	878	875	873	870	868	865	863
2600]	912	910	908	906	904	902	900	897	895	892	889	887	884	881	879	876
2650]	927	925	923	920	918	916	914	911	908	906	903	900	898	895	893	890
2700]	942	939	937	935	933	931	928	925	922	919	917	914	911	909	906	904
2750]	956	954	952	950	947	944	941	939	936	933	930	928	925	922	920	917
2800]	971	968	966	964	961	958	955	952	949	947	944	941	939	936	934	931
2850]	985	983	980	977	974	971	969	966	963	960	958	955	952	950	947	945
2900]	1000	997	994	991	988	985	982	979	977	974	971	968	966	963	961	958
2950]	1014	1011	1007	1004	1001	999	996	993	990	987	984	982	979	977	974	971
3000]	1027	1024	1021	1018	1015	1012	1009	1006	1003	1001	998	995	993	990	987	985
3050]	1041	1037	1034	1031	1028	1025	1022	1020	1017	1014	1011	1009	1006	1003	1001	998
3100]	1054	1051	1048	1045	1042	1039	1036	1033	1030	1027	1025	1022	1019	1017	1014	1011
3150]	1067	1064	1061	1058	1055	1052	1049	1046	1043	1041	1038	1035	1032	1030	1027	1025
3200]	1080	1077	1074	1071	1068	1065	1062	1059	1057	1054	1051	1048	1046	1043	1040	1038
3250]	1094	1090	1087	1084	1081	1078	1075	1073	1070	1067	1064	1061	1059	1056	1053	1051
3300]	1107	1104	1100	1097	1094	1091	1089	1086	1083	1080	1077	1075	1072	1069	1067	1064
3350]	1120	1117	1114	1111	1107	1105	1102	1099	1096	1093	1090	1088	1085	1082	1080	1077
3400]	1133	1130	1127	1124	1121	1118	1115	1112	1109	1106	1103	1101	1098	1095	1093	1090
3450]	1146	1143	1140	1137	1134	1131	1128	1125	1122	1119	1116	1114	1111	1108	1106	1103
3500]	1159	1156	1153	1149	1146	1143	1141	1138	1135	1132	1129	1127	1124	1121	1119	1116
3550]	1172	1169	1165	1162	1159	1156	1153	1151	1148	1145	1142	1139	1137	1134	1131	1129
3600]	1185	1181	1178	1175	1172	1169	1166	1163	1161	1158	1155	1152	1150	1147	1144	1142
3650]	1197	1194	1191	1188	1185	1182	1179	1176	1173	1171	1168	1165	1162	1160	1157	1154
3700]	1210	1207	1204	1201	1198	1195	1192	1189	1186	1183	1181	1178	1175	1172	1170	1167
3750]	1223	1220	1217	1214	1211	1208	1205	1202	1199	1196	1193	1191	1188	1185	1183	1180
3800]	1236	1232	1229	1226	1223	1220	1217	1214	1212	1209	1206	1203	1201	1198	1195	1193
3850]	1248	1245	1242	1239	1236	1233	1230	1227	1224	1221	1219	1216	1213	1211	1208	1205
3900]	1261	1258	1255	1252	1249	1246	1243	1240	1237	1234	1231	1229	1226	1223	1220	1218
3950]	1273	1270	1267	1264	1261	1258	1255	1252	1249	1247	1244	1241	1238	1236	1233	1230
4000]	1286	1283	1280	1277	1274	1271	1268	1265	1262	1259	1256	1254	1251	1248	1245	1242
4050]	1298	1295	1292	1289	1286	1283	1280	1277	1275	1272	1269	1266	1263	1260	1258	1255
4100]	1311	1308	1305	1302	1299	1296	1293	1290	1287	1284	1281	1278	1276	1273	1270	1267
4150]	1323	1320	1317	1314	1311	1308	1305	1302	1299	1297	1294	1291	1288	1285	1282	1279
4200]	1336	1333	1330	1326	1323	1321	1318	1315	1312	1309	1306	1303	1300	1297	1294	1292
4250]	1348	1345	1342	1339	1336	1333	1330	1327	1324	1321	1318	1315	1312	1310	1307	1304
4300]	1360	1357	1354	1351	1348	1345	1342	1339	1336	1333	1330	1327	1325	1322	1319	1316
4350]	1373	1370	1367	1364	1361	1357	1354	1351	1348	1345	1342	1340	1337	1334	1331	1328
4400]	1385	1382	1379	1376	1373	1370	1366	1363	1360	1358	1355	1352	1349	1346	1343	1340
4450]	1397	1394	1391	1388	1385	1382	1379	1376	1373	1370	1367	1364	1361	1358	1355	1353
4500]	1409	1406	1403	1400	1397	1394	1391	1388	1385	1382	1379	1376	1373	1370	1367	1365
4550]	1422	1418	1415	1412	1409	1406	1403	1400	1397	1394	1391	1388	1385	1382	1379	1377
4600]	1434	1430	1427	1424	1421	1418	1415	1412	1409	1406	1403	1400	1397	1394	1391	1389
4650]	1446	1442	1439	1436	1433	1430	1427	1424	1421	1418	1415	1412	1409	1406	1403	1401
4700]	1457	1454	1451	1448	1445	1442	1439	1436	1433	1430	1427	1424	1421	1418	1415	1413
4750]	1469	1466	1463	1460	1457	1454	1450	1447	1444	1442	1439	1436	1433	1430	1427	1425
4800]	1481	1478	1475	1472	1468	1465	1462	1459	1456	1453	1451	1448	1445	1442	1439	1436
4850]	1493	1490	1487	1483	1480	1477	1474	1471	1468	1465	1462	1460	1457	1454	1451	1448
4900]	1505	1502	1498	1495	1492	1489	1486	1483	1480	1477	1474	1471	1469	1466	1463	1460
4950]	1517	1513	1510	1507	1504	1501	1498	1495	1492	1489	1486	1483	1480	1478	1475	1472
5000]	1528	1525	1522	1519	1516	1513	1510	1507	1504	1501	1498	1495	1492	1489	1487	1484

(Left margin vertical label: NONCUSTODIAL PARENT INCOME)

Three Children Monthly Support Schedule

CUSTODIAL PARENT INCOME

	4250	4300	4350	4400	4450	4500	4550	4600	4650	4700	4750	4800	4850	4900	4950	5000
250]	58	58	58	58	58	58	58	58	58	58	58	58	58	58	58	58
300]	58	58	58	58	58	58	58	58	58	58	58	58	58	58	58	58
350]	58	58	58	58	58	58	58	58	58	58	58	58	58	58	58	58
400]	58	58	58	58	58	58	58	58	58	58	58	58	58	58	58	58
450]	58	58	58	58	58	58	58	58	58	58	58	58	58	58	58	58
500]	58	58	58	58	58	58	58	58	58	58	58	58	58	58	58	58
550]	58	58	58	58	58	58	58	58	58	58	58	58	58	58	58	58
600]	58	58	58	58	58	58	58	58	58	58	58	58	58	58	58	58
650]	58	58	58	58	58	58	58	58	58	58	58	58	58	58	58	58
700]	58	58	58	58	58	58	58	58	58	58	58	58	58	58	58	58
750]	70	70	70	70	70	70	70	70	70	70	70	70	70	70	70	70
800]	120	120	120	120	120	120	120	120	120	120	120	120	120	120	120	120
850]	170	170	170	170	170	170	170	170	170	170	170	170	170	170	170	170
900]	220	220	220	220	220	220	220	220	220	220	220	220	220	220	220	220
950]	270	270	270	270	270	270	270	270	270	270	270	270	270	270	270	270
1000]	320	320	320	320	320	320	320	320	320	320	320	320	320	320	320	320
1050]	370	370	370	370	370	370	370	370	370	370	370	370	370	370	370	370
1100]	420	419	417	416	415	414	413	412	411	410	409	408	407	406	405	404
1150]	436	435	434	433	431	430	429	428	427	426	425	424	423	422	421	420
1200]	452	451	450	449	448	446	445	444	443	442	441	440	439	438	437	436
1250]	469	467	466	465	464	462	461	460	459	458	457	456	455	453	452	451
1300]	485	483	482	481	480	478	477	476	475	474	473	471	470	469	468	467
1350]	501	499	498	497	496	494	493	492	491	489	488	487	486	485	484	483
1400]	517	515	514	513	511	510	509	508	506	505	504	503	502	501	499	498
1450]	533	531	530	528	527	526	525	523	522	521	520	518	517	516	515	513
1500]	548	547	546	544	543	541	540	539	538	536	535	534	533	531	530	528
1550]	564	563	561	560	558	557	556	554	553	552	551	549	548	546	545	543
1600]	580	578	577	575	574	573	571	570	569	567	566	565	563	561	560	558
1650]	595	594	592	591	590	588	587	585	584	583	581	580	578	576	575	573
1700]	611	609	608	606	605	604	602	601	599	598	596	594	593	591	589	588
1750]	626	625	623	622	620	619	618	616	615	613	611	609	607	606	604	602
1800]	642	640	639	637	636	634	633	631	629	627	626	624	622	620	618	617
1850]	657	655	654	652	651	650	648	646	644	642	640	638	637	635	633	631
1900]	672	671	669	668	666	664	662	660	659	657	655	653	651	649	647	646
1950]	688	686	684	683	681	679	677	675	673	671	669	667	665	664	662	660
2000]	703	701	700	698	696	694	691	689	687	686	684	682	680	678	676	674
2050]	718	716	714	712	710	708	706	704	702	700	698	696	694	692	690	689
2100]	733	731	729	727	724	722	720	718	716	714	712	710	708	706	705	703
2150]	748	745	743	741	739	737	734	732	730	728	726	724	722	721	719	717
2200]	762	760	757	755	753	751	749	747	745	742	740	739	737	735	733	731
2250]	776	774	772	769	767	765	763	761	759	757	755	753	751	749	747	745
2300]	790	788	786	783	781	779	777	775	773	771	769	767	765	763	761	759
2350]	804	802	800	797	795	793	791	789	787	785	783	780	778	777	775	773
2400]	818	816	814	811	809	807	805	803	801	798	796	794	792	790	788	786
2450]	832	830	828	825	823	821	819	817	814	812	810	808	806	804	802	800
2500]	846	844	842	839	837	835	833	830	828	826	824	822	820	818	816	814

(Left margin vertical label: NONCUSTODIAL PARENT INCOME)

Effective July 1, 2003

Three Children Monthly Support Schedule

CUSTODIAL PARENT INCOME

	4250	4300	4350	4400	4450	4500	4550	4600	4650	4700	4750	4800	4850	4900	4950	5000
2550]	860	858	855	853	851	849	846	844	842	840	838	836	834	832	830	828
2600]	874	872	869	867	865	862	860	858	856	854	851	849	847	845	843	841
2650]	888	885	883	881	878	876	874	871	869	867	865	863	861	859	857	855
2700]	901	899	897	894	892	890	887	885	883	881	879	876	874	872	870	868
2750]	915	913	910	908	905	903	901	899	896	894	892	890	888	886	884	882
2800]	929	926	924	921	919	917	914	912	910	908	906	903	901	899	897	895
2850]	942	940	937	935	932	930	928	926	923	921	919	917	915	913	911	909
2900]	956	953	951	948	946	944	941	939	937	935	932	930	928	926	924	922
2950]	969	966	964	962	959	957	955	952	950	948	946	944	941	939	937	935
3000]	982	980	977	975	973	970	968	966	963	961	959	957	955	953	950	948
3050]	996	993	991	988	986	984	981	979	977	974	972	970	968	966	964	962
3100]	1009	1006	1004	1001	999	997	994	992	990	988	985	983	981	979	977	975
3150]	1022	1020	1017	1015	1012	1010	1008	1005	1003	1001	999	996	994	992	990	988
3200]	1035	1033	1030	1028	1025	1023	1021	1018	1016	1014	1012	1009	1007	1005	1003	1001
3250]	1048	1046	1043	1041	1039	1036	1034	1032	1029	1027	1025	1022	1020	1018	1016	1013
3300]	1061	1059	1056	1054	1052	1049	1047	1045	1042	1040	1038	1035	1033	1031	1029	1026
3350]	1075	1072	1070	1067	1065	1062	1060	1058	1055	1053	1051	1048	1046	1044	1041	1039
3400]	1087	1085	1082	1080	1078	1075	1073	1071	1068	1066	1063	1061	1059	1056	1054	1052
3450]	1100	1098	1095	1093	1091	1088	1086	1083	1081	1079	1076	1074	1071	1069	1067	1065
3500]	1113	1111	1108	1106	1103	1101	1099	1096	1094	1091	1089	1087	1084	1082	1080	1077
3550]	1126	1124	1121	1119	1116	1114	1111	1109	1106	1104	1102	1099	1097	1095	1092	1090
3600]	1139	1137	1134	1132	1129	1126	1124	1121	1119	1117	1114	1112	1110	1107	1105	1103
3650]	1152	1149	1147	1144	1142	1139	1137	1134	1132	1129	1127	1124	1122	1120	1118	1115
3700]	1165	1162	1159	1157	1154	1152	1149	1147	1144	1142	1139	1137	1135	1132	1130	1128
3750]	1177	1175	1172	1169	1167	1164	1162	1159	1157	1154	1152	1150	1147	1145	1143	1140
3800]	1190	1187	1185	1182	1179	1177	1174	1172	1169	1167	1164	1162	1160	1157	1155	1153
3850]	1202	1200	1197	1194	1192	1189	1187	1184	1182	1179	1177	1175	1172	1170	1168	1165
3900]	1215	1212	1210	1207	1204	1202	1199	1197	1194	1192	1189	1187	1185	1182	1180	1178
3950]	1227	1225	1222	1219	1217	1214	1212	1209	1207	1204	1202	1199	1197	1195	1192	1190
4000]	1240	1237	1234	1232	1229	1227	1224	1222	1219	1217	1214	1212	1209	1207	1205	1202
4050]	1252	1249	1247	1244	1242	1239	1236	1234	1231	1229	1227	1224	1222	1219	1217	1215
4100]	1264	1262	1259	1256	1254	1251	1249	1246	1244	1241	1239	1236	1234	1232	1229	1227
4150]	1277	1274	1271	1269	1266	1264	1261	1259	1256	1254	1251	1249	1246	1244	1242	1239
4200]	1289	1286	1284	1281	1278	1276	1273	1271	1268	1266	1263	1261	1259	1256	1254	1252
4250]	1301	1299	1296	1293	1291	1288	1286	1283	1281	1278	1276	1273	1271	1268	1266	1264
4300]	1313	1311	1308	1305	1303	1300	1298	1295	1293	1290	1288	1285	1283	1281	1278	1276
4350]	1326	1323	1320	1318	1315	1312	1310	1307	1305	1302	1300	1298	1295	1293	1290	1288
4400]	1338	1335	1332	1330	1327	1325	1322	1319	1317	1315	1312	1310	1307	1305	1303	1300
4450]	1350	1347	1344	1342	1339	1337	1334	1332	1329	1327	1324	1322	1319	1317	1315	1312
4500]	1362	1359	1357	1354	1351	1349	1346	1344	1341	1339	1336	1334	1331	1329	1327	1324
4550]	1374	1371	1369	1366	1363	1361	1358	1356	1353	1351	1348	1346	1344	1341	1339	1336
4600]	1386	1383	1381	1378	1375	1373	1370	1368	1365	1363	1360	1358	1356	1353	1351	1349
4650]	1398	1395	1393	1390	1387	1385	1382	1380	1377	1375	1372	1370	1368	1365	1363	1361
4700]	1410	1407	1405	1402	1399	1397	1394	1392	1389	1387	1384	1382	1379	1377	1375	1372
4750]	1422	1419	1416	1414	1411	1409	1406	1404	1401	1399	1396	1394	1391	1389	1387	1384
4800]	1434	1431	1428	1426	1423	1421	1418	1416	1413	1411	1408	1406	1403	1401	1399	1396
4850]	1446	1443	1440	1438	1435	1432	1430	1427	1425	1422	1420	1418	1415	1413	1411	1408
4900]	1457	1455	1452	1450	1447	1444	1442	1439	1437	1434	1432	1429	1427	1425	1422	1420
4950]	1469	1467	1464	1461	1459	1456	1454	1451	1449	1446	1444	1441	1439	1437	1434	1432
5000]	1481	1478	1476	1473	1471	1468	1465	1463	1460	1458	1456	1453	1451	1448	1446	1444

(Left margin label, top to bottom: NONCUSTODIAL PARENT INCOME)

Four Children Monthly Support Schedule

CUSTODIAL PARENT INCOME

	0	250	300	350	400	450	500	550	600	650	700	750	800	850	900	950	1000
250]	64	64	64	64	64	64	64	64	64	64	64	64	64	64	64	64	64
300]	69	69	69	69	69	69	69	69	69	69	69	66	66	66	64	64	64
350]	74	74	74	74	74	74	74	74	74	74	74	71	71	71	67	67	67
400]	79	79	79	79	79	79	79	79	79	79	79	75	75	75	71	71	71
450]	84	84	84	84	84	84	84	84	84	84	84	80	80	80	75	75	75
500]	89	89	89	89	89	89	89	89	89	89	89	84	84	84	79	79	79
550]	94	94	94	94	94	94	94	94	94	94	94	89	89	89	83	83	83
600]	99	99	99	99	99	99	99	99	99	99	99	93	93	93	87	87	87
650]	104	104	104	104	104	104	104	104	104	104	104	98	98	98	91	91	91
700]	109	109	109	109	109	109	109	109	109	109	109	102	102	102	95	95	95
750]	125	125	125	125	125	125	125	125	125	125	125	118	118	118	110	110	110
800]	175	175	175	175	175	175	175	175	175	175	175	168	168	168	160	160	160
850]	225	225	225	225	225	225	225	225	225	225	225	218	218	218	210	210	210
900]	275	275	275	275	275	275	275	275	275	275	275	268	268	268	260	260	260
950]	325	325	325	325	325	325	325	325	325	325	325	318	318	318	310	310	310
1000]	375	375	375	375	375	375	375	375	375	375	375	368	368	368	360	360	360
1050]	425	425	425	425	425	425	425	425	425	425	425	418	418	418	410	410	410
1100]	475	475	475	475	475	475	475	475	475	475	475	468	468	468	460	460	460
1150]	525	525	525	525	525	525	525	525	525	525	525	518	518	518	510	510	510
1200]	575	575	575	575	575	575	575	575	575	575	575	568	568	568	560	560	560
1250]	625	625	625	625	625	625	625	625	625	625	625	618	618	618	610	610	610
1300]	675	675	675	675	675	675	675	675	675	675	675	668	668	668	660	660	660
1350]	725	725	725	725	725	725	725	725	725	725	725	718	718	718	710	710	707
1400]	775	775	775	775	775	775	775	775	775	775	775	750	746	741	736	732	727
1450]	825	825	825	825	825	825	825	825	825	825	825	771	766	761	756	752	747
1500]	859	859	859	859	859	859	859	859	859	859	859	791	786	781	776	772	768
1550]	885	885	885	885	885	885	885	885	885	885	885	811	806	801	796	792	787
1600]	911	911	911	911	911	911	911	911	911	911	911	831	826	821	816	812	807
1650]	932	932	932	932	932	932	932	932	932	932	932	850	845	840	836	831	827
1700]	952	952	952	952	952	952	952	952	952	952	952	870	865	860	855	851	847
1750]	972	972	972	972	972	972	972	972	972	972	972	889	884	879	875	870	866
1800]	991	991	991	991	991	991	991	991	991	991	991	908	903	899	894	890	886
1850]	1011	1011	1011	1011	1011	1011	1011	1011	1011	1011	1011	927	923	918	914	909	905
1900]	1031	1031	1031	1031	1031	1031	1031	1031	1031	1031	1031	946	942	937	933	928	924
1950]	1051	1051	1051	1051	1051	1051	1051	1051	1051	1051	1051	965	961	956	952	947	942
2000]	1071	1071	1071	1071	1071	1071	1071	1071	1071	1071	1071	984	980	975	970	966	961
2050]	1091	1091	1091	1091	1091	1091	1091	1091	1091	1091	1091	1003	998	993	989	984	980
2100]	1111	1111	1111	1111	1111	1111	1111	1111	1111	1111	1111	1022	1017	1012	1007	1003	999
2150]	1131	1131	1131	1131	1131	1131	1131	1131	1131	1131	1131	1040	1035	1030	1026	1021	1017
2200]	1150	1150	1150	1150	1150	1150	1150	1150	1150	1150	1150	1058	1053	1049	1044	1040	1036
2250]	1167	1167	1167	1167	1167	1167	1167	1167	1167	1167	1167	1077	1072	1067	1063	1058	1054
2300]	1185	1185	1185	1185	1185	1185	1185	1185	1185	1185	1185	1095	1090	1085	1081	1077	1072
2350]	1202	1202	1202	1202	1202	1202	1202	1202	1202	1202	1202	1113	1108	1103	1099	1095	1091
2400]	1219	1219	1219	1219	1219	1219	1219	1219	1219	1219	1219	1131	1126	1122	1117	1113	1109
2450]	1236	1236	1236	1236	1236	1236	1236	1236	1236	1236	1236	1149	1144	1140	1135	1131	1127
2500]	1253	1253	1253	1253	1253	1253	1253	1253	1253	1253	1253	1167	1162	1158	1153	1149	1145

(Row label: NONCUSTODIAL PARENT INCOME)

Four Children Monthly Support Schedule

CUSTODIAL PARENT INCOME

	0	250	300	350	400	450	500	550	600	650	700	750	800	850	900	950	1000
2550]	1270	1270	1270	1270	1270	1270	1270	1270	1270	1270	1270	1185	1180	1176	1171	1167	1163
2600]	1287	1287	1287	1287	1287	1287	1287	1287	1287	1287	1287	1202	1198	1194	1189	1185	1181
2650]	1305	1305	1305	1305	1305	1305	1305	1305	1305	1305	1305	1220	1216	1212	1207	1203	1199
2700]	1322	1322	1322	1322	1322	1322	1322	1322	1322	1322	1322	1238	1234	1229	1225	1221	1217
2750]	1339	1339	1339	1339	1339	1339	1339	1339	1339	1339	1339	1256	1252	1247	1243	1239	1235
2800]	1356	1356	1356	1356	1356	1356	1356	1356	1356	1356	1356	1274	1269	1265	1261	1256	1252
2850]	1373	1373	1373	1373	1373	1373	1373	1373	1373	1373	1373	1291	1287	1282	1278	1274	1269
2900]	1389	1389	1389	1389	1389	1389	1389	1389	1389	1389	1389	1309	1304	1300	1295	1291	1287
2950]	1406	1406	1406	1406	1406	1406	1406	1406	1406	1406	1406	1326	1321	1317	1313	1308	1304
3000]	1422	1422	1422	1422	1422	1422	1422	1422	1422	1422	1422	1343	1339	1334	1330	1326	1322
3050]	1439	1439	1439	1439	1439	1439	1439	1439	1439	1439	1439	1360	1356	1351	1347	1343	1339
3100]	1455	1455	1455	1455	1455	1455	1455	1455	1455	1455	1455	1377	1373	1369	1364	1360	1356
3150]	1472	1472	1472	1472	1472	1472	1472	1472	1472	1472	1472	1394	1390	1386	1382	1377	1374
3200]	1488	1488	1488	1488	1488	1488	1488	1488	1488	1488	1488	1412	1407	1403	1399	1395	1391
3250]	1505	1505	1505	1505	1505	1505	1505	1505	1505	1505	1505	1429	1424	1420	1416	1412	1408
3300]	1522	1522	1522	1522	1522	1522	1522	1522	1522	1522	1522	1446	1441	1437	1433	1429	1425
3350]	1538	1538	1538	1538	1538	1538	1538	1538	1538	1538	1538	1462	1458	1454	1450	1446	1442
3400]	1555	1555	1555	1555	1555	1555	1555	1555	1555	1555	1555	1479	1475	1471	1467	1463	1459
3450]	1571	1571	1571	1571	1571	1571	1571	1571	1571	1571	1571	1496	1492	1488	1484	1480	1476
3500]	1588	1588	1588	1588	1588	1588	1588	1588	1588	1588	1588	1513	1509	1505	1501	1497	1493
3550]	1604	1604	1604	1604	1604	1604	1604	1604	1604	1604	1604	1530	1526	1522	1518	1514	1511
3600]	1621	1621	1621	1621	1621	1621	1621	1621	1621	1621	1621	1547	1543	1539	1535	1531	1528
3650]	1637	1637	1637	1637	1637	1637	1637	1637	1637	1637	1637	1564	1560	1556	1552	1548	1545
3700]	1653	1653	1653	1653	1653	1653	1653	1653	1653	1653	1653	1581	1577	1573	1569	1565	1561
3750]	1669	1669	1669	1669	1669	1669	1669	1669	1669	1669	1669	1597	1593	1590	1586	1582	1578
3800]	1685	1685	1685	1685	1685	1685	1685	1685	1685	1685	1685	1614	1610	1606	1603	1599	1595
3850]	1701	1701	1701	1701	1701	1701	1701	1701	1701	1701	1701	1631	1627	1623	1619	1616	1612
3900]	1717	1717	1717	1717	1717	1717	1717	1717	1717	1717	1717	1648	1644	1640	1636	1633	1629
3950]	1733	1733	1733	1733	1733	1733	1733	1733	1733	1733	1733	1664	1661	1657	1653	1650	1646
4000]	1749	1749	1749	1749	1749	1749	1749	1749	1749	1749	1749	1681	1677	1674	1670	1666	1663
4050]	1765	1765	1765	1765	1765	1765	1765	1765	1765	1765	1765	1698	1694	1690	1687	1683	1680
4100]	1781	1781	1781	1781	1781	1781	1781	1781	1781	1781	1781	1714	1711	1707	1704	1700	1697
4150]	1797	1797	1797	1797	1797	1797	1797	1797	1797	1797	1797	1731	1727	1724	1720	1717	1713
4200]	1813	1813	1813	1813	1813	1813	1813	1813	1813	1813	1813	1748	1744	1741	1737	1734	1729
4250]	1829	1829	1829	1829	1829	1829	1829	1829	1829	1829	1829	1764	1761	1757	1754	1749	1743
4300]	1845	1845	1845	1845	1845	1845	1845	1845	1845	1845	1845	1781	1777	1774	1769	1763	1757
4350]	1861	1861	1861	1861	1861	1861	1861	1861	1861	1861	1861	1798	1794	1789	1783	1777	1770
4400]	1877	1877	1877	1877	1877	1877	1877	1877	1877	1877	1877	1814	1809	1803	1797	1790	1784
4450]	1893	1893	1893	1893	1893	1893	1893	1893	1893	1893	1893	1829	1823	1816	1810	1804	1798
4500]	1909	1909	1909	1909	1909	1909	1909	1909	1909	1909	1909	1843	1836	1830	1824	1818	1812
4550]	1925	1925	1925	1925	1925	1925	1925	1925	1925	1925	1925	1856	1850	1844	1838	1832	1826
4600]	1941	1941	1941	1941	1941	1941	1941	1941	1941	1941	1941	1870	1864	1857	1851	1845	1839
4650]	1957	1957	1957	1957	1957	1957	1957	1957	1957	1957	1957	1883	1877	1871	1865	1859	1853
4700]	1973	1973	1973	1973	1973	1973	1973	1973	1973	1973	1973	1897	1891	1885	1879	1873	1867
4750]	1989	1989	1989	1989	1989	1989	1989	1989	1989	1989	1989	1910	1904	1898	1892	1886	1880
4800]	2005	2005	2005	2005	2005	2005	2005	2005	2005	2005	2005	1924	1918	1912	1906	1900	1894
4850]	2021	2021	2021	2021	2021	2021	2021	2021	2021	2021	2021	1937	1931	1925	1919	1913	1908
4900]	2037	2037	2037	2037	2037	2037	2037	2037	2037	2037	2037	1951	1945	1939	1933	1927	1921
4950]	2053	2053	2053	2053	2053	2053	2053	2053	2053	2053	2053	1964	1958	1952	1946	1941	1935
5000]	2069	2069	2069	2069	2069	2069	2069	2069	2069	2069	2069	1977	1971	1966	1960	1954	1949

NONCUSTODIAL PARENT INCOME

Four Children Monthly Support Schedule

CUSTODIAL PARENT INCOME

NONCUSTODIAL PARENT INCOME

	1050	1100	1150	1200	1250	1300	1350	1400	1450	1500	1550	1600	1650	1700	1750	1800
250]	64	64	64	64	64	64	64	64	64	64	64	64	64	64	64	64
300]	64	64	64	64	64	64	64	64	64	64	64	64	64	64	64	64
350]	67	67	67	67	67	67	64	64	64	64	64	64	64	64	64	64
400]	71	71	71	71	71	71	67	67	67	67	67	67	67	67	67	64
450]	75	75	75	75	75	75	71	71	71	71	71	71	71	71	71	66
500]	79	79	79	79	79	79	74	74	74	74	74	74	74	74	74	69
550]	83	83	83	83	83	83	78	78	78	78	78	78	78	78	78	72
600]	87	87	87	87	87	87	81	81	81	81	81	81	81	81	81	75
650]	91	91	91	91	91	91	85	85	85	85	85	85	85	85	85	78
700]	95	95	95	95	95	95	88	88	88	88	88	88	88	88	88	81
750]	110	110	110	110	110	110	103	103	103	103	103	103	103	103	103	95
800]	160	160	160	160	160	160	153	153	153	153	153	153	153	153	153	145
850]	210	210	210	210	210	210	203	203	203	203	203	203	203	203	203	195
900]	260	260	260	260	260	260	253	253	253	253	253	253	253	253	253	245
950]	310	310	310	310	310	310	303	303	303	303	303	303	303	303	303	295
1000]	360	360	360	360	360	360	353	353	353	353	353	353	353	353	353	345
1050]	410	410	410	410	410	410	403	403	403	403	403	403	403	403	403	395
1100]	460	460	460	460	460	460	453	453	453	453	453	453	453	453	453	445
1150]	510	510	510	510	510	510	503	503	503	503	503	503	503	503	503	495
1200]	560	560	560	560	560	560	553	553	553	553	553	553	553	553	553	545
1250]	610	610	610	610	610	610	603	603	603	603	603	603	603	603	603	595
1300]	660	660	660	660	660	660	653	653	653	651	647	644	641	639	636	633
1350]	703	699	695	691	687	684	680	677	674	671	668	665	662	659	656	653
1400]	723	719	715	711	708	704	701	698	694	691	688	685	682	679	676	673
1450]	743	739	735	732	728	724	721	718	714	711	708	705	702	699	696	693
1500]	763	759	755	752	748	745	741	737	734	731	728	724	721	719	716	713
1550]	783	779	775	772	768	764	761	757	754	750	747	744	741	738	735	733
1600]	803	799	795	792	788	784	780	777	773	770	767	764	761	758	755	752
1650]	823	819	815	811	807	804	800	796	793	790	786	783	780	777	775	772
1700]	843	839	835	831	827	823	819	816	812	809	806	803	800	797	794	791
1750]	862	858	854	850	846	842	839	835	832	828	825	822	819	816	813	811
1800]	881	877	873	869	865	861	858	854	851	848	845	841	838	836	833	830
1850]	900	896	892	888	884	881	877	874	870	867	864	861	858	855	852	849
1900]	919	915	911	907	903	900	896	893	889	886	883	880	877	874	871	868
1950]	938	934	930	926	922	919	915	912	908	905	902	899	896	893	890	887
2000]	957	953	949	945	941	938	934	931	927	924	921	918	915	912	909	905
2050]	976	972	968	964	960	956	953	949	946	943	940	937	933	930	927	924
2100]	994	990	986	982	979	975	972	968	965	962	959	955	952	949	946	943
2150]	1013	1009	1005	1001	997	994	990	987	984	981	977	974	970	967	964	961
2200]	1031	1027	1024	1020	1016	1013	1009	1006	1002	999	995	992	989	986	983	980
2250]	1050	1046	1042	1038	1035	1031	1028	1024	1021	1017	1014	1010	1007	1004	1001	998
2300]	1068	1064	1060	1057	1053	1050	1064	1061	1057	1054	1050	1047	1044	1041	1038	1035
2350]	1087	1083	1079	1075	1072	1068	1082	1079	1075	1072	1068	1065	1062	1059	1056	1053
2400]	1105	1101	1097	1094	1090	1086	1100	1097	1093	1090	1087	1083	1080	1077	1074	1071
2450]	1123	1119	1116	1112	1108	1104	1118	1115	1111	1108	1105	1101	1098	1095	1092	1089
2500]	1141	1137	1134	1130	1126	1122	1118	1115	1111	1108	1105	1101	1098	1095	1092	1089

Four Children Monthly Support Schedule

CUSTODIAL PARENT INCOME

	1050	1100	1150	1200	1250	1300	1350	1400	1450	1500	1550	1600	1650	1700	1750	1800
2550]	1159	1156	1152	1148	1144	1140	1136	1133	1129	1126	1123	1119	1116	1113	1110	1107
2600]	1178	1173	1169	1165	1162	1158	1154	1151	1147	1144	1141	1137	1134	1131	1128	1125
2650]	1195	1191	1187	1183	1179	1176	1172	1169	1165	1162	1158	1155	1152	1149	1146	1143
2700]	1213	1209	1205	1201	1197	1193	1190	1186	1183	1180	1176	1173	1170	1167	1164	1161
2750]	1230	1226	1222	1219	1215	1211	1208	1204	1201	1197	1194	1191	1188	1185	1182	1179
2800]	1248	1244	1240	1236	1232	1229	1225	1222	1218	1215	1212	1209	1206	1203	1200	1197
2850]	1265	1261	1258	1254	1250	1246	1243	1239	1236	1233	1230	1226	1223	1220	1217	1215
2900]	1283	1279	1275	1271	1268	1264	1261	1257	1254	1250	1247	1244	1241	1238	1235	1232
2950]	1300	1296	1293	1289	1285	1282	1278	1275	1271	1268	1265	1262	1259	1256	1253	1250
3000]	1318	1314	1310	1306	1303	1299	1296	1292	1289	1286	1283	1279	1276	1273	1271	1268
3050]	1335	1331	1327	1324	1320	1317	1313	1310	1306	1303	1300	1297	1294	1291	1288	1285
3100]	1352	1348	1345	1341	1338	1334	1331	1327	1324	1321	1318	1315	1312	1309	1306	1303
3150]	1370	1366	1362	1358	1355	1351	1348	1345	1341	1338	1335	1332	1329	1326	1323	1321
3200]	1387	1383	1379	1376	1372	1369	1365	1362	1359	1356	1353	1350	1347	1344	1341	1338
3250]	1404	1400	1397	1393	1390	1386	1383	1380	1376	1373	1370	1367	1364	1361	1358	1356
3300]	1421	1418	1414	1410	1407	1404	1400	1397	1394	1391	1388	1385	1382	1379	1376	1373
3350]	1438	1435	1431	1428	1424	1421	1417	1414	1411	1408	1405	1402	1399	1396	1393	1391
3400]	1456	1452	1448	1445	1441	1438	1435	1432	1428	1425	1422	1419	1416	1414	1411	1407
3450]	1473	1469	1466	1462	1459	1455	1452	1449	1446	1443	1440	1437	1434	1431	1427	1422
3500]	1490	1486	1483	1479	1476	1473	1469	1466	1463	1460	1457	1454	1451	1447	1442	1437
3550]	1507	1503	1500	1496	1493	1490	1486	1483	1480	1477	1474	1471	1467	1462	1457	1452
3600]	1524	1520	1517	1513	1510	1507	1504	1501	1497	1494	1491	1487	1482	1477	1472	1467
3650]	1541	1537	1534	1531	1527	1524	1521	1518	1515	1512	1508	1502	1497	1492	1487	1482
3700]	1558	1554	1551	1548	1544	1541	1538	1535	1532	1528	1522	1517	1512	1507	1502	1497
3750]	1575	1571	1568	1565	1561	1558	1555	1552	1548	1542	1537	1532	1526	1521	1516	1512
3800]	1592	1588	1585	1582	1578	1575	1572	1568	1562	1557	1552	1546	1541	1536	1531	1526
3850]	1609	1605	1602	1599	1596	1592	1588	1582	1577	1571	1566	1561	1556	1551	1546	1541
3900]	1626	1622	1619	1616	1613	1608	1602	1597	1591	1586	1581	1576	1570	1565	1561	1556
3950]	1643	1639	1636	1633	1628	1622	1617	1611	1606	1600	1595	1590	1585	1580	1575	1570
4000]	1659	1656	1653	1648	1642	1637	1631	1626	1620	1615	1610	1605	1600	1595	1590	1585
4050]	1676	1673	1668	1663	1657	1651	1645	1640	1635	1629	1624	1619	1614	1609	1604	1600
4100]	1693	1689	1683	1677	1671	1665	1660	1654	1649	1644	1639	1633	1629	1624	1619	1614
4150]	1709	1703	1697	1691	1685	1680	1674	1669	1663	1658	1653	1648	1643	1638	1633	1629
4200]	1723	1717	1711	1705	1699	1694	1688	1683	1678	1672	1667	1662	1657	1652	1648	1643
4250]	1737	1731	1725	1719	1713	1708	1702	1697	1692	1687	1682	1677	1672	1667	1662	1657
4300]	1751	1745	1739	1733	1727	1722	1717	1711	1706	1701	1696	1691	1686	1681	1677	1672
4350]	1764	1759	1753	1747	1742	1736	1731	1725	1720	1715	1710	1705	1700	1696	1691	1686
4400]	1778	1772	1767	1761	1756	1750	1745	1740	1734	1729	1724	1719	1715	1710	1705	1701
4450]	1792	1786	1781	1775	1770	1764	1759	1754	1749	1743	1739	1734	1729	1724	1719	1715
4500]	1806	1800	1795	1789	1784	1778	1773	1768	1763	1758	1753	1748	1743	1738	1734	1729
4550]	1820	1814	1808	1803	1798	1792	1787	1782	1777	1772	1767	1762	1757	1753	1748	1743
4600]	1834	1828	1822	1817	1811	1806	1801	1796	1791	1786	1781	1776	1771	1767	1762	1757
4650]	1847	1842	1836	1831	1825	1820	1815	1810	1805	1800	1795	1790	1786	1781	1776	1771
4700]	1861	1855	1850	1845	1839	1834	1829	1824	1819	1814	1809	1804	1800	1795	1790	1785
4750]	1875	1869	1864	1858	1853	1848	1843	1838	1833	1828	1823	1818	1813	1808	1803	1798
4800]	1888	1883	1878	1872	1867	1862	1857	1852	1847	1842	1837	1832	1827	1822	1817	1812
4850]	1902	1897	1891	1886	1881	1876	1871	1866	1861	1856	1851	1845	1840	1835	1830	1825
4900]	1916	1910	1905	1900	1894	1889	1884	1879	1875	1869	1864	1859	1854	1848	1843	1838
4950]	1929	1924	1919	1913	1908	1903	1898	1893	1888	1883	1877	1872	1867	1862	1857	1852
5000]	1943	1938	1932	1927	1922	1917	1912	1907	1901	1896	1891	1885	1880	1875	1870	1865

NONCUSTODIAL PARENT INCOME

Four Children Monthly Support Schedule

CUSTODIAL PARENT INCOME

	1850	1900	1950	2000	2050	2100	2150	2200	2250	2300	2350	2400	2450	2500	2550	2600
250]	64	64	64	64	64	64	64	64	64	64	64	64	64	64	64	64
300]	64	64	64	64	64	64	64	64	64	64	64	64	64	64	64	64
350]	64	64	64	64	64	64	64	64	64	64	64	64	64	64	64	64
400]	64	64	64	64	64	64	64	64	64	64	64	64	64	64	64	64
450]	66	66	66	66	66	66	66	66	64	64	64	64	64	64	64	64
500]	69	69	69	69	69	69	69	69	64	64	64	64	64	64	64	64
550]	72	72	72	72	72	72	72	72	67	67	67	67	67	67	67	67
600]	75	75	75	75	75	75	75	75	69	69	69	69	69	69	69	69
650]	78	78	78	78	78	78	78	78	72	72	72	72	72	72	72	72
700]	81	81	81	81	81	81	81	81	74	74	74	74	74	74	74	74
750]	95	95	95	95	95	95	95	95	88	88	88	88	88	88	88	88
800]	145	145	145	145	145	145	145	145	138	138	138	138	138	138	138	138
850]	195	195	195	195	195	195	195	195	188	188	188	188	188	188	188	188
900]	245	245	245	245	245	245	245	245	238	238	238	238	238	238	238	238
950]	295	295	295	295	295	295	295	295	288	288	288	288	288	288	288	288
1000]	345	345	345	345	345	345	345	345	338	338	338	338	338	338	338	338
1050]	395	395	395	395	395	395	395	395	388	388	388	388	388	388	388	388
1100]	445	445	445	445	445	445	445	445	438	438	438	438	438	438	438	438
1150]	495	495	495	495	495	495	495	495	488	488	488	488	488	488	488	488
1200]	545	545	545	545	545	545	545	545	538	538	538	538	538	538	538	538
1250]	595	595	595	595	595	595	595	594	588	588	588	586	584	583	581	579
1300]	630	628	625	623	621	619	616	614	612	610	608	606	604	602	600	598
1350]	651	648	646	643	641	639	636	634	632	630	628	626	624	622	620	618
1400]	671	668	666	663	661	659	656	654	652	650	648	646	644	642	640	638
1450]	690	688	685	683	681	678	676	674	672	669	667	665	663	661	659	657
1500]	710	708	705	703	700	698	696	694	691	689	687	685	682	680	678	676
1550]	730	727	725	722	720	718	715	713	711	708	706	704	702	700	698	696
1600]	750	747	745	742	740	737	735	732	730	728	725	723	721	719	717	715
1650]	769	767	764	762	759	756	754	751	749	747	745	742	740	738	736	734
1700]	789	786	783	781	778	776	773	771	768	766	764	761	759	757	755	753
1750]	808	805	803	800	797	795	792	790	787	785	783	780	778	776	774	772
1800]	827	824	822	819	816	814	811	809	806	804	802	799	797	795	793	791
1850]	846	843	841	838	835	833	830	828	825	823	821	818	816	814	812	810
1900]	865	862	859	857	854	851	849	846	844	842	839	837	835	833	831	829
1950]	884	881	878	875	873	870	868	865	863	860	858	856	854	852	849	847
2000]	903	900	897	894	891	889	886	884	881	879	877	875	872	870	868	866
2050]	921	918	916	913	910	908	905	903	900	898	895	893	891	889	887	885
2100]	940	937	934	931	929	926	924	921	919	916	914	912	910	907	905	903
2150]	958	955	953	950	947	945	942	940	937	935	933	930	928	926	924	922
2200]	977	974	971	968	966	963	961	958	956	953	951	949	947	944	942	940
2250]	995	992	989	987	984	982	979	976	974	972	969	967	965	963	961	959
2300]	1013	1011	1008	1005	1002	1000	997	995	992	990	988	985	983	981	979	977
2350]	1032	1029	1026	1023	1021	1018	1016	1013	1011	1008	1006	1004	1002	999	997	995
2400]	1050	1047	1044	1042	1039	1036	1034	1031	1029	1027	1024	1022	1020	1018	1015	1013
2450]	1068	1065	1063	1060	1057	1055	1052	1050	1047	1045	1043	1040	1038	1036	1034	1032
2500]	1086	1083	1081	1078	1075	1073	1070	1068	1065	1063	1061	1058	1056	1054	1052	1050

NONCUSTODIAL PARENT INCOME

Four Children Monthly Support Schedule

CUSTODIAL PARENT INCOME

NONCUSTODIAL PARENT INCOME

	1850	1900	1950	2000	2050	2100	2150	2200	2250	2300	2350	2400	2450	2500	2550	2600
2550]	1104	1101	1099	1096	1093	1091	1088	1086	1083	1081	1079	1077	1074	1072	1070	1068
2600]	1122	1120	1117	1114	1111	1109	1106	1104	1102	1099	1097	1095	1092	1090	1088	1085
2650]	1140	1137	1135	1132	1129	1127	1124	1122	1120	1117	1115	1113	1110	1108	1105	1101
2700]	1158	1155	1153	1150	1147	1145	1142	1140	1138	1135	1133	1131	1128	1125	1121	1118
2750]	1176	1173	1171	1168	1165	1163	1160	1158	1155	1153	1151	1149	1145	1141	1138	1134
2800]	1194	1191	1188	1186	1183	1181	1178	1176	1173	1171	1169	1166	1161	1157	1154	1150
2850]	1212	1209	1206	1204	1201	1199	1196	1194	1191	1189	1186	1182	1177	1173	1170	1166
2900]	1230	1227	1224	1221	1219	1216	1214	1211	1209	1206	1202	1197	1193	1189	1185	1182
2950]	1247	1245	1242	1239	1237	1234	1232	1229	1226	1222	1217	1213	1209	1205	1201	1197
3000]	1265	1262	1260	1257	1254	1252	1249	1246	1242	1237	1233	1229	1225	1221	1217	1213
3050]	1283	1280	1277	1275	1272	1270	1266	1262	1257	1253	1249	1245	1241	1237	1233	1229
3100]	1300	1298	1295	1292	1290	1286	1282	1277	1273	1269	1264	1260	1256	1252	1248	1245
3150]	1318	1315	1313	1310	1306	1302	1297	1293	1289	1284	1280	1276	1272	1268	1264	1260
3200]	1335	1333	1330	1326	1322	1317	1313	1308	1304	1300	1296	1291	1287	1284	1280	1276
3250]	1353	1350	1347	1342	1337	1333	1328	1324	1319	1315	1311	1307	1303	1299	1295	1291
3300]	1370	1367	1362	1357	1353	1348	1344	1339	1335	1331	1326	1322	1318	1314	1311	1307
3350]	1387	1382	1377	1372	1368	1363	1359	1354	1350	1346	1342	1338	1334	1330	1326	1322
3400]	1402	1397	1392	1388	1383	1379	1374	1370	1365	1361	1357	1353	1349	1345	1341	1338
3450]	1417	1412	1407	1403	1398	1394	1389	1385	1381	1377	1372	1368	1364	1360	1357	1353
3500]	1432	1427	1423	1418	1413	1409	1404	1400	1396	1392	1388	1384	1380	1376	1372	1368
3550]	1447	1442	1438	1433	1428	1424	1420	1415	1411	1407	1403	1399	1395	1391	1387	1383
3600]	1462	1457	1453	1448	1444	1439	1435	1430	1426	1422	1418	1414	1410	1406	1402	1399
3650]	1477	1472	1468	1463	1458	1454	1450	1445	1441	1437	1433	1429	1425	1421	1417	1414
3700]	1492	1487	1483	1478	1473	1469	1465	1460	1456	1452	1448	1444	1440	1436	1432	1429
3750]	1507	1502	1497	1493	1488	1484	1480	1475	1471	1467	1463	1459	1455	1451	1448	1444
3800]	1522	1517	1512	1508	1503	1499	1495	1490	1486	1482	1478	1474	1470	1466	1462	1459
3850]	1536	1532	1527	1522	1518	1514	1509	1505	1501	1497	1493	1489	1485	1481	1477	1473
3900]	1551	1546	1542	1537	1533	1528	1524	1520	1516	1512	1508	1504	1500	1496	1492	1487
3950]	1566	1561	1556	1552	1548	1543	1539	1535	1531	1527	1523	1519	1515	1510	1506	1502
4000]	1580	1576	1571	1567	1562	1558	1554	1550	1545	1541	1537	1533	1529	1525	1520	1516
4050]	1595	1590	1586	1581	1577	1573	1568	1564	1560	1556	1552	1548	1543	1539	1535	1530
4100]	1609	1605	1600	1596	1592	1587	1583	1579	1575	1571	1566	1562	1557	1553	1549	1545
4150]	1624	1619	1615	1611	1606	1602	1598	1594	1589	1585	1580	1576	1572	1567	1563	1559
4200]	1638	1634	1629	1625	1621	1617	1612	1608	1603	1599	1594	1590	1586	1581	1577	1573
4250]	1653	1648	1644	1640	1635	1631	1627	1622	1617	1613	1608	1604	1600	1596	1591	1587
4300]	1667	1663	1658	1654	1650	1645	1641	1636	1631	1627	1623	1618	1614	1610	1605	1601
4350]	1682	1677	1673	1669	1664	1659	1655	1650	1645	1641	1636	1632	1628	1624	1619	1615
4400]	1696	1692	1687	1683	1678	1673	1668	1664	1659	1655	1650	1646	1642	1638	1633	1629
4450]	1710	1706	1701	1697	1692	1687	1682	1678	1673	1669	1664	1660	1656	1652	1647	1643
4500]	1725	1720	1715	1710	1705	1701	1696	1692	1687	1683	1678	1674	1670	1666	1661	1657
4550]	1739	1734	1729	1724	1719	1715	1710	1705	1701	1696	1692	1688	1684	1679	1675	1671
4600]	1752	1747	1743	1738	1733	1728	1724	1719	1715	1710	1706	1702	1697	1693	1689	1685
4650]	1766	1761	1756	1751	1747	1742	1737	1733	1728	1724	1720	1715	1711	1707	1703	1699
4700]	1780	1775	1770	1765	1760	1756	1751	1747	1742	1738	1734	1729	1725	1721	1717	1713
4750]	1793	1788	1783	1779	1774	1769	1765	1760	1756	1752	1747	1743	1739	1735	1731	1727
4800]	1807	1802	1797	1792	1788	1783	1778	1774	1770	1765	1761	1757	1753	1748	1744	1740
4850]	1820	1815	1810	1806	1801	1797	1792	1788	1783	1779	1775	1770	1766	1762	1758	1754
4900]	1834	1829	1824	1819	1815	1810	1806	1801	1797	1793	1788	1784	1780	1776	1772	1768
4950]	1847	1842	1837	1833	1828	1824	1819	1815	1810	1806	1802	1798	1794	1790	1786	1782
5000]	1860	1856	1851	1846	1842	1837	1833	1828	1824	1820	1815	1811	1807	1803	1799	1795

Four Children Monthly Support Schedule

CUSTODIAL PARENT INCOME

	2650	2700	2750	2800	2850	2900	2950	3000	3050	3100	3150	3200	3250	3300	3350	3400
250]	64	64	64	64	64	64	64	64	64	64	64	64	64	64	64	64
300]	64	64	64	64	64	64	64	64	64	64	64	64	64	64	64	64
350]	64	64	64	64	64	64	64	64	64	64	64	64	64	64	64	64
400]	64	64	64	64	64	64	64	64	64	64	64	64	64	64	64	64
450]	64	64	64	64	64	64	64	64	64	64	64	64	64	64	64	64
500]	64	64	64	64	64	64	64	64	64	64	64	64	64	64	64	64
550]	67	64	64	64	64	64	64	64	64	64	64	64	64	64	64	64
600]	69	64	64	64	64	64	64	64	64	64	64	64	64	64	64	64
650]	72	65	65	65	65	65	65	65	65	65	64	64	64	64	64	64
700]	74	67	67	67	67	67	67	67	67	67	64	64	64	64	64	64
750]	88	81	81	81	81	81	81	81	81	81	76	76	76	76	76	76
800]	138	131	131	131	131	131	131	131	131	131	126	126	126	126	126	126
850]	188	181	181	181	181	181	181	181	181	181	176	176	176	176	176	176
900]	238	231	231	231	231	231	231	231	231	231	226	226	226	226	226	226
950]	288	281	281	281	281	281	281	281	281	281	276	276	276	276	276	276
1000]	338	331	331	331	331	331	331	331	331	331	326	326	326	326	326	326
1050]	388	381	381	381	381	381	381	381	381	381	376	376	376	376	376	376
1100]	438	431	431	431	431	431	431	431	431	431	426	426	426	426	426	426
1150]	488	481	481	481	481	481	481	481	481	481	476	476	476	476	476	476
1200]	538	531	531	531	531	531	531	531	531	531	526	526	526	526	526	526
1250]	577	575	574	572	570	569	567	566	564	563	561	560	559	557	556	555
1300]	597	595	593	591	590	588	587	585	584	582	581	579	578	577	575	574
1350]	616	614	613	611	609	608	606	605	603	602	600	599	597	596	595	593
1400]	636	634	632	630	629	627	626	624	622	621	619	618	617	615	614	612
1450]	655	653	652	650	648	646	645	643	642	640	639	637	636	634	633	632
1500]	675	673	671	669	667	666	664	662	661	659	658	656	655	653	652	651
1550]	694	692	690	688	687	685	683	682	680	678	677	675	674	672	671	670
1600]	713	711	709	707	706	704	702	701	699	697	696	694	693	691	690	689
1650]	732	730	728	727	725	723	721	720	718	716	715	713	712	710	709	708
1700]	751	749	747	746	744	742	740	739	737	735	734	732	731	729	728	726
1750]	770	768	766	764	763	761	759	757	756	754	753	751	750	748	747	745
1800]	789	787	785	783	782	780	778	776	775	773	771	770	768	767	765	763
1850]	808	806	804	802	800	799	797	795	793	792	790	789	787	785	783	781
1900]	827	825	823	821	819	817	816	814	812	810	809	807	806	804	801	798
1950]	845	843	841	840	838	836	834	832	831	829	827	826	824	821	818	815
2000]	864	862	860	858	856	855	853	851	849	848	846	844	841	838	835	832
2050]	883	881	879	877	875	873	871	870	868	866	864	861	858	855	852	849
2100]	901	899	897	895	893	892	890	888	886	884	881	878	875	872	869	866
2150]	920	918	916	914	912	910	908	907	904	901	898	895	892	889	886	883
2200]	938	936	934	932	930	928	927	924	921	918	915	912	909	906	903	900
2250]	956	954	953	951	949	947	944	941	938	935	932	929	926	923	920	917
2300]	975	973	971	969	967	964	961	958	955	951	948	945	942	939	936	934
2350]	993	991	989	987	985	981	978	974	971	968	965	962	959	956	953	950
2400]	1011	1009	1007	1005	1001	998	994	991	988	985	981	978	975	972	970	967
2450]	1030	1028	1025	1021	1018	1014	1011	1008	1004	1001	998	995	992	989	986	983
2500]	1048	1045	1041	1038	1034	1031	1027	1024	1021	1018	1014	1011	1008	1005	1002	999

NONCUSTODIAL PARENT INCOME

Four Children Monthly Support Schedule

CUSTODIAL PARENT INCOME

	2650	2700	2750	2800	2850	2900	2950	3000	3050	3100	3150	3200	3250	3300	3350	3400
2550]	1065	1061	1058	1054	1051	1047	1044	1040	1037	1034	1031	1028	1025	1022	1019	1016
2600]	1081	1078	1074	1070	1067	1063	1060	1057	1053	1050	1047	1044	1041	1038	1035	1032
2650]	1098	1094	1090	1087	1083	1080	1076	1073	1070	1066	1063	1060	1057	1054	1051	1048
2700]	1114	1110	1106	1103	1099	1096	1092	1089	1086	1083	1079	1076	1073	1070	1067	1064
2750]	1130	1126	1122	1119	1115	1112	1109	1105	1102	1099	1095	1092	1089	1086	1083	1080
2800]	1146	1142	1139	1135	1131	1128	1125	1121	1118	1115	1112	1108	1105	1102	1099	1096
2850]	1162	1158	1155	1151	1147	1144	1141	1137	1134	1131	1128	1124	1121	1118	1115	1112
2900]	1178	1174	1170	1167	1163	1160	1156	1153	1150	1147	1143	1140	1137	1134	1131	1128
2950]	1194	1190	1186	1183	1179	1176	1172	1169	1166	1162	1159	1156	1153	1150	1147	1144
3000]	1209	1206	1202	1199	1195	1192	1188	1185	1181	1178	1175	1172	1169	1166	1163	1160
3050]	1225	1221	1218	1214	1211	1207	1204	1201	1197	1194	1191	1188	1185	1182	1178	1175
3100]	1241	1237	1234	1230	1226	1223	1220	1216	1213	1210	1207	1203	1200	1197	1194	1190
3150]	1256	1253	1249	1246	1242	1239	1235	1232	1229	1225	1222	1219	1216	1212	1209	1206
3200]	1272	1268	1265	1261	1258	1254	1251	1247	1244	1241	1238	1234	1231	1228	1224	1221
3250]	1288	1284	1280	1277	1273	1270	1266	1263	1260	1256	1253	1250	1246	1243	1239	1236
3300]	1303	1299	1296	1292	1289	1285	1282	1278	1275	1272	1268	1265	1261	1258	1254	1251
3350]	1318	1315	1311	1308	1304	1301	1297	1294	1290	1287	1283	1280	1276	1273	1269	1266
3400]	1334	1330	1327	1323	1319	1316	1313	1309	1305	1302	1298	1295	1291	1288	1284	1281
3450]	1349	1345	1342	1338	1335	1331	1328	1324	1320	1317	1313	1310	1306	1303	1299	1296
3500]	1364	1361	1357	1354	1350	1347	1343	1339	1335	1332	1328	1324	1321	1317	1314	1311
3550]	1380	1376	1372	1369	1365	1361	1357	1354	1350	1346	1343	1339	1336	1332	1329	1325
3600]	1395	1391	1388	1384	1380	1376	1372	1368	1365	1361	1357	1354	1350	1347	1344	1340
3650]	1410	1406	1403	1399	1395	1391	1387	1383	1379	1376	1372	1369	1365	1362	1358	1355
3700]	1425	1421	1417	1413	1409	1405	1402	1398	1394	1390	1387	1383	1380	1376	1373	1370
3750]	1440	1436	1432	1428	1424	1420	1416	1412	1409	1405	1402	1398	1394	1391	1388	1384
3800]	1454	1450	1446	1442	1438	1435	1431	1427	1423	1420	1416	1413	1409	1406	1402	1399
3850]	1469	1465	1461	1457	1453	1449	1445	1442	1438	1434	1431	1427	1424	1420	1417	1413
3900]	1483	1479	1475	1471	1467	1464	1460	1456	1452	1449	1445	1442	1438	1435	1431	1428
3950]	1498	1494	1490	1486	1482	1478	1474	1470	1467	1463	1460	1456	1453	1449	1446	1442
4000]	1512	1508	1504	1500	1496	1492	1489	1485	1481	1478	1474	1470	1467	1464	1460	1457
4050]	1526	1522	1518	1514	1510	1507	1503	1499	1496	1492	1488	1485	1481	1478	1475	1471
4100]	1541	1537	1533	1529	1525	1521	1517	1514	1510	1506	1503	1499	1496	1492	1489	1486
4150]	1555	1551	1547	1543	1539	1535	1531	1528	1524	1521	1517	1514	1510	1507	1503	1500
4200]	1569	1565	1561	1557	1553	1549	1546	1542	1538	1535	1531	1528	1524	1521	1518	1514
4250]	1583	1579	1575	1571	1567	1564	1560	1556	1553	1549	1546	1542	1539	1535	1532	1529
4300]	1597	1593	1589	1585	1582	1578	1574	1570	1567	1563	1560	1556	1553	1549	1546	1543
4350]	1611	1607	1603	1600	1596	1592	1588	1585	1581	1577	1574	1570	1567	1564	1560	1557
4400]	1625	1621	1617	1614	1610	1606	1602	1599	1595	1591	1588	1585	1581	1578	1574	1571
4450]	1639	1635	1631	1628	1624	1620	1616	1613	1609	1606	1602	1599	1595	1592	1588	1585
4500]	1653	1649	1645	1642	1638	1634	1630	1627	1623	1620	1616	1613	1609	1606	1603	1599
4550]	1667	1663	1659	1656	1652	1648	1644	1641	1637	1634	1630	1627	1623	1620	1617	1613
4600]	1681	1677	1673	1670	1666	1662	1658	1655	1651	1648	1644	1641	1637	1634	1631	1627
4650]	1695	1691	1687	1683	1680	1676	1672	1669	1665	1662	1658	1655	1651	1648	1645	1641
4700]	1709	1705	1701	1697	1694	1690	1686	1683	1679	1676	1672	1669	1665	1662	1658	1655
4750]	1723	1719	1715	1711	1707	1704	1700	1696	1693	1689	1686	1683	1679	1676	1672	1668
4800]	1737	1733	1729	1725	1721	1718	1714	1710	1707	1703	1700	1696	1693	1689	1686	1682
4850]	1750	1746	1743	1739	1735	1731	1728	1724	1721	1717	1714	1710	1706	1703	1699	1695
4900]	1764	1760	1756	1753	1749	1745	1742	1738	1734	1731	1727	1724	1720	1716	1713	1709
4950]	1778	1774	1770	1766	1763	1759	1755	1752	1748	1745	1741	1737	1733	1730	1726	1722
5000]	1791	1788	1784	1780	1776	1773	1769	1765	1762	1758	1754	1750	1747	1743	1739	1736

NONCUSTODIAL PARENT INCOME

Four Children Monthly Support Schedule

CUSTODIAL PARENT INCOME

	3450	3500	3550	3600	3650	3700	3750	3800	3850	3900	3950	4000	4050	4100	4150	4200
250]	64	64	64	64	64	64	64	64	64	64	64	64	64	64	64	64
300]	64	64	64	64	64	64	64	64	64	64	64	64	64	64	64	64
350]	64	64	64	64	64	64	64	64	64	64	64	64	64	64	64	64
400]	64	64	64	64	64	64	64	64	64	64	64	64	64	64	64	64
450]	64	64	64	64	64	64	64	64	64	64	64	64	64	64	64	64
500]	64	64	64	64	64	64	64	64	64	64	64	64	64	64	64	64
550]	64	64	64	64	64	64	64	64	64	64	64	64	64	64	64	64
600]	64	64	64	64	64	64	64	64	64	64	64	64	64	64	64	64
650]	64	64	64	64	64	64	64	64	64	64	64	64	64	64	64	64
700]	64	64	64	64	64	64	64	64	64	64	64	64	64	64	64	64
750]	76	76	76	76	76	76	76	76	76	76	76	76	76	76	76	76
800]	126	126	126	126	126	126	126	126	126	126	126	126	126	126	126	126
850]	176	176	176	176	176	176	176	176	176	176	176	176	176	176	176	176
900]	226	226	226	226	226	226	226	226	226	226	226	226	226	226	226	226
950]	276	276	276	276	276	276	276	276	276	276	276	276	276	276	276	276
1000]	326	326	326	326	326	326	326	326	326	326	326	326	326	326	326	326
1050]	376	376	376	376	376	376	376	376	376	376	376	376	376	376	376	376
1100]	426	426	426	426	426	426	426	426	426	426	426	426	426	426	426	426
1150]	476	476	476	476	476	476	476	476	476	476	476	476	476	476	476	476
1200]	526	526	526	526	526	526	526	526	525	524	523	522	520	518	517	515
1250]	553	552	551	550	549	548	547	546	544	543	542	540	538	537	535	533
1300]	573	572	570	569	568	567	566	565	564	562	560	558	557	555	553	551
1350]	592	591	590	588	587	586	585	584	582	580	578	576	575	573	571	569
1400]	611	610	609	607	606	605	604	602	600	598	596	594	593	591	589	587
1450]	630	629	628	627	625	624	622	620	618	616	614	612	610	608	607	605
1500]	649	648	647	646	644	643	640	638	636	634	632	630	628	626	624	622
1550]	668	667	666	664	663	660	658	656	654	652	650	648	646	644	642	640
1600]	687	686	685	683	680	678	676	674	672	669	667	665	663	661	659	657
1650]	706	705	703	701	698	696	694	691	689	687	685	683	681	679	677	675
1700]	725	723	721	718	716	713	711	709	707	704	702	700	698	696	694	692
1750]	743	741	738	736	733	731	729	726	724	722	720	718	715	713	711	709
1800]	761	758	756	753	751	748	746	744	741	739	737	735	733	731	729	727
1850]	778	775	773	770	768	766	763	761	759	756	754	752	750	748	746	744
1900]	795	793	790	788	785	783	780	778	776	773	771	769	767	765	763	761
1950]	813	810	807	805	802	800	797	795	793	790	788	786	784	782	780	778
2000]	830	827	824	822	819	817	814	812	810	807	805	803	801	799	796	794
2050]	847	844	841	839	836	834	831	829	827	824	822	820	818	815	813	811
2100]	864	861	858	856	853	851	848	846	843	841	839	837	834	832	830	828
2150]	881	878	875	873	870	868	865	863	860	858	856	853	851	849	847	844
2200]	897	895	892	889	887	884	882	879	877	874	872	870	868	865	863	861
2250]	914	911	909	906	903	901	898	896	893	891	889	886	884	882	880	877
2300]	931	928	925	923	920	917	915	912	910	908	905	903	901	898	896	893
2350]	947	945	942	939	937	934	931	929	927	924	922	919	917	914	912	909
2400]	964	961	958	956	953	950	948	945	943	940	938	936	933	930	928	925
2450]	980	977	975	972	969	967	964	962	959	957	954	952	949	946	944	941
2500]	997	994	991	988	986	983	981	978	976	973	970	968	965	962	960	957

Left margin vertical label: NONCUSTODIAL PARENT INCOME

Four Children Monthly Support Schedule

CUSTODIAL PARENT INCOME

	3450	3500	3550	3600	3650	3700	3750	3800	3850	3900	3950	4000	4050	4100	4150	4200
2550]	1013	1010	1007	1005	1002	999	997	994	992	989	986	983	981	978	976	973
2600]	1029	1026	1024	1021	1018	1016	1013	1010	1007	1005	1002	999	997	994	991	989
2650]	1045	1043	1040	1037	1034	1032	1029	1026	1023	1020	1018	1015	1012	1010	1007	1004
2700]	1061	1059	1056	1053	1050	1048	1045	1042	1039	1036	1033	1031	1028	1025	1023	1020
2750]	1078	1075	1072	1069	1066	1063	1060	1057	1055	1052	1049	1046	1044	1041	1038	1036
2800]	1094	1091	1088	1085	1082	1079	1076	1073	1070	1067	1065	1062	1059	1056	1054	1051
2850]	1109	1107	1104	1101	1098	1095	1092	1089	1086	1083	1080	1077	1075	1072	1069	1067
2900]	1125	1122	1119	1116	1113	1110	1107	1104	1101	1098	1095	1093	1090	1087	1085	1082
2950]	1141	1138	1135	1132	1128	1125	1122	1119	1117	1114	1111	1108	1105	1103	1100	1097
N 3000]	1156	1153	1150	1147	1144	1141	1138	1135	1132	1129	1126	1123	1121	1118	1115	1113
O 3050]	1172	1169	1165	1162	1159	1156	1153	1150	1147	1144	1141	1139	1136	1133	1131	1128
N 3100]	1187	1184	1181	1177	1174	1171	1168	1165	1162	1160	1157	1154	1151	1148	1146	1143
C 3150]	1202	1199	1196	1193	1190	1187	1184	1181	1178	1175	1172	1169	1166	1164	1161	1158
U 3200]	1217	1214	1211	1208	1205	1202	1199	1196	1193	1190	1187	1184	1181	1179	1176	1173
S 3250]	1233	1229	1226	1223	1220	1217	1214	1211	1208	1205	1202	1199	1197	1194	1191	1188
T 3300]	1248	1244	1241	1238	1235	1232	1229	1226	1223	1220	1217	1214	1212	1209	1206	1203
O 3350]	1263	1259	1256	1253	1250	1247	1244	1241	1238	1235	1232	1229	1227	1224	1221	1218
D 3400]	1278	1274	1271	1268	1265	1262	1259	1256	1253	1250	1247	1244	1241	1239	1236	1233
I 3450]	1293	1289	1286	1283	1280	1277	1274	1271	1268	1265	1262	1259	1256	1254	1251	1248
A																
L 3500]	1307	1304	1301	1298	1295	1292	1289	1286	1283	1280	1277	1274	1271	1268	1266	1263
3550]	1322	1319	1316	1313	1309	1306	1303	1300	1297	1294	1292	1289	1286	1283	1280	1278
P 3600]	1337	1334	1331	1327	1324	1321	1318	1315	1312	1309	1306	1304	1301	1298	1295	1293
A 3650]	1352	1348	1345	1342	1339	1336	1333	1330	1327	1324	1321	1318	1315	1313	1310	1307
R 3700]	1366	1363	1360	1357	1354	1351	1348	1345	1342	1339	1336	1333	1330	1327	1325	1322
E 3750]	1381	1378	1375	1371	1368	1365	1362	1359	1356	1353	1350	1348	1345	1342	1339	1337
N 3800]	1396	1392	1389	1386	1383	1380	1377	1374	1371	1368	1365	1362	1359	1357	1354	1351
T 3850]	1410	1407	1404	1401	1397	1394	1391	1388	1385	1382	1380	1377	1374	1371	1368	1366
3900]	1425	1421	1418	1415	1412	1409	1406	1403	1400	1397	1394	1391	1388	1386	1383	1380
I 3950]	1439	1436	1433	1430	1426	1423	1420	1417	1414	1411	1409	1406	1403	1400	1397	1394
N																
C 4000]	1454	1450	1447	1444	1441	1438	1435	1432	1429	1426	1423	1420	1417	1414	1411	1408
O 4050]	1468	1465	1462	1458	1455	1452	1449	1446	1443	1440	1437	1434	1431	1428	1425	1422
M 4100]	1482	1479	1476	1473	1470	1467	1464	1461	1458	1455	1452	1449	1445	1442	1439	1436
E 4150]	1497	1493	1490	1487	1484	1481	1478	1475	1472	1469	1466	1463	1459	1456	1453	1450
4200]	1511	1508	1505	1501	1498	1495	1492	1489	1486	1483	1480	1477	1473	1470	1467	1464
4250]	1525	1522	1519	1516	1513	1510	1507	1503	1500	1497	1494	1491	1487	1484	1481	1478
4300]	1539	1536	1533	1530	1527	1524	1521	1517	1514	1511	1508	1504	1501	1498	1495	1492
4350]	1554	1550	1547	1544	1541	1538	1534	1531	1528	1525	1521	1518	1515	1512	1509	1506
4400]	1568	1565	1561	1558	1555	1552	1548	1545	1542	1539	1535	1532	1529	1526	1523	1520
4450]	1582	1579	1576	1572	1569	1565	1562	1559	1556	1552	1549	1546	1543	1540	1537	1534
4500]	1596	1593	1589	1586	1583	1579	1576	1573	1569	1566	1563	1560	1557	1554	1551	1548
4550]	1610	1607	1603	1600	1596	1593	1590	1586	1583	1580	1577	1574	1570	1567	1564	1561
4600]	1624	1620	1617	1613	1610	1607	1603	1600	1597	1594	1590	1587	1584	1581	1578	1575
4650]	1638	1634	1631	1627	1624	1620	1617	1614	1611	1607	1604	1601	1598	1595	1592	1589
4700]	1651	1648	1644	1641	1637	1634	1631	1627	1624	1621	1618	1615	1612	1609	1605	1602
4750]	1665	1661	1658	1654	1651	1648	1644	1641	1638	1635	1631	1628	1625	1622	1619	1616
4800]	1678	1675	1671	1668	1665	1661	1658	1655	1651	1648	1645	1642	1639	1636	1633	1630
4850]	1692	1688	1685	1681	1678	1675	1671	1668	1665	1662	1659	1655	1652	1649	1646	1643
4900]	1705	1702	1698	1695	1692	1688	1685	1682	1678	1675	1672	1669	1666	1663	1660	1657
4950]	1719	1715	1712	1708	1705	1702	1698	1695	1692	1689	1686	1683	1679	1676	1673	1670
5000]	1732	1729	1725	1722	1719	1715	1712	1709	1705	1702	1699	1696	1693	1690	1687	1684

Four Children Monthly Support Schedule

CUSTODIAL PARENT INCOME

NONCUSTODIAL PARENT INCOME	4250	4300	4350	4400	4450	4500	4550	4600	4650	4700	4750	4800	4850	4900	4950	5000
250]	64	64	64	64	64	64	64	64	64	64	64	64	64	64	64	64
300]	64	64	64	64	64	64	64	64	64	64	64	64	64	64	64	64
350]	64	64	64	64	64	64	64	64	64	64	64	64	64	64	64	64
400]	64	64	64	64	64	64	64	64	64	64	64	64	64	64	64	64
450]	64	64	64	64	64	64	64	64	64	64	64	64	64	64	64	64
500]	64	64	64	64	64	64	64	64	64	64	64	64	64	64	64	64
550]	64	64	64	64	64	64	64	64	64	64	64	64	64	64	64	64
600]	64	64	64	64	64	64	64	64	64	64	64	64	64	64	64	64
650]	64	64	64	64	64	64	64	64	64	64	64	64	64	64	64	64
700]	64	64	64	64	64	64	64	64	64	64	64	64	64	64	64	64
750]	76	76	76	76	76	76	76	76	76	76	76	76	76	76	76	76
800]	126	126	126	126	126	126	126	126	126	126	126	126	126	126	126	126
850]	176	176	176	176	176	176	176	176	176	176	176	176	176	176	176	176
900]	226	226	226	226	226	226	226	226	226	226	226	226	226	226	226	226
950]	276	276	276	276	276	276	276	276	276	276	276	276	276	276	276	276
1000]	326	326	326	326	326	326	326	326	326	326	326	326	326	326	326	326
1050]	376	376	376	376	376	376	376	376	376	376	376	376	376	376	376	376
1100]	426	426	426	426	426	426	426	426	426	426	426	426	426	426	426	426
1150]	476	476	476	476	476	476	476	476	476	476	476	476	476	476	476	475
1200]	513	512	510	509	507	506	504	503	501	500	499	497	496	495	494	492
1250]	532	530	528	527	525	524	522	521	519	518	516	515	514	512	511	510
1300]	550	548	546	545	543	542	540	539	537	536	534	533	531	530	529	527
1350]	567	566	564	562	561	559	558	556	555	553	552	550	549	548	546	545
1400]	585	584	582	580	579	577	575	574	572	571	569	568	566	565	564	562
1450]	603	601	600	598	596	594	593	591	590	588	587	585	584	582	581	579
1500]	621	619	617	615	614	612	610	609	607	606	604	602	601	599	598	596
1550]	638	636	635	633	631	629	628	626	624	623	621	620	618	616	615	613
1600]	656	654	652	650	648	647	645	643	642	640	638	637	635	633	632	630
1650]	673	671	669	667	666	664	662	660	659	657	655	654	652	650	648	647
1700]	690	688	686	685	683	681	679	678	676	674	672	670	669	667	665	663
1750]	707	706	704	702	700	698	696	695	693	691	689	687	685	684	682	680
1800]	725	723	721	719	717	715	713	712	710	708	706	704	702	700	698	697
1850]	742	740	738	736	734	732	730	728	726	724	722	720	718	717	715	713
1900]	759	757	755	753	751	749	747	745	743	741	739	737	735	733	731	729
1950]	775	773	771	770	768	765	763	761	759	757	755	753	751	749	748	746
2000]	792	790	788	786	784	782	780	778	776	774	772	770	768	766	764	762
2050]	809	807	805	803	800	798	796	794	792	790	788	786	784	782	780	778
2100]	826	824	821	819	817	815	812	810	808	806	804	802	800	798	796	794
2150]	842	840	838	835	833	831	829	826	824	822	820	818	816	814	812	810
2200]	859	856	854	852	849	847	845	843	841	838	836	834	832	830	828	826
2250]	875	872	870	868	865	863	861	859	857	854	852	850	848	846	844	842
2300]	891	888	886	884	881	879	877	875	873	870	868	866	864	862	860	858
2350]	907	904	902	900	897	895	893	891	888	886	884	882	880	878	876	874
2400]	923	920	918	916	913	911	909	907	904	902	900	898	896	894	892	890
2450]	939	936	934	932	929	927	925	922	920	918	916	914	912	910	908	906
2500]	955	952	950	947	945	943	940	938	936	934	932	929	927	925	923	921

Four Children Monthly Support Schedule

CUSTODIAL PARENT INCOME

		4250	4300	4350	4400	4450	4500	4550	4600	4650	4700	4750	4800	4850	4900	4950	5000
	2550]	970	968	966	963	961	958	956	954	952	949	947	945	943	941	939	937
	2600]	986	984	981	979	976	974	972	970	967	965	963	961	959	956	954	952
	2650]	1002	999	997	994	992	990	987	985	983	981	978	976	974	972	970	968
	2700]	1017	1015	1013	1010	1008	1005	1003	1001	998	996	994	992	990	987	985	983
	2750]	1033	1031	1028	1026	1023	1021	1018	1016	1014	1012	1009	1007	1005	1003	1001	999
	2800]	1049	1046	1044	1041	1039	1036	1034	1032	1029	1027	1025	1023	1020	1018	1016	1014
	2850]	1064	1061	1059	1057	1054	1052	1049	1047	1045	1042	1040	1038	1036	1034	1031	1029
	2900]	1079	1077	1074	1072	1069	1067	1065	1062	1060	1058	1055	1053	1051	1049	1047	1045
	2950]	1095	1092	1090	1087	1085	1082	1080	1078	1075	1073	1071	1068	1066	1064	1062	1060
N	3000]	1110	1107	1105	1102	1100	1098	1095	1093	1090	1088	1086	1084	1081	1079	1077	1075
O	3050]	1125	1123	1120	1118	1115	1113	1110	1108	1106	1103	1101	1099	1097	1094	1092	1090
N	3100]	1140	1138	1135	1133	1130	1128	1126	1123	1121	1118	1116	1114	1112	1109	1107	1105
C	3150]	1156	1153	1150	1148	1145	1143	1141	1138	1136	1134	1131	1129	1127	1124	1122	1120
U	3200]	1171	1168	1166	1163	1161	1158	1156	1153	1151	1149	1146	1144	1142	1139	1137	1134
S	3250]	1186	1183	1181	1178	1176	1173	1171	1168	1166	1164	1161	1159	1156	1154	1151	1149
T	3300]	1201	1198	1196	1193	1191	1188	1186	1183	1181	1179	1176	1174	1171	1169	1166	1164
O	3350]	1216	1213	1211	1208	1206	1203	1201	1198	1196	1193	1191	1188	1186	1183	1181	1178
D	3400]	1231	1228	1225	1223	1220	1218	1215	1213	1211	1208	1205	1203	1200	1198	1195	1193
I	3450]	1246	1243	1240	1238	1235	1233	1230	1228	1225	1222	1220	1217	1215	1212	1210	1207
A																	
L	3500]	1260	1258	1255	1253	1250	1248	1245	1242	1240	1237	1234	1232	1229	1227	1224	1222
	3550]	1275	1273	1270	1267	1265	1262	1259	1257	1254	1251	1249	1246	1244	1241	1239	1236
P	3600]	1290	1287	1285	1282	1279	1277	1274	1271	1269	1266	1263	1261	1258	1256	1253	1251
A	3650]	1305	1302	1299	1297	1294	1291	1288	1286	1283	1280	1278	1275	1273	1270	1268	1265
R	3700]	1319	1317	1314	1311	1308	1305	1303	1300	1297	1295	1292	1289	1287	1284	1282	1279
E	3750]	1334	1331	1328	1325	1323	1320	1317	1314	1312	1309	1306	1304	1301	1299	1296	1294
N	3800]	1348	1345	1343	1340	1337	1334	1331	1329	1326	1323	1321	1318	1316	1313	1310	1308
T	3850]	1363	1360	1357	1354	1351	1348	1346	1343	1340	1338	1335	1332	1330	1327	1325	1322
	3900]	1377	1374	1371	1368	1365	1363	1360	1357	1354	1352	1349	1346	1344	1341	1339	1336
I	3950]	1391	1388	1385	1382	1380	1377	1374	1371	1369	1366	1363	1361	1358	1356	1353	1351
N																	
C	4000]	1405	1402	1399	1396	1394	1391	1388	1385	1383	1380	1377	1375	1372	1370	1367	1365
O	4050]	1419	1416	1413	1411	1408	1405	1402	1399	1397	1394	1391	1389	1386	1384	1381	1379
M	4100]	1433	1430	1428	1425	1422	1419	1416	1414	1411	1408	1406	1403	1400	1398	1395	1393
E	4150]	1447	1444	1442	1439	1436	1433	1430	1428	1425	1422	1420	1417	1414	1412	1409	1407
	4200]	1461	1458	1456	1453	1450	1447	1444	1442	1439	1436	1434	1431	1428	1426	1423	1421
	4250]	1475	1472	1470	1467	1464	1461	1458	1456	1453	1450	1447	1445	1442	1440	1437	1435
	4300]	1489	1486	1483	1481	1478	1475	1472	1469	1467	1464	1461	1459	1456	1454	1451	1449
	4350]	1503	1500	1497	1494	1492	1489	1486	1483	1481	1478	1475	1473	1470	1468	1465	1462
	4400]	1517	1514	1511	1508	1506	1503	1500	1497	1494	1492	1489	1487	1484	1481	1479	1476
	4450]	1531	1528	1525	1522	1519	1517	1514	1511	1508	1506	1503	1500	1498	1495	1493	1490
	4500]	1545	1542	1539	1536	1533	1530	1528	1525	1522	1519	1517	1514	1512	1509	1506	1504
	4550]	1558	1555	1553	1550	1547	1544	1541	1539	1536	1533	1531	1528	1525	1523	1520	1518
	4600]	1572	1569	1566	1563	1561	1558	1555	1552	1550	1547	1544	1542	1539	1537	1534	1531
	4650]	1586	1583	1580	1577	1574	1572	1569	1566	1563	1561	1558	1555	1553	1550	1548	1545
	4700]	1600	1597	1594	1591	1588	1585	1582	1580	1577	1574	1572	1569	1566	1564	1561	1559
	4750]	1613	1610	1607	1605	1602	1599	1596	1593	1591	1588	1585	1583	1580	1578	1575	1572
	4800]	1627	1624	1621	1618	1615	1613	1610	1607	1604	1602	1599	1596	1594	1591	1589	1586
	4850]	1640	1637	1635	1632	1629	1626	1623	1621	1618	1615	1613	1610	1607	1605	1602	1600
	4900]	1654	1651	1648	1645	1642	1640	1637	1634	1631	1629	1626	1624	1621	1618	1616	1613
	4950]	1667	1665	1662	1659	1656	1653	1650	1648	1645	1642	1640	1637	1634	1632	1629	1627
	5000]	1681	1678	1675	1672	1670	1667	1664	1661	1659	1656	1653	1651	1648	1645	1643	1640

Five or More Children Monthly Support Schedule

CUSTODIAL PARENT INCOME

	0	250	300	350	400	450	500	550	600	650	700	750	800	850	900	950	1000
250]	71	71	71	71	71	71	71	71	71	71	71	71	71	71	71	71	71
300]	76	76	76	76	76	76	76	76	76	76	76	73	73	73	71	71	71
350]	81	81	81	81	81	81	81	81	81	81	81	77	77	77	74	74	74
400]	86	86	86	86	86	86	86	86	86	86	86	82	82	82	78	78	78
450]	91	91	91	91	91	91	91	91	91	91	91	86	86	86	82	82	82
500]	96	96	96	96	96	96	96	96	96	96	96	91	91	91	86	86	86
550]	101	101	101	101	101	101	101	101	101	101	101	95	95	95	90	90	90
600]	106	106	106	106	106	106	106	106	106	106	106	100	100	100	94	94	94
650]	111	111	111	111	111	111	111	111	111	111	111	104	104	104	98	98	98
700]	116	116	116	116	116	116	116	116	116	116	116	109	109	109	102	102	102
750]	131	131	131	131	131	131	131	131	131	131	131	124	124	124	117	117	117
800]	181	181	181	181	181	181	181	181	181	181	181	174	174	174	167	167	167
850]	231	231	231	231	231	231	231	231	231	231	231	224	224	224	217	217	217
900]	281	281	281	281	281	281	281	281	281	281	281	274	274	274	267	267	267
950]	331	331	331	331	331	331	331	331	331	331	331	324	324	324	317	317	317
1000]	381	381	381	381	381	381	381	381	381	381	381	374	374	374	367	367	367
1050]	431	431	431	431	431	431	431	431	431	431	431	424	424	424	417	417	417
1100]	481	481	481	481	481	481	481	481	481	481	481	474	474	474	467	467	467
1150]	531	531	531	531	531	531	531	531	531	531	531	524	524	524	517	517	517
1200]	581	581	581	581	581	581	581	581	581	581	581	574	574	574	567	567	567
1250]	631	631	631	631	631	631	631	631	631	631	631	624	624	624	617	617	617
1300]	681	681	681	681	681	681	681	681	681	681	681	674	674	674	667	667	667
1350]	731	731	731	731	731	731	731	731	731	731	731	724	724	724	717	717	717
1400]	781	781	781	781	781	781	781	781	781	781	781	774	774	774	767	767	767
1450]	831	831	831	831	831	831	831	831	831	831	831	824	824	824	817	817	816
1500]	881	881	881	881	881	881	881	881	881	881	881	863	858	853	848	843	838
1550]	931	931	931	931	931	931	931	931	931	931	931	885	880	875	870	865	860
1600]	981	981	981	981	981	981	981	981	981	981	981	907	901	896	891	887	882
1650]	1020	1020	1020	1020	1020	1020	1020	1020	1020	1020	1020	928	923	918	913	908	904
1700]	1041	1041	1041	1041	1041	1041	1041	1041	1041	1041	1041	949	944	939	934	930	925
1750]	1062	1062	1062	1062	1062	1062	1062	1062	1062	1062	1062	970	965	960	956	951	947
1800]	1084	1084	1084	1084	1084	1084	1084	1084	1084	1084	1084	992	987	982	977	972	968
1850]	1105	1105	1105	1105	1105	1105	1105	1105	1105	1105	1105	1013	1008	1003	998	994	989
1900]	1126	1126	1126	1126	1126	1126	1126	1126	1126	1126	1126	1034	1029	1024	1019	1014	1010
1950]	1148	1148	1148	1148	1148	1148	1148	1148	1148	1148	1148	1054	1050	1045	1040	1035	1031
2000]	1169	1169	1169	1169	1169	1169	1169	1169	1169	1169	1169	1075	1070	1065	1061	1056	1052
2050]	1190	1190	1190	1190	1190	1190	1190	1190	1190	1190	1190	1096	1091	1086	1081	1077	1073
2100]	1211	1211	1211	1211	1211	1211	1211	1211	1211	1211	1211	1116	1112	1107	1102	1098	1093
2150]	1233	1233	1233	1233	1233	1233	1233	1233	1233	1233	1233	1137	1132	1127	1123	1118	1114
2200]	1253	1253	1253	1253	1253	1253	1253	1253	1253	1253	1253	1157	1152	1148	1143	1139	1134
2250]	1272	1272	1272	1272	1272	1272	1272	1272	1272	1272	1272	1178	1173	1168	1164	1159	1155
2300]	1291	1291	1291	1291	1291	1291	1291	1291	1291	1291	1291	1198	1193	1188	1184	1180	1175
2350]	1310	1310	1310	1310	1310	1310	1310	1310	1310	1310	1310	1218	1213	1209	1204	1200	1196
2400]	1329	1329	1329	1329	1329	1329	1329	1329	1329	1329	1329	1238	1233	1229	1225	1220	1216
2450]	1348	1348	1348	1348	1348	1348	1348	1348	1348	1348	1348	1258	1254	1249	1245	1241	1237
2500]	1367	1367	1367	1367	1367	1367	1367	1367	1367	1367	1367	1278	1274	1269	1265	1261	1257

NONCUSTODIAL PARENT INCOME

Five or More Children Monthly Support Schedule

CUSTODIAL PARENT INCOME

		0	250	300	350	400	450	500	550	600	650	700	750	800	850	900	950	1000
	2550]	1386	1386	1386	1386	1386	1386	1386	1386	1386	1386	1386	1298	1294	1289	1285	1281	1277
	2600]	1405	1405	1405	1405	1405	1405	1405	1405	1405	1405	1405	1318	1314	1309	1305	1301	1297
	2650]	1424	1424	1424	1424	1424	1424	1424	1424	1424	1424	1424	1338	1334	1329	1325	1321	1317
	2700]	1442	1442	1442	1442	1442	1442	1442	1442	1442	1442	1442	1358	1354	1349	1345	1341	1337
	2750]	1461	1461	1461	1461	1461	1461	1461	1461	1461	1461	1461	1378	1374	1369	1365	1361	1356
	2800]	1480	1480	1480	1480	1480	1480	1480	1480	1480	1480	1480	1398	1393	1389	1385	1380	1376
	2850]	1499	1499	1499	1499	1499	1499	1499	1499	1499	1499	1499	1417	1413	1409	1404	1400	1395
	2900]	1518	1518	1518	1518	1518	1518	1518	1518	1518	1518	1518	1437	1432	1428	1423	1419	1415
	2950]	1536	1536	1536	1536	1536	1536	1536	1536	1536	1536	1536	1456	1452	1447	1443	1438	1434
N	3000]	1555	1555	1555	1555	1555	1555	1555	1555	1555	1555	1555	1475	1471	1466	1462	1457	1453
O	3050]	1573	1573	1573	1573	1573	1573	1573	1573	1573	1573	1573	1495	1490	1485	1481	1477	1473
N	3100]	1592	1592	1592	1592	1592	1592	1592	1592	1592	1592	1592	1514	1509	1505	1500	1496	1492
C	3150]	1611	1611	1611	1611	1611	1611	1611	1611	1611	1611	1611	1533	1528	1524	1519	1515	1511
U	3200]	1629	1629	1629	1629	1629	1629	1629	1629	1629	1629	1629	1552	1547	1543	1538	1534	1530
S	3250]	1648	1648	1648	1648	1648	1648	1648	1648	1648	1648	1648	1571	1566	1562	1558	1553	1549
T	3300]	1667	1667	1667	1667	1667	1667	1667	1667	1667	1667	1667	1590	1585	1581	1577	1573	1569
O	3350]	1685	1685	1685	1685	1685	1685	1685	1685	1685	1685	1685	1608	1604	1600	1596	1592	1588
D	3400]	1704	1704	1704	1704	1704	1704	1704	1704	1704	1704	1704	1627	1623	1619	1615	1611	1607
I	3450]	1723	1723	1723	1723	1723	1723	1723	1723	1723	1723	1723	1646	1642	1638	1634	1630	1626
A																		
L	3500]	1741	1741	1741	1741	1741	1741	1741	1741	1741	1741	1741	1665	1661	1657	1653	1649	1645
	3550]	1760	1760	1760	1760	1760	1760	1760	1760	1760	1760	1760	1684	1680	1676	1672	1668	1664
P	3600]	1778	1778	1778	1778	1778	1778	1778	1778	1778	1778	1778	1703	1699	1694	1690	1687	1683
A	3650]	1797	1797	1797	1797	1797	1797	1797	1797	1797	1797	1797	1721	1717	1713	1709	1705	1702
R	3700]	1815	1815	1815	1815	1815	1815	1815	1815	1815	1815	1815	1740	1736	1732	1728	1724	1721
E	3750]	1833	1833	1833	1833	1833	1833	1833	1833	1833	1833	1833	1759	1755	1751	1747	1743	1740
N	3800]	1851	1851	1851	1851	1851	1851	1851	1851	1851	1851	1851	1778	1774	1770	1766	1762	1758
T	3850]	1869	1869	1869	1869	1869	1869	1869	1869	1869	1869	1869	1796	1792	1789	1785	1781	1777
	3900]	1887	1887	1887	1887	1887	1887	1887	1887	1887	1887	1887	1815	1811	1807	1803	1800	1796
I	3950]	1905	1905	1905	1905	1905	1905	1905	1905	1905	1905	1905	1834	1830	1826	1822	1819	1815
N																		
C	4000]	1922	1922	1922	1922	1922	1922	1922	1922	1922	1922	1922	1852	1849	1845	1841	1837	1834
O	4050]	1940	1940	1940	1940	1940	1940	1940	1940	1940	1940	1940	1871	1867	1863	1860	1856	1853
M	4100]	1958	1958	1958	1958	1958	1958	1958	1958	1958	1958	1958	1890	1886	1882	1878	1875	1871
E	4150]	1976	1976	1976	1976	1976	1976	1976	1976	1976	1976	1976	1908	1905	1901	1897	1894	1890
	4200]	1994	1994	1994	1994	1994	1994	1994	1994	1994	1994	1994	1927	1923	1919	1916	1912	1907
	4250]	2012	2012	2012	2012	2012	2012	2012	2012	2012	2012	2012	1946	1942	1938	1935	1929	1921
	4300]	2030	2030	2030	2030	2030	2030	2030	2030	2030	2030	2030	1964	1960	1957	1951	1943	1935
	4350]	2048	2048	2048	2048	2048	2048	2048	2048	2048	2048	2048	1983	1979	1973	1965	1957	1949
	4400]	2066	2066	2066	2066	2066	2066	2066	2066	2066	2066	2066	2001	1995	1987	1979	1971	1963
	4450]	2084	2084	2084	2084	2084	2084	2084	2084	2084	2084	2084	2017	2009	2001	1993	1985	1978
	4500]	2102	2102	2102	2102	2102	2102	2102	2102	2102	2102	2102	2031	2023	2015	2007	1999	1992
	4550]	2120	2120	2120	2120	2120	2120	2120	2120	2120	2120	2120	2045	2037	2029	2021	2013	2006
	4600]	2137	2137	2137	2137	2137	2137	2137	2137	2137	2137	2137	2059	2051	2043	2035	2027	2020
	4650]	2155	2155	2155	2155	2155	2155	2155	2155	2155	2155	2155	2072	2064	2057	2049	2041	2034
	4700]	2173	2173	2173	2173	2173	2173	2173	2173	2173	2173	2173	2086	2078	2070	2063	2055	2048
	4750]	2191	2191	2191	2191	2191	2191	2191	2191	2191	2191	2191	2100	2092	2084	2076	2069	2062
	4800]	2209	2209	2209	2209	2209	2209	2209	2209	2209	2209	2209	2113	2106	2098	2090	2083	2076
	4850]	2227	2227	2227	2227	2227	2227	2227	2227	2227	2227	2227	2127	2119	2112	2104	2097	2089
	4900]	2245	2245	2245	2245	2245	2245	2245	2245	2245	2245	2245	2141	2133	2125	2118	2111	2103
	4950]	2263	2263	2263	2263	2263	2263	2263	2263	2263	2263	2263	2154	2147	2139	2132	2124	2117
	5000]	2281	2281	2281	2281	2281	2281	2281	2281	2281	2281	2281	2168	2160	2153	2145	2138	2131

Five or More Children Monthly Support Schedule

CUSTODIAL PARENT INCOME

NONCUSTODIAL PARENT INCOME	1050	1100	1150	1200	1250	1300	1350	1400	1450	1500	1550	1600	1650	1700	1750	1800
250]	71	71	71	71	71	71	71	71	71	71	71	71	71	71	71	71
300]	71	71	71	71	71	71	71	71	71	71	71	71	71	71	71	71
350]	74	74	74	74	74	74	71	71	71	71	71	71	71	71	71	71
400]	78	78	78	78	78	78	74	74	74	74	74	74	74	74	74	71
450]	82	82	82	82	82	82	77	77	77	77	77	77	77	77	77	73
500]	86	86	86	86	86	86	81	81	81	81	81	81	81	81	81	76
550]	90	90	90	90	90	90	84	84	84	84	84	84	84	84	84	79
600]	94	94	94	94	94	94	88	88	88	88	88	88	88	88	88	82
650]	98	98	98	98	98	98	91	91	91	91	91	91	91	91	91	85
700]	102	102	102	102	102	102	95	95	95	95	95	95	95	95	95	88
750]	117	117	117	117	117	117	109	109	109	109	109	109	109	109	109	102
800]	167	167	167	167	167	167	159	159	159	159	159	159	159	159	159	152
850]	217	217	217	217	217	217	209	209	209	209	209	209	209	209	209	202
900]	267	267	267	267	267	267	259	259	259	259	259	259	259	259	259	252
950]	317	317	317	317	317	317	309	309	309	309	309	309	309	309	309	302
1000]	367	367	367	367	367	367	359	359	359	359	359	359	359	359	359	352
1050]	417	417	417	417	417	417	409	409	409	409	409	409	409	409	409	402
1100]	467	467	467	467	467	467	459	459	459	459	459	459	459	459	459	452
1150]	517	517	517	517	517	517	509	509	509	509	509	509	509	509	509	502
1200]	567	567	567	567	567	567	559	559	559	559	559	559	559	559	559	552
1250]	617	617	617	617	617	617	609	609	609	609	609	609	609	609	609	602
1300]	667	667	667	667	667	667	659	659	659	659	659	659	659	659	659	652
1350]	717	717	717	717	717	717	709	709	709	709	709	709	709	709	709	702
1400]	767	767	767	767	767	767	759	759	759	756	753	750	747	744	741	739
1450]	812	808	804	800	796	792	789	785	782	778	775	772	769	766	763	761
1500]	834	830	826	822	818	814	811	807	804	800	797	794	791	788	785	782
1550]	856	852	848	844	840	836	832	829	825	822	819	816	813	810	807	804
1600]	878	873	869	865	862	858	854	851	847	844	841	838	835	832	829	826
1650]	899	895	891	887	883	879	876	872	869	865	862	859	856	853	850	848
1700]	921	917	913	908	905	901	897	894	890	887	884	881	878	875	872	869
1750]	942	938	934	930	926	922	919	915	912	908	905	902	899	896	893	891
1800]	963	959	955	951	947	944	940	937	933	930	927	924	921	918	915	912
1850]	985	980	976	972	969	965	961	958	954	951	948	945	942	939	936	933
1900]	1006	1001	997	993	990	986	982	979	976	972	969	966	963	960	957	954
1950]	1027	1022	1018	1015	1011	1007	1004	1000	997	993	990	987	984	981	978	975
2000]	1047	1043	1039	1035	1032	1028	1025	1021	1018	1015	1011	1008	1005	1002	999	996
2050]	1068	1064	1060	1056	1053	1049	1046	1042	1039	1036	1032	1029	1026	1023	1020	1016
2100]	1089	1085	1081	1077	1073	1070	1066	1063	1060	1056	1053	1050	1047	1043	1040	1037
2150]	1110	1106	1102	1098	1094	1091	1087	1084	1081	1077	1074	1070	1067	1064	1061	1057
2200]	1130	1126	1122	1119	1115	1111	1108	1105	1101	1098	1094	1091	1087	1084	1081	1078
2250]	1151	1147	1143	1139	1136	1132	1129	1125	1122	1118	1115	1131	1128	1125	1122	1119
2300]	1171	1167	1164	1160	1156	1153	1149	1146	1142	1138	1135	1152	1148	1145	1142	1139
2350]	1192	1188	1184	1180	1177	1173	1169	1166	1162	1158	1155	1152	1148	1145	1142	1139
2400]	1212	1208	1205	1201	1197	1193	1190	1186	1182	1179	1175	1172	1168	1165	1162	1159
2450]	1233	1229	1225	1221	1217	1213	1210	1206	1202	1199	1195	1192	1189	1185	1182	1179
2500]	1253	1249	1245	1241	1237	1233	1229	1226	1222	1219	1215	1212	1209	1205	1202	1199

Five or More Children Monthly Support Schedule

CUSTODIAL PARENT INCOME

NONCUSTODIAL PARENT INCOME	1050	1100	1150	1200	1250	1300	1350	1400	1450	1500	1550	1600	1650	1700	1750	1800
2550]	1273	1269	1265	1261	1257	1253	1249	1246	1242	1239	1235	1232	1229	1226	1222	1219
2600]	1293	1289	1285	1281	1277	1273	1269	1266	1262	1259	1255	1252	1249	1245	1242	1239
2650]	1313	1309	1305	1301	1297	1293	1289	1285	1282	1278	1275	1272	1269	1265	1262	1259
2700]	1332	1328	1324	1320	1316	1313	1309	1305	1302	1298	1295	1292	1288	1285	1282	1279
2750]	1352	1348	1344	1340	1336	1332	1329	1325	1321	1318	1315	1311	1308	1305	1302	1299
2800]	1372	1367	1363	1359	1356	1352	1348	1345	1341	1338	1334	1331	1328	1325	1322	1319
2850]	1391	1387	1383	1379	1375	1371	1368	1364	1361	1357	1354	1351	1348	1345	1342	1339
2900]	1410	1406	1402	1399	1395	1391	1387	1384	1380	1377	1374	1371	1367	1364	1361	1358
2950]	1430	1426	1422	1418	1414	1411	1407	1403	1400	1397	1393	1390	1387	1384	1381	1378
3000]	1449	1445	1441	1437	1434	1430	1427	1423	1420	1416	1413	1410	1407	1404	1401	1398
3050]	1468	1465	1461	1457	1453	1450	1446	1443	1439	1436	1433	1429	1426	1423	1420	1417
3100]	1488	1484	1480	1476	1473	1469	1465	1462	1459	1455	1452	1449	1446	1443	1440	1437
3150]	1507	1503	1499	1496	1492	1488	1485	1481	1478	1475	1472	1468	1465	1462	1459	1457
3200]	1526	1522	1519	1515	1511	1508	1504	1501	1498	1494	1491	1488	1485	1482	1479	1476
3250]	1545	1542	1538	1534	1531	1527	1524	1520	1517	1514	1511	1507	1504	1501	1498	1496
3300]	1565	1561	1557	1553	1550	1546	1543	1540	1536	1533	1530	1527	1524	1521	1518	1515
3350]	1584	1580	1576	1573	1569	1566	1562	1559	1556	1552	1549	1546	1543	1540	1537	1535
3400]	1603	1599	1595	1592	1588	1585	1581	1578	1575	1572	1569	1566	1563	1560	1557	1552
3450]	1622	1618	1615	1611	1607	1604	1601	1597	1594	1591	1588	1585	1582	1579	1574	1568
3500]	1641	1637	1634	1630	1627	1623	1620	1617	1613	1610	1607	1604	1601	1597	1590	1584
3550]	1660	1656	1653	1649	1646	1642	1639	1636	1633	1629	1626	1623	1619	1612	1606	1599
3600]	1679	1675	1672	1668	1665	1661	1658	1655	1652	1649	1646	1641	1634	1628	1621	1615
3650]	1698	1694	1691	1687	1684	1681	1677	1674	1671	1668	1663	1656	1650	1643	1637	1630
3700]	1717	1713	1710	1706	1703	1700	1696	1693	1690	1685	1678	1671	1665	1658	1652	1646
3750]	1736	1732	1729	1725	1722	1719	1715	1712	1707	1700	1693	1687	1680	1674	1667	1661
3800]	1755	1751	1748	1744	1741	1738	1735	1729	1722	1715	1709	1702	1695	1689	1683	1676
3850]	1774	1770	1767	1763	1760	1757	1752	1744	1737	1731	1724	1717	1711	1704	1698	1692
3900]	1793	1789	1786	1782	1779	1774	1766	1759	1752	1746	1739	1732	1726	1719	1713	1707
3950]	1811	1808	1805	1801	1796	1789	1781	1774	1767	1761	1754	1747	1741	1734	1728	1722
4000]	1830	1827	1823	1818	1811	1803	1796	1789	1782	1775	1769	1762	1756	1750	1743	1737
4050]	1849	1846	1840	1833	1825	1818	1811	1804	1797	1790	1784	1777	1771	1765	1758	1752
4100]	1868	1862	1855	1847	1840	1833	1826	1819	1812	1805	1799	1792	1786	1780	1773	1767
4150]	1885	1877	1869	1862	1855	1847	1840	1833	1827	1820	1813	1807	1801	1794	1788	1782
4200]	1899	1891	1884	1876	1869	1862	1855	1848	1841	1835	1828	1822	1816	1809	1803	1797
4250]	1913	1906	1898	1891	1884	1876	1870	1863	1856	1849	1843	1837	1830	1824	1818	1812
4300]	1927	1920	1912	1905	1898	1891	1884	1877	1871	1864	1858	1851	1845	1839	1833	1827
4350]	1942	1934	1927	1920	1912	1905	1899	1892	1885	1879	1872	1866	1860	1854	1848	1842
4400]	1956	1948	1941	1934	1927	1920	1913	1906	1900	1893	1887	1881	1875	1869	1863	1857
4450]	1970	1963	1955	1948	1941	1934	1928	1921	1914	1908	1902	1895	1889	1883	1877	1871
4500]	1984	1977	1970	1963	1956	1949	1942	1935	1929	1922	1916	1910	1904	1898	1892	1886
4550]	1998	1991	1984	1977	1970	1963	1956	1950	1943	1937	1931	1924	1918	1912	1907	1901
4600]	2012	2005	1998	1991	1984	1977	1971	1964	1958	1951	1945	1939	1933	1927	1921	1915
4650]	2026	2019	2012	2005	1998	1992	1985	1978	1972	1966	1960	1954	1948	1942	1936	1930
4700]	2040	2033	2026	2019	2013	2006	1999	1993	1986	1980	1974	1968	1962	1956	1950	1944
4750]	2054	2047	2040	2033	2027	2020	2014	2007	2001	1995	1988	1982	1976	1970	1964	1958
4800]	2068	2061	2054	2048	2041	2034	2028	2021	2015	2009	2003	1997	1990	1984	1978	1973
4850]	2082	2075	2068	2062	2055	2048	2042	2036	2029	2023	2017	2011	2005	1999	1993	1987
4900]	2096	2089	2082	2076	2069	2062	2056	2050	2044	2037	2031	2025	2019	2013	2007	2001
4950]	2110	2103	2096	2090	2083	2077	2070	2064	2058	2051	2045	2039	2033	2027	2021	2015
5000]	2124	2117	2110	2104	2097	2091	2084	2078	2072	2065	2059	2053	2047	2041	2035	2029

Five or More Children Monthly Support Schedule

CUSTODIAL PARENT INCOME

	1850	1900	1950	2000	2050	2100	2150	2200	2250	2300	2350	2400	2450	2500	2550	2600
250]	71	71	71	71	71	71	71	71	71	71	71	71	71	71	71	71
300]	71	71	71	71	71	71	71	71	71	71	71	71	71	71	71	71
350]	71	71	71	71	71	71	71	71	71	71	71	71	71	71	71	71
400]	71	71	71	71	71	71	71	71	71	71	71	71	71	71	71	71
450]	73	73	73	73	73	73	73	73	71	71	71	71	71	71	71	71
500]	76	76	76	76	76	76	76	76	71	71	71	71	71	71	71	71
550]	79	79	79	79	79	79	79	79	73	73	73	73	73	73	73	73
600]	82	82	82	82	82	82	82	82	76	76	76	76	76	76	76	76
650]	85	85	85	85	85	85	85	85	78	78	78	78	78	78	78	78
700]	88	88	88	88	88	88	88	88	81	81	81	81	81	81	81	81
750]	102	102	102	102	102	102	102	102	95	95	95	95	95	95	95	95
800]	152	152	152	152	152	152	152	152	145	145	145	145	145	145	145	145
850]	202	202	202	202	202	202	202	202	195	195	195	195	195	195	195	195
900]	252	252	252	252	252	252	252	252	245	245	245	245	245	245	245	245
950]	302	302	302	302	302	302	302	302	295	295	295	295	295	295	295	295
1000]	352	352	352	352	352	352	352	352	345	345	345	345	345	345	345	345
1050]	402	402	402	402	402	402	402	402	395	395	395	395	395	395	395	395
1100]	452	452	452	452	452	452	452	452	445	445	445	445	445	445	445	445
1150]	502	502	502	502	502	502	502	502	495	495	495	495	495	495	495	495
1200]	552	552	552	552	552	552	552	552	545	545	545	545	545	545	545	545
1250]	602	602	602	602	602	602	602	602	595	595	595	595	595	595	595	595
1300]	652	652	652	652	652	652	652	652	645	645	645	645	645	645	645	645
1350]	702	702	702	702	702	702	700	698	695	693	691	689	687	685	683	681
1400]	736	733	731	728	726	724	722	720	717	715	713	711	709	707	705	703
1450]	758	755	753	750	748	746	744	741	739	737	734	732	730	728	726	724
1500]	780	777	775	772	770	768	765	763	761	758	756	754	752	749	747	745
1550]	802	799	797	794	792	789	787	784	782	780	777	775	773	771	769	767
1600]	823	821	818	816	813	811	808	806	803	801	799	796	794	792	790	788
1650]	845	842	840	837	835	832	829	827	825	822	820	818	815	813	811	809
1700]	867	864	861	859	856	853	851	848	846	843	841	839	837	834	832	830
1750]	888	885	883	880	877	874	872	869	867	864	862	860	858	855	853	851
1800]	909	906	904	901	898	895	893	890	888	885	883	881	878	876	874	872
1850]	930	927	924	922	919	916	914	911	909	906	904	902	899	897	895	893
1900]	951	948	945	943	940	937	935	932	930	927	925	922	920	918	916	914
1950]	972	969	966	963	961	958	955	953	950	948	946	943	941	939	937	934
2000]	993	990	987	984	981	979	976	974	971	969	966	964	962	959	957	955
2050]	1013	1010	1008	1005	1002	999	997	994	992	989	987	985	982	980	978	976
2100]	1034	1031	1028	1025	1023	1020	1017	1015	1012	1010	1007	1005	1003	1001	998	996
2150]	1054	1052	1049	1046	1043	1040	1038	1035	1033	1030	1028	1026	1023	1021	1019	1017
2200]	1075	1072	1069	1066	1064	1061	1058	1056	1053	1051	1048	1046	1044	1042	1039	1037
2250]	1095	1092	1089	1087	1084	1081	1079	1076	1074	1071	1069	1066	1064	1062	1060	1058
2300]	1116	1113	1110	1107	1104	1102	1099	1096	1094	1092	1089	1087	1085	1082	1080	1078
2350]	1136	1133	1130	1127	1125	1122	1119	1117	1114	1112	1109	1107	1105	1103	1100	1098
2400]	1156	1153	1150	1148	1145	1142	1140	1137	1135	1132	1130	1127	1125	1123	1121	1119
2450]	1176	1173	1171	1168	1165	1162	1160	1157	1155	1152	1150	1148	1145	1143	1141	1139
2500]	1196	1193	1191	1188	1185	1183	1180	1177	1175	1172	1170	1168	1165	1163	1161	1159

NONCUSTODIAL PARENT INCOME

Five or More Children Monthly Support Schedule

CUSTODIAL PARENT INCOME

	1850	1900	1950	2000	2050	2100	2150	2200	2250	2300	2350	2400	2450	2500	2550	2600
2550]	1216	1214	1211	1208	1205	1203	1200	1197	1195	1193	1190	1188	1186	1183	1181	1179
2600]	1236	1234	1231	1228	1225	1223	1220	1218	1215	1213	1210	1208	1206	1203	1201	1198
2650]	1256	1254	1251	1248	1245	1243	1240	1238	1235	1233	1230	1228	1226	1223	1220	1215
2700]	1276	1273	1271	1268	1265	1263	1260	1258	1255	1253	1250	1248	1246	1242	1237	1232
2750]	1296	1293	1291	1288	1285	1283	1280	1277	1275	1273	1270	1268	1264	1259	1254	1249
2800]	1316	1313	1310	1308	1305	1302	1300	1297	1295	1292	1290	1286	1281	1276	1271	1266
2850]	1336	1333	1330	1328	1325	1322	1320	1317	1315	1312	1308	1303	1298	1293	1288	1283
2900]	1356	1353	1350	1347	1345	1342	1339	1337	1335	1331	1325	1320	1315	1310	1305	1300
2950]	1375	1372	1370	1367	1364	1362	1359	1357	1353	1347	1342	1337	1331	1326	1321	1316
3000]	1395	1392	1389	1387	1384	1382	1379	1375	1369	1364	1359	1353	1348	1343	1338	1333
3050]	1415	1412	1409	1406	1404	1401	1397	1391	1386	1380	1375	1370	1365	1360	1355	1350
3100]	1434	1431	1429	1426	1423	1419	1414	1408	1402	1397	1391	1386	1381	1376	1371	1366
3150]	1454	1451	1448	1446	1441	1436	1430	1424	1419	1413	1408	1403	1397	1392	1387	1383
3200]	1473	1471	1468	1464	1458	1452	1446	1440	1435	1429	1424	1419	1414	1409	1404	1399
3250]	1493	1490	1486	1480	1474	1468	1462	1457	1451	1446	1440	1435	1430	1425	1420	1415
3300]	1512	1508	1502	1496	1490	1484	1478	1473	1467	1462	1457	1451	1446	1441	1436	1431
3350]	1530	1524	1518	1512	1506	1500	1494	1489	1483	1478	1473	1467	1462	1457	1452	1448
3400]	1546	1540	1534	1528	1522	1516	1510	1505	1499	1494	1489	1484	1478	1473	1469	1464
3450]	1562	1555	1549	1543	1538	1532	1526	1521	1515	1510	1505	1499	1494	1489	1485	1480
3500]	1577	1571	1565	1559	1553	1548	1542	1537	1531	1526	1521	1515	1510	1505	1500	1496
3550]	1593	1587	1581	1575	1569	1563	1558	1552	1547	1542	1536	1531	1526	1521	1516	1512
3600]	1609	1602	1596	1591	1585	1579	1574	1568	1563	1557	1552	1547	1542	1537	1532	1527
3650]	1624	1618	1612	1606	1600	1595	1589	1584	1578	1573	1568	1563	1558	1553	1548	1543
3700]	1640	1634	1628	1622	1616	1610	1605	1599	1594	1589	1584	1579	1574	1569	1564	1559
3750]	1655	1649	1643	1637	1632	1626	1620	1615	1610	1604	1599	1594	1589	1584	1579	1575
3800]	1670	1664	1658	1653	1647	1641	1636	1630	1625	1620	1615	1610	1605	1600	1595	1590
3850]	1686	1680	1674	1668	1662	1657	1651	1646	1641	1635	1630	1625	1620	1615	1611	1606
3900]	1701	1695	1689	1683	1678	1672	1667	1661	1656	1651	1646	1641	1636	1631	1626	1621
3950]	1716	1710	1704	1699	1693	1688	1682	1677	1671	1666	1661	1656	1651	1646	1641	1636
4000]	1731	1725	1720	1714	1708	1703	1697	1692	1687	1682	1677	1671	1666	1661	1656	1651
4050]	1746	1741	1735	1729	1724	1718	1713	1707	1702	1697	1692	1687	1681	1676	1671	1667
4100]	1761	1756	1750	1744	1739	1733	1728	1723	1717	1712	1707	1702	1697	1692	1687	1682
4150]	1776	1771	1765	1759	1754	1748	1743	1738	1732	1727	1722	1717	1712	1707	1702	1697
4200]	1791	1786	1780	1774	1769	1763	1758	1753	1747	1742	1737	1732	1727	1722	1717	1712
4250]	1806	1801	1795	1789	1784	1779	1773	1768	1762	1757	1752	1747	1742	1737	1732	1727
4300]	1821	1816	1810	1804	1799	1793	1788	1782	1777	1772	1767	1762	1756	1752	1747	1742
4350]	1836	1830	1825	1819	1814	1808	1803	1797	1792	1787	1781	1776	1771	1766	1762	1757
4400]	1851	1845	1840	1834	1828	1823	1817	1812	1807	1801	1796	1791	1786	1781	1776	1772
4450]	1866	1860	1854	1849	1843	1838	1832	1827	1821	1816	1811	1806	1801	1796	1791	1786
4500]	1880	1875	1869	1863	1858	1852	1847	1841	1836	1831	1826	1821	1816	1811	1806	1801
4550]	1895	1889	1883	1878	1872	1867	1861	1856	1851	1846	1840	1835	1830	1826	1821	1816
4600]	1909	1904	1898	1892	1887	1881	1876	1871	1865	1860	1855	1850	1845	1840	1835	1831
4650]	1924	1918	1912	1907	1901	1896	1890	1885	1880	1875	1870	1865	1860	1855	1850	1845
4700]	1938	1932	1927	1921	1916	1910	1905	1900	1894	1889	1884	1879	1874	1870	1865	1860
4750]	1952	1947	1941	1936	1930	1925	1919	1914	1909	1904	1899	1894	1889	1884	1879	1875
4800]	1967	1961	1955	1950	1944	1939	1934	1929	1923	1918	1913	1908	1903	1899	1894	1889
4850]	1981	1975	1970	1964	1959	1953	1948	1943	1938	1933	1928	1923	1918	1913	1908	1904
4900]	1995	1990	1984	1978	1973	1968	1962	1957	1952	1947	1942	1937	1932	1928	1923	1918
4950]	2009	2004	1998	1993	1987	1982	1977	1972	1967	1961	1957	1952	1947	1942	1937	1933
5000]	2024	2018	2012	2007	2002	1996	1991	1986	1981	1976	1971	1966	1961	1956	1952	1947

NONCUSTODIAL PARENT INCOME

Effective July 1, 2003

Five or More Children Monthly Support Schedule

CUSTODIAL PARENT INCOME

		2650	2700	2750	2800	2850	2900	2950	3000	3050	3100	3150	3200	3250	3300	3350	3400
	250]	71	71	71	71	71	71	71	71	71	71	71	71	71	71	71	71
	300]	71	71	71	71	71	71	71	71	71	71	71	71	71	71	71	71
	350]	71	71	71	71	71	71	71	71	71	71	71	71	71	71	71	71
	400]	71	71	71	71	71	71	71	71	71	71	71	71	71	71	71	71
	450]	71	71	71	71	71	71	71	71	71	71	71	71	71	71	71	71
	500]	71	71	71	71	71	71	71	71	71	71	71	71	71	71	71	71
	550]	73	71	71	71	71	71	71	71	71	71	71	71	71	71	71	71
	600]	76	71	71	71	71	71	71	71	71	71	71	71	71	71	71	71
	650]	78	72	72	72	72	72	72	72	72	72	71	71	71	71	71	71
N	700]	81	74	74	74	74	74	74	74	74	74	71	71	71	71	71	71
O	750]	95	87	87	87	87	87	87	87	87	87	83	83	83	83	83	83
N	800]	145	137	137	137	137	137	137	137	137	137	133	133	133	133	133	133
C	850]	195	187	187	187	187	187	187	187	187	187	183	183	183	183	183	183
U	900]	245	237	237	237	237	237	237	237	237	237	233	233	233	233	233	233
S	950]	295	287	287	287	287	287	287	287	287	287	283	283	283	283	283	283
T																	
O	1000]	345	337	337	337	337	337	337	337	337	337	333	333	333	333	333	333
D	1050]	395	387	387	387	387	387	387	387	387	387	383	383	383	383	383	383
I	1100]	445	437	437	437	437	437	437	437	437	437	433	433	433	433	433	433
A	1150]	495	487	487	487	487	487	487	487	487	487	483	483	483	483	483	483
L	1200]	545	537	537	537	537	537	537	537	537	537	533	533	533	533	533	533
	1250]	595	587	587	587	587	587	587	587	587	587	583	583	583	583	583	583
P	1300]	645	637	637	637	637	637	637	637	637	637	633	633	633	633	633	633
A	1350]	679	677	675	674	672	670	669	667	665	664	662	661	660	658	657	655
R	1400]	701	699	697	695	693	692	690	688	687	685	684	682	681	679	678	677
E	1450]	722	720	718	717	715	713	711	710	708	707	705	704	702	701	699	698
N																	
T	1500]	743	742	740	738	736	734	733	731	729	728	726	725	723	722	720	719
	1550]	765	763	761	759	757	756	754	752	751	749	747	746	744	743	741	740
I	1600]	786	784	782	780	778	777	775	773	772	770	768	767	765	764	762	761
N	1650]	807	805	803	801	800	798	796	794	793	791	789	788	786	785	783	782
C	1700]	828	826	824	822	821	819	817	815	814	812	810	809	807	806	804	803
O	1750]	849	847	845	843	841	840	838	836	834	833	831	830	828	826	825	823
M	1800]	870	868	866	864	862	861	859	857	855	854	852	850	849	847	846	843
E	1850]	891	889	887	885	883	881	880	878	876	874	873	871	869	868	865	862
	1900]	912	910	908	906	904	902	900	898	897	895	893	892	890	888	884	881
	1950]	932	930	928	926	925	923	921	919	917	916	914	912	910	906	903	899
	2000]	953	951	949	947	945	943	942	940	938	936	935	932	928	924	921	917
	2050]	974	972	970	968	966	964	962	960	959	957	954	950	946	943	939	936
	2100]	994	992	990	988	986	984	983	981	979	976	972	968	965	961	957	954
	2150]	1015	1013	1011	1009	1007	1005	1003	1001	998	994	990	987	983	979	975	972
	2200]	1035	1033	1031	1029	1027	1025	1023	1020	1016	1012	1008	1005	1001	997	993	990
	2250]	1056	1053	1051	1049	1048	1046	1043	1038	1034	1030	1026	1022	1019	1015	1011	1008
	2300]	1076	1074	1072	1070	1068	1065	1061	1056	1052	1048	1044	1040	1036	1033	1029	1025
	2350]	1096	1094	1092	1090	1087	1083	1078	1074	1070	1066	1062	1058	1054	1050	1047	1043
	2400]	1116	1114	1112	1109	1105	1100	1096	1092	1088	1084	1080	1076	1072	1068	1064	1061
	2450]	1137	1135	1131	1127	1122	1118	1114	1109	1105	1101	1097	1093	1089	1085	1082	1078
	2500]	1157	1153	1149	1144	1140	1135	1131	1127	1123	1119	1115	1111	1107	1103	1099	1095

Five or More Children Monthly Support Schedule

CUSTODIAL PARENT INCOME

	2650	2700	2750	2800	2850	2900	2950	3000	3050	3100	3150	3200	3250	3300	3350	3400
2550]	1176	1171	1166	1162	1157	1153	1148	1144	1140	1136	1132	1128	1124	1120	1116	1113
2600]	1193	1188	1183	1179	1174	1170	1166	1161	1157	1153	1149	1145	1141	1137	1134	1130
2650]	1210	1205	1201	1196	1192	1187	1183	1179	1174	1170	1166	1162	1158	1155	1151	1147
2700]	1227	1223	1218	1213	1209	1204	1200	1196	1192	1187	1183	1179	1176	1172	1168	1164
2750]	1244	1240	1235	1230	1226	1221	1217	1213	1209	1205	1200	1196	1193	1189	1185	1181
2800]	1261	1257	1252	1247	1243	1238	1234	1230	1226	1221	1217	1213	1210	1206	1202	1198
2850]	1278	1273	1269	1264	1260	1255	1251	1247	1242	1238	1234	1230	1226	1223	1219	1215
2900]	1295	1290	1286	1281	1276	1272	1268	1263	1259	1255	1251	1247	1243	1239	1236	1232
2950]	1312	1307	1302	1298	1293	1289	1284	1280	1276	1272	1268	1264	1260	1256	1252	1248
3000]	1328	1324	1319	1314	1310	1305	1301	1297	1293	1289	1284	1280	1277	1273	1269	1265
3050]	1345	1340	1335	1331	1326	1322	1318	1313	1309	1305	1301	1297	1293	1289	1285	1281
3100]	1361	1357	1352	1347	1343	1339	1334	1330	1326	1322	1318	1314	1310	1306	1302	1298
3150]	1378	1373	1368	1364	1359	1355	1351	1346	1342	1338	1334	1330	1326	1322	1318	1314
3200]	1394	1389	1385	1380	1376	1371	1367	1363	1359	1354	1350	1346	1342	1338	1334	1330
3250]	1410	1406	1401	1397	1392	1388	1383	1379	1375	1371	1367	1362	1358	1354	1350	1346
3300]	1427	1422	1417	1413	1408	1404	1400	1395	1391	1387	1383	1379	1374	1370	1366	1363
3350]	1443	1438	1434	1429	1425	1420	1416	1412	1407	1403	1399	1395	1390	1386	1382	1379
3400]	1459	1454	1450	1445	1441	1436	1432	1428	1423	1419	1415	1411	1406	1402	1398	1394
3450]	1475	1470	1466	1461	1457	1452	1448	1444	1439	1435	1431	1426	1422	1418	1414	1410
3500]	1491	1486	1482	1477	1473	1468	1464	1459	1455	1451	1446	1442	1438	1434	1430	1426
3550]	1507	1502	1498	1493	1489	1484	1480	1475	1471	1466	1462	1458	1454	1450	1446	1442
3600]	1523	1518	1513	1509	1504	1500	1495	1491	1486	1482	1478	1474	1470	1466	1462	1458
3650]	1539	1534	1529	1525	1520	1515	1511	1507	1502	1498	1494	1490	1485	1481	1477	1473
3700]	1554	1550	1545	1540	1536	1531	1527	1522	1518	1514	1509	1505	1501	1497	1493	1489
3750]	1570	1565	1560	1556	1551	1547	1542	1538	1533	1529	1525	1521	1517	1513	1509	1505
3800]	1585	1581	1576	1571	1567	1562	1558	1553	1549	1545	1540	1536	1532	1528	1524	1520
3850]	1601	1596	1591	1587	1582	1577	1573	1569	1564	1560	1556	1552	1548	1544	1540	1536
3900]	1616	1611	1607	1602	1597	1593	1588	1584	1580	1575	1571	1567	1563	1559	1555	1551
3950]	1631	1627	1622	1617	1613	1608	1604	1599	1595	1591	1587	1583	1578	1574	1571	1567
4000]	1647	1642	1637	1633	1628	1623	1619	1615	1610	1606	1602	1598	1594	1590	1586	1582
4050]	1662	1657	1652	1648	1643	1639	1634	1630	1626	1621	1617	1613	1609	1605	1601	1597
4100]	1677	1672	1668	1663	1658	1654	1650	1645	1641	1637	1633	1628	1624	1620	1616	1613
4150]	1692	1687	1683	1678	1674	1669	1665	1660	1656	1652	1648	1644	1640	1636	1632	1628
4200]	1707	1702	1698	1693	1689	1684	1680	1675	1671	1667	1663	1659	1655	1651	1647	1643
4250]	1722	1717	1713	1708	1704	1699	1695	1691	1686	1682	1678	1674	1670	1666	1662	1658
4300]	1737	1732	1728	1723	1719	1714	1710	1706	1701	1697	1693	1689	1685	1681	1677	1673
4350]	1752	1747	1743	1738	1734	1729	1725	1721	1716	1712	1708	1704	1700	1696	1692	1688
4400]	1767	1762	1758	1753	1749	1744	1740	1736	1731	1727	1723	1719	1715	1711	1707	1703
4450]	1782	1777	1772	1768	1764	1759	1755	1751	1746	1742	1738	1734	1730	1726	1722	1718
4500]	1797	1792	1787	1783	1778	1774	1770	1765	1761	1757	1753	1749	1745	1741	1737	1733
4550]	1811	1807	1802	1798	1793	1789	1784	1780	1776	1772	1768	1764	1760	1756	1752	1748
4600]	1826	1821	1817	1812	1808	1804	1799	1795	1791	1787	1783	1779	1775	1771	1767	1763
4650]	1841	1836	1832	1827	1823	1818	1814	1810	1806	1802	1797	1793	1789	1786	1782	1778
4700]	1855	1851	1846	1842	1837	1833	1829	1825	1820	1816	1812	1808	1804	1800	1796	1792
4750]	1870	1865	1861	1856	1852	1848	1843	1839	1835	1831	1827	1823	1819	1815	1811	1807
4800]	1885	1880	1876	1871	1867	1862	1858	1854	1850	1846	1842	1838	1833	1829	1825	1821
4850]	1899	1895	1890	1886	1881	1877	1873	1869	1864	1860	1856	1852	1848	1844	1839	1835
4900]	1914	1909	1905	1900	1896	1892	1887	1883	1879	1875	1871	1866	1862	1858	1854	1850
4950]	1928	1924	1919	1915	1910	1906	1902	1898	1894	1889	1885	1881	1876	1872	1868	1864
5000]	1943	1938	1934	1929	1925	1921	1916	1912	1908	1904	1899	1895	1891	1886	1882	1878

(Left margin, read vertically: NONCUSTODIAL PARENT INCOME)

Effective July 1, 2003

Five or More Children Monthly Support Schedule

CUSTODIAL PARENT INCOME

	3450	3500	3550	3600	3650	3700	3750	3800	3850	3900	3950	4000	4050	4100	4150	4200
250]	71	71	71	71	71	71	71	71	71	71	71	71	71	71	71	71
300]	71	71	71	71	71	71	71	71	71	71	71	71	71	71	71	71
350]	71	71	71	71	71	71	71	71	71	71	71	71	71	71	71	71
400]	71	71	71	71	71	71	71	71	71	71	71	71	71	71	71	71
450]	71	71	71	71	71	71	71	71	71	71	71	71	71	71	71	71
500]	71	71	71	71	71	71	71	71	71	71	71	71	71	71	71	71
550]	71	71	71	71	71	71	71	71	71	71	71	71	71	71	71	71
600]	71	71	71	71	71	71	71	71	71	71	71	71	71	71	71	71
650]	71	71	71	71	71	71	71	71	71	71	71	71	71	71	71	71
700]	71	71	71	71	71	71	71	71	71	71	71	71	71	71	71	71
750]	83	83	83	83	83	83	83	83	83	83	83	83	83	83	83	83
800]	133	133	133	133	133	133	133	133	133	133	133	133	133	133	133	133
850]	183	183	183	183	183	183	183	183	183	183	183	183	183	183	183	183
900]	233	233	233	233	233	233	233	233	233	233	233	233	233	233	233	233
950]	283	283	283	283	283	283	283	283	283	283	283	283	283	283	283	283
1000]	333	333	333	333	333	333	333	333	333	333	333	333	333	333	333	333
1050]	383	383	383	383	383	383	383	383	383	383	383	383	383	383	383	383
1100]	433	433	433	433	433	433	433	433	433	433	433	433	433	433	433	433
1150]	483	483	483	483	483	483	483	483	483	483	483	483	483	483	483	483
1200]	533	533	533	533	533	533	533	533	533	533	533	533	533	533	533	533
1250]	583	583	583	583	583	583	583	583	583	583	583	583	583	583	583	583
1300]	633	632	630	629	628	627	626	625	623	622	619	617	615	612	610	608
1350]	654	653	652	650	649	648	647	646	644	641	639	636	634	632	629	627
1400]	675	674	673	672	670	669	668	666	663	661	658	656	653	651	649	646
1450]	696	695	694	693	691	690	688	685	683	680	678	675	673	670	668	666
1500]	718	716	715	714	712	710	708	705	702	699	697	694	692	689	687	685
1550]	739	737	736	735	732	730	727	724	721	719	716	713	711	708	706	704
1600]	760	758	757	755	752	749	746	743	740	738	735	732	730	727	725	722
1650]	780	779	777	774	771	768	765	762	759	756	754	751	749	746	743	741
1700]	801	799	796	793	790	787	784	781	778	775	772	770	767	765	762	760
1750]	821	818	815	812	808	805	802	800	797	794	791	788	786	783	781	778
1800]	840	837	833	830	827	824	821	818	815	812	810	807	804	802	799	796
1850]	859	855	852	849	846	843	840	837	834	831	828	825	823	820	817	815
1900]	877	874	871	867	864	861	858	855	852	849	846	844	841	838	835	833
1950]	896	892	889	886	883	879	876	873	870	867	865	862	859	856	854	851
2000]	914	911	907	904	901	898	895	891	888	886	883	880	877	874	872	869
2050]	932	929	925	922	919	916	913	910	907	904	901	898	895	892	889	887
2100]	950	947	944	940	937	934	931	928	924	921	919	916	913	910	907	905
2150]	968	965	961	958	955	952	949	945	942	939	936	933	931	928	925	922
2200]	986	983	979	976	973	970	966	963	960	957	954	951	948	945	943	940
2250]	1004	1001	997	994	991	987	984	981	978	975	972	969	966	963	960	957
2300]	1022	1018	1015	1012	1008	1005	1002	999	995	992	989	986	983	981	978	975
2350]	1039	1036	1032	1029	1026	1022	1019	1016	1013	1010	1007	1004	1001	998	995	992
2400]	1057	1053	1050	1047	1043	1040	1037	1034	1030	1027	1024	1021	1018	1015	1012	1009
2450]	1074	1071	1067	1064	1061	1057	1054	1051	1048	1045	1041	1038	1035	1032	1029	1026
2500]	1092	1088	1085	1081	1078	1075	1071	1068	1065	1062	1059	1055	1052	1049	1046	1043

NONCUSTODIAL PARENT INCOME

Five or More Children Monthly Support Schedule

NONCUSTODIAL PARENT INCOME	CUSTODIAL PARENT INCOME															
	3450	3500	3550	3600	3650	3700	3750	3800	3850	3900	3950	4000	4050	4100	4150	4200
2550]	1109	1106	1102	1099	1095	1092	1089	1085	1082	1079	1076	1072	1069	1066	1063	1060
2600]	1126	1123	1119	1116	1112	1109	1106	1102	1099	1096	1093	1089	1086	1083	1080	1077
2650]	1144	1140	1136	1133	1130	1126	1123	1119	1116	1113	1109	1106	1103	1100	1097	1094
2700]	1161	1157	1153	1150	1147	1143	1140	1136	1133	1130	1126	1123	1120	1117	1114	1111
2750]	1178	1174	1170	1167	1163	1160	1156	1153	1150	1146	1143	1140	1137	1134	1130	1127
2800]	1194	1191	1187	1184	1180	1177	1173	1170	1166	1163	1160	1156	1153	1150	1147	1144
2850]	1211	1208	1204	1200	1197	1193	1190	1186	1183	1180	1176	1173	1170	1167	1164	1161
2900]	1228	1224	1221	1217	1213	1210	1206	1203	1199	1196	1193	1190	1186	1183	1180	1177
2950]	1245	1241	1237	1234	1230	1226	1223	1219	1216	1213	1209	1206	1203	1200	1197	1193
3000]	1261	1257	1254	1250	1246	1243	1239	1236	1232	1229	1226	1222	1219	1216	1213	1210
3050]	1278	1274	1270	1266	1263	1259	1256	1252	1249	1245	1242	1239	1236	1232	1229	1226
3100]	1294	1290	1286	1283	1279	1275	1272	1268	1265	1262	1258	1255	1252	1249	1245	1242
3150]	1310	1306	1303	1299	1295	1292	1288	1285	1281	1278	1275	1271	1268	1265	1262	1259
3200]	1326	1323	1319	1315	1312	1308	1304	1301	1297	1294	1291	1287	1284	1281	1278	1275
3250]	1343	1339	1335	1331	1328	1324	1321	1317	1314	1310	1307	1304	1300	1297	1294	1291
3300]	1359	1355	1351	1347	1344	1340	1337	1333	1330	1326	1323	1320	1316	1313	1310	1307
3350]	1375	1371	1367	1363	1360	1356	1353	1349	1346	1342	1339	1336	1332	1329	1326	1323
3400]	1391	1387	1383	1379	1376	1372	1369	1365	1362	1358	1355	1352	1348	1345	1342	1339
3450]	1407	1403	1399	1395	1392	1388	1384	1381	1377	1374	1371	1367	1364	1361	1358	1355
3500]	1422	1419	1415	1411	1407	1404	1400	1397	1393	1390	1387	1383	1380	1377	1374	1370
3550]	1438	1434	1431	1427	1423	1420	1416	1413	1409	1406	1402	1399	1396	1393	1389	1386
3600]	1454	1450	1446	1443	1439	1435	1432	1428	1425	1421	1418	1415	1411	1408	1405	1402
3650]	1470	1466	1462	1458	1455	1451	1448	1444	1441	1437	1434	1430	1427	1424	1421	1418
3700]	1485	1481	1478	1474	1470	1467	1463	1460	1456	1453	1449	1446	1443	1440	1436	1433
3750]	1501	1497	1493	1490	1486	1482	1479	1475	1472	1468	1465	1462	1458	1455	1452	1449
3800]	1516	1513	1509	1505	1501	1498	1494	1491	1487	1484	1481	1477	1474	1471	1467	1464
3850]	1532	1528	1524	1521	1517	1513	1510	1506	1503	1499	1496	1493	1489	1486	1483	1480
3900]	1547	1544	1540	1536	1532	1529	1525	1522	1518	1515	1512	1508	1505	1502	1498	1495
3950]	1563	1559	1555	1552	1548	1544	1541	1537	1534	1530	1527	1524	1520	1517	1513	1510
4000]	1578	1574	1571	1567	1563	1560	1556	1553	1549	1546	1542	1539	1535	1532	1528	1525
4050]	1593	1590	1586	1582	1579	1575	1571	1568	1564	1561	1558	1554	1551	1547	1544	1540
4100]	1609	1605	1601	1597	1594	1590	1587	1583	1580	1576	1573	1569	1566	1562	1559	1555
4150]	1624	1620	1616	1613	1609	1605	1602	1598	1595	1591	1588	1584	1581	1577	1574	1570
4200]	1639	1635	1632	1628	1624	1621	1617	1614	1610	1606	1603	1599	1595	1592	1588	1585
4250]	1654	1650	1647	1643	1639	1636	1632	1629	1625	1621	1618	1614	1610	1607	1603	1600
4300]	1669	1666	1662	1658	1655	1651	1647	1643	1640	1636	1632	1629	1625	1622	1618	1615
4350]	1684	1681	1677	1673	1670	1666	1662	1658	1655	1651	1647	1644	1640	1637	1633	1630
4400]	1699	1696	1692	1688	1684	1681	1677	1673	1669	1666	1662	1658	1655	1651	1648	1644
4450]	1714	1711	1707	1703	1699	1695	1691	1688	1684	1680	1677	1673	1670	1666	1663	1659
4500]	1729	1726	1722	1718	1714	1710	1706	1702	1699	1695	1691	1688	1684	1681	1677	1674
4550]	1744	1740	1736	1732	1728	1725	1721	1717	1713	1710	1706	1702	1699	1695	1692	1688
4600]	1759	1755	1751	1747	1743	1739	1735	1732	1728	1724	1721	1717	1713	1710	1707	1703
4650]	1773	1769	1765	1762	1758	1754	1750	1746	1743	1739	1735	1732	1728	1725	1721	1718
4700]	1788	1784	1780	1776	1772	1768	1765	1761	1757	1753	1750	1746	1743	1739	1736	1732
4750]	1802	1798	1794	1791	1787	1783	1779	1775	1772	1768	1764	1761	1757	1754	1750	1747
4800]	1817	1813	1809	1805	1801	1797	1793	1790	1786	1782	1779	1775	1772	1768	1765	1761
4850]	1831	1827	1823	1819	1815	1812	1808	1804	1800	1797	1793	1790	1786	1783	1779	1776
4900]	1846	1842	1838	1834	1830	1826	1822	1819	1815	1811	1808	1804	1800	1797	1794	1790
4950]	1860	1856	1852	1848	1844	1840	1837	1833	1829	1826	1822	1818	1815	1811	1808	1805
5000]	1874	1870	1866	1862	1859	1855	1851	1847	1844	1840	1836	1833	1829	1826	1822	1819

Five or More Children Monthly Support Schedule

CUSTODIAL PARENT INCOME

	4250	4300	4350	4400	4450	4500	4550	4600	4650	4700	4750	4800	4850	4900	4950	5000
250]	71	71	71	71	71	71	71	71	71	71	71	71	71	71	71	71
300]	71	71	71	71	71	71	71	71	71	71	71	71	71	71	71	71
350]	71	71	71	71	71	71	71	71	71	71	71	71	71	71	71	71
400]	71	71	71	71	71	71	71	71	71	71	71	71	71	71	71	71
450]	71	71	71	71	71	71	71	71	71	71	71	71	71	71	71	71
500]	71	71	71	71	71	71	71	71	71	71	71	71	71	71	71	71
550]	71	71	71	71	71	71	71	71	71	71	71	71	71	71	71	71
600]	71	71	71	71	71	71	71	71	71	71	71	71	71	71	71	71
650]	71	71	71	71	71	71	71	71	71	71	71	71	71	71	71	71
700]	71	71	71	71	71	71	71	71	71	71	71	71	71	71	71	71
750]	83	83	83	83	83	83	83	83	83	83	83	83	83	83	83	83
800]	133	133	133	133	133	133	133	133	133	133	133	133	133	133	133	133
850]	183	183	183	183	183	183	183	183	183	183	183	183	183	183	183	183
900]	233	233	233	233	233	233	233	233	233	233	233	233	233	233	233	233
950]	283	283	283	283	283	283	283	283	283	283	283	283	283	283	283	283
1000]	333	333	333	333	333	333	333	333	333	333	333	333	333	333	333	333
1050]	383	383	383	383	383	383	383	383	383	383	383	383	383	383	383	383
1100]	433	433	433	433	433	433	433	433	433	433	433	433	433	433	433	433
1150]	483	483	483	483	483	483	483	483	483	483	483	483	483	483	483	483
1200]	533	533	533	533	533	533	533	533	533	533	533	533	533	533	533	533
1250]	583	583	582	580	578	576	574	572	571	569	567	565	564	562	560	559
1300]	606	604	601	599	597	595	593	592	590	588	586	584	582	581	579	577
1350]	625	623	621	619	617	615	613	611	609	607	605	603	601	600	598	596
1400]	644	642	640	638	636	634	632	630	628	626	624	622	620	618	616	615
1450]	663	661	659	657	655	652	650	648	646	644	642	641	639	637	635	633
1500]	682	680	678	676	673	671	669	667	665	663	661	659	657	655	653	652
1550]	701	699	697	694	692	690	688	686	684	682	680	678	676	674	672	670
1600]	720	718	715	713	711	709	706	704	702	700	698	696	694	692	690	688
1650]	739	736	734	732	729	727	725	723	721	718	716	714	712	710	708	706
1700]	757	755	752	750	748	745	743	741	739	737	734	732	730	728	726	724
1750]	776	773	771	768	766	764	761	759	757	755	753	750	748	746	744	742
1800]	794	791	789	787	784	782	780	777	775	773	770	768	766	764	762	760
1850]	812	810	807	805	802	800	798	795	793	791	788	786	784	782	780	777
1900]	830	828	825	823	820	818	816	813	811	808	806	804	802	799	797	795
1950]	848	846	843	841	838	836	833	831	828	826	824	822	819	817	815	813
2000]	866	864	861	859	856	853	851	849	846	844	841	839	837	835	832	830
2050]	884	882	879	876	874	871	869	866	864	861	859	857	854	852	850	848
2100]	902	899	897	894	891	889	886	884	881	879	876	874	872	869	867	865
2150]	920	917	914	911	909	906	904	901	899	896	894	891	889	887	884	882
2200]	937	934	932	929	926	924	921	918	916	913	911	909	906	904	902	899
2250]	954	952	949	946	944	941	938	936	933	931	928	926	923	921	919	917
2300]	972	969	966	963	961	958	955	953	950	948	945	943	941	938	936	934
2350]	989	986	983	981	978	975	973	970	967	965	962	960	958	955	953	951
2400]	1006	1003	1001	998	995	992	990	987	985	982	979	977	975	972	970	967
2450]	1023	1020	1018	1015	1012	1009	1007	1004	1001	999	996	994	991	989	987	984
2500]	1040	1037	1035	1032	1029	1026	1024	1021	1018	1016	1013	1011	1008	1006	1003	1001

(Vertical label at left: NONCUSTODIAL PARENT INCOME)

Five or More Children Monthly Support Schedule

CUSTODIAL PARENT INCOME

	4250	4300	4350	4400	4450	4500	4550	4600	4650	4700	4750	4800	4850	4900	4950	5000
2550]	1057	1054	1052	1049	1046	1043	1040	1038	1035	1033	1030	1028	1025	1023	1020	1018
2600]	1074	1071	1068	1066	1063	1060	1057	1055	1052	1049	1047	1044	1042	1039	1037	1034
2650]	1091	1088	1085	1082	1080	1077	1074	1071	1069	1066	1063	1061	1058	1056	1053	1051
2700]	1108	1105	1102	1099	1096	1093	1091	1088	1085	1083	1080	1078	1075	1072	1070	1068
2750]	1124	1121	1119	1116	1113	1110	1107	1105	1102	1099	1097	1094	1092	1089	1087	1084
2800]	1141	1138	1135	1132	1129	1127	1124	1121	1118	1116	1113	1111	1108	1105	1103	1100
2850]	1158	1155	1152	1149	1146	1143	1140	1138	1135	1132	1130	1127	1124	1122	1119	1117
2900]	1174	1171	1168	1165	1162	1159	1157	1154	1151	1149	1146	1143	1141	1138	1136	1133
2950]	1190	1187	1184	1182	1179	1176	1173	1170	1168	1165	1162	1160	1157	1154	1152	1149
3000]	1207	1204	1201	1198	1195	1192	1189	1187	1184	1181	1178	1176	1173	1171	1168	1166
3050]	1223	1220	1217	1214	1211	1208	1206	1203	1200	1197	1195	1192	1189	1187	1184	1182
3100]	1239	1236	1233	1230	1227	1225	1222	1219	1216	1214	1211	1208	1206	1203	1200	1198
3150]	1255	1252	1249	1247	1244	1241	1238	1235	1232	1230	1227	1224	1222	1219	1216	1213
3200]	1272	1269	1266	1263	1260	1257	1254	1251	1248	1246	1243	1240	1238	1235	1232	1229
3250]	1288	1285	1282	1279	1276	1273	1270	1267	1264	1262	1259	1256	1253	1250	1248	1245
3300]	1304	1301	1298	1295	1292	1289	1286	1283	1280	1278	1275	1272	1269	1266	1263	1261
3350]	1320	1317	1314	1311	1308	1305	1302	1299	1296	1293	1290	1288	1285	1282	1279	1276
3400]	1336	1333	1330	1327	1324	1321	1318	1315	1312	1309	1306	1303	1300	1297	1295	1292
3450]	1351	1348	1345	1342	1339	1337	1334	1331	1328	1325	1322	1319	1316	1313	1310	1307
3500]	1367	1364	1361	1358	1355	1352	1349	1346	1343	1340	1337	1334	1331	1328	1326	1323
3550]	1383	1380	1377	1374	1371	1368	1365	1362	1359	1356	1353	1350	1347	1344	1341	1338
3600]	1399	1396	1393	1390	1386	1383	1380	1377	1374	1371	1368	1365	1362	1359	1357	1354
3650]	1414	1411	1408	1405	1402	1399	1396	1393	1389	1386	1383	1381	1378	1375	1372	1369
3700]	1430	1427	1424	1420	1417	1414	1411	1408	1405	1402	1399	1396	1393	1390	1387	1384
3750]	1446	1442	1439	1436	1433	1429	1426	1423	1420	1417	1414	1411	1408	1405	1402	1400
3800]	1461	1458	1454	1451	1448	1445	1442	1438	1435	1432	1429	1426	1423	1421	1418	1415
3850]	1476	1473	1470	1466	1463	1460	1457	1454	1451	1448	1445	1442	1439	1436	1433	1430
3900]	1491	1488	1485	1482	1478	1475	1472	1469	1466	1463	1460	1457	1454	1451	1448	1445
3950]	1507	1503	1500	1497	1493	1490	1487	1484	1481	1478	1475	1472	1469	1466	1463	1460
4000]	1522	1518	1515	1512	1509	1505	1502	1499	1496	1493	1490	1487	1484	1481	1478	1475
4050]	1537	1533	1530	1527	1524	1520	1517	1514	1511	1508	1505	1502	1499	1496	1493	1490
4100]	1552	1548	1545	1542	1539	1535	1532	1529	1526	1523	1520	1517	1514	1511	1508	1505
4150]	1567	1563	1560	1557	1554	1550	1547	1544	1541	1538	1535	1532	1529	1526	1523	1520
4200]	1582	1578	1575	1572	1568	1565	1562	1559	1556	1553	1550	1547	1544	1541	1538	1535
4250]	1597	1593	1590	1587	1583	1580	1577	1574	1571	1568	1565	1562	1559	1556	1553	1550
4300]	1611	1608	1605	1601	1598	1595	1592	1589	1586	1583	1580	1577	1574	1571	1568	1565
4350]	1626	1623	1620	1616	1613	1610	1607	1604	1600	1597	1594	1591	1588	1585	1583	1580
4400]	1641	1638	1634	1631	1628	1625	1621	1618	1615	1612	1609	1606	1603	1600	1597	1594
4450]	1656	1652	1649	1646	1643	1639	1636	1633	1630	1627	1624	1621	1618	1615	1612	1609
4500]	1670	1667	1664	1660	1657	1654	1651	1648	1645	1642	1639	1636	1633	1630	1627	1624
4550]	1685	1682	1678	1675	1672	1669	1666	1662	1659	1656	1653	1650	1647	1644	1641	1639
4600]	1700	1696	1693	1690	1687	1683	1680	1677	1674	1671	1668	1665	1662	1659	1656	1653
4650]	1714	1711	1708	1704	1701	1698	1695	1692	1689	1685	1682	1679	1676	1674	1671	1668
4700]	1729	1726	1722	1719	1716	1713	1709	1706	1703	1700	1697	1694	1691	1688	1685	1682
4750]	1743	1740	1737	1733	1730	1727	1724	1721	1718	1715	1712	1709	1706	1703	1700	1697
4800]	1758	1755	1751	1748	1745	1742	1738	1735	1732	1729	1726	1723	1720	1717	1714	1711
4850]	1772	1769	1766	1762	1759	1756	1753	1750	1747	1744	1741	1738	1735	1732	1729	1726
4900]	1787	1783	1780	1777	1774	1770	1767	1764	1761	1758	1755	1752	1749	1746	1743	1740
4950]	1801	1798	1795	1791	1788	1785	1782	1779	1775	1772	1769	1766	1763	1760	1758	1755
5000]	1816	1812	1809	1806	1802	1799	1796	1793	1790	1787	1784	1781	1778	1775	1772	1769

NONCUSTODIAL PARENT INCOME

Regular Forms

Summons and Complaint	MC 01
Complaint for Divorce	GRP 1a&b
Verified Statement	FOC 23
Uniform Child Custody Jurisdiction Enforcement Act Affidavit	MC 416
Default	GRP 2
Notice of Entry of Default and Request for Default Judgment of Divorce	GRP 3
Judgment of Divorce	GRP 4a-e
Income Withholding Order	FOC 5
Testimony	
Proof of Mailing	MC 302

Note: To remove the forms cleanly from the book, follow these steps: 1) keep the back of the book as flat as possible on a table or other hard surface 2) open the front of the book at the form you want to remove and pull gently on the form, keeping the back of the book flat.

STATE OF MICHIGAN Circuit Court - Family Division COUNTY	DEFAULT Application, Affidavit and Entry	CASE NO.

Plaintiff (appearing *in propria persona*):

v

Defendant:

APPLICATION

1. As shown by the proof of service on file, defendant was served with a summons and complaint on

_____

2. Defendant did not respond to the complaint within 21 days (28 days if served by mail or out of state).

I request the clerk to enter the default of defendant for failure to plead or otherwise defend as provided by law.

Date _____   Plaintiff _____

AFFIDAVIT

Plaintiff, being sworn, says:

3. Defendant is not a minor or an incompetent person.

4. Defendant

☐ is not in active-duty service of the U.S. military. This information is based on
☐ personal knowledge. ☐ attached responses from military locator services.

☐ is in active-duty service of the U.S. military, and ☐ has waived all lawsuit relief rights under the Soldiers' and Sailors' Civil Relief Act of 1940 and/or MCL 32.517 or a similar military relief law from another state in the attached waiver form.
☐ other: _____

Date _____   Plaintiff _____

Subscribed and sworn to before me on _____ , _____ County, Michigan

My commission expires _____ Notary public _____

ENTRY

The default of defendant is entered for failure to plead or otherwise defend.

Date _____   Court clerk _____

GRP 2 (1/04)   DEFAULT, Application, Affidavit and Entry

STATE OF MICHIGAN Circuit Court - Family Division COUNTY	NOTICE OF ENTRY OF DEFAULT AND REQUEST FOR DEFAULT JUDGMENT OF DIVORCE	CASE NO.

Plaintiff (appearing *in propria persona*):

v

Defendant:

NOTICE

TO THE DEFENDANT:

1. Your default was entered on _____ , as shown by the attached Default.

2. I will be requesting a default Judgment of Divorce, and a hearing on this request is scheduled for _____ at _____ in the courtroom of the judge in this case.

3. At the hearing, the judge may enter a Judgment of Divorce granting the relief I requested in my Complaint for Divorce and/or grant other relief.

Date _____   Plaintiff _____

PROOF OF MAILING

On the date below, I sent copies of this notice and the Default entered in this case to defendant at his/her address in the caption above by ordinary first-class mail.

I declare that the statement above is true to the best of my information, knowledge and belief.

Date _____   Plaintiff _____

GRP 3   (1/04)   **NOTICE OF/ DEFAULT/ REQUEST FOR DEFAULT JUDGMENT OF DIVORCE**

Plaintiff (appearing *in propria persona*):

Defendant:

v

Date of hearing _____   Judge _____

After the defendant's default, **IT IS ORDERED**:

1. **DIVORCE:** The parties are divorced.

2. **CHILDREN:** There ☐ are ☐ are not children of the parties or born during their marriage who are under 18 or adult and entitled to support.

☐ 3. **NAME CHANGE:** Wife's last name is changed to _____

4. **SPOUSAL SUPPORT:** Spousal support is ☐ not granted for   ☐ wife. ☐ husband.
   ☐ reserved for   ☐ wife. ☐ husband.
   ☐ granted later in the judgment for ☐ wife. ☐ husband.

5. **PROPERTY DIVISION:**

A. **Real property:** ☐ The parties do not own any real property.
   (Land and buildings) ☐ Real property is divided elsewhere in this judgment.

All real property owned by the parties in joint tenancy or tenancy by the entirety is converted to tenancy in common, unless this judgment provides otherwise.

B. **Personal property:** ☐ Each party is awarded the personal property in his or her possession.
   (All other property) ☐ Personal property is divided elsewhere in this judgment.

6. **STATUTORY RIGHTS:** All interests of the parties in the property of the other, now owned or later acquired, under MCL 700.2201-700.2405, are extinguished, including those known as dower under MCL 558.1-558.29.

7. **BENEFICIARY RIGHTS:** The rights each party has to the proceeds or policies or contracts of life insurance, endowments or annuities upon the life of the other as a named beneficiary or by assignment during or in anticipation of marriage, are ☐ extinguished. ☐ awarded later in the judgment.

8. **RETIREMENT BENEFITS:** Any rights of either party in any pension, annuity or retirement plan benefit of the other, whether these rights are vested or unvested, accumulated or contingent, are ☐ extinguished. ☐ awarded later in the judgment.

9. **DOCUMENTATION:** Each party shall promptly and properly execute and deliver to the other documents to carry out the terms of this judgment. A certified copy of this judgment may be recorded with the register of deeds in any county of this state where property is located.

10. **PRIOR ORDERS:** Except as otherwise provided in this judgment, any nonfinal orders or injunctions entered in this action are terminated.

☐ 11. **SUSPENDED FEES AND COSTS:** The previously suspended fees and costs in this case of _____ shall be ☐ paid by ☐ plaintiff ☐ defendant to the clerk. ☐ waived finally.

12. **EFFECTIVE DATE OF JUDGMENT:** This judgment shall become effective immediately after it is signed by the judge and filed with the clerk.

Plaintiff:

Defendant:

v

IT IS ALSO ORDERED:

13. **INALIENABLE RIGHTS OF CHILDREN:** The children have the right to the love and affection of both parents. The parties shall cooperate during child-rearing to promote the well-being of the children and maintain strong parent-child relationships. The parties must also cooperate in carrying out the child-related provisions of this judgment.

14. **CUSTODY:** Custody of the minor children is granted as follows:

PL = Plaintiff   DF = Defendant   JT = Joint   3rd = Third party, named here:

CHILD'S NAME	DATE Of BIRTH	LEGAL CUSTODY	PHYSICAL CUSTODY

15. **PARENTING TIME:** Any parent without physical custody shall have parenting time as follows:
☐ reasonable   ☐ specific (describe specific parenting time later in this judgment)

16. **RESIDENCE OF CHILDREN:**

a. **Local residences.** A parent whose custody or parenting time of a child is governed by this order shall not change the legal residence of the child except in compliance with section 11 of the "Child Custody Act of 1970," 1970 PA 91, MCL 722.31; or: ☐ After an agreement of the parties, and effective _____ , the residence of the following minor children:

Names _____

shall be changed from their current residence with ☐ plaintiff ☐ defendant

at _____

to _____

b. **State residence (domicile).** The minor children's residences (domicile) shall not be moved from the state of Michigan without the prior approval of the court.

c. **Notice of change of residence.** The person awarded custody shall promptly notify the friend of the court in writing when the minor is moved to another address.

Plaintiff:

Defendant:

v

IT IS ALSO ORDERED:

17. CHILD SUPPORT:

a. **Amount.** Child support shall be paid monthly, in advance on the first day of the month, as follows:

Support payer:		Support payee:			
Children supported:	One	Two	Three	Four	Five or more
Base support:	$	$	$	$	$
Child care:	$	$	$	$	$
Total:	$	$	$	$	$

☐ Base support shall abate 50% after 6 consecutive overnights under sec. IV-C of the MCSF.
☐ Support based on shared economic responsibility was set using payer's general support obligation of
$ _____ and _____ overnights of parenting.

These support provisions ☐ do ☐ do not follow the child support formula.

b. **Duration.** Child support shall last until each child is age 18 or graduates from high school as provided in MCL 552.605b, whichever is later, but no longer than age 19½.

c. **Redirection, assignment and abatement.** Subject to the procedures described in MCL 552.605d: 1) support may be redirected to the person who is legally responsible for the actual care, support and maintenance of a child when that person is different from the payee of support 2) support for a child in foster care shall be assigned to the Family Independence Agency 3) support shall abate for a child who resides on a full-time basis with the payer of support.

18. HEALTH CARE FOR CHILDREN:

a. **Health care coverage.** ☐ Plaintiff ☐ Defendant shall carry insurance (as the term "insurer" is defined in MCL 552.602(o) covering hospital, dental, optical and other health care expenses) when coverage is available at a reasonable cost through an employer or under an existing individual policy.

b. **Uninsured health care expenses:**

1. **Ordinary expenses.** Uninsured health care expenses defined as ordinary by sec. IV-D(2) of the MCSF are paid through the base support amount in paragraph #17.

2. **Extraordinary expenses.** Plaintiff shall pay _____% and defendant shall pay _____% of the uninsured health care expenses defined as extraordinary under MCSF IV-D(3). These expenses must be paid within 28 days of a written payment request or the obligation may be enforced as provided by law.

c. **Qualified medical support order.** This order is a qualified medical support order under 29 USC 1169. To qualify this order, a notice to enroll may be issued to the child support payer under MCL 552.626b. A parent may contest the notice by requesting a review or hearing concerning availability of health care at a reasonable cost.

Plaintiff:

v

Defendant:

IT IS ALSO ORDERED:

19. PAYMENT OF SUPPORT:

a. Child support shall be paid

    by   ☐ immediate income withholding   ☐ without income withholding until past-due support equals or exceeds the monthly amount of support

    to   ☐ state disbursement unit (SDU).   ☐ directly to the payee.   ☐ other:

b. Any spousal support shall be paid

    by   ☐ immediate income withholding   ☐ without income withholding until past-due support equals or exceeds the monthly amount of support

    to   ☐ state disbursement unit (SDU).   ☐ directly to the payee.   ☐ other:

20. PAST-DUE SUPPORT:

a. **Retroactive modification.** Support is an order the date it is due and shall not be modified retroactively except as allowed by MCL 552.603 and 552.603b.

b. **Lien and surcharge.** Unpaid support is a lien on the payer's property by operation of law and the payer's property can be encumbered or seized if past-due support exceeds two times the monthly amount of periodic support payments. In a friend of the court case, a surcharge will be added to past-due support as provided by MCL 552.603a.

c. **Current arrearage.** Past-due support owed from a nonfinal order in this case, including amounts owed to the state of Michigan, is preserved and shall be paid as stated later in this judgment.

21. FRIEND OF THE COURT SERVICES AND FEES:

☐ a. **Friend of the court opt-out.** The friend of the court shall be removed from this case as follows:

☐ The previously ordered opt-out from these friend of the court services: ☐ all friend of the court services   ☐ all friend of the court services except collection and distribution of support through the SDU   ☐ immediate income withholding only ☐ shall remain in effect. ☐ shall terminate.

☐ This case shall be opted out of these friend of the court services: ☐ all friend of the court services   ☐ all friend of the court services except collection and distribution of support through the SDU ☐ immediate income withholding only

b. **Friend of the court fees.** While a friend of the court case, the support payer shall pay friend of the court service fees and other statutory fees.

22. PERSONAL INFORMATION:
The parties' current residence addresses and telephone nos. appear in the main caption of this judgment. Their current sources of income are listed below:

                                         Plaintiff   **Defendant**

Source of income:

Address:

Telephone no:

The parties have previously provided information about their health care coverage, social security nos., driver's and occupational licenses. In a friend of the court case, they must inform the friend of the court of any changes or additions to the personal information cited in this section, reporting changes in their residence information in writing within 21 days of a change.

Plaintiff:

v

Defendant:

IT IS ALSO ORDERED:

This judgment ☐ resolves ☐ does not resolve   the last pending claim in this case, and   ☐ closes ☐ does not close   the case, except to the extent jurisdiction is retained by law.

Reviewed by FOC:

_____

Date _____

Judge _____

GRP 4e (1/04)   JUDGMENT OF DIVORCE, final page

Approved, SCAO

Original - Court
1st copy - Friend of the Court

2nd copy - Plaintiff
3rd copy - Defendant
Additional copies to all sources of income

STATE OF MICHIGAN JUDICIAL CIRCUIT COUNTY	INCOME WITHHOLDING ORDER ☐ Court ordered ☐ Consent	CASE NO.

Friend of the Court address

Court telephone no.

Plaintiff's name and address

Regarding: _____
Payer

_____
Social security number

v

Defendant's name and address

Date of order: _____

Judge: _____

1. The court finds that the above payer owes current support, statutory fees, and/or arrearages in the above case, and notice has been given as required by law.

2. Income is defined as: commissions, earnings, salaries, wages, and other income due now or in the future from an employer and successor employers; any payment due now or in the future from a profit-sharing plan, pension plan, insurance contract, annuity, unemployment compensation, supplemental unemployment benefits, and worker's compensation; any amount of money due the payer under a support order as a debt of any other individual, partnership, association, private or public corporation, the United States or any Federal agency, any state or political subdivision of any state, or any other legal entity indebted to the payer.

IT IS ORDERED:

3. The source of income shall withhold payer's income as specified in the attached notice of income withholding and in any subsequent notices.

4. The State Disbursement Unit shall receive and disburse these funds for the purpose of collecting support, statutory fees, and the payment of all arrearages.

5. Any income withheld under this order shall be paid to the State Disbursement Unit within 3 days after the date of withholding.

6. If the payer's existing support order is modified by an order of the court, the office of the friend of the court shall send a notice of modification to the source of income by ordinary mail. The amount assigned or withheld shall be changed to conform with the court modification within 7 days after receipt of the notice of modification.

_____
Signature of preparer

_____
Judge

Bar no.

☐ I consent to the terms of this order.

_____
Payer's signature

CERTIFICATE OF MAILING

I certify that on this date I mailed a copy of this order to the parties and sources of income by ordinary mail addressed to their last known addresses.

_____
Date

_____
Signature

FOC 5 (4/01) **INCOME WITHHOLDING ORDER**

MCL 552.601 et seq.; MSA 25.164(1) et seq.

Testimony

1) My name is [full name] , my address is [address], and I am the plaintiff in this case.

2) I was married to the defendant on _____ at _____ by a person authorized to
perform marriages.
_____ Date and place of marriage

3) Before the marriage, my/[my wife's] name was _____ .
_____ Wife's former name

4) I filed my complaint for divorce on _____ . Before I filed the complaint, I had resided in Michigan since
_____ Filing date

_____ and in this county since _____ .
State residency   County residency

5) As I said in my complaint, there has been a breakdown in our marriage relationship to the extent the objects of matrimony
have been destroyed because _____and there remains no
_____ Brief facts to support grounds

reasonable likelihood that our marriage can be preserved because _____ .
_____ Brief facts to support grounds

6) The defendant and I have _____minor children _____ .
I/[my wife] am not now pregnant.
_____ Names and ages of minor children

7) The friend of the court has recommended that I should have _____ custody of the children with
_____ Custody

_____ parenting time to the defendant. S/he and I have agreed that this arrangement is satisfactory.
Parenting time

8) The friend of the court has also recommended that I receive _____ monthly in child support and I believe that this
should be sufficient.
_____ Child support

9) I am working at_____ and am able to support myself.
_____ Source of support

10) We own some _____ that we have split between us. We have also agreed that
_____ General description of personal property

the defendant is to give me _____ and I will pay off the debt on it.
_____ Specific items of personal property transferred in judgment

11) We also own_____ worth around_____ .
_____ Description of any real property   Value

We have agreed to _____ .
_____ Manner of division

12) I would like my former name of _____ back.
_____ Wife's name change

13) My court fees were suspended when I filed this divorce. Since then, _____ .
_____ Current financial condition

14) Does the court have any questions?

STATE OF MICHIGAN **JUDICIAL DISTRICT** **JUDICIAL CIRCUIT**	**PROOF OF MAILING**	CASE NO.

Court address _____ Court telephone no.

Plaintiff(s)		Defendant(s)
	v	

On the date below I sent by first class mail a copy of _____

to:
Names and addresses

I declare that the statements above are true to the best of my information, knowledge and belief.

Date _____

Name (typed) _____

Signature _____

MC 302 (5/88) **PROOF OF MAILING**

Optional Forms

Request for Accommodations	MC 70
Motion and Order for Appointment of Foreign Language Interpreter	MC 81
Affidavit and Order, Suspension of Fees/Costs	MC 20
Ex Parte Order	GRP 5a-c
Objection to Referee's Recommended Order	FOC 68
Subpoena	MC 11
Income Withholding Order	FOC 5
Advice of Rights Regarding Use of Friend of the Court Services	FOC 101
Supplemental Notice to Advice of Rights Regarding Use of Friend of the Court Services	FOC 101a
Order Exempting Case from Friend of the Court Services	FOC 102
Request to Reopen Friend of the Court Case	FOC 104
Agreement Suspending Immediate Income Withholding	FOC 63
Order Suspending Immediate Income Withholding	FOC 64
Motion and Verification for Alternate Service	MC 303
Order for Alternate Service	MC 304
Order for Service by Publication/Posting and Notice of Action	MC 307
Notice to Prior Court of Proceedings Affecting Minor(s)	MC 28
Waiver of Military Relief Law Rights	GRP 6
Request for Certification of Military Status	
Military Locator Request	
Dismissal	MC 09
Judgment of Divorce (expansion page)	GRP 4x

REQUEST FOR ACCOMMODATIONS	Court name and location

Today's date	**Instructions for completing form:** *Provide your name, address, and telephone number. Check the boxes which apply to you and provide any necessary details. When you have completed this request, please return it to the court at the above address.*

1.

Name			
Address			
City	State	Zip	Telephone no.

2. Court activity you need accommodations for:

☐ Hearing _____
  Date

☐ Mediation meeting _____
  Date

☐ Jury duty _____
  Date(s)

☐ Other (specify): _____
  include dates if relevant

3. What is the nature of your disability?

☐ Physical mobility impairment (wheelchair, walker, crutches, etc.)

☐ Speech impairment (specify): _____

☐ Visual impairment

☐ Hearing impairment (specify)   ☐ deaf   ☐ hard of hearing

☐ Other (specify): _____

4. What type of accommodation are you requesting?

☐ Interpreter for deaf (specify whether ASL, tactile, oral, etc.) _____

☐ Assistive listening device (specify type of device) _____

☐ Physical location accessible for persons with a physical mobility concern.

☐ Other (specify) _____

For court use only

MC 70 (10/97) **REQUEST FOR ACCOMMODATIONS**

Original - Court file
1st copy - Assignment Clerk/Extra
2nd copy - Friend of the Court/Extra
3rd copy - Opposing party
4th copy - Moving party

Approved, SCAO

STATE OF MICHIGAN JUDICIAL DISTRICT JUDICIAL CIRCUIT COUNTY	MOTION AND ORDER FOR APPOINTMENT OF FOREIGN LANGUAGE INTERPRETER	CASE NO.

Court address   Court telephone no.

Plaintiff name(s) ☐ moving party		Defendant name(s) ☐ moving party
Plaintiff's attorney, bar no., address, and telephone no.	v	Defendant's attorney, bar no., address, and telephone no.

MOTION

1. I state that I am unable to speak English sufficiently to understand and participate in the proceedings in this case.

2. ☐ I am represented by an attorney.   ☐ I am not represented by an attorney.

3. I request the court to appoint a foreign language interpreter to interpret for me.

4. I request an interpreter who speaks the _____ language.

5. If required, place my request on the motion calendar.

_____
Date

_____
Signature

To be completed only if the court
requires a hearing on the motion

NOTICE OF HEARING

You are notified that a hearing has been scheduled on this matter for:

Judge	Bar no.	Date	Time
Hearing location
☐ Court address above   ☐

If you require special accommodations to use the court because of disabilities, please contact the court immediately to make arrangements.

_____
Date

_____
Signature

CERTIFICATE OF MAILING

I certify that on this date I mailed a copy of this motion and notice of hearing (if applicable) to the other party at the last known address.

_____
Date

_____
Signature

ORDER

IT IS ORDERED the above motion is   ☐ granted.   ☐ denied.

_____
Date

_____
Judge

MC 81   (10/01)   **MOTION AND ORDER FOR APPOINTMENT OF FOREIGN LANGUAGE INTERPRETER**

Original - Court 1st copy - Applicant	2nd copy - Opposing party PROBATE OSM CODE: OSF

STATE OF MICHIGAN JUDICIAL DISTRICT JUDICIAL CIRCUIT COUNTY PROBATE	AFFIDAVIT AND ORDER SUSPENSION OF FEES/COSTS	CASE NO.

Court address   Court telephone no.

Plaintiff/Petitioner name, address, and telephone no.		Defendant/Respondent name, address, and telephone no.
	v	
Plaintiff's/Petitioner's attorney, bar no., address, and telephone no.		Defendant's/Respondent's attorney, bar no., address, and telephone no.

☐ Probate   In the matter of _____

NOTE: Requests for waiver/suspension of transcript costs must be made separately by motion.

AFFIDAVIT

1. The attached pleading is to be filed with the court by or on behalf of _____,
Name

applicant, who is   ☐ plaintiff/petitioner.   ☐ defendant/respondent.

2. The applicant is entitled to and asks the court for suspension of fees and costs in the action for the following reason:

☐ a. S/he is currently receiving public assistance: $ _____ per _____ Case No.: _____.

☐ b. S/he is unable to pay those fees and costs because of indigency, based on the following facts:

INCOME: _____
Employer name and address

_____ _____ _____ per ☐ week. ☐ month. ☐ two weeks.
Length of employment   Average gross pay   Average net pay

ASSETS: State value of car, home, bank deposits, bonds, stocks, etc.

OBLIGATIONS: Itemize monthly rent, installment payments, mortgage payments, child support, etc.

☐ 3. (in domestic relations cases only) The applicant is entitled to an order requiring his/her spouse to pay attorney fees.

REIMBURSEMENT: It is understood that the court may order the applicant to pay the fees and costs when the reason for their waiver or suspension no longer exists.

_____
Affiant signature

Subscribed and sworn to before me on _____, _____County, Michigan.
Date

My commission expires: _____ Signature: _____
Date   Deputy clerk/Register/Notary public

(SEE REVERSE SIDE FOR ORDER)

MC 20 (6/03) **AFFIDAVIT AND ORDER, SUSPENSION OF FEES/COSTS**   MCR 2.002

CERTIFICATION OF ATTORNEY

1. I have reviewed the affidavit of indigency, and I certify that its contents are true to the best of my information, knowledge, and belief.
2. I will bring to the court's attention the matter of suspended costs and fees and the availability of funds to pay them before any disposition is entered. I will report at that time any changes in the information contained in the affidavit of indigency or any other information regarding the affiant's financial status or alterations of the fee arrangement.

Date _____ Attorney signature _____

Attorney name (type or print) _____ Bar no. _____

CERTIFICATION BY PERSON OTHER THAN PARTY

1. I have personal knowledge of the facts appearing in the affidavit.
2. The person on whose behalf the petition is filed is unable to sign it because of

☐ minority: _____ Date of birth _____ Nature of disability _____ ☐ other disability:

Relationship: _____

Date _____ Affiant signature _____

Affiant name (type or print) _____

Address _____

City, state, zip _____ Telephone no. _____

ORDER

IT IS ORDERED:

☐ 1. Fees and costs in this action required by law or court rule are waived/suspended until further order of the court. Before any final disposition or discontinuance is entered, the moving party shall bring the fee and costs suspension to the attention of the judge for final disposition.

☐ 2. The applicant's spouse shall pay the fees and costs required by law or court rule.

☐ 3. This application is denied.

Date _____ Judge _____ Bar no. _____

STATE OF MICHIGAN Circuit Court - Family Division COUNTY	EX PARTE ORDER for Custody, Parenting Time, Residence of Children and Support	CASE NO.

Plaintiff (appearing *in propria persona*):

v

Defendant:

Date of order_____   Judge _____

While this case is pending, **IT IS ORDERED:**

1. **CUSTODY:** Custody of the minor children is granted as follows:

PL = Plaintiff   DF = Defendant   JT = Joint   3rd = Third party, named here:

CHILD'S NAME	DATE Of BIRTH	LEGAL CUSTODY	PHYSICAL CUSTODY

2. **PARENTING TIME:** Any parent without physical custody shall have reasonable parenting time.

3. **RESIDENCE OF CHILDREN:**

a. **Local residences.** A parent whose custody or parenting time of a child is governed by this order shall not change the legal residence of the child except in compliance with section 11 of the "Child Custody Act of 1970," 1970 PA 91, MCL 722.31.

b. **State residence (domicile).** The minor children's residences (domicile) shall not be moved from the state of Michigan without the prior approval of the court.

c. **Notice of change of residence.** The person awarded custody shall promptly notify the friend of the court in writing when the minor is moved to another address.

GRP 5a (1/04)   **EX PARTE ORDER, page 1**

STATE OF MICHIGAN Circuit Court - Family Division COUNTY	EX PARTE ORDER for Custody, Parenting Time, Residence of Children and Support	CASE NO.

Plaintiff: **Defendant:**

v

IT IS ALSO ORDERED:

4. CHILD SUPPORT:

a. **Amount.** Child support shall be paid monthly, in advance on the first day of the month, as follows:

Support payer:		Support payee:			
Children supported:	One	Two	Three	Four	Five or more
Base support:	$	$	$	$	$
Child care:	$	$	$	$	$
Total:	$	$	$	$	$

☐ Base support shall abate 50% after 6 consecutive overnights under sec. IV-C of the MCSF.
☐ Support based on shared economic responsibility was set using payer's general support obligation of
$ _____ and _____ overnights of parenting.

These support provisions ☐ do ☐ do not follow the child support formula.

b. **Method of payment.** Child support shall be paid

by ☐ immediate income withholding ☐ without income withholding until past-due support
equals or exceeds the monthly amount of support

to ☐ state disbursement unit (SDU). ☐ directly to the payee. ☐ other:

c. **Duration.** Child support shall last until each child is age 18 or graduates from high school as provided in MCL 552.605b, whichever is later, but no longer than age 19½.

d. **Redirection, assignment and abatement.** Subject to the procedures described in MCL 552.605d: 1) support may be redirected to the person who is legally responsible for the actual care, support and maintenance of a child when that person is different from the payee of support 2) support for a child in foster care shall be assigned to the Family Independence Agency 3) support shall abate for a child who resides on a full-time basis with the payer of support.

5. HEALTH CARE FOR CHILDREN:

a. **Health care coverage.** ☐ Plaintiff ☐ Defendant shall carry insurance (as the term "insurer" is defined in MCL 552.602(o) covering hospital, dental, optical and other health care expenses) when coverage is available at a reasonable cost through an employer or under an existing individual policy.

b. **Uninsured health care expenses.** Uninsured health care expenses defined as ordinary by sec. IV-D(2) of the MCSF are paid through the base support amount in paragraph #4.

Plaintiff shall pay _____% and defendant shall pay _____ % of the uninsured health care expenses defined as extraordinary under MCSF IV-D(3). These expenses must be paid within 28 days of a written payment request or the obligation may be enforced as provided by law.

c. **Qualified medical support order.** This order is a qualified medical support order under 29 USC 1169. To qualify this order, a notice to enroll may be issued to the child support payer under MCL 552.626b. A parent may contest the notice by requesting a review or hearing concerning availability of health care at a reasonable cost.

Plaintiff:		Defendant:
	v	

IT IS ALSO ORDERED:

6. **FRIEND OF THE COURT SERVICES AND FEES:**

☐ a. **Friend of the court opt-out.** This case shall be opted out of the following friend of the court services: ☐ all friend of the court services ☐ all friend of the court services except collection and distribution of child support through the SDU ☐ immediate income withholding only

b. **Friend of the court fees.** While a friend of the court case, the child support payer shall pay friend of the court service fees and other statutory fees.

7. **PERSONAL INFORMATION:** The parties' current residence information appears in the main caption of this order. In a friend of the court case, the parties shall keep the friend of the court informed of residence changes or changes in their sources of income or available health care coverage (including the health care provider, coverage identification no. and persons covered).

8. **EFFECTIVENESS AND ENFORCEABILITY:** This order is effective when entered with the clerk and enforceable after service on defendant.

NOTICE

TO THE DEFENDANT:

9. You may file a written objection to this order or a motion to modify or rescind this order. You must file the written objection or motion with the clerk of the court within 14 days after you were served with this order. You must serve a true copy of the objection or motion on the friend of the court and the party who obtained the order.

10. If you file a written objection, the friend of the court must try to resolve the dispute. If the friend of the court cannot resolve the dispute and if you wish to bring the matter before the court without the assistance of counsel, the friend of the court must provide you with form pleadings and written instructions and must schedule a hearing with the court.

11. The ex parte order will automatically become a temporary order if you do not file a written objection or motion to modify or rescind the ex parte order and a request for a hearing. Even if an objection is filed, the ex parte order will remain in effect and must be obeyed unless changed by a later court order.

Reviewed by FOC:

_____

Date _____   Judge _____

PROOF OF MAILING

On the date below, I sent a true copy of this order to defendant at his/her address in the main caption by ordinary first-class mail.

I declare that the statement above is true to the best of my information, knowledge and belief.

Date _____   Plaintiff _____

Original - Court
1st copy - Moving Party
2nd copy - Objecting Party

3rd copy - Friend of the Court
4th copy - Proof of Service
5th copy - Proof of Service

Approved, SCAO

STATE OF MICHIGAN JUDICIAL CIRCUIT COUNTY	OBJECTION TO REFEREE'S RECOMMENDED ORDER	CASE NO.

Court address

Court telephone no.

Plaintiff's name, address, and telephone no. ☐ Moving party		Defendant's name, address, and telephone no. ☐ Moving party
	v	
Third party's name, address, and telephone no. ☐ Moving party		

I object to the entry of the referee's recommended order dated _____ and
request a de novo hearing by the court. My objection is based on the following reason(s):

I declare that the statements above are true to the best of my information, knowledge, and belief.

_____
Date

_____
Signature of objecting party

_____
Name (type or print)

NOTICE OF HEARING

A hearing will be held on this objection before Hon._____
                                                     Name of judge

on _____ at _____ at _____.
   Date   Time   Place

If you require special accommodations to use the court because of a disability, please contact the court immediately to make arrangements.

CERTIFICATE OF MAILING

I certify that on this date I mailed a copy of this objection and notice of hearing on the other party(ies) by ordinary mail at the above address(es).

_____
Date

_____
Signature of objecting party

FOC 68 (6/98) **OBJECTION TO REFEREE'S RECOMMENDED ORDER**   MCR 3.215(E)

Original - Return
1st copy - Witness
2nd copy - File
3rd copy - Extra

STATE OF MICHIGAN JUDICIAL DISTRICT JUDICIAL CIRCUIT COUNTY PROBATE	SUBPOENA Order to Appear and/or Produce	CASE NO.

Court address	Court telephone no.

Police Report No. (if applicable)

Plaintiff(s)/Petitioner(s)		Defendant(s)/Respondent(s)
☐ People of the State of Michigan ☐ _____ _____	v	
☐ Civil ☐ Criminal		Charge

☐ Probate   In the matter of _____

In the Name of the People of the State of Michigan.   TO:

If you require special accommodations to use the court because of disabilities, please contact the court immediately to make arrangements.

YOU ARE ORDERED:

☐ 1. to appear personally at the time and place stated below: You may be required to appear from time to time and day to day until excused.

   ☐ The court address above   ☐ Other:

Day	Date	Time

☐ 2. Testify at trial / examination / hearing.

☐ 3. Produce/permit inspection or copying of the following items:_____

_____

☐ 4. Testify as to your assets, and bring with you the items listed in line 3 above.

☐ 5. Testify at deposition.

☐ 6. MCL 600.6104(2), 600.6116, or 600.6119 prohibition against transferring or disposing of property is attached.

☐ 7. Other: _____

☐ 8.
Person requesting subpoena	Telephone no.
Address	
City	State Zip

NOTE: If requesting a debtor's examination under MCL 600.6110, or an injunction under item 6. this subpoena must be issued by a judge. For a debtor examination, the affidavit of debtor examination on the other side of this form must also be completed. Debtor's assets can also be discovered through MCR 2.305 without the need for an affidavit of debtor examination or issuance of this subpoena by a judge.

FAILURE TO OBEY THE COMMANDS OF THE SUBPOENA OR APPEAR AT THE STATED TIME AND PLACE MAY SUBJECT YOU TO PENALTY FOR CONTEMPT OF COURT.

	Court use only
	☐ Served ☐ Not served

_____
Date

_____
Judge/Clerk/Attorney

_____
Bar no.

MC 11 (6/99) **SUBPOENA, Order to Appear and/or Produce**

MCL 600.1455, 600.1701, 600.6110, 600.6119;
MSA 27A.1455, 27A.1701, 27A.6110, 27A.6119, MCR 2.506

SUBPOENA	PROOF OF SERVICE	Case No.

TO PROCESS SERVER: You must make and file your return with the court clerk. If you are unable to complete service, you must return this original and all copies to the court clerk.

CERTIFICATE / AFFIDAVIT OF SERVICE / NON-SERVICE

☐ **OFFICER CERTIFICATE**	OR	☐ **AFFIDAVIT OF PROCESS SERVER**
I certify that I am a sheriff, deputy sheriff, bailiff, appointed court officer, or attorney for a party [MCR 2.104(A)(2)], and that: (notary not required)		Being first duly sworn, I state that I am a legally competent adult who is not a party or an officer of a corporate party, and that: (notary required)

☐ I served a copy of the subpoena, together with _____ Attachment

☐ personally (including required fees, if any)

☐ by registered or certified mail (copy of return receipt attached) on:

Name(s)	Complete address(es) of service	Day, date, time

☐ After diligent search and inquiry, I have been unable to find and serve the following person(s): _____

I have made the following efforts in attempting to serve process: _____

☐ I have personally attempted to serve the subpoena and required fees, if any, together with _____ Attachment

on _____
Name

at _____ and have been unable to complete service because the address was incorrect at the time of filing.

		Service fee $	Miles traveled	Mileage fee $	Total fee $

Signature _____

Title _____

Subscribed and sworn to before me on _____ , _____ County, Michigan.
Date

My commission expires: _____   Signature: _____
Date   Deputy court clerk/Notary public

ACKNOWLEDGMENT OF SERVICE

I acknowledge that I have received service of the subpoena and required fees, if any, together with _____ Attachment

on _____
Day, date, time

on behalf of _____

Signature _____

AFFIDAVIT FOR JUDGMENT DEBTOR EXAMINATION

I request that the court issue a subpoena which orders the party named on this form to be examined under oath before a judge concerning the money or property of: _____
for the following reasons: _____

Under penalty of contempt of court, I declare that the above statements are true to the best of my information, knowledge, and belief.

Date _____   Signature _____

MCR 2.105

Approved, SCAO

STATE OF MICHIGAN JUDICIAL CIRCUIT COUNTY	INCOME WITHHOLDING ORDER ☐ Court ordered ☐ Consent	CASE NO.

Friend of the Court address   Court telephone no.

Plaintiff's name and address

Regarding: _____
Payer

_____
Social security number

v

Defendant's name and address

Date of order: _____

Judge: _____

1. The court finds that the above payer owes current support, statutory fees, and/or arrearages in the above case, and notice has been given as required by law.

2. Income is defined as: commissions, earnings, salaries, wages, and other income due now or in the future from an employer and successor employers; any payment due now or in the future from a profit-sharing plan, pension plan, insurance contract, annuity, unemployment compensation, supplemental unemployment benefits, and worker's compensation; any amount of money due the payer under a support order as a debt of any other individual, partnership, association, private or public corporation, the United States or any Federal agency, any state or political subdivision of any state, or any other legal entity indebted to the payer.

IT IS ORDERED:

3. The source of income shall withhold payer's income as specified in the attached notice of income withholding and in any subsequent notices.

4. The State Disbursement Unit shall receive and disburse these funds for the purpose of collecting support, statutory fees, and the payment of all arrearages.

5. Any income withheld under this order shall be paid to the State Disbursement Unit within 3 days after the date of withholding.

6. If the payer's existing support order is modified by an order of the court, the office of the friend of the court shall send a notice of modification to the source of income by ordinary mail. The amount assigned or withheld shall be changed to conform with the court modification within 7 days after receipt of the notice of modification.

_____   _____   _____
Signature of preparer   Judge   Bar no.

☐ I consent to the terms of this order. _____
Payer's signature

CERTIFICATE OF MAILING

I certify that on this date I mailed a copy of this order to the parties and sources of income by ordinary mail addressed to their last known addresses.

_____   _____
Date   Signature

FOC 5 (4/01) **INCOME WITHHOLDING ORDER**   MCL 552.601 et seq.; MSA 25.164(1) et seq.

Approved, SCAO

STATE OF MICHIGAN JUDICIAL CIRCUIT COUNTY	ADVICE OF RIGHTS REGARDING USE OF FRIEND OF THE COURT SERVICES	CASE NO.

Friend of the Court address   **Telephone no.**

1. Right to Refuse Friend of the Court Services

a. You have the right to refuse friend of the court services for custody, parenting time, and support. To prevent friend of the court involvement, you must file with the court, along with your first pleading, a motion requesting that friend of the court services not be required. You must attach a signed copy of this advice of rights to the motion. The court will grant the motion provided both parties agree and have signed this advice of rights and it determines that the following are true:

1) Neither of you receives public assistance for the child(ren) or requests friend of the court services.
2) There is no evidence of domestic violence or uneven bargaining position between you.
3) The court finds that declining to receive friend of the court services is not against the best interests of a child.

b. If you already have a friend of the court case, you can file a motion to discontinue friend of the court services provided both parties agree, and have signed this advice of rights and the court finds that the following are true:

1) Neither of you receives public assistance for the child(ren) or requests friend of the court services.
2) There is no evidence of domestic violence or uneven bargaining position between you.
3) The court finds that declining to receive friend of the court services is not against the best interests of a child.
4) No money is due the state because of past public assistance.
5) No arrearage or a custody or parenting time order violation has occurred in the last 12 months.
6) Neither of you has reopened a friend of the court case in the last 12 months.

2. Friend of the Court Services (you will not receive these services if you choose not to use the Friend of the Court)

The friend of the court must provide the following services for friend of the court cases. You are entitled to these services unless you choose to refuse the services and the court grants that choice.

a. Accounting Services

Friends of the court must collect support and disburse it within 48 hours. Friend of the court accounting services include: 1) friend of the court accounting for payments received and sent; 2) adjustments of support for parenting time or other credits; and 3) annual statements of accounts, if requested.

b. Support Enforcement Services

The friend of the court must begin to enforce support when one month of support is overdue. For friend of the court cases, child support enforcement services include:

- Paying support out of tax refunds.
- Asking the court to order the nonpaying party to come to court to explain the failure to pay.
- Having unpaid support paid out of property the payer owns.
- Reporting support arrearage to a consumer reporting agency or requesting that the payer's licenses be suspended.
- Collecting support by an income withholding order.

If you choose not to receive friend of the court services, any existing income withholding source will be notified that the friend of the court is no longer responsible for income withholding. **The parties will be solely responsible for stopping or changing income withholding as the law allows.** The friend of the court will stop any unfinished collection actions.

c. Medical Support Enforcement Services

The friend of the court is required to recommend how the parents divide health care expenses and to take action to collect the amounts that a parent fails or refuses to pay. When a parent is required to insure the children the friend of the court is authorized to instruct an employer to enroll the children in an insurance plan when the parent fails or refuses to do so.

d. Support Review and Modification Services

Once every two years persons with friend of the court cases may request the friend of the court to review the support amount. After completing the review, the friend of the court must file a motion to raise or lower support, or inform the parties that it recommends no change. It must also review support when changed circumstances lead it to believe that support should be modified.

See other side

FOC 101 (6/03) **ADVICE OF RIGHTS REGARDING USE OF FRIEND OF THE COURT SERVICES**

MCL 552.505,
MCL 552.505a

Advice of Rights Regarding Use of Friend of the Court Services, continued from page 1

e. Custody and Parenting Time Enforcement Services

For friend of the court cases, the friend of the court must enforce custody and parenting time when a party complains that it is violated. Child custody and parenting time enforcement services include:

- Asking the court to order the noncooperating party to come to the court to explain the failure to obey the parenting time order.
- Suspending the licenses of individuals who deny parenting time.
- Awarding makeup parenting time.
- Joint meetings to resolve complaints.

f. Custody and Parenting Time Investigation Services

For disputes about custody or parenting time in friend of the court cases, the friend of the court sometimes must investigate and provide reports to the parties and the court.

g. Mediation Services

Friend of the court offices must provide mediation services to help parties with friend of the court cases settle custody and parenting time disputes.

3. State Disbursement Unit and IV-D Services

a. State Disbursement Unit (SDU)

If you choose not to receive friend of the court services, you may continue to make payments to, and receive payments through, the state disbursement unit (SDU). The SDU will keep track of the amount paid and sent out. However, the SDU cannot provide you with all of the accounting functions the friend of the court provides.

All payments made through the SDU must be distributed to the amounts due as required by federal law. When a payer has more than one case, federal law determines how a payment is divided among the cases. Even if you choose not to receive friend of the court services, payments through the SDU must be divided among all a payer's cases and distributed in the same manner as payments on FOC cases. You cannot discontinue friend of the court services if you want to use the SDU unless you first provide to the SDU all the information that the SDU needs to set up an account.

b. Your Rights Under Title IV-D of the Social Security Act

Title IV-D of the Social Security Act provides federal government resources to collect child support and it allows certain funding to be used for parenting time and custody services. In Michigan, critical title IV-D services are delivered by the friend of the court. If you choose not to receive friend of the court services, you cannot receive most IV-D services.

ACKNOWLEDGMENT REGARDING SERVICES

Check below only if you do not want to receive friend of the court services. Then date and sign. A copy of this document must be attached to your first pleading with the court.

I have read this advice of rights and I understand the friend of the court services I am entitled to receive.

☐ I acknowledge that by signing below I am choosing not to receive any friend of the court services. I understand that before this choice can take effect, a motion requesting this choice and the other party's agreement must be filed with the court for approval. I also understand that the court may deny this choice if certain conditions are not met as stated in this advice of rights.

_____   _____   _____   _____
Signature   Date   Signature   Date

If you did not check the above, you are choosing friend of the court to receive the court services. For the most effective friend of the court services, you can request IV-D services by dating and signing below.

I request IV-D services through the friend of the court office.

_____   _____   _____
Date   Signature   Social security number

STATE OF MICHIGAN JUDICIAL CIRCUIT COUNTY	SUPPLEMENTAL NOTICE TO ADVICE OF RIGHTS REGARDING USE OF FRIEND OF THE COURT SERVICES	CASE NO.

Friend of the Court address	Telephone no.

1. State Disbursement Unit Payments

a. State Disbursement Unit (SDU)

If you opt out of the friend of the court, you may continue to make payments through the State Disbursement Unit (SDU). The SDU uses the friend of the court for most accounting functions and cannot provide you with all of the accounting functions the friend of the court provides.

For friend of the court cases, payments are made through the SDU and distributed to the amounts due as required by federal law. When a payer has more than one case, federal law determines how a payment is divided between the cases. **Even if parties opt out of the friend of the court, payments through the SDU must be divided between all payer's cases and distributed in the same manner as payments on friend of the court cases.**

b. SDU Limitations

The SDU relies on the friend of the court records to determine the amount of income withholding. The SDU also requires the friend of the court to set up any income withholding or change in income withholding. If you choose not to accept friend of the court services, the SDU will not be able to process payments through income withholding if the person paying support changes jobs or the amount withheld changes.

Under federal law, the state of Michigan is converting its friend of the court to a new single child support enforcement computer system. County friend of the court offices will be converted under a schedule that begins in March, 2003 and continues until September 30, 2003. Until the conversion is completed, only the friend of the court can process checks. If you choose not to accept friend of the court services, you will not be able to use the SDU until all of your cases are converted to MiCSES version 2.4 or greater.

2. Your Acknowledgment of System Limitations on Your Right to Opt Out of Friend of the Court Services

Please sign and return this form to the friend of the court.

I have read this form and I want to opt out of the friend of the court. I understand that I cannot opt out of the friend of the court with SDU services until this case is converted to MiCSES version 2.4 or greater.

Date	Signature

STATE OF MICHIGAN JUDICIAL CIRCUIT COUNTY	ORDER EXEMPTING CASE FROM FRIEND OF THE COURT SERVICES	CASE NO.

Friend of the Court address   FAX no.   Telephone no.

Plaintiff's name and address

v

Defendant's name and address

Attorney:

Attorney:

Date of hearing: _____   Judge: _____

Bar no.

THE COURT FINDS:

1. There is no evidence of domestic violence or unequal bargaining position between the parties to the case.
2. Granting the parties the relief they have requested would not be against the best interests of any child in the case.
3. The parties have filed executed copies of a form advising them of the services they will not receive if their motion is granted.
4. Neither party receives public assistance for a child in the case.
5. No money is due the state because of past public assistance for a child in the case.
6. No arrearage or custody or parenting time order violation has occurred in the last 12 months in this case.
7. Neither party has reopened a friend of the court case in the last 12 months.
☐ 8. The parties do not want IV-D services and have requested that any existing IV-D case be closed. (Note: This box should be checked unless exceptional circumstances exist that entitle the IV-D case to remain open.)

IT IS ORDERED:

9. Subject to the provisions of item 14 below, this case is not a friend of the court case.
☐ 10. This case is not a title IV-D case. (Note: This box should be checked if item 8 has been checked.)
11. The friend of the court shall not be involved in the enforcement, investigation, or accounting functions for custody, parenting time, or support in this case.
12. The parties are responsible for all enforcement and accounting functions for custody, parenting time, or support in this case.
13. Except as indicated below, there is no income withholding in this case, support will be paid directly by the payer to the payee, and the friend of the court shall terminate any existing income withholding. Should this case become a friend of the court case, the payer must keep the friend of the court advised of the name and address of the payer's source of income and any health care coverage that is available to the payer as a benefit of employment or that the payer maintains including the name of the insurance company, health care organization, or health maintenance organization; the policy, certificate, or contract number; and the names and birth dates of the persons for whose benefit the payer maintains the coverage.
    ☐ a. Support shall be paid through the State Disbursement Unit (SDU). Support shall be paid by income withholding to the extent allowed by statutes and court rules, however, the friend of the court is not responsible for the income withholding. The friend of the court shall notify the employer that it is no longer involved in the case and that any further information concerning income withholding will be provided by the parties.
    ☐ b. Support shall be paid through the SDU.
    If support payments are to be made through the SDU by income withholding or otherwise, the friend of the court shall not close the friend of the court case until the SDU notifies the friend of the court that it has been provided with the information necessary to process the child support payments. There will be no accounting for support that is not paid through the SDU.
14. The friend of the court shall open a friend of the court case if a party applies for public assistance relating to a child of the parties or either party submits to the friend of the court a written request to reopen the friend of the court case. If this case becomes a friend of the court case for any reason, the provisions on the other side of this order shall apply.

_____
Date

_____
Judge

See provisions on back.

CERTIFICATE OF MAILING

I certify that on this date I mailed a copy of this order to the other party by ordinary mail addressed to the last known address.

_____
Date

_____
Signature

FOC 102 (6/03) **ORDER EXEMPTING CASE FROM FRIEND OF THE COURT SERVICES**   MCL 552.505, MCL 552.505a

If this case becomes a friend of the court case for any reason, the following provisions apply:

1. The parties must cooperate fully with the friend of the court in establishing the case as a friend of the court case.
2. The parties must provide copies of all orders in their case to the friend of the court.
3. The parties must supply any documents that a party to a friend of the court case is required to supply if they have not already done so.
4. The friend of the court is not responsible for determining any support arrearage that is not indicated by payment made through the SDU.
5. Support is payable through the friend of the court effective the date the case becomes a friend of the court case.
6. The friend of the court may prepare and submit, exparte, a uniform child support order that contains all the statutory requirements of a Michigan support order as long as the order does not contradict the existing support order.

STATE OF MICHIGAN JUDICIAL CIRCUIT COUNTY	REQUEST TO REOPEN FRIEND OF THE COURT CASE	CASE NO.

Friend of the Court address   **Telephone no.**

Plaintiff's name and address

Defendant's name and address

Attorney: Attorney:

1. On _____ an order was entered exempting this case from friend of the court services.
   Date

I REQUEST that the friend of the court case be reopened upon filing of this request with the friend of the court office.

CERTIFICATE OF MAILING

I certify that on this date I mailed a copy of this request to the other party by ordinary mail addressed to the last known address.

_____
Date

_____
Signature

FOC 104 (6/03) **REQUEST TO REOPEN FRIEND OF THE COURT CASE**   MCL 552.505, MCL 552.505a

Approved, SCAO

STATE OF MICHIGAN JUDICIAL CIRCUIT COUNTY	AGREEMENT SUSPENDING IMMEDIATE INCOME WITHHOLDING	CASE NO.

Friend of the Court address

Court telephone no.

Plaintiff's name and address

v

Defendant's name and address

NOTE: MCL 552.604(3); MSA 25.164(4)(3) requires that all new and modified support orders after December 31, 1990 include a provision for immediate income withholding and that income withholding take effect immediately unless the parties enter into a written agreement that the income withholding order shall not take effect immediately.

We understand that by law an order of income withholding in a support order shall take effect immediately. However, we agree to the following:

1. The order of income withholding shall not take effect immediately.

2. An alternative payment arrangement shall be made as follows:

3. Both the payer and the recipient of support shall keep the friend of the court informed of the following:
   a. the name, address, and telephone number of his/her current source of income;
   b. any health care coverage that is available to him/her as a benefit of employment or that is maintained by him/her; the name of the insurance company, health care organization, or health maintenance organization; the policy, certificate or contract number; and the name(s) and birth date(s) of the person(s) for whose benefit s/he maintains health care coverage under the policy, certificate, or contract; and
   c. his/her current residence and mailing address.

4. We further understand that proceedings to implement income withholding shall commence if the payer of support falls one month behind in his/her support payments.

5. We recognize that the court may order withholding of income to take effect immediately for cause or at the request of the payer.

_____
Date

_____
Date

_____
Plaintiff's signature

_____
Defendant's signature

FOC 63 (4/01) **AGREEMENT SUSPENDING IMMEDIATE INCOME WITHHOLDING**   MCL 552.604; MSA 25.164(4)

Approved, SCAO

STATE OF MICHIGAN JUDICIAL CIRCUIT COUNTY	ORDER SUSPENDING IMMEDIATE INCOME WITHHOLDING	CASE NO.

Friend of the Court address

Court telephone no.

Plaintiff's name and address

v

Defendant's name and address

1. Date of hearing: _____ Judge: _____

Bar no.

2. **THE COURT FINDS:**

☐ There is good cause for the order of income withholding not to take effect immediately as follows:

   a. It is in the best interest of the child for immediate income withholding not to take effect for the following stated reasons:

   b. Proof of timely payment of previously ordered support has been provided.

   c. Both the payer and the recipient of support will notify the friend of the court in writing of any change in:
   1) the name, address, and telephone number of his/her current source of income;
   2) any health care coverage that is available to him/her as a benefit of employment or that is maintained by him/her, the name of the insurance company, health care organization, or health maintenance organization; the policy, certificate, or contract number; and the names and birth dates of the persons for whose benefit s/he maintains health care coverage under the policy, certificate, or contract; and
   3) his/her current residence and mailing address within 21 days of the change.

☐ The parties have entered into a written agreement that has been reviewed and entered in the record as follows:

   a. The order of income withholding shall not take effect immediately.

   b. An alternative payment arrangement has been agreed upon (attached).

   c. Both the payer and the recipient of support will notify the friend of the court in writing of any change in:
   1) the name, address, and telephone number of his/her current source of income;
   2) any health care coverage that is available to him/her as a benefit of employment or that is maintained by him/her, the name of the insurance company, health care organization, or health maintenance organization; the policy, certificate, or contract number; and the names and birth dates of the persons for whose benefit s/he maintains health care coverage under the policy, certificate, or contract; and
   3) his/her current residence and mailing address within 21 days of the change.

IT IS ORDERED:

3. Income withholding shall not take effect immediately.

4. Income withholding shall take effect if the fixed amount of arrearage is reached, as specified in law.

_____
Date

_____
Judge

MCL 552.511; MSA 25.176(11),
MCL 552.604; MSA 25.164(4) .

FOC 64 (4/01) **ORDER SUSPENDING IMMEDIATE INCOME WITHHOLDING**

STATE OF MICHIGAN **JUDICIAL DISTRICT** **JUDICIAL CIRCUIT**	**MOTION AND VERIFICATION FOR ALTERNATE SERVICE**	**CASE NO.**

Court address   Court telephone no.

Plaintiff name(s), address(es), and telephone number(s)

v

Defendant name(s), address(es), and telephone number(s)

1. Service of process upon _____ cannot reasonably be made as otherwise provided in MCR 2.105, as shown in the following verification of process server.

2. Defendant's last known home and business addresses are:

_____

Home address   City   State   Zip

_____

Business address   City   State   Zip

      a. I believe the ☐ home / ☐ business address shown above is current.

      b. I do not know defendant's current ☐ home / ☐ business address. I have made the following efforts to ascertain the current address: _____

_____

_____

3. I request the court order service by alternate means.

I declare that the statements above are true to the best of my information, knowledge and belief.

_____
Date

_____
Address

_____
City, state, zip   Telephone no.

_____
Attorney signature

_____
Attorney name (type or print)   Bar no.

VERIFICATION OF PROCESS SERVER

1. I have tried to serve process on this defendant as described: State date, place, and what occurred on each occasion

I declare that the statements above are true to the best of my information, knowledge and belief.

_____
Date

_____
Signature

_____
Process Server (type or print)

STATE OF MICHIGAN **JUDICIAL DISTRICT** **JUDICIAL CIRCUIT**	ORDER FOR ALTERNATE SERVICE	CASE NO.

Court address   Court telephone no.

Plaintiff name(s), address(es), and telephone no.(s)		Defendant name(s), address(es), and telephone no.(s)
	v	
Plaintiff's attorney, bar no., address, and telephone no.		

THE COURT FINDS:

1. Service of process upon defendant _____

   cannot reasonably be made as provided in MCR 2.105, and service of process may be made in a manner which is reasonably

   calculated to give defendant actual notice of the proceedings and an opportunity to be heard.

IT IS ORDERED:

2. Service of the summons and complaint and a copy of this order may be made by the following method(s):

   a. ☐ First class mail to _____

   b. ☐ Tacking or firmly affixing to the door at _____

   c. ☐ Delivering at _____

   to a member of defendant's household who is of suitable age and discretion to receive process, with instructions to deliver

   it promptly to defendant.

   d. ☐ Other: _____

   _____

3. For each method used, proof of service must be filed promptly with the court.

_____   _____

Date   Judge   Bar no.

MC 304 (3/00) **ORDER FOR ALTERNATE SERVICE**   MCR 2.103, MCR 2.105

PROOF OF SERVICE

I served a copy of the summons and complaint and a copy of the order for alternate service upon

by: _____

1. First class mail to _____ , on _____
   Date

2. Tacking or firmly affixing to the door at _____ , on _____
   Date

3. Delivering at _____ , on _____
   Date

   to a member of defendant's household who is of suitable age and discretion to receive process, with instructions to deliver

   it promptly to defendant.

4. Other: _____ , on _____
   Date

_____   _____
Date   Signature

Service fee $	Miles traveled	Mileage fee $	Total fee $

_____   Title

Subscribed and sworn to before me on _____ , _____ County, Michigan.
                                      Date

My commission expires: _____ Signature: _____ _____
                       Date   Deputy court clerk/Notary public

Original - Court   2nd copy - Moving party
1st copy - Defendant   3rd copy - Return

STATE OF MICHIGAN JUDICIAL DISTRICT JUDICIAL CIRCUIT	ORDER FOR SERVICE BY PUBLICATION/POSTING AND NOTICE OF ACTION	CASE NO.

Court address   Court telephone no.

Plaintiff name(s) and address(es)		Defendant name(s) and address(es)
	v	
Plaintiff's attorney, bar no., address, and telephone no.		

TO: _____

IT IS ORDERED:

1. You are being sued by plaintiff in this court to _____
_____ . You must file your answer or take other action
permitted by law in this court at the court address above on or before _____ . If you fail to do
                                                                    Date
so, a default judgment may be entered against you for the relief demanded in the complaint filed in this case.

2. A copy of this order shall be published once each week in _____
                                                            Name of publication
   ☐ three consecutive weeks,
   for ☐ _____ , and proof of publication shall be filed in this court.

3. _____ shall post a copy of this order in the courthouse, and
   Name
   at _____ and
      Location
   at _____
      Location
   ☐ three continuous weeks,
   for ☐ _____ , and shall file proof of posting in this court.

4. A copy of this order shall be sent to _____ at the last known address
                                        Name   ☐ date of the last publication,
   by registered mail, return receipt requested, before the   ☐ last week of posting,   and the affidavit of mailing shall be
   filed with this court.

_____   _____   _____
Date   Judge   Bar no.

MC 307 (8/88) **ORDER FOR SERVICE BY PUBLICATION/POSTING AND NOTICE OF ACTION**   MCR 2.106

AFFIDAVIT OF PUBLISHING

Name of _____   ☐ publisher   ☐ agent of publisher

Name of newspaper	County where published

This newspaper is a qualified newspaper. The attached copy was published in this newspaper for at least 3 consecutive weeks on these dates:

_____

Attach copy of publication here

_____   _____
Date   Affiant signature

Subscribed and sworn to before me on _____ , _____ County, Michigan.
                                           Date

My commission expires: _____   Signature: _____
                              Date   Court clerk/Notary public

AFFIDAVIT OF POSTING

I have posted this order in a conspicuous place in the _____ courthouse and the following places as ordered by this court:

_____

_____

It has been posted for ☐ 3 continous weeks   ☐ _____ continous weeks   as ordered by this court.

_____   _____
Date   Affiant signature

Subscribed and sworn to before me on _____ , _____ County, Michigan.
                                           Date

My commission expires: _____   Signature: _____
                              Date   Court clerk/Notary public

AFFIDAVIT OF MAILING

As ordered, on _____ I mailed a copy of the attached summons and
                      Date
complaint and this order to _____
                                          Name
at _____ .
            Address
The mailing receipt and return receipt are attached at right.

Attach mailing receipt and return receipt here

_____   _____
Date   Affiant signature

Subscribed and sworn to before me on _____ , _____ County, Michigan.
                                           Date

My commission expires: _____   Signature: _____
                              Date   Court clerk/Notary public

STATE OF MICHIGAN JUDICIAL CIRCUIT PROBATE COURT COUNTY	NOTICE TO PRIOR COURT OF PROCEEDINGS AFFECTING MINOR(S)	CASE NO.

Court address

Court telephone no.

Name(s) of parent(s)/guardian(s)/plaintiff/defendant	Name(s), alias(es), and dates of birth of minor(s)

_____

Case no. of other court

TO: County of _____
- ☐ Court Clerk or Register
- ☐ Friend of the Court
- ☐ Prosecuting Attorney
- ☐ Juvenile Officer

NOTICE:

1. ☐ a. A complaint/petition/motion was filed with this court that affects the minor(s) who are subject to the continuing

   jurisdiction of your court. A hearing on the complaint/petition/motion is scheduled for

   _____
   Date

   _____
   Time

   _____
   Location

   ☐ b. The attached order was entered on _____ .
   Date

2. The actions of the court in this matter may supersede part or all of the order(s) previously entered by your court as the best
   interests of the minor(s) require.

CERTIFICATE OF MAILING

I certify that on this date I mailed a copy of this notice to the prior court by first class mail.

_____
Date

_____
Signature

Note: If item 1. a. is checked, this notice must be mailed at least 21 days prior to hearing.

Do not write below this line - For court use only

MCL 712A.2(b)(2), MCL 712A.3a, MCR 3.205, MCR 5.112, MCR 3.927

MC 28 (9/03) **NOTICE TO PRIOR COURT OF PROCEEDINGS AFFECTING MINOR(S)**

STATE OF MICHIGAN **Circuit Court - Family Division** COUNTY	WAIVER OF MILITARY RELIEF LAW RIGHTS	CASE NO.

Plaintiff (appearing *in propria persona*):

Defendant:

v

Defendant says:

1. I am in the active duty of the following unit of the U.S. military:

2. I waive all lawsuit relief rights provided to me in this case by the Soldiers' and Sailors' Civil Relief Act of 1940 and/or Michigan's military relief law (MCL 32.517) or a similar military relief law from another state.

Date _____   Defendant _____

Request for Certification of Military Status

TO:

Army Worldwide Locator
U.S. Army Enlisted Records and Evaluation Center
8899 E. 56th St.
Indianapolis, IN 46249-5301
Fee: $3.50 payable by check or money to "Finance Officer"

HQ AFPC/MSIMD
550 C St. West, Suite 50
Randolph AFB, TX 78150-4752
Fee: $3.50 payable by check or money order to "DAO-DE RAFB"

World Wide Locator
Bureau of Naval Personnel
Pers-324D
2 Navy Annex
Washington, DC 20370-3240
Fee: $3.50 payable by check or money to "U.S. Treasurer"

Coast Guard Locator Service
Commanding Officer (RAS)
444 SE Quincy St.
Topeka, KS 66683-3591
Fee: $3.50 payable by check or money order to "U.S. Treasurer"

Headquarters U.S. Marine Corps
Personnel Management Support Branch (MMSB-17)
2008 Elliot Rd.
Quantico, VA 22134-5030
Fee: $3.50 payable by check or money to "U.S. Treasurer"

RE:

Case name _____

Case number _____

Full name of defendant _____

Defendant's date of birth_____

Defendant's social security number _____

Defendant's rank and service number (if known)_____

Defendant's last duty assignment (if known) _____

Defendant's last military address (if known)_____

I am the plaintiff in the above divorce case seeking a default judgment of divorce against the defendant. I must know whether or not the defendant is currently in the active duty of your branch of the U.S. military service, to comply with the Soldiers' and Sailors' Civil Relief Act of 1940 and/or Michigan Compiled Law 32.517 or a similar military relief law from another state.

Please respond with a certificate of the defendant's (non)military status, unit of assignment and military address, if any, as soon as possible. If the defendant is overseas or in a deployed unit, please certify whether the defendant is or is not in active-duty service and omit the other requested information from your response.

A self-addressed stamped envelope is enclosed for your response. A certification fee is also enclosed, but if I qualify for a fee waiver (as spouse), please refund my payment.

Date _____

Signature _____

Name _____

Address _____

_____

Telephone:_____

Military Locator Request

TO:

Army Worldwide Locator
U.S. Army Enlisted Records and Evaluation Center
8899 E. 56th St.
Indianapolis, IN 46249-5301
Fee: $3.50 payable by check or money to "Finance Officer"

HQ AFPC/MSIMD
550 C St. West, Suite 50
Randolph AFB, TX 78150-4752
Fee: $3.50 payable by check or money order to "DAO-DE RAFB"

World Wide Locator
Bureau of Naval Personnel
Pers-324D
2 Navy Annex
Washington, DC 20370-3240
Fee: $3.50 payable by check or money to "U.S. Treasurer"

Coast Guard Locator Service
Commanding Officer (RAS)
444 SE Quincy St.
Topeka, KS 66683-3591
Fee: $3.50 payable by check or money order to "U.S. Treasurer"

Headquarters U.S. Marine Corps
Personnel Management Support Branch (MMSB-17)
2008 Elliot Rd.
Quantico, VA 22134-5030
Fee: $3.50 payable by check or money to "U.S. Treasurer"

RE:

Case name _____

Case number _____

Full name of defendant _____

Defendant's date of birth_____

Defendant's social security number _____

Defendant's rank and service number (if known)_____

Defendant's last duty assignment (if known) _____

Defendant's last military address (if known)_____

   I am the plaintiff in the above case seeking a divorce against the defendant. I request information about the defendant's current rank, service number, unit of assignment and military address. I need this information for service of process, to satisfy the military relief laws and other reasons related to this divorce case.

   A self-addressed stamped envelope is enclosed for your response. A locator fee is also enclosed, but if I qualify for a fee waiver (as spouse), please refund my payment.

Date _____   Signature _____

                            Name _____

                            Address _____

                            _____

                            Telephone:_____

Approved, SCAO

STATE OF MICHIGAN	**DISMISSAL**	**CASE NO.**
JUDICIAL DISTRICT		
JUDICIAL CIRCUIT		
COUNTY PROBATE		

Court address

Court telephone no.

Plaintiff name(s) and address(es)		Defendant name(s) and address(es)
	v	
Plaintiff's attorney, bar no., address, and telephone no.		Defendant's attorney, bar no., address, and telephone no.

☐ **NOTICE OF DISMISSAL BY PLAINTIFF**

☐ with
☐ without   prejudice as to:

1. Plaintiff/Attorney for plaintiff files this notice of dismissal of this case
   ☐ all defendants.
   ☐ the following defendant(s): _____

2. I certify, under penalty of contempt, that:
   a. This notice is the first dismissal filed by the plaintiff based upon or including the same claim against the defendant.
   b. All costs of filing and service have been paid.
   c. **No answer or motion has been served upon the plaintiff by the defendant** as of the date of this notice.
   d. A copy of this notice has been provided to the appearing defendant/attorney by ☐ mail ☐ personal service.

_____   _____
Date   Plaintiff/Attorney signature

☐ **STIPULATION TO DISMISS**

☐ with
☐ without   prejudice as to:

I stipulate to the dismissal of this case
☐ all parties.
☐ the following parties: _____

_____   _____
Date   Plaintiff/Attorney signature

_____   _____
Date   Defendant/Attorney signature

☐ **ORDER TO DISMISS**

☐ with
☐ without

IT IS ORDERED this case is dismissed   prejudice. Conditions, if any: _____

_____

_____

_____   _____   Bar no.
Date   Judge

MC 09 (6/97) **DISMISSAL**   MCR 2.504

Plaintiff:

v

Defendant:

Local Forms

(for Wayne County only)

Certificate on Behalf of Plaintiff Regarding Ex Parte Interim Support Order	
Certificate of Conformity for Domestic Relations Order or Judgment	1225
Certificate of Conformity for Domestic Relations Order or Judgment	1225
Order Data Form-Support	FD/FOC 4002

STATE OF MICHIGAN THIRD JUDICIAL CIRCUIT WAYNE COUNTY	CERTIFICATE ON BEHALF OF PLAINTIFF REGARDING EX PARTE INTERIM SUPPORT ORDER	CASE NO.

PLAINTIFF'S NAME	V.	DEFENDANT'S NAME

REVIEW BOTH SIDES OF THIS FORM BEFORE COMPLETING.
IF YOU ARE PRESENTING AN EX PARTE ORDER, COMPLETE THIS SIDE OF THIS FORM.
IF YOU ARE NOT PRESENTING AN EX PARTE ORDER, COMPLETE THE OTHER SIDE OF THIS FORM.
PLEASE PUT A LARGE 'X' ACROSS THE SIDE YOU ARE NOT COMPLETING.

_____ I AM PRESENTING AN EX PARTE INTERIM SUPPORT ORDER FOR ENTRY, WHICH INCLUDES THE FOLLOWING PROVISIONS: (CHECK THE PROVISION AND/OR CIRCLE THE CORRECT CHOICE)

_____ CUSTODY [with Names and Dates of Birth of minor child(ren)] MCL 552.15

    _____ SOLE LEGAL AND PHYSICAL CUSTODY TO PLT / DFT

    _____ JOINT LEGAL, SOLE PHYSICAL CUSTODY TO PLT / DFT

    _____ JOINT LEGAL AND PHYSICAL CUSTODY

_____ ADDRESSES   (NOTIFY FOC IF THERE IS A CHANGE)   MCR 3.211 (D) (2)

    _____ CHILD'S RESIDENCE

    _____ PARTIES' RESIDENCE

    _____ EMPLOYER'S

_____ DOMICILE   MCR 3.211 (C)(1)

_____ PARENTING TIME   MCL 722.27a

_____ SUPPORT   MCR 3.211 (D) & (E)

    _____ PAYABLE THRU FOC

    _____ IF MORE THAN ONE CHILD, IN FORM OF, e.g., "$100 For two children, $64 for one child...etc."

    _____ IMMEDIATE INCOME WITHHOLDING

    _____ STATUTORY FEES

_____ HEALTH CARE   MCR 3.211 (E)(3), MCL 722.27 and .3.

_____ NOTICE REGARDING OBJECTIONS REQUIRED BY MCR 3.207 B(5).

I CERTIFY THAT I AM PRESENTING A SUPPORT ORDER THAT AGREES WITH THE MICHIGAN CHILD SUPPORT GUIDELINES.

DATE _____   _____ / _____   P _____
                        Attorney's or Party's Printed Name/Signature

Address_____

City_____ State____ Zip Code_____ Telephone_____

A.   Please check the appropriate item(s), sign and serve the original of this certificate, the complaint (or counter-claim or petition) and an MSA 27A.659, MCL 600.659 custody affidavit upon the Court, the County Clerk, the Friend of the Court, and the other party. A 'VERIFIED STATEMENT- FRIEND OF THE COURT' MUST BE SERVED ON THE FRIEND OF THE COURT AND THE OTHER PARTY. DO NOT GIVE THE COUNTY CLERK THE VERIFIED STATEMENT.

B.   Provide the Office of the Friend of the Court with a copy of the PROOF OF SERVICE setting forth that each of the documents referred to in Instruction A have been served upon the other party.

STATE OF MICHIGAN THIRD JUDICIAL CIRCUIT WAYNE COUNTY	CERTIFICATE ON BEHALF OF PLAINTIFF REGARDING EX PARTE INTERIM SUPPORT ORDER	CASE NO.

PLAINTIFF'S NAME	V.	DEFENDANT'S NAME

REVIEW BOTH SIDES OF THIS FORM BEFORE COMPLETING.

IF YOU ARE <u>NOT</u> PRESENTING AN EX PARTE ORDER, COMPLETE THIS SIDE OF THIS FORM.
IF YOU ARE PRESENTING AN EX PARTE ORDER, COMPLETE THE OTHER SIDE OF THIS FORM.
PLEASE PUT A LARGE 'X' ACROSS THE SIDE YOU ARE NOT COMPLETING.

_____ I AM <u>NOT</u> PRESENTING AN EX PARTE INTERIM SUPPORT ORDER FOR ENTRY AT THIS TIME DUE TO THE FOLLOWING REASON(S): (CHECK THE REASON(S) THAT APPLY).

___1.   A prior order for support of the minor child/children is in effect:

      Name of County _____   Case Number _____

___2.   The non-custodial party is not the parent of the child/children named in the complaint and the complaint so states.

___3.   The Court lacks personal jurisdiction over the Defendant because the whereabouts of the Defendant are unknown. Service will be by publication.

___4.   The parties are presently residing together and the child/children are being adequately supported and there is no public assistance or application for public assistance pending.

___5.   I am the custodial parent and the other party is providing appropriate support for the child/children and there is no public assistance or pending application for public assistance pending.

___6.   The child/children are receiving Social Security Dependant Benefits as support.

___7.   The non-custodial parent is unemployed, receives Public Assistance or Supplemental Security Income (SSI) and has no other source of income. A request for a Friend of the Court child support investigation has been made.

___8.   The ability of the non-custodial parent to provide support for the minor child/children has not been determined. A motion for a temporary child support order has been filed.

___9.   Other _____

I CERTIFY THAT THE ABOVE INFORMATION IS CORRECT TO THE BEST OF MY KNOWLEDGE.

DATE _____   _____/_____   P_____
                     Attorney's or Party's Printed Name/Signature

Address_____

City_____State____Zip Code_____Telephone_____

A.   Please check the appropriate item(s), sign and serve the original of this certificate, the complaint (or counter-claim or petition) and an MSA 27A.659, MCL 600.659 custody affidavit upon the Court, the County Clerk, the Friend of the Court, and the other party. A 'VERIFIED STATEMENT- FRIEND OF THE COURT' MUST BE SERVED ON THE FRIEND OF THE COURT AND THE OTHER PARTY. DO NOT GIVE THE COUNTY CLERK THE VERIFIED STATEMENT.

B.   Provide the Office of the Friend of the Court with a copy of the PROOF OF SERVICE setting forth that each of the documents referred to in Instruction A have been served upon the other party.

STATE OF MICHIGAN THIRD JUDICIAL CIRCUIT WAYNE COUNTY	CERTIFICATE OF CONFORMITY FOR DOMESTIC RELATIONS ORDER OR JUDGMENT	CASE NO.

Penobscot Bldg. 645 Griswold Ave. Detroit, MI 48226   *313-224-5372*

PLAINTIFF'S NAME		DEFENDANT'S NAME
	V.	

I certify the attached Order or Judgment as presented for entry to be in full conformity with the requirements set forth by statute, **INCLUDING A PROVISION FOR IMMEDIATE INCOME WITHHOLDING (WHICH SHALL BE IMPLEMENTED BY THE FRIEND OF THE COURT), THE PAYER'S SOCIAL SECURITY NUMBER AND THE NAME AND ADDRESS OF HIS/HER SOURCE OF INCOME IF KNOWN , UNLESS OTHERWISE ORDERED BY THE COURT,** and with Michigan Court Rules 3.201 and following, and if applicable, includes all provisions of the Friend of the Court recommendation or is in conformity with the decision of

_____ rendered on the _____ day of

_____ , 19 _____ .

_____   _____
Date   **Attorney / Bar No.**

Instructions :   Please sign and present this Certificate to the Court Clerk when the Order or Judgment is presented
for entry. If an ex parte interim order is being presented to the Judge, please complete the "Certificate
on Behalf of Plaintiff regarding Ex Parte Interim Support Order" and follow Local Court Rule 3.206.

#1225 (7/95) CERTIFICATE OF CONFORMITY FOR DOMESTIC RELATIONS ORDER OR JUDGMENT

STATE OF MICHIGAN THIRD JUDICIAL CIRCUIT WAYNE COUNTY	CERTIFICATE OF CONFORMITY FOR DOMESTIC RELATIONS ORDER OR JUDGMENT	CASE NO.

Penobscot Bldg. 645 Griswold Ave. Detroit, MI 48226   *313-224-5372*

PLAINTIFF'S NAME	V.	DEFENDANT'S NAME

I certify the attached Order or Judgment as presented for entry to be in full conformity with the requirements set forth by statute, **INCLUDING A PROVISION FOR IMMEDIATE INCOME WITHHOLDING (WHICH SHALL BE IMPLEMENTED BY THE FRIEND OF THE COURT), THE PAYER'S SOCIAL SECURITY NUMBER AND THE NAME AND ADDRESS OF HIS/HER SOURCE OF INCOME IF KNOWN**, **UNLESS OTHERWISE ORDERED BY THE COURT**, and with Michigan Court Rules 3.201 and following, and if applicable, includes all provisions of the Friend of the Court recommendation or is in conformity with the decision of

_____ rendered on the _____ day of

_____ , 19 _____.

_____   _____
Date   Attorney / Bar No.

Instructions :   Please sign and present this Certificate to the Court Clerk when the Order or Judgment is presented for entry. If an ex parte interim order is being presented to the Judge, please complete the "Certificate on Behalf of Plaintiff regarding Ex Parte Interim Support Order" and follow Local Court Rule 3.206.

#1225 (7/95) CERTIFICATE OF CONFORMITY FOR DOMESTIC RELATIONS ORDER OR JUDGMENT

THE CIRCUIT COURT
FOR THE THIRD JUDICIAL CIRCUIT OF MICHIGAN
FAMILY DIVISION – FRIEND OF THE COURT

<u>ORDER DATA FORM-SUPPORT</u>
FOR SUBMISSION OF DOMESTIC RELATIONS ORDER FOR ENTRY INTO
Michigan Child Support Enforcement System (MiCSES) BY FOC

<u>NON-EX PARTE ORDERS:</u>

1.   Complete legibly and attach this form to the Friend of the Court (FOC) True Copy of the Order.

2.   Please note that the FOC worker will not review the order. If required fields are not completed (noted by asterisk *), the Order Data Form and the Order will be returned to you.

3.   Do not submit Orders with non-specific dates, such as orders that start support as of the date of sale of the marital home.

4.   If an order provides for different support amounts for different periods of time, complete an Order Data Form for each period. Label each with "1 of 'n', …, 'n' of 'n', in the upper right corner.

5.   The Judge's Circuit Court Clerk will forward the FOC copy of the Order, with attached Order Data Form, to FOC for entry into the MiCSES System.

<u>EX PARTE ORDERS:</u>

1.   Attach the Proof of Service if the Order is an Ex Parte Order. (The Order will not be entered into the MiCSES System unless the Proof of Service is attached.)

2.   Ex Parte Orders, with completed Order Data Form and Proof of Service, should be faxed or mailed to:

Order Entry Department		Attorney Window
3rd Floor, Penobscot Building		2nd Floor, Penobscot Building
645 Griswold	**or delivered to:**	645 Griswold
Detroit, Michigan 48226		Detroit, Michigan 48226
FAX: (313) 237-9290		FAX: (313) 237-9290

**THE ORDER DATA FORM IS AVAILABLE FOR DOWNLOAD TO YOUR COMPUTER
OR FOR PRINTING
ON THE COURT WEBSITE AT http://3rdcc.org OR FAX LIBRARY: (313) 967-3662**

Rev. 11/06/02

ABOUT THE NEW AND REQUIRED "ORDER DATA FORM-SUPPORT"

Friend of the Court, with the support of the Family Law Bench, has developed a data form, now called ORDER DATA FORM-SUPPORT (ODF-S), (formerly known as Fast Track Form) to assist the FOC in the task of loading the provisions of a support order into the Michigan Child Support Enforcement System. (MiCSES) It is now two pages.

A completed ODF-S must be attached to the FOC copy of any domestic relations order.

The old Fast Track form you have used was developed before and during the transition to the Michigan Child Support Enforcement System and is now obsolete.

Here are some features of the new form, as well as some practical considerations that should be noted when an order is being prepared for entry.

First, please note that it is the responsibility of the party submitting the order to the court for signature to enter all the relevant details of the new order into the ODF-S [ORDER DETAILS). The FOC worker will rely upon that information when loading the order and will not consult the attached order, nor any other previously entered order(s).

Second, the information required on page one, "ORDER DETAILS", of the ODF-S should be garnered only from the order attached. If the order results in a change in a certain element of the account, you check the relevant boxes and complete the relevant text areas.   If the order does not impact a certain element of the account, then you do not check those boxes and no change would be noted on MiCSES for that aspect of the account.

For example: the order modifies child support but not childcare. You would check the relevant boxes and enter the ordered amounts and dates into the text fields in the child support section. You would not check any of the childcare boxes. The worker will load the new child support, with its commencement date, and leave the childcare portion of the account as is.

For example: an order might provide for a certain cycle for one period of time, then a different amount for a subsequent period of time [for example, $10/wk from 04-01-02 to 05-31-02, then $40/wk from 06-01-02 until further order of the court]. You will prepare a "1 of 2" ODF-S (ORDER DETAILS) sheet for the '04-01-02 to 05-31-02 period' and a "2 of 2" ODF-S (ORDER DETAILS) sheet for the '06-01-02 until further order of the court' period of time. Only one copy of page 2, ODF-S (DEMOGRAPHICS) would need to be attached.

The only time an arrearage amount would be entered would be when the order, by its specific terms, sets a specific amount of arrearage for a date certain.

Again, the first page of the form (ORDER DETAILS) should contain the specifics of only the attached order.

The second page, DEMOGRAPHICS is also attached to the new order being submitted for entry. FOC will check and correct/update the account for any changes or errors. The information required is standard information you obtain from your clients. Your client's and the other parties' information should be on the verified statement initially and updated in your client file as you interact with your client and opposing counsel. Family Independence Agency account #'s, children's dates of birth and social security numbers, etc. are known to your clients and should be in your client files.

MiCSES has an automated Income Withholding Notice feature. The worker, as a part of the order loading activity that day, reviews the Demographics page and updates the employer, if necessary. Upon entry into MiCSES of a new support order, the system generates an Income Withholding Notice (IWN) that night, in batch, to the active employer. If the order specifies a certain $ amount to be wage deducted, that amount is loaded into MiCSES and the IWN is generated in that amount. If the order does not specify a certain amount to be withheld, the system calculates the guideline amount and the IWN is generated in that amount.

I believe that, especially if you download the template version of this form from the Website, you will find that it is very straightforward and quick to complete. The boxes and text areas, which are impacted by the order, are checked and filled and the balance of the choices are left blank.

ORDER DETAILS   FOR PERIOD ___ OF ___

| STATE OF MICHIGAN
COUNTY OF WAYNE
THIRD JUDICIAL CIRCUIT COURT
FAMILY DIVISION | **ORDER DATA FORM-SUPPORT**
Re: SUBMISSION FOR LOADING
ATTACHED SUPPORT ORDER INTO
MiCSES ON FOC COMPUTER SYSTEM

THE ORDER WAS ENTERED ON:
_____
(DATE ON ORDER STAMPED BY JUDGE'S CLERK) | (PLACE LABEL HERE)

CASE #:
_____

_____
JUDGE |

*INDICATES REQUIRED INFORMATION

CHECK ONLY THE BOXES WHICH APPLY TO PROVISIONS IN THE SUBMITTED ORDER

| *** PLAINTIFF NAME:** | *** DEFENDANT NAME:** |

*THIS ORDER IS:
☐ EX PARTE (PROOF OF SERVICE REQUIRED)   ☐ TEMPORARY   ☐ JUDGMENT   ☐ MODIFICATION

*WERE CHILD SUPPORT GUIDELINES FOLLOWED?   ☐ YES   ☐ NO

*THE CHILD SUPPORT PAYER IS   ☐ PLAINTIFF   ☐ DEFENDANT   ☐ NOT APPLICABLE.

☐ CHILD SUPPORT.   COMMENCEMENT DATE IS _____   ☐ PAY DIRECT, NOT THROUGH FOC.

| *** 5 CHILDREN PER WEEK**
CHILD SUPPORT AMOUNT
$ | *** 4 CHILDREN PER WEEK**
CHILD SUPPORT AMOUNT
$ | *** 3 CHILDREN PER WEEK**
CHILD SUPPORT AMOUNT
$ | *** 2 CHILDREN PER WEEK**
CHILD SUPPORT AMOUNT
$ | *** 1 CHILD PER WEEK**
CHILD SUPPORT AMOUNT
$ |

☐ **INCOME WITHHOLDING:**   ☐ PROCESS AT GUIDELINE AMOUNT   ☐ PROCESS AT $ _____ PER WEEK

☐ **CHILD SUPPORT ARREARAGE:**
☐ PRESERVED   ☐ CANCELED AS OF DATE: _____   ☐ SET AT $ _____ AS OF DATE: _____

☐ **CHILD CARE EXPENSES:** $ _____ PER WEEK, COMMENCEMENT DATE IS _____ ;
END DATE IS ☐ GUIDELINE DATE **OR** ☐ DATE: _____

☐ **CHILD CARE ARREARAGE:**
☐ PRESERVED   ☐ CANCELED AS OF DATE: _____   ☐ SET AT $ _____ AS OF DATE: _____

☐ **ARREARAGE ADJUSTMENT:**
☐ DIRECT CREDIT IN AMOUNT OF $ _____   ☐ ADD ADDITIONAL OBLIGATION IN AMOUNT OF $ _____

☐ **MEDICAL INSURANCE IN ORDER.**
☐ CHILD SUPPORT PAYER RESPONSIBLE FOR _____ % OF UNINSURED MEDICAL EXPENSES.

☐ **PARENTING TIME ABATEMENT:** ____ % PARENTING TIME CREDIT AFTER ___ CONSECUTIVE OVERNIGHTS.

☐ **PARENTING TIME ORDERED: (CHECK ONE):**
☐ REASONABLE   ☐ SPECIFIC   ☐ SUPERVISED   ☐ RESERVED   ☐ REFER TO FAMILY COUNSELING/OTHER

*THE SPOUSAL SUPPORT PAYER IS   ☐ PLAINTIFF   ☐ DEFENDANT   ☐ NOT APPLICABLE.

☐ **SPOUSAL SUPPORT:** ☐ $ _____ PER WEEK, COMMENCEMENT DATE: _____ .
☐ PERMANENT   ☐ END DATE _____   ☐ **PAY DIRECT, NOT THROUGH FOC**

☐ **SPOUSAL SUPPORT ARREARAGE:**
☐ PRESERVED   ☐ CANCELED AS OF DATE: _____   ☐ SET AT $ _____ AS OF DATE: _____

☐ ORDER REFERS MATTERS TO DIVORCE INVESTIGATION/MODIFICATION FOR FURTHER INVESTIGATION.

I CERTIFY THAT THE ABOVE INFORMATION IS TRUE TO THE BEST OF MY KNOWLEDGE, INFORMATION AND BELIEF, AND IS IN FULL CONFORMITY WITH THE REQUIREMENTS SET FORTH BY STATUTE AND COURT RULE AND THE DECISION OF THE COURT. (NOTE: FOC WILL NOT READ THE ORDER WHEN ENTERING IT ON MiCSES.)

_____   _____   BAR NO.
DATE: SIGNATURE OF ATTORNEY

PLEASE PRINT: _____
                          ATTORNEY NAME

                          _____
                          ADDRESS
                                                                                  TELEPHONE NO.
                          _____
                          CITY/STATE/ZIP

FD/FOC 4002 (11/06/02) **ORDER DATA FORM-SUPPORT**

DEMOGRAPHICS

STATE OF MICHIGAN COUNTY OF WAYNE THIRD JUDICIAL CIRCUIT COURT FAMILY DIVISION	**ORDER DATA FORM-SUPPORT** Re: SUBMISSION FOR LOADING ATTACHED SUPPORT ORDER INTO MiCSES ON FOC COMPUTER SYSTEM	(PLACE LABEL HERE)
	THE ORDER WAS ENTERED ON: _____	CASE #: _____
	(DATE ON ORDER STAMPED BY JUDGE'S CLERK)	JUDGE

*INDICATES REQUIRED INFORMATION

CHECK ONLY THE BOXES WHICH APPLY TO PROVISIONS IN THE SUBMITTED ORDER

* PLAINTIFF NAME:	* DEFENDANT NAME:

* NAME(S) OF CHILDREN (OLDEST TO YOUNGEST)	* DATE(S) OF BIRTH	* SOCIAL SECURITY NUMBER(S)

(ADD ADDITIONAL CHILDREN ON SEPARATE SHEET)

NON-CUSTODIAL PARENT (OR FATHER IF JOINT CUSTODY) ☐ PLAINTIFF ☐ DEFENDANT

* NAME:	* DATE OF BIRTH:	* SOC. SEC. NO.	HOME TELEPHONE NO:
* RESIDENTIAL ADDRESS:	* CITY, STATE, ZIP	OTHER TELEPHONE NUMBERS: ☐ WORK ☐ MOBILE	FIA/TANF N0.: NOW ACTIVE: ☐ YES ☐ NO
* EMPLOYER:	* EMPLOYER ADDRESS:	EMPLOYER TELEPHONE NO.:	EMPLOYER FED I.D. NO.:

CUSTODIAL PERSON (OR MOTHER IF JOINT CUSTODY) ☐ PLAINTIFF ☐ DEFENDANT

* NAME:	* DATE OF BIRTH:	* SOC. SEC. NO.	HOME TELEPHONE NO:
* RESIDENTIAL ADDRESS:	* CITY, STATE, ZIP	OTHER TELEPHONE NUMBERS: ☐ WORK ☐ MOBILE	FIA/TANF N0.: NOW ACTIVE: ☐ YES ☐ NO
* EMPLOYER:	* EMPLOYER ADDRESS:	EMPLOYER TELEPHONE NO.:	EMPLOYER FED I.D. NO.:

I CERTIFY THAT THE ABOVE INFORMATION IS TRUE TO THE BEST OF MY KNOWLEDGE, INFORMATION AND BELIEF, AND IS IN FULL CONFORMITY WITH THE REQUIREMENTS SET FORTH BY STATUTE AND COURT RULE AND THE DECISION OF THE COURT. (NOTE: FOC WILL NOT READ THE ORDER WHEN ENTERING IT ON MiCSES.)

DATE: _____

PLEASE PRINT: _____

SIGNATURE OF ATTORNEY _____

ATTORNEY NAME _____

BAR NO. _____

FD/FOC 4002 (11/06/02) ORDER DATA FORM-SUPPORT